Management Accounting

Management Accounting

Vidhu Bansal
Assistant Professor
Department of Commerce
Sri Guru Tegh Bahadur Khalsa College
University of Delhi
Delhi

N.K. Gupta
Professor
Department of Commerce
Ramjas College
University of Delhi
Delhi

TECHSAR™
NEW DELHI

Published and Printed by
Techsar Pvt. Ltd.
4435-36/7, Ansari Road, Daryaganj
New Delhi-110 002 (India)
E-mail: tech_info@techsarworld.com
Website: www.techsarworld.com

ISBN: 978-93-90620-34-0

Reprint 2025

Preface

This book is an attempt to provide thorough understanding and insights on various concepts of management accounting. The text and problems are presented in simple form to facilitate easy and quick understanding. The book has been divided into six chapters with each chapter being followed by theory and numerical exercise. An attempt has been made to explain that how the techniques of management accounting can be used for cost control and decision making over the series of chapters. It comprehensively covers the syllabus of B.Com (Hons), B. Com of University of Delhi and various courses of similar universities and professional bodies. Valuable suggestions of all colleagues and students are welcome.

Vidhu Bansal
N.K. Gupta

Contents

CHAPTER

1 Introduction to Management

Management Accounting facilitates decisions making as it generates accounting information relating to funds, costs, and profits, etc. Accounting information can be interpreted with it to guide the management for future planning, decision making, control, etc. Information and reports relating to the conducts of the various aspects of a business are provided by management accounting which assist management in efficient decision making, planning and control. It also look after needs of the insiders, e.g., owners, managers and employees. It focuses on assisting the management in rational policy decision and to evaluate the impact of its decision and actions.

Management accounting is interlacing with management itself. Management accounting is not only management rather it helps management to execute effectively. In contrast to conventional financial accounting, management accounting describes modern concept of accounting as a tool of management. The focus is to enlarge the financial and statistical information as to crystallize all stages of the organisational activities. Management accounting is concerned with the provisions and use of accounting information to managers within organisations, to provide them with the basis to make informed business decisions that will allow them to be better equipped in their management and control functions. Financial accounting, cost accounting and financial management when blended together, leads to better conduct of management in planning, coordinating, executing, controlling and motivating. As it provides information to managers, they can utilise the available resources in the best possible manner.

1. The Chartered Institute of Management Accountants (CIMA) of UK has given a very authoritative and comprehensive definition as follows: "Management accounting is an integral part of management concerned with identifying, presenting and interpreting information used for formulating strategy, planning and controlling activities, decision making, optimising the use of resources, disclosure to shareholders and others external to the entity, disclosure to employees, and safeguarding assets".
2. "Management Accounting is concerned with accounting information which is useful to management".
—Robert Antony

3. Management Accounting is "the process of identification, measurement, accumulation, analysis, preparation and communication of financial information used by management to plan, evaluate and control within the organisation and to ensure appropriate use and accountability for its resources".

—National Association of Accountants (USA)

4. "Management Accounting is the presentation of accounting information in such a way as to assist management in the creation of policy and the day-to-day operations of an undertaking. The technique of accounting is of extreme importance as it works in most nearly medium available for the expression of fact so that facts of great diversity can be presented in the same picture. It is NOT the presentation of this picture that is the main function of management but the USE of them".

—Management Accounting Team of Anglo-American Council of Productivity

5. "As an intimate merger of two older professions of accounting and management wherein the informational needs of the manager determine the accounting means for their satisfaction". **—Smith**
6. "Any form of accounting which enables a business to be conducted more efficiently can be regarded as management accounting".

—The Institute of Chartered Accountants of England and Wales

7. "Management Accountancy is the term used to describe the accounting methods, system and techniques which, coupled with special knowledge and ability, assist management in its task of maximising profits or minimising losses". **—Batty**

FEATURES OF MANAGEMENT ACCOUNTING

1. *Futuristic:* Though management accounting uses historic information but forms the basis for future decisions.
2. *Elastic:* Management accounting does not follow rules or formats. The choice of tools and techniques to be used in a particular situation, the form and pattern of presenting information lies in the hand of management. So the analysis and decision taken vary from organisation to organisation.
3. *Accounting information:* Financial and cost accounting are foundations of management accounting. This information is used to guide management in planning, control and decision making.
4. *Cause and effect:* In Management Accounting cause and effect relationship is found, i.e., reason for profit and loss are found and then decisions are made accordingly.
5. *Proficiency:* For the ease of manager's requirement various tools and techniques are used to *make accounting information* compatible. It includes budgetary control, standard costing, ratio analysis, cash flow statement, comparative analysis, etc.
6. *Quantitative and qualitative analysis:* Both quantitative and qualitative information is required to have a wise decision.

MANAGEMENT ACCOUNTING vs. FINANCIAL ACCOUNTING

Accounting information system of a business enterprise has 2 parts, i.e., financial accounting and management accounting. They have two similarities: (i) financial accounts and management accounts are both prepared with the help of operating information, and (ii) financial accounting information forms the basis of management accounting.

The difference between financial accounting and management accounting is because of the purposes the two are expected to serve. The terms 'Financial accounting and management accounting are not precise and mutually exclusive description of the activities they perform. In a way, all accounting is financial, as the most common denomination is money and management decision have directly or indirectly financial implications. Still there are differences between the two in spite of inter-relationship and inter-dependence.

1. *Detailed information:* Financial position and operating results are provided to the users by financial accounting for a given period of time. The task of decision making is helped by the information provided by management accounting.
2. *Range of information:* Financial accounting reports contain the information which can be translated or expressed in money only. However, apart from financial reports management accounting may also produce information of non-financial nature such as physical quantities of stock, output, turnover, etc.
3. *Format restriction:* Accounting and government regulations govern the financial report prepared for various businesses to ensure that they are in the prescribed format. However, managers are free from such restriction.
4. *Mandatory:* Financial accounting is compulsory for all business firms for the tax and external reporting purposes. Whereas for management accounting there is no such rule, sole decision lies in the hands of management.
5. *Usefulness of reports:* Specific-purpose reports are outcome of management accounting, which are designed either with a particular decision in mind or a particular manager. Financial accounting gives general-purpose financial reports useful for a variety of users and decisions.
6. Scope: Financial accounting deals with the enterprise as a whole; various parts of enterprise are looked after by management accounting to pinpoint areas of decision making. Overall position is shown by financial statements like balance sheets and profit and loss account whereas management accounting reports relate to responsibility centres, products, inventories, sales and their subdivision of business entity.
7. *Methodology:* Different methods are followed by financial and management accounting. In management accounting profit centres report cost and revenues. In financial accounting, information is recorded in the form of revenue, income, and expenditure, personal accounts, assets accounts, etc.

MANAGEMENT ACCOUNTING vs. COST ACCOUNTING

Management accounting and cost accounting are two crucial subdivisions of accounting. Accounting information is presented by management accounting and cost accounting in a way that it makes sound planning, correct decision making and effective controlling routine operations easy. Cost accounting is not only the tool of cost ascertainment and cost recording, it is also a good tool for cost control, ascertainment of profit, and decision making for the management. Management accounting and cost accounting have complementary functions. Cost accounting deals with the cost data only whereas both cost and revenue are considered by management accounting. The difference between management accounting and cost accounting is as follows:

1. *Principles:* Management accounting doesn't follow any procedure, so information is prepared and presented as per the manager's requirement. Cost accounting follows principles and procedure.
2. *Object:* Determining and recording the cost of producing a product is the basic objective of cost accounting, whereas that of management accounting is to provide necessary information to the management for planning and coordinating the business activities.
3. *Parties:* Management enjoys the benefits of management accounting whereas both information furnished by cost accounting is useful to both internal as well as external parties.
4. *Nature:* Cost accounting is based on past and present facts and figures while management accounting deals with projections and plans on the basis of past and present cost data.
5. *Data used:* Only quantitative information is recorded by cost accounting while both quantitative as well as qualitative information is recorded by management accounting.

Cost accounting developed out of financial accounting while management accounting evolved out of cost accounting. Basically, both the systems are complementary on nature. Management accounting has no significance without cost accounting. Similarly, in the absence of management accounting, cost data and other information would be useless. A good system of cost accounting is predecessor to management accounting. Cost accounting has limited scope while management accounting draws heavily on cost data and other information.

IMPORTANCE OF MANAGEMENT ACCOUNTING

Management accounting is applying various accounting techniques and concepts in processing historical and projected economic data of a business enterprise to help management in executing plans to materialise its objectives. It facilitates management at every stage. It has the following advantages:

1. An effective control of business management can be achieved with management accounting techniques. Proper utilisation of capital assuring maximum return on capital becomes feasible.
2. The use of management accounting may control or even eliminate wastages, and production defectives, etc.
3. A system is planned for all business activities. Management accounting helps in budgeting and forecasting.

4. The various management accounting tools provide validity, objectivity and reliability in business management.
5. Interested parties get up-to-date information with management accounting in successful working of business operations.
6. The efficiency of various functions is increased. The departmental targets are fixed in advance. It helps in measuring the achievement of such targets.

DRAWBACKS OF MANAGEMENT ACCOUNTING

Management is not a fully developed discipline, which gives rise to its drawbacks. Some of the main drawbacks of management accounting are:

(1) *Expensive affair:* Management accounting requires heavy investment as for setting it up a lot of rules and regulations have to be followed. So only large firms are able to adopt management accounting.

(2) *Resistance to change:* A lot of people working in the organisation get affected due to the setup of management accounting as it led to drastic change in the structure of the organisation and completely new set of rules and regulations have to be followed.

(3) *Does not provide decision:* This is a major limitation of management accounting that it only provides the management with necessary information but the decision making still rests on management's discretion. It cannot replace the management or the administration as it serves just as a tool to management.

(4) *It's just a tool:* Management accounting is just a tool to management. It cannot serve the purpose of an alternative to the management. The ultimate decision has to be taken by the management after analysing the information extracted through management accounting.

(5) *Reliability of data:* Management accounting is basically done by using and modifying the original basic records so the accuracy and correctness of its results depend upon the correctness of the basic records.

EFFECTIVE INSTALLATION OF MANAGEMENT ACCOUNTING SYSTEM

The following points should be considered in setting up management accounting effectively and efficiently:

1. To avoid overlapping of functions, responsibilities and authorities an organisational manual has to be prepared in detail describing the duties and responsibilities of each level of management.
2. Only the required amount of staff should be recruited to work in the system.
3. Only standard techniques of costing and budgetary control must be used.
4. There should be clear differentiation between cost centres, budget centres and investment centres.
5. Standard design of pro forma for various types of statements and reports must be prepared issued in the organisation.

The setting up of management accounting has to be done under the direct supervision of the management accountant who is known as Controller of or Director of finance and accounts.

FUNCTIONS OF MANAGEMENT ACCOUNTING

(1) *Assistance to management:* This is the primary function of management accounting. Management accounting assists the management in the performance of planning, organising, directing, and controlling.

(2) *Source of data:* Management accounting through its various tools provide important data which forms the basis for future forecasting. For management planning data about the past progress of the enterprise is required.

(3) *Data modification for planning:* All the accounting information is useful for managerial planning when it is provided in a proper form to the management. So management accounting ensures that all the requisite information is available to the management in the desired format.

(4) *Interpretation of the analysed data:* Through this process economic information collected from financial statements becomes meaningful for the management. As at this stage the information available is analysed for decision making.

(5) *Communication:* It is the duty of the management accountant to communicate the managerial plans in all the directions in the organisation.

(6) *Instilling coordination:* Coordination between various departments of an organisation is necessary for efficient and effective functioning of the organisation. This coordination is brought about by the management accountant with the help of various tools and techniques. Coordination is required because various departments in an organisation are interdependent and the progress of any activity by one department is dependent upon other department's progress.

(7) *Control:* It is a major function of the management accountant to ensure that the actual performance coincides with the predetermined standards and budgets. Corrective measures should be taken in case of any undesirable deviations.

(8) *Qualitative data:* This data is important for decision making purposes and cannot be measured in monetary terms. This information is gathered by doing surveys, gathering statistical data, etc.

ESSENTIAL TOOLS OF MANAGEMENT ACCOUNTING

Some of the tools and techniques used by management accountant regularly:

(1) *Cost accounting:* A lot of care has to be taken care of while designing the procedures for cost accounting as this information is required by management for cost control. It basically involves the recording, classifying, analysing and summarisation of all cost related aspects of a company.

(2) *Standard costing:* This technique is useful for controlling cost and performance. It involves the establishment of standard costs, their comparison with the actual cost

and analysis of the deviations. So cost control which is the main aim of management accounting is done by using this technique.

(3) *Marginal costing:* It is used for measuring profitability of different product lines. It basically measures the cost resulting from changes in the production volume.

(4) *Financial accounting:* It provides all the data required by the management accountant for analysis and interpretation. Management accounting rearranges the information provided by financial accounting.

(5) *Ratio analysis:* It is the most effective technique used in management accounting. Through this tool mathematical relationships are derived between interrelated figures.

(6) *Cash flow analysis:* This analysis is helpful to the management in managing the cash properly. It gives the reason for the difference between cash balances on two dates in the balance sheet so that the management could take the required actions in this regard.

(7) *Fund flow analysis:* This analysis is helpful to the management in efficiently planning and controlling the funds of the company. This tool brings up the causes of changes in the financial position of a company on two different dates.

(8) *Budgetary control:* Budget is basically the expression of plan of action in terms of quantity. Budgetary control has become the most widely used device for managerial control. Here the targets are predetermined by the management and actual performance is compared by them. The deviations thus arising are analysed in details.

(9) *Interim reporting:* Accurate and updated information needs to be communicated to the management at the right time which requires the preparation of different financial statements like cash flow, fund flow and income statements on a regular basis.

(10) *Revaluation accounting:* This is done to maintain and preserve the capital of the enterprise by overcoming the problems related to replacement of fixed assets. The problems of revaluation of fixed assets mainly arise in the period of rising prices.

(11) *Statistical tools:* A large number of statistical tools are prepared and used by the management to assist in the purpose of management accounting.

RULES FOR MANAGEMENT ACCOUNTING

Conventions act as guide while using managerial tools and techniques. Conventions are basically common practices adopted by the management accountant to deal with different situations. They have evolved through the course of time. Some common conventions are:

1. The methods, procedures and principles used in preparing the financial statements should be consistent, i.e., they should not change.
2. Costs and revenues should be strictly matched.
3. Accounting is concerned with the recording of business transactions only.
4. All the possible losses should be provided in advance.
5. Profit should be credited on the realisation.
6. Analysis should be done to know if the resources of the business are most effectively used.

7. The accounting information should be in a form which meets the specific needs of the business.
8. While reporting to the management, the principle of reporting exceptions should be followed.
9. The control mechanism should be set up at the point where the cost is incurred. This is known as objective of control at source.
10. Distinction between controllable and non-controllable costs must be made before identifying the responsibility.
11. Personal contacts should be maintained with the persons at higher levels of authority and reports and statements should not substitute these contacts.
12. The accounting records should be as objective as possible.
13. Only when the capital employed is maintained intact in real terms is profit said to be earned.

The above list of conventions is not an exhaustive one. There may be additions or deletions in this list as we move forward.

FUNCTIONS OF MANAGEMENT ACCOUNTANT

1. For the control of operations of an organisation an adequate plan has to be established by the management, so management accountant has the duty to establish, coordinate and administer this plan for the organisation. This plan would also provide necessary procedures to execute these plans.
2. The management accountant has to compare the performance with the predetermined plans and analyse and interpret the result to all the levels of management to facilitate the managerial function of controlling. This function includes the compilation of statistical data, preparation of reports, communicating these reports to the management.
3. To prepare reports which have to be submitted to the government agencies.
4. To interpret the effect of appraisal of economic and social forces and government influences on the business.
5. Ensuring proper insurance cover and adequate internal control to assure protection of the business assets.
6. To formulate tax policies for the business organisation so as to minimise the tax liability of the organisation.

Cost Control and Cost Reduction

Meaning of Cost Control

According to the ICWA of India, cost control means “The art of power of controlling or regulating or dominating or commanding costs through the application of management tools and techniques to perform one of any operations to most predetermined objectives of quality, quantity, value and time at an optimum outlay”.

Standard costing, quality control, CVP analysis, etc., are some of the techniques that are used by the management for exercising cost control. Various reports submitted by cost accountant like reports on inventory, variable overheads, etc., will help the management in taking appropriate decision.

Meaning of Cost Reduction

Cost reduction refers to the reduction in the cost of goods produced without affecting their quality. Cost reduction techniques should be real and permanent in nature. For example, lowering the price of raw material may be termed as real or permanent reduction but any wind fall reduction technique shall not be termed as a cost reduction method. Also the quality and the features of the products or services should be maintained.

Comparison between cost control and cost reduction

Basis	Cost Control	Cost Reduction
1. Aim	Cost control aims to regulate the cost of production according to the set standards and objectives	Cost reduction aims to find better methods of achieving the targets by reducing the cost of production and ensuring the quality standards at the same time.
2. Nature	Cost control is proactive or a preventive function	It is a reactive or a corrective function.
3. Assumption	Cost control assumes existence of certain standards which are not challenged	Cost reduction assumes that there are certain standards where there is a scope of cost reduction. Hence, such standards are subject to improvement.
4. Emphasis	The emphasis is on past	It emphasises on present and future
5. Technique	Essential techniques of cost control are budgetary control, quality control, etc.	Essential techniques are quality management, market research, etc.

Cost Reduction Programme

Cost reduction programme aims at improvement of human and material resources at all levels of the organisation which help in reducing costs. Short term programmes sort of immediate problems like components, disposal of waste, etc. Long term cost reduction techniques involve major reduction cost. The prerequisites for successful implementation of a cost reduction programme are:

1. For proper implementation of cost reduction programme, a separate cost reduction cell should be established.
2. Efficient management reporting at all levels of management.
3. Top management support to the cost reduction technique.
4. Co-ordination amongst cost reduction cell members.
5. Continuous appraisal of the programme performed with the actual cost reduction performance performed.
6. Uneconomic and unnecessary activities should be eliminated and there should be an operation and research procedure.

Cost Reduction Techniques

Some of the techniques are:

1. Budgeting control
2. Standard costing
3. Production planning and control
4. ABC analysis
5. Value analysis
6. Job evaluation
7. Work study and motion study
8. Reduction in the variety of products.

Scope of Cost Reduction Programme

The following are the areas covered by cost reduction programme.

1. **Product design** – Product should be designed in a manner that gives maximum value at the minimum cost. The technique of value analysis is greatly helpful in designing the product. A careful analysis of cost must be done before introducing any new product design or innovation.
2. **Product advertising** – Since advertising is a very vital component in the present dynamic environment. Most of the companies spend huge amount in spreading awareness about the product. Companies must look for advertisement tools which are cost effective and also adequately spread information about the product.
3. **Production planning** – Factory location has a great influence on the cost, therefore factory location should be selected on more scientific lines.
4. **Raw materials cost reduction** – Material should be purchased in economical lots at economical prices. Also just in time (JIT) inventory technique must be followed so that holding cost of inventory is minimised.
5. **Labour cost reduction** – Right person should be appointed for right job so that turnover and absenteeism of labour is minimised.
6. **Reduction in overheads** – Factory and office overheads can be minimised by creating cost consciousness amongst employees. For example, minimising paper and stationary
7. **Reduction in training and development programmes cost** – Continuous training of employees is essential for their development. Management should device methods where employees are adequately trained but at a minimised cost.
8. **Finance cost reduction** – It refers to controlling capital expenditure revenue expenditure, proper evaluation of investments in new projects, etc.

REVIEW QUESTIONS

1. What do you understand by the term management accounting?
2. How is management accounting helpful to the business enterprise?
3. Bring out the difference between cost reduction and cost control.
4. What benefit does the organisation derives by following cost control and cost reduction methods?
5. Explain in brief the areas of cost reduction at the level of product designing. *[C.A.]*
6. Distinguish between cost control and cost reduction. *[B.Com (H)]*

7. What do you understand by cost reduction? How is it different from cost control? [*B.Com (H)*]
8. What are the technique/tools of cost reduction and cost control. [*B.Com (H)*]
9. Explain the nature and scope of "Cost control" and "Cost reduction". Which of the two is superior? [*B.Com (H)*]

CASE STUDIES

1. The management accountant of Allywin Automobile Company, situated in Chennai was not satisfied with the historical cost depreciation being used for changing cost of expensive machinery to individual components and products. Therefore, the management accountant calculated each year the replacement cost of each machine and calculated depreciation, based on the machine's replacement cost which was subsequently included in calculating machine hour rate. The machine hour rate calculated in this way was considered to assign machine expenses to the components produced on that machine. The management accountant also included an interest charge, based on 50% of machine replacement value, into the machine hour rate. The interest rate was an average of 7–9% on government securities.

   As a consequence of these two decisions (charging replacement cost rather than historical cost and imputing a capital charge for the use for capital equipment), the product cost figures used internally by company managers were inconsistent with the numbers that were needed for inventory valuation for financial and tax reporting. The accounting staff had to perform a tedious reconciliation process at the end of each year to back out the interest and replacement value costs from the cost of goods sold and inventory values before they could prepare the financial statements.

Required:

Based on his remarks, it is obvious that Vikas's background of accounting is limited to financial accounting. Discuss some of the important differences between financial and management accounting and suggest some way management accounting can help Vikas be a better product manager.

2. The Chief Finance Officer (CFO) of Vivekanand Central University, New Delhi is complaining about the heavy work that he is required to do at the beginning of each month. The Vice Chancellor of the University requires the Chief Finance Officer (CFO) to submit a monthly report by the fifth day of the following month. The monthly report contains financial data. The CFO was heard saying, "why does the Vice Chancellor need all this information? He probably does not read half of the report. He is an old Botany professor and probably does not know the difference between cost and revenue".

Required:

(i) What is the importance of monthly report?

(ii) What is the responsibility of Chief Finance Officer with respect to a Vice Chancellor who does not know much accounting? (*M.Com.*)

CHAPTER 2

Marginal Costing, Cost Volume Profit (CVP) Analysis

MEANING OF MARGINAL COSTING (VARIABLE COSTING)

Marginal costing is a distinct technique of costing. It assumes that the managers can only influence variable costs. It is a technique of recording and reporting costs, such as product cost only, which tends to vary directly with the volume of electricity while all other costs are regarded as period costs. In fact, it is a method for matching costs with revenues to determine periodic profit. The distinction between variable costs and period costs determines when costs are matched with revenues.

Marginal costing can be used in combination with historical costing as well as standard costing. It is synonymous with variable costing or direct costing.

Absorption Costing

Absorption costing is a system, under which fixed as well as variable costs are charged to cost units and total overheads are absorbed according to the level of activity. The other terms for absorption costing are the functional, full costing or financial reporting approach. As it aims at identifying all costs, both fixed and variable, it is known as product/full costing. It allocates costs to finished products and to inventories which have the effect of carrying over the costs incurred in one period to the next period/s through inventories. The real problem arises with the transfer of fixed costs of one period to another. Distortions in the profit and loss account of both the current period and the next period are due to the allocation of fixed costs. This is because fixed costs are related to specific periods and not to actual volume of production. Administration and selling and distribution expenses are period costs and the same are charged to cost units. Product cost includes fixed factory overhead, direct material, direct labour, direct expenses and variable factory overhead. The fixed overhead is absorbed by actual production using a predetermined rate based on normal production.

However, absorption costing is not helpful to the management in making decision problems such as:

(i) Selection of production volume and optimum capacity utilisation

(ii) Selection to buy or make
(iii) Evaluation of performance
(iv) Selection of best alternative

Absorption costing is not helpful in controlling costs or planning and control functions and also in fixing responsibilities for the incurrence of costs.

Essential Features of Marginal Costing

The essential characteristics and mechanism of marginal costing technique are as follows:

(i) Dividing costs into fixed and variable elements—All costs are classified into fixed and variable. Semi-variable costs are also split into fixed and variable elements.

(ii) Period costs—The fixed costs are excluded from the product costs and charged to profit and loss account.

(iii) Product cost—Only variable costs are considered product costs.

(iv) Pricing—Products are priced on the basis of marginal cost plus the contribution.

(v) Valuation of inventory—The inventory of finished goods and work in progress is valued at marginal cost of production.

(vi) Consistency of profit—The profit would be consistent from period to period.

(vii) Contribution margin—Contribution is sales value minus marginal cost of sales. Profitability of processes, products, departments and various managerial decisions are made with reference to contribution margin.

Marginal Cost

It is the variable cost of one unit of a product or a service, which would be avoided if the units were not produced, or service not provided. It relates to the change in output in the particular circumstances under consideration.

Contribution

The amount, which a product generates towards total fixed overheads and profit is known as contribution.

It can be described as either fixed cost plus profit or sales revenue minus marginal cost.

CIMA defines it as:

(i) Contribution per unit: It is the difference between the selling price of a unit of product or service and its marginal cost.

(ii) Contribution in total: It is the difference between the sale value and the marginal cost of such sales. If the sales revenue becomes more than the marginal cost of sales, then it denotes that the amount of each unit is contributing towards absorbing fixed costs and generates profit.

The contribution covers fixed costs and provides profits which is known as marginal income/variable profit or contribution margin.

It can also be obtained by deducting from sales revenue for a particular segment of the business the variable costs that relate to that revenue.

Difference between Contribution and Profit

(i) Contribution includes both fixed cost and profit while profit is devoid of fixed cost.

(ii) Contribution is used for managerial decisions while profit is owner-oriented, static and historical concept for determining the outcome of operation.

(iii) The concept of contribution is used in marginal costing while profit is a residual concept used in accounting.

Difference between Gross Margin and Contribution Margin

(i) Gross margin appears in an absorption costing income statement; contribution margin appears in a variable costing income statement.

(ii) Gross margin is based on a categorisation of costs by function; contribution margin divides cost by cost behaviour.

(iii) Gross margin is revenue less manufacturing cost contribution margin is revenue less all variable costs.

(iv) Gross margin is required for financial reporting, contribution margin is most useful for short term management decisions.

Limitations of Marginal Costing (Variable Costing)

(i) It assumes that all costs should be divided into fixed and variable components. However, always such segregation may not be possible.

(ii) It also assumes that there is a direct relationship between sales and variable costs, and the relationship is linear. However, this assumption is not true under all circumstances, e.g., quantity discounts on materials and labour efficiency variance.

(iii) Total product cost does not depend only on variable costs. Fixed cost should also be considered in determining the product cost and for long range pricing and other long range policy decisions.

(iv) It is difficult to apply this technique to the construction or ship building industry where the value of work in progress is high in relation to the turnover. If fixed expenses are ignored there will be loss in every year and huge profit in the year of completion of the contract to construction.

Variable Costing and Absorption Costing

Variable costing is a technique where only variable costs are considered for purpose of product costing, inventory valuation and other connected vital management decisions. Marginal costing is, "the accounting system in which variable costs are charged to cost units and fixed cost of the period are written off in full against the aggregate contribution. Its special value is in decision making".

— CIMA London

The variable costing technique recognises only variable costs as production costs. Fixed manufacturing costs are treated as period costs, i.e., costs that are a function of time rather than of production. These costs are not affected by changes of quantity of product manufactured and therefore are considered an expense of the period and written off to profit and loss account in the period they are incurred.

In absorption costing, total costs are taken into consideration of production costing, inventory valuation and other important managerial decisions. It absorbs all costs necessary to produce in a saleable form. Therefore, it recognises fixed overheads.

These methods differ only in one respect. Fixed manufacturing overhead is excluded from the cost of product under absorption costing. A variable costing system treats fixed manufacturing overhead as a period cost to be immediately charged against sales and not as a product cost.

So, the only difference between variable and absorption costing is the accounting for fixed manufacturing overhead.

The two techniques are not mutually exclusive and complementary in character. Income statements for external reporting and for tax purposes are to be on full costing basis. The variable costing helps management in arriving at profit maximising decisions in certain situations. This is why it becomes important for internal reporting purposes.

Illustration 1

Details	Year 2019-20	Year 2020-21
Opening inventory	Nil	5,000
Production	35,000	30,000
Sales	30,000	34,000
End inventory	5,000	2,000

Cost structure per unit	(₹)
Direct material	50
Direct labour	80
Variable manufacturing overhead	20
Standard variable cost of production	200
Sales commission @ 4% of sales value	250
Selling price per unit	

Annual budget for fixed manufacturing overhead is ₹20,00,000 for the budgeted production of 20000 cubits. Budgeted fixed selling and administrating overhead is ₹6,00,000. Prepare income statement as per

(i) Variable costing

(ii) Absorption costing

1. Income Statement as per Variable Costing

Details	Year 2019-20	Year 2020-21
A. Sales	₹	₹
(30000 × 250) (34000 × 250)	75,00,000	85,00,000
B. Variable cost of sales variable of manufacturing cost of goods sold opening inventory at standard variable cost of ₹200	Nil	10,00,000
Add: Variable cost of goods manufactured at standard cost ₹200: 35000 and 30000 units respectively.	70,00,000	60,00,000
Available for sale, 35000 each year	70,00,000	70,00,000
Deduct: End inventory at standard variable cost of ₹200	10,00,000	4,00,000
Variable manufacturing cost of goods sold	60,00,000	66,00,000
Add: Variable selling expenses @ 4% of rupee sale	3,00,000	3,40,000
Total variable cost of sales	63,00,000	69,40,000
C. Contributing margin (A–B)	12,00,000	15,60,000
D. Fixed Costs		
Fixed Factory overhead	2,00,000	2,00,000
Fixed selling & Admn. Expenses	6,00,000	6,00,000
Total Fixed Expenses	8,00,000	8,00,000
E. Operating Income (C–D)	4,00,000	7,60,000

2. Income Statement as per Absorption Costing (₹)

Details	Year 2019-20 ₹	Year 2020-21 ₹
A. Sales	75,00,000	85,00,000
B. Cost of goods sold	Nil	10,50,000
Opening inventory at standard absorption cost of ₹210		
Cost of goods manufactured at standard of ₹210	73,50,000	63,00,000
Available for sale	73,50,000	73,50,000
Deduct: End of inventory at standard absorption cost of ₹210	10,50,000	4,20,000
Cost of goods sold at standard	63,00,000	69,30,000
C. Gross profit at standard	12,00,000	15,70,000
D. Production volume variance (Add favourable; deduct unfavourable)	1,50,000	1,00,000
E. Gross margin at actual	9,00,000	9,40,000
G. Operating income	13,50,000	7,30,000

Notes:

(i) Standard absorption cost

Variable cost = 200

Fixed manufacturing cost

$$\frac{2,00,000}{20,000} = \frac{10}{210}$$

(ii) Production volume variance

Year 2019-20	1,50,000	(35,000-20,000) 10
2020-21	1,00,000	(30,000-20,000) 10

Under variable costing, fixed works overheads are not charged to production whereas under absorption costing, fixed works overheads are spread an all the units manufactured.

Note: Selling and administration expenses are not charged to product but are treated as expenses in the period they are incurred, under both the techniques.

Difference in Net Income

Differences in the computation of product cost due to the difference in treatment of fixed worker overheads cause difference in net income figures under both the techniques.

Under variable costing, costs are of two types, fixed cost and variable cost. In the income statement, firstly, only the variable manufacturing costs are deducted from sales and secondly, the variable cost of selling and distribution expenses and administrative overheads are deducted to find the gross margin. Lastly, all the fixed costs overheads, administrative and selling and distribution overheads are deducted from gross margin to get the net income.

Under absorption costing, all costs are divided into 3 categories. In income statement, all manufacturing costs are deducted from sales value to get a gross profit on sales and there from selling and distribution and administrative overheads to get net income.

The format for an absorption costing statement splits cost into the major categories of manufacturing and non-manufacturing whereas the variable costing income statement split costs into 2 major categories of fixed and variable.

In absorption costing, revenue minus manufacturing cost is gross margin and in variable costing statement revenue less all variable costs in the contribution margin.

(i) Standard absorption cost of goods sold plus production – volume variance:

Despite the importance of such differences in most industries, more and more firms are not concerned with the choice between variable and absorption costing as they implement 'Just-in-Time' (JIT) production.

If the inventory level does not change, then there would be no difference between both the costings.

COST CONCEPTS

In order to appreciate marginal costing technique in its proper perspective, it is necessary to understand cost behaviour. One of the classification of cost is on the basis of its behaviour. Cost may be fixed, semi-fixed or semi-variable.

Fixed Cost

It is the cost of those inputs, which do not vary with changes in volume of output/activity within a relevant range of activity or output for a given budget period. As the name suggests, it remains constant but always subject to change over a period of time. It means, any increase in volume amounts to sharing of the cost by greater number of units and consequently fixed cost per unit gets progressively smaller as volume increases. So, fixed cost will not change over a wide range, but will fluctuate beyond that range.

Also sometimes, fixed costs are labelled as capacity costs as they measure the capacity for manufacturing, sales, administration and research.

Fixed costs are subdivided into 'committed' fixed costs and 'discretionary' fixed costs.

Committed Fixed Cost

Fixed costs arising due to the acquisition of capacity producing assets such as plant and equipment are known as committed fixed costs. Salaries of the key personnel, insurance of some are its examples. The company has committed itself to incur such costs by making long range decisions. Such costs cannot be reduced substantially.

These costs are the least responsive of the fixed costs as they tend to be less affected by seasonal decisions. Thus, from the point of the management, the emphasis is on the maximum utilisation of these facilities so as to augment income.

Discretionary Fixed Cost

These costs are also called programmed or managed costs. The managerial decisions in regard to undertake research and development, advertising and sales campaign, charitable or political donations cause such fixed costs which can be reduced substantially or even completely for a given period in difficult times.

Variable Cost

Variable cost as the name suggests varies within relevant range for a given budget period in direct proportion to changes in production activity, sales activity or some other measures of volume. It is so because these inputs are used in the requisite exact quantities. Material cost, labour cost and supplies are some examples of variable cost.

Semi-variable Cost (Mixed Cost)

Semi-variable cost is neither perfectly variable or absolutely fixed in relation to volume of activity/output. The fixed component of the mixed cost represents the cost of providing capacity or facility whereas the variable component is caused by using the capacity/facility.

Methods of segregating semi-variable cost:

Following methods are applied to split the mixed cost into fixed and variable costs.

- Graphic method
- Range method
- Bi-level comparison

- Survey method
- Method of least squares

1. Graphic method (Scatter diagram)

Each dot on the chart represents cost for a particular month in relation to the number of units produced. A 'line of best fit' is drawn in such a manner that the true average relationship between cost and volume can be ascertained.

The positive intercept on the vertical axis represents fixed costs and the variable component of the mixed cost. This method is not considered scientific and objective as two persons will draw different lines of the same data, therefore it is purely subjective.

2. Range Method

This method uses only two extreme observations. The two points selected are:

(a) High cost point

(b) The low cost point, corresponding to specific volume of activity.

Statistically, it is not desirable to make use of the Range method. Two extreme observations may not be in tune with the normal trend of the data.

3. Bi-level comparison

The output of two different levels is compared with the corresponding level of expenses. Variable overheads are derived by the ratio of change in expenses to change in output.

4. Survey method (Analytical method)

Through this method, we see that how far the cost varies with volume of production/activity. Such an analysis is especially useful in building flexible budgets.

5. Method of last squares

This is based on the solution of two linear equations of the formula for drawing straight line regression equation, i.e.,

$$y = a + by$$

This gives rise to two normal equations for

Solution $\text{EY} = na + bEx$

$$\text{EX } y = a\ Ex + bE \times 2$$

Illustration 2

Month	Production (Unit)	Repair & Maintenance (₹)
April	60	10,000
May	40	8000
June	50	7000
July	60	1000
August	40	8000
September	50	7000

Solution:

Month	Production (Unit)	Cost (₹)			
		Y	XY	X^2	Yc
April	60	10,000	6,00,000	3600	
May	40	8000	3,20,000	1600	
June	50	7000	3,50,000	2500	
July	60	1000	6,00,000	3600	
August	40	8000	3,20,000	1600	
September	50	7000	3,50,000	2500	
	300	50,000	25,40,000	15,400	

$$50{,}000 = ba + 300b \quad ...(1)$$

$$25{,}40{,}000 = 300a + 15{,}400b \quad ...(2)$$

From the above equations

We get $a = 3333.33$

$b = 100$

Illustration 3

The analysis of production overheads of SV Limited reveals that there is 20% degree of variability at 100% capacity utilisation on budgeted mixed overheads cost are ₹30,000. What would be they at 50, 75 and 80 per cent capacity utilisation?

Solution:

Variable production overheads = (Budgeted mixed overhead × Degree of variability)

= 30,000 × 0.20 = 6000

Fixed production overheads at 100% capacity utilisation

= Budgeted mixed overheads

– Variable production overheads)

= 30,000 – 6000 = 24,000

Variable production overheads at one per cent capacity.

= Total variable overheads/100

= 6000/100 = ₹60 per one per cent.

Details	Capacity		
	50	75	80
Fixed production overheads	24,000	24,000	24,000
Variable production overheads	3000	4500	4800
Total	27,000	28,500	28,800

Profit/volume ratio (PV Ratio)

P/V ratio is also known as contribution sales ratio or C/s ratio

$$\text{P/V ratio} = \frac{\text{Contribution}}{\text{Sales}} = \frac{\text{Sales} - \text{Variables cost}}{\text{Sales}}$$

or C/S or $\frac{S - VC}{S}$ or $1 - \frac{VC}{S}$

where S = Sales and VC = Variable cost

Since fixed costs are constant, any increase in profit would mean increase in contribution and thereby increase in P/V ratio.

P/V comparison is done by management to find out the profitability level of various products and draw comparison.

Key Factor

The most important factor in taking decisions about profitability of a product is known as key factor.

Profitability can be measured by: $\frac{\text{Contribution}}{\text{Key factor}}$

Cost – Volume – Profit (CVP) Analysis

CVP analysis is an integral managerial tool for profit planning. CVP analysis helps us in analysing:

1. Impact of volume on cost.
2. Volumes of sales where business will earn normal profit or break-even.
3. Effect of output on profit level.
4. Quantity of production and sales for a target profit level.

According to Kohler, the cost-volume-profit relationship is "the area of interest, within an organisation, of management and accountants in observing and controlling the relations between prospective and actual manufacturing costs, both fixed and variable – rates of production and gross profit. Break-even charts optimise these relationship at planning and forecasting stages and various types of comparative cost statements provide information and the basis for action at operating, review and reporting levels".

CVP analysis is of primary importance to financial managers who devise solutions to the problems faced by the businesses. It helps them in the following ways.

1. Profit and sales forecasting
2. Formulation of budget to allocate cost and determine sales and profits at different level of activity.
3. Helps the management in exercising control through performance evaluation.
4. Helps in formulating pricing policy for different products and determining the impact of price on costs and profits.

5. Allocation of overhead cost at various levels of production.
6. Effective cost and price control.

Therefore, we can say that CVP analysis helps the management in taking appropriate decision with respect to cost, price, sales, volume of production which directly will have an impact on profit level of a company.

BREAK-EVEN ANALYSIS

The effect on the profit level due to the variations in fixed and variable cost at different levels of profit are studied through a technique called break-even analysis. This is the most widely used technique for studying cost-volume-profit analysis. In the dynamic environment the selling prices keep fluctuating. It is important for the business to know the impact of such changes on the profit level. Break-even analysis is an important tool that determines these changes and helps the organisation in taking appropriate decisions.

Break-even Point

In layman's term it is a point where total cost and total revenue are equal. At this point the firm neither earns profit nor incurs any loss.

Hence, we can say that the point which breaks the total cost and the selling price evenly to show the level of output or sales at which there shall be neither profit nor loss, is regarded as break-even point. If production is increased beyond this level the firm will earn benefit and if it is decreased below this point, the firm will run into losses. The following diagram shall make it more clear.

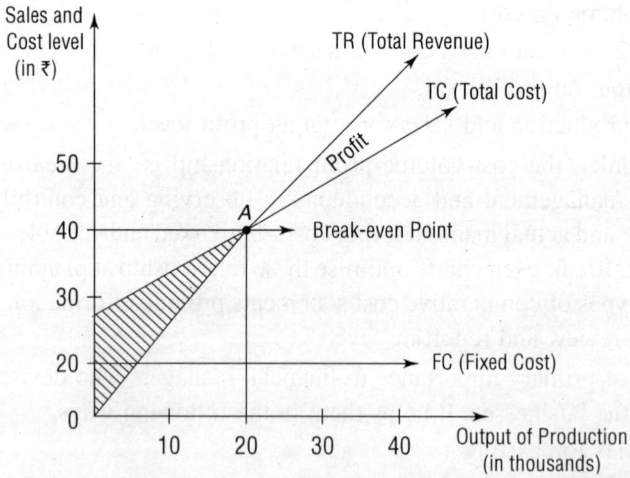

Break-even chart

In the diagram above point *A* is the break-even point where TC = TR. Production below point *A* indicates TC > TR, which implies losses. Beyond *A*, TR > TC which indicates profit.

The break-even point can be expressed as follows:

$$\text{Break-even point (of sales)} = \frac{\text{Fixed cost}}{\text{P/V ratio}} \text{ or } \frac{\text{FC}}{\text{S} - \text{VC}} \times \text{S}$$

$$\text{or } \frac{\text{FC}}{\text{Total contribution}} \times \text{Total sales or } \frac{\text{FC}}{\text{Contribution/Unit}} \times \text{SP/Unit}$$

or Break-even output × SP/Unit

where FC is fixed cost

S is sales

VC is variable cost

SP is selling price

$$\text{Break-even point (of output)} = \frac{\text{Fixed cost}}{\text{Contribution per unit}} \text{ or } \frac{\text{Break-even sales}}{\text{Selling price/unit}}$$

$$\text{At break-even point (BEP), } \frac{\text{Total cost}}{\text{Total sales}} \text{ (Since total cost = Total Sales)}$$

$$\text{At BEP, contribution = Fixed cost or } \frac{\text{Fixed cost}}{\text{Total contribution}} = 1$$

Cost Break-even Point / Cost Indifference Point

When cost under two alternatives is equal, it is known as cost break-even point or cost indifference point. This analysis helps the firm to choose a better alternative for a given level of output.

$$\text{Cost break-even point (in units)} = \frac{\text{Increase in fixed cost}}{\text{Saving in variable cost per unit}}$$

Cash Break-even Point

The level of output or sales where there is no cash profit and no cash loss is known as cash break-even point. At this point the inflow of cash in the firm is just sufficient to meet immediate cash liabilities and expenditure like salary payment, rent, etc.

$$\text{Cash break-even point (of output)} = \frac{\text{Cash fixed costs}}{\text{Cash contribution per unit}}$$

Composite Break-even Point

When a firm dealing with multiple products, a need arises for computation of composite break-even point.

$$\text{Composite break-even point} = \frac{\text{Total fixed costs}}{\text{Cash contribution per unit}}$$

When a firm is dealing with multiple products, a need arises for computation of composite break-even point.

$$\text{Composite Break-even Point (of sales in rupees)} = \frac{\text{Total fixed costs}}{\text{Composite P/C ratio}}$$

$$= \frac{\text{Total fixed costs} \times \text{Total sales}}{\text{Total contribution}}$$

$$\text{Composite Break-even Point (in units)} = \frac{\text{Total fixed costs}}{\text{Composite contribution per unit}}$$

$$\text{Composite P/V Ratio} = \frac{\text{Total contribution}}{\text{Total sales}} \times 100$$

Break-even Chart

When the relationship between cost, revenue, sales and profit is shown on a graph, it is known as break-even chart. This chart shows the costs, revenues and profit at various levels of output and also shows the point where cost is equal to revenue and the firm breaks even. Break-even chart shows:

1. Break-even point
2. Total cost, fixed cost and total revenue
3. Level of cost and revenue at various levels of output
4. Profit and loss at various levels of output
5. Margin of safety
6. Angle of incidence

(The break-even chart diagram is given on (p. 23)).

Margin of Safety

Margin of safety is total sales minus break-even sales.

Margin of safety = Total sales – Sales at break-even point

$$\text{In terms of percentage} = \frac{\text{Margin of safety}}{\text{Total sales}} \times 100$$

Large margin of safety is a sign of soundness of the business. If the margin of safety level is not satisfactory, the management can take any of the following steps to achieve higher safety levels.

1. Production can be increased, without much increase in cost.
2. If the firm is dealing in multiple products, the improfitable products can be substituted by profitable ones.
3. Reducing the cost of production.
4. Increase in the selling price, but ensuring that the demand does not fall as a result of this increment.

Angle of Incidence

The angle formed by the sales line and total cost line at break-even point is known as angle of incidence. A high rate of profit is indicated by large angle of incidence at break-even point. Better understanding of profit, cost and sales can be derived from break-even point, margin of safety and angle of incidence. The following situations will help us understand this better.

Situation 1

High margin of safety, large angle of incidence and low break-even point.

This is the most favourable situation where firm earns maximum profit and is sound in establishment and in financial terms. The chart below shows this situation.

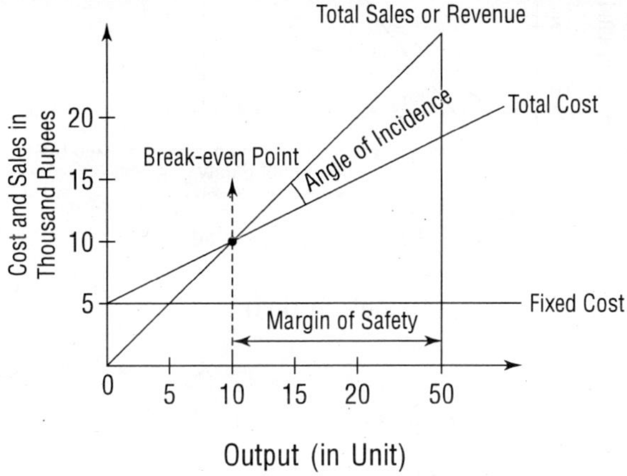

Situation 2

High margin of safety, small angle of incidence and low break-even point.

In this situation the firm makes a low rate of profit over large range of output as compared to the first situation. The following chart shows this situation.

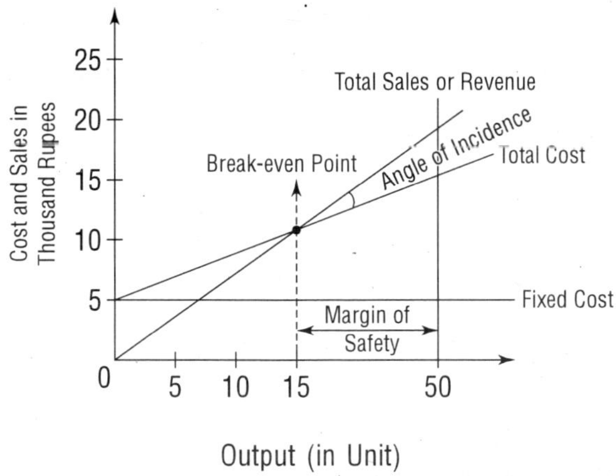

Situation 3

Low margin of safety, large angle of incidence and high break-even point.

Under this situation, even with a small decline in output the firm will run into losses.

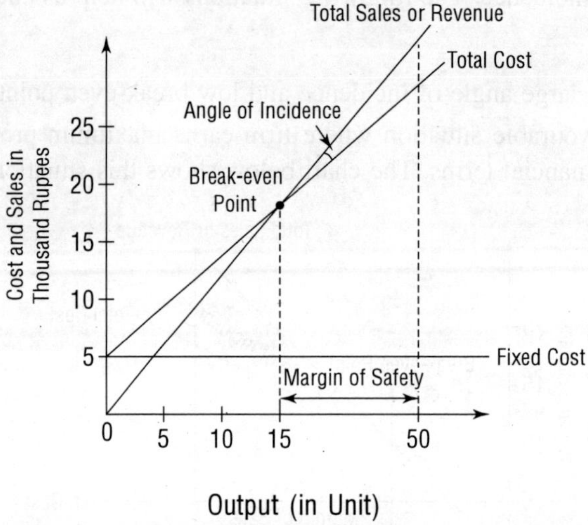

Situation 4

Low margin of safety, small angle of incidence and high break-even point.

This is a situation to understand business financially with high fixed costs.

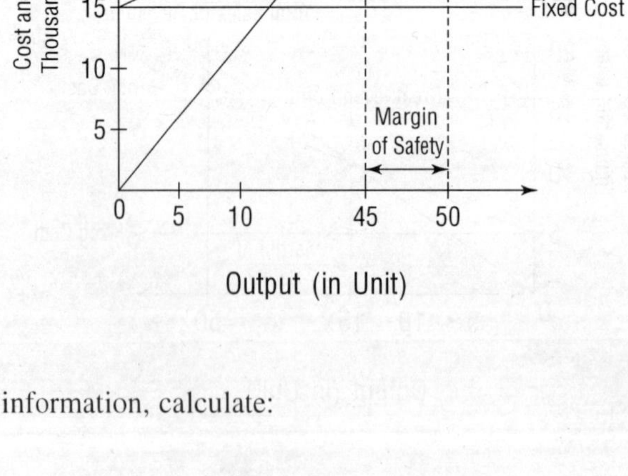

Illustration 4

From the following information, calculate:

(i) P/V ratio

(ii) Break-even point

(iii) Sales required to earn profit of ₹20,000

(iv) Profit when sales are ₹50,000

Selling price per unit is ₹40

Variable cost per unit is ₹20 and fixed expenses are ₹4,000.

Solution: Contribution = Selling Price – Variable Cost

$$= 40 - 20 = 20$$

$$\text{P/V Ratio} = \frac{\text{Contribution}}{\text{Selling price}} \times 100 = \frac{20}{40} \times 100 = 50\%$$

$$\text{Break-even point} = \frac{\text{Fixed cost}}{\text{P/V ratio}} = \frac{4000}{50} \times 100 = ₹8000$$

Sales required to earn profit of ₹20,000

= (Fixed Cost + Desired Profit)/P/V Ratio

$$= (4000 + 20{,}000)/50\% = \frac{24{,}000}{50} \times 100 = ₹48{,}000$$

Profit when sales are 50,000

Profit = Contribution – Fixed cost

= (Sales × P/V ratio – Fixed cost)

= (50,000 × 50% – 4000) = 25,000 – 4000 = ₹21,000.

Illustration 5

A company manufactures and markets three products A, B and C. All the three products are made from the same set of machines. Production is limited by machine capacity. From the data given below indicate priorities for products, A, B and C with a view to maximise profits.

Particulars	Product A (₹)	Product B (₹)	Product C (₹)
Raw material cost per unit	2.25	3.25	4.25
Direct labour cost per unit	0.50	0.50	0.50
Other variable costs per unit	0.30	0.45	0.71
Selling price per unit	5.00	6.00	7.00
Standard machine time required per unit	39 min	20 min	28 min

In the following year the company faces extreme shortage of raw materials. It is noted that 3 kg, 4kg and 5 kg of raw materials are required to produce one unit of A, B and C respectively. How would product priorities change?

Solution:

Comparative Statement of Profitability

Particulars	Product A (₹)	Product B (₹)	Product C (₹)
Selling price per unit	5.00	6.00	7.00
Raw materials	2.25	3.25	4.25
Direct labour	0.50	0.50	0.50
Other variable costs	0.30	0.45	0.71
Total variable costs	3.05	4.20	5.46
Contribution per unit (sales variable costs)	1.95	1.80	1.54
P/V ratio	39%	30%	22%
Contribution per minute of standard machine time	0.05	0.09	0.05
Contribution per kg of raw materials	0.65	0.45	0.31

If the machine capacity is limited, contribution per minute of standard machine time is to be considered for correct decision making. Product B is most profitable, Product C comes next and product A last.

If the key factor is raw materials, contribution per kg of raw materials should be considered for decision making. Thus, product A is most profitable, product B comes next and product C last.

Illustration 6

Assuming raw material as the key factor, availability of which is 10,000 kg and maximum sales potential of each product being 3500 units. Find out the product mix which will yield the maximum profit.

Solution:

3500 units × 2 kg = 7000 kg for product of A (as it is more profitable)

1000 × 3 kg = 3000 kg for B

= 10,000 kg

Profit

A's contribution 3500 × ₹55 = ₹1,92,500

B's contribution 1000 × ₹69 = ₹69,000

= ₹2,61,500

Less: Fixed overheads

(on maximum sales potential) = ₹52,500

Profit = ₹2,09,000

Illustration 7

The following particulars are extracted from the records of AB Ltd.

Particulars	Product A	Product B
Sales (per Unit)	₹100	₹120
Consumption of materials	2 kg	3 kg
Material cost	₹10	₹15
Direct wage cost	₹15	₹10
Direct expenses	₹5	₹6
Machine hours used	3 hours	2 hours
Overhead expenses:		
Fixed	₹5	₹10
Variable	₹15	₹20

Direct wage per hour is ₹15

(a) Comment on the profitability of each product (both use the same raw material) when:

(i) Total sales potential in units is limited

(ii) Total sales potential in value is limited

(iii) Raw material is in short supply

(iv) Production capacity (in terms of machine hours) is the limiting factor.

Solution:

Particulars	Product A (per unit)		Product B (per unit)	
	₹	₹	₹	₹
Selling price		100		120
Less: Variable costs	10	45	15	51
Materials	15		10	
Wages	5		5	
Direct expenses	15		20	
Variable overheads				
Contribution per unit		55		69

P/V Ratio = $\frac{\text{Contribution}}{\text{Sales}} \times 100$	$\frac{55}{100} \times 100 = 55\%$	$\frac{69}{120} \times 100 = 57.5\%$
Contribution per kg of material	$\frac{55}{2\text{ kg}}$ = ₹57.5	$\frac{69}{3\text{ kg}}$ = ₹23
Contribution per hour	$\frac{55}{3}$ = ₹18.33	$\frac{69}{2}$ = ₹34.5

Comments

(i) When total sales potential in units is limited, contribution per unit is higher in B hence product B is more profitable.

(ii) When total sales potential in value is limited, P/V ratio is higher in B, hence product B is more profitable.

(iii) When raw material is in short supply, contribution per kg of material is higher in A, hence product A is more profitable.

(iv) When production capacity is the limiting factor (in terms of machine hours), contribution per hour is higher in B, hence product B is more profitable.

SOLVED PRACTICAL PROBLEMS

MARGINAL COSTING AND ABSORPTION COSTING

Problem 1 Felix Processors produce an item for which the relevant information is given below:

Details	Units
Annual budgeted production	20000
Actual production	22000
Sales @ 15/ Unit	15000
Opening stock	2000

Budgeted details	Amount (₹)
Direct materials	1,00,000
Variable production overheads	20,000
Fixed production overhead	60,000
Fixed selling overhead	40,000
Variable selling overhead	10,000

The company follows absorption costing approach and the overhead absorption rates are based on the budgeted production. Compute the fixed production overhead rate of recovery. Also find out profit as per absorption costing and marginal costing techniques.

Solution: **Working notes**

1. Fixed production overhead rate of recovery:

= Fixed production overhead/Budgeted production

= 60,000/20,000 = ₹ 3/ unit

2. Variable production cost per unit

= Variable production cost/Budgeted production

Variable production cost = Direct materials + Variable production overhead

= 1,00,000 + 20,000

= ₹ 1,20,000

Variable production cost per unit = 1,20,000/20,000 = ₹6/ unit

3. Variable selling overhead per unit:
   Variable selling overhead/Budgeted production
   = 10,000/20,000 = ₹0.50 / unit
4. Fixed selling overhead per unit:
   Fixed selling overhead/Budgeted production
   = 40,000/20,000 = ₹2/ unit
5. Fixed production overhead recovered
   22,000 × ₹3 = ₹66,000
6. Fixed production overhead recovered
   = Fixed production overhead recovered – Fixed production overhead incurred
   = 66,000 – 60,000 = ₹6,000
7. Total cost of production per unit under:
   (a) Absorption costing = ₹19 (₹3 + ₹6) per unit
   (b) Marginal costing = ₹6 per unit

Income Statement (Under Absorption Costing Technique)

Particulars	Amount (₹)	Amount (₹)
A. Sales (15,000 units at 15/Unit)		2,25,000
Opening stock (2000 units @ ₹9)	18,000	
Production cost (22000 units @ ₹9)	1,98,000	
Cost of goods available for sale	2,16,000	
Less: Closing stock (9000 units @ ₹9)	(81,000)	
Cost of goods sold (15000 vits @ ₹9)	1,35,000	
Less: Over recovery of production overheads adjusted cost of goods sold	(6000)	
Add: Fixed: Selling expense	1,29,000	
Variable selling expenses (15000 × ₹.50)	40,000	
B. Cost of sales	7500	1,76,500
C. Profit (A–B)		48,500

Income Statement (under marginal costing)

Particulars	Amount (₹)	Amount (₹)
A. Sales (15000 units at ₹7 15/Unit)		2,25,000
Opening stock (2000 units@ ₹6)	12,000	
Production cost (22000 units @ ₹6)	1,32,000	
Cost of goods available for sale (15000 units @ ₹6)	1,44,000	
Less: Closing stock (9000 units @ ₹6)	54,000	
Variable cost of goods sold (15000 unit @ ₹6)	90,000	
Add: Variable selling cost (15000 unit @ ₹6)	7500	

Table Contd...

Table Contd...

B. Total variable cost of sales		97,500
C. Contribution (A–B)		1,27,500
D. Fixed overhead		
Production	20,000	
Selling	40,000	
Total fixed overhead		60,000
E. Profit (C–D)		67,500

Problem 2 A manufacturing company has an installed capacity of 1,20,000 units per annum. The cost structure of the product is given below:

Particulars	Amount (₹)
Variable cost (per unit material)	8
Labour (subject to minimum ₹56,000 per month)	8
Overheads	3
Fixed overhead	1,68,750 p.a.
Semi-variable overheads	48,000 p.a

At 60% capacity, which increased by ₹T 6,000 p.a. for every 10% increase in the capacity utilisation for any part thereof for the year as a whole.

The capacity utilisation for next year is estimated at 60% for first 2 months, 75% for next six months and 80% for the remaining part of the year. If the company is planning to have a profit of 25% on the selling price, then calculate the selling price per unit for the year under consideration. Assume that there is no opening or closing stock.

Particulars	Fist 2 months	Next 6 months	Last 4 months	Total
Available capacity (in units)	20,000	60,000	40,000	1,20,000
Utilised capacity (in units)	12,000	45,000	32,000	89,000
	(60%)	(75%)	(80%)	
Variable cost (in ₹3)				
Material cost (₹8/unit)	96,000	3,60,000	2,56,000	7,12,000
Labour cost (₹8/ unit subject to a minimum of ₹56,000 per month)	1,12,000	3,60,000	2,56,000	7,28,000
Overheads (₹3/unit)	36,000	1,35,000	96,000	2,67,000
Total variable cost	2,44,000	8,55,000	6,08,000	17,07,000
Fixed overhead				1,68,750
Semi-variable overheads (see working note 1)				58,000
Total cost				19,33,750

Calculation of selling price

Total cost = ₹19,33,750

Total utilised capacity (units) = ₹89,000

Cost per unit = 19,33,750/89,000

= 21.73

According to question, the company should make a profit of 25% on selling price i.e., 1/3 of cost, so

Cost/Unit = 21.73

Add: Expected profit = 7.24

(Profit of 1/3 on cost or $\frac{1}{4}$ pm selling price)

Selling price per unit = 28.97

Working Note:

1. Calculation of semi-variable overheads
 = 48,000 2/12 + 60,000 × 6/12 + 60,000 × 4/12
 = ₹58,000

Problem 3 The following information has been obtained from the books of a company:

Production Volume	40,000 units
Sales volume	38,000 units
Selling price per unit	₹50
Materials cost per unit	₹20
Labour cost per unit	₹10
Manufacturing overheads	
Variable	₹5 per unit
Fixed	₹1,00,000
Administration & Selling Overheads:	
Variable	₹3 per unit
Fixed	₹1,36,000

Prepare an income statement under (a) absorption costing technique and (b) Marginal costing technique.

Solution:

Income Statement under Absorption Costing

Particulars	₹	₹
Sales (38,000 × ₹50)		19,00,000
Less: Manufacturing Cost of Goods Sold:		
Materials (40,000 × ₹20)	8,00,000	
Labour (40,000 × ₹10)	4,00,000	

Table Contd...

Table Contd...

Variable manufacturing overheads (40,000 × ₹5)	2,00,000	
Fixed manufacturing overheads	1,00,000	
Cost of production (COP)	15,00,000	
Less: Closing Stock of Finished Goods		
$\left[₹14,00,00 \dfrac{2,000\text{ units}}{40,000\text{ units}}\right]$	75,000	
Cost of goods sold		
Gross Profit		14,25,000
Less: Administration & Selling Overheads		4,75,000
Variable (38,000 × ₹3)	1,14,000	
Fixed	1,36,000	2,50,000
Net Profit		2,25,000

Income Statement under Variable Costing

Particulars	₹	₹
Sales (38,000 × ₹50)		19,00,000
Less: Variable Cost of Goods sold:		
Materials (40,000 × ₹20)	8,00,000	
Labour (40,000 × ₹10)	4,00,000	
Variable Manufacturing Overheads (40,000 × ₹5)	2,00,000	
Variable Manufacturing Cost	14,00,000	
Less: Closing Stock of Finished Goods		
$\left[₹14,00,000 \times \dfrac{2,000\text{ units}}{40,000\text{ units}}\right]$	70,000	
Variable Manufacturing Cost of Goods Sold		
Add: Variable Administration & Selling Overheads	13,30,000	
(38,000 × ₹3)		
Variable Cost of Goods Sold	1,14,000	14,44,000
Contribution		4,56,000
Less: Fixed Production Overheads	1,00,000	
Fixed Administration & Selling Overheads	1,36,000	2,36,000
Net Profit		2,20,000

Observation: As the production volume is more than the sales volume, the net profit as ascertained under absorption costing is more than the net profit under variable costing. This happens due to higher valuation of closing stock under absorption costing.

Problem 4 The following details have been obtained from the books of a company:

Production Volume	10,000 units
Sales Volume	12,500 units
Opening Stock Volume	5,000 units
Value of Opening Stock (including Variable Cost ₹70,000)	₹95,000
Selling Price per unit	₹40
Variable Production Cost per unit	₹24
Fixed Production Overheads	₹60,000
Administration & Selling Overheads:	
Variable	₹2 per unit
Fixed	₹45,000

Prepare an income statement under: (a) absorption costing technique and (b) variable costing technique.

Solution:

Income Statement under Absorption Costing

Particulars	₹	₹
Sales (12,500 × ₹ 40)		5,00,000
Less: Cost of Goods Sold:		
Variable Production Cost (10,000 × ₹ 24)	2,40,000	
Fixed Production Overheads	60,000	
Cost of Production (COP)	3,00,000	
Add: Opening Stock of Finished Goods	95,000	
Less: Closing Stock of Finished Goods		
$\left[₹3,00,000 \times \dfrac{2,500\text{ units}}{10,000\text{ units}}\right]$	75,000	
Cost of goods sold		3,20,000
Gross Profit		1,80,000
Less: Administration & Selling Over		
Variable (12,500 × ₹ 2)	25,000	
Fixed	45,000	70,000
Net Profit		1,10,000

Income Statement under Variable Costing

Particulars	₹	₹
Sales (12,500 × ₹ 40)		5,00,000
Less: Variable Cost of Goods Sold:		
Production Cost (10,000 × ₹ 24)	2,40,000	

Table Contd...

Table Contd...

Add: Opening Stock of Finished Goods	70,000	
Less: Closing Stock of Finished Goods $\left[₹2,40,000 \times \frac{2,500 \text{ units}}{10,000 \text{ units}}\right]$	60,000	
Variable Manufacturing Cost	2,50,000	
Add: Variable Administration & Selling Overheads (12,500 × ₹2)	25,000	
Variable Cost of Goods Sold		2,75,000
Contribution		2,25,000
Less: Fixed Production Overheads	60,000	
Fixed Administration & Selling Overheads	45,000	1,05,000
Net Profit		1,20,000

Working Notes:

1. Closing Stock of Finished Goods (in Volume) = Production + Opening Stock – Sales = 10,000 + 5000 – 12,500 = 2500 units
2. FIFO method of stock valuation is used.
3. Under absorption costing the opening stock is taken at the total cost, but under variable costing, it is taken at variable cost only.

Observation: As the sales volume is more than the production volume, the net profit as ascertained under absorption costing is less than the net profit under variable costing. This happens due to higher valuation of closing and opening stock under absorption costing.

Problem 5 A company has a production capacity of 1,00,000 units per year. The normal capacity utilisation is reckoned at 80%. The standard variable production costs are ₹15 per unit and fixed production costs are ₹3,20,000 per year. The variable selling costs are ₹4 per unit and fixed selling costs are ₹1,60,000 per year. The unit selling price is ₹30. During the year that ended on 31 March 2019, 75,000 units were produced and 70000 units were sold The closing inventory on 31 March 2019 was 10,000 units. The actual variable production cost for the year was ₹75,000 higher than standard.

Prepare an income statement under: (i) absorption costing technique; and (ii) variable costing technique. [*B. Com. (Hons.)*]

Solution:

(i) Income Statement under Absorption Costing

Particulars	₹	₹
Sales (70,000 × ₹30)		21,00,000
Less: Cost of Goods Sold:		
Variable Production Cost (75,000 × ₹15) + 75,000	12,00,000	
Fixed Production Cost (75,000 × ₹4)	3,00,000	

Table Contd...

Table Contd...

Particulars	₹	₹
Cost of Production (COP)	15,00,000	
Add: Opening Stock of Finished Goods[1]	95,000	
Less: Closing Stock of Finished Goods $\left[₹15,00,000 \times \frac{10,000 \text{ units}}{75,000 \text{ units}}\right]$	2,00,000	
	13,95,000	
Add: Under-absorption of Fixed Production Overheads	20,000	
(₹ 3,20,000 – ₹ 3,00,000)		14,15,000
Gross Profit		6,85,000
Less: Selling Cost:		
Variable (70,000 × ₹ 4)	2,80,000	
Fixed	1,60,000	4,40,000
Net Income		2,45,000

Income Statement under Variable Costing

Particulars	₹	₹
Sales (70,000 × ₹ 30)		21,00,000
Less: Variable Cost of Goods Sold:		
Variable Production Cost (75,000 × ₹ 15) + 75,000	12,00,000	
Add: Opening Stock of Finished Goods (5000 units × ₹ 15)	75,000	
Less: Closing Stock of Finished Goods $\left[₹12,00,000 \times \frac{10,000 \text{ units}}{75,000 \text{ units}}\right]$	1,60,000	
	11,15,000	
Add: Variable Selling Cost (70,000 × ₹ 4)	2,80,000	
		13,95,000
Contribution		7,05,000
Less:		
Fixed Production Cost	3,20,000	
Fixed Selling Cost	1,60,000	4,80,000
Net Profit		2,25,000

Observations: As the production volume is more than the sales volume, the net profit as ascertained absorption costing is more than the net profit under variable costing. This happens due to higher valuation of closing stock under absorption costing

Working Notes:

1. Opening stock of finished goods = Sales closing stock – Production
   = 70,000 + 10,000 – 75,000 = 5000 units.

Standard Overhead rate per unit at Normal Capacity Utilisation = ₹3,20,000/(80% of 1,00,000 units) = ₹4

As explained earlier, under Absorption Costing the Opening Stock is taken at the full cost, but under Variable Costing, it is taken at the Variable Cost only. Therefore, value of Opening Stock under Absorption Costing = 5000 units (₹15 + ₹4) = ₹95,000

2. The Closing Stock is valued according to FIFO method.

Problem 6 The following information relates to a company which makes and sells laptops.

	March 2020	April 2021
Production Volume	10,000 units	5000 units
Sales Volume	5000 units	10,000 units
Selling Price per unit	₹50	₹50
Variable Production Cost per unit	₹25	₹25
Fixed Production Overheads Incurred	₹50,000	₹50,000
Fixed Production Overheads per unit (Being predetermined overhead absorption rate)	₹5	₹5
Selling Distribution & Administration Cost (all fixed)	₹40,000	₹40,000

You are required to present a Comparative Profit Statement for each month using: (a) Absorption costing technique and (b) Marginal Costing technique. Comment on the results obtained.

Solution:

Income Statement under Absorption Costing

Particulars	March 2020		April 2021	
	₹	₹	₹	₹
Sales (5000 × ₹50) and (10,000 × ₹50)		2,50,000		5,00,000
Less: Manufacturing Cost of Goods Sold:				
Variable Production Cost (10,000 × ₹25) and (5000 × ₹25)	2,50,000		1,25,000	
Fixed production Overheads (10,000 × ₹5) and (5000 × ₹25)	50,000		25,000	
	3,00,000		1,50,000	
Add: Opening Stock of Finished Goods $\left[₹3,00,000 \times \frac{5000 \text{ units}}{10,000} \text{ units}\right]$	—		1,50,000	

Table Contd...

Table Contd...

Particulars	**March 2020**		**April 2021**	
	₹	₹	₹	₹
Less: Closing Stock of Finished Goods	3,00,000		3,00,000	
$\left[₹3,00,000 \times \frac{5000 \text{ units}}{10,000 \text{ units}}\right]$	1,50,000		—	
	1,50,000		3,00,000	
Add: Under-Absorption of Fixed Production Overhead (₹50,000 – ₹50,000) and	NIL		25,000	
(₹50,000 – ₹25,000)		1,50,000		3,25,000
Gross Profit		1,00,000		1,75,000
Less: Selling & Administration Costs		40,000		40,000
Net Profit		60,000		1,35,000

Income Statement under Variable Costing

Particulars	**March 2020**		**April 2021**	
	₹	₹	₹	₹
Sales (5000 × ₹50) and (10,000 × ₹50)		2,50,000		5,00,000
Less: Variable Cost of goods sold (10,000 × ₹25) & (5000 × ₹25)	2,50,000		1,25,000	
Add: Opening Stock of Finished Goods $\left[₹2,50,000 \times \frac{5000 \text{ units}}{10,000 \text{ units}}\right]$	—		1,25,000	
	2,50,000		2,50,000	
Add: Closing Stock of Finished Goods	1,25,00		—	
$\left[₹2,50,000 \times \frac{5000 \text{ units}}{10,000 \text{ units}}\right]$			1,50,000	
		1,25,000		2,50,000
Contribution		1,25,000		2,50,000
Less: Fixed Cost:				
Fixed Production Overheads	50,000		50,000	
Fixed Selling & Administration Costs	40,000		40,000	
		90,000		90,000
Net Profit		35,000		1,60,000

Observation: In the month of March, as the production volume is more than the sales volume, the net profit as ascertained under absorption costing is more than the net profit under variable costing. This happens due to higher valuation of closing stock under absorption costing.

In the month of April, when the sales volume is more than the production volume, the net profit as ascertained under absorption costing is less than the net profit under variable costing.

Working Notes:

1. Closing Stock of Finished Goods of March 2021 (in volume) = Production Volume – Sales Volume = 10,000 – 5000 = 5000 units.
2. Opening Stock of Finished Goods of April 2021 (in volume) = Closing Stock of Finished Goods of March 2021 = 5000 units.
3. Under Absorption Costing, the stock is valued at the total cost, but under Variable Costing, it is taken at the variable cost only.

Problem 7 Oriental Ltd. released the figures given ahead from its records for year 1 and year 2:

	Year I	Year II
Sales units	2,40,000	2,40,000
Production units	2,40,000	4,00,000
Selling price per unit	20	20
Variable manufacturing cost per unit (₹)	12	12
Variable fixed manufacturing cost per unit (₹)	12,00,000	12,00,000
Variable marketing and administrative costs per unit (₹)	1.25	1.25
Fixed marketing and administrative costs (₹)	4,20,000	4,20,000

(a) Prepare income statements for both years, using full-absorption costing.

(b) Prepare income statements for both years, using variable costing.

(c) Comment on the different operating profit figures. [*B.Com. (H)*]

Solution:

Absorption Costing

Particulars	Year I	Year II
Sales @ 20/- per unit	48,00,000	48,00,000
Less: Cost of Sales		
Variable Manufacturing Cost @ 12 P.U.	28,80,000	48,00,000
Fixed manufacturing cost	12,00,000	12,00,000
Total Factory of goods produced	40,80,000	60,00,000
Add: Opening stock	Nil	Nil
Less: Closing stock (160,000 units @ ₹15 P.U)	—	24,00,000
Factory cost of goods sold and marketing	40,80,000	36,00,000
+ Variable administration overhead (@ 1.25 per unit)	3,00,000	3,00,000
+ Fixed Administration and marketing overhead	4,20,000	4,20,000
Total cost	48,00,000	43,20,000
Profit	Nil	4,80,000

Marginal Costing

Particulars	Year I	Year II
Sales @ 20/- per unit	48,00,000	48,00,000
Less: Variable cost of sales	28,80,000	48,00,000
+ Opening stock	Nil	Nil
– Closing stock @ 12 per unit (160,000 * 12)	Nil	19,20,000
	28,80,000	28,80,000
Add: Variable Administration and Marketing cost @ ₹1.25 per unit	3,00,000	3,00,000
Total variable cost of sales	31,80,000	31,80,000
Contribution = Sales – Variable cost	16,20,000	16,20,000
Less: Fixed Cost		
Fixed factory cost	12,00,000	12,00,000
Fixed Administration and Marketing cost	4,20,000	4,20,000
Total fixed cost	16,20,000	16,20,000
Profit	Nil	Nil

Comment: When there is no opening and closing stock there is no difference in the profit in the marginal costing and absorption costing. But when production exceeds sales profit will be higher in case of absorption costing by ₹4,80,000.

Problem 8 Expo Mart sells its products at ₹73 per unit. The company uses a First-In First-Out actual costing system. A new fixed manufacturing overhead allocation rate is computed each year by dividing the actual fixed manufacturing overhead cost by the actual production costs. The following simplified data are related to its first two years of operation:

	Year I	Year II
Sales (units)	1000	1200
Production (units)	1400	1000
Costs:	₹	₹
Variable manufacturing	700	500
Fixed manufacturing	700	700
Variable marketing and administration	1000	1200
Fixed marketing and administration	400	400

Required:

(i) Prepare income statements based on:

(a) Absorption costing and

(b) Variable costing for each year. [*B.Com. (H)*]

(ii) Give reasons for the difference in the answer.

Solution:

Income Statement (Absorption Costing)

Particulars			Year I	Year II
Sales @ ₹3 per unit			3000	3600
Cost of manufacture:				
Variable	700	500		
Fixed	700	700	1400	1200
Add: Opening Stock			Nil	400
Less: Closing Stock			400	240
Cost of goods Sold			1000	1360
Add: Marketing and administration				
Variable	1000	1200		
Fixed	400	400	1400	1600
Cost of sales (Total cost)			2400	2960
Profit (Sale – Total cost)			600	640

Income Statement (Variable Costing)

Particulars	Year I	Year II
Sales @ ₹3 per unit (1)	3000	3600
Variable manufacturing	700	500
Add: Opening Stock	Nil	200
Less: Closing Stock	(200)	(100)
Cost of goods sold	500	600
Variable marketing and administration cost	1000	1200
Variable cost of sales (2)	1500	1800
Contribution (1) – (2)	1500	1800
Less: Fixed Cost		
Manufacturing	700	700
Marketing and administration	400	400
Income	400	700

Reasons for Difference:

1. Difference in valuation of stock

   Year I: Closing stock is more in absorption costing ₹200 [400 – 200]

   Year II: Opening stock exceeds by ₹200 in absorption costing and the closing stock exceeds by ₹140. Thus, the net difference is ₹60.

Problem 9 The following is the cost information of a production of plastic glass

Variable manufacturing costs ₹4 per unit

Fixed manufacturing costs ₹2,00,000 per year

The normal capacity is set at 2,00,000 units. There are no work-in-progress inventories. In the test year the firm produced 2,00,000 units and sold 90% at a price of ₹7 per unit. In the current year, the firm produced 9,10,000 units and sold 2,15,000 units at the same price. Prepare income statements for both the years based on:

(a) Absorption costing, and (b) Variable costing. [*B.Com. (H)*]

Solution:

Absorption Costing

Particulars	Year I	Year II
Sales @ ₹7/- per unit	12,60,000	15,05,000
Less: Cost of Sales		
Variable Manufacturing Cost @ 4 per unit	8,00,000	8,40,000
Fixed manufacturing cost	2,00,000	2,10,000
Total Factory cost of goods produced	10,00,000	10,50,000
Add: Opening stock	Nil	1,00,000
Less: Closing stock (20,000 and 15,000 units @ ₹5 per unit)	1,00,000	75,000
Factory cost of goods sold	9,00,000	10,75,000
Profit	3,60,000	4,30,000

Marginal Costing

Particulars	Year I	Year II
Sales @ ₹7/- per unit	12,60,000	15,05,000
Less: Variable Cost of Sales		
Variable Manufacturing Cost @ 4 per unit	8,00,000	8,40,000
Add: Opening stock	NIL	80,000
Less: Closing stock (20,000 and 15,000 units @ ₹4 per unit)	80,000	2,10,000
Total Variable cost of sales	7,20,000	8,45,000
Contribution	5,40,000	6,60,000
Less: Fixed Manufacturing Cost	2,00,000	2,00,000
Profit	3,40,000	4,60,000

SOLVED PRACTICAL PROBLEMS

COST-VOLUME-PROFIT ANALYSIS

CONTRIBUTION

- P/V RATIO
- BREAK-EVEN POINT (BEP)
- MARGIN OF SAFETY (MOS)

Problem 1 Calculate the break-even point from the following data, and determine profit if sales are 20% above the break-even point.

Details	Amount (₹)
Direct labour (per unit)	30
Direct material (per unit)	45
Total fixed overhead	1,70,000
Trade discount	5%
Selling price (per unit)	200
Variable overhead	100% on direct labour

Solution:

Details		Amount (₹)
Net sales (200–(0.05 x 200)]		190
Variable cost:		
Direct labour	45	
Direct material	30	
Variable overhead(100% of 30)	30	105
Contribution, i.e., (190–105) [Selling price – Variable cost]		85

Break-even point = Fixed cost/Contribution per unit

= 1,70,000/85 = 2000 units

Break-even point (in ₹) = 2000 × 200 = 400000

Less: Trade discount @ 5% = 20,000

Net sales proceeds (₹) = 3,80,000

When sales are 20% above the break point:

Sales = 2000 + 0.20 × 2000 = 2400 units

Contribution (2400 × 85) = ₹2,04,000

Less: Fixed cost ₹1,70,000

Profit ₹34,000

Problem 2 Find out the break-even point in quantity and value when the monthly fixed cost of Blues Ltd. is ₹4,00,000 and the selling price of the single product is ₹95 and the variable cost of sales is 45.

Solution:

BEP (units) Fixed cost/Contribution per unit

Contribution per unit = SP – V.C.

95 – 45 = ₹50

BEP (in units) = ₹4,00,000/₹50 = 8000 units

BEP (in value) = BEP (units) × Selling price = 8000 × 95 = 7,60,000

OR

BEP (Value) Fixed cost divided by P/V ratio

P/V ratio = Contribution per unit divided by selling price per unit multiplied by 100

= (50/95) × 100 52.63% BEP (Value) = 4,00,000/52.63%

= 7,60,000 (approximately)

Problem 3 Mare Ltd. earned a contribution of ₹4,00,000 and net profit of ₹3,00,000 on sales of ₹16,00,000. Determine margin of safety here.

Solution:

Margin of safety = Profit divided by P/V ratio

P/V = contribution/sales = 4,00,000/14,00,000 = 25 margin of safety 3,00,000/.25 ₹12,00,000

Verification:

M.S. (₹) = Actual sales – Break-even sales

BES Fixed cost/P/V

Fixed cost = Contribution – Profit

= 4,00,000 – 3,00,000 = 1,00,000

B.E.S. = 1,00,000/.25

= 4,00,000 M.S. (₹) = 16,00,000 – 4,00,000

= 12,00,000

Problem 4 Following information about JK Ltd. is given:

Annual fixed cost ₹3,00,000

Selling price ₹153

Variable cost ₹102

Next year cost shall increase by 20%. By what percentage BEP will go up?

Solution:

BEP for the current year:

$$\text{BEP} = \text{Fixed cost/P/V ratio}$$

$$\text{P/V} = 153 - 102 = 51/153\ 1/3\ 153$$

₹30,00,001(1/3) ₹9,00,000

BEP for next year:

$$\text{Fixed cost} = 3,00,000\ (1 + 0.2) = 3,60,000$$

$$\text{P/V} = 1/3$$

(It remains same as in current year because there is no change either in selling price or in variable cost.)

$$\text{BEP}\ 3,60,000/(1/3) = ₹10,80,000$$

Change in BEP difference in two BEP values divided by current year BEP value = 1,80,000/9,00,000 = 0.2 = 20%.

The change in BEP value is exactly the same as the % change in annual fixed cost.

Problem 5 XYZ Ltd. sold 20,000 units during 2020-21 at a price of 500 each. The cost structure is given:

Details	Amount (₹)
Fixed overheads	225
Variable overheads	60
Variable cost	200
Materials	100
Labour	75
Total cost	660

Due to competition, price has to be reduced to ₹400 for the year 2021-2022. Find out additional units to be sold to ensure the same amount of profit as in 2020-2021, assuming that there will be no change in cost.

Solution:

Details	Amount (₹) per unit	Amount (₹) Total
Sales(S)	500	1,00,00,000
Materials	100	20,00,000
Labour	75	15,00,000
Variable overheads	60	12,00,000
Total variable cost: V	200	40,00,000
Contribution: C = S–V	300	60,00,000
Fixed overheads: F	225	45,00,000
Profit: PC–F	75	15,00,000

Contribution at new selling price (per unit) = 400 – 200 = 200 Sales to earn a desired

$$\text{profit} = \frac{\text{Fixed cost + Desired profit}}{\text{Contribution per unit}}$$

Sales to earn a profit of ₹15,00,000 at reduced selling price:

= (45,00,000 + 15,00,000)/200 = 30000 units

Additional units to be sold in 2021-22:

Units to be sold in 2021-22	30,000
Units sold in 2020-21	20,000
Additional units required:	10,000

Problem 6 During the current year Larry's Ltd showed a profit of ₹2,50,000 on a sale of ₹45,00,000. The variable expenses were 32,00,000. Find:

(1) Break-even sales at present

(2) Break-even sales if variable cost increases by 3%

(3) Break-even sales to maintain the profit as at present, if selling price is reduced to 3%

Solution:

Sales = Fixed Cost + Variable Cost + Profits

4,50,00,000 = Fixed Cost + 32,00,000 + 2,50,000

Fixed cost = 10,50,000

P/V ratio = 18,00,000/45,00,000 = 0.4

BEP = 10,50,000/0.4 = 26,25,000

Break-even sales when variable cost is increased by 3%:

P/V ratio (new) = 12,04,000/45,00,000 = 0.268

BEP (new) = 10,50,000/0.268 ₹39,17,910.4

Required sales price when selling price is reduced by 3%:

Sales (modified) = ₹45,00,000 (1 – 0.03) 43,65,000

Contribution (modified) = 43,65,000 – 32,00,000 = ₹11,65,000

P/V ratio (revised) = 11,65,000/43,65,000

Required sales volume = 13,00,000/(11,65,000/43,65,000) = ₹48,70,815.45

Problem 7 P/V ratio for a product is 30%. By what percentage sales value and sales quantity should increase so that even after 10% reduction in selling price the firm continues to earn same profit as before? Assume data to verify.

Solution Assumptions:

(1) Fixed cost is constant.

(2) Maintaining same profit as before means earning same total contribution as before.

	Amount (₹)
Let existing sales be (200 units @ ₹1)	200
Existing variable cost 200 × (1 – 0.3)	140
Existing total contribution	60

The firm should continue to earn contribution of ₹60 even after 10% reduction in unit price.

	Amount (₹)
So new sales (200 × .9)	180
New variable cost = Existing variable cost	140
New contribution	40

New P/V ratio new contribution/New sales = 40/180 2/9

New desired sales value:

Desired contribution/New P/V ratio 60/2/9) = 270

Percentage increase in sales value (270 – 200/200) × 100 = 35% increase

Since price has declined to 90% the quantity should increase by 100/90 to neutralise the effect of price reduction.

Thus, increased quantity to be sold = 270 × 100/90 = 300

Percentage increase in quantity to be sold = (300 – 200)/100 × 100 × 50%

Verification: (assumed data with P/V ratio 30%)

Fixed cost	3,00,000
Selling price per unit	40
Variable cost per unit	28
Existing sales (i.e., 17,500 units @ ₹80 each)	14,00,000

Existing profit = 1,20,000 (14,00,000 × 0.34200001 and (4,20,000 – 3,00,000)

Reduced selling price 72 (0.9 × 80)

New contribution = ₹16 (72 – 56)

New P/V ratio = New contribution/new sales = 16/72

Required sales to earn a profit of ₹1,20,000 = (F + P)/New P/V

(3,00,000 + 1,20,000)/(2/9) = ₹18,90,000

Percentage increase in sales value (18,90,000 – 1,40,00,00)/14,00,000]

0.35, i.e., 35%

New sales units to earn profit of ₹1,20,000 = (F + P)/contribution per unit [(3,00,000 + 1,20,000)/16] = 26,250

Percentage increase in sales units [(25,250 – 17,500)/14,00,000) = 0.5, i.e., 50%

Thus, the results: 35% increase in sales value and 50% increase in sales quantity stand verified.

Problem 8 A firm is earning a profit of ₹4,00,000 at a sale of ₹25,00,000, the P/V ratio being 35%. What should be the requisite sale for maintaining this profit after fixed cost goes up by 25% and the variable cost by 20%?

Solution: RS = [F + P]/(P/V)

25,00,000 = [F + 4,00,0001/0.4

F = 6,00,000

New fixed cost = 6,00,000 × 1.25 = ₹7,50,000

New variable cost:

Let selling price = ₹100, so variable cost = ₹50

New variable cost = 50 × 1.20 = ₹60

New P/V ratio = (100 – 60)/100 = 40%

New RS = [New F + P]/(new P/V ratio)

= (7,50,000 + 4,00,000)/.4

= ₹28,75,000

Problem 9 A company breaks even at sale of ₹5,00,000 whereas its actual sale is ₹6,00,000. The company enjoys P/V ratio of 30%. Calculate:

1. Margin of safety (absolute)
2. Margin of safety (percentage)
3. Fixed cost
4. Additional profit and profit percentage after margin of safety gets doubled

Solution:

(1) Margin of safety (absolute) = Actual sales – Break-even sales

= 6,00,000 – 5,00,000 = 1,00,000

(2) Margin of safety (%age) = Margin of safety (absolute) actual sale

= 1,00,000/6,00,000 = 16.66%

(3) Fixed cost = BEP sale × P/V ratio

= 5,00,000 × 3 = 1,20,000

(4) Profit % on sales = M/S ratio × P/N ratio = .17 × .3 = .051 = 5% (Approximately)

Reconciliation:

Profit MS × P/V ratio

1,00,000 × 0.3 = 30,000

Profit % on sales = 30,000/6,00,000 = 5%

(5) Margin of safety doubles = 2,00,000

Additional margin of safety = 1,00,000

New sales = Break-even sales + New margin of safety

5,00,000 + 2,00,000 = 7,00,000

New sales = Existing sales + Additional margin of safety

6,00,000 + 1,00,000 = 7,00,000

New MS ratio = New ms/New sales 2,00,000/7,00,000

= 2/7 Additional profit = Additional MS

× P/V ratio = 1,00,000 × 0.3 = 30,000

Total profit = existing profit + Additional profit

= 3,00,000 + 3,00,000 = 6,00,000

New profit percentage on sales = New MIS ratio × PN ratio = 2/7 × 0.3 = 8.6%

Problem 10 PN ratio is 20% and MIS ratio is 35%. What is the net profit and break-even point if sales volume is 4,00,000?

Solution: Break-even sales and profit:

Sales	4,00,000
Less: M/S ratio (35% of sales)	1,40,000
Break-even sales	2,60,000

or

Break-even ratio = 1 – M/S ratio = 1 – 0.35 = .65

Break-even sales = 0.65 × 4,00,000 2,60,000

Profit ratio = P/V ratio × M/S ratio = 0.2 × 0.35 = .07 of sales

Net profit 0.07 × 4,00,000 ₹28,000

Alternatively:

Contribution on sales = 4,00,000 × 0.2 = ₹80,000

Contribution on break-even sales = 2,60,000 × .02 = 52,000

At break-even sales

Contribution = Fixed cost

Thus, the fixed cost is ₹52,000

Net profit on sales of 4,00,000 is ₹28,000 (i.e., 80,000 – 52,000)

Problem 11 Sales and profit of BK Ltd. during two periods are given:

Period	Sales (₹)	Profit (₹)
2020	2,00,000	30,000
2021	3,00,000	50,000

(1) Find out the break-even point.

(2) What amount of sales would generate a profit of 80,000?

(3) What will be profit if the sales are ₹3,50,000?

Solution: When sales increase by ₹1,00,000 total cost increases by ₹80,000. Assuming that fixed costs have remained unchanged, the change in total costs is equal to variable cost. Further it is assumed that selling price has not changed. The relationship between differential sales and variable costs provides the ratio of variable costs to sales, i.e., 80,000/1,00,000 = 0.8 or 80%. Thus, the P/V ratio is 1 – 0.8 = 0.2 or 20%. Fixed cost is as under:

Fixed cost = Total costs – (Sales × Variable costs to sales ratio)

= 1,70,000 – (2,00,000 × 0.8)

= 1,70,000 – 1,60,000 = ₹10,000 OR

= 2,50,000 – (3,00,000 × 0.8)

= 2,50,000 – 2,40,000 ₹10,000

Break-even point = Fixed cost (P/V ratio)
= 10,000/0.2
= ₹ 50,000

Sales volume to earn a profit of ₹ 80,000:
= (Fixed cost + Required profit)/(P/V ratio)
= 10,000 + 80,000/0.2
= 90,000/0.2 = ₹ 4,50,000

Profit at the sales volume of 350000
= (350000 × 0.2) – 10000
= 70000 – 10000
= 60000

Problem 12 A firm has ₹ 5,00,000 invested in its plant and sets a goal of 18% annual return of investment. Fixed cost in the factory presently amount to ₹ 1,50,000 per year and variable costs amount to 50 per unit. In the past year the firm produced and sold 4000 units at ₹ 80 each and earned a profit of ₹ 8000. How can the management achieve the budgeted profit by varying different variables like fixed costs, variable costs, quantity sold or increasing the selling price per unit?

Solution: Profit to be earned = 5,00,000 × 0.18 ₹ 90,000

Profit equation = (Quantity × Selling price per unit) – (Quantity × Variable cost per unit)

Fixed costs

Case 1: Achievement of budget profit by varying fixed costs. Let the fixed costs be F

90,000 = [4000 × 80] – [4000 × 50] – F
F ₹ 30,000

Thus, the management must make efforts to reduce the existing fixed cost by ₹ 1,20,000 (i.e., 1,50,000 – 30,000)

Case 2: Achievement of budget profits by varying variable costs

Let the variable costs be V

90,000 = [4000 × 801 – [4000 × VI – 1,50,000]
V = ₹ 20

Thus, the management must make efforts to reduce the existing variable cost by ₹ 30 (i.e., 50 – 20)

Case 3: Achievement of budget profit by varying quantity sold

Let the quantity be Q

90,000 = [Q × 80] – [Q × 50] – 1,50,000
Q = 8000 units

So the management must make efforts to increase the existing quantum of sales by 4000 units (8000 – 4000)

Case 4: Achievement of target profit by varying selling price

Let the selling price be S

$$90{,}000 = [4{,}000 \times 5]\ [4{,}000 \times 50] - 1{,}50{,}000$$

$$S = ₹111$$

So the management must make efforts to increase the selling price by ₹31 (i.e., 111 – 80)

Problem 13 Calculate contribution in each of the following alternative cases:

(a) Sales ₹50,000; Variable Cost ₹20,000
(b) Fixed Costs ₹19,600; Profit ₹12,400
(c) Sales 60,000; P/V Ratio 60%
(d) Break-even sales ₹60,000, P/V ratio 40%, Profit ₹9,000
(e) Fixed Cost ₹25,000; Margin of safety 1800 units, Contribution per unit ₹6
(f) Fixed Cost ₹28,000; Margin of safety ₹12,000; P/V Ratio 50%
(g) Profit ₹25,000; Margin of safety 40%.

Solution:

(a) Contribution = Sales – Variable cost = ₹50,000 – ₹20,000 = ₹30,000
(b) Contribution = Fixed Cost + Profit = ₹19,600 + ₹12,400 = ₹32,000
(c) Contribution = Sales × P/V Ratio = ₹60,000 × 60% = ₹36,000
(d) Contribution = [BEP (in value) × P/V ratio] + Profit
= (₹60,000 × 40%) + ₹9,000 = ₹33,000
(e) Contribution = Fixed cost + [Margin of safety (in units) contribution per unit]
= ₹25,000 + [1,800 units × ₹6] = ₹35,800
(f) Contribution = Fixed cost + [Margin of safety (in value) × P/V ratio]
= ₹28,000 + [₹12,000 × 50%] = ₹34,000
(g) Contribution = Profit/Margin of safety (%) = ₹25,000/40% = ₹62,500

Problem 14 Calculate P/V ratio in each of the following alternative cases :

(a) Selling Price ₹20 and Marginal Cost ₹12.
(b) Marginal Cost ₹78 and Contribution ₹12.
(c) Variable Cost to Sales Ratio 40%.
(d) Fixed Costs ₹20,000, Profit ₹5,000, Sales ₹40,000.
(e) BEP ₹60,000 and Fixed cost ₹20,000.
(f) Margin of safety ₹8,000, Fixed cost ₹10,000 and Actual Sales ₹48,000.
(g) Margin of Safety Ratio 40%, Profit ₹4,800 and Actual Sales ₹80,000.
(h)

	Year 1	Year 2
Total Sales	20,000	30,000
Total Cost	17,600	21,600

Solution:

$$\text{(a) P/V Ratio} = \frac{\text{Contribution}}{\text{Sales}} \times 100 = \frac{\text{Contribution}}{\text{Marginal cost + Contribution}} \times 100$$

$$= \frac{8}{(8+12)} \times 100 = 40\%$$

(b) $\text{P/V Ratio} = \frac{\text{Contribution}}{\text{Sales}} \times 100 = \frac{\text{Contribution}}{\text{Marginal cost} + \text{Contribution}} \times 100$

$$= \frac{₹12}{₹8 + ₹12} \times 100 = 60\%$$

(c) P/V Ratio = 100 – Variable cost to Sales ratio = 100% – 40% = 60%.

(d) $\text{P/V Ratio} = \frac{\text{Fixed cost} + \text{Profit}}{\text{Sales}} \times 100 = \frac{₹20{,}000 + ₹5{,}000}{₹40{,}000} \times 100 = 62.5\%$

(e) $\text{P/V Ratio} = \frac{\text{Fixed cost}}{\text{BEP (in value)}} \times 100 = \frac{₹20{,}000}{₹60{,}000} \times 100 = 33\frac{1}{3}\%$

(f) BEP = Actual sales – Margin of safety = ₹ 48,000 – ₹ 8,000 = ₹ 40,000

$\text{P/V Ratio} = \frac{\text{Fixed cost}}{\text{BEP}} \times 100 = \frac{₹10{,}000}{₹40{,}000} \times 100 = 25\%$

(g) $\text{M.S. Ratio} = \frac{\text{Margin of safety}}{\text{Sales}} \times 100$

Margin of Safety = Sales × M.S. ratio = ₹ 80,000 × 40% = ₹ 32,000

$\text{P/V Ratio} = \frac{\text{Profit}}{\text{Margin of safety}} \times 100 = \frac{₹4{,}800}{32{,}000} \times 100 = 15\%$

(h) Profit = Total sales – Total cost

For year 1 : ₹ 20,000 – ₹ 17,600 = ₹ 2,400

For year 2 : ₹ 30,000 – ₹ 21,600 = ₹ 8,400

$\text{P/V Ratio} = \frac{\text{Change in profit}}{\text{Change in sales}} \times 100$

$$= \frac{₹8{,}400 \quad ₹2{,}400}{₹30{,}000 \quad ₹20{,}000} \times 100 = \frac{₹6{,}000}{₹10{,}000} \times 100 = 60\%$$

Problem 15 Calculate break-even point in each of the following situations:

(a) Margin of safety 1500 units and Actual sales 5000 units

(b) Margin of safety 40% and Actual sales ₹ 50,000

(c) P/V ratio 40%, Profit ₹ 2000 and margin of safety $33\frac{1}{3}\%$

(d) Variable cost to sales ratio 60%, Profit ₹ 2,400 and Margin of safety 60%

Solution:

(a) BEP = Actual sales – Margin of safety = 5000 units – 1500 units = 3500 units

(b) BEP = Actual sales – Margin of safety = ₹ 50,000 – 40% of ₹ 50,000 = ₹ 30,000

(c) $\text{Margin of safety} = \dfrac{\text{Profit}}{\text{P/V ratio}} = \dfrac{₹2000}{40\%} = ₹15{,}000$

$\text{Actual sales} = \dfrac{\text{Margin of safety}}{\text{MS ratio}} = \dfrac{₹5{,}000}{33\frac{1}{3}} = ₹15{,}000$

BEP (in ₹) = Actual sales – Margin of safety
= ₹ 15,000 – ₹ 5000 = ₹ 10,000

(d) P/V ratio = 100% – Variable cost to sales ratio
= 100% – 60% = 40%

$\text{Margin of Safety} = \dfrac{\text{Profit}}{\text{P/V ratio}} = \dfrac{₹2400}{40\%} = ₹6000$

$\text{Actual Sales} = \dfrac{\text{Margin of safety}}{\text{MS ratio}} = \dfrac{₹6000}{60\%} = ₹10{,}000$

BEP (in ₹) = Actual Sales – Margin of safety
= ₹ 10,000 – ₹ 6000 = ₹ 4000

Problem 16 Calculate margin of safety in each of the following situation:

(a) Break-even sales 11600 units, actual sales 20000 units
(b) Profit ₹ 10,000, P/V ratio 40%
(c) Break-even sales 40%, actual sales ₹ 20,000
(d) Break-even sales 70%.

Solution:

(a) Margin of safety = Actual sales (in units) – BEP (in units)
= 20000 units – 11600 units = 8400 units

(b) $\text{Margin of safety} = \dfrac{\text{Profit}}{\text{P/V ratio}} = \dfrac{10{,}000}{40\%} = ₹25{,}000$

(c) Margin of safety = Actual sales – BEP
= ₹ 20,000 – 40% of 20,000 = ₹ 12,000

(d) Margin of safety = 100% – BEP (in %) = 100% – 70% = 30%

Problem 17

(a) From the following information of a firm for the year ended March 2020, calculate the P/V ratio, break-even point and margin of safety at this level.
Sales ₹ 80,000; Variable Cost ₹ 60,000; Fixed Cost ₹ 15,000.

(b) The ratio of variable cost to sales is 80%. The break-even point occurs at 40% of the capacity sales. Find the capacity sales when fixed costs are ₹ 1,00,000. Also compute profit at 60% of the capacity sales.

(c) X Ltd. has earned contribution of ₹1,00,000 and net profit of ₹75,000 on sales of ₹4,00,000. What is its margin of safety?

(d) If margin of safety is 40% of sales, find fixed costs when profit is ₹50,000.

Solution:

(a) $\text{P/V Ratio} = \dfrac{\text{Contribution}}{\text{Sales}} \times 100 = \dfrac{S - V}{S} \times 100$

$= \dfrac{80{,}000 - 60{,}000}{80{,}000} \times 100 = 25\%$

$\text{Break-even point} = \dfrac{\text{Fixed cost}}{\text{P/V ratio}} = \dfrac{15{,}000}{25\%} = ₹60{,}000$

Margin of safety = Sales – Break-even point

= 80,000 – 60,000 = ₹20,000

(b) P/V Ratio = 100 – Variable cost to sales = 100 – 80% = 20%

$\text{Break-even sales} = \dfrac{\text{Fixed costs}}{\text{P/V ratio}} = \dfrac{₹1{,}00{,}000}{20\%} = ₹5{,}00{,}000$

$\text{Actual capacity sales} = \dfrac{\text{Break-even sales (in ₹)}}{\text{Break-even sales (\%)}}$

$= \dfrac{₹5{,}00{,}000}{40\%} = ₹12{,}50{,}000$

Statement showing Profit at 60% of Capacity Sales

Sales (60% of ₹12,50,000)	₹7,50,000
Less: Variable costs (80% of ₹7,50,000)	₹6,00,000
Contribution	₹1,50,000
Less: Fixed costs	₹1,00,000
Profit	₹50,000

(c) $\text{P/V Ratio} = \dfrac{\text{Contribution}}{\text{Sales}} \times 100 = \dfrac{₹1{,}00{,}000}{₹4{,}00{,}000} \times 100 = 25\%$

$\text{Margin of Safety} = \dfrac{\text{Profit}}{\text{P/V ratio}} = \dfrac{₹75{,}000}{25\%} = ₹3{,}00{,}000$

(d) Margin of safety = 40% of sales

Break-even sales = 60% of sales.

$$\text{Margin of Safety} = \frac{\text{Profit}}{\text{P/V ratio}}$$

$$\text{Break-even sales} = \frac{\text{Fixed cost}}{\text{P/V ratio}}$$

$$\frac{40\%}{60\%} = \frac{\text{Profit}}{\text{Fixed cost}} \div \frac{\text{Fixed cost}}{\text{P/V ratio}}$$

$$\frac{40\%}{60\%} = \frac{\text{Profit}}{\text{Fixed cost}}$$

$$\frac{2}{3} = \frac{₹50{,}000}{\text{Fixed Cost}}$$

$$\text{Fixed Cost} = \frac{(50{,}000 \times 3)}{2} = ₹75{,}000$$

Problem 18

(a) Margin of safety 40%, Fixed cost ₹ 1,50,000, Variable cost ratio to sales 80%. Compute the amount of actual sales.

(b) Fixed cost ₹ 20,000, Actual sales ₹ 1,60,000, Margin of safety ₹ 10,000. Compute the P/V ratio?

(c) If MS is 40% of sales, find the fixed cost when profit is ₹ 20,000.

(d) Compute margin of safety ratio when Profit is ₹ 8,000 and total contribution is ₹ 20,000.

Solution:

(a)

$$\text{P/V ratio} = 100 - 80\% = 20\%$$

$$\text{Break-even point} = \frac{\text{Fixed cost}}{\text{P/V ratio}} = \frac{1{,}50{,}000}{20\%} = ₹7{,}50{,}000$$

$$\text{Sales} = \frac{\text{BE point in ₹}}{60\%} = \frac{7{,}50{,}000}{60\%} = ₹12{,}50{,}000$$

(b)

$$\text{Break-even point} = \text{Actual sales} - \text{Margin of safety}$$

$$= 60{,}000 - 10{,}000 = ₹50{,}000$$

$$\text{P/V ratio} = \frac{\text{Fixed cost}}{\text{B.E. point}} = \frac{20{,}000}{50{,}000} \times 100 = 40\%$$

(c) Here,

$$\text{M/S} = 40\% \text{ of Sales}$$

$$\therefore \quad \text{BEP} = 100 - 40 = 60\% \text{ of Sales}$$

$$\text{Margin of safety} = \frac{\text{Profit}}{\text{P/V ratio}}$$

$$40\% \text{ of sales} = \frac{20{,}000}{\text{P/V ratio}} \qquad \text{...(i)}$$

$$\text{BEP} = \frac{\text{Fixed cost}}{\text{P/V ratio}}$$

$$60\% \text{ of sales} = \frac{F}{\text{P/V ratio}} \qquad \text{...(ii)}$$

Now, dividing Eq. (ii) by Eq. (i), we get:

$$\frac{60\% \text{ of sales}}{40\% \text{ of sales}} = \frac{F}{\text{P/V ratio}} \times \frac{\text{P/V ratio}}{20{,}000}$$

or

$$\frac{60}{40} = \frac{F}{20{,}000}$$

$$\therefore \quad \text{Fixed Cost} = \frac{60 \times 20{,}000}{40} = ₹30{,}000$$

(d)

$$\text{Margin of safety ratio} = \frac{\text{Profit}}{\text{Total contribution}} \times 100$$

$$= \frac{8000}{20{,}000} \times 100 = 40\%$$

Problem 19

(a) Find out the Break-even point when P/V ratio 40%, Margin of safety 20%, Profit ₹50,000.

(b) What is the amount of margin of safety when profit is ₹20,000, contribution ₹30,000 and sales ₹2,00,000. Also determine the break-even point.

(c) Calculate the amount of actual sales when profit ₹10,000, break-even point ₹50,000 and fixed cost ₹20,000.

(d) Variable cost is 60% of sales and margin of safety is 20%. What is the amount of fixed cost if sales are ₹5,00,000.

(e) When the volume is 3000 units, the average cost is ₹4 per unit. When the volume is ₹4000 units, the average cost is ₹3.50. The BEP is 5,000 units. Find the P/V ratio.

Solution:

(a)

$$\text{Profit} = \text{Actual sales} \times \text{Margin of safety \%} \times \text{P/V ratio}$$

$$\therefore \quad \text{Actual sales} = \frac{\text{Profit}}{\text{M/S ratio} \times \text{P/V ratio}} = \frac{50{,}000}{40\% \times 20\%} = ₹6{,}25{,}000$$

$$\text{Break-even point} = \text{Actual sales} - \text{Margin of safety}$$

$$= 6{,}25{,}000 - (20\% \times 6{,}25{,}000) = ₹5{,}00{,}000$$

(b)

$$\text{P/V ratio} = \frac{\text{Contribution}}{\text{Sales}} \times 100 = \frac{30{,}000}{2{,}00{,}000} \times 100 = 15\%$$

$$\text{Margin of safety} = \frac{\text{Profit}}{\text{P/V ratio}} = \frac{20{,}000}{15\%} = ₹\,1{,}33{,}333$$

$$\text{Fixed cost} = \text{Contribution} - \text{Profit}$$

$$= ₹\,30{,}000 - ₹\,20{,}000 = ₹\,10{,}000$$

$$\text{Break-even point} = \frac{\text{Fixed Cost}}{\text{P/V ratio}} = \frac{10{,}000}{15\%} = ₹\,66{,}667$$

(c) $$\text{P/V ratio} = \frac{\text{Fixed Cost}}{\text{B.E. Point}} = \frac{20{,}000}{50{,}000} = 40\%$$

$$\text{Sales} = \frac{\text{Fixed cost + Profit}}{\text{P/V ratio}} = \frac{20{,}000 + 10{,}000}{40\%} = ₹\,75{,}000$$

(d) $$\text{P/V ratio} = 100 - 60\% = 40\%$$

$$\text{Break-even point} = ₹\,5{,}00{,}000 - (20\% \times ₹\,5{,}00{,}000) = ₹\,4{,}00{,}000$$

$$\text{Break-even point} = \frac{\text{Fixed cost}}{\text{P/V ratio}}$$

$$\text{Fixed cost} = \text{Break-even point} \times \text{P/V ratio}$$

$$= ₹\,4{,}00{,}000 \times 40\% = ₹\,1{,}60{,}000$$

(e) Total Cost at 4000 units = 4000 units × ₹ 3.50 ₹ 14,000

Total Cost at 3000 units = 3000 units × ₹ 4.00 ₹ 12,000

$$\therefore \quad \text{Variable Cost per unit} = \frac{\text{Increase in cost}}{\text{Increase in output}} = \frac{₹2000}{₹1000} = ₹\,2$$

$$\text{Fixed Cost} = \text{Total Cost} - \text{Variable Cost}$$

$$= 14{,}000 - (4{,}000 \text{ units} \times ₹\,2) = 6{,}000$$

$$\text{Now, Contribution per unit} = \frac{\text{Fixed cost}}{\text{BEPS in units}} = \frac{₹6000}{5000 \text{ units}} = ₹\,1.20$$

$$\text{Selling Price} = \text{VC} + \text{Contribution per unit}$$

$$= 1.20 + 2 = ₹\,3.20$$

$$\text{P/V Ratio} = \frac{\text{Contribution}}{\text{Sales}} \times 100 = \frac{1.20}{3.20} \times 100 = 37.50\%$$

Problem 20

(a) When sales increase from ₹ 40,000 to ₹ 60,000 and profit increases by ₹ 5000. Compute the P/V ratio.

(b) A company which has a margin of safety of ₹ 4 lakhs makes a profit of ₹ 80,000. Its fixed cost is ₹ 5 lakhs. What is break-even sales? *[B.Com. (H)]*

Solution:

(a) $$\text{P/V ratio} = \frac{\text{Change in profit}}{\text{Change in sales}} \times 100$$

$$= \frac{5{,}000 \times 100}{20{,}000} = 25\%$$

(b) $$\text{Margin of Safety} = \frac{\text{Profit}}{\text{P/V ratio}}$$

$$₹4{,}00{,}000 = \frac{₹80{,}000}{\text{P/V ratio}}$$

$$\text{P/V Ratio} = \frac{₹80{,}000}{₹4{,}00{,}000} = 20\%$$

$$\text{Break-even Sales} = \frac{\text{Fixed cost}}{\text{P/V ratio}}$$

$$= \frac{₹5{,}00{,}000}{20\%} = ₹25{,}00{,}000$$

Problem 21 Attempt the following:

(i) If Margin of Safety is ₹3,60,000 (40% of sales and P/V ratio is 30% of AB Ltd., calculate its:

(1) Break-even sales; and

(2) Amount of profit on sales of ₹10,00,000.

(ii) If fixed costs are ₹4000, variable costs ₹32,000 and break-even point ₹20,000, find out:

(1) Sales

(2) Net profit

(iii) The ratio of variable cost to sales is 70%.

The break-even point occurs at 60% of the capacity sales. Find the capacity sales when fixed costs are ₹90,000. Also compute profit at 75% of the capacity sales.

[*B.Com. (H.)*]

Solution:

(i) Margin of Safety (MS)	40%
Actual sales (3,60,000 ÷ 40%)	₹9,00,000
Break-even sales (9,00,000 (1 – MS) = (₹9,00,000 × (1 – 4)	₹5,40,000
Profit volume ratio (P/V ratio)	0.3
Fixed cost (5,40,000 × 0.3)	₹1,62,000
Profit on sales of ₹10,00,000	
(Sales × P/V ratio) – Fixed cost	
(₹10,00,000 × 0.3) – ₹1,62,000	₹1,38,000

(ii)

$$\text{P/V ratio} = \frac{\text{Fixed cost}}{\text{BE sales}}$$

= ₹4000 ÷ ₹20,000 = 20%

Variable cost = 1 – 20% = 80%

Sales = Variable cost ÷ 80%

= ₹32,000 ÷ 80% = ₹40,000

Net profit = Contribution – Fixed cost

= (₹40,000 × 20%) – ₹4,000

= ₹4,000

(iii)

Variable cost = 70%

P/V ratio (1 – .70) = 30%

BE sales (90,000 – 30%) = ₹3,00,000

Capacity sales (3,00,000 ÷ .6) = ₹5,00,000

Profit at 75% of capacity sales = (₹5,00,000 × .75 × .3) – ₹90,000

= ₹22,500

Problem 22 T-Tunes Ltd. is selling music players for which the following information is available:

Selling price per unit	₹150
Trade discount	10%
Direct material cost per unit	₹60
Direct labour cost per unit	₹30
Fixed overheads	₹1,20,000
Variable overheads based on direct labour cost	100%

If sales are 20% above the BEP, you are required to compute the net profits.

Solution:

	₹	₹
Selling Price per unit:		150
Less: Trade Discount (10% of ₹150)		15
Net selling price per unit		135
Less: Variable Cost per unit:		
Direct material	60	
Direct labour	30	
Variable overhead (100% of ₹30)	30	120
Contribution per unit		15

Total fixed cost = ₹1,20,000

$$\therefore \quad \text{BEP (in units)} = \frac{\text{Total fixed cost}}{\text{Contribution per unit}} = \frac{1,20,000}{15} = 8,000 \text{ units}$$

$$\therefore \quad \text{BEP (in value)} = 8,000 \text{ units} \times ₹135 = ₹10,80,000$$

When sales are 20% above BEP:

Sales (in units) = 8000 units + 20% = 9600 units

	₹
Total Contribution at this level of sales (9,600 units × ₹15)	1,44,000
Less: Fixed cost	1,20,000
Profit	24,000

Problem 23 A company provides you the following information regarding its performance for the last two years:

	Sales	Profit
Year 2019	₹2,00,000	12,000
Year 2020	₹2,50,000	17,000

Find:

(a) P/V ratio

(b) Fixed cost

(c) Profit when sales are ₹1,80,000

(d) Sales required to earn a profit of ₹5000.

Solution:

	Sales	Profit
Year 2019	₹2,00,000	12,000
Year 2020	₹2,50,000	17,000
Change	₹50,000	5000

(a) $\text{P/V ratio} = \frac{\text{Change in profit}}{\text{Change in sales}} \times 100 = \frac{5000}{50,000} \times 100 = 10\%$

(b) Contribution in 2019 = (2,00,000 × 10%)	₹20,000
Less: Profit	₹12,000
Fixed cost	₹ 8000

(c) Contribution (₹1,80,000 × 10%)	₹18,000
Less: Fixed costs	₹ 8000
Profit	₹10,000

(d) $\text{Desired sales} = \frac{\text{Fixed cost + Desired profit}}{\text{P/V ratio}} = \frac{8000 + 5000}{10\%} = ₹1,30,000$

Problem 24 A company had incurred fixed expenses of ₹2,50,000 with a sales of ₹10,00,000 and earned a profit of ₹1,50,000 during the first half-year. In the second half, it suffered a loss of ₹50,000. You are required to calculate:

(i) P/V ratio, BEP and margin of safety for the first half-year.

(ii) Sales for the second half-year assuming that the Selling Price and fixed expenses remained unchanged.

(iii) The BEP and MS for the whole year. [*C.S Inter, Modified*]

Solution:

(i)
$$\text{P/V ratio} = \frac{\text{Contribution}}{\text{Sales}} \times 100 = \frac{F+P}{S} \times 100$$

For the first half-year:

$$\text{P/V ratio} = \frac{(2{,}50{,}000 + 1{,}50{,}000)}{10{,}00{,}000} \times 100 = 40\%$$

$$\text{BEP (in ₹)} = \frac{\text{Total fixed cost}}{\text{P/V ratio}} = \frac{2{,}50{,}000}{40\%} = ₹6{,}25{,}000$$

$$\therefore \quad \text{MS} = \text{Total sales} - \text{BEP} = ₹10{,}00{,}000 - ₹6{,}25{,}000 = ₹3{,}75{,}000$$

(ii)
$$\text{P/V ratio} = \frac{\text{Contribution}}{\text{Sales}} \times 100 = \frac{F+P}{S} \times 100$$

$$40 = \frac{(2{,}50{,}000 - 50{,}000)}{S} \times 100 = ₹5{,}00{,}000$$

∴ Sales for the second half-year = ₹5,00,000

(iii) Total Fixed Cost for the whole year = ₹2,50,000 + ₹2,50,000 = ₹5,00,000

P/V Ratio remains constant throughout the year = 40%

$$\therefore \text{BEP for the whole year} = \frac{\text{Total fixed cost}}{\text{P/V ratio}} \times 100$$

$$= ₹5{,}00{,}000/40\% = ₹12{,}50{,}000$$

∴ MS for the whole year = Total sales for the whole year – BEP for the whole year

= (₹10,00,000 + ₹5,00,000) – ₹12,50,000 = ₹2,50,000

Problem 25 Given below are the sales and profits of the two halves of the year:

	1st half	2nd half
Sales	₹1,00,000	₹1,20,000
Profit	₹30,000	₹38,000

Fixed cost remains same for the two periods. Selling price and variable cost per unit remain unchanged. Calculate the following:

(i) P/V ratio for each half and for the year.

(ii) Fixed cost for each half and for the year.
(iii) BEP for each half and for the year.
(iv) Half-yearly sale to earn half-yearly profit of ₹40,000.
(v) Annual sale to earn annual profit of ₹90,000. [*B.Com. (Hons.)*]

Solution:

	Sales ₹	Profit ₹
1st half	1,00,000	30,000
2nd half	1,20,000	38,000
Change	20,000	8,000

(i) $\text{P/V ratio} = \dfrac{\text{Change in profit}}{\text{Change in sales}} \times 100$

(for each half year and for the year) $= \dfrac{₹8000}{20,000} \times 100 = 40\%$

(ii) *Fixed cost for each half year*

Sales	1,00,000
Contribution (40% of sales)	40,000
Less: Profit	30,000
Fixed Cost	10,000

Fixed Cost for the whole year = 10,000 + 10,000 = ₹20,000

(iii) *BEP for each half year and for the year*

$$\text{BEP (₹)} = \frac{\text{Fixed cost}}{\text{P/V ratio}}$$

$$= \frac{10,000}{40\%} = ₹25,000$$

$$\text{For the year} = \frac{20,000}{40\%} = ₹50,000$$

(iv) *Half-yearly sale to earn half-yearly profit of 40,000*

$$\text{Desired sales} = \frac{\text{Fixed cost + Desired profit}}{\text{P/V ratio}}$$

$$= \frac{₹10,000 + 40,000}{40\%} = ₹1,25,000$$

(v) *Annual Sales to earn annual profit of ₹90,000*

$$\text{Desired sale} = \frac{\text{Fixed cost + Desired profit}}{\text{P/V ratio}}$$

$$= \frac{₹20,000 + 90,000}{40\%} = ₹2,75,000$$

Problem 26 G.S. Ltd. manufactures a single product for which market demand exists for additional quantity. Present sale of ₹60,000 per month utilises only 60% capacity of the plant. Sales Manager assures that with a reduction of 10% in the price, he would be in a position to increase the sale by about 25% to 30%.

The following data are available:

Selling Price	₹10 per unit
Variable Cost	₹ 3 per unit
Semi-variable Cost	₹6000 fixed plus ₹0.50 per unit
Fixed Cost	₹20,000 at present level which is estimated to increase to ₹24,000 at 80% output.

You are required to submit the following statements to the Board showing:

1. The operating profits at 60%, 70% and 80% levels (a) at current selling price and (b) at proposed selling price.
2. The percentage increase in the present output which will be required to maintain the present profit margin at the proposed selling price.

[*B.Com. (Hons.)*]

Solution:

1. (a) Statement of Profit at Current Selling Price

Particulars	6000 units (60%)	7000 units (70%)	8000 units (80%)
Sales @ 10 per unit	60,000	70,000	80,000
Less: Variable cost (working note 1)	21,000	24,500	28,000
Contribution	39,000	45,500	52,000
Less: Fixed cost (working note 1)	26,000	26,000	30,000
Profit	13,000	19,500	22,000

1. (b) Statement of Profit at Proposed Selling Price

Particulars	6000 units (60%)	7000 units (70%)	8000 units (80%)
Sales @₹9 per unit	54,000	63,000	72,000
Less: Variable cost	21,000	24,500	28,000
Contribution	33,000	38,500	48,000
Less: Fixed cost	26,000	26,000	30,000
Profit	7,000	12,500	18,000

2. Increase in output to maintain same profit :

$$\text{Desired sales} = \frac{\text{FC} + \text{P}}{\text{Revised CPU}}$$

$$= \frac{26{,}000 + 13{,}000}{(9 - 3.50)}$$

$$= \frac{39{,}000}{5.50} = 7091 \text{ units}$$

$$\text{Increase in sales} = 7{,}091 - 6000 = 1091 \text{ units}$$

$$\% \text{ Increase} = \frac{1{,}091}{6{,}000} \times 100 = 18.18\%$$

Working Note:

1. The semi-VC is split into fixed and variable and is added to the respective costs.

VC	= 3 + 0.50	= ₹3.50 per unit
FC	= ₹20,000 + ₹6,000	= ₹26,000

Problem 27 In a purely competitive market 10,000 units of a product can be manufactured and sold and a certain amount of profit is generated. It is estimated that 2000 units of that product need to be manufactured and sold in a monopoly market to earn the same amount of profit. Profit under both the conditions is targeted at ₹2,00,000. The variable cost per unit is ₹100 and total fixed cost is ₹60,000. You are required to determine the selling prices under both monopoly and competitive conditions. [*B.Com (Hons.)*]

Solution:

Let the selling price per unit be = x

Monopoly Market

Total Sales =	2000 x
Variable cost = 2,000 × 100 =	₹ 2,00,000
Fixed cost	₹ 60,000
Total cost	₹ 2,60,000
Desired profit	₹ 2,00,000

$$\text{Selling price} = \frac{(\text{Total cost} + \text{Desired profit})}{\text{Number of units}}$$

$$= \frac{2{,}60{,}000 + 2{,}00{,}000}{2000}$$

$$= ₹230$$

Competitive Market

Total sales = 10,000x

Variable cost = 10,000 × 100 =	₹ 10,00,000
Fixed cost	₹ 60,000
Total cost	₹ 10,60,000
Desired profit	₹ 2,00,000

$$SP = \frac{10,00,000 + 60,000 + 2,00,000}{10,000} = ₹126$$

Problem 28 A product is earning a post-tax profit of ₹90,000 when rate of income tax is 40%. Selling price of the product is ₹50 and per unit variable cost is ₹30. How many more units should he sell to earn the same post-tax profit when tax rate goes up to 50%? The total fixed cost of the firm is ₹2 lakhs for the period. Also verify your answer.

Solution:

$$\text{Present sale} = \frac{F + \frac{P}{1-t}}{S-V} = \frac{2,00,000 + \frac{60,000}{1-.4}}{50-30} = 17500 \text{ units}$$

$$\text{Desired sale} = \frac{2,00,000 + \frac{60,000}{1-.5}}{50-30} = 19000 \text{ units}$$

Additional units to be sold = 19,000 – 17,500 = 1500 units.

Verification:

	17,500 units Tax rate 40%	19,000 units Tax rate 50%
Sale @ ₹50	₹8,75,000	₹9,50,000
Less: Variable cost @ ₹30	(5,25,000)	(5,70,000)
Contribution	3,50,000	3,80,000
Less: Fixed cost	–2,00,000	–2,00,000
Profit before tax	1,50,000	1,80,000
Less: Tax @ 40% & 50%	–60,000	(90,000)
Profit after Tax	₹90,000	₹90,000

Problem 29 A producer is earning a post-tax profit of ₹80,000 at sale of 10000 units. Per unit contribution is ₹12. What will be the post-tax profit at sale of 15000 units if income tax rate is 20%?

Solution: Pre-tax profit at sale of 10000 units $= \frac{80,000}{1-t} = \frac{80,000}{1-.2} = ₹1,00,000$

Change in pre-tax profit = Change in sale units × Per unit contribution

= (15,000 – 10,000) × 12 = ₹60,000

∴ Pre-tax profit at sale of 15,000 units = 1,00,000 + 60,000 = ₹1,60,000

$$\text{Post-tax profit} = 1{,}60{,}000 \times \frac{80}{100} = ₹1{,}28{,}000.$$

Problem 30 A company budgets for a production of 1,00,000 units. The variable cost per unit is ₹15 and fixed cost ₹5 per unit. The company fixes its selling price to fetch a profit of 20% on cost.

(i) What is the P/V ratio?

(ii) What is the BEP?

(iii) If it reduces its Selling Price by 5%, how much does the revised selling price affect the BEP and the P/V ratio?

(iv) If a profit increase of 10% is desired more than the budget, what should be the sales at the reduced prices? [*B.Com. (Hons) Modified*]

Solution:

Statement showing Sales for 100000 units

Particulars	₹
Variable cost (1,00,000 × ₹15)	15,00,000
Fixed cost (1,00,000 × ₹5)	5,00,000
Total cost	20,00,000
Add: Budgeted Profit (20% on 20,00,000)	4,00,000
Sales Value of Budgeted Production of 1,00,000 units	24,00,000

$$\therefore \text{Selling price per unit} = \frac{24{,}00{,}000}{1{,}00{,}000} = ₹24$$

∴ Contribution per unit = S – V = ₹24 – ₹15 = 9

$$\text{(i) P/V Ratio} = \frac{\text{Contribution}}{\text{Sales}} \times 100 = \frac{9}{24 \times 100} = 37.5\%$$

$$\text{(ii) BEP (in units)} = \frac{\text{Fixed cost}}{\text{Contribution per unit}} = \frac{5{,}00{,}000}{9} = 55{,}556 \text{ units}$$

$$\text{BEP (in ₹)} = \frac{\text{Total fixed cost}}{\text{P/V ratio}} = \frac{5{,}00{,}000}{37.5\%} = ₹13{,}33{,}333$$

(iii)

	₹
Current selling price per unit	24
Less: Reduction in selling price (5% of 24)	1.20
New selling price per unit	22.80
Less: Variable cost per unit	15.00
New contribution per unit	7.80

$$\therefore \text{New BEPS (in units)} = \frac{\text{Fixed cost}}{\text{New contribution per unit}} = \frac{500000}{7.80} = 64103 \text{ units}$$

$$\therefore \quad \text{New P/V ratio} = \frac{\text{New contribution per unit}}{\text{New selling price per unit}} \times 100 = \frac{7.80}{22.80} \times 100 = 34.21\%$$

(iv) Desired Profit = 4,00,000 + 40,000 = ₹4,40,000

$$\text{Desired sales (units)} = \frac{\text{Fixed cost + Profit}}{\text{Contribution per unit}}$$

$$= \frac{(5{,}00{,}000 + 4{,}40{,}000)}{7.80} = ₹1{,}20{,}513 \text{ units}$$

$$\text{Desired sales (₹)} = \frac{\text{Fixed cost + Desired profit}}{\text{P/V ratio}}$$

$$= \frac{(5{,}00{,}000 + 4{,}40{,}000)}{34.21\%} = ₹27{,}47{,}735$$

Problem 31 Delta Corporation provides you the following information:

	Year 2019	Year 2020
Total sales	₹40,000	₹60,000
Total cost	₹35,200	₹43,200

Calculate the following:

(a) The Variable cost to sales ratio; (b) the Profit/volume ratio; (c) Fixed costs; (d) Break-Even Point; (e) Margin of safety; (f) the amount of profit/loss when sales are ₹50,000; (g) the amount of sales required to earn a profit of ₹15,800; (h) the amount of sales required to earn profit @ 10% on sales; (i) the amount of profit for the year 2021 after taking into consideration the 10% decrease in selling price but 20% increase in physical sales volume and fixed costs.

Solution:

(a) $$\text{Variable Cost to Sales Ratio} = \frac{\text{Difference in total cost}}{\text{Difference in total sales}} \times 100$$

$$= \frac{(43{,}200 - 35{,}200)}{(60{,}000 - 40{,}000)} \times 100 = 40\%$$

(b) Profit/Volume Ratio = 100% – Variable cost to Sales ratio

= 100% – 40% = 60%

(c) Fixed costs = Contribution – Profit

Taking the figures relating to 2019

Contribution = 60% of ₹40,000 = ₹24,000

Less: Profit = ₹40,000 – ₹35,200 = ₹4,800

Fixed Costs = ₹19,200

(d) $$\text{Break-even Point} = \frac{\text{Fixed costs}}{\text{P/V ratio}} = \frac{₹19{,}200}{60\%} = ₹32{,}000$$

(e) Margin of Safety = Actual Sales – Break-even sales

For 2019 = ₹40,000 – ₹32,000 = ₹8,000

For 2020 = ₹60,000 – ₹32,000 = ₹28,000

(f) Profit/Loss at sales of ₹50,000

Profit = Contribution – Fixed costs

= 60% of ₹50,000 – ₹19,200 = ₹10,800

(g) Sales required to earn a profit of ₹15,800

$$\text{Desired sales} = \frac{\text{Fixed costs + Desired profit}}{\text{P/V ratio}}$$

$$= \frac{₹19{,}200 + ₹15{,}800}{60\%} = ₹58{,}333$$

(h) Sales required to earn profit @ 10% on sales.

Suppose, sales = x

Sales	x
Less : Variable cost	$0.4x$
Contribution	$0.6x$
Less : Fixed costs	19200
Profit	$0.6x - 19200$

⇒ $0.6x - 19200 = 10\%$ of x (given)

or, $.5x = 19200$

$x = 19200/.5 =$ ₹38,400

(i) Sales (90% of 60,000 + 20% of (90% of 60,000)]	64,800
Less : Variable cost [40% of (60,000 × 120%)]	28,800
Contribution	36,000
Less : Fixed costs (19,200 + 20% of ₹19,200)	23,040
Profit	12,960

Problem 32 The following information is obtained from the records of a production unit

Sales (4000 units)		₹2,00,000
Material consumed	₹80,000	
Variable overheads	₹20,000	
Labour charges	₹40,000	

Fixed overheads	₹36,000	1,76,000
Net profit		24,000

Compute:

(i) The number of units by selling which the company will neither lose nor gain anything

(ii) The sales needed to earn a profit of 20% on sales.

(iii) The extra units which should be sold to obtain the present profit it is proposed to reduce the selling price by 20% and 10%.

(iv) The selling price to be fixed to bring down its Break-even Point to 500 units under present conditions.

Solution:

(i) Number of units where there is no profit no loss

$$\text{Break-even Point} = \frac{\text{Fixed cost}}{\text{Contribution per unit}} = \frac{₹36{,}000}{₹50 - ₹35} = 2400 \text{ units}$$

(ii) Sales to earn a net profit of 20% on sales

Let the sales be x.

Sales	x
Less : Variable Cost	.7x
Contribution	.3x
Less : Fixed Cost	36,000
Profit	.3x - 36,000

$$\Rightarrow \quad .3x - 36{,}000 = .2x$$

$$\text{or} \quad .3x - 2x = 36{,}000$$

$$x = 3{,}60{,}000$$

(iii) Extra units to be sold to maintain present profit

Particulars	Reduction in Selling Price	
	By 20%	By 10%
Present selling price	50	50
Less : Reduction	10	5
New Selling price	40	45
Less : Variable Cost	35	35
Contribution per unit	5	10
Units to be sold = $\frac{\text{Fixed cost + Desired profit}}{\text{Contribution per unit}}$ =	$\frac{36{,}000 + 24{,}000}{5}$	$\frac{36{,}000 + 24{,}000}{10}$
=	12,000 units	6000 units
Existing sales of units =	4000 units	4000 units
Extra units to be sold =	8000 units	2000 units

(iv) Selling price for break-even point of 500 units

$$\text{BEP} = \frac{\text{Fixed costs}}{\text{Contribution per unit}}$$

Let the contribution per unit be x

$$500 = \frac{36{,}000}{x}$$

or $$500\,x = 36{,}000$$

or $$x = ₹72$$

$$\text{Selling price per unit} = \text{Variable cost per unit} + \text{Contribution per unit}$$
$$= ₹35 + ₹72 = ₹107 \text{ per unit.}$$

Note: $$\text{Variable cost per unit} = \frac{(₹80{,}000 + ₹40{,}000 + ₹20{,}000)}{4000}$$
$$= ₹35 \text{ per unit}$$

Problem 33 Falcon Engineering is operating at 70 per cent capacity and presents the following information:

Break-even point	₹200 crores
P/V Ratio	40 per cent
Margin of safety	₹50 crores

Falcon's management has decided to increase production to 95 per cent capacity level with the following modifications:

(i) The selling price will be reduced by 8 per cent.

(ii) The variable cost will be reduced by 5 per cent on sales.

(iii) The fixed cost will increase by ₹20 crores, including depreciation on additions, but excluding interest on additional capital.

(iv) Additional capital of ₹50 crores will be needed for capital expenditure and working capital. Required: (a) Indicate the sales figure that will be needed to earn ₹10 crores over and above the present profit and also meet 20 per cent interest on the additional capital. (b) What will be the revised. (i) Break-even point; (ii) P/V Ratio; (iii) Margin of safety

Solution: Assuming that the present selling price is ₹100 crores

	₹ (crores)
(a) Revised selling price will be (8% less)	92.00
Revised variable costs (55% of ₹92)	50.60
Contribution (₹92.00 – ₹50.60)	41.40

$$\text{New P/V ratio} = \frac{41.40}{92.00} \times 100 = 45\%$$

Revised fixed costs :

Present fixed costs	80
Increase in fixed costs	20
Interest at 20 per cent on additional capital (₹50 crores × 20%)	10
Total revised fixed costs	110

$$\text{Revised required sales} = \frac{\text{Revised fixed cost + Expected profit}}{\text{P/V Ratio}}$$

$$= \frac{₹110 \text{ crores} + ₹30 \text{ crores}}{45\%} = ₹311.11 \text{ crores}$$

(b) (i) $\text{Revised break-even point} = \frac{\text{Fixed costs}}{\text{P/V ratio}} = \frac{₹110 \text{ crores}}{45\%} = ₹244.44 \text{ crores}$

(ii) P/V ratio = 45%

(iii) Revised margin of safety = Revised sales – Revised break-even sales
= ₹311.11 crores – ₹244.44 crores
= ₹66.67 crores

Working Notes:

(i) Total sales = Break-even sales + Margin of safety
= ₹200 crores + ₹50 crores = ₹250 crores

(ii) P/V ratio = 40%

(iii) Variable cost 60% of Sales = 60% of ₹250 crores = ₹150 crores

(iv) Fixed cost = Break-even sales × P/V Ratio = ₹200 crores × 40%
= ₹80 crores

(v) Total cost = ₹150 crores + ₹80 crores = ₹230 crores

(vi) Profit = Total sales – Total costs = ₹250 crores – ₹230 crores
= ₹20 crores.

Alternatively,

Profit = Margin of Safety × P/V Ratio = 50 × 40% = ₹20 crores

Problem 34 Alpha Ltd. manufactures a product for which is generally sold in the market at 10 per unit. The variable cost per unit is ₹2.50 per unit. The firm has the capacity to produce 10000 units. Fixed costs are estimated at ₹30,000 up to the capacity utilisation level of 50%; ₹36,000 above that level but ₹42,000 if the level of capacity utilisation is 80% or above. You are required to compute:

(a) The break-even point.

(b) The operating profits of the firm, if the levels of capacity utilisation are 70%, 80% and 90% respectively.

(c) The level of activity at which the firm can make an operating profit of ₹18,000.

(d) The margin of safety, if the firm manufactures and sells only 6000 units in a year due to market constraints.

(e) Is it worthwhile to reduce the selling price—when management of the firm is advised that, if the selling price is reduced to ₹9 per unit, sales will go up from 7000 units to 7500 units.

(f) Management of the firm is also advised that sales of 7500 units at the present selling price can also be achieved, if a sum of ₹5000 is spent on advertisement.
Which alternative-reducing the selling price to ₹9 per unit or spending ₹5000 on advertisement will generate more profits? *(ICWA Inter, Modified)*

Solution:

1. Contribution per unit = ₹10 – ₹2.50 = ₹7.50

$$\text{P/V ratio} = \frac{\text{Contribution}}{\text{Selling price}} \times 100 = \frac{₹7.50}{₹10} \times 100 = 75\%$$

$$\text{Break-even sales} = \frac{\text{Fixed cost}}{\text{P/V ratio}} = \frac{₹30{,}000}{75\%} = ₹40{,}000$$

Break-even sales (units) = 40,000 ÷ 10 = 4000 units.

2. **Statement of Profit**

Particulars	70%	80%	90%
Production and Sale (in units)	7000	8000	9000
Sales @ 10 per unit	₹70,000	₹80,000	₹90,000
Less : Variable Cost @₹2.50 per unit	₹17,500	₹20,000	₹22,500
Contribution	₹52,500	₹60,000	₹67,500
Less : Fixed cost	₹36,000	₹42,000	₹42,000
Operating profit	₹16,500	₹18,000	₹25,500

3. $$\text{Desired sales} = \frac{\text{FC} + \text{P}}{\text{P/V ratio}}$$

$$\text{Required sales} = \frac{₹36{,}000 + ₹18{,}000}{75\%} = ₹72{,}000$$

Required sales (in units) = ₹72,000 ÷ ₹10 = 7200 units

i.e., 72% capacity utilisation.

4. Margin of safety = Total sales – Break-even sales
= (₹6000 × ₹10) – (₹4000 × ₹10)
= ₹20,000.

5. **Statement of Profit**

Particulars	Amount
Sales 7500 × ₹19	₹67,500
Less : Variable costs (7500 × ₹2.50)	₹18,750
Contribution	₹48,750
Less : Fixed cost	36,000
Profit	12,750

It is not worthwhile to reduce the selling price to ₹9 because profit will decline substantially. At 75% capacity, profit is only ₹12,750 after reduction, whereas at 70% capacity level profit is ₹16,500.

6. **Statement of Profit**

Particulars		Amount
Sales (7500 × ₹10)		₹75,000
Less : Variable costs (7500 × ₹2.50)		₹18,750
Contribution		₹56,250
Less: Fixed cost (more than 50% capacity tilisation)	₹36,000	
Advertisement	₹ 5000	41,000
Profit		15,250

The advertisement expenditure increases the profit by ₹2,500, i.e., ₹15,250 – ₹12,750), therefore, spending on advertisement is recommended.

Problem 35 When volume is 3000 units, average cost is ₹4 per unit whereas the average cost comes down to ₹3.50 per unit when volume increases to 4000 units. The Break-even point is 5000 units. Find the P/V ratio. [*B.Com. (H)*]

Solution:

Total cost of 3000 units of output (3000 × 4)	₹12,000
Total cost of 4000 units of output (4000 × 3.5)	₹14,000
Increase in output	1000
Increase in cost	₹2000

$$\text{Variable cost per unit} = \frac{\text{Change in cost}}{\text{Change in output}} = \frac{2000}{1000} = ₹2 \text{ per unit}$$

Total cost for 3000 units	₹12,000
Variable cost for 3000 units (3,000 × 2)	6000
Total Fixed Cost (TC – TVC)	6000

$$\text{Break-even level} = \frac{\text{Fixed cost}}{\text{Contribution per unit}}$$

$$5{,}000 = \frac{6000}{\text{Contribution per unit}}$$

$$\text{Contribution per unit} = \frac{6000}{5000} = ₹1.20$$

$$\begin{aligned}\text{Selling price} &= \text{Variable cost} + \text{Contribution}\\ &= ₹2 + 1.20\\ &= ₹3.20\end{aligned}$$

$$\text{P/V ratio} = \frac{\text{Contribution per unit}}{\text{Price per unit}} \times 100 = \frac{1.20}{3.20} \times 100 = 37.5\%$$

Problem 36

(a) A company sells its product at ₹15 per unit. In a period, if it produces and sells 8000 units, it incurs a loss of ₹5 per unit. If the volume is raised to 20,000 units, it earns a profit of 4 per unit. Calculate break-even point both in terms of rupees as well as in units

(b) ABC Ltd has a fixed cost of ₹2,00,000. It has two products that it can sell, A and B. The company sells these products at a rate of 2 units of A and 1 unit of B, the unit contribution is ₹1 per unit for A and ₹2 per unit of B, how many units of A and B would be sold at the BEP?

(c) The ratio of variable cost to sales is 80%. The BEP occurs at 60% of the capacity sales. Find the capacity sales when the fixed costs are ₹1,20,000. Also compute the profit at 70% of the capacity. [*C.A. Inter, Modified*]

Solution:

(a)

$$\begin{aligned}\text{Average cost (at 8000 units)} &= \text{Selling price per unit} + \text{Loss component per unit}\\ &= ₹15 + ₹5 = ₹20\\ \text{Average cost (at 20,000 units)} &= ₹15 - ₹14 = ₹111\\ \text{Total Cost of 8000 units} &= ₹8000 + ₹20 = ₹1{,}60{,}000\\ \text{Total Cost of 20,000 units} &= ₹11 \times 20{,}000 = ₹2{,}20{,}000\end{aligned}$$

$$\text{Variable Cost per unit} = \frac{\text{Change in total cost}}{\text{Change in volume of production}}$$

$$= \frac{₹60{,}000}{12{,}000} = ₹5$$

$$\begin{aligned}\text{Fixed Cost} &= \text{Total cost} - \text{Variable cost}\\ &= ₹1{,}60{,}000 - (5 \times 8000) = ₹1{,}20{,}000\end{aligned}$$

$$\text{P/V ratio} = \frac{\text{Contribution}}{\text{Sales}} \times 100 = \frac{₹10}{₹15} \times 100 = 66\frac{2}{3}\%$$

$$\text{Break-even point (₹)} = \frac{\text{Fixed cost}}{\text{P/V ratio}} = \frac{₹1,20,000}{66\frac{2}{3}\%} = ₹1,80,000$$

$$\text{Break-even point (in units)} = \frac{\text{Fixed cost}}{\text{Contribution per unit}} = \frac{₹1,20,000}{₹10} = 12,000 \text{ units}$$

(b)

	₹
Contribution from 2 units of A = 2 × ₹1	2
Contribution from 1 unit of B = 1 × ₹2	2
Contribution from 3 units	4

$$\text{Weighted average CPU} = \frac{₹4}{3 \text{ units}} = 1.33$$

$$\therefore \quad \text{Total BEPS (in units)} = \frac{\text{Total Fixed Cost}}{\text{Contribution per unit}} = \frac{2,00,000}{1.33}$$

$$= 1,50,000 \text{ units}$$

$$\therefore \quad \text{BEP (units) for A} = \frac{2}{3} \times 1,50,000 = 1,00,000 \text{ units}$$

$$\therefore \quad \text{BEP (units) for B} = \frac{1}{3} \times 1,50,000 = 50,000 \text{ units}$$

(c) (i) $\text{Variable Cost to Sales Ratio} = \frac{\text{Variable cost}}{\text{Sale}} \times 100 = 80\%$

$$\therefore \quad \text{P/V Ratio} = 20\% \text{ (P/V ratio + V/C ratio = 1)}$$

$$\text{Break-even Point} = \frac{\text{Fixed cost}}{\text{P/V ratio}}$$

$$= \frac{1,20,000}{20}\% = ₹6,00,000$$

As the BEP is attained at 60% of the capacity sales,

Therefore, full capacity sales = 6,00,000 × 100 ÷ 60 = ₹ 10,00,000

(ii) Sales at 70% of capacity = 70% of 10,00,000 = ₹ 7,00,000

Contribution = 20% of 7,00,000 = ₹ 1,40,000

Less fixed cost = ₹ 1,20,000

Profit = ₹ 20,000

Problem 37 A company has a P/V ratio of 40 per cent. By what percentage must sales be increased to offset—

1. 10 per cent reduction in selling price, and
2. 20 per cent reduction in selling price? [*B.Com. (Hons.)*]

Solution: Let the present units sold be 100 @ ₹1 per unit

Present total sales	₹ 100
Present variable cost	60
Present contribution (P/V ratio 40%)	40
1. If selling price is reduced by 10%, selling price per unit	0.90
Variable cost per unit	0.60
Contribution per unit	0.30

$$\text{New P/V ratio} = \frac{0.30}{0.90} \times 100 = 33.33\%$$

In order to maintain the same contribution, i.e., ₹40, the desired sales would be:

$$\text{Desired Sales (in units)} = \frac{\text{Fixed cost + Profit}}{\text{Contribution per unit}} = \frac{40}{0.30} = 133\frac{1}{3}\text{ units}$$

$$\text{Desired sales (₹)} = \frac{\text{Fixed cost + Profit}}{\text{P/V ratio}} = \frac{40}{33.33\%} = ₹\,120$$

Thus, the volume of sales will have to be increased by $33\frac{1}{3}\%$ from the existing level if the selling price is reduced by 10%

2. Selling price is reduced by 20%

Selling price per unit	₹0.80
Variable cost per unit	₹0.60
Contribution per unit	₹0.20

$$\text{New P/V ratio} = \frac{0.20}{0.80 \times 100 = 25\%}$$

In order to maintain the same contribution, i.e., ₹40, the desired sales would be:

$$\text{Desired Sales (in units)} = \frac{\text{Fixed cost + Profit}}{\text{Contribution per unit}} = \frac{40}{0.20} = 200\text{ units}$$

$$\text{Desired sales (₹)} = \frac{\text{Fixed cost + Profit}}{\text{P/V ratio}} = \frac{40}{25\%} = ₹\,160$$

Thus, the volume of sales will have to be increased by 100% from the existing level if the selling price is reduced by 20%.

Problem 38 The Comfort Enterprises sells five different styles of ladies chappals with identical purchase costs and selling prices. The company is trying to find out the profitability of opening another store, which will have the following expenses and revenues:

	Per Pair (₹)
Selling price	30.00
Variable Cost	19.50
Salesmen's commission	1.50
Total Variable cost	21.00
Annual fixed costs:	
Rent	60,000
Salaries	2,00,000
Advertising	80,000
Other fixed expenses	20,000
	3,60,000

(a) Calculate the annual break-even point in units and in value. Also determine the profit or loss if 35,000 pairs of chappals are sold.

(b) The sales commissions are proposed to be discontinued, but instead a fixed amount of ₹90,000 is to be incurred in fixed salaries. A reduction in selling price of 5% is also proposed. What will be the break-even point in units?

(c) It is proposed to pay the store manager 50 paise per pair as further commission. The selling price is also proposed to be increased by 5%, what would be the break-even point in units?

(d) Refer to the original data. If the store manager were to be paid 30 paise commission on each pair of chappals sold in excess of the break-even point, what would be the store's net profit if 50,000 pairs were sold?

Solution:

(a) (i) Break-even point (in units)

$$\text{BEP (in units)} = \frac{\text{Fixed cost}}{\text{Contribution per pair of chappals}}$$

$$= \frac{₹3,60,000}{(₹30 - ₹21)} = 40,000 \text{ pairs}$$

$$\text{P/V ratio} = \frac{\text{Contribution}}{\text{Sales}} \times 100 = \frac{9}{30} \times 100 = 30\%$$

$$\text{Break-even Point} = \frac{\text{Fixed cost}}{\text{P/V ratio}} = \frac{3,60,000}{30\%} = ₹12,00,000$$

(ii) Profit (Loss) on the sale of 35,000 pairs of chappals

	₹
Sales Revenue (35,000 × ₹30)	10,50,000
Less: Variable Cost (35,000 × ₹21)	7,35,000
Contribution	3,15,000
Less: Fixed costs	3,60,000
Loss	(45,000)

(b) Break-even point (in units)

	₹
New selling price per pair	28.50
New variable cost per pair	19.50
Contribution (per pair)	9.00

$$\text{BEP (in units)} = \frac{\text{New fixed costs}}{\text{New contribution per unit}}$$

$$= \frac{₹4,50,000}{9} = 50,000 \text{ pair of chappals}$$

(c) Break-even point (in units)

	₹
Selling price (per pair)	31.50
Less: Variable cost (per unit)	21.50
Contribution (per pair)	10.00

$$\text{Break-even point} = \frac{\text{Fixed cost}}{\text{Contribution per unit}}$$

$$= \frac{₹3,60,000}{₹10} = 36,000 \text{ pairs of chappals}$$

(d) BEP (in units) as per part (a) = 40,000 pairs of chappals

Total pairs of chappals sold = 50,000

Expected number of pairs of chappals sold above the BEP are 10,000

Sales Revenue (10,000 pairs @ ₹230)	3,00,000
Less: Total variable cost (10,000 @ ₹21.30)	2,13,000
Less: Fixed cost	Nil
Profit	87,000

Problem 39 Classic Clothing is currently selling 24,000 shirts annually. He supplies the following details for the year ended 31st December, 2020:

	₹
Selling price per shirt	40
Variable cost per shirt	25
Fixed cost: Staff salaries for the year	1,20,000
General office costs for the year	80,000
Advertising costs for the year	40,000

As a cost accountant of the firm you are required to answer the following each part independently:

1. Calculate the break-even point and margin of safety in sales revenue and number of shirts sold.
2. Assume that 20,000 shirts were sold in a year. Find out the net profit of the firm.
3. If it is decided to introduce selling commission of ₹3 per shirt, how many shirts would require to be sold in a year to earn a net income of ₹15,000.
4. Assuming that for the year 2021 an additional staff salary of ₹33,000 is anticipated, and price of a shirt is likely to be increased by 15%, what should be the break-even point in the number of shirts and sales revenue?

Solution:

1. Contribution per unit = 40 – 25 = 15

$$\text{P/V ratio} = \frac{\text{Contribution}}{\text{Sales}} \times 100$$

$$= 15/40 \times 100 = 37.5\%$$

$$\text{BEP (in units)} = \frac{\text{Total fixed cost}}{\text{Contribution per unit}}$$

$$= 2,40,000/15 = 16,000 \text{ units}$$

$$\text{BEP (in ₹)} = \frac{\text{Total fixed cost}}{\text{P/V ratio}}$$

$$= \frac{2,40,000}{37.5\%} = ₹6,40,000$$

$$\text{Margin of safety (MS)} = \text{Actual sales} - \text{Break-even sales}$$

$$= (24,000 \times 40) - 6,40,000$$

$$= 9,60,000 - 6,40,000 = ₹3,20,000$$

2. *Net Profit when 20,000 shirts are sold:*

Sales 20,000 × 40	8,00,000
Contribution (37.5% of sales)	₹23,00,000
Less: Fixed costs	₹ 2,40,000
Profit	₹ 60,000

3. *Sales for Desired Profit:* $= \dfrac{\text{Fixed cost + Desired profit}}{\text{New contribution per unit}}$

$$= \frac{2{,}40{,}000 + 15{,}000}{15 - 3}$$

$$= \frac{2{,}55{,}000}{12} = 21250 \text{ shirts}$$

4. *New Break-even Point:* (in units) $= \dfrac{\text{New fixed cost}}{\text{New contribution per unit}}$

$$= \frac{2{,}40{,}000 + 33{,}000}{46 - 25}$$

$$= \frac{2{,}73{,}000}{21} = 13000 \text{ shirts.}$$

New Break-even Point: (in ₹) = 13,000 × 46 = ₹5,98,000

Problem 40 A garment exporter earning a profit of ₹1,50,000 on a sale of ₹15,00,000. Selling price ₹40 per garment and variable cost is ₹30 per garment. He incurs an additional fixed cost of ₹3,75,000 on product improvement which also enables him to economise ₹5 in per unit variable cost. As per trade agreements the sale of his garments is restricted to the old figure of ₹15,00,000. What would be the selling price per garment so that he earns the same profit at the same sales value? [*B.Com. (Hons.)*]

Solution: $\text{P/V ratio} = \dfrac{\text{Contribution p.u.}}{\text{Selling price}} \times 100$

$$\frac{(40 - 30)}{40} \times 100 = 25\%$$

$$\text{Desired Sales (₹)} = \frac{\text{Fixed cost + Desired profit}}{\text{P/V ratio}};$$

or $$₹15{,}00{,}000 = \frac{(\text{Fixed cost} + 1{,}50{,}000)}{25\%}$$

$$15{,}00{,}000 \times 25\% = \text{Fixed cost} + 1{,}50{,}000;$$

$$\text{Fixed cost} = 3{,}75{,}000 - 1{,}50{,}000 = ₹2{,}25{,}000$$

$$\text{New FC} = 2{,}25{,}000 + 3{,}75{,}000 = ₹6{,}00{,}000$$

Desired profit is same ₹1,50,000 when variable cost comes down by ₹5 per unit and sales remains unchanged

$$\text{New Desired Sales (₹)} = \frac{\text{New FC + New profit}}{1 - \dfrac{\text{New VC}}{\text{New sales}}}$$

$$15,00,000 = \frac{6,00,000 + 1,50,000}{1 - \dfrac{25}{\text{Sales}}}$$

$$15,00,000\left(1 - \frac{25}{S}\right) = 6,00,000 + 1,50,000$$

$$S = ₹50.$$

Thus, New Selling Price = ₹50

Problem 41 Sale value of a product is ₹10,00,000 at selling price of ₹50 per unit, variable cost of ₹30 per unit and fixed cost of ₹2,00,000. The producer can increase sales value by 35% by reducing price by 10%. Such increase in sale would also require 20% increase in fixed cost. Should he adhere to the existing costs and sales or he should affect proposed changes?

Solution:

$$\text{P/V ratio} = \frac{\text{Contribution}}{\text{Sales}} \times 100 = \frac{(50 - 30)}{50} \times 100 = 40\%$$

$$\text{Sales (₹)} = \frac{\text{Fixed cost + Desired profit}}{\text{P/V ratio}}$$

$$10,00,000 = \frac{(2,00,000 + \text{Profit})}{40\%}$$

$$\text{Profit} = ₹2,00,000$$

Proposed selling price = 50 – 5 = ₹45, VC = ₹30;

Therefore, revised P/V ratio = 33.33%

Proposed sales = ₹10,00,000 + 35% = ₹13,50,000

New fixed cost = 2,00,000 + 20% = ₹2,40,000

$$\text{Desired sales (₹)} = \frac{\text{Fixed cost + Desired profit}}{\text{P/V ratio}}$$

$$13,50,000 = \frac{(2,40,000 + \text{Profit})}{33.33\%}$$

$$\text{Profit} = ₹4,50,000 - 2,40,000 = ₹2,10,000$$

Budgeted profit goes up from ₹22,00,000 to ₹2,10,000 due to proposed changes. Hence, the proposed changes should be implemented.

Problem 42 Rawat Ltd. is manufacturing and selling snacks in the market for which the following information is available:

	(₹ per Unit)
Materials	10.00
Conversion costs (variable)	₹4.00
Dealer's margin	2.00
Selling price	20.00
Fixed cost	₹2,20,000
Capacity utilisation	60%

The company is currently making a sales 80,000 units. Due to intense competition in the market, the manager of the company has suggested following alternatives to improve the sales:

(1) Reduce sales price by 5%

(2) Increase dealer's margin by 25% over the existing rate.

Which of the two suggestions would you recommend if the company desires to maintain the present profit? Give reasons. *(CS Inter, Modified)*

Solution:

Statement showing present profit

Particulars	₹
Selling price	20
Materials	10
Conversion cost (variable)	4
Dealer's margin	2
Variable cost	16
Contribution per unit	4
Total contribution: (4 × 80,000)	3,20,000
Less: Fixed cost	2,20 000
Profit	1,00,000

Suggestion 1: *Increasing sales by reducing sales price by 5%*

	₹
Revised selling price (20 – 5%)	19
Variable cost	16
Contribution per unit	3

$$\text{Desired Sales (Units)} = \frac{\text{Fixed cost + Profit}}{\text{Contribution per unit}} = \frac{(2,20,000 + 1,00,000)}{3}$$

$$= \frac{3,20,000}{3} = 1,06,667 \text{ units.}$$

Therefore, 106667 units should be sold to maintain the present profit of ₹1,00,000.

The company will operate at $\frac{1,06,667}{80,000} \times 60\% = 80\%$ capacity utilisation

Suggestion 2: *Increasing sales by increasing dealer's margin by 25%*

	₹
Selling price	20.00
Materials	8
Conversion cost	6
Dealer's margin (2 + 25%)	2.50
Variable cost	16.50
Contribution per unit	₹3.50

$$\text{Desired Sales (units)} = \frac{\text{Fixed cost + Profit}}{\text{Contribution per unit}}$$

$$= \frac{(2,20,000 + 1,00,000)}{3.5} = \frac{3,20,000}{3.50} = 91,429 \text{ units}$$

Therefore, 91,429 units should be sold to maintain the present profit of ₹1,00,000. i.e., the company will operate at

$$\frac{91,429}{80,000} \times 60\% = 68.57\% \text{ capacity utilisation}$$

On the basis of comparison of the two suggestions, the desired profit is achieved at lower sales of 91429 units under the second suggestion. Therefore, dealer's margin should be increased.

Problem 43 An analysis of Oman Pvt. Ltd. led to the following information:

Cost element	*Variable cost (% of sales)*	*Fixed cost*
Direct material	32	
Direct labour	28	
Factory overheads	12	₹1,89,900
Distribution overheads	4	58,400
General administration overheads	3	66,700

Budgeted Sales are ₹18,50,000. You are required to determine:

1. Break-even sales
2. Profit at the budgeted sales volume
3. Profit if actual sales:
   (a) drops by 10%
   (b) increases by 10% from budgeted sales. [*B.Com. (Hons)*]

Solution:

Total Variable cost as % of sales = 79

$$\text{P/V ratio} = \frac{100 - 79}{100} = 21\%$$

Total fixed costs = ₹3,15,000

1. $$\text{Break-even sales} = \frac{₹3,15,000}{21} \times 100$$

$$= ₹15,00,000$$

2. Contribution (Sales × P/V ratio) ₹18,50,000 × 21% = ₹3,88,500

Less: Fixed cost = (₹3,15,000)

Profit = ₹73,500

3. (a) Profit when actual sales drops by 10%

Actual sales = ₹18,50,000 – ₹1,85,000

= ₹16,65,000

Contribution (Sales × P/V ratio) ₹16,65,000 × 21% = ₹3,49,650

Less: Fixed cost = (₹3,15,000)

Profit = ₹34,650

(b) Profit when actual sales increase by 10% from budgeted sales

Actual sales = ₹18,50,000 + ₹1,85,000

= ₹20,35,000

Contribution (Sales × P/V ratio) ₹20,35,000 × 21%= ₹4,27,350

Less: Fixed cost = (₹3,15,000)

Profit = ₹1,12,350

Problem 44 Colourmax Ltd. manufactures and sells a paper, the selling price and raw material cost of which have remained unchanged during the past two years. The following are the relevant data :

Particulars	*Year 1*	*Year 2*
Quantity sold (kg.)	200	300
	₹	₹
Sales value	40,000	?
Raw materials	20,000	?
Direct wages	6000	?
Factory overheads	10,000	11,400
Profit	4000	5100

During the second year, direct wage rates increased by 50% but there was a saving of ₹600 in fixed factory overheads.

You are required to compute the quantity (in kg.) that the company should have produced and sold in the second year in order to maintain the same amount of net profit per kg as it earned during the first year? (*CA Inter, Modified*)

Solution: **Statement of Quantity to be Produced during Second Year**

Particulars	₹	₹
Selling price per kg (Note 1)		200
Less : Variable costs per kg.		
Raw materials	100	
Direct wages (Note 2)	45	
Variable Factory Overheads (Note 3)	20	165
Contribution per kg		35
Less : Profit required per kg (at 200 kg of sales)		20
Balance contribution per kg for meeting fixed costs		15

Total fixed cost (Note 4) = 5400

$$\text{Quantity (in kg) to be produced and sold} = \frac{₹5400}{15} = 360 \text{ kg}$$

Working Notes:

1. $$\text{Selling price per kg} = \frac{₹40{,}000}{200 \text{ kg}} = ₹200 \text{ per kg}$$

2. $$\text{Direct wages per kg} = \frac{6000}{200 \text{ kg}} = \frac{150}{100} = ₹45$$

3. Variable factory overheads per kg:

	₹
Total factory overheads in second year	11,400
Add : Saving in fixed factory overheads	600
	12,000
Less : Total factory overheads in year 1	10,000
Increase in factory overhead	2000
Increase in quantity (300 kg – 200 kg)	100 kg

$$\text{Variable factory overhead per kg } \frac{2000}{100 \text{ kg}} = ₹20$$

4. *Fixed factory overheads :*	*Year 1 (₹)*	*Year 2 (₹)*
Total factory overheads	10,000	11,400
Less : Variable factory overheads	4000	6000
Fixed factory overheads	6000	5400

Problem 45 Jolly Ltd. prepares a cost volume profit budget analysis for each point as per details below:

(a) Profit plan for plant 1 shows annual budgeted fixed costs ₹12,00,000, variable costs ₹8,40,000; and sales value of production ₹22,00,000. Allocated head office budgeted fixed costs are ₹3,20,000. You are asked to prepare an analysis indicating the break-even points before and after cost allocation. Explain why the break-even point change (in ₹) is greater than allocated amount.

(b) Plant 2 produces a product that sells at ₹40. It costs ₹42.50 when 15,000 units are produced. At a production level of 20,000, the cost per unit is ₹38.125. What is the break-even point in ₹ and in units?

(c) Plant 3: Budgeted income and cost estimates are follows:

Sales (annual)		₹10,00,000
Costs:		
Fixed	₹4,00,000	
Variable	₹3,00,000	
Head office allocated	₹3,50,000	₹10,50,000
Loss		₹50,000

Sale of plant 3 is under consideration. What is your recommendation based on the data given? Justify your recommendation.

(d) Plant 4 produces one product. The budgeted income and cost estimates are as follows:

Sales (annual) @ ₹200		₹20,00,000
Costs:		
Fixed	₹ 7,47,500	
Variable	₹13,50,000	
Head office allocated	₹ 5,02,500	₹26,00,000
Loss		₹ 6,00,000

How many additional units must be manufactured in the plant in order to break-even? What would be the profit pick up per unit above break-even? [*B.Com. (H)*]

Solution:

(a) *Plant 1:*

$$\text{Contribution} = \text{Sales} - \text{Variable cost} = 22{,}00{,}000 - 8{,}40{,}000$$

$$= 13{,}60{,}000$$

$$\text{P/V ratio} = \frac{\text{Contribution}}{\text{Sales}} \times 100 = 13,60,000/22,00,000 \times 100$$

$$= 61.81\%$$

$$\text{BEP (before allocation)} = \frac{\text{Total fixed cost}}{\text{P/V ratio}} = 12,00,000/61.81\% = ₹19,41,176$$

$$\text{BEP (after allocation)} = \frac{\text{Total fixed cost}}{\text{P/V ratio}} = 15,20,000/61.81\% = ₹24,58,751$$

The P/V ratio of 61.81% implies that every 100 rupee of additional sales will recover only ₹61.81 of additional fixed cost. Therefore, the break-even sales increase by more than the increase in fixed cost.

(b) *Plant 2:*

Total cost of 15000 units = ₹15,000 × ₹42.50 = ₹6,37,500

Total cost of 20000 units = ₹38.125 × 20,000 = ₹7,62,500

$$\text{Variable cost per unit} = \frac{\text{Change in total cost}}{\text{Change in volume of production}}$$

$$= \frac{7,62,500 - 6,37,500}{5,000} = ₹25$$

Fixed cost = Total cost – Variable cost

= ₹6,37,500 – (25 × 15,000) = ₹2,62,500

$$\text{P/V ratio} = \frac{\text{Contribution}}{\text{Sales}} \times 100 = \frac{15}{40} \times 100 = 37.5\%$$

$$\text{Break-even point (₹)} = \frac{\text{Fixed cost}}{\text{P/V ratio}} = \frac{2,62,500}{37.5\%} = ₹7,00,000$$

$$\text{Break-even point (in units)} = \frac{\text{Fixed cost}}{\text{Contribution per unit}} = \frac{2,62,500}{15} = 17,500 \text{ units}$$

(c) *Plant 3:*

Recommendation: Since there is contribution of 7,00,000, the management should not sell the plant. If Head Office allocations are ignored (because they are going to be there even if the plant is sold) there is still profit of ₹3,00,000 (₹7,00,000 – 4,00,000)

(d) *Plant 4:*

Current sales 20,00,000/200 = 10,000 units

$$\text{Break-even point} = \frac{12,50,000}{65} = 19,230 \text{ units}$$

Additional units to be manufactured to break-even = 19,230 – 10,000 = 9230 units.

Problem 46 Pet Bottles Ltd. sells its products at ₹60 per unit. In 2019, the company operated at a margin of safety of 40%. The fixed costs amounted to ₹3,60,000 and the variable cost ratio to sales was 80%.

In 2020, it is estimated that the variable cost will go up by 10% and the fixed costs will increase by 5%.

You are required to (a) find the selling price to be fixed in 2020 to earn the same P/V ratio as in 2019. (b) Assuming the same selling price of ₹60 per unit in 2020, find the number of units to be produced and sold to earn the same profit as in 2019.

Solution:

(a) *Selling price to be fixed in 2020*

Variable cost per unit in 2020 = 52.80 (i.e. ₹48 + ₹4.80)

Fixed cost in 2020 = ₹3,78,000 (i.e. ₹3,60,000 + ₹18,000)

P/V ratio in 2019 = 20%

Since P/V ratio is 20%, therefore variable cost is 80%.

$$\text{Hence, the required selling price} = \frac{₹52.80}{80\%} = ₹66$$

(b) *Number of units to be produced and sold in 2020 to earn the same profit as in 2019.*

Profit in 2019	₹2,40,000
Fixed cost in 2020	₹3,78,000
Desired contribution in 2020 (₹2,40,000 + ₹3,78,000)	₹6,18,000

Contribution per unit in 2020 = Selling price per unit – Variable cost per unit

= ₹60 – ₹52.80 = ₹7.20

$$\text{Number of units to be produced and sold in 2020} = \frac{\text{Fixed cost in 2020 + Desired profit}}{\text{Contribution per unit in 2020}}$$

$$= \frac{₹6,18,000}{₹7.2} = 85,833.33 \text{ units}$$

Working Notes:

1. $$\text{P/V ratio} = \frac{(\text{Selling price} - \text{Variable cost})}{\text{Selling price}} \times 100$$

$$= \frac{(₹60 - ₹48)}{₹60} \times 100 = \frac{₹12}{₹60} \times 100 = 20\%$$

2. Number of units sold (in 2019)

$$\text{Break-even point} = \frac{\text{Fixed cost}}{\text{Contribution per unit}} = \frac{₹3,60,000}{₹12} = 30,000 \text{ units}$$

Since, margin of safety is 40%, therefore break-even point is 60% of units sold.

or, $\text{No. of units sold} = \frac{\text{Break-even point}}{60\%} = \frac{30{,}000 \text{ units}}{60\%} = 50{,}000 \text{ units}$

3. *Profit earned in 2019*

Profit = [Total contribution on the sale of 50,000 units – Fixed costs]
= [(50000 units × ₹12) – ₹3,60,000]
= [₹6,00,000 – ₹3,60,000] = ₹2,40,000

Problem 47 The comparative profit statement of a firm for two years is given as under:

	Year 2019	*Year 2020*
Units sold	2500	3750
	₹	₹
Direct materials	87,500	?
Direct wages	62,500	?
Factory overheads (Fixed and variable)	75,000	1,00,000
Sales	2,75,000	?
Profit	50,000	66,250

In the year 2020, the direct material price has increased by 20%, wage rates have gone down by 8% and the fixed cost reduced by ₹5,000. The other costs and selling price remained the same. You are required to determine the quantity to be sold in the year 2020 to maintain the same amount of profit per unit as in the year 2019. *(CA. Inter, Modified)*

Solution: **Statement showing Cost for Year 2020**

Particulars		₹
Selling price per unit[1]		110
Less : Variable Cost	₹	
Direct materials[2] (35 + 20% of ₹35)	42	
Direct wages[3] (25 – 8% of ₹25)	23	
Variable overheads[4]	20	85
Contribution per unit		25

Let the number of units to be sold = x

Desired profit (profit per unit[5] × No. of units sold) = $20\,x$

$$\text{Desired Sales (units)} = \frac{\text{Fixed cost + Profit}}{\text{Contribution per unit}}$$

$$\Rightarrow \qquad x = \frac{(20{,}000 + 20\,x)}{25}$$

$$x = \frac{20{,}000}{5} = 4000 \text{ units}$$

Working Notes:

1. Selling price per unit in 2019 = $\frac{₹2{,}75{,}000}{2500 \text{ units}} = ₹110$

2. Direct material per unit in 2019 = $\frac{₹87{,}500}{2500 \text{ units}} = ₹35$

3. Direct wages per unit in 2019 = $\frac{₹62{,}500}{2500 \text{ units}} = ₹25$

4. Variable factory overheads per unit = $\frac{\text{Change in overheads}}{\text{Change in production volume}}$

$$= \frac{₹1{,}00{,}000 - ₹75{,}000}{3750 \text{ units} - 2500 \text{ units}}$$

$$= \frac{₹25{,}000}{1{,}250 \text{ units}} = ₹20$$

5. Profit per unit in 2019= $\frac{₹50{,}000}{2500 \text{ units}} = ₹20$

6. Fixed overheads for 2019= Total overheads – Variable overheads

$$= 75000 - (2500 \text{ units} \times ₹20) = ₹25{,}000$$

Fixed overheads for 2020 = 25,000 – 5000 = ₹20,000

Problem 48 An Indian company manufactures plastic buckets. The following information was available from the records of the company:

Variable cost per bucket	₹20
Fixed cost	₹50,000 for the year
Capacity	₹2000 buckets per year
Selling price per bucket	₹70

You are required to:

(a) Find the break-even point.

(b) Find the number of buckets to be sold to get a profit of ₹30,000.

(c) If the company can manufacture 600 buckets more per year with an additional cost of ₹2000, what should be the selling price to maintain the profit per bucket as in (b) above?

Solution:

(a)

$$\text{Break-even point} = \frac{\text{Fixed cost}}{\text{Contribution per unit}}$$

$$= 50{,}000/50 = 1000 \text{ buckets.}$$

(b) Buckets to be sold for desired profit of ₹ 30,000.

$$\text{Desired Sales (units)} = \frac{\text{Fixed cost + Profit}}{\text{Contribution per unit}}$$

$$= 80{,}000/50$$

$$= 1600 \text{ buckets}$$

(c) Profit per bucket at sales of 1600 buckets = 30,000/1600 = ₹ 18.75

Total Sales 1,600 + 600 = 2200 buckets

Total profit desired = 2200 × 18.75 = ₹ 41,250

Let Selling price be x

$$\text{Total sales} = \text{VC} + \text{FC} + \text{Profit}$$

$$2200x = (20 \times 2200) + 52{,}000 + (2200 \times 18.75)$$

$$2200x = 1{,}37{,}250$$

$$x = ₹62.39 \text{ per bucket.}$$

Problem 49 Payroll Ltd. manufactures a document reproducing machine which has a variable cost structure as follows:

Material	₹ 40
Labour	₹ 10
Overheads	₹ 4
Selling price of the machine	₹ 90.

Sales during the current year are expected to be ₹ 13,50,000 and Fixed overheads ₹ 1,40,000.

Under a wage agreement, an increase of 10% is payable to all direct workers from the beginning of the forthcoming year, while material costs are expected to increase by 7.5%, Variable Overhead Costs by 5% and Fixed Overhead Costs by 3%.

You are required to calculate:

1. The new selling price if the current profit/volume ratio is to be maintained; and
2. The quantity to be sold during the forthcoming year to yield the same amount of profit as in the current year assuming the selling price to remain at ₹ 90. *(C.A. Inter)*

Solution:

1. *Computations of new selling price*

Particulars	Current Year ₹	Increase	Next Year ₹
Selling price	90.00		x
Material	40.00	7½%	43.00
Labour	10.00	10%	11.00

Table Contd...

Table Contd...

Particulars	Current Year ₹	Increase	Next Year ₹
Overheads	4.00	5%	4.20
Total variable cost	54.00		58.20
Contribution	36.00		x – 58.20

$$\text{P/V ratio}\left(\frac{\text{Contribution per unit}}{\text{Selling per unit}} \times 100\right) = \frac{₹36}{₹90} \times 100 = 40\%$$

In the next year, the current profit/volume ratio of 40% is to be maintained. Therefore,

$$40 = \frac{(x - 58.20)}{x} \times 100$$

$$x = ₹97.00.$$

The new selling price should be ₹97

2. Computation of quantity to be sold during the forthcoming year at ₹90 to yield the same amount of profit as in the current year.

Statement showing profit for current year

Particulars	₹
Contribution (40% of 13,50,000)	5,40,000
Less: Fixed cost	1,40,000
Profit	4,00,000

	₹
Desired sales for next year	
Profit required (as per current year)	4,00,000
Fixed overhead costs (₹1,40,000 + 3% of ₹1,40,000)	1,44,200

$$\text{Per unit contribution} = \text{Selling price} - \text{Variable cost}$$

$$= ₹90 - ₹58.20 = ₹31.80$$

$$\text{Desired sales (Units)} = \frac{(\text{new fixed cost + profit})}{\text{Contribution per unit}} = \frac{₹5,44,200}{₹31.80}$$

$$= ₹17,113 \text{ machines.}$$

Problem 50 Fast Track Ltd. is producing sports shoes for the past several years, which are sold at ₹30 per pair. Higher costs in recent years have forced the management to consider about the adequacy of this selling price.

The labour rate has increased from ₹2.50 per hour to ₹3.50 per hour and the cost of leather has gone up from ₹2 per sq. ft. foot to ₹3 per sq. ft. Fixed expenses have increased by 33 $\frac{1}{3}$% from the level of ₹27,000 five years ago. Over the same period, the variable overheads have increased by 30% or ₹3 per pair of shoes. Each shoe requires 1.5 sq. ft. of leather and one hour of direct labour.

Calculate the selling price that the company has to charge under the new cost structure to break-even at the same number of units as five years ago.

Solution:

Statement showing contribution

Particulars	Current year	Next year
Selling price	30	X
Material (leather cost)	1.5 × 2 × 2 = 6	1.5 × 3 × 2 = 9
Labour	1 × 2.5 × 2 = 5	1 × 3.5 × 2 = 7
Variable overhead	10	10 + 3 = 13
Variable cost per unit	21	29
Contribution (SP – VC)	9	X – 29
Fixed Cost	27,000	27,000 + 9000 = 36,000
Break-even Point $\left(\frac{\text{Fixed cost}}{\text{Contribution per unit}}\right)$	$\frac{27,000}{9}$ = 3000 units	

$$\text{Therefore,} \quad 3,000 = \frac{36,000}{x-29}$$

$$x = ₹41$$

New Selling price = ₹41

Problem 51 Bisleri Ltd. is planning to establish a subsidiary company in India to produce mineral water. Based on the estimated annual sales of 40000 bottles of the mineral water, cost studies produced the following estimates for the Indian subsidiary:

	Total Cost	*Variable Cost (% of TC)*
Material	1,93,600	100%
Labour	90,000	70%
Factory overhead	80,000	64%
Administration overheads	30,000	30%

The Indian production will be sold by the manufacturer's representatives who will receive a commission of 8% of the sale price. No portion of the British Office expenses is to be allowed to the Indian subsidiary.

You are required to:

(i) Compute the sale price per bottle to enable management to realise an estimated 10% profit on sale proceeds in India, and

(ii) Calculate the break-even point in rupee sales for the Indian subsidiary on the assumption that the sale price is ₹11 per bottle. (*B. Com. Hons.*)

Solution:

Particulars	Variable Cost (₹)	Fixed Cost (₹)
Materials	1,93,600	–
Labour	63,000	27,000
Factory overheads	51,200	28,800
Administration overheads	9000	21,000
Total	3,16,800	76,800

(i) Let the selling price per bottle be x

Total sales = $40{,}000x$

Total commission (8% of sales) $3{,}200\,x$

Total profit (10% of sales) $4{,}000x$

$$\text{Selling Price per unit} = \frac{\text{Total sales}}{40{,}000}$$

$$= \frac{(\text{Fixed cost} + \text{Variable cost} + \text{Profit})}{40{,}000}$$

$$x = \frac{[(3{,}16{,}800 + 3{,}200\,x) + 76{,}800 + 4000\,x]}{40{,}000}$$

$$40{,}000x = 3{,}93{,}600 + 7200x$$

$$32{,}800x = 3{,}93{,}600$$

$$x = ₹\,12$$

Thus, selling price of ₹ 12 gives a profit of 10% on sales.

(ii)

$$\text{Selling Price} = ₹\,11$$

$$\text{Fixed Cost} = 76{,}800$$

$$\text{Variable Cost per unit} = \frac{(3{,}16{,}800)}{40{,}000} + 8\%\text{ of }₹\,11 = ₹\,8.80$$

$$\text{Contribution per unit} = 11 - 8.80 = ₹\,2.20$$

$$\text{P/V ratio} = \frac{\text{Contribution per unit}}{\text{Selling per unit}} \times 100 = \frac{2.20}{11 \times 100} = 20\%$$

$$\text{BEP (in units)} = \frac{\text{Total fixed cost}}{\text{Contribution per unit}} = \frac{76{,}800}{2.20} = 34909 \text{ units}$$

$$\text{BEP (in ₹)} = \frac{\text{Total fixed cost}}{\text{P/V ratio}} = \frac{76{,}800}{20\%} = ₹\,3{,}84{,}000$$

Problem 52 Lakme India is manufacturing and selling two products A at and B, at selling prices of ₹3 and ₹4 per unit respectively. The following sales strategy has been outlined for the current year:

- Sales planned for the year will be ₹7.20 lakh in case of A and 3.50 lakh in case of B.
- To meet competition, the selling prices of A will be reduced by 20% and that of B by 12.5%.
- Break-even is planned at 60% of the total sales of each product.
- Profit to be achieved for the year is planned as ₹69,120 in case of A and ₹17,500 in case of B. This would be possible by launching a cost reduction programme and reducing the present annual fixed expenses of ₹1,35,000, allocated as ₹1,08,000 to A and ₹27,000 to B.

You are required to present the proposal in financial terms giving clearly the following information:

(a) Number of units to be sold for each of the product to break-even.

(b) Total number of units to be sold during the year.

(c) Reduction in fixed expenses product-wise as envisaged by the cost reduction programme.

Solution:

(a) & (b) Statement showing units to be sold during the year (product-wise) as well as the break-even units required

Particulars	Products	
	A	B
	₹	₹
Current selling price per unit	3	4
Less : Reduction in price	0.60	0.50
Revised selling price (RSP)	2.40	3.50
Budgeted sales (BS) during the year at revised selling price	7,20,000	3,50,000
Number of units to be sold to achieve budgeted sales (BS ÷ RSP)	3,00,000	1,00,000
Break-even sales in units (0.60 x total sales unit)	1,80,000	60,000

(c) Statement showing reduction in Fixed Expenses (product-wise) envisaged in the cost-reduction programme

Particulars	Products	
	A	B
Budged sales during the year	₹7,20,000	₹3,50,000
Break-even sales (60% x total sales)	4,32,000	2,10,000
Margin of safety (MS) [BS – BES]	2,88,000	1,40,000

Table Contd...

Table Contd...

Particulars	Products	
	A	B
Planned profit of the year	69,120	17,500
P/V (Planned profit/MS) (%)	24	12.5
Variable cost ratio (%)	76	87.5
Variable costs at break-even sales	₹3,28,320	₹1,83,750
Fixed costs (break-even sales – VC)	1,03,680	26,250
Present fixed cost	1,08,000	27,000
Reduction in fixed costs envisaged	4320	750

Problem 53 There are two plants under the same management. The management desires to merge these two plants. The following particulars are available:

	Plant I	*Plant II*
Capacity operation	100 per cent	60 per cent
Sales	₹300 lakhs	₹120 lakhs
Variable costs	₹220 lakhs	₹ 90 lakhs
Fixed costs	₹ 40 lakhs	₹ 20 lakhs

You are required to calculate:

(i) What would be the capacity of the merged plant to be operated for the purpose of breaking even?

(ii) What would be the capacity of the marked plant to earn a profit of ₹60 lakhs?

(iii) What would be the profit on working at 80 per cent of the merged capacity?

[*B.Com. (H)*]

Solution:

Statement of Profit (Figure in lakhs)

Particulars	Plant I	Plant II	Merged Plants
Sales (at 100%)	300	200	500
—Variable cost	220	150	370
Contribution	80	50	130
—Fixed cost	40	20	60
Net income	40	30	70

(i) P/V Ratio: $\frac{\text{Contribution}}{\text{Sales}} \times 100 = \frac{130}{500} \times 100 = 26\%$

(ii) $\text{Break-even level} = \frac{\text{Fixed cost}}{\text{P/V ratio}} = \frac{60}{.26} = 230.77 \text{ lakhs}$

(iii) % capacity at BE level = ₹230.77 ÷ ₹500 = 46.15%

(iv) To earn Profit of ₹60 lakhs = (₹60 lakhs + ₹60 lakhs) ÷ 26
= ₹461.54 lakhs

(v) % capacity = ₹461.54 lakhs/₹500 lakhs
= 92.31%

(vi) Profit at 80% capacity = (₹500 lakhs × .80 × .26) – ₹60 lakhs
= ₹44 lakhs

Problem 54 A, B and C are three similar plants under the same management who want them to be merged for better operation. The details are as under:

Plant	*A*	*B*	*C*
Capacity operated	100%	70%	50%
	₹ lakhs	₹ lakhs	₹ lakhs
Sales turnover	300	280	150
Variable cost	200	210	75
Fixed cost	70	50	62

Find out :

(i) The capacity of the merged plant for break-even.

(ii) The profit at 75% capacity of the merged plan.

(iii) The turnover from the merged plant to give a profit of ₹28 lakhs.

Solution:

Statement showing contribution

	A	B	C	Merged Plant
Capacity	100%	100%	100%	100%
Turnover	300	400	300	1,000
Less: Variable cost	200	300	150	650
Contribution	100	100	150	350
Fixed cost	70	50	62	182

(i) $$\text{P/V Ratio of merged plant} = \frac{\text{Contribution of merged plant}}{\text{Turnover of merged plant}} \times 100$$

$$= \frac{₹350 \text{ lakhs}}{1000 \text{ lakhs}} \times 100 = 35\%$$

$$\text{Break-even point} = \frac{\text{Fixed Cost}}{\text{P/V Ratio}} = \frac{₹182 \text{ lakhs}}{35\%} = 7520 \text{ lakhs}$$

$$\text{Capacity utilisation} = \frac{\text{Turnover at break-even point}}{\text{Total turnover}} \times 100$$

$$= \frac{₹520 \text{ lakhs}}{₹1000 \text{ lakhs}} \times 100 = 52\%$$

(ii) Sales at 75% capacity = ₹750 lakhs.

Contribution at 75% capacity = 750 × 35%	₹262.50 lakh
Less: Fixed cost	₹ 182 lakhs
Profit	₹80.50 lakhs

(iii)

$$\text{Desired Sales} = \frac{\text{Fixed cost + Profit}}{\text{P/V ratio}}$$

$$= \frac{182 + 28}{35} \times 100 = 600 \text{ lakhs.}$$

Problem 55 A company has a fixed cost of ₹2,00,000. It sells two products: X and Y in the ratio of 2 : 1. If contribution of X is ₹10 per unit and of Y is ₹20 per unit, how many units of each X and Y would be sold at break-even point? [*B.Com. (H)*]

Solution:

$$\text{Break-even Point} = \frac{\text{Fixed cost}}{\text{Contribution per unit}}$$

Contribution of mix = Ratio of sales mix × Contribution per unit

X (2 × 10)	₹20
Y(1 × 20)	₹20
Total contribution from mix	₹40

$$\text{Break-even level} = \frac{\text{Fixed cost}}{\text{Contribution from mix}} = \frac{₹2,00,000}{40} = 5,000 \text{ mix}$$

Units X to be sold (5,000 × 2)	10,000
Units Y to be sold (5,000 × 1)	5,000

Problem 56 A company has three factories in North, East and South with its head office in Mumbai. The management has received the following summary report on the operations of each factory for a period:

Zone	Sales Over/(Under)		Profit Over/(Under)	
	Actual (₹)	Budget (₹)	Actual (₹)	Budget (₹)
North	11,00,000	(4,00,000)	1,35,000	(1,80,000)
East	14,50,000	1,50,000	2,10,000	90,000
South	12,00,000	(2,00,000)	3,30,000	(1,10,000)

Calculate for each factory and for the company as a whole for the period:

(i) Fixed cost; and (ii) Break-even point.

Solution:

(i) Computation of P/V ratio:

North:	*Sales (₹)*	*Profit (₹)*
Actual	11,00,000	1,35,000
Add: Under-budgeted	4,00,000	1,80,000
Budgeted	15,00,000	3,15,000

P/V Ratio = Difference in profit/Difference in sales
= [(3,15,000 – 1,35,000)/(15,00,000 – 11,00,000)) × 100
= (1,80,000/ 4,00,000) × 100 = 45% or 0.45

East:	*Sales (₹)*	*Profit (₹)*
Actual	14,50,000	2,10,000
Less: Over-budgeted	1,50,000	90,000
Budgeted	13,00,000	1,20,000

P/V Ratio = Difference in profit/ Difference in sales
= [(2,10,000 – 1,20,000)/(14,50,000 – 13,00,000)] × 100
= (90,000/1,50,000) × 100 = 60% or 0.60

South:	*Sales (₹)*	*Profit (₹)*
Actual	12,00,000	3,30,000
Add: Under-budgeted	2,00,000	1,10,000
Budgeted	14,00,000	4,40,000

P/V Ratio = Difference in profit/ Difference in sales
= [(4,40,000 – 3,30,000) 14,00,000 – 12,00,000)] × 100
= (1,10,000/2,00,000) × 100 = 55% or 0.55

Computation of Fixed Cost:

Fixed Cost = (Actual Sales × P/V Ratio) – Profit

North: = (11,00,000 × 0.45) – 1,35,000 = ₹3,60,000

East: = (14,50,000 × 0.60) – 2,10,000 = ₹6,60,000

South: = (12,00,000 × 0.55) – 3,30,000 = ₹3,30,000

(ii) Computation of Break-even Point:

BEP (₹) = Fixed Cost/P/V Ratio

North: = (3,60,000/0.45) = ₹8,00,000

East: = (6,60,000/0.60) = ₹11,00,000

South: = (3,30,000/0.55) = ₹6,00,000

Total = ₹25,00,000

Problem 57 Tata Ltd. is presently selling 1,00,000 units at a selling price of ₹8 per unit. The following are the cost estimates for three prospective plants A, B & C:

	Plant A	*Plant B*	*Plant C*
Annual fixed cost (₹)	1,20,000	2,16,000	2,40,000
Variable cost per unit (₹)	5	4.4	4.20
Annual capacity (units)	75,000	1,20,000	1,50,000

1. Calculate the range of output over which each plant would be most economical.

2. What is the present profit earned with each of the plants? Assume that Plant A can be worked double shift with an additional expense of 10% in fixed costs and 5% in variable costs of all units. *(CS Inter, Modified)*

Solution:

1. Statement of Economic Range of Output

	Plant A ₹	Plant B ₹	Plant C ₹
Selling Price per unit	8.00	8.00	8.00
Variable Cost per unit	5.00	4.40	4.20
Contribution per unit	3.00	3.60	3.80
Annual Fixed Costs	1,20,000	2,16,000	2,40,000
BEP (Units)	1,20,000/3	2,16,000/3.6	2,40,000/3.80
	= 40,000	= 60,000	= 63,158
Annual Capacity (units)	75,000	1,20,000	1,50,000
Economical range of Output beyond BEP	40,001–75,000	60,000–1,20,000	63,159–1,50,000

2. Statement of Profits on the Sale of 1,00,000 Units

Particulars	A (₹)	B (₹)	C (₹)
Contribution per unit[1]	2.75	3.60	3.80
Total Contribution on 100000 units	2,75,000	3,60,000	3,80,000
Less : Fixed Cost	(1,32,000)	(2,16,000)	(2,40,000)
Profit	1,43,000	1,44,000	1,40,000

Working Note:

1. Annual capacity of Plant A is 75,000 units. For the required sales of 1,00,000 units, Plant A has to work double shift. This will increase 10% in fixed costs and 5% in variable costs of all units :

Revised annual fixed cost = 1,20,000 + 10% = ₹ 1,32,000

Revised variable cost = 5 + 5% of ₹ 5 = ₹ 5.25 per unit

Contribution per unit = 8 – 5.25 = ₹ 2.75 per unit

Problem 58 A Ltd., owns two factories, one at Noida and the other at Gurugram. Both factories produce same product which is sold in the market at ₹ 200 per unit. The following are the other cost details:

	Noida Factory	*Gurugram Factory*
Capacity (units)	20,000	30,000
Fixed cost	₹ 14,00,000	₹ 4,00,000
Variable cost per unit	₹ 120	₹ 160

Determine BEP for the company as a whole assuming:

(a) Constant sales-mix in the ratio of capacities of the plants.

(b) Variable sales-mix producing from more profitable plant first.

(c) Using actual sales ratio as the basis assuming that actual output and sale from Noida plant is 15,000 units and from Gurugram plant 25,000 units.

Solution:

(a) *Constant sales-mix in the ratio of capacity of plants*

Particulars	Noida Factory	Gurugram Factory	Total
Sales value @ ₹200	40,00,000	60,00,000	1,00,00,000
Less: Variable Cost	24,00,000	48,00,000	72,00,000
Contribution	16,00,000	12,00,000	28,00,000
P/V Ratio	$\frac{16}{40} \times 100 = 40\%$	$\frac{12}{60} \times 100 = 20\%$	$\frac{28}{100} \times 100 = 28\%$
Fixed Cost	14,00,000	4,00,000	18.00.000
BEP $\left(\frac{FC}{P/V\ Ratio}\right)$	35,00,000	20,00,000	64,28,571

One may notice that the overall BEP is greater than the total of the individual BEP. This is so because the overall BEP assumes that the sales from the two plants must be in the given constant sales mix, i.e., 40,00,000 : 60,00,000.

(b) *Variable sales-mix producing from more profitable plant first.*

The plant with a higher contribution per unit should be used first.

Noida plant gives higher per unit contribution of ₹80 compared with only ₹40 per unit from Gurugram Plant.

Total contribution from full capacity of Noida plant = 20,000 × 80 = ₹16,00,000

At overall BEP, the contribution should be sufficient to recover the total fixed cost of both the plants. Therefore, remaining fixed cost shall be recovered by producing from Gurugram Plant.

Remaining contribution to be realised from Gurugram Plant

= Combined FC – 16,00,000

= (14,00,000 + 4,00,000) – 16,00,000 = ₹2,00,000

Units to be produced from Gurugram Plant = 2,00,000 ÷ p.u. contribution from Gurugram Plant

= 2,00,000 ÷ 40 = 5000 units.

Total Sales at BEP = (20,000 × 200) + (5000 × 200) = ₹50,00,000

One may notice that the overall BEP is achieved at the lowest level of sales in this case. This is so because most profitable plant is utilised first which helps to recover the fixed cost at the earliest.

(c) Using actual sales-mix as the basis:

Particulars	Noida Factory ₹	Gurugram Factory ₹	Total
Sales value @ ₹200	30,00,000	50,00,000	80,00,000
Variable Cost	18,00,000	40,00,000	58,00,000
Contribution	12,00,000	10,00,000	22,00,000
P/V Ratio			$\left(\frac{22}{80} \times 100 = 27.5\%\right)$
Fixed Cost	14,00,000	4,00,000	18,00,000
BEP $\left(\frac{FC}{P/V\ Ratio}\right)$			65,45,454

Problem 59 A producer has two plants–one in Faridabad and another in Delhi, producing same product. Cost details regarding the two plants are given below:

	Faridabad Plant	Delhi Plant
Maximum capacity (units)	30,000	50,000
Total fixed cost	1,60,000	3,00,000
Depreciation	₹40,000	₹75,000
Variable cost per unit	₹12	₹11
Selling price per unit	₹20	₹20
Output and sales (units)	20,000	40,000

You are required to determine the following:

(a) Break-even for each of the two plants; (b) Cash break-even for each of the two plants; (c) Combined P/V ratio; (d) In case total output is to be increased by 12,000 units, how much output should be increased from which plant and why; (e) In case total output is to be curtailed by 7000 units, from which plant should it be curtailed and why?

Solution:

	Faridabad Plant ₹	Delhi Plant ₹	Combined
Sales value @₹20	4,00,000	8,00,000	12,00,000
Variable cost	2,40,000	4,40,000	6,80,000
Contribution	1,60,000	3,60,000	5,20,000
(c) P/V ratio	40%	45%	$\frac{52}{120} \times 100 = 43.33\%$
Fixed cost	1,60,000	3,00,000	4,60,000

Table Contd...

Table Contd...

Depreciation	40,000	75,000	1,15,000
Cash Fixed Cost	1,20,000	2,25,000	3,45,000
(a) BEP $\left(\dfrac{FC}{P/V\ Ratio}\right)$	4,00,000	6,66,667	10,61,538
(b) Cash BEP = $\dfrac{Cash\ FC}{P/V\ Ratio}$	3,00,000	5,00,000	8,00,000

(d) The output should be first increased from Delhi plant as it has a higher contribution per unit. But this can be increased only by 10000 units which makes the capacity utilisation to 100%. Remaining 2000 units should be increased from Faridabad Plant.

(e) The output should be curtailed from Faridabad plant as the contribution per unit is lower from this plant.

Problem 60 Pink Ltd. manufactures a single product having a marginal cost of ₹0.75 per unit. Fixed costs are ₹12,000. The market is such that up to 40000 units can be sold at ₹1.50 a unit, but any additional sales must be made at ₹1 a unit only. The company is planning to earn a profit of ₹20,000. How many units should be produced and sold by the company to earn the planned profit? [*B.Com. (Hons)*]

Solution: First, let us find out the profit on the sale of the first 40000 units.

Statement showing profit from 40000 units

Particulars		Amount (₹)
Sales	(40,000 × 1.50)	60,000
Variable cost	(40,000 × 0.75)	30,000
Contribution		30,000
Fixed cost		(–) 12,000
Profit		18,000

∴ Out of the total planned profit of ₹20,000, a profit of ₹18,000 is earned from the sale of first 40000 units.

∴ Balance of the planned profit, i.e., ₹20,000 – ₹18,000 = ₹2000, which is to be earned from the additional sales over 40,000 units.

The contribution per unit from the additional sales over 40000 units = ₹1 – ₹0.75 = ₹0.25.

∴ Additional sales required to earn the balance profit of ₹2,000

$$= \frac{\text{Total contribution}}{\text{Contribution per unit}} = \frac{₹2{,}000}{₹0.25} = 8000 \text{ units}$$

∴ Total number of units to be sold to earn a profit of ₹20,000 = 40,000 + 8000 = 48,000 units.

Problem 61 Calculate BEP for a train journey between Delhi and Bangalore where cost of an engine is ₹80,000, and of a bogie ₹16,000. Capacity of a bogie is 70 passengers and each ticket for the journey is priced at ₹500. There is no variable cost of passenger.

[*B.Com. (Hons.)*]

Solution: The contribution generated by a full bogie = 500 × 70 – 16,000 = ₹19,000

No. of bogies required to recover engine cost of 80,000 = 80,000 ÷ 19,000 = 4.21 bogies i.e., 5 bogies.

Total cost of the train with 5 bogies = 80,000 + (5 × 16,000) = ₹1,60,000

Break-even (passengers) = 1,60,000 ÷ 500 = 320 passengers.

Break-even (₹) = 320 × 500 = ₹1,60,000

Problem 62 Sagar Ltd. manufactures a product, currently utilising 80% capacity with a turnover of ₹8,00,000 at ₹25 per unit. The cost data are as follows:

Material cost is ₹7.50 per unit, labour cost is ₹6.25 per unit, semi-variable cost (including the variable cost of ₹3.75 per unit) is ₹1,80,000. The fixed cost is ₹90,000 up to 80% level of the output; and beyond this, an additional amount of ₹20,000 will be incurred.

You are required to compute:

(i) Activity level at BEP.

(ii) Number of units to be sold to earn a net income of 8% of sales.

(iii) Activity level needed to earn a profit of ₹95,000.

(iv) What should be the selling price per unit, if BEP is to be brought down to 40% activity level?

Solution:

Statement showing contribution

Particulars	₹
Selling Price per unit	25.00
Material Cost	7.50
Labour Cost	6.25
Variable Portion within Semi-Variable Cost	3.75
Variable Cost per unit	17.50
Contribution per unit	7.50

$$\therefore \text{ P/V Ratio} = \frac{C}{S} \times 100 = \frac{7.50}{25} \times 100 = 30\%$$

$$\text{Number of units produced and sold currently utilising 80\% capacity} = \frac{₹8,00,000}{₹25}$$

$$= 32,000 \text{ units}$$

Fixed portion included in the Semi-variable Cost:

Total semi-variable cost at 32,000 units of output	1,80,000
Less: Variable Portion of semi-variable cost (32,000 units × 73.75)	1,20,000
Fixed Portion of semi-VC at 32,000 units of output (i.e., at 80% capacity)	60,000

Total Fixed Cost up to 80% capacity:

Fixed cost	90,000
Add: Fixed portion of semi-variable cost	60,000
Total fixed cost up to 80% capacity	1,50,000

(i)
$$\text{BEP (in units)} = \frac{₹1,50,000}{₹7.50} = 20000 \text{ units}$$

$$\therefore \quad \text{Activity level at BEP} = \frac{80}{32,000} \times 20,000 = 50\%$$

(ii) Let the sale be ₹x.

$$\therefore \quad \text{Profit} = 8\% \text{ of } ₹x = 0.08x$$

$$\text{We know that P/V ratio} = \frac{\text{Contribution}}{\text{Sales}} \times 100 = \frac{F+P}{S} \times 100$$

$$\Rightarrow \quad 30 = \frac{₹1,50,000 + 0.08x}{x} \times 100$$

$$\Rightarrow \quad \frac{30x}{100} = 1,50,000 + 0.08x$$

$$\Rightarrow \quad 0.3x - 0.08x = 1,50,000$$

$$\Rightarrow \quad 0.22x = 1,50,000$$

$$\therefore \quad x = \frac{1,50,000}{0.22} = 6,81,818$$

∴ Required sales value = ₹6,81,818

∴ Required number of units to be sold to earn a net income of 8% sales

$$= \frac{₹6,82,818}{₹25} = 27273 \text{ units (approx.)}$$

(iii) As the profit of ₹95,000 is higher than the existing profit, this amount of profit will be achieved by operating beyond the mentioned 80% capacity.

$$\therefore \quad \text{New fixed cost} = \text{Existing fixed cost} + ₹20,000$$

$$= ₹1,50,000 + ₹20,000 = ₹1,70,000$$

$$\therefore \quad \text{Desired Sales (Units)} = \frac{FC + P}{\text{Contribution per unit}} = \frac{1{,}70{,}000 + 95{,}000}{7.50}$$

$$= 35333 \text{ units}$$

$$\therefore \text{Activity level needed to earn a profit of ₹95,000} = \frac{80}{32{,}000} \times 35333 \text{ units} = 88.33\%$$

(iv) Output at 40% activity level = 32,000 × 40 ÷ 80 = 16,000 units

Particulars	₹
∴ Variable cost at 40% activity level (₹17.50 × 16,000 units)	2,80,000
∴ Fixed cost at 40% activity level	1,50,000
Total cost at 40% activity level	4,30,000

At BEP, total cost = Total sales = ₹4,30,000

$$\therefore \text{Selling price per unit} = \frac{₹4{,}30{,}000}{16{,}000 \text{ units}} = ₹26{,}875$$

Problem 63 Ranfort Pharmaceutical Company produces formulations having a shelf life of one year. The company has an opening stock of 5000 boxes on 1st January, 2019 and expects to produce 75,000 boxes in the current year. Sales expected during the year are 70,000 boxes.

Cost accounting department has worked out escalation in cost by 20% on variable cost and 10% on fixed cost for the year 2019. Fixed costs are estimated at ₹12,00,000. New price planned for 2019 is 250 per box. Variable cost of the opening stock is ₹20 per box.

You are required to find out (a) break-even volume for the year 2019, and (b) the estimated profits on the sale for the year 2019.

Solution:

(a) Break-even Sales:

Since the product has a shelf life of one year, the company will fist liquidate the opening stock.

Contribution on the sale of opening stock (5000 boxes) = 5000 × (50 – 20)

= ₹1,50,000

Balance of fixed cost to be recovered = 12,00,000 – 1,50,000 = ₹10,50,000.

Revised variable cost = ₹20 + ₹4 = ₹24

Contribution on the additional units sold = 50 – 24 = ₹26

$$\text{Required sales volume to recover the balance fixed cost} = \frac{10}{50{,}000{,}26} = 40{,}385 \text{ boxes.}$$

Break-even volume for the year = 5000 + 40,385 = 45,385 boxes.

(b) Estimation of profit for the year 2019:

Sales (70,000 × ₹50)	₹35,00,000
Less : Variable cost (5000 × ₹20)	1,00,000
Variable cost (65,000 × ₹24)	15,60,000
Contribution	18,40,000
Less : Fixed cost	12,00,000
Profit	6,40,000

Problem 64 Vinod Ltd. manufactures pressure cookers with the selling price being ₹300 per unit. Currently the capacity utilisation is 60 per cent with a sales turnover of 18 lakh. The company proposes to reduce the selling price by 20 per cent but desires to maintain the same profit position by increasing the output. Assuming that all the increased output could be made and sold, determine the level at which the company should operate to achieve the desired objective assuming the following additional information:

(i) Variable costs per unit, ₹60.

(ii) Semi-variable costs (including a variable element of 10 per unit), ₹1,80,000.

(iii) Fixed costs, ₹3,00,000 will remain constant up to 80 per cent level. Beyond this an additional amount of ₹60,000 will be incurred.

Solution: **Profitability Statement at 60% capacity**

Particulars	Amount (₹)
Sales revenue (6000 units[1] × ₹300)	18,00,000
Less : Variable costs :	
Variable costs (6000 units × ₹60)	3,60,000
Variable component in semi-variable costs (6000 units × ₹10)	60,000
Total contribution	13,80,000
Less : Fixed costs	3,00,000
Less : Fixed components in semi-variable costs	1,20,000
Profit	9,60,000

When Sales Price is reduced by 20 per cent.

Revised selling price [₹300 – (20)] per unit	₹240
Less : Variable costs	70
Revised contribution per unit	170

Desired sales volume to maintain profit = (₹4,20,000 + ₹9,60,000) ÷ ₹170 = 8118 units or 81.2 per cent. Capacity expansion beyond 80 per cent will require additional fixed costs of ₹60,000.

Therefore, the desired sales volume to maintain profit = (₹4,80,000 + ₹9,60,000) ÷ ₹170 = 8,471 units 84.7 per cent. Therefore, the company should operate at 84.7 per cent level of capacity to maintain the existing profit of ₹9,60,000.

Working Notes:

1. 60 per cent capacity = (₹18,00,000 ÷ ₹300) = 6000 units
   At 100 per cent capacity = 10,000 units

Problem 65 Calculate the break-even number of candidates from the following information:

	₹
Fee collected per candidate	100
Variable cost per candidate	80
One supervisor for every 100 candidates at the rate of	500
Fixed cost	20,000

Solution:

Fees collected		100
Less : Variable cost		
Variable cost	80	
Supervision cost	5	85
Contribution		15
Fixed cost		20,000

$$\text{BEP} = \left[\frac{\text{Fixed costs}}{\text{Contribution per unit}}\right] = \left[\frac{20{,}000}{15}\right] = 1333.33$$

In BEP is taken as 1333.33 candidates, there would be under recovery of supervisors cost to the extent of 333.35 as follows:

Supervision Cost recovered (1333.33 × 5)	6666.65
Actual Supervision Cost (1400 × 5)	7,000
Under recovery	333.35

To recover ₹333.35, 16.67 candidates $\left[\text{i.e., } \frac{₹333.35}{₹20}\right]$ should be added to the above BEP

Hence, BEP is – 1333.33 + 16.67 = 1351 candidates

Verification:

Fees collected for 1351 candidates [1351 × ₹100]		1,35,100
Less : Variable cost [1351 × ₹80]	1,08,100	
Supervision cost [14 × 500]	7,000	1,15,100
Contribution		20,000
Less : Fixed cost		20,000
Profit		Nil

Problem 66 Bright Management School teaches wholly through the correspondence method. This is done by the development of self-study packages which enable students to prepare for professional qualifications.

Each course of study was sold at the price of ₹ 15 last year and a total of 10,000 units were produced and sold. The production costs of the various courses offered by the School are the same.

The variable cost of producing a study course last year was:

	₹
Direct materials	5.00
Direct labour	6.00
Other direct costs (mainly postage)	0.60
Variable overheads	0.40

The fixed overhead for the institute during the year was ₹ 20,000.

During the coming year the costs of the organisation are expected to increase by the following:

	%
Direct materials	20.00
Direct labour	16.67
Other direct costs	66.67
Variable overhead	25.00
Fixed overhead	5.00

Market research has shown that the increase in the prices of the course package up to 17.5% will have no effect on the number of units sold. However, for every 1% increase in price above 17.5%, the number of units sold is expected to fall by 2%.

You are required to compute:

(a) The new selling price of the study courses if the number of study courses sold and the annual profits are to remain as before.

(b) The number of units to be sold to maintain the same profit as earlier, assuming the selling price to remain same.

Solution:

(a) *Computation of Selling Price*	₹
Contribution per unit [₹ 15 – 12]	3
Total contribution [10,000 × ₹ 3]	30,000
Less : Fixed cost	20,000
Profit	10,000
New Variable Cost: Material (5 × 1.2)	6.00

	₹
Labour (6 × 1.1667)	7.00
Other direct costs (0.60 × 1.667)	1.00
Variable overhead (0.40 × 1.25)	0.50
	14.50

$$\text{New contribution required} = \frac{\text{Profit + Fixed costs}}{10{,}000}$$

$$= \frac{[₹10{,}000 + (₹20{,}000 \times 1.05)]}{10000} = ₹3.10 \text{ per unit}$$

$$\text{New selling price} = \text{New variable cost + New contribution}$$
$$= ₹14.50 + ₹3.10 = ₹17.60$$

Thus, an increase of ₹2.60 on the previous price of ₹15, i.e., 17.33% increase is required. This is below 17.5%, therefore, no change in the number of units sold.

(b) $$\text{Number of units to be sold} = \frac{\text{New fixed costs + Desired profit}}{\text{New contribution per unit}}$$

$$= \frac{21000 + 10000}{₹15 - ₹14.50}$$

$$= 62{,}000 \text{ units}$$

Problem 67 From the following information relating to a firm, you are required to calculate the cash break-even point.

Selling price per unit ₹80

Variable cost per unit ₹70.

Total fixed cost for the year ₹6,00,000 which includes depreciation amounting to ₹60,000, notional salary for proprietor's supervision ₹24,000, write off of deferred revenue expenditure ₹16,000.

Solution: $$\text{Cash BEP (units)} = \frac{\text{Cash fixed cost}}{\text{Cash contribution per unit}}$$

$$= \frac{6{,}00{,}000 - (60{,}000 + 24{,}000 + 16{,}000)}{80 - 70}$$

$$= 5{,}00{,}000 \div 10 = 50000 \text{ units}$$

$$\text{Cash BEP (₹)} = 50{,}000 \times 80 = ₹40{,}00{,}000$$

Problem 68 The product of a firm is sold at ₹150 per unit, which has the following cost structure:

Direct materials	40	Variable overheads	10
Direct labour	30	Fixed overheads	50,000
Direct expenses	20		

The overheads mentioned above consisted of:

			₹
Salary (fixed)	10,000	Electricity (fixed)	15,000
Telephone charge (fixed)	5000	Maintenance (2/3rd fixed)	12,000
Depreciation (2/3rd fixed)	18,000		

Assuming an activity level of 1000 units, compute the cash break-even point.

Solution:

$$\text{Selling price} = ₹\,150$$

$$\text{Variable Cost} = ₹\,40 + 30 + 20 + 10 = 100$$

$$\text{Fixed overheads} = ₹\,50{,}000$$

$$\text{Non-cash VC (Depreciation) per unit} = ₹\,6000/1000 = 6$$

$$\text{Non cash FC (Depreciation)} = ₹\,12{,}000$$

$$\text{Cash VC} = 100 - 6 = 94$$

$$\text{Cash FC} = ₹\,50{,}000 - 12{,}000 = 38{,}000$$

$$\text{Cash BEP} = \frac{\text{Cash fixed cost}}{\text{Cash contribution per unit}} = 38{,}000/94 = 405 \text{ units}$$

Problem 69 A producer is contemplating purchase of either Machine A or Machine B. The following are the cost details:

	Machine A	*Machine B*
Fixed cost	₹5,00,000	₹3,00,000
Variable cost per unit	₹30	₹40
Selling price	₹50	₹50

Calculate cost break-even (i.e., point of indifference). Explain its implications. Verify the result.

Solution:

$$\text{Cost break-even} = \frac{\text{Difference in fixed cost}}{\text{Difference in per unit contribution}}$$

$$= \frac{5{,}00{,}000 - 3{,}00{,}000}{[50 - 30] - [50 - 40]}$$

$$= 20{,}000 \text{ units}$$

At output and sale of 20,000 units, the producer's profit will be same from Machine A and Machine B so that he is indifferent between the two machines. In case his expected sale is below 20,000 units, his profits will be higher with Machine *B* (i.e., one with a lower fixed cost). If actual or anticipated sale is above 20,000 units, profits will be higher with Machine A (One with a lower VC per unit).

Problem 70 Roxy Ltd. has been offered choice to buy a plant between P_1 and P_2. The following information is available:

	P_1	P_2
Annual output in units	10,000	10,000
Fixed Cost	₹60,000	₹32,000
Profit at above level	₹60,000	₹48,000

The market price of the product is expected to be ₹20 per unit.

You are required to compute:

(a) Break-even point of each plant.

(b) The level of sales at which both the plants earn equal profit.

(c) The range of sales at which one is more profitable than the other.

Solution:

(a)

Particulars	P_1	P_2
	₹	₹
Sales value (10,000 × ₹20)	2,00,000	2,00,000
Contribution (Fixed Cost + Profit)	1,20,000	80,000
Variable Cost	80,000	1,20,000
P/V Ratio $\left(\frac{\text{Contribution}}{\text{Sales}}\right)$	60%	40%
Break-even Point $\left(\frac{\text{Fixed Cost}}{\text{P/V ratio}}\right)$	1,00,000	80,000
Break-even Point (Units)	5000	4000
Contribution per unit (₹)	12	8
Variable Cost per unit	8	12

(b) Since the selling price of the product produced by plant P_1 and P_2 are same, the plants will earn equal profit when the total costs of operation of both the plants are same.

Let the number of units be x.

$$\text{Total cost of } P_1 = 8x + 60{,}000$$

$$\text{Total cost of } P_2 = 12x + 32{,}000$$

Therefore, at cost break-even point,

$$8x + 60000 = 12x + 32{,}000$$

or, $$4x = 28{,}000$$

or, $$x = 7000 \text{ units}$$

At a production level of 7000 units the profits made by P_1 and P_2 would be same.

(c) 6999 units: Plant P_2 is more profitable as the total cost is lower with the plant having a lower fixed cost.

At 7000: Both the plants give equal profits.

7001 and above: Plant P_1 is more profitable as the total cost is lower with the plant having a lower variable cost per unit.

Problem 71 Service provider now spends 9 per km on taxi fares for his clients work. He is considering two other alternatives, the purchase of a new small car or an old bigger car.

Items	New Small Car	Bigger Car
	₹	₹
Purchase Price	3,50,000	2,00,000
Sales Price, after 5 years	1,90,000	1,20,000
Repairs and Servicing, per annum	10,000	12,000
Taxes and Insurance, per annum	17,000	7,000
Mileage per kg of CNG	10 km	7 km
CNG Price, per kg	35	35

(a) Which of the three alternatives will be cheapest, if he is expected to travel 10,000 km annually?

(b) If his practice expands and has to travel 19,000 km per annum, what should be his decision?

(c) At how many km per annum will the cost of the two cars break-even? Ignore interest and income tax.

Solution: (a) & (b) **Statement showing comparative costs under each alternative**

Particulars	New Small Car (₹)	Old Bigger Car (₹)	Taxi (₹)
Fixed costs per annum:			
Depreciation	32,000	16,000	
Repairs & Servicing	10,000	12,000	
Taxes & Insurance	17,000	7,000	
	59,000	35,000	
Variable costs per annum:			
(a) CNG 10,000 km	35,000	50,000	
(b) CNG 19,000 km	66,500	95,000	
Total Cost :			
(a) 10,000 km	94,000	85,000	90,000
(b) 19,000 km	1,25,500	1,30,000	1,71,000

Recommendation:

The old bigger car is the cheapest for his present practice. However, if his practice expands, new small car will be the cheapest.

(c) $$\text{Cost break-even point} = \frac{\text{Difference in fixed cost}}{\text{Difference in variable cost of two cars}}$$

$$\frac{₹59{,}000 - ₹35{,}000}{₹5 - ₹3.50} = \frac{₹24{,}000}{₹1.50}$$

Working Note:

1. $$\text{Depreciation} = \frac{3{,}50{,}000 - 1{,}90{,}000}{5} = 32{,}000$$

Problem 72 Two companies, M Ltd. and N Ltd. sell the same type of product. Their budgeted profit and loss accounts for the year show the following: (₹ '000)

Particulars	M Ltd.		N Ltd.	
Sales		150		150
Less: Variable cost	120		100	
Fixed cost	15	135	35	135
Budgeted profit		15		15

You are required to calculate the break-even point of each company. Also state which company is likely to earn greater profit for its product if there is:

(i) Heavy demand

(ii) Poor demand

Solution:

$$\text{Break-even Point} = \frac{\text{Fixed cost}}{\text{P/V ratio}}$$

$$\text{P/V Ratio} = \frac{\text{Contribution}}{\text{Sales}} \times 100$$

$$\text{Contribution} = \text{Sales} - \text{Variable cost}$$

Statement showing P/V ratio, BEP and Margin of Safety

Particulars	M Ltd. (₹)	N Ltd. (₹)
Sales	1,50,000	1,50,000
Less: Variable cost	1,20,000	1,00,000
Contribution	30,000	50,000
P/V Ratio	$\frac{₹30{,}000}{₹1{,}50{,}000} \times 100 = 20\%$	$\frac{₹50{,}000}{₹1{,}50{,}000} \times 100 = 33½\%$
Break-even Point	$\frac{₹15{,}000}{0.20} = ₹75{,}000$	$\frac{₹35{,}000}{0.333} = ₹1{,}05{,}000$

Table Contd...

Table Contd...

Margin of Safety (Actual sales – Break-even sales)	₹1,50,000 – ₹75,000 = ₹75,000	₹1,50,000 – ₹1,05,000 = ₹45,000

Comments:

(i) In case of heavy demand, a firm with the higher P/V ratio will give the higher profits, i.e., firm N Ltd.

(ii) In case of low demand, a firm with the lower BEP will recover the total cost earlier and will have the lower chances of losses. Therefore, M Ltd. with low break-even point will be able to sustain.

Problem 73 Two firms A & Co. and B & Co. sell the same type of product in the same market. Their budgeted Profit & Loss Account for the year ending 31st March 2021 are as follows:

Particulars	₹	A & Co.	₹	B & Co.
Sales		5,00,000		6,00,000
Variable cost	4,00,000		4,00,000	
Fixed cost	30,000	4,30,000	70,000	4,70,000
Net Profit		70,000		1,30,000

Required:

1. Calculate at which sales volume both the firms will earn equal profits.
2. State which firm is likely to earn greater profits in conditions of heavy demand.
3. Low demand for the product. (*C.A. Inter*)

Solution:

Particulars	A & Co. (3)	B & Co. (₹)
Sales	5,00,000	6,00,000
Less: Variable costs	4,00,000	4,00,000
Contribution	1,00,000	2,00,000
P/V ratio	$\frac{1,00,000}{5,00,000} \times 100 = 20\%$	$\frac{2,00,000}{6,00,000} \times 100 = 33.33\%$
Break-even sales	$\frac{30,000}{20\%} = ₹1,50,000$	$\frac{70,000}{31.33\%} = ₹2,10,000$

1. Sales volume (At which both the firm will earn equal profits)

$$= \frac{\text{Difference in fixed costs}}{\text{Difference in P/V ratio}}$$

$$= \frac{₹70,000 - 30,000}{33.33\% - 20\%} = 3,00,000$$

2. In conditions of heavy demand for the product, the firm which is having higher P/V ratio is likely to earn more profits. The P/V ratio of B & Co. at 33.33% is higher than that of A & Co. at 20%. Therefore, B & Co. is likely to earn more profits if the sales volume exceeds ₹3,00,000.
3. In conditions of low demand for the product, the firm which breaks even earlier, is likely to earn more profits. As the break-even point of A & Co. at ₹1,50,000 is lower than that of B & Co. at ₹2,10,000, therefore, A & Co. is likely to earn higher profits.

Problem 74 Following is the data taken from the records of an Autocrat Ltd. manufacturing a special part of engine.

Selling price per unit	₹20
Direct material cost per unit	₹ 5
Direct labour cost per unit	₹ 3
Variable overhead cost per unit	₹ 2
Budgeted level of output and sales	20,000 units
Budgeted recovery rate of fixed overheads cost per unit	₹ 5

You are required to:

(a) Draw a break-even chart showing the break-even point, and

(b) In the same chart show the impact on break-even point if selling price per unit is reduced by 25%.

Solution:

Selling price per unit = ₹20

VC per unit = 5 + 3 + 2 = 10

Contribution per unit = 10

Fixed cost = 20,000 × 5 = 1,00,000

$$\text{Break-even point} = \frac{1,00,000}{10} = 10,000 \text{ units}$$

Now, to draw the sales line and total cost line, compute the sales and total cost at different levels of output. The output levels should be selected in such a way that 10,000 units lie in it.

Output (units)	Sales @ ₹20	Variable cost	Fixed cost	Total cost
0	–	–	1,00,000	1,00,000
5,000	1,00,000	50,000	1,00,000	1,50,000
10,000	*2,00,000*	*1,00,000*	*1,00,000*	*2,00,000*
15,000	3,00,000	1,50,000	1,00,000	2,50,000
20,000	4,00,000	2,00,000	1,00,000	3,00,000
25,000	5,00,000	2,50,000	1,00,000	3,50,000

The above table shows that at 10,000 units of production, the total revenue is equal to total costs. Therefore, 10,000 units is break-even level of production. At this level, the break-even sales are ₹2,00,000.

Now to show the impact of 25% decrease in selling price, a new BEP is computed.

$$\text{Break-even point} = \frac{\text{Fixed cost}}{\text{Contribution per unit}} = \frac{1,00,000}{(15-10)} = 20,000 \text{ units.}$$

Now, to draw the new break-even chart, the sales and total cost at different levels of output is computed again.

Output (units)	Sales @ 15	Variable cost	Fixed cost	Total cost
0	–	–	1,00,000	1,00,000
5,000	75,000	50,000	1,00,000	1,50,000
10,000	1,50,000	1,00,000	1,00,000	2,00,000
15,000	2,25,000	1,50,000	1,00,000	2,50,000
20,000	*3,00,000*	*2,00,000*	*1,00,000*	*3,00,000*
25,000	3,75,000	2,50,000	1,00,000	3,50,000

The above table shows that at 20,000 units of production, the total revenue is equal to total costs. Therefore, 20,000 units is the new break-even point. At this level, the break-even sales are ₹3,00,000. The new break-even point is shown in the graph with the dotted lines.

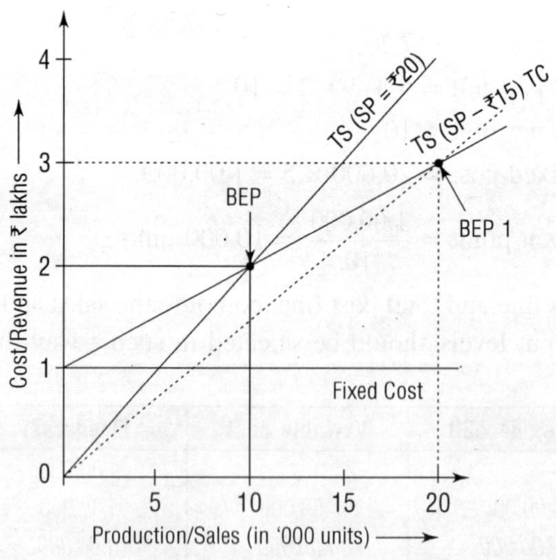

It may be observed that break-even point is 10,000 units when the selling price is ₹20 per unit which increases to 20,000 units when the selling price is reduced to ₹15 shown by the dotted lines.

Problem 75

Period	Sales (₹)	Profit (₹)
2019	12,40,000	80,000
2020	14,20,000	1,30,000

Calculate:

(i) P/V Ratio

(ii) Break-even sales

(iii) Profit when sales is ₹ 18,00,000

(iv) Sales required to earn a profit of ₹ 1,20,000

(v) Margin of safety for the year 2019 [*B.Com (H)*]

Solution:

1. $$\text{P/V ratio} = \frac{\text{Change in profit}}{\text{Change in sales}} \times 100$$

$$= 5{,}00{,}00/2{,}00{,}000 \times 100$$

$$= 25\%$$

2. $$\text{Break-even sales} = \frac{\text{Fixed cost}}{\text{P/V ratio}}$$

Calculation of fixed cost

Contribution = Sales × P/V ratio

In 2019 contribution = 12,00,000 × 0.25	=	3,00,000
Less: Profit	=	(80,000)
Fixed cost	=	2,20,000
In 2020 contribution = 14,00,000 × 0.25	=	3,50,000
Less: Profit		(1,30,000)
Fixed cost		2,20,000

$$\text{Break-even sales} = \frac{\text{Fixed cost}}{\text{P/V ratio}}$$

= 2,20,000/0.25 = 8,80,000

3. Profit when sales is ₹ 18,00,000

18,00,000 × 0.25	=	4,50,000
Less: Fixed cost	=	(2,20,000)
Profit	=	2,30,000

4. Required sales = (Fixed cost + Desired profit)/P/V ratio

$$= \frac{2,20,000 + 1,20,000}{0.25}$$

= ₹ 13,60,000

5. Margin of safety for the year 2019

= Actual sales in 2019 – Break-even sales.

= 12,00,000 – 80,000

= 3,20,000

Problem 76 Vardhan Limited manufactures four products A, B, C, D. The data regarding cost sales and profits are as under:

Product	Sale (Unit)	Selling price per unit (₹)	Variable cost per unit (₹)	Contribution per unit (₹)
A	3000	10	5	5
B	4000	10	6	4
C	2000	10	7	3
D	1000	10	8	2

The fixed costs are ₹ 25,000. The company wants to change the mix from the existing proportion of 3:4:2:1 to 4:3:2:1 of A, B, C and D respectively. Calculate the number of units of each product which the company should produce and sell to maintain the existing profit.

Solution: Existing profit:

Total contribution

[(3,000 × 5) + (4,000 × 4) + (2,000 × 3) + (1,000 × 2) = ₹ 39,000

Less: Fixed costs ₹ 25,000

= ₹ 14,000

Number of units to be sold for a profit of ₹ 1400 as per new mix:

If the number of units to be sold of product D is taken as X

Units sold of product A = 4X

B = 3X

C = 2X

Total sales in ₹ 40X + 30X + 20X + 10X = 100X

Total variable costs in ₹ 20X + 18X + 14X + 8X = 60X

Total sales: Total cost + Profit

$$100X = 60X + 25000 + 14000$$

$$40X = 39000$$

$$X = 975 \text{ units}$$

Number of units to be produced and sold:

A	3900
B	2925
C	1950
D	975

Verification:

Total contribution:

A	3900 × 5 =	19500
B	2925 × 4 =	11700
C	1950 × 3 =	5850
D	975 × 2 =	1950
		39000

Less: Fixed costs 25,000

Profit ₹ 14,000

Problem 77

(a) Total fixed cost ₹25,000

Contribution ₹35,000

Number of units sold 20,000

Variable cost 60% of sales

Determine selling price per unit and also the total profit/loss.

Solution:

(a)

Contribution = Fixed cost + Profit

Profit = Contribution – Fixed cost = ₹35,000 – ₹25,000

= ₹ 10,000

P/V ratio 1 – P/V ratio = 1 – 0.6 = 0.4 or 40%

Sales = [Fixed cost + Profit]/[P/V ratio]) = ₹ 87,500

Selling price per unit = Sales/number units sold = 87,500/20,000 = ₹ 4.375

(b) Total fixed cost ₹ 25,000

Actual sales ₹ 80,000

Margin of safety ₹ 30,000

Determine the P/V ratio.

Break-even sales = Actual sales – Margin of safety

= 80,000 – 30,000 = 50,000 break-even sales

= Fixed cost/P/V ratio

P/V ratio = Fixed cost/Break-even sales = 25,000/50,000

= 1/2 or 50%

(c) When output is 500 units, the average cost per unit is ₹4. When output is increased to 700 units, the average cost is ₹3.5 per unit. The break-even point is 800 units. Find the P/V ratio.

Solution:

Production unit	Production cost (₹)
500	500 × 4 = 2000
700	700 × 3.5 = 2450
Difference 200 units	450

Variable cost per unit = [Change in cost/Change in production units]

450/200 = ₹2.25

Variable component in semi-fixed cost

= Production units × Variable cost per unit

= 500 × 2.25

= 1,125

Fixed cost = Total semi-fixed cost – Variable component in semi-fixed cost

= 2,000 – 1,125

= ₹875

At BEP = Fixed cost + Variable cost

= 875 + [800 × 2.25]

= ₹2,675

Selling price per unit = Sales/number of units sold

= ₹2,675/800

= ₹3.34

Contribution per unit = Selling price per unit variable cost per unit

= 3.34 – 2.25

= 1.09

P/V ratio = Contribution per unit/Selling price per unit

= 1.09/3.34

= 0.326

= 32.6%

Problem 78 After a study of cost volume relationships, a company TFS Ltd. concluded that its cost for any given volume of sales could be expressed as ₹1,00,000 for fixed costs plus variable costs equal to 60% of sales. The company's range of sales was from zero to 60% of sales. The company's range of sales was from zero to ₹6,00,000. Break-even sales of TFS Ltd. are ₹2,50,000. A company operating a plant of the same size as TFS Ltd. also has fixed cost of ₹1,00,000 per annum, but its break-even point is ₹3,00,000 of sales. What may be the probable causes of difference between the break-even points of the TFS Ltd. and its competitors?

Solution: Possible causes for the differences in break-even points:

1. The competitors are having higher variable cost to volume ratio than TFS Ltd. It is $\frac{1}{3}$ for the competitors, assuming the selling price per unit same for both the companies.

$$\text{BEP} = \text{Fixed cost/(P/V) ratio}$$
$$3,00,000 = 1,00,000\text{/P/V) ratio}$$
$$\text{(Ply) ratio} - 1,00,000/3,00,000 = \frac{1}{3}$$

2. The competitors are having lower price per unit. Their prices per unit are 1/15 lower than those of the TFS Ltd. as shown below:

$$\begin{aligned} \text{BEP} &= \text{Fixed cost/(P/V) ratio} \\ &= 10,00,001\text{l}(14/15) - (3/5) \\ &= 10,00,001(1/3) \\ &= ₹3,00,000 \end{aligned}$$

3. Partly due to higher variable cost to volume ratio or partly due to lower selling price, the sum of the differences is 1/15, i.e., 6.67%.

Problem 79 Stag Ltd. is operating at 100% capacity and its annual sales are ₹15 lakhs. Fixed cost is ₹5 lakhs, and total variable cost ₹7.5 lakhs. Calculate the following:

(1) BEP in terms of % capacity
(2) Margin of safety
(3) New BEP point of fixed cost is increased by ₹1 lakh

Solution:

$$\begin{aligned} \text{Contribution} &= \text{Sales} - \text{Variable cost} \\ &= 15,00,000 - 7,50,000 \\ &= ₹7,50,000 \\ \text{P/V ratio} &= \text{Contribution/Sales} \\ &= 7,50,000/15,00,000 = 0.5 \text{ or } 50\% \\ \text{BEP fixed cost! (P/V) ratio} &= 5,00,000/0.5 \\ &= ₹10,00,000 \end{aligned}$$

BEP (% capacity) BEP sales/actual sales

$$\begin{aligned} &= 10,00,000/15,00,000 = 2/3 \text{ or } 66.67\% \\ \text{Margin of safety} &= \text{Actual sales} - \text{Break-even sales} \\ &= 15,00,000 - 10,00,000 = ₹5,00,000 \\ \text{BEP (new)} &= \text{New fixed cost/(P/V) ratio} \\ &= 6,00,000/0.5 = ₹12,00,000 \end{aligned}$$

(New) BFP (% capacity) New BEP sales' Actual sales

= 12,00,000/15,00,000

= 4/5 or 80%

Problem 80 The following particulars are extracted from the records of a company.

Particulars	Product X	Product Y
Sales per unit	₹200	₹240
Direct expenses	₹10	₹12
Direct wage cost	₹30	₹20
Machine hours used	3 hours	2 hours
Consumption of materials (kg.)	2 kg	3 kg
Material cost	₹20	₹30
Overhead expenses:	₹20	₹30
Fixed	₹10	₹20
Variable	₹30	₹40

Direct wages per hour is ₹10.

Comment on the profitability of each product (both of the same raw materials) when:

(1) Total sales potential in units is limited
(2) Total sales in value is limited
(3) A raw material is in short supply
(4) Production capacity (in terms of machine hours) is the limiting factor
(5) Assuming raw material as the key factor, availability of which is 10,000 kg and maximum sales potential of each product being 3500 units, find out the product mix which will yield the maximum profit.

Solution:

Particulars	Product X		Product Y	
Selling price		200		240
Less: Variable costs				
Materials	20	90	30	102
Wages	30		20	
Direct expenses	10		12	
Variable overheads	30		40	
Contribution per unit		110		138
P/V ratio = (Contribution/Sales) × 100		(110/200) × 100 = 55%		(138/240) × 100 = 57.5%
Contribution per kg of material		110/2 = ₹55		138/3 = ₹46
Contribution per kg		110/3 = ₹36.67		138/2 = ₹69

Comments:

(1) Total sales potential in units is limited: Contribution per unit for product Y is higher, so the product Y is more profitable.

(2) Total sales potential in value is limited: P/V ratio for product Y is higher, so the product Y is more profitable.

(3) Raw material is in short supply: Contribution per kg. Of material for product X is higher, so the product X is more profitable.

(4) Production capacity (in terms of machine hours) is the limiting factor: Contribution per hour for product Y is higher, so the product Y is more profitable.

(5) Raw material consumption:

Product (Unit)	Consumption per unit (kg)	Total consumption (kg) per hour
X: 3500	2	7000
Y: 100 (balancing figure)	3	3000
	Total available and consumed	10,000

Statement of profitability

Product (Unit)	Contribution per unit (₹)	Contribution (₹)
X: 3500	110	3,85,000
Y: 100 (balancing figure)	138	1,38,000
	Total contribution	5,23,000
	Less: Fixed cost	1,05,000
	[3,500 (5 + 10)] profit	4,18,000

Problem 81 Calculate the effect of sales mix from the following data by comparing the P/V ratio and break-even point:

Details	P-I (₹)	P-II (₹)	P-III (₹)	P-IV (₹)
Sales	30,000	37,500	20,000	12,500
Variable cost	15,000	22,500	15,000	5000
Revised sales mix	20,000	30,000	22,500	27,500

Fixed cost = ₹25,500

Solution:

Existing sales mix

Details	P-I (₹)	P-II (₹)	P-III (₹)	P-IV (₹)	Total
Sales	30,000	37,500	20,000	12,500	1,00,000
Variable cost	15,000	20,000	15,000	5,000	57,500
Contribution	37,500	22,500	5000	7500	42,500
P/V ratio	0.5	0.4	0.25	0.6	0.425

Break-even point = Fixed cost (P/V) ratio
= 25,500/0.425
= ₹60,000

Revised sales mix

Details	P-I (₹)	P-II(₹)	P-III(₹)	P-IV (₹)	Total (₹)
Sales	20,000	30,000	22,500	27,500	1,00,000
Variable cost	10,000	18,000	16,875	11,000	55,875
Contribution	10,000	12,000	5625	16,500	44,125
P/V ratio	0.6	0.4	0.25	0.6	0.44125

Break-even point = Fixed cost/P/V ratio = 26,500/0.44125 = ₹57,790

Comments: Revised sales mix is favourable because it raises the P/V ratio from 0.425 to 0.44125 and brings the break-even point from ₹60,000 to ₹57,790.

Problem 82 ABC Ltd. manufactures and sells a product, the selling price and raw materials costs of which have remained unmoved during the past two years. The following details are relevant:

Details	Year 2019	Year 2020
Units sold (kg)	250	400
Sales value	2,50,000	74,000
Direct wages	40,000	46,000
Factory overheads	60,000	
Raw materials	1,25,000	
Profit	25,000	

During the year 2020, direct wage rates increased by 25% but there was a saving of ₹4000 in fixed factory overheads.

Find out the quantity the firm should have produced and sold in year 2020 in order to maintain the same amount of net profit per kg as it earned during the year 2019.

Solution:

Details	Amount (₹)	Amount (₹)
Selling price per kg (2,50,000/250)		1000
Variable costs per kg:		
Raw materials (1,25,000/250)	500	
Direct wages [(40,000/250)(1.25)]	200	
Variable factory overhead	120	
Total variable cost		820
Contribution per kg (2,50,000/250)		180

Table Contd...

Table Contd...

Details	Amount (₹)	Amount (₹)
Less: Profit required per kg (@ ₹100 per kg)		100
Balance contribution per kg for meeting costs		80
Total fixed costs		74000
Quantity to be produced and sold (₹74,000/80)		925

Working Notes:

Variable factory overheads per kg:

Total factory overheads during the year 2020	₹74,000
Add: Saving in fixed factory overheads	₹4,000
Total factory overheads should have been	
During the year 2020	₹78,000
Less: Total factory overheads during the year 2019	₹60,000
Increase in factory overheads	₹18,000
Increase in quantity (400 kg – 250 kg) 150 kg.	
Variable factory overheads per kg: (₹18,000/150)	₹120

Fixed factory overhead:

Details	Year 2019 Amount (₹)	Year 2020 Amount (₹)
Total factory overheads	60,000	74,000
Less: Variable factory overheads	30,000	48,000
Fixed factory overheads	30,000	26,000

Problem 83 Following details are obtained from the costing records of a factory:

Details	Product P-1 (per unit)	Product P-2 (per unit)
1000	1000	2500
200	200	800
240	240	480
120	120	240

Total fixed overheads ₹1,60,000

Comment of the profitability of each product when:

(1) Raw material is in short supply

(2) Production capacity is limited

(3) Sales quantity is limited

(4) Sales value is limited

(5) Only 2000 kg of raw materials is available for both the products in total. Maximum sales quantity of each product is 400 units

Solution:

Details	Product P-1 (per unit)	Product P-2 (per unit)
Selling price	1000	2500
Less: Variable costs:		
Materials	200	800
Labour	240	480
Variable overheads	120	240
Total variable cost	560	1520
Contribution per unit	440	980
P/V ratio = (Contrib./ sales) × 100	44%	39.2%
Contribution per kg	₹440/2 kg = 220	₹980/8 kg = ₹122.5
Contribution per hour	₹440/5 hour = 88	₹980/10 hour = ₹98

(1) In case raw materials are in scarcity, contribution per kg of product P-1 is higher and hence product P-1 is more profitable.

(2) In case production capacity is limited, contribution per hour of product P-2 is higher and hence product P-2 is more profitable.

(3) In case sales quantity is limited, contribution per unit of product P-2 is higher and hence product P-2 is more profitable.

(4) In case sales value is limited, the P/V ratio of product P-I is higher and hence product P-l is more profitable.

(5) In case raw material as well as sales quantity is limited, raw materials should first be used for maximum number of units of product P-I, i.e., for 400 units. This will consume 800 kg of raw material and the balance 1200 kg shall be utilised for producing 150 units (1200/8) of product P-2. The profit in each case would be as under:

Contribution from product P-1 (400 × 440)	₹1,76,000
Contribution from product P-2 (150 × 980)	₹1,47,000
Total contribution	₹3,23,000
Less: Fixed overheads	₹1,60,000
Maximum profit	₹1,63,000

REVIEW QUESTIONS

1. Distinguish between absorption and variable costing.
2. Define marginal costing and explain its main characteristics. *[B.Com (H)]*
3. What are marginal uses of marginal costing?
4. Explain the advantages and disadvantages of marginal costing?

5. Write short note on the application of marginal costing.
6. "Absorption costing obscures the total amount of fixed costs whereas variable costing highlights it". Comment.
7. What is meant by margin of safety and angle of incidence? Show these on a break-even chart.
8. Write short notes on:
   (a) Key factor and its significance
   (b) CVP analysis
9. What are the limitations of break-even analysis?
10. What is break-even point? What are its advantages?
11. (a) Enumerate the factors which can change the break-even point?
    (b) How can P/V ratio be improved.
12. Profit is a product of P/V ratio and margin of safety. Explain giving a suitable example.
13. (a) What is CVP analysis? What are its objectives.
    (b) Distinguish between "cost indifference point" and "break-even point"
14. What is meant by "angle of incidence" and "margin of safety" in a break-even chart? Explain their significance.
15. What are the assumptions made in drawing a break-even chart?
16. Briefly explain the concepts of contribution.

UNSOLVED PRACTICAL QUESTIONS

1. JK Co. Pvt. Ltd. has prepared the following budget estimates for year 2019–20:

Sales units	15,000
Fixed expenses	₹34,000
Sales value	₹1,50,000
Variable costs	₹6 per unit

   You are required to
   (a) Find the P/V ratio, break-even point and margin of safety.
   (b) Calculate the revised P/V ratio, break-even point and margin of safety in each of the following cases:
      (i) Decrease of 10% in selling price
      (ii) Increase of 10% in variable costs
      (iii) Increase of sales volume by 2,000 units
      (iv) Increase of 6,000 in fixed costs.

[*Ans.* [(a) 40%; 8,500 units (₹85,000); 6,500 units (₹65,000), (b)(i) 33.3%; 11,333 units (₹10,01,997); 3,667 units (₹33,003), (ii) 34%; 10,000 units (₹1,00,000); 5,000 units (₹50,000), (iii) 40%; 8,500 units (₹85,000); 8,500 units (₹85,000), (iv) 40%; 10,000 units (₹1,00,000, 5,000 units (₹50,000))]

2. The following information is available from the books of PVC Ltd.

Year	2019	2020
Sales	4,00,000	5,00,000
Loss	30,000	–
Profit	–	20,000

Calculate:

(i) Fixed cost.
(ii) BEPS.
(iii) MS for 2020.
(iv) Sales required to earn a profit of ₹ 60,000.
(v) Profit or loss at a sales of 7,50,000.

[*Ans.* (i) Fixed cost ₹ 2,30,000, (ii) BEP ₹ 4,60,000, (iii) MS for 2013 ₹ 40,000, (iv) Desired sales ₹ 5,80,000, (v) Profit ₹ 1,45,000]

3. Fab Mart furnished the following information:

	2019 (₹)	2020 (₹)
Sales (10/unit)	2,00,000	2,50,000
Profit	30,000	50,000

You are required to compute:

(i) P/V ratio.
(ii) BEP.
(iii) Total variable cost for the year 2019 and 2020.
(iv) Sales required to earn a profit of ₹ 60,000.
(v) Profit/loss when sales are ₹ 1,00,000.
(vi) MS when profit is ₹ 80,000.
(vii) During 2019-20, due to an increase in cost, the variable cost is expected to rise to ₹7/unit and fixed cost to 55,000. If the selling price cannot be increased, what will be the amount of sales to maintain the profit of 2018-19? [*B.Com. (Hons)*]

Ans. (i) P/V ratio = 40%, (ii) ∴ BEP = ₹ 1,25,000, (iii) Total variable cost for 2017-18 ₹ 1,20,000, for 2018-19 = ₹ 1,50,000, (iv) Required sales = ₹ 2,75,000, (v) Variable cost as a percentage of selling price = 66.67%, (vi) Fixed cost = ₹ 35,000]

4. A Ltd. furnishes you the following information relating to half year ended 30th Sept. 2020

	₹
Fixed expenses	45,000
Sales value	1,50,000
Profit	30,000

During the second half of the year, the company has projected a loss of ₹ 10,000.

Calculate:

(i) The margin of safety for six months ending on 30th Sept. 2020.

(ii) Expected sales volume for the second half of the year assuming that the P/V ratio and fixed expenses remain constant in the second half year also.

(iii) The break-even point and margin of safety for the whole year 2021-22

[***Ans.*** (i) ₹3,60,000 (ii) ₹70,000 (iii) ₹40,000]

5. A producer is earning a post-tax profit of ₹4,20,000. Fixed cost is ₹4,00,000, selling price is ₹200 and per unit variable cost is ₹120. The prevailing tax rate is 30%. By what percentage sales volume should increase so that he is able to earn same post-tax profit after tax rate goes up to 40%?

[***Ans.*** Current sales 12,500 units, revised sales 13,750 units, percentage increase 10%]

6. A manufacturer incurs an annual fixed cost of ₹8,00,000 and per unit variable cost is ₹60. He sells the product at ₹80 per unit. At what volume of annual sale he will earn a post-tax profit of ₹2,10,000 if the income tax rate is 30%?

[***Ans.*** 55,000 units, ₹44,00,000]

7. GAS agency receives 10% commission on all sales effected by it. The establishment cost is ₹18,000 p.a. and other fixed expenses amounted to ₹16,500 p.a. The cost of after-sales service is 3% of sales, which is borne by the agency. Casual labour is employed at ₹5 per day for handling the forwarding work. This work out to one-man day labour for every ₹5,000 sales. Calculate the BEP.

[***Ans.*** BEP ₹5,00,000]

8. ABC has a P/V ratio of 40%. By what percentage must selling price be increased to offset 25% increase in variable cost?

[***Ans.*** 15%]

9. Synergy Ltd. decides to effect a 10% reduction in the price of its product because it is felt that such a step may lead to a greater volume of sales.

It is anticipated that there are no prospects of a change in total fixed costs and variable cost per unit. The directors wish to maintain net profits at the present level. The following information has been obtained from its books:

Sales	10,000 units	₹2,00,000
Variable costs		15 per unit
Fixed costs		₹40,000

How would management proceed to implement this decision? [*B.Com. (Hons.), DU*]

[***Ans.*** Increase sales by 6,667 units]

10. The following is a summary of the cost and sales data of a company selling an electrical appliances for the year ended 31st December 2020 during which 80,000 units were sold :

		₹ *(Lakhs)*
Sales		96
Costs :		
Material	36	

Labour :		
Direct	15	
Indirect	6	
Other costs	18	75
Profit		21

In the forthcoming year, it is anticipated that:

(a) The selling price is to be reduced by ₹7.50.

(b) Sales volume is expected to be increased by 40%.

(c) Suppliers have agreed to give a discount of 5% on all purchases of materials.

(d) Direct workmen are to be paid an incentive bonus of 2½% in order to stimulate production.

(e) Other costs vary directly with production except to the extent of 3 lakhs which is considered 'fixed' and an additional expense of ₹1 lakh will arise due to rent in respect of an extension to the factory.

(f) You are to assume that there are no stock or work-in-progress as at 31st December. You are required to compute the profit for the next year after incorporating the changes as given above.

[***Ans.*** Profit ₹23,19,500]

11. The Pepperfry Ltd. furnishes you the following information:

Year	2019	2020
Sales	8,10,000	10,26,000
Profit earned	21,600	64,800

Assuming that fixed cost remains same in both the years you are required to compute: (i) P/V ratio (ii) Fixed cost (iii) The amount of profit or loss where sales is ₹6,48,000 (iv) The amount of sales required to earn a profit of ₹1,08,000.

[***Ans.*** (i) 20% (ii) ₹1,40,400 (iii) Loss ₹10,800 (iv) Sales ₹12,42,000]

12. The accounts of a company manufacturing the plastic buckets revealed the following information:

Capacity	2000 buckets p.a.
VC per bucket	₹20
Fixed cost	₹50,000 p.a.
Selling price per bucket	₹70

(a) Find out the BEP

(b) Find the number of buckets to be sold to get a profit ₹30,000.

(c) If the company can manufacture 600 buckets more per year with an additional fixed cost of ₹2000, what should be the SP for the additional 600 units to maintain the same profit per bucket as in (b) above.

(d) What minimum price would be acceptable for additional units during competition?

[***Ans.*** (a) 1000 units (b) 1600 units (c) ₹42.08 (d) ₹23.33]

13. A company is manufacturing product A, which has the following cost structure (per unit):

    Materials cost ₹80; Labour ₹20;Variable overheads ₹8; SP ₹180.

    For the current year sales are at ₹27 lakhs and fixed overheads as ₹2,80,000.

    Under a wage agreement, an increase of 10% is payable to all direct workers from the beginning of the forthcoming year, while materials costs are expected to increase by 7.5%, variable overheads by 5% and fixed overheads by 3%.

    Calculate: (a) the new selling price, if the current P/V ratio is to be maintained. (b) The quantity to be sold during the forthcoming year to yield the same amount of profits as in the current year assuming the selling price to remain at ₹180.

    [*Ans.* (a) SP ₹194, (b) Sales 17,113 units]

14. The variable cost structure of a product manufactured by Best Quality Ltd. during the current year is as under.

	₹ per unit
Material	160
Labour	40
Overheads	16

    The selling price per unit is ₹360 and the fixed cost and sales during the current year are ₹5.60 lakhs and ₹54 lakhs respectively.

    During the forthcoming year, the direct workers will be entitled to a wage increase of 10% from the beginning of the year and the material cost, variable overhead and fixed overhead are expected to increase by 7.5%, 5% and 3% respectively.

    You are required to compute:

    (a) The new selling price, if the current P/V ratio is to be maintained,

    (b) The quantity to be sold during the forthcoming year to yield the same amount of profits as in the current year assuming the selling price to remain at ₹360.

    Ans. [(a) SP ₹388, (b) Sales 17,113 units]

15. The variable cost structure of a product manufactured by Infocomm Ltd. during the current year is as under

	₹ per unit
Material	120
Labour	30
Variable overheads	12

    The selling price per unit is ₹270 and the fixed cost and sales during the current year are ₹14 lakhs and ₹40.5 lakhs respectively.

    During the forthcoming year, the direct workers will be entitled to a wage increase of 10% from the beginning of the year and the material cost, variable overheads and fixed overhead are expected to increase by 75%, 5% and 3% respectively.

You are required to compute the following:

(i) New price in the forthcoming year, if the current P/V ratio is to be maintained.

(ii) Number of units that would require to be sold during the forthcoming year so as to yield the same amount of profit as in the current year assuming that selling price per unit will remain same. [*CA Inter*]

[***Ans.*** (a) SP ₹291, (b) Sales 17,113 units]

16. Aqua Ltd. is planning to establish a subsidiary company in India to produce mineral water. Based on the estimated annual sales of 40,000 bottles of the mineral water, cost studies produced the following estimated for the Indian subsidiary:

	Total annual costs	*Percent of total annual cost which is variable*
Material	2,10,000	100%
Labour	1,50,000	80%
Factory overheads	92,000	60%
Administration expenses	40,000	35%

The Indian production will be sold by manufacturer's representatives who will receive a commission of 8% of the selling price. No portion of the Japanese office expenses is to be allocated to the Indian subsidiary.

You are required to: (i) Compute the selling price per bottle to enable the management to realise an estimated 10% profit on sale proceeds in India. (ii) Calculate the break-even point in ₹ sales as also in number of bottles for the Indian subsidiary on the assumption that the selling price is ₹14 per bottle.

[*B.Com. (H)*]

[***Ans.*** (i) SP ₹15, (ii) BEP ₹4,48,000, 32,000 bottle)

17. A company prepared the profit plans for different plants as given below:

Profit plan for Plant I shows annual budgeted fixed costs ₹12 lakhs, variable costs ₹8,40,000, sales value ₹22 lakhs, allocated head office budgeted fixed costs ₹3,20,000. You are required to compute the BEP before and after the allocation of fixed costs by the head office. Explain why the BEP change in rupees is greater than the allocated fixed costs.

Plant II produces a product that sells at ₹40. It costs ₹42.50 when 15,000 units are produced. At a production level of 20,000 units, the cost per unit is ₹38.125. What is the BEP in units and in ₹?

Plant III, the budgeted income statement:

Sales	10,00,000
Costs: Fixed	4,00,000
Variable	3,00,000
Allocated by HO	3,50,000
Total cost	10,50,000
Loss	(50,000)

Sale of plant III is under consideration. Give your recommendations.

Plant IV produces one product, the budgeted income statement of which is as given below:

Sales @ ₹200 per unit		20,00,000
Costs: Fixed	7,47,500	
Variable	13,50,000	
HO allocated	5,02,500	26,00,000
Loss		6,00,000

How many additional units must be manufactured in the plant in order to break-even? What would be the profit pick-up per unit above break-even?

18. Everlook Inn is a small bed-and-breakfast inn located in Shimla. The charge is ₹50 per person for one night's lodging and a full breakfast in the morning. The retired couple who own and manage the estimate that the variable expense per person is ₹20. This includes such expenses as food, maid service and utility. The inn's fixed expenses total ₹42,000 per year. The inn can accommodate 10 guests each night.

    You are required to compute:

    (a) Contribution margin per unit of service.

    (b) Contribution margin ratio.

    (c) Annual break-even point in units of service and in rupee terms.

    (d) The number of units of service required to earn a target net profit of ₹60,000 for the year. (Ignore income tax)

    [*Ans.* (a) ₹30 (b) 60% (c) 1,400 units and ₹70,000 (d) 3,400 units]

19. Cico Ltd. manufactures pressure cookers the selling price of which is ₹300 per unit. Currently the capacity utilisation is 60% with a sales turnover of ₹18 lakhs. The company proposes to reduce the selling price by 20% but desires to maintain the same profit position by increasing the output. Assuming that the increased output could be made and sold, determine the level at which the company should operate to achieve the desired object.

    The following further data are available:

    (i) Variable cost per unit ₹60.

    (ii) Semi-variable cost (including a variable element of ₹10 per unit) ₹1,80,000.

    (iii) Fixed cost ₹3,00,000 will remain constant up to 80% level. Beyond this an additional amount of ₹60,000 will be incurred.

    [*Ans.* 8,471 units i.e., 84.71% capacity utilisation]

20. A company has an opening stock of 5000 units of output. The production planned for the current period is 25,000 units and expected sales for the current period amount to 28,000 units. The selling price per unit of output is ₹20. Variable cost per unit is expected to be ₹13 per unit while it was only ₹10 per unit during the previous period. What is the break-even volume for the current period if the total fixed costs for the current period is ₹1,20,000?

    Assume that the first-in-first-out system is followed.

    [*Ans.* 15,000 units, ₹3,00,000]

21. There are three similar plants under the same management. The management desires to merge these three plants. The following particulars are available:

	Plant A	*Plant B*	*Plant C*
Capacity operation	100%	70%	50%
Sales (Lakhs)	300	280	150
Variable cost	200	210	75
Fixed costs	70	50	62

You are required to compute:

(a) The capacity of the merged plant to be operated for the purpose of break-even.

(b) What would be the profitability on working at 75% of the merged capacity?

(c) The turnover from the merged plant to give a profit of ₹28 lakhs.

[*Ans.* (a) 52% (b) 80.5 lakhs (c) 600 lakhs]

22. A Ltd. has two factories X and Y producing the same article whose selling price is ₹150 per unit. The following area has the other particulars:

	Factory - X	Factory - Y
Capacity (units)	10,000	15,000
Variable cost per unit	₹100	₹120
Fixed costs	₹3,00,000	₹2,10,000

Determine the BEP for the two factories and for the company as a whole assuming: (a) Constant sales mix (b) Variable sales mix.

[*Ans.* (a) ₹9,00,00, ₹10,50,000 and ₹20,13,423 (b) ₹15,50,000]

23. Sigma Ltd. has just been incorporated and plans to produce a product that will sell for 10 per unit. Market surveys show that demand will be around 10,000 units per year. The company has the choice of buying one of two machines, each of which has a capacity of 10,000 units per year. Machine A would have fixed costs of ₹30,000 per year and would yield a profit of ₹30,000 per year on the sale of 10,000 units. Machine B would have fixed costs of ₹18,000 per year and will yield a profit of ₹22,000 per year on the sale of 10000 units. Variable costs behave linearly for both machines. You are required to compute:

(a) Break-even sales for each machine, (b) Sales level where both machines are equally profitable, (c) Range of sales where one machine is more profitable than the other.

[*Ans.* (a) 5000 units, 4500 units, (b) 6000 units, (c) up to 6000 units, A is profitable and beyond 6000 units, B is more profitable.]

24. Foot Print Ltd. has been offered a choice to buy a plant between X and Y. You are required to compute:

(a) The break-even point for each of the machines.

(b) The level of sales of which both the machines earn equal profits.

(c) The range of sales at which one is more profitable than the other.

The relevant information is as given below:

	X	*Y*
Annual output (units)	10000	10000
Fixed costs	₹ 30,000	₹ 16,000
Profits at above level of production	₹ 30,000	₹ 24,000

The market price of the product is expected to be ₹ 10 per unit.

[***Ans.*** (a) 5000 units and 4000 units, (b) 7000 units (c) upto 7000 units, B is profitable and beyond 6000 units A is more profitable]

CHAPTER

3 Decision Making

When an organisation has more than one option, the decision is taken on a certain monetary evaluation. This process is known as decision making. Decision making is related to planning about future and is aimed at achieving a desired goal. The option that gives the highest profit is preferred. The most profitable decision will be the one which has lowest cost because lower cost will, in return, give higher profits.

VARIOUS COST CONCEPTS

Relevant Cost. Costs which are relevant or relate to any decision making process are known as relevant costs.

Opportunity Cost. Opportunity costs are the decision making costs. It is the benefit that would have been received from an asset if it would have been put to its next best use.

Differential Costs. Differential cost is the difference of cost between two alternatives. It is the difference between two costs between two volumes. When the decision leads to increased costs, it means incremental cost. Incremental cost includes both variable as well fixed costs. If fixed costs do not change then it will be treated as irrelevant. Only the variable cost is taken into account for decision making if the fixed cost remain constant. Relevant costs change with different alternatives for decision making.

Sunk Cost. It is the cost that has already been incurred. It is called unavoidable cost.

Out of Pocket Costs. These costs signify the cash cost incurred on an activity.

Mostly, differential cost analysis or opportunity cost analysis is used for decision making.

Variable costing is an important tool of profit planning and cost control. The preceding section has established that the contribution margin/marginal contribution is the core of variable costing. It is out of the marginal contribution that the fixed costs are to be met; and the excess of the marginal contribution over fixed costs represents profit. From the above it follows that maximising the marginal contribution would lead to the maximisation of profit. The marginal contribution approach can be applied in making decisions with regard to:

(a) price fixing on special orders,

(b) optimal sales mix,

(c) adding a new product line,
(d) dropping a product line,
(e) developing a production plan if certain input (material or labour) is in short supply,
(f) making or buying component parts, and
(g) selling of a product in a limited market.

Throughout the discussion, it will be assumed that fixed costs will remain unchanged within the relevant range. Thus, as output is changed, within the relevant range, changes will be only in variable costs and revenue; fixed costs, on the other hand, will not change and, therefore, are irrelevant costs for decision-making. Thus, sales revenue and variable costs are the only relevant variables for decisions.

ACCEPTING A SPECIAL ORDER

A company may have a production capacity which is not fully utilised. In that case, the total profit of the company can be increased by using the unutilised capacity to produce and sell goods which yield a positive marginal income. The following example is illustrative of this situation.

Example: The management of a company is to decide whether to accept an export order for 500 units per month at ₹7 per unit. Its present position is as follows:

Present sales	1,500 units per month
Production capacity	2,000 units per month
Selling price	₹10 per unit
Total cost	₹8 per unit
Fixed cost	

The result of accepting the export order may be tabulated as follows:

	Present Sale	Proposed Expert Sale	Total
Sales (units)	1,500	5,000	22,000
Sales revenue (₹)	15,000	3,500	18,500
Variable costs @ ₹5 per unit 7,500	7,500	2,500	10,000
	7,500	1,000	8,500
Additional cost for export order	–	500	500
Contribution margin	7,500	500	8,000
Fixed costs (₹)	4,500	–	4,500
Profit (₹)	3,000	500	3,500

Note. Calculation of variable cost per unit:

Fixed cost per unit = ₹4500/1500 = ₹3

Total cost = ₹8 per unit

Variable cost = ₹8 – ₹3 = ₹5 per unit

In the above example, the use of marginal costing technique reveals that the company will be better off by accepting the offer of export sales and the total profit will improve by ₹ 500. If the total cost were only considered, the contribution to profit of this additional sale would not be known except by recalculating all costs and breaking up, the fixed expenses which cannot be promptly done. Otherwise the decision may be to reject the offer as the selling price is ₹ 1 per unit less than the total cost.

Similarly, during a period of economic depression when sales are low and tend to decline, it may be wrong to consider total cost while deciding whether production should be continued or not. If production is stopped and no sale is made, there will be no recovery of fixed cost and the firm will suffer a loss. However, if orders are accepted at a price below the total cost but above the variable cost, it will lead to some contribution towards the fixed cost and the loss will be reduced to that extent.

Marginal costing is also helpful in developing data to show which sales-territory or customers, or other segment are contributing most towards fixed cost and in what proportions.

Let us consider the following example:

	Total	Sales Districts ('000)			
		I	II	III	IV
Sales revenue (₹)	3,700	1,200	1,000	800	700
Variable costs:					
Production	1,650	550	450	350	300
Selling	795	190	205	200	200
	2,445	740	655	550	500
Contribution margin	1,255	460	345	250	200
Fixed costs (districts)	955	560	242	250	240
Profit (loss) by districts	260	200	100	0	(40)
Fixed cost (total)	160				
Total profit	100				

From the above Table, it is obvious that the elimination of sales district IV would increase the overall profit of the company by ₹40,000 a year.

REPLACEMENT DECISION

Whether it would be more profitable to replace existing machinery by a new and improved one is a question which management in every concern has to face from time to time. The differential cost of keeping the old machine in use and using new machinery is the proper basis of making decisions of this kind.

PRICING DECISIONS (SELLING AT BELOW NORMAL PRICE)

The marginal contribution approach can help management in arriving at correct pricing decisions under special circumstances like the following.

Situations: When it may be Necessary to Sell at or Below Unit Cost

(a) If the firm has already purchased large quantities of raw materials and if the attempt to sell the raw materials will result in heavy loss or if continued storage will result in deterioration in quantity or quality thus giving rise to an extraordinary loss, it may be better to turn the raw materials into finished stock and sell it at a price below the marginal cost.

(b) If the closure of the business though temporary will mean discharge of old trusted employees and experienced workers the management must continue the production and sell at below marginal cost. If business is closed and restarted late, the services of these experienced hands may not be available. It will create the need of new recruitment and fresh selection of inexperienced persons which may entail expenditure on training, etc.

(c) If there is a threat of even a temporary closure of the business which may result into breaking the connection with the customers, the sale may be made at a lower price.

(d) When the goods are of perishable nature, they may be sold at a lower price also. It is better to sell the perishable goods at a lower price whatever they can realise otherwise these goods will perish and nothing will be, realised if they remain unsold.

(e) In the case of a new product it may be sold at a low price to make it popular and acceptable. This is done with the hope that sales will increase with the passage of time and cost of production will come down as a result of increase in sales. Ultimately, cost of production will be in line with the selling price and the concern will start earning profit from the new line of production.

(f) When a foreign market has to be explored to foreign exchange, the price may be quoted at a lower value. The same thing also applies to sale to special customers like the government who can be offered price concessions. The concessional price below the total cost but above the marginal cost will bring additional profits if additional sales are made. Several monthly magazines and journals work on the same principle when they offer specially low subscription rate to new customers.

(g) Sometimes prices below cost are charged in the event of keen competition also. When competitors are to be eliminated from the market, losses may be deliberately incurred to defeat and eliminate rivals. It is done in hope that after sometime the quantity of sales will considerably go up and shall be able to earn profit and cover the loss.

(h) When the sale of one product at a price below the marginal cost will push up the sales of other profitable products, one product maybe sold at below prices too. The loss in one product will be made up by profits in other products.

(i) There are certain expenses of closing and reopening the business. At the time of closing the works machinery has to be dismantled and greased up. At the time of reopening machinery will have to be reassembled again overhauled thoroughly. These expenses can be avoided if production is continued.

MAKE OR BUY DECISIONS

Most firms have to decide sometimes or the other whether they should buy a part from the market and stop making it themselves or whether they should stop buying it and start making it. There are various considerations affecting such a decision, chief of which is cost. As in any other case, the decision will mostly turn, in case the part is already being made, and the decision is whether or not to buy it from outside, on the comparison of the price that has to be paid and the saving that can be effected in cost. This, as can be realised, is only the marginal cost or the variable cost normally no saving is possible in fixed expenses.

However, if the decision is whether or not to produce a part being bought at present from outside suppliers, the comparison will have to be between the price being paid to outsiders and all the additional cost that will have to be incurred. Such additional cost will comprise not only materials and wages on the production of the part but also salaries of additional supervisors to be engaged, if any, interest on the capital that will have to be used for buying the necessary equipment as well as the depreciation on it, rent of premises, if present premises are not sufficient to house the new activity.

Besides the comparison of price demanded by the outsiders and the marginal cost, other considerations as below are also important:

(A) Opportunity Cost. It may be that the price quoted by the outsider may be higher than the marginal cost and thus the indicated decision may be for 'own' production. But before the decision is taken, the alternative use to which the machines and facilities can be put should also be considered. To take a simple, suppose a machine produces 10,000 units at a total cost of ₹5 of which ₹4 is variable. The article can be purchased from outside at ₹4.25. Suppose, if the machine is released from this article, it can be hired out at an annual rent of ₹3600. It would be cheaper to hire out the machine and buy the article from outside.

(B) The Fixed Expenses Burden. In case a part is produced by the firm itself, it will mean an outlay on machines and other facilities and also employment of staff some of which may be permanent and fixed in nature. Thus, the fixed expenses burden increases. Some firms deliberately buy from outside to keep this burden as low as possible even if the price to be paid is a little more than the cost of 'own' manufacture. A compromise is also often adopted own production is kept at the estimated minimum requirement, keeping in view possible fluctuations in demand, and the excess quantity required is purchased from outside. The effect of such a policy is that should demand fall, orders on outsiders can be cut down; the costs to be incurred will then be in proportion to the effective demand. In other words, the bulk of the cost then becomes controllable.

(C) Non-Cost Consideration. It is usually a mistake to arrive at make a decision only on the basis of costs. Factors which do not affect costs directly are important. Of these the under mentioned are noteworthy:

(i) Quality. Given the quality of the final product, there is a certain quality for the various parts and components about which there should be no compromise. If quality cannot be ensured in own production, the article concerned should be purchased from outside; if outside suppliers cannot be relied upon in this respect, the article should be produced by the firm itself, whatever the cost.

(ii) Regularity of Supply. Interruption of production process is very costly and therefore, before reliance is placed on outside sources of supplies, one must be sure that supplies will be regular and timely.

(iii) Expected Fluctuations in Demand. When there are large fluctuations in demand, it is better to purchase from outside; but if demand is likely to increase substantially, own production may lead to lower costs.

(iv) Reliability of Supplier. Except points (i) and (ii) made above, the supplier may land the firm in serious trouble if later on he runs into difficulties himself or adopts an attitude of non-cooperation or tries to extract a high price, knowing that production facilities that previously existed have been dismantled. For checking the dependability of the supplier, the under mentioned points may be kept in mind:

(a) the general reputation enjoyed by the supplier for reliability;
(b) his financial position and reputation in this regard;
(c) the technical know-how and production facilities at his disposal; and
(d) his relation with his workmen, etc.

Example A firm purchases 20000 units of a spare part from an outside source @₹3.00 per unit. There is a proposal that the spare be produced in the factory itself. For the purpose a machine costing ₹50,000 with a capacity 30,000 units and a lift of 5 years, will be required. A foreman with a monthly salary of ₹1000 p.m. will have to be engaged. Materials leaned will be 60 paise per unit and wages 45 paise per unit. Variable overheads are 150% of labour and fixed expenses are recovered @ 200% of wages. The firm can raise funds @ 16% p.a.

Advise the firm whether the proposal should be accepted.

Solution: The decision should be based on the comparison of the price being paid at present and the additional costs to be incurred if manufacture is undertaken. This comparison is made below:

(i) Price being paid at present (₹20,000 × ₹3000) ₹60,000
(ii) Cost to be incurred if manufacture is undertaken:

	₹
Materials @ 60 p.	12,000
Labour @ 45 p.	9000
Variable overheads	13,500
Additional foreman's salary	12,000
Depreciation (50,000 + 5)	10,000
Interest (16% on ₹50,000)	8000
	64,500

The cost of making 10,000 units will be higher than the price being paid at present. Hence, the proposal is not acceptable.

OPERATE OR SHUT-DOWN DECISIONS

If the demand of the products is not adequate enough to cover fixed costs, it is better to shut-down the business temporarily. There may be some fixed costs, which can be substantially reduced due to this temporary closing down of operations. Hence, management will have to make a comparison between two situations whether to continue or "suspend the production". Marginal costing helps the management in the decisions of such type also.

Example Rainbow Paint and Varnish Works, manufactures 2,00,000 medium-size tins of 'spray lac paints' when working at normal capacity. It incurs the following costs of manufacturing per unit.

	₹
Direct material	7.80
Direct labour	2.10
Variable overheads	2.50
Fixed overheads	4.00
Product cost per unit	16.40

Each unit of product is sold for ₹21 with variable selling and administrative expenses of 60 paise per unit of product.

During the next three months, only 10,000 units can be produced and sold. Management plans to shut down the plant estimating that the fixed manufacturing costs can be reduced to ₹74,000 for the quarter.

When the plant is operating, the fixed overhead costs are incurred at a uniform rate throughout the year. Additional cost of plant shut down for the three months are estimated at ₹14,000.

You are required:

(i) to express your opinion, along with calculations, whether the plant should be shut down for three months, and

(ii) to calculate the shut-down point for three months in units of products.

Solution:

(i) Variable cost of the product = ₹7.80 + ₹2.10 + ₹2.50 + ₹0.60 + ₹13 per unit

Contribution = ₹21 – ₹13 = ₹8 per unit

Calculation of Loss, if the Plant is Operated

	₹
Total contribution on 10,000 units	80,000
Total fixed costs for three months	
(200000 × 4 × 3/12)	2,00,000
Expected loss on operation	1,20,000

Calculation of Loss, if the Plant is Shut Down

	₹
Unavoidable fixed cost	74,000
Additional cost of shut down	14,000
Total loss on shut down	88,000

As is clear from the above calculations, the plant should be shut down for three months. If this decision is carried down, the management can reduce its loss from ₹1,20,000 (loss on operation) to ₹88,000 (loss on shut down).

(ii) Calculation of shut down point

Avoidable fixed for the period

= Total fixed costs for the period – (Unavoidable fixed costs – Additional cost of shut down)

₹2,00,000 – (₹74,000 + ₹14,000) = ₹1,12,000.

Shut down point = Avoidable fixed cost/Contribution per unit = ₹1,12,000/₹8

= 14000 units

KEY FACTOR

The limiting factor which prevents an enterprise from earning unlimited profit is known as the key factor. In a multi-product company or seasonal business, the question may arise as to which product should be pushed more in the peak season (where production, capacity is limited) so that the company can maximise profits. The concept of contribution; margin helps and guides management to determine which products are most profitable to sell and highlights the key factor.

The key factor may be the market for sales (as is usually the case) or scarce raw material, skilled labour, machine capacity, etc. If there is a key factor or constraint, the best position is reached when the gross margin (i.e., contribution) is maximised per unit of the key factor. For example, if the available labour supply is inadequate to permit manufacture of all the products, the most profitable course of action would be to use the available manpower to make the products which contribute the largest marginal income per hour of labour. Similarly, if materials are in short supply, management has to generate maximum marginal income per unit of material used. Thus, the contribution per unit of the key factor of production may be ascertained and the products ranked according to the descending order of contribution for selective attention. Consideration of total cost cannot be expected to reveal the significance of this aspect of business policy, nor help in decision making which is appropriate.

FIXATION OF SELLING PRICES

The fixation selling prices is one of the important functions of management. The technique of marginal costing can be applied to the pricing of products. The theory is that only those products should be produced or sold which make the largest contribution towards the recovery of fixed costs. The selling price fixation is also done under different circumstances. Some important circumstances are as follows:

(i) **Under Normal Circumstances.** Under normal situation the product giving more contribution should be produced and sold. The selling price of the product should be fixed, covering the total cost as otherwise profits cannot be earned.

For example,

Product A selling price ₹10: p.u. V.C. ₹6/- p.u.

Product B selling price ₹12: p.m. V.C. ₹10/- p.u.

If the maximum number of units of Product A and/or Product B which can be produced and sold by the firm is 100 unit B. The comparison should be made in this manner:

Contribution p.u. Product A = ₹4/- p.u.
Product B = ₹2/- p.u.
Profit + F.C. Product A = ₹4,000 total (1,000 × 4)
Product B = ₹2,000 total (1,000 × 2)

If the number of fixed costs is ₹1500 p.a. it is clear that the product of production A is profitable as maximise the profit ₹2500 as against ₹5000 only in case of product B.

(ii) **Pricing in Depression.** Price fall during depression and the product may be sold below the total cost. In case there is a serious but temporary fall in the demand on account of depression leading to the need for a drastic reduction in prices temporarily, the minimum selling price should be equal to the marginal cost. If the selling price at which the goods can be sold is equal to marginal cost or more than marginal cost, the product should be continued. Fixed expenses will be incurred even if the products discontinued during depression for a short period. If the product can be sold at a price, which is a little more than marginal cost, loss on account of fixed expenses will reduce because price will recover fixed expenses to some extent. This will be clear from the following example.

Suppose, marginal cost per unit is ₹10 and fixed expenses amount to ₹150,000. Selling price per unit is ₹11 and 40000 units can be sold at this price.

	₹
Marginal cost: 40000 units @ ₹10	= 4,00,000
Fixed expenses	= 1,50,000
Total cost	5,50,000
Cost p.u. ₹13.75	

Here, at the selling price of ₹10 is below the total cost, yet it is advantageous to sell the product at the selling price of ₹11 which is more than the marginal cost of ₹10. This will reduce the loss on account of fixed expenses (if the product is discontinued) by ₹40,000 as below:

	₹
Selling price of 40000 units @ ₹11	= 4,40,000
Less: Total cost (calculated earlier)	= 5,50,000
Loss:	= 1,10,000
Loss if the product is discontinued (fixed expenses)	= 1,50,000
Loss reduced if the product is continued	40,000

PRODUCTION MIX WITH AND WITHOUT CONSTRAINTS

If there are no production contraints, that is, raw material and labour are in abundant supply, the product with the highest contribution margin per unit should be produced until demand is satisfied. Next, relate the next product with the next highest contribution margin per unit and so on. This criterion will maximise profit.

Let us suppose that the management of a hypothetical company has the following data relating to its two products per unit basis.

Table

	Product X	Product Y
Selling price	₹330	₹500
Direct material	₹40	₹240
Direct labour (skilled)	₹150	₹100
Variable overheads (20% of labour) ₹30	₹20	
Fixed overheads	₹2,80,000 per annum	

Problem 1 How much of each product should be produced if there are no production and sales constraints?

Decision. The management should concentrate on producing product Y only because it gives a higher (₹140) marginal contribution per unit than product X (₹110).

Problem 2 How much of each product should be produced if there are no production but sales constraints in terms of volume of rupees?

Decision. Management should produce X units exclusively because its profit volume ratio (marginal contribution to sales ratio) is higher ($33\frac{1}{3}$ %, i.e., ₹110 + ₹330) than that of product Y (28%, i.e., ₹140 + 500).

Let us further suppose that the sales level is ₹3,00,000. Then, product X will generate a marginal contribution of ₹1,00,000, while the corresponding amount will be ₹84,000 in the case of product Y. 1.

Let us incorporate some more information to explain the problem of production mix with a scarce supply of inputs.

Further information	Product X	Product Y
Materials used (per unit)	2 kg	12 kg
Labour hours (per unit)	30 hours	20 hours
Power consumed (per unit)	20 kWh	28 kWh
Demand for products	5000 units	4000 units

Problem 3 How much of each product should be, produced if capacity is limited to 1,40,000 labour hours?

Decision. The production mix will depend on which product has a higher contribution per hour (see the following Table)

	Product X	Product Y
Selling price	₹330	₹500
Less: Variable costs:		
Direct material	40	240
Direct labour	150	100
Variable overheads		
Told variable costs:	–₹220	–₹360
Marginal contribution per unit	₹110	₹140
Labour hours	30	20
Marginal contribution per hour	₹3.67	₹7.0

The basis of our decision should be the marginal contribution per direct labour hour. The firm should produce as many units of product Y as it can sell. If any labour hours still available, they should be used in manufacturing the product which gives the next higher marginal contribution per direct labour hour. Accordingly, the following solution emerges:

(Time taken in producing a unit × Expected sales in units)

= Total hours left (Capacity used – Hours used)

Product Y	20 hours × 4000 = 80000	60000
Product X	30 hours × 2000 = 60000	Nil

Accordingly, a production mix of 4000 units of product Y and 2000 units of X is the most suitable under the circumstances. Such a combination will yield income greater than any other combination, given labour hours as a key factor. The amount of income generated by such a combination will be ₹5,00,000 as shown in Table 1.

Table 1

	Product X	Product Y	Total
Marginal contribution per unit	₹110	₹140	
Total units sold	2000	4000	
Total marginal contribution	₹2,20,000	₹5,60,000	₹7,80,000
Less: Fixed cost			(–) 2,80,000
Net income			₹5,00,000

Problem 4 How much of each product should be produced if only 22,000 kg of material is available?

Decision. Maximising, marginal contribution per kilogram of material will be the guiding criterion for the decision.

(i) *Maintaining Desired Level of Profits.* Management may be interested in maintaining a desired level of profit. The volume of sales needed to have a desired level of profits can be ascertained by the marginal costing technique. As per formulae,
Desired sales = Fixed cost + Desired profit/P/V ratio

(ii) *Evaluation of Profitability of Departments.* The decision whether a department should continue or be closed depends to a costing technique helps the management in taking such decisions.

PRODUCT DECISIONS

The concept of marginal contribution guides management to determine which products are most profitable to sell and highlights the key factor of production. Such a key factor may be some scarce raw material, skilled labour, machine capacity, etc. If the available labour supply is inadequate to permit manufacture of all products the most profitable course of action is to use the available manpower to make the products which contribute the largest material income per hour of labour. If materials are in short supply, management should produce according to the largest marginal contribution per input of material. Thus, the contribution per unit of the key factor of production should be determined and the products ranked according to descending order of contribution for selection. Absorption costing just cannot explain such an important aspect of a production decision affecting the total profits of the enterprise. This is illustrated in the following examples.

(i) Dropping a Product Line

Example A hypothetical company makes a profit of ₹40,000 from the manufacture and sale of three products in the following Table.

Table

Products	X (₹)	Y(₹)	Z(₹)	Total
Sales	50,000	60,000	80,000	1,90,000
Less costs:				
Variable costs	–16,000	–40,000	26,000	82,000
Fixed costs (allocated)	–2,000	–36,000	–20,000	–68,000
Profit (loss)	22,000	(16,000)	34,000	40,000

Problem 5 On the basis of the income statement prepared under absorption costing and supplied to management, management is considering dropping product Y because it is incurring a loss of ₹16,000. Should the management carry out the proposal?

Decision. The decision would depend on the fact whether the facilities represented by ₹36,000 fixed costs allocated to product Y can be better used elsewhere in the company, that is, new sales line may be added or it may be possible to produce and sell existing more profitable products X and Z. If neither of the things is possible, management will be advised not to eliminate product Y, otherwise profits will be reduced by ₹20,000 as shown in this Table.

Table

	Products X(₹)	Z (₹)	Total
Sales	50,000	80,000	1,30,000
Less: Variable costs	(–)16,000	(–)26,000	(–)42,000
Marginal contribution	34,000	54,000	88,000
Less: Fixed costs net profit			(–)68,000
Net profit			20,000

Although product Y is an unprofitable line, its elimination has converted ₹40,000 profit to a much lower figure of ₹20,000. The reason is that this product was making a marginal contribution of ₹20,000 (US 60,000 sales ₹40,000 variable costs) to fixed costs which are to be incurred, irrespective of the fact whether product Y is continued or eliminated.

(ii) Adding a New Product Line

Let us modify the example on the assumption that management has found a substitute product W in place of product Y. The marketing and production departments of the company have furnished to management the following information regarding the new product, W:

Sales revenue: ₹1,00,000

Variable costs: ₹60,000

No additional fixed costs will be required.

Problem 6 Advise the management whether product W should be introduced.

Decision. Yes, product W should be introduced because it will increase the existing profit by ₹20,000 as shown in this Table.

Table

	Products X(₹)	Z(₹)	W (₹)	Total
Sales	50,000	8,000	1,00,000	2,30,000
Less: Variable costs	(–)16,000	(–)26,000	60,000	(–)1,02,000
Marginal contribution				1,28,000
Less: Fixed costs				(–)68,000
Net profit				60,000

(iii) Decisions on Product Priorities

It often happens that a firm has to decide on the relative importance to be attached to various products; in other words, the priorities for various products are to be fixed. If the output of only single product can be increased, which product should be chosen? If the production of one of the products is to be curtailed, again which product should suffer the curtailment?

Normally, on the assumption that fixed expenses will remain unaffected, the question posed above is answered on the basis of contribution per unit of each product. The product which produces the highest contribution should be accorded, the highest priority and that whose contribution is the least should come at the bottom of the list. Of course, if product produces no or minus contribution, its production and sale should be immediately given up unless there are other advantages.

(iv) Scarcity of Factor of Production

Though normally priorities for various products cannot be decided on the basis of contribution of each product, the principle has to be modified when a particular factor is in short supply and it is necessary that the available supplies should be put to the best use. In such a case, the proper thing to do is to work out the contribution of per unit of scarce factor and accord the highest priority to that product which produces the highest contribution.

Consider the following figures of cost and profit:

	A	B
	₹	₹
Materials	10.00	15.00
Labour	6.00	8.00
Overheads–Varialble	3.00	5.00
Fixed	5.00	7.00
Total cost	24.00	35.00
Profit	3.00	4.00
Selling price	27.00	39.00
Contribution	8.00	11.00

On the basis of contribution shown above B will be more profitable than A. But suppose both products use imported raw materials and that the foreign exchange allotment is limited to ₹9000 per period. In that case one can either produce 900 units of A or 600 units of B and one can see that the total contribution thus will be ₹7200 (i.e., 900 × ₹8) if all the materials used for production of A and ₹6600 in the other case. Thus A becomes more profitable than B. This conclusion could also be arrived at by ascertaining the contribution per rupee spent on materials. The figures are:

A ₹0.80, i.e., ₹8.00 ÷ 10

B ₹0.73, i.e., ₹11.00 4 ÷ 15

Thus, one of the principles to remember, when relative product priorities are being fixed, is that contribution per unit of scarce factor or production should be the highest for products selected for preferential treatment.

Selection of an Optimum Sales Mix

When a factory produces more than one product, a problem is faced by the management as to which product-mix will give the maximum profits. The best product mix is that which yields the maximum contribution. For example, a company produces X and Y. The following are the facts regarding costs:

	Products	
	X	Y
Contribution per unit	₹2	₹3
Required production hours per unit	1	2
Sales potential (in units)	1,500	800
Available production hours	2,000	hours
Determine the optimum product mix.		

Solution:

	Products	
	X	Y
Contribution per unit	₹2	₹3
Required hours per unit	1	2
Contribution per hour	₹2	₹1.50
(Contribution/Key factor)		

Since product X has the greatest contribution per hour, the optimum solution would be to produce all the X that can be sold and then if there are any hours left over, product Y. As such 1500 units of X (1500 hours) and 250 units of Y (500 hours) is the optimum product mix.

Sales Mix with no Input Constraint

The management of a hypothetical company is considering the sales budget for the next budget period. The sales manager of the company has made the following sales forecasts:

(i) 2250 units of A and 1500 units of B.

(ii) 4500 units of A only.

(iii) 3000 units of B only.

(iv) 3000 units of A and 1000 units of B.

The costing department has provided the relevant information shown in this Table relating to products on a per unit basis.

Table

	Product A (₹)	Product B (₹)
Selling price	300	500
Direct materials	100	125
Direct labour	50	75
Variable overheads	50	75
Fixed costs	₹2,00,000 per annum	

Problem 7 Recommend the optimal sales mix.

Decision. The sales alternative which yields the highest marginal contribution leading to the highest profit will be recommended. The marginal contributions for products A and B are 100 and ₹225 respectively as shown in their Table A B.

Table Marginal Contrinution Per Unit (Products A and B)

	Product A (₹)	Product B (₹)
Selling price	300	500
Less: Variable costs: Direct materials (DM)		
DM	–100	–125
DL	–50	–75
VD	–50	–75
Marginal contribution	100	225

Table Net Income in Various Alternative

	Product A (₹)	Product B (₹)	Total (₹)
Sales alternatives:			
(i) (2,250 units of A and 1,500 units of B			
Marginal contribution	2,25,000	3,37,500	5,62,000
Less: Fixed costs			(–)2,00,000
Net income			3,62,000
(ii) 4500 units of A only			
Marginal contribution	4,50,000		4,50,000
Less: Fixed costs			(–)2,00,000
Net income			2,50,000
(iii) 3000 units of B only			
Marginal contribution	—	6,75,000	6,75,000

Table Contd...

Table Contd...

Less: Fixed costs	—		(−)2,00,000
Net income			4,75,000
(iv) 3000 units of A and 1000 units of B			
Marginal contribution	3,00,000	2,25,000	5,25,000
Less: Fixed costs			(−)2,00,000
Net income			3,25,000

Thus, a sales mix consisting of selling only 3000 units of B is the best as it yields the highest profit.

Illustration 1 Mrs. Jain, an architect has been employed by a firm for ₹1,50,000 p.a. She is considering an alternative use of her time.

Details	Alternative options		
	Remain an employee	Open an independent firm	Difference
Revenues	15,00,000	30,00,000	15,00,000
Outlay costs (operating expenses)	Nil	10,00,000	10,00,000
Income effects per year	15,00,000	20,00,000	5,00,000

Solution: Mrs. Jain has revenue of ₹30,00,000, which is greater than she would have made as an employee. However, she also had to pay ₹10,00,000 to operate the firm. ₹20,00,000 is the operating income which is more than the salary received by her.

Illustration 2 XYZ Limited has been working under normal capacity due to recession. Management have been approached by an enquiry for a special purpose job the costing department estimated the following in respect of the job:

Direct materials ₹1,20,000, Direct labour hour 400 @ ₹25 per hour

Overhead costs : (normal rates of recovery)

Variable ₹10 per hour

Fixed ₹15 per hour

The directors of the company seek your advice on the minimum price to charge.

Solution:

Details	Amount
Direct materials	20,000
Direct labour	10,000
Variable overhead costs	8000
Variable costs	1,38,000

The absolute minimum price is ₹ 1,38,000, i.e., total of variable costs' proportion of fixed costs of ₹ 6000 may be added to make the job worthwhile circumstances.

Illustration 3 Dropping a product): Crystal electronics manufacture 3 products S1, S2, and S3. Following are the details.

Details	Product S1	Product S2	Product S3
Direct material	50	40	46
Direct wages	30	32	30
Variable overhead	20	24	19
Fixed expenses	16	14	12
Total cost	116	110	106
Profit	44	40	24
Selling price	160	150	10
Number of units produced and sold	20000	12000	17000

Production arrangements are such that if one product is given tip the production of others can be raised by 50%. Finance department proposes that product S3 should be given up because the contribution from the product S3 is the lowest. Do you think the proposal should be entertained.

Solution:

Calculation of Current Profit

Details	Amount (₹)
Product S1 (20,000 × 44)	8,80,000
Product S2 (12,000 × 40)	4,80,000
Product S3 (17,000 × 24)	4,08,000
Total profit	17,68,000

Calculation of Fixed Cost

Details	Amount (₹)
Product S1 (20,000 × 16)	8,80,000
Product S2 (12,000 × 40)	4,80,000
Product S3 (17,000 × 24)	4,08,000
Total	3,46,000

Calculation of Proposed Profit

Details	Amount (₹)
Cost: Variable	
Product S1 (30,000 × 100)	15,00,000
Product S2 (18,000 × 96)	8,64,000
Cost: (fixed) as above	3,46,000
Total cost	27,10,000
Sales: Product S1 (3000 × 160)	48,00,000
Sales : Product S2 (18,000 × 150)	13,50,000
Total sales value	61,50,000
Profit	34,40,000

Since the profit has increased by 16,72,000 (34,40,000 – 17,68,000). The proposed should be accepted.

Expansion of production

The new product should be introduced if it can add to the contribution of the business.

Illustration 4 Following are the details about LCD's manufactured by Videocon Ltd.

Sales	₹5,00,000
Variable cost	₹30,000
Fixed overheads	₹1,20,000

The company proposes to introduce production of LED so that sales may be increased by ₹1,25,000. The production of this new product does not involve fixed cost and the estimated variable cost is ₹1,05,000. Find whether the production of product S2 will be profitable or not.

Solution:

Profit Level of LCD's

Details	Amount (₹)
Sales	5,00,000
Variable cost	3,00,000
Contribution	2,00,000
Less: Fixed cost	1,20,000
Profit	8,000

Profit Statement after Introduction of LEDs

Details	LCD	LED	Total
Sales	5,00,000	1,25,000	6,25,000
Variable cost	3,00,000	1,05,000	4,05,000

Table Contd...

Table Contd...

Details	LCD	LED	Total
Contribution	2,00,000	20,000	2,20,000
Less: Fixed cost			1,20,000
Profit			1,00,000

The total contribution has increased by ₹20,000 with the introduction of LED's. Hence, it will benefit the firms to manufacture LED's.

Make or Buy Decision

A firm may have idle capacity which may be utilised in manufacturing components/parts or similar items instead of buying them from market. If the manufacturers marginal cost is less than the purchase price it is better to make in the factory but on the other hand if the marginal cost is more than the purchase price it is desirable to purchase the same from the market. Fixed cost are ignored on the assumption that such cost will not increase with the manufacturing the components.

Illustration 5 Cine Art Ltd. has prepared the following cost estimate for the manufacture of a camera which can brought from an outside supplier at ₹580 per unit and the company is to incur ordering cost ₹20 per unit. The company has idle capacity and no extra costs will be required to be incurred. The annual requirement is 15000 units.

Element of cost	Amount (₹) details
Direct material	200
Direct wages	100
Variable overheads	125
Fixed overbeads	180
Total	615

Give your suggestion whether to make or buy the camera.

Solution: Since fixed cost shall remain the same, irrespective of whether the firm is manufacturing the camera itself or buying from outside, the decision shall be taken on the basis of difference in the variable cost.

Decision Analysis

Details	Per unit cost (₹)		Total cost of 15,000 units (₹)	
	Manufacture	Buy	Manufacture	Buy
Direct material	200		30,00,000	
Direct wages	100		15,00,000	
Variable Overheads	125		20,00,000	
Purchase price		580		87,00,000
Ordering cost		20		30,00,000
Total	505	600	65,00,000	1,17,00,000

The company should manufacture camera as the cost of manufacturing is much lower than buying from outside.

Key Factor

It is the most important factor.

Illustration 6 The following information show the profitability of two products during labour shortage. Production of which product would be more profitable for the organisation.

Details	Product Z	Product Y
Selling price	1125	1440
Direct material	900	900
Direct labour hours @ ₹8 (per hour)	40	8
Variable overheads @125% of direct wages		
Fixed overheads ₹5,00,000*		

Solution: Since fixed cost is same and does not changes, the decision shall be taken on the basis of contribution per labour hour.

Details	Product Z	Product Y
Selling price	2,250	1,440
Less: Variable cost	900	900
Direct material	320	64
Direct wages	400	80
Variable overheads		
	1,620	1,044
Contribution per unit	620	396
Profitability: Contribution/labour hours	620/40 = 15.75 per hour	396/8 = 49.80 per hour

Decision: Product Y is more profitable than product Z during labour shortage. Since its contribution per labour hour is higher.

Plant shut down decision. Shut down of the plant means closure of the plant for such a decision other points of consideration are given due importance. When the existing plant becomes obsolete or is not giving the minimum desired level of output, the company decides to shut down the plant.

Illustration 7 Departmental store has 3 departments, furniture, grocery and clothing. However clothing department is not giving desired profit level. So the proposal of closing this department is under consideration. Do you agree?

Details	Furniture	Grocery	Clothing	Total (₹)
Sales	38,00,000	28,00,000	8,00,000	74,00,000
Variable cost	30,00,000	18,00,000	6,40,000	54,40,000
Contribution	8,00,000	10,00,000	1,60,000	19,60,000
Less: Fixed costs				

Table Contd...

Table Contd...

Details	Furniture	Grocery	Clothing	Total (₹)
Unavoidable	1,90,000	4,40,000	80,000	7,10,000
Avoidable	4,00,000	2,60,000	75,000	7,35,000
Net income	2,10,000	3,00,000	5,000	51,500

Solution: The unavoidable costs would continue to be incurred and no other department can be installed at the place of furniture department is the assumption.

Shut Down Decision Analysis

Details	Total of all three departments	Clothing department	Net
Sales	74,00,000	8,00,000	66,00,000
Variable cost	54,40,000	6,40,000	48,00,000
Contribution	19,60,000	1,60,000	18,00,000
Less: Avoidable fixed costs	7,35,000	75,000	6,40,000
Gross income	11,25,000	85,000	10,40,000
Less: Unavoidable fixed costs	7,10,000		7,10,000
Net income	4,15,000	3,30,000	85,000

Decision: The total income of departmental store initially is ₹5,15,000. Moreover if the clothing department is shut down, total income falls to ₹3,30,000. Therefore, it is not adjustable for the firm to shut down the clothing department.

SOLVED PRACTICAL PROBLEMS

Problem 1 A college spends ₹10 per kilometre on taxi fare for their chief guest. They are considering two alternatives, the purchase of a Indica or Accent. The estimated cost data is as under:

Details	Indica (₹)	Accent (₹)
Purchase price	4,00,000	2,50,000
Sale price after five years	2,50,000	1,50,000
Repairs and servicing (annual)	20,000	25,000
Taxes and insurance (annual)	25,000	10,000
Petrol consumption per litre	45	45
Kilometres run per litre	16 km	10 km

College estimates that it has to travel 10,000 km annually. Which of the three alternatives will be the cheapest? If the car runs 22,000 km per annum, what would be your decision? At how many km, will the costs of two cars break-even. Ignore interest and income tax.

Solution:

Details	Indica	Accent	Taxi (₹)
Purchase price	4,00,000	2,50,000	
Less: Sale price (scrap)	2,50,000	1,50,000	
Balance as depreciation for five years	1,50,000	1,00,000	
Annual depreciation	30,000	20,000	
Repairs and servicing	20,000	25,000	
Taxes and insurance	25,000	10,000	
Total fixed expenses	75,000	5,000	
Variable expenses: new small car:			
(a) Petrol for 10,000 km @ ₹2.8125	28,125	45,000	
(b) Petrol for 22,000 km @ ₹2.8125 old bigger car:	61,875	99,000	
(c) Petrol for 10,000 km @ ₹4.50			
(d) Petrol for 22,000 km @ ₹4.50			
Total cost			
(a) 10,000 km	1,03,125	1,00,000	1,00,000
(b) 22,000 km	1,36,875	1,54,000	2,20,000

Comments for decision

(1) The Accent is the cheapest for his present need. However, if the car runs more, Indica will be cheaper.

(2) The difference in the variable cost of running the two cars is ₹1.6875. The difference of fixed cost is ₹20,000. Hence, the break-even point between the two cars is 11,852 km (i.e., 20,000/1.6875).

Details	Indica	Accent
Fixed cost	75,000	55,000
Variable cost	33,334	53,334
	1,08,334	1,08,334

Problem 2 Handloom Corporation is at present operating at 75% capacity level, the production being 4200 units per year. The company operates a flexible budgetary control system. The following relevant cost data are obtained from the company's budget at different capacity utilisation levels:

Details	75%	100%
Sales	40,00,000	53,33,333
Variable overheads	5,00,000	6,66,667
Semi-variable overheads	2,10,000	2,80,000

Table Contd...

Table Contd...

Details	75%	100%
Fixed overheads	6,00,000	8,00,000
Output (unit)	4200	5600

Material and labour costs per unit are constant under the existing conditions. The management expects a profit margin of 15% on sales.

You are required to compute the differential cost of producing the additional 1400 units by increasing the capacity utilisation to 100% and the minimum price per unit at 15% of profit on cost.

Solution:

		₹
Sales at 75% capacity		40,00,000
Less: Profit 15% [40,00,000 × 0.15]		6,00,000
Cost of goods sold		34,00,000
Less: Expenses:		
Variable overheads	₹5,00,000	
Semi-variable overheads	₹2,10,000	
Fixed overheads	₹ 6,00,000	20,90,000
Cost of material and labour at 75% capacity		13,10,000
Cost of material and labour at 100% capacity		17,46,667

Particulars	75% capacity uitilization (4200 units (₹)	100% capacity utilisation (5600 units (₹)	Differential cost of (1400 units)
Material and labour	13,10,000	17,46,667	4,36,667
Variable overheads	5,00,000	6,66,667	1,66,667
Semi-variable overheads	2,10,000	2,80,000	70,000
Fixed overheads	6,00,000	8,00,000	2,00,000
Total cost	26,20,000	34,93,334	8,73,334

Differential cost per unit = 873334/1400 = ₹623.81

Minimum price = 623.81 (1.4) = ₹873.334

Problem 3 Spencers production has a capacity of selling 600 units at ₹100 per quarter. Marginal cost per unit is ₹60 and fixed costs are ₹10,000. It is proposed to reduce the selling price by 15%. Find the additional sales required to earn the same profit as before.

Solution: Contribution per unit = Selling price per unit – Marginal cost per unit

= 100 – 60 = ₹40

Existing profit [(600 × 40) – 10,000)= ₹14,000

At reduced price, to earn the same amount of profit, the sales required are:

= [Fixed cost + Existing profit]/New contribution per unit 1)

= [10,000 + 1,40,001/25 = 960 units. Additional sale units

= Required sale units – Existing sale units

= 960 – 600 = 360 units

or

₹30,600 (i.e., 360 × 85)

Working Note:

[100 – (0.15 × 100)] = ₹85 is the new selling price

Problem 4 Expansion decision is under consideration by ABC Corporation. Fixed costs amount to ₹5,00,000 and are expected to increase by ₹2,00,000 when plant expansion is completed. The existing plant capacity is 40,000 units a year. Capacity will increase by 50% with the expansion. Variable costs are currently ₹20 per unit and are expected to go down by ₹2 per unit with the expansion. The current selling price is ₹40 and is expected to remain same under either alternative. What are the break-even points under either alternative? Given a choice amongst both the alternatives which alternative do you think the company will select.

Solution:

Particulars	Present level	Post expansion level
Fixed cost	5,00,000	7,00,000
Capacity (unit)	40,000	60,000
Selling price per unit	40	40
Less: Variable cost	20	18
Contribution per unit	20	22
Break-even point (units)	5,00,000/20 = 25,000	7,00,000/22 = 31818
(Fixed cost/contribution per unit)		

Assuming that the production up to plant capacity can be sold, profit under the two alternatives would be as under:

Particulars	Present level	Post expansion level
Sales:	16,00,000	2,40,000
40,000 units ₹40		
60,000 units @ ₹40		
Less: Variable cost:		
40,000 units @ ₹20	8,00,000	10,80,000
60,000 units @ ₹18		
Contribution	8,00,000	13,20,000
Less: Fixed cost	5,00,000	7,00,000
Profit	3,00,000.	6,20,000

The above analysis shows that profit after expansion is more than double. Hence, ABC Corporation should accept the expansion plans.

Problem 5 Sweety manufacturers produced Jim Jam biscuits in the previous year 2020.

Information	Amount (₹)
Units produced and sold (30,000)	
Fixed overhead	3,00,000
Variable cost per unit	
Labour	25
Material	15
Overheads	5
Selling price per unit	60

Sweety Corporation prepared the current year's budget and incorporated the following changes in 2021.

Information	Amount (₹)
Units produced and sold (65,000)	
Fixed overhead increased by	20,000
Fall in labour efficiency	20%
Special discount for bulk purchase of material	10%
Variable overhead per unit reduced by fall in selling price : (4%)	5%

Calculate:

(i) The number of units which must be sold to break-even in the year 2020 and 2021.

(ii) The number of units which would have had to be sold in 2020 to double its profits.

(iii) The number of the units which would have to be sold in 2021 to maintain the profit level of the year 2020.

Solution:

Units produced and sold	Year 2020 (30,000)		Year 2021 (65,000)	
	Per unit (₹)	Amount (₹)	Per unit (₹)	Amount (₹)
Sales	60	18,00,000	57.6	37,44,000
Variable cost: Direct wages				
Direct materials	25	7,50,000	31.25	20,31,250
Variable overheads	15	4,50,000	13.5	8,77,500
Total variable costs	5	1,50,000	4.75	3,08,750
Contribution	45	13,50,000	49.5	32,17,500
Fixed overheads	15	4,50,000	8.1	5,26,500

Table Contd...

Table Contd...

		3,00,000		3,20,000
Net profit/loss		1,50,000		2,06,500

(i) Units to be sold for break-even 2020

= Fixed overheads / Contribution per unit

= ₹ 3,00,000/₹ 15

= 20,000 Units

Units to sell for break-even 2021

= Fixed overheads / Contribution per unit

= 3,20,000/8.1

= 39,506 units (approx.)

(ii) Units to sell for doubling profit in year 2020

(2 profit + fixed overhead)' contribution per unit) of year 2020 + Fixed overhead of the year 2020/ Contribution per unit

= ₹ (2 × 1,50,000 + 3,00,000)/₹ 8.1

= 40,000 units

Problem 6 From the following particulars, find the most profitable product mix and prepare a statement of profitability of that product mix:

Particulars	Product A	Product B	Product C
Units budgeted to be produced	1800	3000	1200
Selling price per unit ₹	60	55	50
Cost of direct materials per kg	₹ 4	₹ 4	4
Direct labour hour rate	₹ 2	₹ 2	2
Variable overheads	₹ 7	₹ 13	8
Fixed overheads	₹ 10	₹ 10	₹ 10
Requirement per unit:			
Direct materials	5 kg	3 kg	4 kg
Direct labour	4 hr	3 hr	2 hr
Maximum possible sales (units)	4000	5000	1500

All the three products are produced from the same material using the same type of machines and labour. Direct labour, which is the key factor, is limited to 18,600 hours. (*B.Com Hons*)

Solution:

Statement Showing Contribution

Particulars	A (₹)	B (₹)	C (₹)
(i) Selling price	60	55	50

Table Contd...

Table Contd...

Particulars	A (₹)	B (₹)	C (₹)
Direct materials @ ₹4 per kg	20	12	16
Direct labour @ ₹2 per hr	8	6	4
Variable overheads	7	13	8
(ii) Total variable costs	35	31	28
(iii) Contribution (i)–(ii)	25	24	22
(iv) Direct labour hours per unit	4 hrs	3 hrs	2 hrs
(v) Contribution per direct labour hr. (iii) ÷ (iv)	6.25	8.00	11.00
Ranking	III	II	I

Product Mix:

Maximum possible units of each product should be produced according to ranking shown above. 18,600 labour hours will be utilised in the following manner:

		Labour hours
Product C (1500 units × 2 hr)		3000
Product B (5000 units × 3 hr)		15000
Product A (600 hr ÷ 4 hrs = 150 units) Balance hours		600
	Total	18600

Profitability Statement

Particulars	A (₹)	B (₹)	C (₹)	Total (₹)
Sales	150 × 60	5,000 × 55	1,500 × 50	3,59,000
Less: Variable cost	150 × 35	5,000 × 31	1,500 × 28	2,02,250
Contribution	3,750	1,20,000	33,000	1,56,750
Less: Fixed cost[1]				60,000
Profit				96,750

Working Notes:

1. As the labour hour is the key factor, the product with the highest contribution per labour hour should be produced first to maximise the profits.
2. Calculation of fixed cost is based on budgeted units:

A	1800 units @ ₹10	= ₹18,000
B	3000 units @ ₹10	= ₹30,000
C	1200 units @ ₹10	= ₹12,000
Total		= ₹60,000

Problem 7 Alpha Ltd. which produces three products furnishes you the following data for the year 2021:

	Products		
	A	B	C
Selling price per unit (₹)	100	75	50
Profit/volume ratio	10%	20%	40%
Maximum sales potential (units)	40000	25000	10000
Raw material content as percentage of variable costs	50%	50%	50%

The fixed expenses are estimated at ₹6,80,000. The company uses a single raw material in all the three products. Raw material is in short supply and the company has a quota for the supply of raw materials of the value of ₹18,00,000 for the year for the manufacture of its products to meet its sales demand.

You are required to: (i) set a product mix which will give the maximum overall profit keeping the short supply of raw material in view. (ii) Compute that maximum profit. [*B.Com. (H)*]

Solution:

Statement Showing Contribution

Particulars	A	B	C
Selling price	100	50	75
P/V ratio	10%	20%	40%
Contribution per unit	10	15	20
Variable cost per unit	90	60	30
Raw material per unit (50% of variable cost)	45	30	15
Contribution per rupee of material cost	₹0.22	0.50	1.33
Ranking	III	II	I

Statement of Product Mix

Products	No. of units	Material cost per unit	Total material cost ₹
C	10,000	15	1,50,000
B	25,000	30	7,50,000
A	20,000	45	9,00,000 (Balance)
Total			18,00,000

Profitability Statement

Particulars	A	B	C	Total
Sales	20,00,000	18,75,000	5,00,000	43,75,000
Variable cost	18,00,000	15,00,000	3,00,000	36,00,000
Contribution	2,00,000	3,75,000	2,00,000	7,75,000
Fixed cost				6,80,000
Profit				95,000

Problem 8 Saya Co. produces three products A, B, and C, from the same manufacturing facilities. The cost and other details of the three products are as follows:

	A	B	C
Selling price/unit (₹)	200	160	100
Variable cost/unit (₹)	120	120	40
Fixed expenses/month (₹)			2,76,000
Maximum production per month (units)	5000	8000	6000
Total hours available for the month : 200 hours			
Maximum demand per month (units)	2000	4000	2400

The processing hours cannot be increased beyond 200 hours per month

You are required to:

(a) Compute the most profitable product-mix.

(b) Compute the overall break-even sales of the company for the month based on the mix calculated in (a) above.

Solution:

(a) Statement Showing Contribution

Particulars	A	B	C
Selling price per unit (₹)	200	160	100
Variable cost per unit (₹)	120	120	40
Contribution per unit	80	40	60
Maximum production per hour (units)	5000/200 = 25	8000/200 = 40	6000/200 = 30
Contribution per hour (₹)			
(Maximum production per hour × Contribution per unit)	= 2000	= 1600	= 1800
Ranking	I	III	II
Units to be produced	2000	1600	2400
Time required for the units to be produced (hr.)	2000/25 = 80	1600/40 = 40	2400/30 = 80

Profitability Statement of M/s Saya Co.

Particulars	A	B	C	Total
Units	2000	2400	1600	
Selling price	200	160	100	
Sales	4,00,000	2,56,000	2,40,000	8,96,000
Less : Variable cost	2,40,000	1,92,000	96,000	5,28,000
Contribution	1,60,000	64,000	1,44,000	3,68,000
Fixed cost				2,76,000
Profit				92,000

(b)

$$\text{Break-even sales} = \frac{\text{Fixed costs} \times \text{Total sales}}{\text{Total contribution}}$$

$$= \frac{₹2,76,000}{₹3,68,000} \times 8,96,000$$

$$= ₹6,72,000$$

Problem 9 Tata Co. provides you the following data for three products :

Particulars	A	B	C	Total
Selling price per unit (₹)	20	20	20	
Variable costs to sales ratio	40%	50%	60%	
Possible maximum sales (units)	1000	200	2000	
Fixed costs (₹)				12,000
Raw material required per unit (kg)	8	5	3.2	
Minimum sales	20 units	40 units	—	

Comment on the profitability in the following alternative cases:

(a) Sales demand is the limiting factor.

(b) If contribution per unit is the deciding factor.

(c) If sales value is the key factor.

(d) On the basis of BEP

(e) In case the raw material is in short-supply

(f) If maximum availability of raw material is 8000 kg, suggest that product mix which will yield maximum profit and also ascertain profit at suggested product mix.

Solution:

Statement Showing Contribution

Particulars	Product A		Product B		Product C	
	Per unit	Total	Per unit	Total	Per unit	Total
Sales (₹)	20.00	20,000	20.00	4,000	20.00	40,000
Less: Variable cost (₹)	8.00	8,000	10.00	2,000	12.00	24,000
Contribution (₹)	12.00	12,000	10.00	2,000	8.00	16,000
P/V ratio	60%		50%		40%	
BEP (₹) $\left[\frac{\text{Fixed cost}}{\text{P/V ratio}}\right]$		20,000		24,000		30,000
Raw material required per unit	8.00		5.00		3.20	
Contribution per unit of raw Material (₹)	1.50		2.00		2.50	

Comments:

(a) The profitability should be judged on the basis of contribution per unit: A, B and lastly C.

(b) The profitability should be judged on the basis of contribution per unit: i.e., again A, B and lastly C.

(c) On the basis of P/V ratio: A, B and lastly C.

(d) On the basis of BEP A, B and lastly C.

(e) In case raw material is in short supply, contribution per kg of raw material is the deciding factor and accordingly first C, then B and lastly A should be produced.

Statement Showing the Allocation of Raw Material

Particulars		kg
Total raw material available		8,000 kg
Less : Raw material required for – 20 units of product A [20 × 8]	160 kg	
– 40 units of product B [40 × 5]	200 kg	360 kg
Balance raw material		7640 kg
Less : Raw material required for 2000 units of C (i.e., maximum sales) [2,000 × 3.2 = 6,400 kg]		6400 kg
Balance raw material [7640 kg – 6400 kg]		1240 kg
Less : Raw material required for 160 units of B [160 × 5 kg]		800 kg
Balance raw material [1240 kg – 800 kg]		440 kg
Maximum possible production of product A with the balance [440/8]		55 units

Thus, product mix should be A 55 units, B 200 units, C 2000 units.

Statement Showing the Profitability (Suggested Product Mix)

Particulars	Product A	Product B	Product C	Total
Units	75	200	2,000	
Selling price per unit	20	20	20	
Total sales (₹)	1500	4000	40,000	45,500
Less : Variable cost (₹)	600	2000	24,000	26,600
Contribution (₹)	900	2000	16,000	18,900
Less : Fixed costs (₹)				12,000
Profit (₹)				6,900

Problems 10 The following information is given in respect of an Gamma Company,

Products	A	B	C
Raw material cost per unit (₹)	200	120	300
Labour cost per unit (₹)	12	20	16
Variable overhead per unit (₹)	3	5	4
Selling price per unit (₹)	250	200	400
Maximum sales demand (units)	6000	4000	3000

The maximum raw material available is 1,00,000 kg @ ₹20 per kg. The maximum labour hours available are 1,84,000 @ ₹0.80 with facility for a further 15,000 hours on overtime basis at twice the normal wage rate.

You are required to:

(a) suggest the attainable product mix which will give the highest profit?

(b) advise on the overtime working?

Solution:

(a) Statement Showing Contribution

Particulars	A	B	C
Selling Price per unit (₹)	250	200	400
Less : Variable cost per unit (₹)			
Material cost	200	120	300
Labour cost	12	20	16
Variable overheads	3	5	4
	215	145	320
Contribution per unit (₹)	35	55	80
Raw material required per unit (kg) material cost/₹20	10	6	15
Labour hour required per unit (hr) [labour cost ₹0.80]	15	25	20

Table Contd...

Table Contd...

Particulars	A	B	C
Contribution per kg of raw material	3.5	9.2	5.3
Contribution per labour hour	2.3	2.2	4
Ranking according to contribution per kg of material	III	I	II
Ranking according to contribution per labour hour	II	III	I

Note: As there are two limiting factors on the input side, profitability should be compared taking each of the input as the limiting factor one by one.

Statement Showing Total Contribution

(On the basis of contribution per kg of raw material as priority)

Particulars	Raw Material used	Labour hours used	Contribution
Total available	1,00,000	1,84,000	
Required for 4000 units of B	24,000	1,00,000	36,800
Balance available	76,000	84,000	
Required for 3000 units of C	45,000	60,000	15,900
Balance available	31,000	24,000	
Required for 1600 units of A	16,000	24,000	5600
Unused material	15,000	Nil	58,300

Statement showing Total Contribution

(on the basis of contribution per labour hour as priority)

Particulars	Labour Hrs.	Raw Mat.	Contribution
Total available	1,84,000	1,00,000	—
Required for 3000 units of C	60,000	45,000	12,000
Balance	1,24,000	55,000	
Required for 5500 units of A	82,500	55,000	12,650
Unused labour hours	41,500	Nil	24,650

Total contribution is higher when product mix on the basis of contribution per kg of raw material is adopted. Therefore, the product mix- A – 1600 units, B – 4000 units and C – 3000 units is most profitable.

(b) Evaluation of Overtime Working

Since B and C have already been produced to the maximum possible demand, the available raw material of 15,000 kg and 15,000 hours on overtime basis can be utilised to produce A. If this is done, the contribution per unit of A will be as follows:

	₹
Raw material per unit	200
Normal labour cost per unit	12
Overtime labour cost per unit	12
Variable overhead per unit	3
Total variable cost	227
Selling price per unit	250
Profit per unit	23

Recommendation : As the additional units contribute positively to the profits, overtime working is recommended.

Problem 11 Falcon Ltd. is manufacturing three household products A, B and C, and selling them in a competitive market. Details of current demand, selling price and cost structure are given below:

	A	B	C
Expected demand (units)	10,000	12,000	20,000
Selling price per unit (₹)	20	16	10
Variable cost per unit (₹):			
Direct materials (10/kg)	6	4	2
Direct labour (₹ 15/hr)	3	3	1.50
Variable overheads	2	1	1
Fixed overhead per unit (₹)	5	4	2

The company is frequently affected by acute scarcity of raw material and high labour turnover. Suggest the optimal product mix in each of the following situations:

(a) Assuming that raw material is the limiting factor availability of which is restricted to only 12,100 kg.

(b) Assuming that availability of labour is the key factor and the supply of labour is restricted to only 5000 hr.

(c) It may be possible to increase sales of any one product by 25% without any additional fixed costs. However, a cost of ₹ 20,000 will have to be incurred on advertisement to achieve the higher sales. Further assume that there will be no shortage of materials and labour for additional production.

You are also required to show the profit in each case as per your recommendation.

Solution: The profitable production mix is decided according to contribution per unit of key factor.

Statement Showing Contribution

Particulars	Products		
	A	B	C
	₹	₹	₹
Selling price per unit	20	16	10
Variable costs:			
Material	6	4	2
Labour	3	3	1.50
Variable overhead	2	1	1
Variable cost per unit	11	8	4.50
Contribution per unit	9	8	5.50
P/V ratio	45%	50%	55%
Raw material required per unit (kg)	0.60	0.40	0.20
(Material cost ÷ price per kg)			
Contribution per kg of raw material ₹	15	20	27.50
Ranking (material is the key factor)	III	II	I
Labour hours required per unit (Labour cost ÷ Wages per hour)	$\frac{1}{5}$	$\frac{1}{5}$	$\frac{1}{10}$
Contribution per labour hour ₹	45	40	55
Ranking (labour hours is the key factor)	II	III	I

(a) *Producer mix, when raw material is available 12,100 kg only.*

When raw material is the limiting factor, the product with the highest contribution per kg, of raw material should be produced first. In the above Table, the ranking of products should be C, B and in the last A.

Statement Showing Product Mix and Profit

Product	No. of units	Raw material required (kg)	Contribution per unit (₹)	Total contribution (₹)
C	20,000	4000	5.50	1,10,000
B	12,000	4800	8.00	96,000
A (Balance)	5500	3300	9.00	49,500
Total				2,55,500
Less: Fixed cost[1]				1,38,000
Profit				1,17,500

(b) *Product mix when labour hours available only 5000*

When labour hours is the limiting factor, the product with the highest contribution per labour hour should be produced first. In the above table, the ranking of products should be C, A and in the last B.

Statement Showing Comparative Contribution

Product	No. of units	Labour hours required	Contribution per unit (₹)	Total contribution (₹)
C	20000	2000	5.50	1,10,000
A	10000	2000	9.00	90,000
B (Balance)	5000	1000	8.00	40,000
Total				4,40,000
Less: Fixed cost				1,38,000
Profit				1,02,000

(c) *Increase in sales by 25% when there is no shortage of material and labour.*

25% increase in output should be made only for the product which generates maximum additional contribution. Therefore, the decision should be taken on the basis of comparison of contribution of each product from 25% increase in output.

Statement Showing Product Mix and Profit

Particulars	A	B	C
Additional units (25%)	2500	3000	5000
Contribution per unit (₹)	9	8	5.50
Total contribution	22,500	24,000	27,300

Recommendation: As the additional contribution generated is highest in case of product C, therefore, the production of C should be increased by 25%.

Statement Showing Product Mix and Profit.

Product	No. of units	Contribution per unit (₹)	Total contribution (₹)
A	10,000	9	90,000
B	12,000	8	96,000
C	25,000	5.50	1,37,500
Total			3,23,500
Less: Fixed cost			(1,38,000)
Advertisement			(20,000)
Profit			1,65,500

Working Notes:

1. Calculation of total fixed cost

A = 10,000 units × ₹5	= ₹50,000
B = 12,000 units × ₹4	48,000
C = 20,000 units × ₹2	40,000
Total fixed cost	₹1,38,000

Problem 12 A farmer owns a piece of land which has an area of 300 acres on which he grows apples, apricots, cherries and plums. The marketing policy requires that in each season all the four types of fruits must be grown and the quantity of any one type should not be less than 12,000 boxes. There are no physical or marketing limitations and there is an adequate supply of all types of labour. The other relevant information was as given below:

	Apples	Apricots	Cherries	Plums
Selling price per box (₹)	10	10	20	30
Seasons yield (boxes per acre)	500	150	100	200
Weight per box (kg)	30	30	40	20
Costs:				
Materials per acre	180	70	60	100
Wages per box (₹)	1	1	2	3
Transport per kg	0.10	0.10	0.05	0.20

Fixed overheads per season are ₹1,05,000. How the area should be allocated in terms of complete acres) to each fruit in order to maximise the profits when

(a) 200 acres of land is unsuitable for growing apples and plums.

(b) 210 acres of land is unsuitable for growing apples and plums.

Also give a statement showing profit in each case on the basis of area allocation recommended by you.

Solution: The availability of area in acres is the limiting factor. The area should be allocated to those fruits which give the highest contribution per acre of land.

Statement Showing Contribution per acre

Particulars	Apples	Apricots	Cherries	Plums
Selling price per box (₹)	10	10	20	30
Season's yield in boxes per acre	500	150	100	200
	₹	₹	₹	₹
Sales per acre (SP × Yield)	5,000	1,500	2,000	6,000
Variable costs per acre:				
Material	180	70	60	100
Wages (boxes × wages per box)	500	150	200	600
Transport per acre	1,500	450	200	800

Table Contd...

Table Contd.

Variable cost per acre	2180	670	460	1500
Contribution per acre	2820	830	1540	4500
Ranking	II	IV	III	I

(a) The 200 acres of land is suitable for apricots and cherries which is fully allocated out of the remaining 100 acres suitable for all, 24 + 60 are allocated to apples and plums. Remaining 16 acres are allocated to fruit which gives highest contribution per acre, i.e., plums.

Statement Showing Area Allocation (Acres)

Particulars	Minimum area	Additional	Total
Apples	12,000/500 = 24	—	24
Apricots	12,000/150 = 80	—	80
Cherries	12,000/100 = 120	—	120
Plums	12,000/200 = 60	16	76
	284		300

Statement Showing Profit (Proposed Area Allocation)

Particulars	Apples	Apricots	Cherries	Plums	Total
Sales per acre (SP × Yield)	5000	1,500	2,000	6000	
Variable cost per acre	2180	670	460	1500	
Contribution per acre (a)	2820	830	1540	4500	
Acres allotted (b)	24	80	120	76	
Total contribution (a) × (b)	67,680	66,400	1,84,800	3,42,000	6,60,880
Less: fixed cost					1,05,080
Profit					5,55,800

(b) The 210 acres of land is suitable for apricots and cherries out of which 200 is allocated. remaining 10 acres will be allocated to cherries as it has higher contribution as compared to apricots. Of the remaining 90 acres, 24 + 60 = 84 acres is allocated to other two fruits as per minimum production criteria. Balance 6 acres will be allocated to plums as it has the highest contribution per acre.

Statement Showing Area Allocation (Acres)

Particulars	Minimum Area	Additional	Total
Apples	12,000/500 = 24		24
Apricots	12,000/150 = 80		80
Cherries	12,000/100 = 120	10	130
Plums	12,000/200 = 60	6	66
	284		300

Statement Showing Profit (Proposed Area Allocation)

Particulars	Apples	Apricots	Cherries	Plums	Total
Sales per acre (SP × Yield)	5000	1500	2000	6000	
Variable cost per acre	2180	670	460	1500	
Contribution per acre (a)	2820	830	1540	4500	
Acres allotted (b)	24	80	130	66	
Total contribution (a) × (b)	67,680	66,400	2,00,200	2,97,000	6,31,280
Less: Fixed cost					1,05,000
Profit					5,26,280

Working Note:

Transport cost is calculated by multiplying number of boxes by the weight and the cost per kg.

Problem 13 Agro Ltd. engaged in plantation activities has 200 hectares of virgin land which can be used for growing jointly or individually tea, coffee and cardamom. The yield per hectare of the different crops and their selling price per kg are as under:

	Yield kg	Selling price per kg
Tea	2000	20
Coffee	500	40
Cardamom	100	250

The relevant cost data are given below:

Variable Cost per kg	Tea (₹)	Coffee (₹)	Cardamom (₹)
Labour charges	8	10	120
Packing materials	2	2	10
Other costs	4	1	20
Total cost	14	13	150

Fixed Cost per Annum (₹)

	(₹)
Cultivation and growing cost	10,00,000
Administrative cost	2,00,000
Land revenue	50,000
Repairs and maintenance	2,50,000
Other costs	3,00,000
Total cost	18,00,000

The policy of the company is to produce and sell all the three kinds of products and the maximum and minimum area to be cultivated per product is as follows:

	Hectares	
	Maximum	Minimum
Tea	160	120
Coffee	50	30
Cardamom	30	10

Calculate the most profitable product mix and the maximum profit which can be achieved

Solution:

Statement Showing Contribution

Particulars	Tea (₹)	Coffee (₹)	Cardamom (₹)
Selling price per kg	20	40	250
Variable cost per kg	14	13	150
Contribution per kg	6	27	100
Yield per hectare	2000 kg	500 kg	100 kg
Contribution per hectare	₹ 12,000	₹ 13,500	₹ 10,000
Ranking	II	I	III

Thus, the coffee is most profitable, followed by tea and cardamom.

Statement Showing Area Allocation (Hectares)

Particulars	Minimum Area	Additional	Total
Tea	120	20	140
Coffee	30	20	50
Cardamom	10	Nil	10
	160		200

Statement Showing Profit (Proposed Area Allocation)

Particulars	Tea	Coffee	Cardamom	Total
Contribution per hectare (a)	12,000	13,500	10,000	
Hectares allocated (b)	140	50	10	
Total contribution (a) × (b)	16,80,000	6,75,000	100,000	₹ 24,55,000
Less: Fixed cost				18,00,000
Profit				₹ 6,55,000

Problem 14 Star Ltd. manufactures 10,000 units of a product at a cost of ₹ 4 per unit. There is home market for consuming the entire volume of production at the sale price of ₹ 4.25 per unit. In the next year there is a fall in the demand for home market which can consume 10,000 units only at a sale price of ₹ 3.70 per unit The analysis of the cost per 10000 units is:

Material	₹ 15,000	Fixed overheads	₹ 8,000
Wages	₹ 11,000	Variable overheads	₹ 6,000

The foreign market is explored and it is found that this market can consume 20,000 units of the product if offered at a sale of ₹3.55 per unit. It is also discovered that for additional 10,000 units of the product (over initial 10,000 units) the fixed overheads will increase by 10%. Is it worthwhile to try to capture the foreign market? [*B.Com. (H)*]

Solution: There are two alternatives:

A: Status quo, i.e., reject the foreign order

B: Accept the foreign order, i.e., Home market + Foreign order

Statement Showing Profit under each Alternative

Particulars	A	B
Sales:	₹	₹
Domestic market (3.70 × 10,000)	37,000	37,000
Foreign market (3.55 × 20,000)	–	71,000
Total sales	37,000	1,08,000
Costs:		
Material	15,000	45,000
Wages	11,000	33,000
Variable overheads	6000	18,000
Fixed overheads	8000	9600
Total cost	40,000	1,05,600
Profit	(3000)	2400

Recommendation: If the sale is continued only in the home market, the company is in losses. However, if the export order as accepted and the company sells in both the markets, the company becomes profitable. Hence, export order should be accepted.

Problem 15 Happy Ltd. manufacturing toys is currently selling at a price of ₹200. The following are the cost particulars:

	₹
Direct material cost	70
Direct labour cost	20
Variable factory overhead	10
Other variable cost	10
Fixed overhead	2,50,000 per annum
Commission	30% on selling price

The company is producing only 10,000 units according to the demand in the domestic market. However, the company has the capacity to produce another 1000 units without any additional fixed overheads. One of the distributors has offered that he will take 1000 units in addition to his normal quota, but at a selling price of ₹160 per unit. He is also prepared to accept only half of his regular commission for this transaction.

The Managing Director wants your expert opinion regarding this offer. Prepare a statement showing all calculations and give your recommendations based on those calculations.

Solution: There are two alternatives:

A: Status quo, i.e., reject the offer.

B: Accept the offer and produce additional 1000 units.

Statement Showing Profit under each Alternative

Particulars	A: Present production	Additional production	B: Present + Aditional production
Production & sales (units)	10,000	1000	11,000
Sales	20,00,000	1,60,000	21,60,000
Direct material at ₹70 per unit	7,00,000	70,000	7,70,000
Direct labour at 20 per unit	2,00,000	20,000	2,20,000
Variable factory overhead at 10 per unit	1,00,000	10,000	1,10,000
Other variable cost at 10 per unit	1,00,000	10,000	1,10,000
Commission : at 30% on sales value	6,00,000		6,00,000
: at 15% on sales value		24,000	24,000
Total variable cost	17,00,000	1,34,000	18,34,000
Contribution (Sales – Variable cost)	3,00,000	26,000	3,26,000
(*Less*) Fixed overhead	(2,50,000)	(–)	(2,50,000)
Profit	₹50,000	₹26,000	₹76,000

Recommendation: The profit of the company increases from ₹50,000 to ₹76,000. Therefore, the proposal given by the distributor should be accepted. However, before taking a final decision, the impact on the existing market should also be studied.

Problem 16 The following extracts are taken from sales budget of a company for a current year.

		Rupees in '000
Sales : 40,000 units @ ₹25 per unit		1,000
Selling costs:		
Advertising	100	
Salesmen's salaries	80	
Travelling expenses	50	
Rent of sales office	10	
Others	10	250

The management is considering a proposal to establish a new market in the eastern region in the next year. It is proposed to increase the advertising expenditure by 25% and appoint an additional sales supervisor at a salary of ₹30,000 per year to establish a market. This will involve additional travelling and travelling expense shall increase by 10%.

Target annual sales volume at the existing selling price for the new market is 10,000 units. The estimated variable cost of production is ₹12 per unit.

Should the company try to establish the new market?

Solution: There are two alternatives:

A: Status quo, i.e., Maintain the present sales only, i.e., 40,000 units.

B: Establish the new market and sell in both the markets, i.e., 40000 + 10000 = 50000 units.

Statement Showing Profit under each Alternative

Particulars	A (Present)	B (Proposed)
Sales units	40,000	50,000
(a) Sales ₹'000	1,000	1,250
Variable costs of production @ ₹12 per unit	480	600
Selling Costs: Advertising	100	125
Sales salaries	80	110
Travelling exp.	50	55
Rent	10	10
Others	10	10
(b) Total cost	730	910
Profit (a)–(b)	270	340

Recommendation: The total profits of the company are higher under alternative B, therefore the company should try to establish the new market. The profits have increased from 2,70,000 to 3,40,000, therefore the proposal should be accepted.

Problem 17 A company is currently working at 90% capacity and is producing 13,500 units per year. It operates a flexible budgetary control system. The following figures are obtained from its budget.

	90%	*100%*
	₹	₹
Sales	15,00,000	16,00,000
Fixed expenses	3,00,500	3,00,600
Variable expenses	1,45,000	1,49,500
Semi-fixed expenses	97,500	1,00,400
Units manufactured	13,500	15,000

Labour and material cost per unit are constant under present conditions. Profit margin is 10% of sales at 90% capacity.

(a) You are required to determine the differential cost of producing 1500 units by increasing capacity to 100%.

(b) What price would you recommend for export of these 1500 units, taking into account that overseas prices are much lower than indigenous prices. [*B.Com. (H)*]

Solution:

Statement of Different Cost Analysis

	90%	100%	Differential
Production (units)	13500	15000	1500
Labour and material cost	₹8,07,000[1]	8,96,667[2]	89,667
Variable expenses	₹1,45,000	1,00,500	4,500
Semi-fixed expenses	₹97,500	1,00,400	2,900
Fixed expenses	₹3,00,500	3,00,600	100
Total	13,50,000	14,47,167	97,167

$$\text{Differential cost per unit} = \frac{\text{Differential cost}}{\text{Differential units}} = \frac{₹97,167}{1,500 \text{ units}} = ₹64.78$$

At a price of ₹64.78, there will be no additional profit. Therefore, any price above ₹64.78 which gives at least reasonable profit should be acceptable for export, assuming that export will not affect the domestic sales.

Working Notes:

1. The material and labour cost may be computed by working in the reverse order. It is computed as follows:

		At 90% capacity
		₹
Sales (13,500 units)		15,00,000
Less: Profit (10% of sales)		1,50,000
Cost of goods sold		13,50,000
Less: Variable expenses	1,45,000	
Semi-fixed expenses	97,500	
Fixed expenses	3,00,500	5,43,000
Cost of labour and material (prime cost)		8,07,000

2. Labour and material costs are variable in nature and thus at 100% capacity these will be calculated as under:

$$8,07,000 \times \frac{100}{90} = ₹8,96,667 \text{ (approx.)}$$

Problem 18 T Ltd. operating at 80% level of capacity, provides you the following information:

Units produced & sold	2000
	₹
Direct materials	20,000
Direct labour	20,000
Direct expenses	16,000
Overheads (80% fixed)	1,20,000
Total cost	1,76,000
Total cost per unit (1,76,000 ÷ 2,000)	88
Profit per unit	12
Selling price per unit	100

This company receives an offer from Canada for the purchase of above product to be produced on idle capacity at present at a price of ₹70 per unit.

If this export order is executed, the company will have to incur the following expenses:

(i) Special packing charge of ₹2 per unit;

(ii) Insurance ₹5000

(iii) Freight ₹7500

The company will also receive an incentive of 10% of the revenue realised in foreign exchange. Should the company accept or reject the export order?

Solution:

I. *Benefits associated with acceptance of export order*		
Revenue realised [(500 × ₹70)]		₹35,000
Entitlement to an export incentive		₹3,500
Total revenues		₹38,500
II. *Costs associated with acceptance of export order*		
Variable cost of manufacturing		₹
Direct material (₹20,000 × 500/2000)	5000	
Direct labour (₹20,000 × 500/2000)	5000	
Direct expenses (₹16,000 × 500/2000)	4000	
Overheads (₹24,000 × 500/2000)	6000	20,000
Extra out of pocket costs		
Packing (500 × ₹2)	1000	
Insurance	5000	
Freight	7500	13,500
Total out of pocket costs		33,500
III. Net Benefits associated (I – II)		5,000

Recommendation: Yes, the company should accept the export order as it gives an additional gain of ₹5000.

Problem 19 Pet Ltd is producing 60,000 units at 60 per cent of potential capacity and selling these in domestic market on a selling price of ₹14.30 per unit.

Its cost of sales per unit is as follows:

Direct materials	₹3.50
Direct wages	₹1.25
Factory overhead	₹6.25 (50% fixed)
Sales overhead	₹0.80 (25% variable)

During the coming year 2020-2021, it intends to produce the same number but estimates that his fixed cost would go up by 10% while the rates of direct wages and direct materials will increase by 8% and 6% respectively. However, the selling price will not be changed.

(A) Prepare a Statement of Marginal Cost and Profit for the year 2011-12.

(B) Answer the following, explaining the relevant cost and non-cost factors in the following independent situations, assuming that existing domestic sales will continue:

(i) The company obtains an export order for a further 30% of the potential capacity at a price of ₹9 per unit. Should this order be accepted?

(ii) What will be your answer if export order is at ₹8.25 per unit (instead of ₹9 per unit) for a further 30% of the potential capacity?

(iii) What will be your answer if instead of export order, the offer is from a domestic market for a bulk supply of 30,000 units at ₹10 per unit? *[B.Com. (H)]*

Solution:

Statement of Profit for the year 2020-21

Details			Amount (₹)
Sales (60,000 × 14.30)			8,58,000
Less: Variable cost:			
Direct materials (increase by 6%)	3.50 (1.06) = 3.710		
Direct wages (increase by 8%)	1.25 (1.08) = 1.350		
Factory overheads (50% fixed)	6.25 (0.5) = 3.125		
Sales overhead (25% Variable)	0.8 (0.25) = 0.200		
		8.385 × 60,000	5,03,100
Contribution			3,54,900
Fixed overheads:			
Factory overheads			2,06,250
Selling overheads			39,600
Profit			1,09,050

Working Notes:

(1) Fixed overheads:

Factory	3.125 × 60,000 = 1,87,500 (1.10) =	2,06,250
Sales	0.6 × 60,000 = 36,000 (1.10) =	39,600
Total		2,45,850

(2) (i) Yes, the export order may be accepted as the export price exceeds by ₹0.615 per unit, i.e., 9.00 – 8.385). Acceptance of the order will increase the profits by ₹18,450.

(ii) Non-cost factors may be given due weightage at the time of taking decision. Purely on cost basis, the order may be rejected since the export price is less than the variable cost of sales (8.250 – 8.385) = ₹0.135 per unit.

(iii) Bulk supply order from the domestic market may be accepted as it will increase the profits by ₹48,450. However, before taking the final decision, non-cost factors may be given due weightage.

Problem 20 Sigma Ltd. having an installed capacity of 100000 units is currently operating at 70% utilisation. At current level of prices, the unit cost works out as follows:

Capacity Utilisation (%)	Unit Cost
70	₹97
92	₹87
80	₹90
100	₹82

The company has received three foreign offers from the different sources as under:

Source A: 5000 units at ₹55 per unit.

Source B: 10000 units at ₹52 per unit.

Source C: 10000 units at ₹51 per unit.

Advise the company as to whether any or all the export offers should be accepted or not. [*B.Com. (H)*]

Solution: There are seven alternatives:

A: Accept order A only.

B: Accept order B only.

C: Accept order C only.

D: Accept A and B but reject C.

E: Accept B and C but reject A.

F: Accept A and C but reject B.

G: Accept all the three A, B and C.

Statement showing Profit under each alternative

Particulars	A	B	C	D	E	F	G
Sales[1]	2,75,000	5,20,000	5,10,000	7,95,000	10,30,000	7,85,000	13,05,000
Less: Variable cost	2,85,000	5,70,000	5,70,000	8,05,000	10,40,000	8,05,000	12,25,000
Profit	(10,000)	(50,000)	(60,000)	(10,000)	(10,000)	(20,000)	80,000

Recommendation: One may observe that there is a loss under each alternative except the last one. But when all the three orders are accepted, the company makes a profit. Thus, the company should accept all the orders. However, before taking a final decision, other non-cost factors should also be considered.

Working Notes:

1. Sales

   A: 5000 units @ 55 = ₹2,75,000

   B: 10,000 units @ 52 = ₹5,20,000

   C: 10,000 units @51 = ₹75,10,000

   D: (5000 units @55) + (10,000 units @52) = ₹7,95,000

   E: (10,000 units @52) + (10,000 units @51) = ₹10,30,000

   F: (5000 units @ 55) + (10,000 units @ 51) = ₹7,85,000

   G: (5000 units @ 55) + (10,000 units @ 52) + (10,000 units @ 51) = ₹13,05,000

2. The differential cost of the additional units produced may be computed as given below:

Statement Showing Differential Cost (D.C.)

Capacity %	Production units	Cost per unit ₹	Total Cost ₹	D.C. Total ₹	D.C. per unit ₹
70	70000	97	67,90,000	–	–
80	80000	92	73,60,000	5,70,000	57
90	90000	87	78,30,000	4,70,000	47
100	100000	82	82,00,000	3,70,000	37

3. Variable cost

   A: 5000 units @ 57 = ₹72,85,000

   B: 10,000 units @57 = ₹5,70,000

   C: 10,000 units @ 57 = ₹5,70,000

   D: (10,000 units @ 57) + (5000 units @47) = ₹8,05,000

   E: (10,000 units @57) + (10,000 units @ 47) = ₹10,40,000

   F: (10,000 units @ 57) + (5000 units @ 47) = ₹8,05,000

   G: (10,000 units @ 57) + (10,000 units @ 47) + (5000 units @ 37) = ₹12,25,000

Problem 21 Genuine Auto Products produces and sells two small components, P and Q, used in automobiles. The details regarding unit income and costs of these components are as under:

Particulars	P (₹)	Q (₹)
Selling price	24	30
Direct material	4	10
Direct labour	6	2
Variable factory overhead	8	8
Fixed factory overhead	2	4
Total cost of goods sold	20	24
Gross profit per unit	4	6

Factory overheads, both fixed and variable, have been accounted for on a machine hour basis which is ₹ 5. Both P and Q are processed through the same cost centres. Selling costs are fixed.

Which of the two products, the company should produce to maximise the profit? Supplement your suggestion with appropriate calculations.

Solution:

Statement Showing the Contribution and Ranking of the Product

Particulars	P	Q
Selling Price per unit (₹)	24	30
Less: Variable costs per unit (₹):		
Direct material	4	10
Direct labour	6	2
Variable factory overheads	8	8
Marginal cost per unit (₹)	18	20
Contribution per unit (₹)	6	10
Machine hours per unit[1]	2	2.4
Contribution per machine hour (₹)	3	4.2
Ranking	II	I

Recommendation: It is clear from the above that the contribution per machine hour of component Q is more than component P. Since, there are no sales constraints, management should prefer product Q over product P.

Working Note:

1. Since it is given that factory overheads, both variable and fixed, have been absorbed on the basis of machine hours. Machine hours used for each unit may be computed as:

$$\text{P requires} = \frac{8+2}{5} = 2 \text{ hours, and}$$

$$\text{Q requires} = \frac{8+4}{5} = 2.4 \text{ hours}$$

Problem 22 A Ltd. operating at 75% level of activity, produces and sells two products, X and Y. The cost sheets of these products are as follows:

	Product X	Product Y
Units produced and sold	3,000	2,000
	Per unit	Per unit
	₹	₹
Direct materials	10	20
Direct labour	20	20
Factory overhead (40% fixed)	25	15
Administration and selling overhead (60% fixed)	40	25
Total cost per unit	95	80
Selling price per unit	115	95

Factory overheads are absorbed on the basis of machine hour which is the limiting factor. The machine hour rate is 10 per hour.

The company receives an offer from Japan for the purchase of product X at a price of ₹87.50 per unit. Alternatively, the company has another offer from Bangkok for the purchase of product Y at a price of ₹77.50 per unit. In both the cases, a special packing charge of ₹2.50 per unit has to be borne by the company. The company can accept either of the two export orders by utilising the balance of 25% of its capacity.

Advise the company with detailed working as to which proposal should be accepted and prepare a statement showing the overall profitability of the company after incorporating the export proposal suggested by you. [*B.Com. (H)*]

Solution: The company has two alternatives to use the spare machine hours of 3,500. The spare capacity should be used for the export order which gives higher contribution per machine hour.

Statement showing contribution under each export offer

Particulars	Japan Product X Per unit ₹	Bangkok Product Y Per unit ₹
Direct materials	10.00	20.00
Direct labour	20.00	20.00
Variable factory overhead	15.00	9.00
Variable adm. and selling overhead	16.00	10.00

Table Contd...

Table Contd...

Particulars	Japan Product X Per unit ₹	Bangkok Product Y Per unit ₹
Special packing cost	2.50	2.50
(a) Variable cost per unit	63.50	61.50
(b) Export price per unit	87.50	77.50
Contribution (b–a)	24.00	16.00
Machine hours per unit	2.5	1.5
Contribution per machine hour	24 ÷ 2.5 = 9.6	16 ÷ 1.5 = 10.67

Recommendation: Contribution per unit of key factor (i.e., machine hour) is higher in product Y. Thus, export offer from Bangkok should be accepted.

Total number of units of Y that can be produced with surplus machine hours is calculated as:

$$\text{Units} = \frac{\text{Surplus machine hours}}{\text{Machine hr per unit}} = \frac{3500}{1.5} = 2333 \text{ units of Y}$$

Statement Showing Overall Profit

Particulars	Home Market		Export to Bangkok	Total
	X	Y	Y	₹
Units sold (a)	3,000	2,000	2,333	
Selling price per unit	115	95	77.50	
Less: Variable cost per unit:				
Direct material	10	20	20	
Direct labour	20	20	20	
Factory overhead	15	9	9	
Adm. and selling overhead	16	10	10	
Special packing cost	Nil	Nil	2.50	
Variable cost per unit	61	59	61.50	
Contribution per unit (b)	54	36	16	
Total contribution (a) × (b)	1,62,000	72,000	37,328	2,71,328
Less: Fixed cost				1,44,000
Profit				1,31,328

Working Notes:

1. Calculation of surplus machine hours available

As the availability of machine hours is the limiting factor, the spare capacity shall be measured in terms of unused machine hours. Factory overheads are charged on the basis of machine hour rate, therefore, the hours used for each unit of output may be computed as given below:

	X	*Y*
Factory overhead per unit (a)	₹ 25	15
Machine hour rate (b)	₹ 10	10
(c) Machine hours per unit (a ÷ b)	2.5	1.5
(d) Units produced	3000	2000
Total machine hours used (c × d)	7500	3000

Total machine hours used for products X and Y at 75% (7500 + 3000)	10,500 hours
Machine hours available at 100% capacity (10,500 ÷ 75%)	14,000 hours
Surplus machine hours (14,000 – 10,500)	3500 hours

2. Calculation of fixed cost

		₹
Fixed factory overhead:		
X: 3000 units @ ₹ 10		30,000
Y: 2000 units @₹ 6	12,000	42,000
Fixed administration and selling overhead:		
X: 3000 units @ ₹ 24	72,000	
Y: 2000 units @ ₹ 15	30,000	1,02,000
Total fixed cost		1,44,000

Problem 23 A Ltd. Company is operating at 75% level of activity produces and sells two products A and B. The cost sheets of the two products are as under:

	Product A	*Product B*
	₹	₹
Units produced and sold	600	400
Direct materials	₹ 200	₹ 400
Direct labour	400	400
Factory overheads (40% fixed)	500	300
Selling and administration overheads (60% fixed)	800	500
Total cost per unit	1900	1600
Selling price per unit	2300	1900

Factory overheads are absorbed on the basis of machine hour which is the limiting (key) factor. The machine hour rate is 200 per hour.

The company receives an offer from Canada for the purchase of product A at a price of ₹ 1750 per unit.

Alternatively, the company has another offer from the Middle East for the purchase of product B at a price of ₹ 1550 per unit.

In both the cases, a special packing charge of 50 per unit has to be borne by the company.

The company can accept either of the two export orders and in each case the company can supply such quantities as may be possible to produce by utilising the balance 25% of its capacity.

You are required to prepare:

(i) A statement showing the economics of the two export proposals giving your recommendations as to which proposal should be accepted.

(ii) A statement showing the overall profitability of the company after incorporating the export proposal recommended by you. [*M.Com.*]

Solution:

(i) The company has two alternatives to use the spare machine hours of 700. The spare capacity should be used for the export order which gives higher contribution per machine hour.

Statement showing contribution under each export offer

Particulars	Canada Product A Per unit ₹	Middle East Product B Per unit ₹
Direct materials	200.00	400.00
Direct labour	400.00	400.00
Variable factory overhead	300.00	180.00
Variable adm. and selling overhead	320.00	200.00
Special packing cost	50.00	50.00
(a) Variable cost per unit	1,270	1,230
(b) Export price per unit	1,750	1550
Contribution (b – a)	480	320
Machine hours per unit	2.5	1.5
Contribution per machine hour	480 ÷ 2.5 = 192	320 ÷ 1.5 = 210

Recommendation: Contribution per unit of key factor (i.e., machine hour) is higher in product B. Thus, export offer from Middle East should be accepted.

Total number of units of B that can be produced with surplus machine hours is calculated as:

$$\text{Units} = \frac{\text{Surplus machine hours}}{\text{Machine hours per unit}} = \frac{700}{1.5} = 466 \text{ units of B}$$

Working Notes:

1.

Particulars	A(₹)	B(₹)	Total (₹)
Factory overheads per unit	500	300	
Machine hour rate per hour	200	200	

Table Contd...

Table Contd...

Machine hour per unit	2.5	1.5	
Units produced	600	400	
Machine hours utilised	1500	600	2100
Level of activity			75%

$$\text{Maximum hours at 100\% activity: } \frac{2100}{75} \times 100 = 2800 \text{ hr}$$

Capacity hours available for export 2800 – 2100 = 700 hr.

Statement of overall profitability

Particulars	Product A	Product B	Total
Units	600	867	
Materials	1,20,000	3,46,100	4,66,800
Labour	2,40,000	3,46,800	5,86,800
Factory overhead: Variable	1,80,000	1,56,100	3,36,800
Fixed	1,20,000	48,000	1,68,000
Selling & admn. overheads:	1,92,000	1,73,400	3,65,400
Variable			
Fixed	2,88,000	1,20,000	4,08,000
Special packing	—	23,400	23,400
Total costs	11,40,000	12,14,500	23,54,500
Sales	13,80,000	14,83,900	28,63,900
Profit	2,40,000	2,69,400	5,09,400

Working Notes:

1. Number of units of B:

	₹
Sales in the home market	400
Export market $\frac{700 \text{ hr}}{1.5}$	467
Total	867

2. Sales value of B:

	₹
400 units in the home market @ ₹ 1900	7,60,000
467 units for export @ ₹ 1550	7,23,900
Total :	14,83,900

Problem 24 A company currently operating at 80% capacity has the following particulars:

	₹
Sales	32,00,000
Direct material	10,00,000
Direct labour	4,00,000
Variable overheads	2,00,000
Fixed overheads	13,00,000

An export order has been received that would utilise half the capacity of the factory. The order cannot be split, i.e., it has either to be taken in full and executed at 10% below the normal domestic price or rejected totally.

The alternatives available to the management are:

(1) reject the order and continue with the domestic sales only (as at present), or

(2) accept the order, split capacity between overseas and domestic sales and turn away excess domestic demand, or

(3) increase capacity to accept the export order and maintain the present domestic sales by:

(a) buying equipment that will increase capacity by 10%. This will result in an increase of 1,00,000 in fixed costs, and

(b) work overtime to meet balance of required capacity. In that case, labour will be paid at one and a half time the normal wage rate.

Prepare a comparative statement of profitability and suggest the best alternative.

Solution: There are three alternatives:

A: Status quo, i.e., operate at 80% in home market.

B: Accept the overseas order, i.e., 50% Home market + 50% Overseas order

C. Increase the capacity, i.e., 80% Home market + 50% Overseas order

Statement showing profit under each alternative

Particulars	A: Present position 80% Home market	B: 50% Home Market + 50% Overseas Order	80% Home Market + 50% Overseas Order
	₹	₹	₹
Sales			
Home market	32,00,000	20,00,000	32,00,000
Overseas	—	18,00,000	18,00,000
Total sales (A)	32,00,000	38,00,000	50,00,000
Direct materials	10,00,000	12,50,000	16,25,000
Direct labour	4,00,000	5,00,000	7,00,000
Variable overhead	2,00,000	2,50,000	3,25,000

Table Contd...

Table Contd...

Total variable cost (B)	16,00,000	20,00,000	26,50,000
Contribution (A – B)	16,00,000	18,00,000	23,50,000
Less: Fixed overheads	13,00,000	13,00,000	14,00,000
Profit	3,00,000	5,00,000	9,50,000

Recommendation: As the profit of the company is highest under alternative C, the capacity should be expanded to 130% so as to operate in both the markets.

Working Notes:

1. Sales

   Home market $\frac{32,00,000 \times 50\%}{80\%}$ = ₹20,00,000

   Overseas 20,00,000 – 10% = ₹18,00,000

   Total 38,00,000

2. Sales

   Home market at 80% 32,00,000

   Overseas at 50% (20,00,000 – 10%) = ₹18,00,000

   Total 50,00,000

3. Direct material cost for alternative B (100% capacity)

   $$10,00,000 \times \frac{100}{80} = ₹12,50,000$$

4. Direct material cost for alternative C (130% capacity)

   $$10,00,000 \times \frac{130}{80} = ₹16,25,000$$

5. Thus, labour cost for alternative B.

   $$\text{At } 100\% = 4,00,000 \times \frac{100}{80} = ₹5,00,000.$$

6. Labour cost for alternative C

   $$\text{At } 130\% = \left(4,00,000 \times \frac{110}{80}\right) + \left(4,00,000 \times \frac{20}{80} \times \frac{3}{2}\right)$$

   $$= 5,50,000 + 1,50,000 = ₹7,00,000.$$

Problem 25 Sulphur Engineering Company has received an export order for its sole product that would require the use of half of the factory's total capacity, which is estimated at 4 lakh units per annum. The condition of the export order is that it has to be accepted in full; acceptance of part quantity is not allowed.

The factory is currently operating at 60% level to meet the demand of its domestic customers. As against the current price of ₹6.00 per unit, the export offer is ₹4.70 per unit, which is less than the cost of production.

Direct material	₹2.50 per unit
Direct labour	₹1.00 per unit
Variable expense	₹0.50 per unit
Fixed overhead	₹1.00 per unit
Total cost	₹5.00

The company has the following options:

(a) Accept the export order and cut back domestic sales as necessary.

(b) Remove the capacity constraint by installing necessary balancing equipment and also by working overtime to meet both domestic and export demand. This will increase fixed overheads by ₹15,000 annually, and additional cost for overtime work will amount to ₹40,000 for the year.

(c) Appoint a subcontractor to manufacture the additional requirement and meet the domestic and export requirement in full by supplying raw materials, paying a conversion charge @ 2.00 per unit and appointing a supervisor at a salary of ₹3000 per month for checking the quality of the product and controlling operations at the manufacturing unit.

(d) Refuse the order.

Required:

(i) A statement of costs and profits under each of the above four options.

(ii) Your recommendation, with reasons, as to which of these options the company should decide upon.

Solution: There are four alternatives:

A: Accept the export order and cut back domestic sales as necessary.

B: Remove capacity constraints.

C: Appoint a subcontractor.

D: Refuse the order and maintain the *status quo*.

Statement showing profit under alternative A

Particulars	Amount (₹)
Sales:	
Export 2,00,000 units @ ₹4.70	9,40,000
Domestic 2,00,000 units @ ₹6	12,00,000
Total	21,40,000
Less: Variable cost: 4,00,000 units @ ₹4	16,00,000

Table Contd...

Table Contd...

Contribution		5,40,000
Less: Fixed overheads		2,40,000
Profit		3,00,000

Statement showing profit under alternative B

Particulars		Amount
Sales:		
Export 2,00,000 units @ ₹ 4.70		9,40,000
Domestic 2,40,000 units @ ₹ 6		14,40,000
Total		23,80,000
Less: Variable cost:		
4,40,000 units @ ₹ 4	17,60,000	
Overtime payment	40,000	
		18,00,000
Contribution		5,80,000
Less: Fixed overheads (2,40,000 + 15,000)		2,55,000
Profit		3,25,000

Statement showing profit under alternative C

Particulars			Amount
Sale as in option B			23,80,000
Less: Variable cost on own production of			
4,00,000 units @ ₹ 4		16,00,000	
Subcontract for 40,000 units:			
Material on 40,000 units @ ₹ 2.50 per unit	₹ 1,00,000		
Conversion Cost 40,000 × ₹ 2	₹ 80,000		
		1,80,000	
			17,80,000
Contribution:			6,00,000
Less: Fixed overheads as at present		2,40,000	
Fixed Overheads at present.		2,40,000	
Supervision charges		36,000	
Profit			2,76,000
			3,24,000

Statement showing profit under alternative D (refusing export order)

Particulars	Amount ₹
Sales: Domestic 2,40,000 units @ ₹6	14,40,000
Less: Variable Cost: 2,40,000 units @ ₹4	9,60,000
Contribution	4,80,000
Less: Fixed overheads	2,40,000
Profit	2,40,000

Recommendation: Export offer should not be rejected because it gives an additional profit of ₹60,000 (i.e., ₹3,00,000 – ₹2,40,000) in option A, ₹85,000 (i.e., ₹3,25 000 – ₹2,40,000) in Option B and ₹84,000 (i.e., ₹3,24,000 – ₹2,40,000) in Option C. It should also be kept in mind that domestic sales (as has been done in Option A) should not be curtailed as other competitors may soon capture your market. Hence, the choice is between Option B and Option C which are almost equally profitable. Out of the two options, Option C is preferable because substantial amount of investment in balancing equipment is required in Option B. Overtime is also required in Option B which may pose a problem. If future export order is not repeated, investment in balancing equipment will result in under utilisation of capacity. Hence, it is advisable to appoint a subcontractor to manufacture the additional requirement.

Working Notes:

1. Calculation of Variable Cost and Fixed Cost

	₹
Variable cost per unit:	
Material	2.50
Labour	1.00
Expenses	0.50
	4.00

2. Fixed overheads : At 60% level @ ₹1 each = $\frac{60}{100} \times 4{,}00{,}000 \times ₹1 = ₹2{,}40{,}000$

Problem 26 Beta Ltd. produces a range of products and absorbs production overheads at the rate of 300% of direct labour costs. The rate is based on the following budgeted figures:

Variable overheads	₹2,16,000
Fixed overheads	₹3,24,000
Direct labour cost	₹1,80,000

One of the company's products 'Snowhite' has a normal selling price of 52.50 and a unit production cost of ₹42 (direct materials ₹18, direct labour ₹6 and overheads ₹18).

A customer has offered to buy 5000 units of 'Snowhite' at a price of ₹33 each. If the order is accepted, the normal sales would be unaffected, and the company has the existing capacity to make the extra units. Should the offer be accepted?

Solution:

Statement showing profit if the order is accepted

Direct materials	5,000
Direct labour	18
Variable overhead (120% of labour cost)	6
Fixed overhead	7.20
Total cost	Nil
Selling Price	31.20
Profit per unit	33
Total profit (5,000 × 1.80)	1.80
Units	9,000

Recommendation: As the company earns an additional profit of ₹9000 on this order, the offer should be accepted.

Working Notes:

1. Direct labour cost ₹2,16,000

   Variable overheads (% of labour cost) $\frac{2{,}16{,}000}{180{,}000} \times 100 = 120\%$

   Fixed overheads (% of labour cost) $\frac{3{,}24{,}000}{1{,}80{,}000} \times 100 = 180\%$

2. Total fixed cost of the company remains same and no additional fixed overheads are incurred for this order using the spare capacity.

Problem 27 AB 360 Ltd. produces product P in its production shop A. The overhead recovery rate is 100% of direct wages based on the following budgeted figures:

	₹
Direct wages	1,60,000
Variable overhead	64,000
Fixed overheads	96,000

The production plan for the same budget period envisages an output of 18,000 units of product P whose sales and cost data are as under:

	₹ per unit
Selling price	42
Direct materials	12

	₹
Direct wages	8
Total overheads	8

The company proposes to use the balance capacity of Shop A after completing the above said production plan, for the manufacture of component Q whose cost data are as under:

	₹ per unit
Direct materials	8
Direct wages	16
Total overheads	16

The component Q is used by the company in the manufacture of some other product in another production department.

The company receives an export order from abroad for the purchase of 2000 units of Product P at ₹30 each. This offer can be accepted by diverting the capacity from component Q. In that event the company has to buy the component which is available from an outside supplier at a price of ₹40 each.

You are required to evaluate the alternative of action and state with reasons whether the spare capacity should be lised for the manufacture of:

(a) The component Q or

(b) 2000 units of product P for the export and buying of the component Q from a outside supplier

Soution: There are two alternatives:

A: Manufacture Q

B: Manufacture P for export.

Statement Showing Benefit of Manufacturing, Q.

Particulars	Amount ₹
Units	1,000
Savings in cost of purchasing component Q from the market	40.00
Less: Manufacturing cost	
Direct Material	8
Direct Wages	16
Variable Overheads (40% of Direct wages)	6.40
Manufacturing cost	30.40
Benefit per unit	9.60
Total benefit (1,000 × 9.60)	9,600

Statement Showing Benefit of Manufacturing, P

Particulars	Amount
Selling price per unit	30.00
Manufacturing cost per unit of Product P:	₹
Direct material	12
Direct labour	8
Variable overheads (40% of direct labour)	3.20
	23.20
Contribution per unit (₹ 30.00 – ₹ 23.20)	6.80
Total contribution for 2,000 units (2000 × 6.80)	13,600
Less: Fixed cost	Nil
Profit	13,600

Recommendation: As the benefits are higher under alternative B, the product P for export should be produced and the component Q should be purchased from the market. This will give an additional benefit of ₹13,600 – 9600 = ₹4000

Working Notes:

	₹
1. Total direct wages (given)	1,60,000
Variable overhead (given)	64,000
Variable overhead recovery rate: $\frac{64{,}000 \times 100}{1{,}60{,}000}$ = 40% of direct wages	
Fixed overheads	96,000
2. Production of P as per budget	18,000 units
Direct wages per unit	8
Total wages cost of P	1,44,000

3. Spare capacity available in terms of wages cost: 1,60,000 – 1,44,000 = 16,000

Using this spare capacity, the company can either produce Q or may produce P for export. Each unit of Component Q cost ₹16 in direct wages and Product P has a wage cost of ₹8. Therefore,

No. of units of Q that can be produced; 16000/16 = 1000 units

Alternatively, No. of units of P that can be produced; 16000/8 = 2000 units

Problem 28 Comfort Ride Ltd. currently purchasing 10,000 horns per annum from an outside supplier at ₹50 each. The management feels that these horns can be manufactured and not purchased. A machine costing ₹2,50,000 will be required to manufacture the item within the factory. The machine has an annual capacity of 15,000 units and life of 5 years. The following additional information is available:

Material cost per unit	₹20.00
Labour cost per unit	₹10.00
Variable overheads	100% of labour cost

You are required to advise whether

(i) the company should continue to purchase the horns from the outside supplier or should make them in the factory, or

(ii) the company should accept an order to supply 2500 horns to the market at a selling price of ₹45.00 per unit?

Solution:

(i) Statement showing the cost of manufacture of one unit (horn)

		Per Unit ₹
Material		20.00
Labour		10.00
Variable overheads		10.00
Depreciation $\frac{2,50,000/5}{10000}$		5.00
	Total cost	45.00
Purchase cost		50.00
Saving per horn		5.00

Therefore, the company should manufacture the horns resulting in a saving of ₹50,000 annually for 10,000 units.

(ii) Marginal cost per unit is ₹40.00 as shown above. As depreciation of the machine is already recovered on 10,000 horns, there will be no additional depreciation on the extra 2500 units to be sold in the market. Further the machine has spare capacity too. Therefore, the company is advised to supply 2500 horns to the market at ₹45.00 per unit and make a profit or ₹5.00 per unit, i.e., total profit ₹12,500.

Problem 29 D Ltd, has got a Machine No. AB01. It manufactures Component X with its selling price ₹100 and marginal cost ₹60. The machine takes 20 hours to produce it.

The company uses a component Y that can be manufactured on Machine No. AB01 in 3 hours at a marginal cost of ₹5. However, the Component Y can be brought from the market at a price of ₹10. Should the Component 'Y' be made on Machine No. AB01.

[*B.Com. (H)*]

Solution:

Statement showing contribution

Component X: Selling price	₹ 100
– Marginal cost	₹ 60
Contribution per unit	₹ 40
Machine hours required	20
Contribution per hour (₹ 40 ÷ 20)	₹ 2
Component Y:	
Purchase price	₹ 10
Less: Marginal cost	₹ 5
Contribution per unit	₹ 5
Hours required to produce	3
Contribution per machine hour (₹ 5 ÷ 3)	₹ 1.67

Recommendation: Since component X gives the higher contribution per hour and better utilisation of limited machine hours, it is recommended that component Y should not be produced. It is assumed that capacity in terms of machine hours is limited.

Problem 30 Sigma Ltd. manufactures automobile accessories and parts. The following are the total costs and the unit costs of processing a component:

Cost element	Total cost for 50,000 units	Unit cost
Direct material	₹ 5,00,000	10
Direct labour	8,00,000	16
Variable factory overhead	6,00,000	12
Fixed factory overhead	5,00,000	10
	24,00,000	48

Another manufacturer has offered to sell the part to Sigma Ltd., for ₹ 44 each. The fixed overhead would continue to be incurred even when the component is bought out although there would be a reduction to the extent of ₹ 1,50,000 following the savings in salaries of supervisory personnel that could be avoided if the company opts to 'Buy' rather than 'Make'

(a) Should the part be made or bought considering the present facility when released following a buying decision would remain idle?

(b) In case the release facility can be rented to another manufacturer for ₹ 1,00,000, as there is a good demand for 'spare facilities', what will be the position?

Solution: There are three alternatives:

A: Manufacture it.

B: Buy the component but facility remains idle.

C: Buy the component and lease out the facility.

Statement showing the Relevant Cost under each alternative

Particulars	A Manufacture	B Buy at ₹44 Per unit (facility remains idle)	C Buy the part (when released facility is rented out)
Variable cost of production	₹19,00,000	–	–
Cost of buying from outside @ ₹44 per unit	–	₹22,00,000	₹22,00,000
Fixed cost	5,00,000	3,50,000	3,50,000
Rent receipts when the idle facility is rented out	–	–	(1,00,000)
Total relevant cost	24,00,000	25,50,000	24,50,000

Recommendation: The cost is lowest under alternative A, therefore it is advisable to manufacture the part.

Problem 31 A company manufactures four components, the cost particulars of which are given below:

	Components			
	A (₹)	B (₹)	C (₹)	D (₹)
Direct material	80	100	100	120
Direct labour	20	25	25	30
Variable overhead	10	12	15	10
Fixed overhead	15	23	20	20
	125	160	160	180
Output per machine hour (units)	4	2	3	3
The key factor is shortage of machine capacity.				

Advise the management as to whether they should continue to produce all or some of these components (which are used in its main product) or they should buy them from a supplier who has quoted the following prices:

A = ₹115; B = ₹175; C = ₹135; D = ₹185.

Solution:

Statement showing Contribution

Particulars	Components			
	A	B	C	D
Purchase Price per unit (₹)	115	175	135	185
Less: Variable cost of manufacturing per unit (₹)				
Direct material	80	100	100	120
Direct labour	20	25	25	30
Variable overhead	10	12	15	10
Marginal cost per unit	110	137	140	160
Contribution per unit (₹)	5	38	(5)	25
Machine hour per unit	0.25	0.50	0.33	0.33
Contribution per machine hour (₹)	20	76	(15)	75
Ranking for manufacturing	III	I		II
Decision	Mfg.	Mfg.	Buy	Mfg.

On the basis of the above computations, it may be concluded that:

(i) Component C should be purchased from outside as the contribution is negative and the marginal cost is more than its purchase price. Purchasing from outside will improve the profitability by ₹15 per machine hour.

(ii) In the present case, machine capacity is the key factor (as given in the question). Therefore, the product giving highest contribution per machine hour should be produced first. The recommended order of the products for manufacturing should be B, D and A.

Problem 32 A company has been using a part in the assembly of a product manufactured. Under the current scheme the company is purchasing this component from an outside supplier. The current price of this part is ₹300. Transportation and other delivery costs account for ₹37.50 per piece. Sales tax at 10% is added to the invoice price.

Now the company is planning to manufacture this part and there is sufficient spare capacity. Annual requirements of the part are 5000 units.

You are required to advise the company regarding manufacturing decision and submit the supportive statements. The following estimates are available:

	Cost per unit (₹)
Raw material	240
Direct wages	20
Overheads at 800% of direct wages	160
Total cost	420
Mark up for return on investment	30
	450

In additional special tools, jigs and fixtures required to manufacture this part are needed to be acquired at a cost of ₹3,75,000. These are to be amortised over 5 years. Assume rate of interest is 16% p.a.

The overhead rate is the budgeted recovery rate for products manufactured by the company. The variable portion of this amounts to 100 per cent of direct wages.

Solution: There are two alternatives:

A. Manufacture the component.

B. Buy it from outside

Statement showing cost under each alternative

Particulars	Buy	Make
Current purchase price	300.00	
Add: Sales tax 10%	30.00	
Add: Transportation and other delivery cost	37.50	
Raw materials		240.00
Direct wages		20.00
Variable overheads (100% of direct wages)		20.00
Special tools, jigs and fixtures—Depreciation (3,75,000/5) = 75,000		15.00
Interest at 16% per annum on the cost of special tools (16% of 75,000/1000 (per annum))		12.00
Total	367.50	307.00

Recommendation: From the above statements, it is clear that there is saving of 60.50 per unit (i.e., ₹367.50 – ₹307) in case of manufacturing. Hence, it is recommended that the part should be manufactured instead of buying it from outside.

Problem 33 SDT Ltd. manufactures three products. The respective cost and sales information for the three products is as given below:

Particulars	A	B	C
Capacity engaged	(20%)	(40%)	(40%)
Units produced	2000	5000	6000
Cost per unit:	(₹)	(₹)	(₹)
Material cost	20	32	36
Wages	10	12	16
Variable overheads	7	9	11
Fixed overheads	6	9	10
Total	43	62	73
Selling price per unit	40	75	85
Profit per unit (loss)	(3)	13	12

The management proposes to discontinue line A as for the last few years it is showing a loss. Future prospects of the other two lines being good, it is intended to utilise the disengaged capacity in line A, in line B and line C equally.

	B	C
Expected rise in prices and cost (%):		
Material	10%	10%
Wages	25%	5%
Selling price	20%	25%

Fixed overheads shall remain the same. You are required to prepare a statement of projected profitability and advise the management as to whether the scheme may be adopted.

[*M.Com*]

Solution: There are two alternatives:

A: *Status quo,* i.e., continue with all the three products A, B and C.

B: Discontinue A and divide the released capacity between B and C equally.

Statement showing Profit under alternative A (Products A, B and C)

Particulars	A	B	C	Total
Capacity engaged	20%	40%	40%	100%
Units produced	2000	5000	6000	—
Sales revenue[1]	₹	₹	₹	₹
Less: Variable costs (new)	80,000	4,50,000	6,37,500	11,67,500
Contribution	74,000	2,96,000	4,04,400	7,74,100
Less: Fixed costs	6000	1,54,000	2,33,100	3,93,100
Net profit				1,17,000
				2,76,100

Statement showing Profit under alternative B (Products B and C only)

Particulars	B	C	Total
Capacity engaged	50%	50%	100%
Units produced	6250	7500	–
	₹	₹	₹
Sales revenue	5,62,500	7,96,875	13,59,375
Less: Variable costs (new)	3,70,000	5,05,500	8,75,500
Contribution	1,92,500	2,91,375	4,83,875
Less: Fixed costs			1,17,000
Net profit			3,66,875

Working Notes:

1. The sales revenue and variable cost are computed based on the following calculations:

Statement showing New Variable Cost and Selling Price

Particulars	A	B	C
Materials	20	35.20	39.60
Wages	10	15	16.80
Variable overheads	7	9	11
Variable cost per unit	37	59.20	67.40
New selling price	40	90	106.25

2. Fixed cost:

A	2000 × 6	=	₹12,000
B	5000 × 9	=	₹45,000
C	6000 × 10	=	₹60,000
Total			₹1,17,000

3. All the profits have been calculated based on the new cost and new selling price. The decision making is always for the future, therefore, the new prices are relevant.

Problem 34 The cost per unit of the three products A, B and C of a company are given below.

	A (₹)	B (₹)	C (₹)
Direct materials	20	16	18
Direct labour	12	14	12
Variable expenses	8	10	6
Fixed expenses	6	6	4
Total cost	46	46	40
Profit	23	19	17
Selling price	69	65	57
No. of units produced	10000	5000	8000

Production arrangements are such that if one product is given up, the production of the others can be raised by 50%. The directors propose that C should be given up because the profit from that product is the lowest

Present suitable analysis of the data indicating whether the proposal should be accepted or not?

Solution:

Statement showing the Current Productwise Contribution

Particulars	Products		
	A (₹)	B (₹)	C (₹)
Selling price per unit	69	65	57
Marginal cost per unit	40	40	36
Contribution per unit	29	25	21
Total contribution	2,90,000	1,25,000	1,68,000

(a) Statement showing the Profitability if A is given up

Particulars	A	B	C	Total
Present units	–	5000	8000	
Additional units	–	2500	4000	
Total units	–	7500	12000	
Contribution per unit		25	21	
Total contribution (₹)	–	1,87,500	2,52,000	4,39,500
Less : Fixed cost (₹)				1,22,000
Total profit (₹)				3,17,500

(b) Statement showing the Profitability if B is given up

Particulars	A ₹	B ₹	C ₹	Total ₹
Present units	10,000	–	8000	
Additional units	5000	–	4000	
Total units	15,000	–	12,000	
Contribution per unit	29	–	21	
Total contribution (₹)	4,35,000	–	2,52,000	6,87,000
Less: Fixed cost				1,22,000
Total profit				5,65,000

(c) Statement showing the Profitability if C is given up

Particulars	A ₹	B ₹	C ₹	Total ₹
Present units	10,000	5,000	–	
Additional units	5,000	2,500	–	
Total units	15,000	7,500	–	
Contribution per unit	29	25	–	
Total Contribution (₹)	4,35,000	1,87,500	–	6,22,500
Less : Fixed cost				1,22,000
Total profit				5,00,000

Recommendation: The profit is highest if product B is given up. The proposal to give up product C is therefore, not advisable.

Working Notes:

1. *Fixed cost:*

	Units	Rate	Amount
A	10000	× ₹6	= ₹60,000
B	5000	× ₹6	= ₹30,000
C	8000	× ₹4	= ₹32,000
			₹1,22,000

Problem 35 Style Ltd. is engaged in 3 distinct lines of production. Their production cost per unit and selling prices are as under:

	A	B	C
Production (units)	3000	2000	5000
Material cost	18	26	30
Wages	7	9	10
Variable overheads	2	3	3
Fixed overheads	5	8	9
Total cost	32	4652	
Selling price	40	60	61
Profit	8	14	9

The management wants to discontinue one line and gives you the assurance that production in two other lines shall rise by 50%. They intend to discontinue the line which produces Article A as it is less profitable.

(a) Do you agree to the scheme in principle? If so, do you think that the line which produces A should be discontinued.

(b) Offer your comments and show the necessary statements to support your decision. Make three separate statements.

Solution: There are four alternatives:

A: *Status quo,* i.e., maintain the current status and produce all the three products.

B: Discontinue A and produce 50% extra of other products (3000 units of B + 7500 units of C).

C: Discontinue B and produce 50% extra of other products (4500 units of A + 7500 units of C).

D: Discontinue C and produce 50% extra of other products (4500 units of A + 3000 units of B).

Statement showing Profit under alternative A

Particulars	A	B	C	Total
Units	3000	2000	5000	
Selling price per unit	40	60	61	
Materials	18	26	30	
Wages	7	9	10	
Variable overheads	2	3	3	
Variable cost per unit	27	38	43	
Contribution per unit	13	22	18	
Total contribution (Units × Contribution per unit)	39,000	44,060	90,000	1,73,000
Less: Fixed cost				76,000
Profit				97,000

Statement showing Profit under alternative B

Particulars	B	C	Total
Units	3000	7500	
Selling price per unit	60	61	
Materials	26	30	
Wages	9	10	
Variable overheads	3	3	
Variable cost per unit	38	43	
Contribution	22	18	
Total contribution (Units × Contribution per unit)	66000	135000	201000
Less: Fixed cost			76,000
Profit			1,25,000

Statement showing Profit under alternative C

Particulars	A	C	Total
Units	4500	7500	
Selling price per unit	40	61	
Materials	18	30	
Wages	7	10	
Variable overheads	2	3	
Variable cost per unit	27	43	
Contribution	13	18	
Total contribution (Units × Contribution per unit)	58,500	1,35,000	1,93,500
Less: Fixed cost			76,000
Profit			1,17,000

Statement showing Profit under alternative D

Particulars	A	B	Total
Units	4500	3000	
Selling price per unit	40	60	
Materials	18	26	
Wages	7	9	
Variable overheads	2	3	
Variable cost per unit	27	38	
Contribution	13	22	
Total contribution (Units X Contribution per unit)	58,500	66,000	1,24,500
Less: Fixed cost			76,000
Profit			48,500

Recommendation: The total profit of the company is highest under alternative B where product A is discontinued. Hence, the decision of the management to discontinue A is correct.

Working Notes :

1. Total fixed overheads:

	₹
A (3000 units @ ₹5)	15,000
B (2000 units @ ₹8)	16,000
C (5000 units @ ₹9)	45,000
Total fixed overhead	76,000

2. Contribution = Selling price – Variable cost

   Article A = 40 – 27 = ₹13 per unit

   B = 60 – 38 = ₹22 per unit

   C = 61 – 43 = ₹18 per unit

Problem 36 Agri Co. Ltd. is currently producing three products. It recently introduced a cost accounting system in the organisation and appointed a cost accountant. The cost accountant observed that out of the three products which were being produced independent of each other, loss were being incurred on product B. He immediately decides to advise the management to discontinue manufacture of this product supported by the following statement:

Particulars	Product A	Product B	Product C
Sales	₹1,00,000	₹65,000	₹4,90,000
Variable manufacturing cost	52,000	26,000	1,40,000
Fixed manufacturing overheads (apportioned)	6500	19,000	1,05,000
Variable selling and administration costs	18,000	17,000	18,000
Fixed selling and administration cost	4600	4600	4000
Total cost	81,100	66,600	2,67,000
Net loss	18,900		2,23,000
Net profit		1600	

Do you agree with the suggestion given by the cost accountant? Also give the supportive calculation

Solution: In order to comment on the profitability of the different products, the income statement is re-arranged as given below:

Statement showing Contribution and Profit

Particulars	A (₹)	B (₹)	C (₹)
Sales (a)	1,00,000	65,000	4,90,000
Variable cost :			
Manufacturing	52,000	26,000	1,40,000
Selling and distribution	18,000	17,000	18,000
Total variable cost (b)	70,000	43,000	1,58,000
(c) Contribution (a) – (b)	30,000	22,000	3,32,000
Fixed costs:			
Manufacturing	6500	19,000	1,05,000
Selling and distribution	4600	4600	4000
(d) Total fixed cost	11,100	23,600	1,09,000
Profit/loss (c) – (d)	18,900	(1,600)	2,23,000
Profit/volume ratio	30%	34%	67.8%

Recommendation: The product B should not be discontinued as the contribution of the product is positive. The following reasons for the continuation of B may be considered:

(1) In case product B is discontinued, the contribution of ₹22,000 will not be available to meet the fixed costs. Thus, the burden of ₹23,600 (fixed costs charged to product B) will fall on the remaining two products A and C.

(2) Product B is showing a loss because of the arbitrary manner in which the fixed manufacturing costs and selling and distribution costs have been charged to it.

(3) Product B has higher P/V ratio (34%) as compared to product A (30%).

Problem 37 A plate manufacturer makes an average profit of ₹2.50 per unit on a selling price of ₹17.50 by producing and selling 60,000 units at 60 per cent of potential capacity

Cost of sales per unit is as follows:

Direct materials	₹3.50
Direct wages	₹1.25
Factory overhead	₹6.50 (50% fixed)
Sales overhead	₹0.80 (25% variable)

During the current year, he intends to produce the same number but estimates that his fixed cost would go up by 10 per cent while the rates of direct wages and direct materials will increase by 8% and 10% respectively. However, the selling price cannot be changed.

Under this situation, he obtains an offer for a further 20% of his potential capacity.

What minimum price would you recommend for acceptance of the offer to ensure the manufacturer and overall profit of ₹4,00,000? [*B.Com. (H)*]

Solution:

Statement of Marginal Cost and Profit

Particulars	Per unit	60000 units
	₹	₹
Sales	17.50	10,50,000
Direct materials (3.50 +10%)	3.85	2,31,000
Direct wages (1.25 + 8%)	1.35	81,000
Variable overhead		
Factory	3.25	1,95,000
Selling	0.20	12,000
Variable cost	8.65	5,19,000
Contribution (Sales – Variable cost)		5,31,000
Fixed cost		4,48,800
Profit		82,200

$$\text{Selling price for 20000 units} = \frac{\text{Sales}}{20{,}000}$$

$$= \frac{(\text{Variable cost} + \text{Fixed cost} + \text{Profit})}{20{,}000}$$

$$= \frac{(8.65 \times 20{,}000) + \text{Nil} + 3{,}17{,}800}{20{,}000} = ₹24.54$$

Working Notes:

1. In this case, the hidden administration overhead is ₹2.95 per unit.
   [i.e., 15 – (3.5 + 1.25 + 6.5 + 0.8)]
2. Fixed factory overheads:

60,000 units @ ₹3.25 =	₹1,95,000
Add: 10% increase	19,500
Total (a)	2,14,500

Fixed administration overheads:	
60,000 units @ ₹2.95 =	₹1,77,000
Add: 10% increase	17,700
Total (b)	1,94,700
Fixed selling overheads:	
60,000 units @ ₹0.60 =	₹36,000
Add: 10% increase	3,600
Total (c)	39,600
Total fixed cost (a) + (b) + (c) = 2,14,500 + 1,94,700 + 39,600 =	₹4,48,800
3. Total desired profit	₹4,00,000
Profit from 60,000 units	₹ 82,200
Desired profit from new order	₹3,17,800

Problem 38 Cookware Private Limited, manufacturing pressure cookers has drawn up the following budget for the year 2021-22.

		₹
Raw materials		20,00,000
Labour, stores, power and other variable costs		6,00,000
Manufacturing overheads		7,00,000
Variable distribution costs		4,00,000
General overheads including selling		3,00,000
	Total	40,00,000
Income from sales		50,00,000
Budgeted profit		10,00,000

The General Manager suggests reducing selling prices by 5% and expects to achieve an additional volume of 50%. There is sufficient manufacturing capacity. More intensive manufacturing programme will involve additional costs of ₹50,000 for production planning. It will also be necessary to open an additional sales office at a cost of ₹1,00,000 per annum.

The Sales Manager, on the other hand, suggests increasing selling price by 10% which is estimated to reduce sales volume by 10%. At the same time, saving in manufacturing overheads and general overheads at ₹50,000 and ₹1,00,000 per annum respectively is expected on this reduced volume.

Which of these two proposals would you accept and why? *[B.Com. (H)]*

Solution: There are two alternatives:

A: Reduce the selling price by 5%.

B: Increase the selling price by 10%.

Statement showing Profit under each alternative

Particulars	A (₹)	B (₹)
Sales	71,25,000	49,50,000
Cost of sales:		
Raw materials	30,00,000	18,00,000
Labour, stores, power and other variable costs	9,00,000	5,40,000
Manufacturing overheads	7,50,000	6,50,000
Variable distribution cost	6,00,000	3,60,000
General overheads including selling	4,00,000	2,00,000
Total cost	56,50,000	35,60,000
Profit (Sales – Cost of sales)	14,75,000	14,00,000

Recommendation: Proposal A gives a higher profit of ₹ 14,75,000 and thus should be accepted. The company should reduce the selling price by 5%.

Working Notes:

1. Sales: Proposal A ₹ 50,00,000 $\times \frac{95}{100} \times \frac{150}{100}$ = ₹ 71,25,000

   B ₹ 50,00,000 $\times \frac{110}{100} \times \frac{90}{100}$ = ₹ 49,50,000

2. Raw material: Proposal A ₹ 20,00,000 + 50% = ₹ 30,00,000

   B ₹ 20,00,000 – 10% = ₹ 18,00,000

3. Labour: Proposal A ₹ 6,00,000 + 50% = ₹ 9,00,000

   B ₹ 6,00,000 – 10% = ₹ 5,40,000

Problem 39 A company engaged in manufacturing glasses is working at 40% capacity and produces and sells 10000 units per annum. The other relevant information were:

Selling price	₹ 20
Material	₹ 10
Labour	₹ 3
Overhead (60% fixed)	₹ 5

The marketing manager informs that the sales may be increased to 50% capacity level but the selling price will have to be reduced by 3% accompanied by a similar fall in the prices of materials. The sales may be increased to 90% if selling price is reduced by 5% with a similar fall in materials cost.

You are required to comment on the pricing strategies of the firm on the basis of the profitability in each case. Also determine the break-even points at each of the production levels.

[*B.Com.*]

Solution:

Profitability Statement

Particulars	50% (12500 buchets)		90% (22,500 buchets)	
	Per unit ₹	Total ₹	Per unit ₹	Total ₹
Sales	19.40	2,42,500	19.00	4,27,500
Material cost	9.70	1,21,250	9.50	2,13,750
Labour cost	3.00	37,500	3.00	67,500
Variable overheads	2.00	25,000	2.00	45,000
Total variable cost	14.70	1,83,750	14.50	3,26,250
Contribution (Sales – V.C.)	4.70	58,750	4.50	1,01,250
Less : Fixed cost	2.40	30,000	1.33	30,000
Profit	2.30	28,750	3.17	71,250

Since the profit is highest under 90% capacity utilisation, the selling price should be reduced by 5%.

$$\text{Break-even point (in units)} = \frac{\text{Fixed cost}}{\text{Contribution per unit}}$$

$$\text{At 50\% capacity} = \frac{₹30{,}000}{₹4.70} = 6383 \text{ units}$$

$$\text{At 90\% capacity} = \frac{₹30{,}000}{₹4.50} = 6667 \text{ units}$$

Problem 40 A company has a capacity of producing 50,000 units of a product in a month. The sales department reports that the following schedule of selling prices is possible:

Volume of Sales (% Capacity)	Selling Price per unit
50%	2.00
60%	1.90
70%	1.85
80%	1.80
90%	1.70
100%	1.60

Total fixed cost at 100% capacity is ₹20,000 per month and variable cost per unit is ₹1 per unit.

Prepare a statement showing total and differential costs and incremental revenue at each of the above levels of production and sales. At which level the profit will be maximum? Give reasons. [*B.Com. (H)*]

Solution:

Statement of Differential Cost & Incremental Revenue

Capacity	Units of Output	Variable Cost @ ₹1	Fixed Cost(₹)	Total Cost (₹)	Differentia Cost (₹)	Sales (₹)	Incremental Revenue (₹)
50%	25,000	25,000	20,000	45,000	–	50,000	–
60%	30,000	30,000	20,000	50,000	5000	57,000	7000
70%	35,000	35,000	20,000	55,000	5000	64,750	7750
80%	40,000	40,000	20,000	60,000	5000	72,000	7250
90%	45,000	45,000	20,000	65,000	5000	76,500	4500
100%	50,000	50,000	20,000	70,000	5000	80,000	3500

Recommendation: The profit is maximum at 70% volume of production where incremental revenue is ₹7,750 and incremental cost is ₹5000.

Problem 41 A company produces 50,000 units of a product representing 50% of the total capacity. The product is sold at a price of ₹75 per unit. The cost incurred in producing the product is: variable costs per unit ₹50; fixed costs per month ₹10 lakhs.

To improve the profitability, the management has three proposals under consideration:

Proposal A: To accept an export supply order for 40,000 units per month at a reduced price of ₹60 per unit. The export order will attract additional variable costs of ₹5 per unit towards export packing, duties, etc.

Proposal B: To increase the domestic market sales by selling to a domestic chain store 50,000 units at ₹55 per unit, retaining the existing sales at the existing price.

Proposal C: To reduce the selling price for the increased domestic sale as advised by the sales department as under:

Reduce selling price by ₹ (per unit)	Increase in sales expected (in units)
5	25000
8	10000
10	40000

You are required to give your expert opinion regarding the three alternative proposals.

Solution: There are four alternatives:

A: *Status quo,* i.e., maintain the current sales.

B: Accept an export order for 40,000 units.

C: Accept the additional domestic order for 50,000 units.

D: Reduce the selling price.

Profitability Statement under alternative A (Existing)

Particulars	Amount
Units	50,000
Selling price ₹	75
Less: Variable cost ₹	50
Contribution per unit ₹	25
Total contribution	12,50,000
Less: Fixed cost	10,00,000
Profit	2,50,000

Profitability statement under alternative B

Particulars	Existing	Export	Total
Units	50,000	40,000	
Selling price ₹	75	60	
Less: Variable cost ₹	50	55	
Contribution per unit ₹	25	5	
Total contribution	12,50,000	2,00,000	14,50,000
Less: Fixed cost			10,00,000
Profit			4,50,000

Profitability statement under alternative C

Particulars	Existing	Domestic	Total
Units	50,000	50,000	
Selling price ₹	75	55	
Less: Variable cost ₹	50	50	
Contribution per unit	25	5	
Total contribution	12,50,000	2,50,000	15,00,000
Less: Fixed cost			10,00,000
Profit			5,00,000

Profitability Statement under alternative D

Particulars	Price ₹ 5	Price ₹ 8	Price ₹ 10
Units	60000	75000	90000
Selling price	70	67	65
Less: Variable cost	50	50	50
Contribution per unit	20	17	15
Total contribution	12,00,000	12,75,000	13,50,000
Less: Fixed cost	10,00,000	10,00,000	10,00,000
Profit	2,00,000	2,75,000	3,50,000

Recommendation: As the profit is highest under alternative C, it is recommended to sell additional 50,000 units @ ₹ 55 to the domestic chain store.

Problem 42 Shreya Ltd. has prepared the following budget estimates for the year 2020.

	Product A	Product B
Sales (in units)	6000	16000
	per unit (₹)	per unit (₹)
Selling price	40	64
Direct materials	12	22
Direct wages @ ₹ 1 per hour	8	12
Variable overheads	4	6
Fixed overheads	8	12
Total cost	32	52
Profit	8	12

After finalisation of the above budget estimates, it is observed that one-third of the production capacity is still idle. In order to improve the performance, the following proposals are under consideration:

(i) Product A will be discontinued and the capacity so released will be used for product B. The selling price of product B will, however, have to be reduced by 2 per unit in order to increase the volume of sales.

(ii) Product B will be discontinued and the capacity so released will be diverted to the production of product C. The particulars relating to per unit of product care as under:

Selling price	₹ 52
Direct materials	₹ 15
Direct labour	₹ 10
Variable overheads	₹ 5

(iii) The idle capacity will be utilised for meeting an export demand for product D. The particulars relating to per unit of product D are as under:

Selling price	₹72
Direct materials	₹40
Direct labour	₹20
Variable overheads	₹10

(iv) The idle capacity will be hired out by fixing a price in such a way that the same rate of profit per direct labour hour as obtained in the budget estimates is achieved.

Prepare a statement showing the profitability of the products A and B as envisaged in the budget estimates. Also evaluate each of the above four proposals separately and prepare statement showing the profitability under each proposal.

Solution:

1. Idle capacity

	Product A	Product B
Labour hours required per unit	8 (₹8 @ ₹1)	12 (₹12 @ ₹1)
No. of units	6,000	16,000
Labour hours utilised	48,000	1,92,000

Total labour hours utilised (2/3^{rds} capacity) = 48,000 + 1,92,000 = 2,40,000

$$\text{Idle capacity in terms of labour hours} = 2,40,000 \times \frac{3}{2} \times \frac{1}{3} = 1,20,000 \text{ hours}$$

2. Total fixed cost

Product A = 6000 units @ ₹8=	₹ 48,000
Product B = 16,000 units @ ₹12 =	₹1,92,000
Total fixed overheads	₹2,40,000

Profitability Statement on the basis of Budget Estimates

Particulars	Product A	Product B	Total
Sales (in units)	6000	16000	
Selling price per unit (₹)	40	64	
Less: Variable cost per unit			
Direct material (₹)	12	22	
Direct wages (₹)	8	12	
Variable overheads	4	6	
V.C. per unit	24	20	

Table Contd...

Table Contd...

Particulars	Product A	Product B	Total
Contribution per unit (₹)	16	24	
Total contribution:			
On product A = 6,000 × ₹16 =			
On product B = 16,000 × ₹24 =		₹3,84,0000	
Total contribution			₹4,80,0000
Less: Fixed cost			₹4,40,0000
Profit			₹2,40,0000

Proposal (I):

Capacity released by discontinuing A = 48,000 hr

Additional units of product B from released capacity $= \frac{48,000}{12} = 4000$ units

Therefore total production of product B

= 16,000 units existing + 4000 additional

= 20,000 units

Product Mix

Product A = Nil

Product B = 20,000 units

Profitability statement on the Basis of Proposal (II)

Particular	Amount (₹)
Sales: 20,000 units of product B @ ₹62 (i.e., ₹64 – ₹2)	12,40,000
Less: Variable cost of 20,000 units @ ₹40 per unit	8,00,000
Total contribution	4,40,000
Less: Fixed overheads	2,40,000
Profit	2,00,000

Proposal (II):

Capacity released by discontinuing product B = 16000 units 12 hours

= 1,92,000

Capacity released will produce product C $= \frac{1,92,000}{10} = 19,200$ units

Product mix = Product A 6000 units

Product C 19,200 units

Profitability statement on the Basis of Proposal (II)

Particulars	Product A ₹	Product C ₹	Total ₹
Sale: A (6000 × ₹40) & B (19200 × ₹52)	2,40,000	9,98,400	12,38,400
Less: Variable Cost: A (6000 × ₹24) B (19200 × ₹30)	1,44,000	5,76,000	7,2,000
Contribution	96,000	4,22,400	5,18.400
Less: Fixed overheads			2.40,000
Profit			2,78,400

Proposal (III):

Idle capacity of 1,20,000 hours will be utilised by producing product D which takes 20 hours to complete one unit.

$$\text{Production of product D} = \frac{120000}{20 \text{ hours}} = 6000 \text{ units}$$

Product mix = A 6000 units, B 16000 units and D 6000 units.

Profitability statement on the basis of Proposal (III)

Particulars	Product A ₹	Product B ₹	Product D ₹	Total ₹
Sale A(6000 × 40) B (16000 × 60) and D (6000 × 72)	2,40,000	10,24,000	4,32,000	16,96,000
Less: Variable cost: A (6000 × 24) B(16000 × 40) & D (6000 × 70)	1,44,000	6,40,000	4,20,000	12,04,000
Contribution	96,000	3,84,000	12,000	4,92,000
Less: Fixed overheads				2,40,000
Profit				2,52,000

Proposal IV (Hiring out the idle capacity):

Profit as per budget estimates	₹2,40,000 hrs
Labour hours utilised as per budget estimates	₹1,20,000 hrs
Profit per labour hour	₹1
Idle capacity as per budget estimates	1,20,000 hrs
Additional profit by hiring out idle capacity at the same rate of profit as per budget estimates	₹1,20,000
Add: Profit as per budget estimates	₹2,40,000
Total profit	₹3,60,000

Recommendation: Proposal (IV) is recommended as it gives the highest profit of ₹3,60,000.

Problem 43 Tata Product Co. manufactures product. The company is expect to show a profit of ₹14,00,000 from the production of this product after charging fixed cost of ₹10,00,000. Product is sold for ₹50 per unit and has variable cost of ₹20 per unit.

Market research suggests the following responses to price charges:

Alternative	Selling price reduced by	Quantity sold increased by
A	5%	10%
B	7%	20%
C	10%	25%

Evaluate these alternatives and suggest on profitability considerations, which alternative should be adopted for the next year assuming there is no change in the cost structure.

[*B.Com. (H)*]

Solution:

Total contribution = FC + P = 14,00,000 + 10,00,000 = ₹24,00,000.

Contribution per unit = SP – VC = 50 – 20 = ₹30

$$\text{Quantity produced} = \frac{\text{Total contribution}}{\text{Contribution per unit}}$$

$$= \frac{24,00,000}{₹30}$$

$$= 80,000 \text{ units}$$

There are three alternatives

A: Reduce the price by 5% and increase output by 10% (units = 80,000 + 8000 = 88,000)

B: Reduce the price by 7% and increase output by 20% (units = 80,000 + 16,000 = 96,000)

C: Reduce the price by 10% and increase output by 25% (units = 80,000 + 20,000 = 1,00,000)

Statement showing profit under each alternative

Units	A 88,000 ₹	B 96,000 ₹	C 1,00,000 ₹
Selling price (a)	50.00	50.00	50.00
Less: Price reduction	2.50	3.50	5.00
Revised selling price (b)	47.50	46.50	45.00
Less: Variable cost	20.00	20.00	20.00
Contribution per unit	27.50	26.50	25.00
Total contribution (a × b)	24,20,000	25,44,000	25,00,000
Less: Fixed cost	10,00,000	10,00,000	10,00,000
Profit	14,20,000	15,44,000	15,00,000

Recommendation: The profit is highest under alternative B, therefore the price should be reduced by 7%.

Problem 44 Ola Ltd. Co. manufactures three different products and the following information has been collected from the books of accounts:

Particulars		S	T	Y
Sales mix		35%	35%	30%
		₹	₹	₹
Selling price		30	40	20
Variable cost		15	20	12
Total fixed costs	1,80,000			
Total sales	6,00,000			

The company has currently under discussion, a proposal to discontinue the manufacture of product Y and replace it with product M, when the following results are anticipated:

Particulars		S	T	M
Sales mix		50%	25%	25%
		₹	₹	₹
Selling price		30	40	30
Variable cost		15	20	15
Total fixed costs	1,80,000			
Total sales	6,40,000			

Will you advise the company to change over to production of M? Give reasons for your answer.

Solution:

Statement showing profit under existing sales mix

Particulars	S	T	Y	Total
Selling price (₹)	30	40	20	
Less: Variable cost (₹)	15	20	12	
Contribution per unit (₹)	15	20	8	
P/V Ratio	50%	50%	40%	
Sales mix	35%	35%	30%	
Contribution per rupee of sales (P/V ratio × Sales mix)	17½%	17½%	12%	47%

Present total sales	6,00,000
Present total contribution (6,00,000 × 47%)	2,82,000

Less: Fixed cost	1,80,000
Present profit	1,02,000

Present break-even sales:

$$\frac{\text{Fixed cost}}{\text{P/V ratio}} = \frac{1,80,000}{47\%} = \quad 3,83,000$$

Statement showing profit under proposed change in sales mix

Particulars	S	T	M	Total
Selling price (₹)	30	40	30	
Less: Variable cost (₹)	15	20	15	
Contribution per unit (₹)	15	20	15	
P/V Ratio	50%	50%	50%	
Sales mix	25%	25%	50%	
Contribution per rupee of sales (P/V ratio × Sales mix)	25%	12½%	12½%	50%

	₹
Proposed total sales	6,40,000
Proposed total contribution (6,40,000 × 0.50)	3,20,000
Less: Fixed costs	1,80,000
Profit	1,40,000

Proposed break-even point: $\frac{\text{Fixed cost}}{\text{P/V ratio}} = \frac{1,60,000}{0.50} = 3,60,000$

The new proposal to replace product Y with M can be accepted because of the following reasons:

(i) The break-even point of the company under the new proposal reaches at a lower level of the total sales as compared to the present situation.

(ii) The profit under the new proposal also increases by ₹38,000.

Problem 45 A multi-product company provides the following costs and output data for the last year.

	Products		
	X	Y	Z
Sales mix	40%	35%	25%
	₹	₹	₹
Selling price	20	25	30
Variable cost per unit	10	15	18

Total fixed cost	₹ 3,00,000
Total sales	₹ 10,00,000

The company proposes to replace Product Z by Product S. Estimated cost and output data are :

	X	Y	S
Sales mix	50%	30%	20%
	₹	₹	₹
Selling price	20	25	28
Variable cost per unit	10	15	14
Total fixed cost			₹ 3,00,000
Total sales			₹ 10,00,000

Analyse the proposed change and suggest what decision the company should take.

Solution: There are two alternatives

A. *Status quo,* i.e., maintain the current sales mix.

B. Replace product Z with product S and change the sales mix as proposed.

The sales mix which gives higher profit to the company should be selected.

Statement showing profit under alternative A (Present Position)

Particulars	X	Y	Z	Total
Selling price	20	25	28	
Less: Variable cost	10	15	18	
Contribution	10	10	12	
P/V ratio	50%	40%	40%	
Sales mix	40%	35%	25%	100%
Sales	4,00,000	3,50,000	2,50,000	10,00,000
Contribution (Sales x P/V ratio)	2,00,000	1,40,000	1,00,000	4,40,000
Less: Fixed cost				3,00,000
Profit				1,40,000

$$\text{Overall P/V ratio} = \frac{\text{Contribution}}{\text{Sales}} \times 100 = \frac{4,40,000}{10,00,000} \times 100 = 44\%$$

$$\text{Overall BEP (in ₹)} = \frac{\text{Total fixed cost}}{\text{P/V ratio}} = \frac{₹3,00,000}{44\%} = 6,81,818$$

Statement showing profit under alternative B (Change in Mix)

Particulars	X	Y	S	Total
Selling price	20	25	28	
Less: Variable cost	10	15	14	
Contribution	10	10	14	
P/V ratio	50%	40%	40%	
Sales mix	50%	30%	20%	100%
Sales	5,00,000	3,00,000	2,00,000	10,00,000
Contribution (Sales × P/V ratio)	2,50,000	1,20,000	1,00,000	4,70,000
Fixed cost				1,70,000
Profit				3,00,000

$$\text{Overall P/V ratio} = \frac{\text{Contribution}}{\text{Sales}} \times 100 = \frac{4,70,000}{10,00,000} \times 100 = 47\%$$

$$\text{Overall BEP (in ₹)} = \frac{\text{Total fixed cost}}{\text{P/V ratio}} \quad (₹3,00,000 \div 47\%) = 6,38,297$$

Recommendation: The profit of the company is higher under alternative B, therefore the replacement of Product Z by Product S is recommended. The proposed change will result into:

(a) Increased profit by ₹30,000 (i.e., 1,70,000 – 1,40,000);

(b) Lower BEP from ₹6,81,818 to ₹6,38,297.

Problem 46 The budgeted income statement by product lines of Maharaja Ltd. is as follows:

Particulars	Product A ₹	Product B ₹	Product C ₹
Sales	2,00,000	5,00,000	3,00,000
Variable expenses:			
Cost of goods sold	1,10,000	2,80,000	1,35,000
Selling expenses	20,000	90,000	45,000
Fixed expenses			
Overheads	30,000	75,000	45,000
Administrative expenses	12,000	30,000	18,000
Income before tax	28,000	25,000	57,000
Income tax @ 40%	11,200	10,000	22,800
Net income	16,800	15,000	34,200

All products are manufactured with the same facilities under common administrative control. Fixed expenses are allocated among the product in proportion to their budgeted sales value. Required:

(a) to compute the budgeted break-even point of the company as a whole from the data provided;

(b) to draft an income statement productwise to ascertain the effect on budgeted income if half of the budgeted sales value of product B were shifted to product A and C in equal rupee amounts so that the total V sales in rupees remain the same; and

(c) to show the effect on the shift suggested in point (b) above on the budgeted break-even point of the whole company.

Solution:

(a) Break-even Point of the Company

Particulars	Product A	Product B	Product C	Total
Sales	2,00,000	5,00,000	3,00,000	10,00,000
Less: Variable cost	1,30,000	3,70,000	1,80,000	6,80,000
Contribution	70,000	1,30,000	1,20,000	3,20,000

$$\text{Composite P/V ratio} = \frac{\text{Total contribution}}{\text{Total sales}} \times 100 = \frac{₹3,20,000}{₹10,00,000} \times 100 = 32\%$$

$$\text{Break-even point of the company} = \frac{\text{Total fixed expenses}}{\text{Composite P/V ratio}} = \frac{₹2,10,000}{32\%} = ₹6,56,250$$

(b) Statement showing profit

(Sales of B shifted to Products A and C in equal rupee amount)

Particulars	A	B	C	Total
Revised budgeted sales	3,25,000	2,50,000	4,25,000	10,00,000
Less: Variable cost:				
Cost of goods sold	1,78,750	1,40,000	1,91,250	5,10,000
Selling expenses	32,500	45,000	63,750	1,41,250
Variable cost	2,11,250	1,85,000	2,55,000	6,51,250
Contribution (a)	1,13,750	65,000	1,70,000	3,48,750
Less: Fixed cost:				
Overheads	48,750	37,500	63,750	1,50,000
Administrative expenses	19,500	15,000	25,500	60,000
Total fixed expenses (b)	68,250	52,500	89,250	2,10,000
Profit before tax (a) – (b)	45,500	12,500	80,750	1,38,750

Table Contd...

Table Contd...

Particulars	A	B	C	Total
Less: Tax @ 40%	18,200	5,000	32,300	55,500
Profit after tax	27,300	7,500	48,450	83,250
Budget Income as given	16,800	15,000	34,200	66,000
Increase in Income over budgeted income (83,250 – 66,000)				17,250

Recommendation: It is recommended to divert the sales of B to products A and C.

(c) *BEP after the revised sales mix*

$$\text{Composite P/V ratio} = \frac{\text{Total contribution}}{\text{Total sales}} \times 100 = \frac{₹3,48,750}{₹10,00,000} \times 100 = 34.875\%$$

$$\text{BEP} = \frac{\text{Total fixed expenses}}{\text{P/V}} \times 100 = \frac{₹2,10,000}{34.875\%} = 6,02,150$$

Working Note:

1. $$\text{Cost of goods sold} = \left(\frac{\text{Budgeted cost of goods sold}}{\text{Budgeted sales}} \times \text{Revised budgeted sales}\right)$$

A	B	C
$\frac{1,10,000}{2,00,000} \times 3,25,000$	$\frac{2,80,000}{5,00,000} \times 2,50,000$	$\frac{1,35,000}{3,00,000} \times 4,25,000$
= 1,78,750	= 1,40,000	= 1,91,250

Like cost of goods sold, all other expenses are calculated.

2. Total fixed cost:

	A	B	C	Total
	₹	₹	₹	₹
Overheads	30,000	75,000	45,000	1,50,000
Administrative expenses	12,000	30,000	18,000	60,000
Total fixed expense				2,10,000

Problem 47 A company manufactures 2,00,000 units per annum of paints when working at normal capacity. It incurs the following cost of manufacturing per unit.

Direct material	₹7.80
Direct labour	2.10
Variable overhead	2.50
Fixed overhead	4.00
Product cost (per unit)	16.40

Each unit of the product is sold for ₹21 with variable selling and administrative expenses of 60 paise per unit. During the next quarter only 10,000 units can be produced and sold.

Management plans to shut down the plant estimating that the fixed manufacturing cost can be reduced to ₹74,000 for the quarter. When the plant is operating, the fixed overheads are incurred at a uniform rate throughout the year. Additional costs of plant shut-down for the quarter are estimated at ₹14,000.

Required:

(a) Advise along with calculation, as to whether the plant should be shut down during the quarter.

(b) Calculate the shut-down point for quarter in units.

Solution: There are two alternatives:

A: Continue the production.

B: Shut-down.

Statement showing losses under each alternative

Particulars	Continue	Shut-Down
Sales (1000 × ₹21)	2,10,000	
Direct material cost	78,000	
Direct labour costs	21,000	
Variable overheads	25,000	
Selling & adm. expenses	6,000	
Fixed costs	2,00,000	74,000
Cost of shut-down	–	14,000
Total cost	3,30,000	88,000
Loss	1,20,000	88,000

(a) ***Recommendation:*** As the losses are lower in case of shut down, it is recommended to shut down. However, before taking a final decision, the non-cost factors should also be considered.

(b) Shut-down point (units) = $\dfrac{\text{Fixed costs (if continued) - Fixed costs (if shut down)}}{\text{Contribution per unit}}$

$$= \frac{₹2,00,000 - ₹88,000}{₹8} = 14,000 \text{ units}$$

Working Note:

Fixed cost for the quarter = $\dfrac{4 \times 2,00,000 \text{ units} \times 3 \text{ months}}{12} = 2,00,000$

Problem 48 A firm has capacity to manufacture 15,000 units of a product per annum. Presently, it produces 10,000 units which are sold in domestic market at ₹25 per unit. The production cost of it per unit is as under:

Material	₹8.00
Labour	6.00
Factory overheads :	
Fixed	2.00
Variable	1.50
Office overheads (fixed)	1.00
Selling overheads :	
Fixed	0.50
Variable	1.00
Total	20.00

A foreign customer is interested in the product and he is willing to buy 5000 units (one order) but at a price of ₹17.50 per unit. Should the order be accepted by the firm? If yes, what possibly be the underlying assumptions?

Will your advice be different if the price offered is 16 per unit? [*B.Com. (H)*]

Solution:

Statement of Profit (for domestic market of 10,000 units)

Sales		₹25.00
Less : Variable cost		
Material	8.00	
Labour	6.00	
Factory overhead (variable)	1.50	
Selling overhead (variable)	1.00	16.50
Contribution per unit		8.50
Total contribution (10,000 × 8.50)		₹85,000
Less : Fixed cost		
Factory overhead (10,000 × 2)	₹20,000	
Office overhead (10,000 × 1)	10,000	
Selling overhead (10,000 × 0.5)	5,000	35,000
Profit		50,000

Statement of Profit (after accepting the foreign offer)

Particulars	Domestic	Foreign	Total
Units	10,000	5,000	15,000
Sales per unit	25.00	17.50	
Less : Variable cost per unit	16.50	16.50	
Contribution per unit	8.50	1.00	
Total contribution	85,000	5,000	90,000
Less : Fixed cost			35,000
Profit			55,000

Recommendation: The order from foreign customer is acceptable for 5000 units at a price of ₹17.50 per unit because the profit increases by ₹5000. However, the following factors should be considered before taking a final decision:

(1) The acceptance of foreign offer at lower price does not impact the domestic market.

(2) Variable cost per unit does not change.

(3) Fixed cost will remain same.

If the price offered by the foreign customer is ₹15 per unit, then the proposal should be accepted. The additional variable cost per unit is less than the offered price, which implies losses on the foreign offer.

Problem 49 XYZ limited received an order for 15,000 units for its product from a large retail store at a price of ₹70 per unit. The company sells this product to its customers at ₹100 per unit but it has a surplus capacity and can take the special order without adversely affecting its regular operations for the ensuing festive season.

The income statement of the company for the preceding quarter is as under:

Details	Amount in ₹
Net sales 1,00,000 @ ₹100 per unit	1,00,00,000
Costs:	
Direct materials @ ₹20 per unit	20,00,000
Direct labour @ ₹15 per unit	15,00,000
Factory overheads	10,00,000
Selling and administrative overheads	10,00,000
Total cost	55,00,000
Net profit	45,00,000

Direct material and labour incurred on the special order are estimated to be of the same amount per unit as for the regular business. Special tools costing ₹1,75,000 would be required to meet the specifications of the retail house. You are required to prepare a differential cost statement for deciding about the acceptance of the order.

Solution: Differential cost statement

Differential cost of 15000 units:

Details	*Amount (₹)*
Direct materials @ 20 per unit	3,00,000
Direct labour @ ₹ 15 per unit	2,25,000
Cost of special tools	1,75,000
	7,00,000
Incremental revenue of 15,000 units:	
15,000 units @ ₹ 70 per unit	10,50,000
Incremental gain	3,50,000

Problem 50 Jagdish Chand Limited manufactures a product the cost structure of which is as under:

Fixed: ₹ 2,25,000 per month and variable cost is 9 per unit

Sales are at present 30,000 units per month ₹ 30 per unit. Following proposals have been made to augment the profitability of the enterprise.

1. Sales to a foreign market which has demand of 15,000 units per month. To meet this additional demand it will be necessary to absorb the additional shipping costs and duties amounting to ₹ 12 per unit.
2. A domestic chain store has offered to take 15000 units per month at ₹ 18 per unit.
3. The sales department proposes to sell at the reduced selling price at various volumes ₹ 25 per unit 34,000 per month at ₹ 21 per unit for 40,000 units per month.

Assuming the above estimates are correct, would you recommend the company to go for the proposed price cut?

Solution:

1. Differential cost of 15,000 units:

Details:	*Amount (₹)*
Variable costs ₹ 9 per unit	1,35,000
Additional shipping cost ₹ 12 per unit	1,80,000
	3,15,000
Incremental revenue of 15,000 units:	
15,000 units ₹ 30 per unit	4,50,000
Incremental gain	1,35,000

The foreign business will be profitable since it gives an incremental gain of 1,35,000

2. Supply to a domestic chain store:

Differential cost of 15,000 units ₹ 9 per unit	1,35,000

	(₹)
Incremental revenue of 15000 units @ ₹ 18 per unit	2,70,000
Incremental gain	1,35,000

On the basis of incremental gain, to sell the additional 15000 units to a foreign customer or a domestic chain store is equally profitable as the incremental gain in both the cases is same at ₹ 1,35,000. However, it is preferable to sell in the foreign market because otherwise the price differential may affect the existing domestic sales at ₹ 30 per unit.

3. Reduction of price:

Comparative Profitability Statement

Details	Existing (3000 units)	Option 1 (34000 units)	Option 2 (40000 units)
Sales	9,00,000	8,50,000	8,40,000
Variable	2,70,000	3,06,000	3,60,000
Contribution	6,30,000	5,46,000	4,80,000
Less: Fixed cost	2,25,000	2,25,000	2,25,000
Net profit	4,05,000	3,21,000	2,55,000

As the profit of ₹ 4,05,000 at the original level of 30,000 units per month, the price should be the same as to ₹ 30 per unit.

REVIEW QUESTIONS

1. Write short notes on
   (a) Relevant cost
   (b) Differential costing vs. marginal costing *[B.Com]*
   (c) Out of pocket cost
2. Write note on make or buy decisions.
3. What do you understand by relevant cost and irrelevant cost in decision making? Give examples. *[B.Com. (H)]*
4. Explain the interrelationship between price, cost and volume in taking a decision.
5. Which illustrations and examples explain the concept of opportunity cost and sunk cost. *[B.Com. (H)]*
6. What factors are considered in taking a decision under shut-down or continue situation.
7. Explain the cost and non-cost consideration which shall govern the decision to make or buy a component. *[B.Com. (H)]*

UNSOLVED PRACTICAL QUESTIONS

1. Flora Ltd. provides you the following information:

	X	Y	Z
Selling price per unit	₹550	₹630	₹690
Direct material cost per unit	₹180	₹160	₹380
Direct labour cost per unit	₹160	₹220	₹140
Variable overheads per unit	₹110	₹140	₹145
Specific fixed overheads	–	2000	4,780
General fixed overheads ₹20,000			

Required: Find out the most profitable product mix

(a) If maximum labour hours available are 1617 hours @ ₹20 per hour.

(b) If demand is limited to 100 units of X, 115 units of Y and 135 units of Z with production facility being limited to 215 units X, Y and Z put together.

[*Ans.* (a) X 202 units, (b) X 100 units, Y 115 units]

2. Fab Mart makes and sells two products: X and Y. The budgeted selling price of X is ₹1800 and that of Y is ₹2160. Variable costs associated with producing and selling the X are ₹900 and with Y ₹1800.

The company has two production/sales option. X and Y can be sold either in the ratio of two X to three Y or in the ratio of one X to two Y. Find the optimal product mix.

[*Ans.* X 2 units, Y 3 units]

3. Tata manufactures and markets two products A and B, the demand in the market of which fluctuates with the prices quoted. As a result of the deliberations of its recent sales conference the following data were agreed upon as a working basis:

	Product A			Product B		
Selling price per unit (3)	32	30	28	22	20	19
Expected demand per month (Nos.)	900	1000	1500	1600	2000	3000

Eight labour hours are required to produce product A and 4 labour hours to produce product B and the maximum capacity of the factory is restricted to 20,000 labour hours per month. The variable cost per unit for product A and product B are ₹20 and ₹14 respectively.

Fixed overheads are ₹32,400 per quarter.

You are required to compute the possible combinations and arrive at a proper price mix for maximum profitability.

[*Ans.* Price Mix. A ₹32, B ₹19]

4. Reliance manufactures 10,000 units of component X per month. The total cost of a manufactured component is 100 as follows:

₹

Materials	10
Labour @ 10 per hour	40
Overheads (40% variable)	50
	100

An outside supplier has offered the same component at ₹80 plus 10% GST *plus* delivery cost of ₹2. If the component is bought, fixed overheads to the extent of 60% could be avoided, if the capacity remains idle.

Required:

(a) Should the component be made or bought assuming that the released capacity remains idle.

(b) Determine the level of production of component X at which VB Ltd. would be indifferent between buying and producing the component. If the future volume level where predicted to decrease, would that influence the decision taken in part (a)?

(c) Evaluate the following two alternatives available to the manufactures :

(i) Rent out the released capacity at ₹1 per hour.

(ii) Manufacture a new product Y which can be sold at ₹73 per unit. The unit cost of product Y is ₹60 as follows:

	₹
Material	30
Labour @ ₹10 per hour	20
Variable overheads	10
	60

[***Ans.*** (a) Mfg. (b) 9000 units, (c) Buy and produce Y]

5. Provides you the following data for three products:

	A	B	C	Total
Selling price per unit (₹)	10	10	10	
Raw material cost per unit @ ₹0.50 Per kg)	2.00	1.25	0.80	
Direct labour [₹2 per hour]	1.00	3.00	4.00	
Variable overheads per hour	2.00	0.50	0.60	
Possible maximum sales (units)	2,000	200	4,000	
Fixed costs (₹)				9,600
Minimum committed sales	20 units	40 units	–	

Required: If maximum availability of raw material is 7000 kg, suggest that product mix which will yield maximum profit and also ascertain profit at suggested product mix.

[***Ans.*** A–25 units, B–200 units, C–4,000 units]

6. Balbir of Punjab presently operates its plant at 80% of the normal capacity to manufacture a product only to meet the demand of Government of Tamil Nadu under a rate contract.

He supplies the product for ₹4,00,000 and earns a profit margin of 20% on sale realisations. Direct cost per unit is constant.

The indirect costs as per his budget projections are:

Indirect cost	20,000 units (80% capacity) ₹	22,500 units (90% capacity) ₹	25,000 units (100% capacity) ₹
Variable	80,000	90,000	1,00,000
Semi-variable	40,000	42,500	45,000
Fixed	80,000	80,000	80,000

He has received an order for the product equal to 20% of its present operations. Additional packing charges on this order will be ₹1000. Arrive at the price to be quoted for the export order to give him a profit margin of 10% on the export price.

[*Ans.* ₹12.50]

7. Petals Ltd. can produce three different products from the same raw material using the same production facilities. The relevant details are as follows:

Particulars	X	Y	Z
Maximum market demand (units)	600	400	300
Selling price per unit (₹)	125	100	200
Raw material as % of sales value	80%	60%	75%
Labour cost per unit	12	20	6

Overhead rate is ₹5 per hour of which 60% is fixed. Maximum raw material available 1,00,000 kg @ ₹10 kg. Maximum production hours available 18400 @ ₹8 per hour.

Required:

(a) Find out the product max to yield maximum profit and determine the profit at the selected product mix.

(b) Assume, in above situation 1500 hours of overtime working is possible and additional 7000 kg of raw material is available at 5% extra rate. It will result in additional fixed overheads of ₹1,000, 50% increase in labour rates and 20% increase in variable overheads. Do you recommend the overtime working?

[*Ans.* (a) X 3943 units, Y 2594 units, Z 3000 units (b) No]

8. Anurag manufactures two products P and Q and sells them at ₹215 and ₹320 per unit respectively. The variable costs per unit are as under:

	Product P	Product Q
Raw materials:		
Material X	22.00	28.00
Material Y	8.00	32.00
Direct wages (₹6 per labour hour) :		
Department A	36.00	54.00
Department B	18.00	36.00
Department C	54.00	–
Department D	–	72.00
Variable overheads	23.00	14.30

The company procures raw materials against import licence. The company operates at single shift a day of 8 hours for 300 days in a year. The number of workmen engaged are 30, 16, 18 and 24 departments A, B, C and D respectively. Neither the workers are subject to transfer from one department to another nor any new recruitment is possible at present. Fixed costs are ₹ 12,000 per month.

You are required to find out the following:

(a) The product-mix to yield maximum profit.

(b) The most profitable product if only one product is to be manufactured. When the answer will differ if licence to import raw materials is released only for ₹ 1,80,000

[*Ans.* (a) P 4800 units, Q 4000 units (b) P is to be preferred]

9. Polo Ltd. is engaged in the manufacturing of three products in its factory. The following budget estimates are prepared for 2020-21:

	Product		
	A	B	C
Sales (units)	10000	25000	20000
Selling price per unit (₹)	40	75	85
Direct material per unit (₹)	10	14	18
Direct wages per unit @ ₹2 per hour	8	12	10
Variable overhead per unit (₹)	8	9	10
Fixed overhead per unit (₹)	16	18	20
Profit/(loss)	(2)	22	27

After the finalisation of the above manufacturing schedule, it is observed that presently only 80% capacity being utilised by these three products. The production activities are made at the same platform and it may be interchangeable among products according to requirement. In order to improve the profitability of the company, the following three proposals are put for consideration:

(a) Discontinue Product A and capacity released may be used for either Product B or C or equally shared. The fixed cost of product A is avoidable. Expected changes in material cost and selling price subject to the utilisation of Product A's capacity are as under:

Product B: Material cost increased by 10% and selling price reduced by 2%.

Product C: Material cost increased by 5% and selling price reduced by 5%.

(b) Discontinue Product A and divert the capacity to released and the idle capacity to produce a new Product D for meeting export demand whose per unit cost data are as follows:

	₹
Selling price	60
Direct material	28
Direct wages @ ₹3 per hour	12
Variable overheads	6
Fixed cost (Total)	1,05,500

(c) Product A, B and C are continuously run and hire out the idle capacity fixing a price in such a way that the same rate of profit per direct labour hour is obtained in the original budget estimates.

Required:

(i) Prepare a Statement of Profitability of Products A, B and C in existing situation.

(ii) Evaluate the above proposals independently and calculate the overall profitability of the company under each proposal.

(iii) Which proposal should be accepted, if the company wants to maximise its Profits?

[*Ans.* (i) A loss 20,000, B ₹5,50,000, C ₹5,40,000,
(ii) (a) Proposal I ₹12,64,846, II ₹10,69,800, III ₹9,89,554
(b) ₹13,78,250, (c) ₹2,88,250, (iii) Proposal (b)]

10. A company at present manufactures component X one unit of which is required for each unit of Product A. The budgeted output of Product A are 1,20,000 units. The cost details for 10,000 units of component X are as under:

Direct materials	₹24,000
Direct labour @ ₹5 per hour	30,000
Variable overheads	18,000
Fixed overheads	18,000
Total	90,000

The component X however is available for purchase at the market at ₹8.00 each. In the event of the company deciding to purchase the component X from market, the company has two alternatives for the use of the capacity so released as under.

(a) Rent out the released capacity at ₹1 per hour.

(b) Manufacture component "Y" which can be sold at ₹8.00 per unit. The cost data of this component for 10,000 units are:

Direct materials	₹30,000
Direct labour @ ₹5 per hour	15,000
Factory variable overheads	9,000
Other variable overheads	21,000
Total	75,000

Required:

(i) Make an appraisal of proposal to manufacture component X and state whether the component X should be manufactured in the factory or purchased from the market. Assume that no alternative use of spare capacity is available.

(ii) Evaluate the alternative use of the spare capacity and state whether to manufacture or buy the component X and if your decision is to buy the component X, which of the two alternatives for the use of share capacity will you prefer

[***Ans.*** (i) Mfg. (b) buy and produce Y]

11. Sharma Ltd. manufactures four products P, Q, R and S. The direct cost of production are estimated at

	P	Q	R	S
Materials	₹36	₹38	₹42	₹24
Labour :				
Assembly (at 4 per hour)	8	12	16	16
Machinists (at 6 per hour)	12	24	18	36

Total fixed costs are dependent on output levels, as follows:

Production (units)	**Total fixed costs**
Up to 50,000	₹4,00,000
50,001 to 75,000	5,00,000
75,001 to 1,00,000	6,00,000

The Sales Director estimates that demand for that their products in the next year will be as follows:

	P	Q	R	S
Units	18,000	30,000	27,000	15,000
Selling price per unit (₹)	68	90	91	94

The Production Manager states that the capacity of existing machines is 2,10,000 hours per annum, though this will be increased to 3,00,000 hours in two years time when new plant which is currently on order will be delivered. Meanwhile, a local firm has offered to manufacture any of the products on a subcontract basis at the following prices: P ₹63; Q ₹80; R ₹72; S ₹82

Required:

(a) Advise the management to what extent the services of the subcontractor should be utilised in order to meet the expected demand of P, Q, R and S.

(b) Prepare a statement showing the profit you would expect if your advice is followed.

(c) What will be your advice if existing fixed costs are fully avoidable on subcontracting?

[*Ans.* (a) Mfg. P&Q, S 9,000, Subcontract R 27,000, S 6,000 (b) ₹9,43,000 (c) Subcontract all units]

12. The ratio of variable cost to sales is 70%. The break-even point occurs at 60% of the capacity sales. Find the capacity sales when fixed costs are ₹90,000. Also compute profit at 75% of the capacity sales.

[*Ans.* Break-even point ₹3,00,000; Capacity sales at 100% ₹5,00,000; Profit at 75% capacity sales ₹22,500]

13. After a study of cost-volume-relationships, the Paul Limited concluded that its costs for any given volume of sales could be expressed as ₹2,50,000 for fixed costs plus variable costs equal to 60% of sales. The company's range of sales was from zero to ₹12,00,000 of sales. Prepare a graph which will illustrate this cost-volume-relationship. Also draw a proper sales line to the graph to form a break-even chart. Determine the break-even point. A company operating a plant of the same size as Paul Limited also has fixed cost of ₹2,50,000 per annum, but its break-even point is ₹8,00,000 of sales. What may be the probable causes of the difference between the break-even points of the Paul Limited and its competitor?

[*Ans.* Competitor's P/V ratio ; 5/16 and the difference is 7/80]

14. Timeline produces and sells watches of high quality over an extensive market, utilising the services of skilled artists who are paid on an average rate of ₹15 per hour. The total number of skilled labour hours available in a year is only 14,000. The details of planned production for the year 2019-20; estimated cost and unit selling prices are given below:

		Cost of Production (Per Unit) (₹)			
Product	**Production Planned (Unit)**	**Direct Material**	**Direct Wages (₹)**	**Fixed Overheads (₹)**	**Selling Price (Per Unit) (₹)**
P-1	3000	20	10	15	70
P-2	4000	24	12	18	92
P-3	4000	3	12	18	95
P-4	3000	40	16	24	60
P-5	2400	60	20	30	180

Variable overhead costs amount to 50% of the direct wages cost.

The company has estmated the following maximum and minimum demand for each product:

Details	P-1	P-2	P-3	P-4	P-5
Maximum (unit)	5000	6000	6000	4000	4000
Minimun (unit)	1000	1000	500	500	

Determine:

Estimated profit for the year 2019-20; and suggest a plan for maximum profit.

[*Ans.* Existing estimated planned profit : ₹5,06,000; Estimated planned profit (considering the key factors) : ₹5,34,895]

15. Calculate the effect of sales mix form the following data by comparing the P/V ratio and break-even point and make your comments and the acceptability of the revised sales mix.

Details	P-I (₹)	P-II (₹)	P-III (₹)	P-IV (₹)
Sales	1,00,000	1,25,000	50,000	25,000
Variable cost	60,000	85,000	40,000	10,000
Revised sales mix	75,000	1,10,000	1,00,000	15,000

Fixed cost (₹): 73,500.

[*Ans.* Existing : Composite P/V ratio : 0.35; Break-even point : ₹2,10,000; Revised : Composite P/V ratio : 0.314; Break-even point : ₹2,34,075; Comments : Revised sales mix is UNFAVOURABLE]

16. Attempt the following (working notes should form part of the answer):
    (i) Total fixed cost is ₹12,000; contribution ₹20,000, number of units sold 10000, variable cost is 60% of sales. Determine the selling price per unit and also the total profit/loss.
    (ii) Total fixed cost is ₹2000; Actual sales ₹48,000, Margin of safety ₹8,000. Determine the P/V ratio.
    (iii) When output is 3000 units, the average cost per unit is ₹4. When output is increased to 4000 units, the average cost is ₹3.50. The break-even pint is 5000 units. Find the P/V ratio.

[*Ans.* (i) Profit ₹8,000; Selling price per unit ₹5; (ii) 30%; (iii) 37.5%]

17. Alisha Limited provides the following information:

Details	Product A	Product B	Product C
Units planned to be produced and sold	18000	30000	27000
Selling price per unit (₹)	60	55	50
Direct material required per unit (kg)	5	3	4
Direct labour per unit (hr.)	4	3	2

Table Contd...

Table Contd...

Details	Product A	Product B	Product C
Variable overheads (₹)	7	13	8
Fixed overheads (₹)	10	10	10
Cost of direct material per kg (₹)	4	4	2
Direct labour hour rate (₹)	2	20	2
Maximum possible units of sale	4000	5000	1500

All the three products are produced from the same direct material using the same type of machines and labour. Direct labour, which is the principal factor (i.e., the key factor), is limited to 18,600 hours.

Find the most profitable product mix and prepare a statement of profitability of that product mix.

[*Ans.* Product mix : Product A 150 units; Product B 5,000 units; Product C 1,500 units; Profit ₹96,750]

18. Mr. Das has ₹2,00,000 investments in his business firm. He desires a 15% return on his money. From an analysis of recent cost figures, he finds that his variable cost of operating is 60% of sales. His fixed costs are ₹80,000 per annum. Show computations to answer the following questions:
    (i) What sales volume must be obtained to break-even?
    (ii) What sales volume must be obtained to even 15% returns on his investment?
    (iii) Mr. PKG estimates that even if he closed the doors of the business, he would incur ₹30,000 as expenses per year. At what sales would he be better off by locking his business up?

    [*Ans.* (i) ₹2,00,000; (ii) ₹2,75,000; (iii) ₹75,000]

19. Tomco is operating at 100% capacity and its annual sales are ₹60,00,000. Fixed cost is ₹15,00,000 and total variable cost ₹36,00,000. Prepare a break-even chart showing the following:
    (i) Break-even point as a percentage of total capacity;
    (ii) Margin of safety.

    New break-even point if fixed cost is increases by ₹3,00,000.

    Hint. P/V ratio: 40% Break-even point : ₹37,50,000; Break-even point (in % capacity); 62.5%; New Break-even point : ₹45,00,000; New Break-even point (in % capacity); 75; Margin of safety: 37.5%)

20. The trading results of PJ for the two years have been:

Year	Sales Amount (₹)	Profit Amount (₹)
2005	5,40,000	12,000
2006	6,00,000	30,000

Compute the following:
(i) P/V ratio
(ii) Fixed cost
(iii) Break-even sales
(iv) Margin of safety at a profit of ₹48,000
(v) Variable costs during the two years.

[*Ans.* (i) 30%; (ii) ₹1,50,000; (iii) ₹5,00,000; (iv) ₹6,60,000; (v) ₹3,78,000 and ₹40,20,000]

21. (a) From the following details, draw a break-even chart and find out break-even units as well as value in ₹:

Details	Amount (₹)
Fixed overheads	1,00,000
Variable cost per unit	30
Selling price per unit	50

(b) What should be the selling price per unit, if the break-even unit should be brought down to 4000 units?

(c) If the present value of the sales is ₹4,00,000, what is the margin of safety on the basis of data given in (a) above.

[*Ans.* (a) 5000 units, ₹2,50,000; (b) ₹55; (c) ₹1,50,000]

22. The following data relate to one year work in a manufacturing business:

Details	Amount (₹)
Fixed overheads	60,000
Variable overheads	1,00,000
Direct wages	75,000
Direct materials	2,05,000
Sales	5,00,000

Prepare break-even chart and determine break-even capacity.

[*Ans.* 50%]

23. A retail dealer in garments is currently selling 2400 shirts annually. He supplies the following details for the year ended December 31, 2021:

Details	Amount (₹)
Selling price per unit	40
Variable cost per shirt	25
Fixed cost :	
Staff salaries for the year	1,20,000
General office cost for the year	80,000
Advertising cost for the year	40,000

As a managerial consultant of the firm you are required to answer the following each part independently:

(i) Calculate the break-even point and margin of safety in sales revenue and number of shirts sold.

(ii) Assume that 20,000 shirts were sold in a year. Find out the net profit of the firm.

(iii) If it is decided to introduce selling commission of ₹3 per shirt, how many shirts would require to be sold in a year to earn a net income of ₹15,000?

(iv) Assuming that for the year 2021 an additional salary of ₹33,000 is anticipated, and price of a shirt is likely to be increased by 15%, what should be the break-even point in number of shirts and sales revenue?

[*Ans.* (i) BEP (unit) 16,000 shirts and margin of safety at current sales : ₹3,20,000; (ii) Profit ₹60,000; (ii) 21,250 shirts; (iv) BEP (unit) 13000 shirts]

24. From the following results of a company, determine by how much the value of sales must be increased by the company to break-even.

Details	Amount (₹)
Fixed costs	4,00,000
Variable costs	3,75,000
Net sales (60% capacity)	7,50,000

Use a break-even chart to illustrate the case.

[*Ans.* Break-even sales ₹8,00,000; Sales must increase by ₹50,000]

25. (A) Prepare a profit graph using the following data:

Details	Amount (₹)
Fixed overheads	1,20,000
Variable cost per unit	3
Selling price per unit	7
Output: 50,000 units	

(B) Also prepare break-even chart and determine the profit for each of the following situations:

(a) Increase in output by 10%;

(b) Increase in fixed cost by 10%;

(c) Increase in variable cost by 10%;

(d) Increase in selling price by 10%.

[*Ans.* (A) 30,000 units; ₹2,10,000; (B) (a) ₹1,00,000, (b) ₹68,000, (c) ₹65,000, (d) ₹1,15,000]

26. Given below are the sales and profits of the two halves of the year:

Details	First Half Amount (₹)	Second Half Amount (₹)
Sales	1,00,000	1,20,000
Profit	30,000	38,000

Fixed cost during the first half is equal to that during the second half. Selling price and per unit variable cost remain unchanged.

(i) P/V ratio for each half and for the year.

(ii) Fixed cost for each half and for the year.

(ii) BEP for each half and for the year.

(iv) Half yearly sale to earn half yearly profit of ₹40,000.

(v) Annual sale to each annual profit of ₹90,000. [*B.Com. (H)*]

[*Ans.* (i) 40%; (ii) ₹10,000 each and ₹20,000 for year; (iii) ₹25,000 each and ₹250,000 for year; (iv) ₹1,25,000: (v) ₹2,75,000)

27. From the following data compute:

(i) Break-even sales in ₹

(ii) Number of units that must be sold to earn a profit of ₹60,000

(iii) How many units must be sold to earn a net income of 10% of sales? DATA:

Details	Amount (₹)
Selling price per unit	20
Variable manufacturing costs (per unit)	12
Variable selling costs (per unit)	2
Fixed factory overheads	5,40,000
Fixed selling costs	2,58,000

[*Ans.* (i) ₹26,60,000; (ii) 143000 units; (iii) 199500 units]

28. A company wants to buy a new machine to replace one which is having frequent break-down. It received offers for two models NM-1 and NM-2. Additional details regarding these models are furnished for your analysis.

Details	NM-1	NM-2
Installed capacity (units)	12,500	12,500
Annual fixed overheads (₹)	6,00,000	2,50,000
Estimated profit at the above capacity (₹)	4,00,000	2,50,000

The product manufactured using this type of machine (NM-1 or NM-2) is sold at ₹200 per unit. You are required to determine:

(i) break-even level of sales for each model;

(ii) the level of sales at which both the models will earn the same profit; and

(iii) the model suitable for different levels of demand for the product.

29. A company sells its products at ₹5 per unit. In a period if it produces and sells 10,000 units, it incurs a loss of ₹5 per unit. If the volume is doubled, it earns a profit of ₹5.50 per unit. Calculate the break-even point.

[*Ans.* ₹3,28,125]

30. A company earned a profit of ₹30,000 during the year 2018. If the marginal cost and selling price of the product are ₹8 and ₹10 per unit respectively, find out the amount of margin of safety. [C.A.]

[*Ans.* ₹1,50,000]

31. When volume is 1500 units, average cost is ₹8 per unit. When volume is 2000 units, average cost is ₹7. The break-even point is 2500 units. Find P/V ratio.

[*Ans.* 38 or 37.5%]

32. Sales 1000 units @ ₹25 per unit
Variable costs ₹10 per unit
Fixed cost (total) ₹60,000
Find out: (i) Break-even units
(ii) Profit earned
(iii) Sales required earning a profit of ₹1,20,000.

[*Ans.* (i) 4,000 units; (ii) ₹60,000; and (ii) 11,000 units]

33. A manufacturer makes a profit of 2.50 per unit on a selling price of 15 producing and selling 60,000 units at 60 per cent of potential capacity.
His cost of sales per unit is as follows:
Direct wages ₹3.60
Direct materials ₹1.50
Factory overhead ₹6.40 (50% fixed)
Sales overhead ₹1.00 (25% variable)
During the current year, he intends to produce the same number but estimates that his fixed costs would go up by 10% while the rates of direct wages and direct materials will increase by 8% and 6% respectively. However, the selling price cannot be changed. Under this situation, he obtains an offer for a future 20% of his potential capacity. What minimum price would you recommend for acceptance of the offer to ensure the manufacturer an overall profit of ₹1,67,420?

[*Ans.* ₹11.80]

34. Santa Limited which launched a new product reviewed the operational performance after six months. The profit statement relating to last two quarters is as under:

Details	Quarter I Amount (₹)	Quarter II Amount (₹)
Sales : Quarter I: 1,25,000 @ 24		
Quarter II : 1,75,000 @ 24	3,0,000	4,20,000
Direct materials	6,18,750	8,66,250
Direct wages	5,06,250	7,08,750

Table Contd.

Table Contd...

Production overheads	7,75,000	9,25,000
Total	19,00,000	25,00,000
Gross profit	11,00,000	17,00,000
Selling and administration overheads	11,50,000	15,10,000
Net profit/(Loss)	5,000	1,90,000

Required:

1. Compute break-even point in units as well as in ₹.
2. If the company supplies 50,000 units over and above the sales of the second quarter to a special customer (this sale will not affect the regular market) what selling price should be quoted to earn a profit of ₹1,00,000 after meeting special expenses of ₹50,000?
3. If the selling commission is raised by 5% on sales, what quarterly unit sales will be required to earn a return of 18% on the investment of ₹20,00,000 in this line of product?
4. If in the third quarter, the company reduces the selling price by ₹1.20 and increase the advertisement expenses by ₹1,00,000, the sales volume will increase by 20% over that of the second quarter. Should this plan be implemented?

[***Ans.*** (1) ₹32,50,000; 1,35,417 units; (2) ₹27; (3) 2,05,558 units; (4) the proposed plan gives profit ₹6,000, so it should be accepted]

35. The following particulars are taken from the records of a company engaged in manufacturing two products, P-1 and P-2, from a certain material:

Details	Product P-1 per unit (₹)	Product P-2 per unit (₹)
Sales	2,500	5,000
Material cost (₹50 per kg)	500	1,250
Direct labour (₹30 per hr)	750	1,500
Variable overhead	250	500

Total fixed overheads : ₹10,00,000.

Comment on the profitability of each product when :

(i) Total sales in value is limited

(ii) Raw materials is in short supply

(iii) Production capacity is the limiting factor

(iv) Total availability of raw materials is 20,000 kg and maximum sales potential of each product is 1000 units, find the product mix to yield maximum profits.

[***Ans.*** (i) Product P-1 is more profitable; (ii) Product P-1 is more profitable; (iii) Product P-1 is more profitable; (iv) ₹7,00,000]

36. It has been found that the Product P is making losses to the firm. It is proposed that the production of this product should be stopped. Give your considered suggestion. The loss of product Px was ascertain as under:

Details		Amount (₹)	Amount (₹)
(I) Sales revenue			7,00,000
(II) Cost of goods sold:			
Direct material		1,60,000	
Variable labour expenses	₹3,00,000		
Fixed labour expenses	₹ 36,000		
Fringe benefits : (15% of labour costs)	₹ 50,400	3,86,400	
Variable factory costs		18,400	
Depreciation (SLM)		14,200	
Machine maintenance (Fixed)		4,000	5,83,000
(iii) Gross profit			1,17,000
(iv) Selling and distribution expenses :			
Sales commission		51,000	
Salaries (Fixed)		10,600	
Fringe benefits : (15% of salaries and commission)		9,240	
Miscellaneous expenses (fixed)		41,260	
Advertising		52,000	1,64,100
(v) Operating losses			(47,100)

All costs classified as fixed have been allocated to products and no change is expected if product Px is eliminated. Advertising is a direct traceable cost to product Px. Revise the statement given above to give correct profitability of product Px.

[*Ans.* It is advisable to continue the production of Px]

37. Standard Products Limited manufactures three different products from a single raw material and by a common process. Budgeted data for the year 2020–21 are given below. The production costs with the individual products are only the separate processing costs incurred after the slit-off point.

Details	P-1 (₹)	P-2 (₹)	P-3 (₹)	Joint Cost (₹)
Output (unit)	45000	30000	15000	
Selling price per unit	30	60	100	
Production costs:				
Direct materials				15,00,000

Table Contd...

Table Contd...

Direct labour	1,20,000	1,80,000	1,50,000	7,50,000
Variable manufacturing overheads	30,000	50,000	30,000	2,40,000
Fixed manufacturing overheads	45,000	75,000	60,000	4,80,000

A new sales-basket has been suggested: P-1: 30,000; P-2: 40,000; and P-3: 20,000 involving additional joint processing costs of ₹3,50,000. Comment on the economic viability of the proposed sales-mix.

[*Ans.* Decision: The proposed sales-mix is economically viable]

38. At present an auditor spends ₹9 per kilometre on taxi fares for his client's works. He is considering two alternatives, the purchase of a new small car or an old bigger car. The estimated cost data is as under:

Details	New Small Car (₹)	Old Bigger Car (₹)
Purchase price	3,50,000	2,00,000
Sale price after five years	1,90,000	1,20,000
Repairs and servicing (annual)	10,000	12,000
Taxes and insurance (annual)	17,000	7,000
Petrol consumption per litre	35	35
km run per litre	10 km	7 km

He estimates that he has to travel 10,000 km annually. Which of the three alternatives will be the cheapest? If his practice expands and if he has to travel 19,000 km per annum, what would be your decision? At how many km will the costs of two cars break-even. Ignore interest and income tax.

[*Ans.* The old bigger car is the cheapest for his present practice. However, if his practice expands, a new small car will be the cheapest. At 16,000 km, the costs of the two cars will break-even]

39. XY Limited manufactures auto parts. The following costs are incurred for processing 1,00,000 units of a component:

Details	*Amount (₹)*
Direct material cost	5,00,000
Direct labour cost	8,00,000
Variable factory overhead	6,00,000
Fixed factory overhead	5,00,000

The purchase price of the component is ₹22. The fixed overhead would continue to incur even when the component is bought from outside although there would be reduction to the extent of ₹2,00,000.

Required:

(i) Should the part be made or bought, considering that the present facility when released following a buying decinion would remain idle?

(ii) In case the released capacity can be rented out to another firm for ₹ 1,50,000, what would be the decision?

[*Ans.* (i) Make the component as the relevant cost to make is less than the relevant to buy, (ii) buy the component as the relevant cost to buy is less than the relevant cost to make]

40. The following details are taken from the records of a company engaged in manufacturing two products P-1 and P-2 from a certain material:

Details	Product P-1 (per unit) (₹)	Product P2 (per unit) (₹)
Sales	2,500	5,000
Material cost @ ₹ 50 per kg	500	1,250
Direct labour (₹ 30 per hour)	250	1,500
Variable overheads	750	500
Total fixed overheads (₹ 10,00,000)		

Comment on the profitability of each product when

(1) Total sales in value is limited.
(2) Raw materials is in short supply.
(3) Production capacity is the limiting factor.
(4) Total availability of raw materials is 20000 kg and a maximum sales potential of each product is 1000 units, find the product mix to yield maximum profits.
(*CA*)

[*Ans.* (1) Product A is more profitable as its P/V ratio is higher; (2) Product A is more profitable as its contribution per kg of raw materials is higher; (3) product A is more profitable as its contribution per hour is higher; (4) product mix: P-1:1000 units and P-2: 100 units]

41. A machine shop in a factory is working to its full capacity and earning a contribution of ₹ 50 per hour. The management receives a high priority order which it wants to execute immediately. Material will be supplied by the customer and the special order will take a minimum of 10 hours. Wages payable will be ₹ 15 per hour and variable overhead will be 1509% of wages. If the customer is prepaid to pay ₹ 8000 for the order, should the order be accepted?

[*Ans.* Cost of special order exceeds the price offered by the customer by ₹ 75. In view of this, the offer of ₹ 800 should be rejected]

42. Firefox purchased 20,000 bells of an essential component for its product from an outside supplier @ ₹ 5 each. The management feels that these be manufactured and not purchased. A machine costing ₹ 50,000 will be required to manufacture the item within the factory. The machine has annual capacity of 30,000 units and the life of 5 years. The following additional information is available:

Details:	**Amount (₹)**
Material cost per unit of the component	2.00
Labour cost	1.00
Variable overheads	100% of labour cost

Advise the company for the following:

(i) The company should continue to purchase the component from outside supplier or should make it in the factory itself?

(ii) The company should accept an order to supply 5000 units of the component to the market at a selling price of ₹4.50. (*CS*)

[*Ans.* (i) The company should make the bells in the factory, (ii) The company should accept the order to supply in the market @ ₹4.50 per bell]

43. Fastrun Auto Products produces and sells two small components P and Q used in automobiles.

The details regarding unit income and costs of these components are as under:

Details	Product P Amount (₹)	Product Q Amount (₹)
Selling price	12	20
Direct materials	2	4
Direct labour	2	1
Variable factory overheads	2	4
Fixed factory overheads	2	4
Total cost of goods sold	8	13
Gross profit	4	7

Factory overheads, both fixed and variable, have been accounted for on a machine hour basis.

As far as car be determined, the sales outlook is such that the plant could operate at full capacity on either or both products. Both P and Q are processed through the same cost centre. Selling costs are all fixed.

Which product should be preferred ?

Give a brief explanation in support of your answer.

[*Ans.* Product Q should be preferred as the P/V ratio is higher for it. In case machine hour is the key factor, product P should be preferred as the contribution per hour is higher for it]

44. Uflex Limited is engaged in three distinct lines of production. Their production cost per unit and selling prices are as under:

Details	Product A	Product B	Product C
Production units	3000	2000	5000
Per unit	Amount (₹)	Amount (₹)	Amount (₹)

Table Contd...

Table Contd...

Details	Product A	Product B	Product C
Material cost	18	26	30
Wages	7	9	10
Variable overheads	2	3	3
Fixed overheads	5	8	9
Total cost	32	46	52
Profit	8	14	9
Selling price	40	60	61

The management wants to discontinue one of the three products and gives you assurance that production in rest of the two products shall rise by 50%. It intends to discontinue product A as it is less profitable.

(1) Do you agree to the scheme in principle? If so, do you think that the product A should be discontinued?

(2) Offer your comments and show the necessary statements to support your decision

[***Ans.*** The decision of the management to drop product line A is correct]

CASE STUDIES

1. Hitkari Ceramic Ltd. produces ceramic coffee mugs. The company has the capacity to produce 50 lakh mugs per year but the results of a downturn has cut production and sales in the current year to 15 lakh mugs. The operating statement for the year 2020 is as follows:

Income statement for the year ending 2020

	₹ (lakhs)
Sales (15 lakhs @ ₹ 20)	300
Less: Cost of goods sold : Variable cost 15 lakhs @ ₹ 5	(75)
Fixed cost	(200)
Gross margin	25
Less: Selling and administration	(40)
Operating profit	(15)

At the end of 2020, there was no ending inventory of finished goods.

The board of directors is very concerned about the ₹ 16 lakhs operating loss and hires an outside consultant who reports that the company suffers from two problems. First, Hitkari Ceramic's chairman receives a fixed salary and since he does not hold any share in the company, he does not worry about profits. Second, the company has not aggressively marketed its product. The board of director makes an offer to the chairman to retire so that the company can hire a new chief general manager to turn the company around.

The new chairman is to get a fixed salary to ₹5,00,000 a year *plus* 15% of the firm's operating profits, if any, operating profits are calculated using absorption costing. In 2020, the new chairman doubles selling and administrative budget to ₹80 lakhs (which includes his salary of ₹5,00,000). He expands inventory and the number of distributors handling the mugs. Production is increased to 45 lakhs mugs and sales of mugs climb to 18 lakhs at ₹/ 20 each. Variable cost per mug in 2020 remain at ₹5 and fixed cost at ₹200 lakhs. At the end of 2023, the new chairman meets with the board of directors, and announces that he has accepted another job. He believes that he has successfully put Hitkari back on track and thanks the board for giving him the opportunity. His new job is helping to turn around another struggling company.

Required:

(i) Calculate the new chairman's bonus for 2020, using appropriate income statement.

(ii) Evaluate the new chairman's performance for 2021. Did he do as good a job as the numbers in part (i) suggest.

(iii) Which technique(s)—absorption costing or variable costing or both is (are) correct measures(s) of profit and performance. Give reasons. [*M.Com.*]

2. ABC Company manufactures pharmaceutical products that are sold through a network of sales agents located in India and Sri Lanka. The agents are currently paid an 18 per cent commission on sales; this percentage was used when the company prepared the following pro forma income statement for the fiscal year ended June 30, 2021.

ABC Company

PRO FORMA INCOME STATEMENT

for the ear ending June 30, 2021

(₹000) omitted)

	₹	₹
Sales		26,000
Cost of goods sold:		
Variable	11,700	
Fixed	2870	14,570
Gross profit		11,430
Selling and administration costs:		
Commission	4680	
Fixed advertising cost	750	
Fixed administrative cost	18,750	7280
Operating income		4150
Fixed interest cost		650
Income before income taxes		3500
Income taxes (40%)		1400
Net income		2100

Since the completion of this statement, the company has learnt that its agents require an increase in the commission rate to 23 per cent for the upcoming year. As a result, the company's president has decided to investigate the possibility of hiring its own sales staff in place of the network of sales agents. He has asked Ramaswamy, the company's management accountant to gather information on the costs associated with this change.

Ramaswamy estimates that the company will have to hire eight sales people to cover the current market area, and the annual payroll cost of each of these employees will average ₹ 80,000, excluding fringe benefit expenses. Travel and entertainment expenses are expected to total ₹ 6,00,000 for the year and the annual cost of hiring a sales manager and sales secretary will be ₹ 1,50,000. In addition to their salaries, the eight salespeople will each earn commissions at the rate of 10 per cent on the first ₹ 20,00,00 in sales and 15 per cent on all sales over ₹ 20,00,000. For planning purpose, Ramaswamy expects that all eight salespeople will exceed the ₹ 20,00,00 market and that sales will be at the level previously projected. Ramaswamy believes that the company should also increase its advertising budget by ₹ 5,00,000.

Required:

(a) Calculate ABC Company's break-even point in sales rupees for the fiscal year ending June 30, 2021, if the company hires is own sales force and increases its advertising costs.

(b) A ABC Company continues to sell through its network of sales agents and pays the higher commission rate, determine the estimated volume in sales ₹ for the fiscal year ended June 30, 2021, that would be required to generate the same net income as that projected in the pro forma income statement presented.

(c) Describe the general assumptions underlying break-even analysis that might limit its usefulness in this case.

Answer:

(a) ₹ 1,80,25,000

(b) ₹ 3,00,63,000

3. In the beginning of the year 2020, Prosoft Technology Ltd. developed and marketed business applications software for minicomputers, achieving a significant market share and a secure position in the industry. After maturing at this level of success, the company's mission became less clear. Further, software development for minicomputers was seen as costly with little value to the company, as the market for major business applications was saturated and the minor applications have limited markets.

   In order to maintain Prosoft's market share, management decided to enter the growing personal computer field. While major programming would be required to make the company's existing software compatible with personal computes (PCs), management viewed the commitment of all personnel to this project as critical to the continued growth of Prosoft.

After weeks of executive strategy sessions regarding product specifications, management imposed the task deadlines and set the date for the introduction of its first PC product, an accounting package for general ledger, accounts payable, and accounts receivable applications. Three months prior to the introduction date, Prosoft began an advertising and dealer promotion campaign announcing the new product and setting the introduction date. Several technical problems arose during development, but the staff believed that a few time saving measures would enable them to complete the package in time to meet the announced date. Management felt considerable pressure to meet this date as Prosoft had previously missed an announced date and suffered the consequences. Two weeks before the announced date, Prosoft's new package was designed to interact with, was to be released shortly. The marketing staff knew that features could quickly be added to Prosoft's new product to take advantage of the new features in the operating software; however, there would not be time to field test the programme changes. The technical personnel warned the marketing staff of the dangers of releasing a product without proper field testing. But these warnings were not heeded. Management with encouragement from the marketing staff, made the decision to incorporate the features necessary to take advantage of the new operating software and introduce the product on the scheduled date.

Not long after Prosoft despatched the first lots of its new software, customers began complaining about processing problems in the accounts payable and accounts receivables modules. Very quickly, it was determined that portions of Prosoft's new package were not compatible with the updated operating software. To correct the problem, the company had to rewrite the software and manuals and replace all existing products. The technical personnel were not dedicated to the development at the next PC product and this problem fragmented their efforts. The revised product was not available for three months, causing a loss of sales. The financial impact of the ₹5 crore error on the company with annual profits of ₹4 crore was devastating.

Required:

(a) Identify the steps in the general decision-making process.

(b) Using the steps identified in requirement (a), describe the weaknesses in Prosoft's decision making process.

(c) Recommend changes to correct the weaknesses identified in requirement (b).

4. Sportway Inc, is a wholesale distributor supplying a wide range of moderately priced sporting equipment to large chain stores. About 600 per cent of Sportway's products are purchased from other companies, while the remainder of the products are manufactured by Sportway. The company's plastics department is currently manufacturing molded fishing tackle boxes. Sportway is able to manufacture and sell 8000 tackle boxes annually, making full use of its labour capacity at available workstations. Following are the selling price and costs associated with Sportways's tackle boxes.

	₹	₹
Selling price per box		8600
Costs per box:		
Molded plastic	800	
Hinges, latches, handle	900	
Direct labour (₹1,500/hour)	1875	
Manufacturing overheads	1250	
Selling and administrative expenses	1700	6525
Profit per box		2075

Because Sportway believes it could sell 12,000 tackle boxes if it had sufficient manufacturing capacity, the company has looked into the possibility of purchasing the tackle boxes for distribution. Maple Products, a steady supplier of quality products, would be able to provide up to 9000 tackle boxes per year at a price of ₹6800 per box delivered to Sportway's facility.

Bart Johnson, Sportway's product manager, has suggested that the company could make better use of its plastic department by manufacturing skateboards. To support his position, Bart had a market study that indicates an expanding market for skateboards and a need for additional suppliers. He believes that Sportway could expect to sell 17,500 skateboards annually at a price of ₹4500 per skateboard. Bart's estimate of the costs to manufacture the skateboards follows:

	₹	₹
Selling price per skateboard		4500
Costs per skateboard:		
Molded plastic	550	
Wheels, hardware	700	
Direct labour (₹1,500/hour)	750	
Manufacturing overheads	500	
Selling and administrative expenses	900	3400
Profit per skateboard		1100

In the plastic department, Sportway uses direct laboủr hours as the application base for manufacturing overhead. Included in the manufacturing overhead for the current year is ₹50,00,000 of factorywide, fixed manufacturing overhead that has been allocated to the plastic department. For each unit of product that Sportway sells, regardless of whether the overhead cost per unit for distribution is included in the selling and administrative expenses product has been purchased or is manufactured by Sportway, an allocated ₹600 fixed overhead cost per unit for distribution is included in the selling and admisitrative expenses for all products. Total selling and administrative expenses for the purchased tackle boxes would be ₹1000 per unit.

Required:

(a) In order to maximise the company's profitability, prepare an analysis based on the date presented that will show which product or products Sportway, Inc. should manufacture and/or purchase. It should also show the associated financial impact. Support your answer with appropriate calculations.

(b) Discuss some qualitative factors that might impact on Sportway's decision.

Answer:

(a) To maximise the company's profitability, Sportway should purchase 9000 tackle boxes from Maple Products, manufacture 17,500 skateboards.

(b) Improvement in total contribution margin ₹2,36,25,000.

5. Auto Corporation manufactures automobiles, vans, and trucks. Among the various Gian Auto plants around the United States is the Denver Cover plant, where vinyl covers and upholstery fabric are sewn. These are used to cover interior seating and other surfaces of Gian Auto products.

Pam Vosilo is the plant manager for Denver Cover. The plant was the first Gian Auto plant in the region. As other area plants were opened, Pam, in recognition of her management ability, was given the responsibility of managing them. She functions as a regional manager although the budget for her and her staff is charged to the Denver plant.

Pam has just received a report indicating that Gian Auto could purchase the entire annual output of Denver Cover from outside suppliers for ₹300 lakhs. Pam is astonished at the low outside price because the budget for Denver Cover's operating costs was set at ₹520 lakhs. She believes that Denver Cover will have to close down operations in order to realise the ₹220 lakhs in annual cost savings.

The budget (in thousands) for Denver Cover's operating costs for the coming year follows:

	₹	₹
Materials		12,000
Labour :		
Direct	13,000	
Supervision	3000	
Indirect plant	4000	20,000
Overhead:		
Depreciation (equipment)	5000	
Depreciation (building)	3000	
Pension expenses	4000	
Plant manager and staff	2000	
Corporate allocation	6000	20,000
Total budgeted costs		52,000

Additional facts regarding the plant's operations are as follows:

- Due to Denver Cover's commitment to use high-quality fabrics in all its products, the purchasing department was instructed to place blanket orders with major suppliers to ensure the receipt of sufficient materials for the coming year. If these orders are cancelled as a consequence of the plant closing, termination charges would amount to 15 per cent of the cost of direct materials.
- Approximately 700 plant employees will lose their jobs if the plant is closed. This includes all direct labourers and supervisors as well as the plumbers, electricians, and other skilled workers classified as indirect plant workers. Some would be able to find new jobs, but many others would have difficulty. All employees would have difficulty matching Denver Cover's base pay of ₹9.40 per hour, the highest in the area. A clause in Denver Cover's contract with the union may help some employees; the company must provide employment assistance to its former employees for 12 months after a plant closing. The estimated cost to administer this service would be ₹10 lakhs for the year.
- Some employees would probably elect early retirement because Denver Cover has an excellent pension plan. In fact, ₹30 lakhs of next year's pension expense would continue whether Denver Cover is open or not.
- Pam and her staff would not be affected by the closing of Denver Cover. They would still be responsible for administering three other area plants.
- Denver Cover considers equipment depreciation to be a variable cost and uses the units-of-production method to depreciate its equipment; Denver Cover is the only Gian Auto plant to use this depreciation method.

Required:

Prepare a quantitative analysis to help in deciding whether or not to close the Denver Cover plant. Explain how do you treat the non recurring relevant costs.

Consider the analysis in Requirement 1 and add to it the qualitative factors that you believe are important to the decision. What is your decision? Would you close the plant? Explain.

Answer

	Make	**Buy**
First year	₹36,000	35,800
Subsequent years	₹36,000	33,000

Denver Cover plant should be closed.

6. Ashwani Kumar is manager of the Delhi Public Schools in national capital region (NCR) of Delhi. He is preparing for the upcoming meeting of the D.P. School Board. In addition to presenting reports on the routine operations of schools in the NCR, Ashwani will be expected to make recommendations on two special agenda items. The first item addresses the number of high school classroom teachers for the next school year; the second involves the inclusion of computer courses in the education programme. Both of these items have budget implications that must be addressed. Ashwani is responsible for developing the NCR budget under the direction of, and

within the guidelines, established by the Delhi Public School Board. Once the board approves the budget, it is voted on by the citizens representatives in the NCR, i.e., the citizens accept or reject the budget.

Ashwani must determine the number of teachers that will be needed to teach classes 10, 11, and 12 at Delhi Public School next year. The salary line is always the largest single item in the school budget and will be the subject of intense discussion before it is voted on by the citizens representatives. To aid in making his recommendations, Ashwani has the following information available: the current high school enrollment, the current ninth class enrollment, historical data on students transferring in and out of the region, and statistics on the number of students that can be expected to drop out of Delhi Public School. The Delhi Public School has always maintained a teacher-student ratio that is at or above the state average.

The principal at Delhi Public Schools have proposed that the computer facilities at the school be utilised in the evenings to conduct adult education courses to gain increased benefits from the investment in these facilities. Ashwani has been given little information about this programme although he has been told that additional materials would be required (e.g., additional software and training manual) which could be expensive. There is little formal information available about local interest in a programme of this nature, and Ashwani is not sure that the programme will generate enough revenue to defray the costs. Based on Ashwani's recommendation, a decision about this programme will be reached at the next meeting

Required:

(a) Identify the steps in the general decision-making process under rational and objective conditions.

(b) Citing examples from the situation given above, identify the areas and steps which would require comprehensive investigation and decision in the decision-making process.

CHAPTER

4

Budgeting and Budgetary Control

MEANING OF A BUDGET

A budget is a blueprint and plan for futuristic management action. It is a detailed plan of operations for some specific period. It is a numerical statement showing the plans, policies and goals of the enterprise for a definite period in the future. It is a plan laying down the targets to be achieved within a specific period. It is expressed in monetary terms. It shows the planned level of income, which the firm is expected to generate, and the expenditure that is expected to be incurred. It is prepared for a specific period of time and approved prior to the commencement of the specific period.

It defines the objectives of the firm and each responsibility centre in concrete and quantitative terms and prescribes guidelines for the accomplishment of said objectives.

According to Brown and Howard, "A budget is a pre-determined statement of policy of the management during a given period which provides a standard of comparison with the results actually achieved".

EFFECTIVE BUDGETING

The fundamentals are concerned directly with effective implementation of budget plans as the management process. The fundamentals tend to represent desirable management orientations, activities, and approaches that are basically necessary conditions for proficient, sophisticated and effective application of the concept of budgeting. These are environmental conditions that need to be established on a sound foundation of managerial commitment. The more important fundamentals, some of which have been referred to as essentials may be enumerated thus:

(a) **Responsibility accounting system**, tailored first and foremost to the organisational responsibilities.

(b) **Goal orientation**, entailing the acceptance on the part of management of the concept of management by objectives (MBO).

(c) **Realistic expectations**, by avoiding both under conservation and irrational over-optimism.

(d) **Full communication understanding**, ensuring full and clear understanding, by the executive and subordinates alike, of responsibilities and goals as well as full and open reporting in performance reports.

(e) **Individual and group recognition**, identifying and recognising in the management process individual accomplishment, both outstanding and substandard performance. The system of individual evaluation must be fair, understandable, and accurate.

(f) **Flexible application**, to avoid rigidity and "straitjackets" so that budgets do not act as a severe constraint on the decision-making freedom of managers and supervisors.

(g) **Timeliness**, that is, a definite time schedule for formal planning performance reports and certain other related activities.

(h) **Follow-up**. This fundamental holds that both good and substandard performance should be carefully investigated, the purpose being threefold: (i) in the case of substandard performance, to lead in a constructive manner to immediate corrective action; (ii) in the case of outstanding performance, to recognise it and perhaps provide for transfer of knowledge to similar operations, and (iii) to provide a basis for better planning and control in the future.

(i) **Organisational adaptation**, to ensure sound and clearly defined organisational structure with a clearing designation of lines if authorities and responsibilities.

(j) **Managerial involvement and participation**, including top-management support.

FEATURES OF A BUDGET

1. It is a financial blueprint.
2. It is prepared for a definite future period.
3. It is prepared to advance detailing the measures for future course of action.
4. It is a statement in monetary and/or physical terms.
5. It indicates the business policy of the management which has to be followed so as to achieve a given objective. Organisation cannot function in the absence of a budget.
6. It provides the basic yardstick for comparison of performance.
7. It helps the organisation in arranging funds, in case it is falling short of money well in time.
8. It is primarily a planning and control device.
9. It details planned income and expenditure and also the resources to be employed.
10. The purpose of the budget is to implement the policies formulated by management for attaining the given objective.
11. At the end of the specific period, actual performance is compared with the budget and deviations are ascertained and corrective actions are taken by the management.

FORECASTING AND BUDGETING

According to CIMA, forecast is "a statement of probable events" at the planning stage it is necessary to prepare forecasts of probable courses of action for the business in future. A budget is a statement of planned events generally expressed in monetary and/or quantitative terms. It is generally evolved from the forecast. Budget denotes a definite target.

The purpose of preparing a budget is called budgeting.

Forecasting	Budgeting
Forecasting is a process of predicting events and their effects on the budget.	Budget is a process of preparing budgets.
It is subject to change.	It remains unchanged for the budget period.
It concerns the event over which there is no control.	It is concerned with planned events.

Thus, budgeting is not merely forecasting of a particular event. It is not simply estimation or prediction: it is a plan of action.

ADVANTAGES OF BUDGETING

1. Budgeting helps the management to make an early attempt to analyse and study of its financial problems and also they know the direction in which they are heading.
2. It facilitates most optimal utilisation of capital and other resources of the firm.
3. It provides a basis for measuring performance of all departments in organisation.
4. It provides an important tool to control income and expenditure of a business as it is a plan of spending. Also certain contingency funds are created to meet exigencies, if any.
5. It provides a tool through which managerial policies and goals are periodically reviewed.
6. It promotes cost consciousness and stimulates the effective use of resources within the organisation.
7. Budgeting, if executed in almost every organisation, helps the national economy by providing stability of employment, economic use of resources and effective prevention of waste and also adhering to the rules and regulations relating to the environment protection.
8. Budgeting bridges the gap between the financial plans and financial targets and goals.
9. **Optimum use of Available Resources.** Budgeting entails in itself the most effective use of physical equipment and other facilities. It helps in checking waste related to their uneconomical use.
10. **Relation of Business Activities to General Economic Trend**. The plans of the business must reflect courage or caution depending upon the expected general trend of business or economic conditions. Budgeting assists the management to coordinate the activities of the business to the signals of high and low economic trends. Particularly, the danger signals which act as forewarners to the business are reflected in budgeting which cautions the entire organisation well in advance.
11. **Elimination of Uncertainty.** The organisation should be schooled in basic policies, which are the real guide to a business. The budget procedure provides a vehicle through

which basic policies are periodically re-examined, restated and set forth as guiding principles for the organisation at large.

12. **Fixation of Objectives.** When the objectives are not the product of hope but rather the logical sequence of carefully laid plans, the executives can command the cooperation and loyalty of their associates. This leads to successful execution of the programmes.
13. **Combined Judgement of Entire Organisation.** The budgeting process takes the assistance of the entire organisation in determining the most profitable course, thus the bias or prejudice is eliminated and the final plans are expressive of the combined judgement of entire organisation.
14. **Early Study of Problems.** Most of us prefer to postpone difficult decisions until necessity compels. In the business also, people are normally opportunists, they wait till a decision is forced.

Budgetary Control. Comparing actual budget with the planned budget and then analysing the deviations and the corrective actions to be taken thereafter in budgetary control.

It is a means of control in which the actual state of affairs is compared with the budget so that the corrective action may be taken before it is too late. The use of budget to control a firm's activities is known as budgetary control. Budgetary control is a system of controlling costs which includes the preparation of budgets, coordinating the departments and establishing responsibilities, comparing actual performance with the budgeted; and acting upon results to achieve maximum profitability.

1. It provides means of ascertaining the deviations from the planned targets and to provide information on the basis of which necessary remedial action may be taken.
2. It gives a detailed plan of action for a business over a definite period of time and at a glance the financial allocation can be known.
3. It facilitates coordination of all the activities of various departments of a business firm.

Thus, budgetary control has the objective of controlling costs and since cost allocation is optimally done, harmony amongst various departments is maintained.

ADVANTAGES OF BUDGETARY CONTROL SYSTEM

Following are the advantages that accrue to the management of the concern:

1. Provides basis for controlling the cost.
2. It helps the management in execution of standard costing system in the organisation.
3. It helps in spreading cost awareness among the workforce of the organisation since they are aware of cost allocated to a particular department or activity.
4. It helps the management to conduct its business activities in the effective and efficient manner.
5. Planning and controlling of financial activities.
6. It helps the management in framing of future policies and programmes.
7. Current performance comparison with the defined level helps the management in framing policies and regulations.
8. Facilitates management by objectives.

OBJECTIVES OF BUDGETING

1. To ensure that adequate working capital is available for the efficient operation of the business.
2. To show management where action is needed to remedy a situation.
3. To centralise management control.
4. To obtain a more economical use of capital.
5. To aid in controlling cash.
6. To provide a method of measurement of operating activities and financial position both where standards are and are not used.
7. To provide more definite assurance of earning the proper return on capital invested.
8. To aid an obtaining better inventory control and turnover.
9. To forecast operating activities and financial position.
10. To prevent waste, to reduce expenses and to obtain the income desired.
11. To establish divisional and departmental responsibilities.
12. To operate most efficiently the divisions, departments and cost centres of a plant.
13. To coordinate the various divisions of a business, namely, production, marketing, financial and administrative divisions, by consultation among the divisional heads and mutual agreement on company policies.
14. To smooth out seasonal variations in production by developing new 'fill-in' products and thereby accomplishing one phase of economic planning.
15. To conform why good business practice by planning for the future.

GUIDELINES FOR A GOOD BUDGETING

The success of the budget programme may well hinge upon proper administration, for the human element is so important. To assist the budget officer of any company in initiating and selling a sound budget system, on the Management Planning and Control of the Institute of America prepared the following check list of do's and don'ts" (The Controller, Vol. XVIII, No. 12 (Controllers Institute of America), pp. 550-553.)

1. The following points should be considered to budgeting organisation and preparation:

(i) (Budgeting Policy)

PROS	CONS
1. Adapt the budget procedure to the needs of the organisation, viz., cash requirements, inventories, capital assets, sales, expense control, etc.	Don't divide responsibility below the level of policy determinations.
2. Make certain that the final responsibility for execution of the budget rests with top management. If top management does not really desire a budget, and your efforts to promote the principle are unavailing, better abandon the thought altogether.	Don't fail to secure executive approval of budgets before issuing statements.

Table Contd...

Table Contd.

3. Remember that it is a basic principle of budgeting procedure that the preparation of and responsibility for a sound budget rest with the respective department heads and not with the budget officer. The budget should, at all times, be considered a consultant or to advisor to the operating heads of a business.	Don't let the budget a creation of the budget officer alone. It is essentially an operation function of department heads. The officer is the coordiantor and advisor. Variances from budget are then the responsibility of the department supervisor to explain.
4. Use an organisation or operation chart to show the functional responsibility of each executive whose activities justify a separate budget.	Dont's install a budget system if management is unwilling to accept or comply with full cooperation.
5. Determine management's objectives as to the economy as a whole, competition within industry, internal expansion, and operating efficiency before establishing the forecast.	Don't place budget authority in hands of anyone with partisan influences.
6. Arrange educational meeting to obtain cooperation in the successful operation of a budget.	Don't force budgets on department heads. Make the budget a joint venture. Work out the results together.
7. Plan ways and means of keeping everyone interested in the planning and control programme. For example, use "easier" reports to stimulate interest in budgeting.	Don't present a master budget plan without consulting all parties concerned.
8. Provide for detailed review and approval of programme before expenditure are permitted for items included in budget. Accept approvals of divisional supervisors up to specified limits to save time of general executives.	Don't classify all capital expenditures on the same basis. Consider as "Urgent", or "Desirable" project.
9. Require specific approval for projects not budgeted and for`expenditures in excess of stated amount or percentage compared with budgeted amount.	

(ii) Preparation

PROS	CONS
1. Budget accounts must correspond with the established chart of accounts.	Don't fail to praise individuals who are responsible for good planning and performance and don't fail to assist those whose planning is below par.
2. Express budget objectives and plans in writing. Supplement written material with verbal instructions when necessary.	Don't fail to keep and circulate an up-to-date writing. Supplement written material budget procedure or budget manual. Refer to it frequently.
3. Prepare master budgets from summarise of departmental budgets.	Don't depend entirely upon a tailormade budget from a publication. A general outline of a budget may be available for a particular industry but usually this from will require an adaptation to your specific requirements.
4. Make the budget easy to accept. Offer to test or trial run your ideas.	
5. Select the toughest foreman or division head in the company and sell him on it, then watch the gospel spread.	

Table Contd...

Table Contd...

PROS	CONS
6. Classify expenditures carefully and diligently. Avoid arbitrary allocation of expenses between departments.	Don't permit anyone on the budget staff to have an indifferent attitude towards budgeting. An enthusiastic attitude is a requisite of a successful budget staff.

(iii) Organisation of Budget Department

PROS	CONS
1. Vigorously and continually sell the values of practical budgeting. Promote it up the line of authority and down the line of authority. Design it. Dress it. Enthusiastically tout it at every opportunity written and spoken.	Don't try to perfect the budget immediately.
2. Be properly staffed for the budgeting job. Judicious expenditures for this department will pay dividends.	Don't overlook the unique opportunity afforded to the budget direct to act as a liaison officer between the various operating and staff departments.

(A) Planning

PROS	CONS
1. Make provisions in the budget for every principal activity.	Don't depend exculsively on past experience. Keep an open and inquiring mind for cost reduction, otherwise inefficiencies are cultivated.
2. Furnish past performance guides to each department executive for preparation of future budgets. Explain unusual and non-recurring items.	Don't oppose current and future trends in forecasting without adeqate reasons therefor.
3. Budget net results in point of cost per unit when possible. Reach the lowest possible common denominator that will highlight the results of budgeting.	
4. Have alternate plans available for emergencies. Variables budgets are widely used for this purpose.	Don't release your forecasts without through study.
5. Carefully consider discontinuance of low margin lines or the effect of new product lines.	Don't set budgets on variable rates too tight. To be stimulating, rates must be on a basis that will permit a better-than-even chance of attainment. Don't criticise too often. Don't recommend planning as a panacea for all evils.
6. Do an adequate job of research before starting to forecast.	Don't budget too far in advance. Short-term budgets (usually for one year of less) permit more realistic comparisons with actual results and they also permit closer adjustment to charging conditions.
7. Classify expenses realistically as between variable, semi-variable and fixed categories	Don't prepare budgets until determination of plant production goals is established.

(B) Forecasting

PROS	CONS
1. Use budget period which coincides with sale's and production cycles.	Don't fail to consider the favourable effect of capital expenditures on operating budgets. Stress the advisability of capital additions which will increase production improve product or rejduce operating costs.
2. Set production budgets on sales, volume after considering existing inventories and the effect of inventory fluctuations and purchasing policies.	Don't overlook external statistic and assistance.
3. Base the sales budget on a reasonably attainable and expected : volume of sales, neither too optimistic nor pessimistic.	Don't establish a budget that is too elablorate at the outset. It is better to start with a basic operation set up and enlarge the scope as conditions warrant.
4. Determine and record the reasons, or statistics behind each forecast.	Don't compute all budget expenditures on the same basis. Usually there are three classifications as follows:
	(i) Variable (vary with volume)
	(ii) Semi-variable-(increase and decrease not usually in proportion to volume)
	(iii) Fixed (rent, taxes, etc.)
5. Anticipate trade, seasonal and economic changes in the establishment of expense budgets.	Don't resort to bromidic euphemisms. Be realistic and to the point. Slangy sayings sometimes rebound to your own embarrassment.
6. Make certain that each executive clearly outlines the practical objectives that are expected to be accomplished in the budget period.	Don't forecast to the last detail. Concentrate on items of importance.
7. Point out prior and proposed forecast errors tactfully.	Don't be misled by executive optimism or pessimism in forecasting.
	Don't disregard ideas of others affected by the plan.
8. Use these vital factors in forecasting sales:	Don't fail to recognise that certain departments operate at various stages of capacity.
(a) Past experience	
(b) Pricing policy	
(c) Production capacity and cost	
(d) General business conditions	
(e) Position in business cycle	
(f) Nature of competition	
(g) Consumer demand	
(h) Consumer purchasing power	
(i) Relate probable results from varying advertising appropriations	

Table Contd...

Table Contd...

PROS	CONS
(j) Sales promotico plans	
(k) Gross profit margins by product, operating profit and net profit.	

(C) When comparing results following considerations should be made

PROS	CONS
1. Study budget and operating data carefully for recommendations, suggestions and future action.	Don't set controls too tight at first. Revise controls as experience is gained.
2. Make reports that are clear and concise. They will command greater executive respect and attention.	Don't accept variances without reasonable explanation.
3. Make certain that budget reports are issued on a timely schedule.	Don't present reports at such a late date they are ineffective.
4. Review results regularly with management, department heads, supervisors and others.	Don't forget that a budget is based on estimates.
5. Check operating results and budgeting methods with contemporaries for new ideas and techniques.	
6. Present progress reports of capital expenditures with emphasise on cumulative costs, completion dates and resulting economies or improvement of product.	
7. Issue daily, weekly, monthly or other regular reports showing the conforming actuals with budget as well as explanations of principal variances.	Don't issue budget statements without comparison to prior periods or without measurements of departmental efficiency.
8. Consider the advisability of using functional charts and graphs for readable interpretations. Compare results of one division or department with another to develop a competitive spirit with respect to results.	Don't hesitate to recommended vigorous corrective action when necessary.

(D) Checklist

PROS	CONS
1. Eliminate transfer of labour between departments except when absolutely necessary.	Don't overlook the objective viewpoint. Sit in the other fellow's chair when making recommendations: department head, banker, stock-holder, executive, (Board of Directors, etc.)
2. Remember that budgets and budget reports are essentially tools of management, not merely accounting reports.	Don't stop trying to improve results with new methods, procedures and ideas.
3. Provide for possible curtailment because of unforeseen adverse changes in business conditions or prospects.	Don't allow the budget to take the place of management and administration.
4. Observe, record and consider those daily incidents that are likely to develop into future variations.	Don't fail to establish definite objectives of performance within the budget.

(E) Follow-up

PROS	CONS
1. Compare results with benefits anticipated before expenditure to see if mechanical or engineering faults may be remanded at little extra cost and thus fully realise the intended objectives.	Don't fail to forecast the effect of management's current decisions on future results. Don't be content and conclude that your job is done after publication of the budget.
2. Reflect savings resulting from capital expenditures in the operating expense budget.	Don't forget that good budget performance does not occur as a matter, of course but is brought about by constant surveillance.
3. Regularly analyse transfers of direct to indirect labour and expense and *vice versa*.	Don't fail to stimulate the development of newer land better ways and means of obtaining' results from department executives.
4. Review corrective action with the department head respecting those daily incidents that are likely to result in budget variations.	Don't take credit for all the favourable results.

ESSENTIALS OF AN EFFECTIVE BUDGETING

(1) **A Degree of Flexibility.** It is always desirable to provide for both possible and unforeseen circumstances. In fact, control is increased and strengthened though the provision of an arrangement whereby differences are automatically catered for, as in flexible budgets, rather than an amendment to the budget plan as would be necessary in the case of fixed budget.

(2) **Motivation.** Budget is a device to control costs through people; hence human relations aspects are of paramount importance in dealing with the subject. No management tool can be used to maximum effectiveness without motivation.

(3) **Well Defined Organisation.** In order to carry out budgeting in a manner that will provide maximum benefits, organisation within the business is essential. There should be a sound plan with responsibilities well defined and adequately maintained. Further, records should be clear, consistently departmentalised and established in such a manner as will indicate definite responsibility on each unit or section of the business.

(4) **Coordination.** One of the important prerequisites in effective budgeting is willingness on the part of each echelon of management to participate in the preparation of a budget and to be judged against it. The budget must be viewed, not as a pressure tool, but as a challenge, a goal, an objective, that can be attained.

(5) **Human Recognition.** For the most effective budgeting the best human engineering is needed. If any plans are to be made, the departmental heads and minor executives should, also participate. Most people want recognition and therefore those who are made responsible for execution of the plans must have a role in making them. Men must be dealt with as human beings.

(6) **Responsibility Accounting.** The transactions or events should be recorded in such a manner as to identify them with the individual in the organisation who controls the

activity and is to be held accountable for it. The business plan must be developed by the responsibility centres.

(7) Support Management. Though a budget programme, in order to be successful, must have the whole-hearted support of every member of management, the impetus and direction must come from the top. This requires commitment of top management to the budget idea as well as to the principles, policies and philosophy underlying it.

(8) Accurate Accounting. The historical facts must be made available in such a manner so as to determine the relationship of costs and results and the efficiency of individual divisional and functional performance.

Moreover, the information system must provide the data in usable form to assist in making sound management decisions.

(9) Clear Policy. A budget programme is always based on certain fundamentals, the collection of which is called the 'policy' of the business. Naturally, therefore, no programme can be prepared without the knowledge of the business policy to be adopted during the period covered by the budgets.

(10) Budget Knowledge. An essential condition for the success of budgeting is that it must be able to sustain the interest of those who shoulder the responsibility of putting budget proposals into effect. This needs continuous 'budget education' which is concerned with briefing the employees of the undertaking on the objectives, potentials and techniques of budgeting as well as making them understand its uses and limitations.

BUDGETARY CONTROL SYSTEM IMPLEMENTATION

Budgetary control system is a cost controlling technique that includes both budget and budgeting.

Following steps are essential for successful implementation of a good budgetary control in system in an organisation.

1. **Setting of Objectives.** The organisation should develop a system of long-term planning process which facilitates the preparation of long-term objectives. The objectives should be analysed under the following categories.
   (a) Present product and production capacities.
   (b) Proposed new products and production capacities.
   (c) Profit planning and budgeting are complementary to each other.
2. **Reconciling Departmental Estimate with the Organisational Budget.** The departmental heads provide estimates of future conditions and activities that will have an impact on the performance of the company. Estimates of sales, expected costs and availability of resources are required. The organisation coordinate departmental estimated with the overall organisational budget.
3. **Preparation of Budget Manual.** It is a document which contains the essential information required for the framing and execution of the budget. It is a rule book for the preparation of budgets. It may also include a time schedule specifying the order in which different budgets should be prepared and the time frame within these budgets

should be prepared. It also provides the periodical review and the forms and procedures for such reviews for exercising budgetary control. It specifies the objectives of budgeting organisation and the methods to be adopted.

4. **Budgeting administration.** For the overall responsibility of the budgetary process lies with the following
   (A) **Budget Committee:** In case of large organisation a budget committee consisting of chief executive, budget officer and heads of the main departments or budget centres shall be established. Overall policy matters relating to budget programmed are looked after by the committee.
   (B) **Budget Controller:** The budget committee is headed by the budget controller. He himself is not expected to prepare the budget, his duty is merely to supervise and direct the budget programme and recommend charges.
5. **Budgeted Period.** A budget period is the period of time for which a budget is prepared and implemented. The budget period is usually the accounting year. A continuous or a rolling budget is a twelve months budget prepared two or more times a year. A basic budget is established for use over a long period of time. A current budget is established for use over a short period of time.
6. Establishing authority and responsibility relationship across the organisation and within the departments.

Limitations of Budgetary Control

Budgetary control is a sound technique of control. However, it is not a perfect tool. It has its own limitations:

1. Budgets are future oriented and based on forecast and estimates are not always accurate.
2. The success largely depends upon accuracy of the estimates and unpredictable future conditions.
3. It is not a substitute of management.
4. It is a decision making instrument and it helps the management in taking sound decision. It acts as an assistant to management.
5. The success of the budgetary control mainly depends upon cooperation of all concerned.
6. **Danger of rigidity.** As budgets are prepared by quantifying all relevant data, there is tendency to attach sort of finality to budget figures but, as they are meant to deal with business conditions which are constantly changing, they would lose much of their usefulness if they acquire rigidity. Therefore, it is essential that budgetary programme must be continuously adapted to changing conditions in and off a business unit.
7. **Thinking too ahead.** If forecasting is practised too for into the future, the budgetary control technique may not be that fruitful. Appropriate techniques must be developed before the purpose.
8. **Prohibited cost.** It is quite common to find that the structure of the budgetary system becomes top heavy and costly so much so that small concerns cannot afford to adopt

it. However, it is essential that there must be some correlation between the cost of the system and the benefits obtained from it. No cast iron rules can be laid down for this as much depends on the size and nature of the activities of individual business.

9. **Managers discretion in submitting budget estimates may be fatal.** If it is left entirely in the hands of managers to submit budget estimates and the same are accepted as such the performance may not improve since the estimates may not be too demanding on their performance.
10. **Misplacement of motivation.** Managers may be satisfied with budget performance when better performance is possible and could reasonable be attained if a low level of attainment had not been in the budget.
11. **Regarded as a pressure instrument.** The technique is regarded by staff as a pressure instrument rather than a procedure to assist the executive to do a better job. Thus, there is opposition against the very spirit of budgeting.
12. **Gestation period not allowed.** The system itself, demands some time to be developed fully within the organisation. The required experience, if not there, can lead to a failure of the system in its initial stages.
13. **Ineffective accounting system.** If the accounting system, which is the bedrock of successful budgeting is not effective, the control technique would not work.
14. **Weak organisation structure.** The entire organisational structure should be very solid and sound. Wherever there are inherent weaknesses in the organisational structure, no control system would prove to be effective. Delegation of authority and responsibility should be very specific.
15. **No action or delayed action.** If even after knowing that particular person or department is responsible for off-budget performance, no action is taken or the action is delayed, the technique of budgetary control could be blamed unnecessarily for unsatisfactory achievements of targets in future also.
16. **Budget plan is based on estimates.** Absolute accuracy is not possible in forecasting and budgeting though a high standard is always aimed at. The adequacy or otherwise of a budgetary programme depends to a very large extent on the accuracy with which estimates are made. If the budgeted figures are removed from reality, very little purpose would be served by them.
17. **The budgetary plan is bound to become rigid.** Hence, the employees have a feeling that the unpredictable charges which may be because of upgraded R&D or any other reason may not be incorporated.

Objectives of Budgetary Control

The following are the objectives of a budgetary control system:

1. **Planning.** A budget is a detailed plan of actions regarding the policies to be pursued over the budget period. Budgeting makes it mandatory for the management at all levels to plan the future activities in advance. Many problems are anticipated well in advance

before they arise at the time of preparing the detailed plans relating to the different functional areas of management. The solutions for these anticipated problems can be found in advance.

2. **Coordination.** One of the prerequisite for the effective budgeting is the coordination among the different departments within the organisation. It is the coordinated effort of all the divisions that a budget can be prepared. For example, in the preparation of a materials purchase budget, the information regarding budgeted sales, budgeted production and budgeted usage of the material in the production activities is required. A coordinated effort of all the concerned departments will only ensure the correct materials purchase budget. Therefore, budgeting will ensure that all the individuals and departments work as a team in the attainment of the common goals.
3. **Communication.** A budget is an effective means of communication between the top level management and the operative level. Generally, these budgets become an important source of information regarding policies to be implemented in the attainment of organisational goals. It brings clarity to the middle and lower levels of management regarding the policies to be pursued.
4. **Motivation.** An active involvement of the staff in the preparation of the budgets will increase its acceptability among the staff. It works as a strong motivation for them in achieving the set goals.
5. **Control.** Budgetary control technique is based on the premises that the actual performance should be compared with the budgeted performance and the deviations found, should be reported to the top level management for their action. A continuous monitoring and comparison of the performance ensures a stricter control in the organisation.
6. **Performance evaluation.** The performance of the individual can be rated on the basis of their actual performance in comparison with the budgets set. This performance evaluation becomes the basis for many HR decisions relating to transfers, promotions and bonuses.

Prerequisites for an Effective Budgetary Control

An effective budgetary control system requires the following:

1. **Support of top management.** Budgetary control system shall be installed in an organisation only if the management is convinced about its usefulness. For the success of the system, the support of the top level management is required.
2. **Involvement of the staff.** The staff of the organisation should be actively involved in the budgeting process. It improves the acceptability of the targets among the employees and creates a feeling of belongingness it works as a motivation for them in the implementation of these budgets.
3. **Realistic goals.** The goals and targets set in the budgets should be reasonable and feasible to attain.

4. **Efficient accounting system.** An effective budgeting requires a strong and efficient accounting system. In the preparation of budgets, one has to depend on the accounting department for reliable historical data which is the basis for many estimates.
5. **Well defined responsibility centres.** The performance of the individual departments can be measured only if the centres are well defined. A comparison of the actual cost incurred and the expected cost (controllable) of that department will allow the meaningful performance appraisal.
6. **Updation.** To keep the interest of the executives alive, they should be informed about the objectives, potentials and updates of budgeting on continuous basis. An effective communication with the executives through manuals, meetings, etc., is necessary.
7. **Cost-benefit analysis.** The budgetary control system attracts additional cost for the Organisation. For its implementation, the cost of the system should be much lower than the benefits to be derived from the system.

Advantages of Budgetary Control System

Budgetary control offers the following advantages:

1. The use of budgetary control system enables the management of a business concern to conduct its business activities in the efficient manner.
2. It ensures the effective utilisation of the resources as the plans are made keeping in mind those resources.
3. It reports the significant deviations to the top level management and thus follows the principle of management by exception.
4. It is an effective tool for cost control.
5. It helps in the review of the current trends and in making the policies for the future.
6. It creates suitable environment and conditions for the implementation of the standard costing system in the organisation
7. It inculcates the feeling of cost consciousness among the workers.
8. The companies following the budgetary control system and which operate accordingly find favour from the credit agencies.

Limitations of Budgetary Control System

Budgetary control system suffers from certain limitations as given below:

1. **Based on estimates.** Budgets are based on forecasts and forecasting cannot be perfect. Absolutely accurate projections about the future are not possible. The strength or weakness of the budgetary control system depends to a large extent, on the accuracy with which estimates are made. Thus, while using the system, the fact that budget is based on estimates must be kept in mind.
2. **Rigidity.** Budgets are considered rigid documents and lose their usefulness unless these are revised from time to time according to the changing business environment.

3. **Budgeting is a tool, not a substitute of management.** Budgeting in itself cannot be effective unless it is properly implemented by the management. Sometimes it is believed that introduction of a budget programme alone is sufficient to ensure its success.
4. **Expensive technique.** The installation and operation of a budgetary control system is a costly affair. It requires the involvement of the staff with an expertise which attracts a substantial cost. A proper cost benefit analysis of the system should be made before introducing it in the organisation.

Types of Budgets

Functional/Coverage

- Sales Budget
- Production Budget
- Production Cost Budget
- Input (Raw Material) Usage Budget
- Input (Material) Purchase Budget
- Cash Budget
- Master Budget

Capacity

- Fixed Budgets
- Flexible Budgets

FUNCTIONAL BUDGETS

A functional budget relates to the functional area of the management, e.g., sales budget, production budget, purchase budget, etc. Some of the functional budgets are explained below.

1. Sales Budget The sales budget shows the expected sales during the budget period in terms of quantity and value. The sales budget may show the sales of the different products, territories and periods. It is the key budget that provides the basis for preparation of all other budgets. The following factors are generally considered in the preparation of this budget:

(a) **Past sales.** Past sales figures help the management to analyse the future trend and seasonal and cyclical fluctuations.

(b) **Future projections.** Future projections based on the analysis of market demand, trends and competition in the market.

(c) **Available resource.** The resources available with the firm in terms of installed capacity, availability of input, regulatory approvals, etc.

(d) **Business environment.** An uncertain business environment forces the management to cut down the scale of operation.

Illustration 1 The following data relate to the sales forecast for the next year in respect of three products produced and sold by Fireworks Ltd.

Product	Quantity (units)	Selling price per unit (₹)
A	20000	200
B	30000	250
C	40000	300

You are required to prepare a sales budget from the above information:

Solution:

Sales Budget of Fireworks Ltd.

Product	Sales Quantity	Selling price (₹)	Sales value (₹)
A	20,000	200	40,00,000
B	30,000	250	75,00,000
C	40,000	300	1,20,00,000
Total			2,35,00,000

2. Production Budget The production budget gives an estimate of the quantity to be produced during the budget period. The principal considerations involved in preparing this budget are expected sales, inventory requirements, production capacity, etc.

Production = Sales + Closing Stock – Opening Stock

Illustration 2 The following data relate to the three products produced and sold by Fireworks Ltd.

1. **Sales forecast**

Products	Quantity (units)
A	20,000
B	30,000
C	40,000

2. The following further information in respect of opening and closing and stock is available.

Opening Stock of Finished Goods

Product	Quantity (units)
A	3000
B	6000
C	9000

It is proposed to increase the closing stock quantity by 20% in each case. Prepare production budget.

Solution:

Production Budget

Product	A	B	C
Budgeted sales	20,000	30,000	40,000
Add: Closing stock (after 20% increase)	3,600	7,200	10,800
Less: Opening stock	3,000	6,000	9,000
Units to be produced	20,600	31,200	41,800

3. Production Cost Budget This budget shows the estimated cost of the production budgeted as per the production budget. This budget shows summary of different items of cost to be incurred for the budgeted output. Production cost budget consists of a series of budgets for every element of cost such as materials, labour, overheads and so on. The different sub-budgets such as material purchase budget, material cost budget, labour cost budget, factory overheads cost budget, etc., provides the basis for the preparation of the production cost budget.

4. Input (Raw Material) Usage Budget This budget shows the estimated quantities of all the raw materials and components to be used for the budgeted production. The cost of material used can also be incorporated in this budget. This budget may be prepared for the different inputs such as raw material, labour hours, machine hours, etc.

$$\text{Material Usage} = \text{Production units} \times \text{Material consumption per unit}$$

Illustration 3 The following data relate to the three products produced and sold by Fireworks Ltd.

1. **Production (Units)**

A	20,600
B	31,200
C	41,800

2. The following quantity of raw materials for each unit of finished product is required:

Product	Raw material (kg)			
	M_1	M_2	M_3	M_4
A	3	2	2	5
B	4	4	4	3
C	5	3	4	2
Price per kg (₹)	5	4	3	2

Based on the above information, prepare the direct material usage budget.

Solution:

Direct Material usage Budget

Product	Production (units)	Materials							
		M_1		M_2		M_3		M_4	
		Per unit	Total units	Per unit	Total units	Per unit	Total units	Per unit	Total units
A	20600	3	61800	2	41200	2	41200	5	103000
B	31200	4	124800	2	62400	4	124800	3	93600
C	41800	5	209000	3	125400	4	167200	2	83600
Total usage kgs.			395600		229000		333200		280200
Price per unit (₹)			5		4		3		2
Material usage cost (₹)			1978000		916000		999600		560400

Total material usage cost:

= (₹ 19,78,000 + ₹ 9,16,000 + ₹ 9,99,600 + ₹ 5,60,400) = ₹ 44,54,000.

5. Input (Material) Purchase Budget The purchase budget shows the quantity of input to be purchased and its corresponding cost during the budget period. The quantity of raw material to be purchased depends upon the usage of material and the inventory policy of the firm. The various other factors which affect the purchase budget are economic order quantity, storage facility available, fund availability, etc.

Purchase units = Usage + Closing Stock – Opening Stock

Purchase Cost = Purchase units × Cost per kg

Illustration 4 The following data relate to the four raw materials used in the manufacturing of a product by Fireworks Ltd.

1. The usage and opening stock of raw materials at the beginning of the budget period an under:

Raw material	Usage (kg)	Opening (kg)
M_1	395600	50000
M_2	229000	
M_3	333200	10000
M_4	280200	20000

2. The quantity of raw material of closing stock at the end is to be reduced by 10%.
   Prepare the raw material purchase budget.

Solution:

Direct Material Purchase Budget

	M_1 (kg)	M_2 (kg)	M_3 (kg)	M_4 (kg)
Raw material usage for production	3,95,600	2,29,000	3,33,200	2,80,200
Add: Closing stock (10% less of opening stock)	45,000	18,000	9000	18,000
Less: Opening stock	50,000	20,000	10,000	20,000
Purchase quantity (i)	3,90,600	2,27,000	3,32,200	2,78,200
Cost per unit (₹) (ii)	5	4	3	2
Total purchase cost (₹) (i) × (ii)	19,53,000	9,08,000	9,96,600	5,56,400

Illustration 5 The following data relate to the cost incurred in the manufacturing of three ducts by Fireworks Ltd. You are required to prepare the production cost budget.

	Products		
	A	B	C
	10400	20800	31200
Production (units)			
Direct material cost:			
M_1	30	40	50
M_2	16	32	24
M_3	18	24	24
M_4	20	12	8
Direct labour cost per unit of output	50	67	86
Factory overhead per unit of output	17.60	24.20	30.80

Solution:

Production Cost Budget

Production units	Product						
	A 10,400		B 20,800		C 31,200		Total 62,400
	Per unit ₹	Total ₹	Per unit ₹	Total ₹	Per unit ₹	Total ₹	₹
Direct material*	78.00	8,11,200	108.00	22,46,400	106.00	33,07,200	63,64,800
Direct labour	50.00	5,20,000	67.00	13,93,600	86.00	26,83,200	45,96,800
Factory overhead	17.60	1,83,040	24.20	5,03,360	30.80	9,60,960	16,47,360
Total	145.60	15,14,240	199.20	41,43,360	222.80	69,51,360	1,26,08,960

Working Notes:

*Direct material cost:

	A	B	C
M_1	30	40	50
M_2	16	32	24
M_3	18	24	24
M_4	20	12	8
Direct material cost per unit of output	78	108	106

6. Capital Expenditure Budget This budget represents the expenditure to be made on all fixed assets during the budget period. It includes items such as new buildings, machinery, land and intangible items (patents), etc., generally this budget requires the approval of the top level management as the significant amount is involved in this type of budget.

7. Cash Budget The cash budget gives an estimate of cash receipts and cash payments during the budget period. It considers all receipts during the budget period irrespective of their nature-capita; *or revenue*. All the receipts are added to the opening balance of cash and all payments are subtracted to get the closing balance of cash during the budget period. Cash budget serves the following purposes:

1. To know the period and the amount of cash surplus. It allows the firm to plan about the investment of surplus cash.
2. To know the period and amount of cash deficit. It allows the firm to plan in advance about the sources from where the funds need to be arranged.
3. It establishes a sound basis for control of cash position.

Illustration 6 A company is expecting to have ₹30,000 cash in hand on 1st Jan 2020 and it requires you to prepare cash budget for the three months Jan to March 2020. The following information is provided to you.

	Sales ₹	Purchase ₹	Wages ₹	Expenses ₹
November	1,00000	50,000	10,000	7000
Dec.	1,20,000	60,000	10,000	8000
Jan.	1,12,000	62,000	12,000	8000
Feb.	1,20,000	70,000	12,000	9000
March	1,40,000	65,000	14,000	10,000

Additional information:

(a) Period of credit allowed by suppliers is two months;

(b) 25% of sale is for cash and the period of credit allowed to customers for credit sale is one month;

(c) Wages and expenses are paid in the following month;

(d) Income tax ₹ 15,000 is to be paid in March, 2020.

Solution:

Cash Budget
(for three months ending March 2020)

Particulars	Jan ₹	Feb ₹	March ₹
Opening balance	30,000	80,000	1,14,000
Add receipts:			
Cash sales	28,000	30,000	35,000
Debtors	90,000	84,000	90,000
Total	1,48,000	1,94,000	2,39,000
Less payments:			
Creditors	50,000	60,000	62,000
Wages	10,000	12,000	12,000
Expenses	8000	8000	9000
Income tax:	–	–	15,000
Total	68,000	80,000	98,000
Closing balance	80,000	1,41,000	1,14,000

Illustration 7 The following data relate to Bookshop Ltd.

The financial manager has made the following sales forecasts for the first five months of the coming year, commencing from 1st April, 2021:

Month	*Sales (₹)*
April	40,000
May	45,000
June	55,000
July	60,000
August	50,000

Other data:

(i) Debtor's and creditors' balance at the beginning of the year are ₹ 30,000 and ₹ 14,000 respectively. The balance of other relevant assets and liabilities are:

Cash balance	₹ 7500
Stock	₹ 51,000
Accrued sales commission	₹ 3500

(ii) 40% sales are on cash basis. Credit sales are collected in the month following the sale.
(iii) Cost of sales is 60 per cent on sales.
(iv) The only other variable cost is 5% commission to sales agents. The sales commission is paid in a month after it is earned.
(v) Inventory (stock) is kept equal to sales requirements for the next two months budgeted sales.
(vi) Trade creditors are paid in the following month after purchases.
(vii) Fixed costs are ₹5,000 per month including ₹2,000 depreciation.

You are required to prepare a cash budget for the months of April, May and June, 2021 respectively. *[B.Com. (H)]*

Solution:

Cash Budget
(April—June 2021)

Particulars	April ₹	May ₹	June ₹
Opening balance	7,500	33,000	37,000
Add: Receipts			
Cash sales (40% of sales)	16,000	18,000	22,000
Receipts from debtors	30,000	24,000	27,000
Total Receipts	53,500	75,000	86,000
Less: Payments			
Creditors	14,000	33,000	36,000
Fixed costs (5,000 – 2000)	3000	3000	3000
Commission to sales agents	3500	2000	2250
Total payments	20,500	38,000	41,250
Closing balance	33,000	37,000	44,750

Working Notes:

1. Calculation of receipts from debtors, purchases and payment to creditors (assuming that all purchases are on credit basis).

Particulars	April	May	June	July	August
(1) Receipts from debtors credit sales (60% of total sales)	24,000	27,000	33,000	36,000	30,000
(2) Payments to creditors Cost of sales 60% of total sales	24,000	27,000	33,000	36,000	30,000
Desired closing inventory at cost	60,000	69,000	66,000		
	84,000	96,000	99,000		

Table Contd...

Table Contd.

Particulars	April	May	June	July	August
Less: Opening inventory	51,000	60,000	69,000		
Purchases	33,000	36,000	30,000		
Payment to creditors	14,000	33,000	36,000		

8. Master Budget Master budget is the summary of all the functional budgets of the firm. According to the Chartered Institute of Management Accountants (CIMA), London, "it is a summary of the budget schedules in capsule form made for the purpose of presenting, in one report, the highlights of the budget forecast". A master budget generally includes sales budget, production budget, input cost budget, cash budget and the budgeted income statement.

FIXED BUDGET AND FLEXIBLE BUDGET

On the basis of level of activity or capacity, budgets are classified into fixed budget and flexible budget.

Fixed Budget

A fixed budget is prepared for one level of activity and one set of conditions. It is defined as a budget which is designed to remain unchanged irrespective of the level of activity attained. It is a rigid budget prepared on the assumption that the actual level of activity will be same as the budgeted level of activity. It is suitable for the conditions when output and sales can be estimated with a fair degree of accuracy.

Flexible Budget

A flexible budget is designed to change in relation to the change in the level of activity, by recognising the difference between fixed and variable costs. In the flexible budget, a series of budgets are prepared at different levels of activity. Thus, a budget might be prepared for various levels of activity, say, 60%, 80% and 100% capacity utilisation. Such a budget is useful for cost control, performance appraisal and cost ascertainment for the tenders and quotations. The flexible budget is considered superior to the fixed budget in the following cases:

(a) Where the capacity utilisation differs from period to period either due to seasonal factors or due to variation in demand.
(b) Where the business is new and it is difficult to forecast the demand.
(c) Where sales are affected by changes in fashion, e.g., readymade garments.
(d) Where company frequently makes changes in the product or introduces new products
(e) Where the company is engaged in make-to-order business.

On the basis of above discussion, the difference between these budgets may be summarised as given below:

Points of Distinction	Flexible Budget	Flexible Budget
1. Budget	Only one budget at a fixed level of activity is prepared assuming that given conditions will not change.	Series of budgets are prepared under the assumption of different levels of activity.
2. Flexibility	It is not flexible enough to change with the change in actual volume of output.	It can be suitably redeveloped quickly according to the change in level of activity.
3. Classification of costs	The different items of cost are not classified according to variability, i.e., fixed, variable and semi-variable.	Costs are classified according to variability.
4. Condition	It is applicable only under the given static conditions.	It is modified according to changed conditions.
5. Comparison	Comparison of actual and budgeted performance is not meaningful if the volume of output changes.	Comparisons are meaningful as the modified budgets are placed against actual ones.

Illustration 8 The following information relates to a company:

	At 80% capacity
Variable cost:	
Direct labour	18,000
Materials cost	6,000
Semi-variable cost:	
Power (30% fixed, 70% variable)	40,000
Repairs and maintenance (80% fixed, 20% variable)	6,000
Fixed overheads:	
Depreciation	11,000
Insurance	5,000
Salaries	10,000

Draw up a flexible budget at 70%, 80% and 90% plant capacity.

Solution:

Flexible Budget for the period..................

Particulars	70%	80%	90%
Variable cost:	₹	₹	₹
Direct Labour	15,750	8000	20,250
Materials cost	5250	6000	6750
Semi-variable cost:			
Power: Fixed	12,000	12,000	12,000
Variable	24,500	28,000	31,500
Repairs and maintenance:			

Table Contd...

Table Contd...

Particulars	70%	80%	90%
Fixed	4,800	4,800	4,800
Variable	1,050	1,200	1,350
Fixed cost:			
Depreciation	11,000	11,000	11,000
Insurance	5,000	5,000	5,000
Salaries	10,000	10,000	10,000
Total cost	89,350	86,000	1,02,650

Working Notes:

1. Direct labour cost

$$\text{At } 70\% = 18{,}000 \times \frac{70}{80} = 15{,}750$$

$$\text{At } 90\% = 18{,}000 \times \frac{90}{80} = 20{,}250$$

In the same manner, calculation for materials is done.

2. Power

Fixed (30%) = ₹ 12,000,

Variable = ₹ 28,000.

$$\text{At } 70\% = 28{,}000 \times \frac{70}{80} = ₹\,24{,}500$$

$$\text{At } 90\% = 28{,}000 \times \frac{90}{80} = ₹\,31{,}500$$

In the same manner, calculation for repairs and maintenance is done.

Illustration 9 The budget manager of Jupiter Electricals Limited is preparing flexible budget for the accounting year starting from 1 July, 2020.

The company produces one product --- DETX II. Direct material costs ₹ 7 per unit. Direct labour averages ₹ 2.50 per hour and requires 1.6 hours to produce one unit of DETX II. Salesmen are paid a commission of ₹ 1 per unit sold. Fixed selling and administrative expenses amount to ₹ 85,000 per year.

Manufacturing overhead is estimated in the following amounts under specified volumes:

Volume of production (in units)	1,20,000	1,50,000
	₹	₹
Expenses :		
Indirect material	2,64,000	3,30,000
Indirect labour	1,50,000	1,87,500

Table Contd...

Table Contd...

Inspection	90,000	1,12,500
Maintenance	84,000	1,02,000
Supervision	1,98,000	2,34,000
Depreciation of plant and equipment	90,000	90,000
Engineering services	94,000	94,000
Total manufacturing overhead	9,70,000	11,50,000

Prepare a Total Cost Budget for 1,40,000 units of production. [*B.Com. (H)*]

Solution: Budget for the year ending 30th June, 2020

Particulars	**Amount**
Output (units)	1,40,000
Variable costs:	₹
Direct material @ ₹7 per unit	9,80,000
Direct labour @ ₹4 per unit	5,60,000
Salesmen's commission @ ₹1 per unit	1,40,000
Indirect materials @ ₹2.20 per unit	3,08,000
Indirect labour @ ₹1.25 per unit	1,75,000
Inspection @ ₹0.75 per unit	1,05,000
Semi-variable costs:	
Variable @ ₹1.20 per unit	1,68,000
Maintenance	
Fixed	12,000
Variable @ ₹0.60 per unit	84,000
Fixed costs:	
Depreciation	90,000
Engineering services	94,000
Selling and distribution expenses	85,000
Total cost	28,55,000

Working Notes:

Fixed and variable components of each item of cost are determined as follows:

1. Indirect material

$$\text{Variable cost per unit} = \frac{\text{Change in cost}}{\text{Change in output}} = \frac{₹3,30,000 - ₹2,64,000}{1,50,000 - 1,20,000 \text{ units}}$$

$$\frac{66,000}{30,000} = ₹2.20$$

Variable indirect material = 1,20,000 × ₹2.20 = ₹2,64,000 for 1,20,000 units.

Hence, there is no fixed cost element and this item is purely variable.

2. Indirect labour

$$\text{Variable cost per unit} = \frac{\text{Change in cost}}{\text{Change in output}} = \frac{(1{,}87{,}500 - 1{,}50{,}000)}{(1{,}50{,}000 - 1{,}20{,}000 \text{ units})}$$

$$= \frac{37{,}500}{30{,}000} = ₹1.25$$

Variable indirect labour = 1,20,000 × ₹1.25 = ₹1,50,000 for 1,20,000 units.

Hence, there is no fixed cost element and this item is purely variable.

3. Inspection

$$\text{Variable cost per unit} = \frac{\text{Change in cost}}{\text{Change in output}} = \frac{(1{,}12{,}500 - 90{,}000)}{(1{,}50{,}000 - 1{,}20{,}000 \text{ units})}$$

$$\frac{22{,}500}{30{,}000} = ₹0.75$$

Variable inspection = 1,20,000 × ₹0.75 = ₹90,000 for 1,20,000 units.

Hence, there is no fixed cost element and this item is purely variable.

4. Maintenance

$$\text{Variable cost per unit} = \frac{\text{Change in cost}}{\text{Change in output}} = \frac{(1{,}02{,}000 - 84{,}000)}{(1{,}50{,}000 - 1{,}20{,}000 \text{ units})}$$

$$\frac{18{,}000}{30{,}000} = ₹0.60$$

Variable maintenance cost = 1,20,000 × ₹0.60 = ₹72,000 for 1,20,000 units.

Fixed maintenance cost = 84,000 – (1,20,000 × 0.60) = ₹12,000

5. Supervision

$$\text{Variable cost per unit} = \frac{\text{Change in cost}}{\text{Change in output}} = \frac{₹2{,}34{,}000 - 1{,}98{,}000}{1{,}50{,}000 - 1{,}20{,}000 \text{ units}}$$

$$= \frac{36{,}000}{30{,}000} = ₹1.20 \text{ per unit}$$

Variable supervision cost = 1,20,000 × 1.20 = ₹1,44,000

Fixed supervision cost = 1,98,000 – (1,20,000 × 1.20) = ₹54,000

6. Depreciation and engineering services costs are the same at two levels of production. Thus, these are fixed costs.

Illustration 10 ABC Ltd. manufactures a single product for which market demand exists for additional quantity. Present sales of ₹60,000 per month utilises only 60% capacity of the plant. Marketing Manager assures that with the reduction of 10% in the price he would be in a position to increase the sale by about 25% to 30%.

The following data are available:

(i) Selling price	₹10 per unit
(ii) Variable cost	₹3 per unit
(iii) Semi-variable cost	₹6,000 fixed + 50 paise per unit
(iv) Fixed cost	₹20,000 at present level estimated to be ₹24,000 at 80% output.

You are required to prepare the following statements:

(1) The operating profits at 60%, 70% and 80% levels at current selling price, and

(2) The operating profits at proposed selling price at the above levels.

[*B.Com. (H)*]

Solution:

Profitability statement at current price ₹10

Particulars	60%	70%	80%
Sales	60,000	70,000	80,000
Less: Variable cost @(₹3 +0.50)	21,000	24,500	28,000
Contribution	39,000	45,500	52,000
Less: Fixed cost (20,000 + 6,000)	26,000	26,000	30,000
Profit	13,000	19,500	22,000

Profitability statement at reduced price of ₹9

Particulars	60%	70%	80%
Sales	54,000	63,000	72,000
Less: Variable cost	21,000	24,500	28,000
Contribution	33,000	38,500	44,000
Less: Fixed cost	26,000	26,000	30,000
Profit	7,000	12,500	14,000

PROGRAMME BUDGETING

It is used by the Central Government and the State Governments in India. It is used by Government departments and Non-for-profit organisations (NPOs) where budget objectives are not laid down in monetary terms but in physical units. For example, polio programme focuses on the number of children given the drops and not the cost. Programme budgeting is also known as output budgeting and is used for social welfare programmes.

Characteristic

1. Profit orientation is not the criteria. Rather focus is on resulting in public well-being.
2. Targets are physical units.

3. Success in implementing the budget is measured in terms of (a) over and under achievement of the targets, and (b) resources spend in achieving the targets.
4. The shortcomings in implementation and the difficulties faced should be thoroughly analysed so that these are avoided while extending the similar programme or taking up new programmes.
5. Identification of national goals with greater precision.
6. Long-term costs are projected and related with the benefit of each programme.
7. It fails to reflect the operation and execution process of the programme. Since targets are not defined in monetary terms.
8. It does not serve as an operating tool for the executives who are responsible for the implementation of the policy and programme decisions.
9. The process of funding the programmes and fixation of priorities for different levels of effect are not stated in the programme budgeting.
10. Evaluation of the activities and operations of on-going programmes is not focused and the emphasis is on the new programmes. This is the reason why it is so commonly used by the Government and NPOs.

PERFORMANCE BUDGETING

Performance budget is the comparative analysis of actual costs incurred with the planned allocation of cost in achieving the set target. It relates the monetary cost and corresponding benefit of a particular activity.

Characteristics

1. It simplifies budget formulation process.
2. Coordinates departmental, objectives with the objectives of the organisation.
3. Ensures optimal utilisation of resources and also optimal allocation of the resources.
4. Financial activities are well controlled with the performance budgeting.
5. Performance budgeting ignores qualitative variables. Only quantitative variables which can be expressed in monetary terms are entertained.

Comparison between Programme Budgeting and Performance Budgeting

	Basis	Programme Budgeting	Performance Budgeting
1.	Meaning	It is output budgeting	It is comparative analysis of planned and actual cost.
2.	Approach	It is forward looking	It evaluates projects completed.
3.	Emphasis	It emphasis on the achievement of objectives.	It emphasises on the way the objectives can be achieved.
4.	Management	More relevant to top level management.	More relevant to middle and lower level management.

ZERO BASE BUDGETING (ZBB)

A budgeting technique where all activities are revaluated each time a budget is set. Discretre levels of each activity are valued and a combination is chosen to match funds available. ZBB tries to locate these activities which are not essential and they do not form part of the future operations of the organisation.

Characteristics

1. It starts budgeting of all items from the scratch. All items are considered afresh.
2. It focuses on why the organisation or the department needs to spend on any particular activity.
3. Its main purpose is to eliminate the not very useful activities and diverts fund allocation to the more useful activities.
4. A meticulous cost-benefit analysis is conducted before allocation.
5. Results in efficient and effective allocation of resources.
6. Non-profitable activities are identified and eliminated.
7. Generates psychological pressure on the employees to avoid wasteful expenditure.
8. Since all the activities are analysed on cost-benefit basis, managers may resist new ideas.

ZBB is a cost-benefit approach whereby it is assumed that the cost allowance for an item is zero, and will remain so until the manager responsible justifies the existence of the cost item and the benefits the expenditure brings. In this way a questioning attitude is developed whereby each cost item and its level has to be justified in relation to the way it helps to meet objectives and hew the expenditure benefits the organisation. This is a forward looking approach as opposed to the all too common method of extrapolating past activities and costs, which is a feature of the incremental budgeting approach.

ZBB is formally defined by the CIMA as a method of budgeting whereby all activities are re-evaluated each time a budget is formulated. Each functional budget starts with the assumption that the function does not exist and is at zero cost. Increments of cost are compared with increments of benefit, culminating in the planning maximum benefit for a given budgeted cost.

ZBB can be applied in both profit seeking and non-profit seeking organisations. The technique gained wide publicity when the then President Carter directed that all US government departments adopt zero base budget.

In a manufacturing firm. It is best applied to service and support expenditure including, administration, marketing, personnel, information and computer services, research and development, finance and accounting, production planning and so on. These activities are less easily quantifiable by conventional methods and are more discretionary in nature. Manufacturing costs such as direct materials and labour and production overheads can be more easily controlled by well established methods which compare production outputs with resource inputs rather than using ZBB. Budgeting and controlling manufacturing expenditure uses techniques such as work study and standard costing which are described later in the manual.

Zero base budget can successfully be applied to service industries and to a wide range of non-profit seeking orgnisations. For example, local and central government departments, educational establishments, hospitals and so on. It could be applied in any organisation where alternative levels of provision for each activity are possible and the costs and benefits can be separately identified. It is concerned with alternatives and means that established activities have to be compared with alternative uses of the same resources. It takes away the implied right of existing activities to continue to receive resources, unless it can be shown that this is the best use of those resources.

There are several formal stages involved in implementing this type of budget but of greater importance is the appropriate questioning attitude by all be a 'value for money' approach which challenges existing practices and expenditures and searching questions must be asked at each stage.

The overall process of implementing this type of budget can be subdivided into three stages thus.

I. Definition of Decision Packages

A decision package is a comprehensive description of a facet of the organisation's activities or functions which can be individually evaluated. The decision package is specified by the managers concerned and must show details of the anticipated costs and result expected expressed in terms of tasks accomplished and benefits achieved.

Two types of decision packages are possible:

(a) **Mutually-exclusive Decision Packages.** These are alternative forms of activity, tasks and expenditure to carry out the same job. The best option among the mutually exclusive packages is selected by comparing costs and benefits, and the other packages are then discarded. Naturally, mutually–would only be prepared when the different approaches for dealing with the same function. As an example, an organisation with a distribution problem might cons: decision packages: Package 2 m fleet of lorries, whereas Package 2 could involve contracts with independent hauliers.

(b) **Incremental Decision Packages.** These packages reflect different levels of effort > in dealing with a particular activity. There will be what is known as the base package, which represents the minimum feasible level of activity, and other packages which describe higher activity levels at given costs and resulting benefits. As an example, a base package for a personnel department might provide for staff engagement and termination procedures and payroll administration. Incremental packages might include: education and training, welfare and social activities, pension administration, trade union liaison and negotiations, etc. Each package would have its costs and benefits clearly tabulated.

II. Packages are Evaluated and Ranked

When the decision packages have been prepared, management will then rank all the packages or the basis of their benefits to the organisation. This is a process of allocating scarce resources between different activities, some of which already exist and other than that are new.

Minimum requirements which are essential to get the job done and activities necessary to meet legal or safety obligation will naturally receive high priority. It will be found that the ranking process focuses management's attention on discretionary or optional activities.

Because of the large number of packages prepared throughout the organisation the ranking process can become onerous and time consuming for senior management. One way of reducing this problem is for lower level managers to rank the packages for their own budget centre and for these rankings to be consolidated, with others, at the next level up the hierarchy. Alternatively, there could be a cut-off-limits for expenditure so that packages for a lower amount say less than £2000, could be ranked within the department and need not be referred higher.

III. Resources are Allocated

When the overall budgeted expenditure level is decided upon the packages would be accepted in the ranked priority. Sequence up to the agreed expenditure level.

Where the ranking of lower cost packages has been delegated to departments the proportion of the expenditure budget remaining after the more expensive packages have been ranked would be allocated to individual departments. The departments would then rank their own small package up to their allocated expenditure level.

Advantages of Zero Base Budget

(a) It is a systematic way of challenging the *status quo* and obliges the organisation to examine alternative activities and existing cost behaviour patterns and expenditure levels.

(b) This leads to greater staff and management knowledge of the operations and activities of the organisations and can increase motivation.

(c) It develops a questioning attitude and makes it easier to identify ineficient, obsolete or less cost-efective operations.

(d) It focuses attention on the value for money and makes explicit the relationship between the input of resources and the output of benefits.

(e) Properly carried out, it should result in more efficient allocation of resources to activities and departments.

Disadvantages of Zero Base Budget

(a) It may emphasise short term benefits to the detriment of longer term ones which in the end may be more important.

(b) ZBB is not always acceptable to staff or management or trade unions who may prefer the cosy *status quo* and who see the detailed examination of alternatives, costs and benefits as a threat not a challenge.

(c) There are considerable problems in ranking packages and there are inevitable many subjective judgements. Political pressures within organisations also contribute to the problem of ranking diferent types of activity, especially where there are qualitative rather than quantitative benefits.

(d) It may encourage the wrong impression that all decisions have to be made in the budget. Circumstances change and new opportunities and threats can arise at any time and organisations must be flexible enough to deal rapidly with these circumstances when they occur.
(e) There is considerable management skill required in both drawing up decision packages and for the ranking process. These skills may not exist in the organisation.
(f) It is a time consuming process which can generate volumes of paper work especially for the decision packages.

SOLVED PRACTICAL PROBLEMS

Problem 1 Okay Limited has prepared a budget for the production of 50000 units of the only commodity manufactured by them as a period as under:

Details (Per Unit)	Amount (₹)
Raw materials	65.00
Direct wages	18.75
Direct expenses	3.75
Works overhead (60% fixed)	60.50
Administration overhead (20% variable)	10.00
Selling overhead (50% fixed)	5.00

The actual production during the period was only 30,000 units. Calculate revised budget cost per unit.

Solution:

Details	Per unit (₹)	Total for 50,000 units	Per unit (₹)	Total for 30,000 units
Raw material	65.00	325000	65.00	1950000
Direct wages	18.75	937500	18.75	562500
Direct expenses	3.75	137500	3.75	82500
Variable overheads: • Works 24.20 • Adm. 2.00 • Selling 2.50	28.70	1475000	28.70	861000
Total variable cost	116.20	5760000	116.20	3456000
Fixed overheads: • Works 36.20 • Adm. 8.00 • Selling 2.50	46.80	234000	46.80	1404000
Total	163	8100000	163	4860000

Problem 2 From the following figures of the previous quarters, prepare a production overhead budget for the quarter ending on June 30, the budgeted output during this quarter is 4000 units.

Expenses	Amount (₹)
Fixed overheads	3,00,000
Variable overheads @ 40 unit	1,00,000
Semi fixed overheads (40% Fixed, 60% Variable @ 30 per unit)	1,00,000

Solution:

Production Overhead Budget
(For the quarter ending on 30.06 ....)

Expenses		Amount (₹)
Fixed overheads		3,00,000
Variable overheads (40 × 4000)		1,60,000
Semi-fixed overheads		
• Fixed	40,000	
• Variable	1,20,000	1,60,000
Total overheads		6,20,000

Problem 3 Anderson Limited has estimated the percentage of total production and percentage of total production cost for each month in relation to the total for the second quarter to be as follows:

July	40%
August	30%
September	30%

The estimated costs for the second quarter are:

Direct materials	₹2,50,000
Direct labour	₹1,50,000
Factory overhead	₹1,00,000

Estimated ending inventories of finished goods are:

June	₹1,00,000
July	₹ 80,000
August	₹1,20,000
September	₹1,30,000

Solution:

Anderson Ltd. Cost of Goods Sold Budget

Details	July	August	September	Total
Direct material	1,00,000	75,000	75,000	2,50,000
Direct labour	60,000	45,000	45,000	1,50,000
Factory overhead	40,000	30,000	30,000	1,00,000
Total manufacturing cost	2,00,000	1,50,000	1,50,000	5,00,000
Add: Finished goods (beginning)	1,00,000	80,000	1,20,000	1,00,000
Finished goods available for sale	3,00,000	2,30,000	2,70,000	6,00,000
Less: Finished goods (ending)	80,000	1,20,000	1,30,000	1,30,000
Cost of goods sold	2,20,000	1,10,000	1,40,000	4,70,000

Problem 4 Trans India Corporation anticipates Sales ₹ 50,00,000 for the current year. The percentage of gross profit from sales has been 30% in past years. Operating expenses are expected to be ₹ 10,00,000 of which 40% is administrative expenses and 60% is selling and distribution expenses. Assuming a 30% tax rate, prepare a budget income statement for the Multi Sales Corporation for the year 2021-22

Solution:

Multi Sales Corporation

BUDGET INCOME STATEMENT for 2021-22

Details	Amount (₹)	Percentage
Sales	50,00,000	100
Cost of goods sold	35,00,000	70
Gross profit	15,00,000	30
Operating expenses		
Selling & distribution expenses	6,00,000	13.40
Administrative	4,00,000	10.60
Total	10,00,000	24.00
Net Income before Taxes	5,00,000	10.00
Income of TZX @ 30%	1,50,000	3
Net income after taxes	3,50,000	7

Problem 5 Following data pertains to Mr. Sharma for the monthly budget for October 2020.

Item	Amount (₹)
Direct material used	845
Beginning finished goods inventory	?

Table Contd...

Table Contd...

Item	Amount (₹)
Ending finished goods inventory	94
Direct manufacturing labour	380
Manufacturing overhead	?
Cost of goods manufactured	1875
Cost of goods sold	?
Cost of goods available for sale	1950

Prepare the cost of goods sold budget for the month of October 2020 by filling the missing figures.

Solution:

(i) Cost of goods manufacture = Direct materials + Direct manufacturing labour + Manufacturing overhead.

$$1875 = 845 + 380 + \text{MOH}$$

$$\text{MOH} = 1875 - 845 - 380 = 650$$

(ii) Cost of goods available for sale = Cost of goods manufactured + Beginning finished goods inventory

$$1950 = 1875 + \text{Beginning finished goods inventory}$$

$$\text{B.F.I.} = 1950 - 1875$$

$$= 75$$

(iii) C.G.S. = Cost of goods available for sale – Ending finished goods inventory

$$= 1950 - 94$$

$$\text{Cast of goods} = ₹\,1856$$

COST OF GOODS SOLD FOR THE MONTH OCTOBER 2020

Elements of Cost	Amount (₹)
Direct material used	845
Direct manufacturing labour	380
Manufacturing overhead	650
Cost of goods manufactured	1875
Add: Beginning finished goods inventory	75
Cost of goods available for sale	1950
Less: Ending finished goods inventory	94
Cost of goods sold	1856

Problem 6 With the following data for 70% capacity utilisation prepare a budget for 60%, 80% and 100% capacity, production at 90% capacity = 1820 units, material 100, labour ₹ 50

expenses ₹20, factor overheads ₹1,50,000 (60% fixed), administration overheads ₹1,40,000 (80% fixed).

Solution:

Details	60% (1560)	70% (1820)	80% (2080)	100% (2600)
Material @ 100/unit	1,56,000	1,82,000	2,08,000	2,60,000
Labour @ 50/unit	78,000	91,000	104,000	1,30,000
Expenses @ 20/unit	31,200	36,400	41,600	52,000
Factory overhead @ 32.96	51,428	60,000	68,571	85,714
Adm. overhead @ 15.38	24,000	28,000	32,000	40,000
Total variable cost	3,40,628	3,97,400	4,54,171	5,67,714
Per unit	(218.35)	(218.35)	(218.35)	(218.35)
Fixed cost				
Factory overheads	90,000	90,000	90,000	90,000
Adm. overheads	1,12,000	1,12,000	1,12,000	1,12,000
Total fixed cost	2,02,000	2,02,000	2,02,000	2,02,000
Per unit	(129.48)	(110.98)	(97.11)	(77.69)
Total cost	54,628	59,400	6,56,171	7,69,714
Per unit	(347.83)	(329.34)	(315.46)	(296.04)

Problem 7 Kohan Ltd. requires you to calculate and present the master budget for the next year from the following information:

Sales:	
Produet P1	₹8,00,000
Product P2	₹5,00,000
Product P3	₹5,00,000
Direct materials	50% of Sales
Direct wages	10 workers@ ₹2500 p.m.
Factory overheads	
Salary of works manager	₹20,000 p.m.
Supervisor's salary	₹12000 p.m.
Stores & spares	2% of sales
Depreciation of machine	₹50,000
Light & power	₹25000
Repairs and maintenance	₹20,000

Administration, selling and distribution expenses 50,000 per year

Solution:

MASTER BUDGET

For the year ending on ....

Details			Amount (₹)
Sales (As per sales budget)			
Product P1		₹8,00,000	
Product P2		₹5,00,000	
Product P3		₹5,00,000	1,80,000
Less: Cost of production			
Direct materials		₹9,00,000	
Direct wages		₹3,00,000	
Prime cost		₹12,00,000	
Factory overheads			
Variable			
Stores & spares	36000		
Light & power	25000		
Repair & maintenance	15000	76000	
Fixed			
Salary of works manager	2,40,000		
Supervisor's salary	1,44,000		
Depreciation on machine	50,000	4,34,000	
Total works cost			17,10,000
Gross profit			90,000
Less: Adm. selling & administration expenses			50,000
Net profit			40,000

Problem 8 ABC Ltd. has supplied the following summary of its operating results for the year ending 31.03.2020

Details	Amount (₹)
Sales (80,000 units)	96.00
Less: Trade discount	4.80
Net sales	91.20
Cost of sales	
Direct materials	28.80
Direct wages	25.20
Factory overhead	12.60
Administrative overhead	7.20
Selling & distribution overhead	9.00

Te following changes are to be incorporated in the budget for the year ending 31.03.2021.

(i) Sales quantity to be increased by 25%

(ii) Material prices are to be increased by 15%

(iii) Factory overhead will increase by 15%. In addition a new facility will be added to the factory at a recurring cost of ₹ 30,000.

(iv) Administration & selling and distribution overheads are estimated to go up by 10% and 15% respectively.

(v) Direct wages rates to go up by 12%.

You are required to present the budget for the year ending 31.03.2021 showing the details of total cost, sales and profit.

Solution: Budget quantity = 80,000 (1.25) = 1,00,000

Rate of trade discount $\frac{4.80}{96} \times 100 = 5\%$

Selling price per unit = 120

Budget for the year ending 31.03.2021

Details	Amount (₹)
Sales (1,00,000 × 120)	120,00,000
Less: Trade discount @ 5%	6,00,000
Net sales	1,14,00,000
Less: Cost of sales	
Direct material (28,80,000 × 1.25 × 1.15)	41,40,000
Direct wages (25,20,000 × 1.25 × 1.12)	35,28,000
Factory overhead (12,60,000 × 1.15)	14,49,000
Additional factory overhead	30,000
Administrative overhead (7,20,000 × 1.10)	7,92,000
Selling & distribution overhead (9,00,000 × 1.15)	10,35,000
Total cost	1,09,74,000
Profit	4,26,000

Problem 9 For production of 10,000 blenders, the following are budgeted expenses:

	Per unit (₹)
Direct materials	60
Direct labour	30
Variable overheads	25
Fixed production overheads (₹ 1,00,000)	10

	(₹)
Direct expenses	5
Selling expenses (10% fixed)	15
Administration expenses (₹ 50,000 fixed for all levels of production)	5
Distribution expenses 20% fixed	5
Cost per unit	155

Prepare a production cost budget for 6000, 7000 and 8000 blenders.

Solution:

Flexible budget

	Output 6000 units		Output 7000 units		Output 8000 units	
	Cost per unit	Total Cost	Cost per unit	Total Cost	Cost per unit	Total Cost
	₹	₹	₹	₹	₹	₹
Variable Cost:						
Direct materials	60.00	3,60,000	60.00	4,20,000	60.00	4,80,000
Direct labour	30.00	1,80,000	30.00	2,10,000	30.00	2,40,000
Variable overheads	25.00	1,50,000	20.00	1,75,000	25.00	2,00,000
Direct expenses	5.00	30,000	5.00	35,000	5.00	40,000
Semi-Variable Cost:						
Selling expenses variable (90% of ₹ 15)	13.50	81.000	13.50	94,500	13.50	1,08,000
Fixed (10% of ₹ 15 × 10,000)	2.50	15,000	2.14	15,000	1.88	15,000
Distribution expenses						
Variable (80% of ₹ 5)	4.00	24,000	4.00	28,000	4.00	32,000
Fixed (20% of ₹ 5 × 10,000)	1.67	10,000	1.43	10,000	1.25	10,000
Fixed Overheads:						
Production overheads	20.00	1,20,000	17.14	1,20,000	15	1,20,000
Administration expenses	8.33	50,000	7.14	50,000	6.25	50,000
Total Cost	170.00	10,20,000	165.35	11,57,500	161.88	12,95,000

Problem 10 B Ltd. incurs the following expenses to produce 2000 units of an article:

	₹
Direct materials	60,000
Direct labour	30,000
Power [20% fixed]	20,000
Repairs & maintenance [15% fixed]	16,000
Depreciation (40% variable)	12,000
Administrative expenses (100% fixed]	30,000

Prepare a flexible budget showing the individual expenses of production levels at 3000 units and 4000 units.

Solution:

Flexible Budget of B Ltd.

Particulars	At 3000 units		At 4000 units	
	Per Unit (₹)	Total (₹)	Per Unit (₹)	Total (₹)
Direct materials[1]	30.00	90,000	30	1,20,000
Direct labour[2]	15.00	45,000	15	60,000
Power[3]	9.33	28,000	9	36,000
Repairs & maintenance[4]	7.60	22,800	7.40	29,600
Depreciation[5]	4.80	14,400	4.20	16,800
Administrative expenses[6]	10.00	30,000	7.50	30,000
Total Cost	121.73	2,30,200	73.10	2,92,400

Working Notes:

1. Power

At the production level of 2000 units, power = ₹20,000, which includes 20% fixed portion and balance 80% variable portion.

(a) *At the production level of 2000 units*

Fixed power [20% of ₹20,000]	4000
Variable power [80% of ₹20,000]	16,000
Total power	20,000

∴ Variable power per unit = ₹16,000 ÷ 2000 = ₹8

(b) *At the production level of 3000 units,*

Variable power [13000 unit]	24,000
Fixed power [as it was at 2000 units]	4000
Total power at 3000 units of production	28,000

(c) *At the production level of 4000 unts*

Variable power [4000 units × ₹8]	32,000
Fixed power [as it was at 2000 units]	4000
Total power at 4000 units of production	36,000

2. Repairs and Maintenance

At the production level of 2000 units, repairs and maintenance is ₹16,000, which includes 15% of fixed portion and balance 85% of variable portion.

(a) *At the production level of 2000 units*

Fixed repairs & maintenance (15% of ₹16,000)	2,400
Variable repairs & maintenance (85% of ₹16,000)	13,600
Total repairs & maintenance	16,000

∴ Variable repairs and maintenance per unit = ₹13,600 ÷ 2000 = ₹6.80

(b) *At the production level of 3000 units*

Variable repairs & maintenance (3000 units × ₹6.80]	20,400
Fixed repairs & maintenance (as it was at 2000 units]	2,400
Total repairs & maintenance at 3000 units of production	22,800

(c) *At the production level of 4000 units*

Variable repairs & maintenance (4000 units ₹6.80]	27,200
Fixed repairs & maintenance (as it was at 2000 units]	2,400
Total repairs & maintenance at 4000 units of production	29,600

3. Depreciation

At the production level of 2000 units, depreciation is ₹12,000, which includes 40% of variable portion and balance 60% of fixed portion.

(a) *At the production level of 2000 units*

Fixed depreciation (60% of 12000]	7,200
Variable depreciation [40% of 12000]	4,800
Total depreciation	12,000

∴ Variable depreciation per unit = ₹4800 – 2000 = ₹2.40

(b) *At the production level of 3000 units*

Variable depreciation [3000 units × 2.40]	7,200
Fixed depreciation (as it was at 2000 units)	7,200
Total depreciation at 3000 units of production	14,400

(c) *At the production level of 4000 units*

Variable depreciation [4000 units × ₹2.40]	9,600
Fixed depreciation (as it was at 2000 units)	7,200
Total depreciation at 4000 units of production	16,800

4. Administrative Expenses

Administrative expenses are ₹30,000, which is 100% fixed. It remains same at all levels of production.

Problem 11 The information relating to the budget prepared for two levels of capacity utilisation is given as follows:

Capacity Output (units)	60% 36000	100% 60000
Direct materials	3,60,000	6,00,000
Direct wages	2,16,000	3,60,000
Production overhead	5,40,000	7,56,000
Administrative overhead	1,80,000	1,80,000
Selling overhead	1,44,000	1,92,000

Prepare a flexible budget for 70%, 80% and 90% capacity utilisation showing clearly the unit fixed cost, unit variable cost and total cost. [*B.Com. (H)*]

Solution:

Flexible Budget

Particulars	At 70% Capacity (42,000 Units)		At 80% Capacity (49,000 Units)		At 90% Capacity (54,000 Units)	
	p.u.	Total	p.u.	Total	p.u.	Total
Variable Cost:						
Direct materials	10	4,20,000	10	4,80,000	10	5,40,000
Direct wages	6	2,52,000	6	2,88,000	6	3,24,000
Variable production overheads	9	3,78,000	9	4,32,000	9	4,86,000
Variable selling overheads	2	84,000	2	96,000	2	1,08,000
	27	11,34,000	27	12,96,000	27	14,58,000
Fixed Cost:						
Administrative overheads	4.29	1,80,000	3.75	1,80,000	3.33	1,80,000
Fixed production overheads	5.14	2,16,000	4.50	2,16,000	4.00	2,16,000
Fixed selling overheads	1.71	72,000	1.50	72,000	1.33	72,000
	11.14	4,68,000	9.75	4,68,000	8.66	4,68,000
Total Cost	38.14	16,02,000	36.75	17,64,000	35.66	19,26,000

Working Notes:

1. Production at 100% capacity = 60,000 units

 ∴ Production at 70% capacity = 70% of 60,000 = 42,000 units

 ∴ Production at 80% capacity = 80% of 60,000 = 48,000 units

 ∴ Production at 90% capacity = 90% of 60,000 = 54,000 units

2. Production Overheads

Total production overheads at 60000 units of output	7,56,000
Total production overheads at 36000 units of output	5,40,000
Difference in cost	₹2,16,000

$$\text{Variable cost per unit} = \frac{\text{Difference in cost}}{\text{Difference in units}}$$

∴ Variable production overhead per unit = ₹2,16,000 ÷ 24,000 units = ₹9

Now, at 60,000 units of output

Total production overheads	7,56,000
Less: Variable production overheads [60000 units × ₹9]	5,40,000
∴ Fixed production overheads	2,16,000

3. Selling Overheads

Total selling overheads at 60000 units of output	1,92,000
Total selling overheads at 36000 units of output	1,44,000
Difference in cost	₹48,000

$$\text{Variable cost per unit} = \frac{\text{Difference in cost}}{\text{Difference in units}}$$

Variable selling overheads per unit = ₹48,000 ÷ 24000 units = ₹2

Now, at 60,000 units of output:

Total selling overheads	1,92,000
Less: Variable selling overheads [60000 units × ₹2]	1,20,000
Fixed selling overheads	72,000

Problem 12 Flip Flop Ltd. attains sales of ₹6,00,000 at 80% of its normal capacity. Its expenses are given below:

	₹
Administration Costs:	
Office salaries	90,000
General expenses	2% of sales
Depreciation	7,500
Rent and rates	8,750
Selling Costs:	
Salaries	8% of sales
Travelling expenses	2% of sales
Sales office	1% of sales
General expenses	1% of sales

Distribution Costs:

Wages	15,000
Rent	1% of sales
Other expenses	4% of sales

Draw up flexible administration, selling and distribution costs budget, operating at 90%, 100% and 110% of normal capacity. [*B.Com.*]

Flexible Budget for the period ....

	80% (₹)	90% (₹)	100% (₹)	110% (₹)
Sales	6,00,000	6,75,000	7,50,000	8,25,000
Administration Costs:				
Office salaries (fixed)	90,000	90,000	90,000	90,000
General expenses (2% of sales)	12,000	13,500	15,000	16,500
Depreciation (fixed)	7500	7500	7500	7500
Rent and rates (fixed)	8750	8750	8750	8750
(a) Total Adm. Costs	1,18,250	1,19,750	1,21,250	1,22,750
Selling Costs:				
Salaries (8% of sales)	48,000	54,000	60,000	66,000
Travelling expenses (2% of sales)	12,000	13,500	15,000	16,500
Sales office (1% of sales)	6000	6750	7500	8250
General expenses (1% of sales)	6000	6750	7500	8250
(b) Total selling costs	72,000	81,000	90,000	99,000
Distribution Costs:				
Wages (fixed)	15,000	15,000	15,000	15,000
Rent (1% of sales)	6000	6750	7500	8250
Other expenses (4% of sales):	24,000	27,000	30,000	33,000
(c) Total distribution costs	45,000	48,750	52,500	56,250
Total Cost (a + b + c)	2,35,250	2,49,500	2,63,750	2,78,000

Working Note:

All fixed costs are assumed to remain unchanged even at 110% capacity. However, in practice, fixed costs may also change when capacity utilisation exceeds 100%.

Problem 13 The following data are available in a manufacturing company for a year period :

Fixed Expenses

	₹ (Thousands)
Wages and salaries	950
Rent, rates and taxes	660

	₹
Depreciation	740
Sundry administrative expenses	650
Semi-variable Expenses (at 50% capacity)	
Maintenance and repairs	350
Indirect labour	790
Sales department salaries, etc.	380
Sundry administrative expenses	280
Variable Expenses (at 50% of capacity)	
Materials	2170
Labour	2040
Other expenses	790
	9,800

Assume that the fixed expenses remain constant for all levels of production, semi-variable expenses remain constant between 45% and 65% of capacity increasing by 10% between 65% and 80% capacity and by 20% between 80% and 100% capacity.

Sales at various levels are :

	(₹ lakhs)
50% capacity	100
60% capacity	120
75% capacity	150
90% capacity	180
100% capacity	200

Prepare a flexible budget for the year and forecast the profits at 60%, 75%, 90% and 100% of capacity.

Solution:

Flexible Budget **₹ (Thousands)**

Particulars	50% Capacity	60% Capacity	75% Capacity	90% Capacity	100% Capacity
A. Sales	10000	12000	15000	18000	20000
Variable Expenses :					
Materials	2170	2604	3255	3906	4340
Labour	2040	2448	3060	3672	4080
Other expenses	790	948	1185	1422	1580
Semi-variable Expenses					
Maintenance and repairs	350	350	385	420	420
Indirect labour	790	790	869	948	948

Table Contd...

Table Contd...

Sales department salaries, etc.	380	380	418	456	456
Sundry administrative expenses	280	280	308	336	336
Fixed Expenses :					
Wages and salaries	950	950	950	950	950
Rent, rates and taxes	660	660	660	660	660
Depreciation	740	740	740	740	740
Sundry administrative expenses	650	650	650	650	650
B. Total cost	9800	10,800	12,480	14,160	15,160
Profit (A – B)	200	1200	2520	3840	4840

Problem 14 Dreamline Ltd. produces 4000 shirts per month of a certain product at 100% capacity. The following information is obtained:

	Aug.	Sept.
Units produced	2800	3600
	₹	₹
Repairs and maintenance	500	560
Power	1,800	2,000
Shop labour	700	900
Consumable stores	1,400	1,800
Salaries	1,000	1,000
Inspection	200	240
Depreciation	1,400	1,400

Rate of production per hour is 10 units. Direct material cost per unit is ₹1 and direct wages per hour is ₹4.

You are required to:

(i) Compute the cost of production at 100%, 80% and 60% capacity showing the variable, fixed and semi-variable items under the flexible budget.

(ii) Find out the overhead absorption rate per unit at 80% capacity. [*B.Com. (H)*]

Solution:

(i) Flexible Budget of Dreamline Ltd. for the period.....

Particulars	100% 4000 units	80% 3200 units	60% 2400 units
Variable costs :			
Direct materials (@₹1 per unit)	4000	3200	2400
Direct wages [@₹4 per hour for 10 units]	1600	1280	960
Shop labour	1000	800	600

Table Contd...

Table Contd...

Particulars	100% 4000 units	80% 3200 units	60% 2400 units
	₹	₹	₹
Consumable stores	2000	1600	1200
Total (a)	8600	6880	5160
Semi-variable overheads:			
Power	2100	1900	1700
Inspection	260	220	180
Repairs and maintenance	590	530	470
Total (b)	2950	2650	2350
Fixed costs:			
Salaries	1000	1000	1000
Depreciation	1400	1400	1400
Total (c)	2400	2400	2400
Total cost (a + b + c)	13,950	11,930	9910

(ii) *Overhead absorption rate (at 80% capacity)*

$$\text{Overhead cost} = \text{Total cost} - \text{Direct material} - \text{Direct wages}$$
$$11{,}930 - 3{,}200 - 1{,}280 = ₹7{,}450$$
$$\text{Overhead rate per unit} = ₹7{,}450 \div 3200 \text{ units} = ₹2.33$$

Working Notes:

1. Power cost

$$\text{Variable power cost per unit} = \frac{\text{Difference in cost}}{\text{Difference in units}} = \frac{₹2000 - ₹1800}{3600 - 2800 \text{ units}}$$
$$= \frac{200}{800} = ₹0.25$$

$$\text{Fixed power cost (at 70\%)} = \text{Total cost} - \text{Variable cost}$$
$$= 1800 - (2800 \times 0.25) = ₹1100$$
$$\text{Total power cost at 100\%} = 1100 + (4000 \text{ units} \times 0.25) = ₹2100$$
$$\text{Total power cost at 80\%} = 1100 + (3200 \text{ units} \times 0.25) = ₹1900$$
$$\text{Total power cost at 60\%} = 1100 + (2400 \text{ units} \times 0.25) = ₹1700$$

2. In the same manner, calculation for inspection cost and repairs and maintenance cost is done.

Problem 15 X Ltd. is currently operating at 75% of its capacity. In the past two years the level of operations were 55% and 65% respectively. Presently, the production is 75,000 units. The company is planning for 85% capacity level during 2021–22. The cost details are as follow:

Particulars	55%	65%	75%
	₹	₹	₹
Direct materials	11,00,000	13,00,000	15,00,000
Direct labour	5,50,000	6,50,000	7,50,000
Factory overheads	3,10,000	3,30,000	3,50,000
Selling overheads	3,20,000	3,60,000	4,00,000
Administrative overheads	1,60,000	1,60,000	1,60,000
	24,40,000	28,00,000	31,60,000

Profit is estimated @ 20% on sales. The following increases in costs are expected during the year:

	(%)
Direct materials	10
Direct labour	20
Variable factory overheads	5
Variable selling overheads	5
Fixed factory overheads	7.5
Fixed selling overheads	10
Administrative overheads	25

Prepare a flexible budget for the period 2021–22 at 85% level of capacity and ascertain the profit on sales [*B.Com. (H)*]

Solution:

Flexible budget for the period 2020-21

(Production: 85,000 units)

Particulars	Amount (₹)
Direct materials[1] @ (₹20 + 10% = 22)	18,70,000
Direct labour[1] @ (₹10 + 20% =12)	10,20,000
Factory overhead[2]:	
Fixed (2,00,000 + 7.5%)	2,15,000
Variable (₹2 + 5% = 2.10)	1,78,500
Administration overhead[3] (1,60,000 + 25%)	2,00,000
Selling overhead:	
Fixed (1,00,000 + 10%)	1,10,000
Variable (₹4 + 5% = 4.20)	3,57,000
Total cost	39,50,500
Profit (20% on sales or 25% on cost)	9,87,625
Sales	49,38,125

Working Notes:

1. Direct material cost and direct labour cost are increasing in the same proportion as the level of output, therefore are variable costs.
2. Factory overhead and selling overhead are semi-variable items and are segregated by the following methods:

$$\text{Variable overhead per unit} = \frac{\text{Difference in overhead at two levels}}{\text{Difference in output}}$$

$$\text{Variable factory overhead} = \frac{₹3{,}30{,}000 - 3{,}50{,}000}{10000 \text{ units}} = ₹2 \text{ per unit}$$

$$\text{Fixed factory overhead} = ₹3{,}30{,}000 - (65000 \text{ units} \times ₹2)$$
$$= ₹2{,}00{,}000$$

Similar calculation may be made for selling overhead.

3. The administration overheads remain constant at all levels, hence is a fixed cost.

Problem 16 The performance of a company at two levels of operations during a financial year is as follows:

Capacity utilisation	50%	60%
Direct materials	₹1,50,000	1,80,000
Direct wages	₹2,40,000	2,88,000
Production overheads	₹9,00,000	9,75,000
Administration overheads	₹1,80,000	1,80,000
Selling overheads	₹3,30,000	3,60,000

The company produced 12,000 units at 60% capacity utilisation. The profit margin is 20% on sales.

During the next financial year, the company is poised for increasing the capacity utilisation to 75%. The company desired to have the same profit margin as in the last financial year. The following percentage changes in costs are expected to be applicable in the next year.

- Direct material prices will increase by 5%
- Direct wage rates will increase by 3%
- Direct labour efficiency will fall by 4%
- Variable production overheads will increase by 6%
- Fixed production overheads will increase by 10%, up to 80% capacity utilisation and by 22% thereafter.
- Variable selling expenses will increase by 10%
- Fixed selling expenses will increase by 8%
- Administrative overheads will increase by 15%

The company expects to receive an export order for 3000 units while operating at 75% capacity utilisation, the anticipated export price offer is ₹138 per unit.

1. Prepare a flexible budget for the next year and determine the cost per unit of output at the capacity utilisation levels of 75% and 90%.
2. Calculate the sales value and profit for the next year at 75% capacity.
3. Advise the manager as to whether or not the export order at the price of ₹138 per unit should be accepted.

Solution:

1. Analysis of semi-variable overheads into fixed and variable elements

Particulars	50% Capacity	60% Capacity	Difference
Production quantity	10,000 units	12,000 units (given)	2000 units
Total production overhead	₹9,00,000	₹9,75,000	₹75,000
Total selling overhead	₹3,30,000	₹3,60,000	₹30,000

Hence, variable production overhead

= Change in production overheads ÷ Change in output

= ₹75,000 + 2000 units = ₹37.5 per unit

Fixed production overhead

= ₹9,00,000 – (10000 units × ₹37.6) = ₹5,25,000

Also variable selling overhead

= Change in selling overhead ÷ Change in output

= ₹30,000 ÷ 2000 units = ₹15 per unit

Fixed selling overhead

= ₹3,60,000 – (12000 units × ₹15) = ₹1,80,000

2. Flexible budget for next year

Particulars	60%	75%	90%
Output (Units)	12,000	15,000	18,000
Materials	1,89,000	2,36,250	2,83,500
Labour	3,08,550	3,85,632	4,62,758
Production overheads			
Variable	4,77,000	5,96,250	7,15,500
Fixed	5,77,500	5,77,500	6,40,500
Admn. overhead (fixed)	2,07,000	2,07,000	2,07,000
Selling overhead (variable)	1,98,000	2,47,500	2,97,000
Fixed	1,94,400	1,94,400	1,94,400
Total costs	21,51,450	24,44,532	28,00,658
Cost per unit	179.29	162.97	155.59

3. Computation Sales Value at 75% Capacity:

Since profit is 20% on sales = 1/5 on sales = 1/4 on cost.

Sales value at 75% capacity level = ₹24,44,532 + 25% of ₹24,44,532
= ₹30,55,665

Profit at 20% thereon = 20% × 30,55,665
= ₹6,11,133

4. Incremental cost of 3,000 units:

= (28,00,658 – 24,44,532) = 3,56,126

Average incremental cost per unit = ₹53,56,126/3000 units = 118.70 per unit

Since the export price offered ₹138 is more than the incremental costs per unit, it may be accepted.

Additional profit = (₹138 × 3,000) – ₹3,56,126 = ₹57,874

Problem 17 The following are the details of the budget and the actual costs in a factory for the six months from January–June 2021. From the following information, prepare a production cost budget for Jan–June 2022.

	Budget	**Actual**
Production (units)	20,000	18,000
Materials cost	₹40,00,000	₹39,90,000
	(2,000 MT@ ₹2,000)	(1,900M'T@ ₹2,100)
Labour cost	₹8,00,000	7,99,920
	(@ ₹20 per hour)	(@ ₹22 per hour)
Variable overheads	₹2,40,000	₹2,16,000
Fixed overheads	₹4,00,000	₹4,20,000

In the first half of 2022, the production is budgeted for 25,000 units. Materials cost per tonne will increase by ₹100 from last year's actual but the consumption efficiency is proposed to be maintained as budgeted in 2021. Labour efficiency will be lower by another 1% and labour rates will be ₹22 per hour.

Variable and fixed overheads are expected to go up by 20% over 2021 actuals.

[*B.Com. (H)*]

Solution:

Production Cost Budget

(for the six months ending 30th June, 2022) **25000 units**

Particulars	Amount (₹)
Material cost[1]	55,00,000
Labour cost[2]	11,22,000
Variable overheads[3]	3,60,000
Fixed overheads[4]	5,04,000
Total cost	74,86,000

Working Notes:

1. Materials cost = $\frac{2000}{20,000}$ × 25,000 units × ₹2200 = ₹55,00,000

2. Labour cost

   2020:

   Total labour hours = $\frac{8,00,000}{20}$ = 40,000

   Labour hour per unit = $\frac{40,000}{20,000}$ = 2 hr.

   Actual labour hours = $\frac{7,99,920}{22}$ = 36,360 hr.

   Actual labour hour per unit = 36,360/18,000 = 2.02 hr.

   Hence, time per unit for 2021 (efficiency lower by another 1%) = 2.04 hr.

   Labour cost = 2.04 × 25000 units × 22

   = ₹11,22,000

3. Variable overheads:

   = $\frac{2,40,000}{20,000}$ × 25,000 × 120% 3,60,000

4. Fixed overheads:

   4,20,000 × 120% 5,04,000

Problem 18 Production costs of a factory for a year are as follows:

	₹
Direct wages	90,000
Direct materials	1,20,000
Production overheads — fixed	40,000
— variable	60,000

During the forthcoming year it is anticipated that:

(a) The average rate for direct labour remuneration will fall from ₹90 per hour to ₹75 per hour.

(b) Production efficiency will be reduced by 10%.

(c) Price per unit for direct material and of other materials and services which comprise overheads will remain unchanged.

(d) Direct labour hours will increase by 25%.

Draw up a budget and compute a factory overhead rate when the overheads are absorbed on the basis of direct wages.

Solution:

Output last year	100%
Increase due to 25% increase in labour hours	25%
	125%
Less: 10% decline in production efficiency $\left(125\% \times \frac{100}{10}\right)$	12.5%
Output in the forthcoming year	112.5%
Increase in output	12.5%

$$\text{Labour hours} = \frac{\text{Wages}}{\text{Rate per hour}} = \frac{90,000}{90} \qquad 1,000 \text{ hrs.}$$

Budget for the Forthcoming Year

Particulars	Amount (₹)
Direct material cost (1,20,000 × 112.5%)	1,35,000
Direct wages (1,000 × 125% × 75)	93,750
Prime cost	2,28,750
Production overheads:	
Fixed	40,000
Variable (₹60,000 × 112.5%)	67,500
Estimated works cost	3,36,250

$$\text{Factory overhead rate based on direct wages} = \left(\frac{\text{Production overheads}}{\text{Wages}}\right)$$

$$= \frac{1,07,500}{93,750} \times 100 = 114.66\%$$

Problem 19 From the following, prepare a production budget of Cine Vision Ltd. for the year that ended on 31 March 2022

Products	Sales as Per Sales Budget (units)	Stock on 1 April 2021 (units)	Estimated Stock on 31 March 2022 (units)
X	40,000	5000	20,000
Y	60,000	15,000	10,000
Z	30,000	10,000	5000

Solution:

Production Budget of Cine Vision Ltd.
(for the year that ended on 31 March 2022)

Particulars	X (units)	Y(units)	Z (units)
Sales as per sales budget	40000	60000	30000
Add: Closing stock [on 31 March 2022]	20000	10000	5000

Table Contd...

Table Contd...

	60,000	70,000	35,000
Less: Opening stock [on 1 April 2021]	5000	15,000	10,000
Production for the year	55,000	55,000	25,000

Problem 20 From the following particulars, prepare a purchase budget for the year 2022 when the estimated prices per kg of materials are: A: ₹5, B: ₹10 and C: ₹4.

Materials	Estimated Consumption of Materials (kg)
A	1,00,000
B	1,50,000
C	2,00,000

	Estimated Stock (kg)	
	On 1 January 2022	On 31 December 2022
A	20,000	25,000
B	40,000	30,000
C	50,000	40,000

Solution:

Materials Purchase Budget
(for the year 2022)

Particulars	Material A (kg)	Material B (kg)	Material C (kg)	Total
Consumption for the year	1,00,000	1,50,000	2,00,000	
Add: Closing stock (on 31 Dec. 2014)	25,000	30,000	40,000	
	1,25,000	1,80,000	2,40,000	
Less: Opening stock [on 1 January 2014]	20,000	40,000	50,000	
Purchase for the year	1,05,000	1,40,000	1,90,000	
Price per kg	₹5	₹10	₹4	
Cost of purchase for the year (Purchase × Price per kg)	₹5,25,000	₹14,00,000	₹7,60,000	₹26,85,000

Problem 21 The sales director of a manufacturing company reports that next year he expects to sell 80,000 units of a certain product.

The production manager consults the storekeeper and costs his figures as follows:

Two kinds of raw materials, A and B, are required for manufacturing the product. Each unit of the product requires 2 units of A and 3 units of B. The estimated opening balances at the commencement of the next year are:

Finished product—10,000 units ; A—12,000 units ; B—15,000 units.

The desirable closing balance at the end of the next year are :

Finished product—14,000 units ; A—13,000 units; B—16,000 units.

Draw up quantitative chart showing the material purchases budget for the next year.

Solution:

Material Purchases Budget

Particulars	Material A Units	Material B Units
Material usage for the production:		
Material A @ 2 units for 84,000 finished units	1,68,000	
Material B @ 3 units for 84,000 finished units		2,52,000
Add: Desired closing balance of materials at the end	13,000	16,000
	1,81,000	2,68,000
Less: Opening balances of materials at the beginning	12,000	15,000
Materials to be purchased during the budget period	1,69,000	2,53,000

Working Note:

Production = Sales + Closing stock of finished goods – Opening stock of goods

= 80000 units + 14000 units – 10000 units

= 84000 units.

Problem 22 The following are the estimated sales of Samsung Co. for about 8 months that is ending on 30 November 2021:

2021	Units	2021	Units
April	10,000	August	10,000
May	11,000	September	12,000
June	9000	October	15,000
July	8000	November	12,000

As a matter of policy, the company maintains the closing balance of finished goods and raw materials as follows:

(i) Finished goods—The closing stock of a month will be 50% of the estimated sales for the next month.

(ii) Raw material—The closing stock of a month will be equal to be estimated consumption for the next month. Each unit of production consumes 4 kg of raw material costing ₹5 per kg.

Prepare the following budgets for the half-year that is ending on 30 September 2021:

(i) Production budget (month-wise in units).

(ii) Raw material purchase budget (month-wise in units and cost).

Solution:

Production Budget
(for the half-year ending on 30 September 2021)

Particulars	April (units)	May (units)	June (units)	July (units)	August (units)	Sept. (units)	Total (units)
Sales	10,000	11,000	9000	8000	10,000	12,000	60,000
Add: Closing stock of finished goods [50% of next months' sales][1]	5500	4500	4000	5000	6000	7500	32,500
	15,500	15,500	13,000	13,000	16,000	19,500	92,500
Less: Opening stock of finished goods [150% of current months' sales]	5000	5500	4500	4000	5000	6000	30,000
Production	10,500	10,000	8500	9000	11,000	13,500	62,500

Raw Material Purchase Budget 2021
(for the half-year ending on 30 September 2021)

Particulars	April (kg)	May (kg)	June (kg)	July (kg)	August (kg)	Sept. (kg)	Total (kg)
Consumption of material [@ 4 kg per unit of production]	42,000	40,000	34,000	36,000	44,000	54,000	2,50,000
Add: Closing stock of raw material [@4 kg per unit of next months' production]	40,000	34,000	36,000	44,000	54,000	54,000	2,35,000
Less: Opening stock of raw material [@4 kg per unit of current months' estimated production][4]	42,000	40,000	34,000	36,000	44,000	54,000	2,50,000
Purchases	40,000	34,000	36,000	44,000	54,000	54,000	2,35,000
Cost of purchases @ ₹5 per kg (₹)	2,00,000	1,70,000	1,80,000	2,20,000	2,70,000	2,70,000	11,75,000

Working Notes:

1. Closing stock of finished goods is equal to the 50% of the sales for the next month.
2. Opening stock of finished goods of the current month is nothing but the closing stock of the previous month. Opening stock of April is nothing but the closing stock of March and it is equal to 50% of sales of April.

3. Closing stock of raw materials is equal to the estimated consumption of next month.
4. Opening stock of raw materials is nothing but the closing stock of the previous month. Opening stock of April is nothing but the closing stock of March and it is equal to consumption of month of April.

Problem 23 From the following information as furnished by Tesla Ltd., prepare a month-wise production budget and a summarised production cost budget for the 6 months that end on 31st December 2021.

(i) Estimated units to be sold:

	Units		Units
July 2021	3000	November 2021	7000
August 2021	4000	December 2021	9000
September 2021	6000	January 2022	8000
October 2021	7000		

(ii) Estimated finished stock at the end of each month is equal to half of the estimated sales for the next month.

(iii) Budgeted units to be produced during the year 2021 and details of production cost for the year that end on 31 December 2021 are as follows:

Production for the year	1,00,000 units
Direct material cost per unit	₹ 25
Direct wage cost per unit	₹ 15
Variable factory overhead cost per unit	₹ 5
Total fixed factory overhead for the year	₹ 3,08,000

Solution:

Production Quantity Budget
(for 6 Months ending on 31 December 2021)

	July (units)	Aug. (units)	Sept. (units)	Oct. (units)	Nov. (units)	Dec. (units)	Total (units)
Sales	3000	4000	6000	7000	7000	9000	36,000
Add: Closing stock[1] [1/2 of next months' sales]	2000	3000	3500	3500	4500	4000	20,500
Less: Opening stock[2] [1/2 of current months' sales]	1500	2000	3000	3500	3500	4500	18,000
Estimated production	3500	5000	6500	7000	8000	8500	38,500

Production Cost Budget
(for 6 months ended on 31 December 2021) **(Output = 38500 units)**

Particulars	Amount (₹)
Direct materials @ ₹ 25	9,62,500
Direct wages @ ₹ 15	5,77,500
Factory overhead:	
Variable factory overhead @ ₹ 5	1,92,500
Fixed factory overhead[3] (1/2 of ₹ 3,08,000)	1,54,000
Total Production Cost	18,86,500

Working Notes:

1. Closing stock of finished goods is equal to the 50% of the sales for the next month.
2. Opening stock of finished goods of the current month is nothing but the closing stock of the previous month. Opening stock of April is nothing but the closing stock of March and it is equal to 50% of sales of April.
3. Fixed overheads have been considered for six months.

Problem 24 From the following information, prepare the following budgets for the year 2021: (a) Production budget; (b) Material usage budget; and (c) Material purchase budget.

	Product (units)		
	A	B	C
Sales	15,000	25,000	20,000
Finished stock on 1, January 2021	5000	8000	5000
Finished stock on 31 December 2021	7000	3000	10,000

	M_1	M_2	M_3
Stock of materials on 1 January 2021 (kg)	20,000	50,000	20,000
Stock of materials on 31 December 2021 (kg)	60,000	35,000	55,000
Quantities used in (kg):			
Product A	3	5	5
Product B	7	8	4
Product C	3	6	9
Rate of materials per kg (₹)	5	4	6

Solution:

(i) Production Budget for the year 2021

	Product A (units)	Product B (units)	Product C (units)
Sales for the year	15,000	25,000	20,000
Add: Closing stock of finished goods [on 31 December 2021]	7000	3000	10,000
Less: Opening stock of finished goods [on 1 January 2021]	5000	8000	5000
Production for the year	17,000	20,000	25,000

(ii) Material Usage Budget for the year 2021

Particulars	Material M_1		Material M_2		Material M_3	
	Usage per unit (kg)	Total (kg)	Usage per unit (kg)	Total (kg)	Usage per unit (kg)	Total (kg)
Production of 17,000 units of A	3	51,000	5	85,000	5	85,000
Production of 20,000 units of B	7	1,40,000	8	1,60,000	4	80,000
Production of 25,000 units of C	3	75,000	6	1,50,000	9	2,25,000
Usage of materials for the year		2,66,000		3,95,000		3,90,000

(iii) Material Purchase Budget for the year 2021

Particulars	Material M_1 (kg)	Material M_2 (kg)	Material M_3 (kg)	Total
Usages of materials for the year [(ii) above]	2,66,000	3,95,000	3,90,000	
Add: Closing stock of materials	60,000	35,000	55,000	
Less: Opening stock of materials	20,000	50,000	20,000	
Purchase quantity of materials for the year	3,06,000	3,80,000	4,25,000	
Rate of materials per kg	₹5	₹4	₹6	
∴ Cost of purchase for the year [Purchase quantity × rate per kg]	15,30,000	15,20,000	25,50,000	56,00,000

Problem 25 The following information relating to the 3rd and last quarter of 2020–21 is furnished by a company which manufactures and sells a single product.

Sales	3rd Quarter (Actual)		Last Quarter (Estimate)
	₹6,24,000		₹6,60,000
	Opening Balance	Closing Balance	Opening Balance
Inventory:			
Raw material A (kg)	25,000	23,500	25,000
Raw material B (kg)	12,650	13,400	15,000
Finished goods (units)	670	700	1000

Units cost data:

Raw material A = 10 kg @ ₹3 = ₹30
Raw material B = 5 kg @ ₹2 = ₹10

Direct labour

Machine shop [Machine time of 5 hr @₹4] = ₹20
Assembly [Labour time of 2 hr @ ₹5] = ₹10

Production overheads:

Machine shop @ ₹12 per machine hour
Assembly @ ₹10 per labour hour
Selling and administration overheads: 20% of production cost
Profit margin 10% on selling price

Production and sales occur evenly during the budget period.

You are required to prepare the following budgets for the last quarter of the year.

(a) Production budget (in units)
(b) Purchase budget (in quantity and value)
(c) Production cost budget.

Solution:

(i) Production budget for the last quarter of 2020–21

Particulars	Units
Sales for the last quarter of 2020–21 [₹660000 ÷ ₹200[1]]	3300
Add: Closing stock of finished goods at the end of the last quarter	1000
Less: Opening stock of finished goods at the beginning of the last quarter	700
Production for the last quarter of 2020–21	3600

(ii) Purchase budget for the last quarter of 2020–21

Particulars	Material A (kg)	Material B (kg)	Total (kg)
Usage of material for the last quarter:			
Material A: 3600 units × 10 kg	36,000		
Material B: 3600 units × 5 kg		18,000	
Add: Closing stock of materials at the end of last quarter	25,000	15,000	
Less: Opening stock of materials at the beginning	23,500	13,400	
Estimated purchase for the last quarter	37,500	19,600	
Price of materials per kg	₹3	₹2	
Cost of purchase for the last quarter	1,12,500	39,200	1,51,700
[Purchase quantity × Price per kg]			

(iii) Production cost budget for the last quarter of 2020–21

Particulars	Amount ₹
Raw Materials:	
A: 36,000 kg × ₹ 3	1,08,000
B: 18,000 kg × ₹ 2	36,000
Direct Labour:	
Machine shop: 5 hr × 3600 units × ₹ 4	72,000
Assembly: 2 hr × 3600 units × ₹ 5	36,000
Prime Cost	2,52,000
Production Overheads:	
Machine shop: 5 hr × 3600 units × ₹ 12	2,16,000
Assembly: 2 hr × 3600 units × ₹ 10	72,000
Total Production Cost	5,40,000

Working Note:

1. Calculation of selling price per unit of the product

	₹
Raw Materials:	
A: 10 kg × ₹ 3	30
B: 5 kg × ₹ 2	10
Direct Labour:	
Machine shop: 5 hr × ₹ 4	10
Assembly: 2 hr × ₹ 5	20
Production Overheads:	
Machine shop: 5 hr × ₹ 12	60
Assembly: 2 hr × ₹ 10	20
Production Cost	150
Selling & Administration Overheads: 20% of ₹ 150	30
Total cost	180
Profit Margin (1/10 on selling price or 1/9 on Total cost = 1/9 on ₹ 180)	20
Selling price per unit	200

Problem 26 B. Pharma manufactures two products (A and B) and operates two sales divisions for selling them in the market. From the following information, prepare a sales budget for the year 2021 which is to be presented to the budget committee:

Market	Product	Budgeted Sales for the Year 2020	Actual Sales for the Year
Division I	A	2000 units @ ₹4 each	2500 units @ ₹4 each
	B	1500 units @ ₹6 each	1000 units @ ₹6 each
Division II	A	3000 units @ ₹4 each	3500 units @ ₹4 each
	B	2500 units @ ₹6 each	2000 units @ ₹6 each

In a meeting of the zonal sales managers, the following courses of action have been agreed:

(a) The sales managers contend that there is a high potential demand for product A and there is a scope for increase in the price of the product. Therefore, the price of product A should be increased by 2.

(b) The sale of product B is not picking up and therefore, the selling price of this product should be reduced by ₹1. Price sensitivity analysis suggest that the demand will positively respond to the fall in price.

On the basis of these price changes and impact of additional advertisement, the following estimates are made:

Market	Product	% Increase in Sales for Price Changes	% Increase in Sales for Additional Advertisement
Division I	A	15%	5%
	B	5%	5%
Division II	A	20%	5%
	B	10%	15%

Solution:

Sales budget for the year 2021

Division	Product	Budgeted Sales for the Year 2020			Actual Sales for the Year 2020			Budgeted Sales for the Year 2021		
		Qty. (Units)	Rate (₹)	Amount (₹)	Qty. (Units)	Rate (₹)	Amount (₹)	Qty. (Units)	Rate (₹)	Amount (₹)
I	(a) A	2000	4	8000	2500	4	10,000	3000	6	18,000
	(b) B	1500	6	9000	1000	6	6000	1100	5	5500
		3500		17,000	3500		16,000	4100		23,500
II	(c) A	3000	4	12,000	3500	4	14,000	4375	6	26,250
	(d) B	2500	6	15,000	2000	6	12,000	2500	5	12,500
		5500		27,000	5500		26,000	6875		38,750
Total Sales	A(a + c)	5000		20,000	6000		24,000	7375		44,250
	B(b + d)	4000		24,000	3000		18,000	3600		18,000
		9000		44,000	9000		42,000	10,975		62,250

Working Notes:

1. Budget sales for the year 2021 in Division I

Product	A (units)	B (units)
Actual sales for the year 2020	2500	1000
Add: Proposed increase in sales for price changes and additional advertisement	500	100
Budgeted total sales for the year 2021	3000	1100

2. Budgeted sales for the Year 2021 in Division II

	A (units)	B (units)
Budgeted sales for the year 2020	3500	2000
Add: Proposed increase in sales for price changes and additional advertisement	875	500
Budgeted total sales for the year 2021	4375	2500

Problem 27 Colour Max is manufacturing for sale four models of TV sets. The major accessories, viz., cabinet and transformers are bought out by the company. Four cabinet styles (A, B, C and D), and two kinds of transformers (X and Y), are assembled in the following ways in the final product:

1.

Model	*Cabinet*		*Transformer*
Standard	A @ ₹	400	X @ ₹400
Deluxe	B @ ₹	600	X @ ₹400
Aristocrat	C @ ₹	1000	Y @ ₹600
Royal	D @ ₹	1400	Y @ ₹600

2. The company expects the following inventories in hand on 1st July:

Finished sets: Standard 46; Deluxe 73; Aristocrat 64; Royal 69.

Sub-assemblies : Cabinet : A 30; B 40; C 20;D 25

Transformers : X 31; Y 17

3. The sales manager estimates that sales for the quarter, July–September will be:

Model	*Quantity*
Standard	200
Deluxe	600
Aristocrat	500
Royal	300

4. The following inventory quantities have been budgeted for 30th September.

Finished sets : 25 in each model

Sub-assemblies : Cabinet — 15 (each model)

Transformers — 20 (each type)

You are required to prepare the production budget (in units) for various TV models and the purchase budget (in units) and consolidated purchase budget for the two items of accessories for the quarter July–September.

Solution:

Production budget (TV sets in units)
(for the period July–September)

Model	Sale budget	Closing stock	Opening stock	Production[1]
Standard	200	25	46	179
Deluxe	600	25	73	552
Aristocrat	500	25	64	461
Royal	300	25	69	256

Material purchase budget (for cabinets and transformers)
(for the period July–September)

Cabinets Type	Model	Production	Closing stock	Opening stock	Purchases[2]
A	Standard	179	15	30	164
B	Deluxe	552	15	40	527
C	Aristocrat	461	15	20	456
D	Royal	256	15	25	246

Transformers

Type	Model	Production	Closing stock	Opening stock	Purchases
X	Standard	179 }	20	31	720
	Deluxe	552 }			
Y	Aristocrat	461 }	20	17	720
	Royal	256 }			

Purchase budget (consolidated) for cabinets and transformers
(for the period July–September)

Items	Type	Quantity	Rate (₹)	Amount (₹)
Cabinets:	A	164	400	65,600
	B	527	600	3,16,200
	C	456	1,000	4,56,000
	D	246	1,400	3,44,400

Table Contd...

Table Contd...

Items	Type	Quantity	Rate (₹)	Amount (₹)
Transformers	X	720	400	2,88,000
	Y	720	600	4,32,000
Total				19,02,200

Working Notes:

1. Production = Sales + Closing stock – Opening stock.
2. Purchases = Usage + Closing stock – Opening stock.
3. Cost of purchase = Quantity × Rate

Problem 28 JK Furnishings has prepared the following sales budget for the first five months of 2021

	Sales Budget (in units)
January	10,800
February	15,600
March	12,200
April	10,400
May	9800

The inventory of finished products at the end of every month is to be equal to 25 per cent of the sales estimate for the next months. On 1 January 2021, there were 2700 units of product on hand. There is no work-in-process at the end of any month.

Every unit of product requires two types of materials in the following quantities:

Material A	4 kg
Material B	5 kg

Materials equal to one-half of the next month's production are to be in hand at the end of every month. This requirement was met on 1 January, 2021.

Budgeted prices for the purchase of materials are :

Material A — ₹3 per kg, Material B — ₹2 per kg.

Prepare a materials budget for the first quarter of 2021 in a logical form showing the quantities of each type of materials to be purchased every month. Also prepare a purchase budget [*B.Com. (H)*]

Solution: Before preparing material budget, production has to be estimated by preparing a production budget.

Production Budget 2021

(For the 1st Quarter Jan–March, 2021)

Particulars	Jan. units	Feb. units	March units	April
Estimated sales	10,800	15,600	2600	10,400
Add: Closing stock[1]	3900	3050	2450	12,200
Less: Opening stock[2]	2700	3900	3050	2600
Production	12,000	14,750	11,750	10,250

Material Usage Budget

(For the Quarter Jan. 1 to March............)

Particulars	Jan.		Feb.		March	
Production (units)	12000		14750		11750	
	A	B	A	B	A	B
Materials usage per unit	4 kg	5 kg	4 kg	5 kg	4 kg	5 kg
Total consumption	48,000	60,000	59,000	73,750	47,000	58,750

Material Purchase Budget (Quantity)

(For the Quarter Jan. 1 to March ....)

	Feb.		Feb.		March	
	A kg	B kg	A kg	B kg	A kg	B kg
Materials consumption	48,000	60,000	59,000	73,750	47,000	58,750
Add: Closing stock[3]	29,500	36,875	23,500	29,375	20,500	25,625
Less : Opening stock[4]	24,000	30,000	29,500	36,875	23,500	29,375
Quantity to be purchased	53,500	66,875	53,000	66,250	44,000	55,000

Purchases Budget (Amount)

(For the Quarter Jan. 1 to March 31, 2021 ....)

Material	Jan.			Feb.			Mar.			Total
	Qty. kg.	Price ₹	Amt. ₹	Qty. kg.	Price ₹	Amt. ₹	Qty. kg.	Price ₹	Amt. ₹	Amt. ₹
A	53,500	3	1,60,500	53,000	3	1,59,000	44,000	3	1,32,000	4,51,500
B	66,875	2	1,33,750	66,250	2	1,32,500	55,000	2	1,10,000	3,76,250
Total			2,94,250			2,91,500			2,42,000	8,27,750

Working Note:

1. **Closing Stock of Finished Goods**

Closing stock is 25% of sales of next month.

Jan.	25% of 15,600 units	= 3900
Feb.	25% of 12,200 units	= 3050
March	25% of 10,400 units	= 2600

2. **Opening Stock of Finished Goods**

Opening stock for Jan. is closing stock of Dec. which is 25% of sales of Jan. Therefore, the opening stock becomes 25% of current month sales. Closing stock of Jan. is opening stock of Feb. and closing stock of Feb. is opening stock of March.

Jan.	25% of 10,800 units	= 2700
Feb.	25% of 15,600 units	= 3900
March	25% of 12,200 units	= 3050

3. **Closing Stock of Raw Material**

Closing stock is .... of next month's production requirement.

Material A

Jan.	50% of 59,000 kg	= 29,500 kg
Feb.	50% of 47,000 kg	= 23,500 kg
March	50% of (10,250 × 4 kg)	= 20,500 kg

Material B

Jan.	50% of 73,750 kg	= 36,875 kg
Feb.	50% of 58,750 kg	= 29,375 kg
March	50% of (10,250 × 5 kg)	= 25,625 kg

4. **Opening Stock of Raw Material**

Opening stock for Jan. is closing stock of Dec. which is 50% of usage of Jan. Therefore, the opening stock becomes 50% of current month's consumption. Closing stock of Jan. is opening stock of Feb. and closing stock of Feb. is opening stock of March.

Material A

Jan.	50% of 48,000 kg	= 24,000 kg
Feb.	50% of 59,000 kg	= 29,500 kg
March	50% of 47,000 kg	= 23,500 kg

Material B

Jan.	50% of 60,000 kg	= 30,000 kg
Feb.	50% of 73,750 kg	= 36,875 kg
March	50% of 58,750 kg	= 29,375 kg

Problem 29 Spring Ltd. estimated its sales for the next year, quarter-wise as under:

Quarter	Sales
I	30,000
II	37,500
III	41,250
IV	45,000

The opening stock finished goods is 10,000 units and the company expects to maintain the closing stock of finished goods at 16,250 units at the end of the year. The production pattern in each quarter is based on 80% of the sales of the current quarter and 20% of the next quarter.

The opening stock of raw materials in the beginning of the year is 10,000 kg and the closing stock at the end of the year is required to be maintained at 5000 kg. Each unit of finished output requires 2 kg of raw materials.

The company proposes to purchase the entire annual requirement of raw materials in the first three quarters in the proportion and at the prices given below:

Quarter	Purchase of raw materials % of total annual requirement in quantity	Price per kg
I	30%	2
II	50%	3
III	20%	4

The value of the opening stock of raw materials in the beginning of the year is ₹20,000.

You are required to present the following for the next year, quarter-wise :

(i) Production budget in units.

(ii) Raw material consumption budget in quantity.

(iii) Raw material purchase budget in quantity and value.

(iv) Priced stores ledger card of the raw material using first-in-first-out method.

[*B. Com. (H)*]

Solution:

1. As the sales for the first quarter of the next year is not given, it is necessary to compute the annual production first of all.

Estimated sales per year (30,000 + 37,500 + 41,250 + 45,000)	1,53,750
Add : Closing stock	16,250
Less : Opening stock	10,000
Estimated production	1,60,000

(i) Production Budget (Quarter-wise)

Particulars	Quarters				Total
	I	II	III	IV	
Sales (unit)	30,000	37,500	41,250	45,000	1,53,750
Production (80% of sales of current quarter)	24,000	30,000	33,000	36,000	
Production (20% of sales of next quarter)	7500	8250	9000	12,250	
Production	31,500	38,250	42,000	48,250	1,60,000

(ii) Raw Material Consumption Budget (Quantity)

Raw material consumption in kg = Units of production × Usage per unit

Quarter				
Quarter	I	31500 × 2 kg	=	63,000 kg
	II	38250 × 2 kg	=	76,500 kg
	III	42000 × 2 kg	=	84,000 kg
	IV	48250 × 2 kg	=	96,500 kg
	Total			3,20,000 kg

(iii) Raw Material Annual Purchase Budget (Quantity)

Raw material required for production	3,20,000 kg
Add: Closing stock	5000 kg
Less: Opening stock	10,000 kg
Materials to be purchased	3,15,000

Raw Material Purchase Budget (in ₹)

Quarter	Qty. to be purchased	Rate per kg. ₹	Amount ₹
I	3,15,000 × 30% = 94,500 kg	2	1,89,000
II	3,15,000 × 50% = 1,57,500 kg	3	4,72,500
III	3,15,000 × 20% = 63,000 kg	4	2,52,000
Total	3,15,000 kg		9,13,500

(iv) Stores Ledger Card (FIFO Method)

Quarter Particulars	Receipts			Issues			Balance		
Date	Qty. kg	Rate ₹	Amount ₹	Qty. kg	Rate ₹	Amount ₹	Qty. kg	Rate ₹	Amount ₹
I. Opening	–	–	–				10,000	2	20,000
purchases	94,500	2	1,89,000	–	–	–	1,04,500	2	2,09,000
Issues	–	–	–	63,000	2	1,26,000	41,500	2	83,000
II. Purchase	1,57,500	3	4,72,500	–	–	–	41,500 1,57,500	2&3	5,55,500
Issues	–	–	–	41,500 35,000	2 3	83,000 1,05,000	1,22,500	3	3,67,500
III. Purchase	63,000	4	2,52,000	–	–	–	1,22,500 63,000	3 4	3,67,500 2,52,000
Issues	–	–	–	84,000	3	2,52,000	38,500 63,000	3 4	1,15,500 2,52,000

Table Contd...

Table Contd...

Quarter Particulars	Receipts			Issues			Balance		
Date	Qty. kg	Rate ₹	Amount ₹	Qty. kg	Rate ₹	Amount ₹	Qty. kg	Rate ₹	Amount ₹
IV. Issues	–	–	–	38,500 58,000	3 4	1,15,500 2,32,000	5000	4	20,000

Problem 30 Fab Mart produces and sells a single product. Sales budget for the calendar year 2022 quarter-wise is as under:

Quarter	*No. of units to be sold*
I	1200
II	1500
III	1650
IV	1800

The year 2022 is expected to open with an inventory of 400 units of finished product and close with an inventory of 650 units.

Production is customarily scheduled to provide for two-thirds of the current quarter's sales demand plus one-third of the following quarter's demand. Thus, production anticipates sales volume by about one month.

The standard cost details for one unit of the product is as follows:

Direct materials 10 kg @ ₹5 per kg

Direct labour 1 hour 30 minutes @ ₹8 per hour

Variable overheads 1 hour 30 minutes @ ₹10 per hour.

Fixed overheads 1 hour 30 minutes @ ₹10 per hour based on a budgeted production volume of 9000 direct labour hours for the year.

(i) Prepare a production budget for 2022, by quarters, showing the number of units to be produced, and the total costs of direct material, direct labour, variable overheads and fixed overheads.

(ii) If the budgeted selling price per unit is ₹97, what would be the budgeted profit for the year as a whole?

(iii) In which quarter of the year, the company is expected to break-even?

Solution:

(i) Production Budget

(for the year 2022 quarter-wise)

Units to be produced in each quarter	Quarter I	Quarter II	Quarter III	Quarter IV	Total
	Units	Units	Units	Units	Units
2/3rds of the current sales	800	1000	1100	1200	4100
1/3rd of next quarter's sales	500	550	600	650	2300
	1300	1550	1700	1850	6400

Production Cost Badget

	Quarter I	Quarter II	Quarter III	Quarter IV	Total
Units to be produced	1300	1550	1700	1850	6400
	₹	₹	₹	₹	₹
Direct material @ ₹ 50 per unit	65,000	77,500	85,000	92,500	3,20,000
Direct labour @ ₹ 12 per unit	15,600	18,600	20,400	22,200	76,800
Variable overheads @ ₹ 15 per unit	19,500	23,250	25,500	27,750	96,000
Fixed overheads	22,500	22,500	22,500	22,500	90,000
Total cost	1,22,600	1,41,850	1,53,400	1,64,950	5,82,300

(ii) Statement of Budgeted Profit
(for the year 2022 as a whole)

Particulars	Amount (₹)
Total sales (6150 units @ ₹ 97 per unit)	5,96,550
Less : Total variable cost (6,150 units @ ₹ 77 per unit)	4,73,550
Contribution	1,23,000
Less : Fixed cost for the year	90,000
Loss for the year 2022 as a whole	23,000

(iii)

$$\text{Break-even point} = \frac{\text{Fixed overheads}}{\text{Selling price per unit} - \text{Variable cost per unit}}$$

$$= \frac{90{,}000}{(97 - 77)} = 4500 \text{ units}$$

Total sales in units by the end of 4th quarter will be 6150 (i.e., 1200 + 1500 + 1650 + 1800). Therefore, the company will break-even in the early part of the 4th quarter.

Working Notes:

1. Variable cost per unit

	₹
Direct material: 10 kg @ ₹ 5 per kg	50
Direct labour : 1 hour @ ₹ 8 per hour	12
Variable overheads : 1½ hours @ ₹ 10 per hour	15
	77

2. Fixed overheads per annum : 9000 hr @ ₹ 10 90,000

   ∴ Fixed overheads per quarter (divided equally) 22500

3. Number of units to be sold during the year 2022

Quarter I	1200 units
Quarter II	1500 units
Quarter III	1650 units
Quarter IV	1800 units
Total Sales during the year	6150 units

Problem 31 Mac Ltd. manufactures three products, namely A, B, and C. The current pattern of sales of A, B, and C is in the ratio of 8:2:1 respectively. The relevant data are as follows:

Products	A	B	C
Selling price per unit (₹)	100	130	210
Raw materials per unit (kg)	0.50	1.2	2.5
Direct materials per unit (kg)	0.25	–	–
Skilled labour hours per unit	4	6	8
Semi-skilled labour hours per unit	2	2	3
Variable overheads (₹ per unit)	20	40	40

Prices of raw materials and direct materials respectively are ₹50 and ₹20 per kg. Wage rates of skilled and semi-skilled labour respectively are ₹3 and ₹2.50. Each operator works 8 hours a day for 25 days in a month.

The positions of inventories are as under:

Particulars	Raw Materials (units)	Direct Materials (units)	A (units)	B (units)	C (units)
Opening	600	400	400	100	50
Closing	650	260	200	300	50

The fixed overhead amounts to ₹1,00,000 per month. The company desires a profit of ₹60,000 per month.

Prepare the following for the month:

1. Sales budget in quantity and value.
2. Production budget showing the quantity to be manufactured.
3. Purchase budget showing the quantity and value.
4. Direct labour budget showing the number of workers and wages.

Solution:

1. Sales budget in quantity

Particulars	Product A	Product B	Product C
Selling price per unit	₹100	₹130	₹210
Variable costs per unit			
Raw materials at ₹50/kg	0.5 × 50 = ₹25	1.2 × 50 = ₹60	2.5 × 50 = ₹125

Table Contd...

Table Contd...

Particulars	Product A	Product B	Product C
Direct materials at ₹40/kg	0.25 × 20 = ₹5	Nil	Nil
Skilled labour at ₹3 per hour	4 × 3 = ₹12	6 × 3 = ₹18	8 × 3 = ₹24
Unskilled labour at ₹2.50 per hour	2 × 2.50 = ₹5	2 × 2.50 = ₹5	3 × 2.50 = ₹7.50
Variable overheads (given)	₹20	₹40	₹40
Total variable costs per unit	₹67	₹123	₹196.50
Contribution per unit	₹33	₹7	₹13.50
Sales mix ratio	8	2	1
Total weighted contribution	33 × 8 = ₹264	7 × 2 = ₹14	13.5 × 1 = ₹13.50

Desired profit per month = ₹60,000

Add: Fixed overhead per month = ₹1,00,000

Desired contribution per month = ₹1,60,000

Total of weighted contribution = 264 + 14 + 13.5 = ₹291.50

Hence, number of batches of A, B and C = ₹1,60,000 / 291.50 = 548.88

So, the sales quantities are : A : 548.88 × 8 = 4391 units; 548.88 × 2 = 1098 units; C: 548.88 × 1 = 549 units.

1. Sales Budget in Value

Particulars	Product A	Product B	Product C	Total
Budgeted quantity	4391 units	1098 units	549 units	6038 units
Budgeted price	₹100	₹130	₹210	
Budgeted sales value	₹4,39,100	₹1,42,740	₹1,15,290	₹6,97,130

2. Production Budget

Particulars	Product A	Product B	Product C	Total
Budgeted sales quantity	4391 units	1098 units	549 units	6038 units
Add: Closing stock	200 units	300 units	50 units	550 units
Less: Opening stock	400 units	100 units	50 units	550 units
Budgeted production	4191 units	1298 units	549 units	6038 units

3. Raw Material Usage Budget

Particulars	Product A	Product B	Product C	Total
(a) Budgeted production	4191 units	1298 units	549 units	6038 units
(b) Raw material required per unit	0.50 kg	1.20 kg	2.50 kg	
(c) Total raw materials required	2096 kg	1558 kg	1372 kg	5026 kg
(d) Direct materials required per unit	0.25 kg	–	–	
(e) Total direct materials required	524 kg	–	–	524 kg

4. Materials Purchase Budget

Particulars	Raw Materials	Direct Materials	Total
Budgeted usage	5026 kg	524 kg	
Add : Closing stock	650 kg	260 kg	
Less : Opening stock	600 kg	400 kg	
Budgeted purchases	5076 kg	384 kg	
Price of materials	₹50 per kg	₹20 per kg	
Cost of purchase	2,53,800	7,680	₹2,61,480

5. Direct Labour Budget
(Note: Hours per worker = 25 × 8 = 200)

Particulars	Product A	Product B	Product C	Total
Budgeted production	4191 units	1298 units	549 units	6038 units
Skilled labour-hours per unit	4	6	8	
Total skilled DLH required	16,764	7788	4392	83,600
Cost of skilled labour at ₹3 p.h.	₹50,292	₹23,364	₹13,176	₹5,01,600
Skilled workers required	16,764/200 = 84	39	22	45
Semi-skilled labour hours per unit	2	2	3	
Total semi-skilled DLH required	8382	2596	1,647	12,625
Cost of semi-skilled labour at ₹2.50	₹20,955	₹6490	₹4118	₹31,563
Semi-skilled workers required	42	130	9	181
Total labour cost	₹71,247	₹29,854	₹17,294	₹1,18,395

Problem 32 A company has ₹3750 cash in hand on 1st April, 2021 and requires you to prepare an estimate of cash position during the three months, April to June, 2021. The following information is supplied to you:

	Sales	Purchases	Wages	Factory Expenses	Office Expenses	Selling Expenses
February	7500	4500	900	750	600	450
March	8400	4800	975	825	600	450
April	9000	5250	1050	900	600	525
May	12,000	6000	1350	1125	600	657
June	13,500	6000	1425	1400	700	700

Other information:

(1) Period of credit allowed by suppliers–2 months.

(2) 20% of sales is for cash and period of credit allowed to customers for credit sales is one month.

(3) Delay in payment of all expenses is one month.
(4) Income-tax of ₹5750 is due to be paid on June 15, 2021.
(5) The company is to pay dividends to shareholders and bonus to workers of ₹1500 and ₹2250 respectively in the month of April.
(6) Plant has been ordered to be received and paid in May. It will cost ₹12,000.

The company wants to maintain a cash balance of ₹10,000 at the end of each month for day to day requirements. Determine the amount of surplus or deficit of cash in each month.

Solution:

Cash Budget

Particulars	April 2021	May 2021	June 2021
	₹	₹	₹
Opening balance (cash in hand)	3750	1170	(9105)
Add: Receipts			
Cash sales (20% of current month's sales)	1800	2400	2700
Debtors (80% of previous month's sales)	6720	7200	9600
Total	12,270	10,770	3195
Less: Payments			
Creditors (2 month's previous purchases)	4500	4800	5250
Wages (previous month's wages)	975	1050	1350
Factory expenses (previous month's expenses)	825	900	1125
Office expenses (previous month's expenses)	600	600	600
Selling expenses (previous month's expenses)	450	525	657
Dividend to shareholders	1500	–	–
Bonus to workers	2250	–	–
Purchase of plant	–	12,000	–
Income tax	–	–	5750
Total of payments	11,100	19,875	14,732
Closing balance (receipts - payments)	1170	(9105)	(11,537)

Observation: Comparing with the desired cash balance of ₹10,000, the company will face a cash deficit of ₹8,830 in the month of April, ₹19,105 in May and ₹21,537 in the month of June.

Problem 33 Freight Ltd. has given the following particulars. You are required to prepare a cash budget for the three months ending 31st December, 2021.

(a) *Months*	*Sales*	*Materials*	*Wages*	*Overheads*
	₹	₹	₹	₹
August	20,000	10,200	3800	1900
September	21,000	10,000	3800	2100

	₹	₹	₹	₹
October	23,000	9800	4000	2300
November	25,000	10,000	4200	2400
December	30,000	10,800	4500	2500

(b) A plant will be installed in August, 2021 at a cost of ₹ 1,00,000. The monthly instalment of ₹ 15,000 is payable from October onwards.

(c) Dividend at 10% on preference share capital of ₹ 3,00,000 will be paid on 1st December, 2021.

(d) Advance to be received for sale of equipment ₹ 20,000 in December.

(e) Income-tax (advance) to be paid in December ₹ 5,000.

(f) Credit terms are:

Sales/debtors: 10% sales are on cash basis, 50% of the credit sales are collected next month and the balance in the following month:

Creditors: Materials 2 months

20% of wages are paid in the following month.

Overheads ½ months

(g) Cash balance on 1st October, 2021 is expected to be ₹ 8000.

(h) The company desires to maintain a closing balance of ₹ 7500 at the end of every month.

Solution:

Cash budget for three months ended 31st December 2021

Particulars	October	November	December
	₹	₹	₹
Opening cash balance	8000	7390	8180
Add: Receipts :			
Cash sales (10% of Sales)	2300	2500	3000
Collection from debtors[1]	18,450	19,800	21,600
Advance from sale of equipment	–	–	20,000
Total (a)	28,750	29,690	52,780
Payments :			
Creditors (materials)[2]	10,200	10,000	9800
Wages[3]	3960	4160	4440
Overheads[4]	2200	2350	2450
Monthly instalment of plant	5000	5000	5000
Preference dividend (10%)	–	–	30,000
Advance Income tax	–	–	5000
Total (b)	21,360	21,510	56,690
Closing cash balance (a)–(b)	7390	8180	(–) 3910

Observation: Comparing with the desired cash balance of ₹7500, the company will need overdraft facility in the month of October ₹110 and in the month of December ₹11,410. But there will be a surplus of ₹680 in November as is evident from the cash budget.

Working Notes:

1. Cash collected from debtors

Particulars	Aug. ₹	Sept. ₹	Oct. ₹	Nov. ₹	Dec. ₹
Cash sales (10%)	2000	2100	2300	2500	3000
Credit sales (90%)	18,000	18,900	20,700	22,500	27,000
Total sales	20,000	21,000	23,000	25,000	30,000
Collections from debtors:					
1st month (50%)			9450	10,350	11,250
2nd month (50%)			9000	9450	10,350
Total			18,450	19,800	21,600

2. Since the period of credit allowed by suppliers is two months, the payment for purchases of materials in August will be paid in October and so on.
3. 4/5 of wages of the current month will be paid in the month itself and 1/5 wages of the previous month will be paid in the current month.
4. 1/2 of overheads of September and 1/2 of those of October will be paid in the month of October. Similarly, calculations are made for months of November and December.

Problem 34 From the following information, prepare the cash budget for the 3 months, September to November of 2021.

Month	Sales ₹	Purchase ₹	Wages ₹	Factory Expenses ₹	Office Expenses ₹
July	50,000	28,000	3400	3200	4000
August	65,000	32,500	3700	3300	4200
September	70,000	37,200	3900	3450	4350
October	60,000	29,500	4200	3600	4420
November	84,000	39,700	4500	3700	3700

Additional Information:

(i) A sales commission at 5% on sales, which is due in the month following the month in which the sales dues are collected, is payable in addition to the office expenses.

(ii) The period of credit allowed to debtors is 2 months.

(iii) A month's credit is obtained from the creditors.

(iv) Wages are paid on the 1st and 16th of each month in respect of dues for a period of 15 days, preceding those days.

(v) Other expenses are paid in the month in which they are due.

(vi) For purchase of an asset under instalment-payment system, an instalment of ₹1250 per month is paid.

(vii) Bank balance on 1st September is ₹15,200. [B.Com. (H)]

Solution:

Cash Budget 2021

(September–November 2021)

Particulars	September ₹	October ₹	November ₹
Opening Bank Balance	15,200	19,850	31,830
Add: Cash receipts			
Collection from debtors[1]	50,000	65,200	70,000
	65,000	84,850	1,01,830
Less: Cash Payments			
Creditors	32,500	37,200	29,500
Wages[2]	3800	4050	4350
Factory expenses[3]	3450	3600	3700
Office expenses[3]	4350	4420	4800
Sales commission[5]	–	2500	3250
Instalment for the purchase of asset	1250	1250	1250
	45,350	53,020	46,850
Closing bank balance	19,850	31,830	54,980

Working Notes:

1. Collection from debtors: As the period of credit allowed to debtors is 2 months, the sales for July, August and September will be collected in September, October and November respectively.
2. Payment to creditors: One month credit is allowed by creditors; therefore, the payment to creditors is made in the next month.
3. Payment of factory expenses and office expenses: Factory and office expenses are paid in the month during which these expenses are incurred.
4. Payment of wages: As wages are paid on 1st and 16th of each month; Half of the wages are paid in the same month and the remaining half are paid in the next month.

	September ₹	October ₹	November ₹
Wages for August (½ of ₹33,700)	1,850	–	–
Wages for September (½ of ₹73,900)	1,950	1,950	–

Table Contd...

Table Contd...

	September ₹	October ₹	November ₹
Wages for October (½ of ₹4,200)	–	2,100	2,100
Wages for November (½ of ₹4,500)	–	–	2,250
Total wages	3,800	4,050	4,350

5. Sales commission: It is paid in the month following the month in which debtors are collected.

	September	October	November
Sales Commission payable	5% on sales for June = Sales for June is not given in the problem (assumed nil)	5% on sales for July = 5% on ₹50,000 = ₹2,500	5% on sales for August = 5% on ₹65,000 = ₹3,250

Problem 35 From the following information, prepare a cash budget for the quarter that is ending on 30 June 2021:

Month	Sales ₹	Purchases ₹	Wages ₹	Misc. Exp. ₹
February	1,20,000	84,000	10,000	7000
March	1,30,000	1,00,000	12,000	8000
April	80,000	1,04,000	8000	6000
May	1,06,000	1,16,000	10,000	12,000
June	88,000	80,000	8000	6000

Additional Information:

(a) Cash on hand on 1 April 2021 is ₹5000.

(b) 20% of sales are realised in the month of sale, discount allowed is 2% and balance is realised after 2 months.

(c) Purchases are paid in the following month.

(d) 25% of wages are paid in the following month and the balance 75% is paid in the same month.

(e) There is a time lag of one month in the payment of other expenses.

(f) Income tax of ₹25,000 due on or before 30 June 2021.

Solution:

Cash Budget

(for the quarter ending on 30 June 2021)

Particulars	April (₹)	May (₹)	June (₹)
Opening cash & bank balance	5000	(–)320	6916
Add: Cash receipts			

Table Contd...

Table Contd...

Cash sales[1]	15,680	22,736	17,248
Collection from debtors[2]	96,000	1,04,000	64,000
	1,16,680	1,26,416	88,164
Less: Cash Payments			
Payment to creditors for goods	1,00,000	1,04,000	1,06,000
Payment of wages	9000	9500	8500
Payment of other expenses	8000	6000	12,000
Income tax payment	–	–	25,000
	1,17,000	1,19,500	1,51,500
Closing Cash & Bank Balance	(–)320	6,916	(–)163,336

Working Notes:

1. Receipts from cash sales:
   In April = (20% of ₹80,000) – {2% of (20% of ₹80,000)} = ₹15,580
   In May = (20% of ₹1,16,000) – {2% of (20% of ₹1,16,000)} = ₹22,736
   In June = (20% of ₹88,000) – {2% of (20% of ₹88,000)} = ₹17,248
2. Collection from debtors: 80% of total sales are collected after 2 months.
   April = 80% of total sales in February = 80% of ₹1,20,000 = ₹96,000
   May = 80% of total sales in March = 80% of ₹1,30,000 = ₹1,04,000
   June = 80% of total sales in April = 80% of ₹80,000 = ₹1,06,000
3. Payment to creditors is made in the next month.
   April = Payment for purchases in March = ₹1,00,000
   May = Payment for purchases in April = ₹1,04,000
   June = Payment for purchases in May = ₹1,06,000
   = 5% of wages payable for the previous month + 75% of the wages payable for the current month.
4. Payment of wages: 25% of wages payable for the previous month + 75% of the wages payable for the current month.

	₹
∴ Payment of wages in April:	
25% of wages of March [i.e., 25% of ₹12,000]	3000
75% of wages of April [i.e., 75% of ₹8000]	6000
	9000
Payment of wages in May:	
25% of wages of April [i.e., 25% of ₹8000]	2000
75% of wages of May [i.e., 75% of ₹10,000]	7500

Table Contd...

Table Contd...

	9500
Payment of wages in June:	
25% of wages of May [i.e., 25% of ₹8000]	2500
75% of wages of June [i.e., 75% of ₹10,000]	6000
	8500

5. Payment of other expenses in the next month.
   Payment in April = Other expenses of March = ₹8000
   Payment in May = Other expenses of April = ₹6000
   Payment in June = Other expenses of May = ₹12,000

Problem 36 Sunrise Ltd. will commence business on 1 January when it will issue equity share of ₹10 each at a premium of 30% payable in cash to finance:

(a) Capital expenditure:
  1 January—₹5 lakh
  31 March—₹1.01 lakh by cash payment

(b) Working capital for the first six months on the basis of:
  (i) Sales (gross profit rate being 25% on sales)
    January and February—₹60,000 p.m.
    March—₹80,000; April—₹1 lakh
    May to July—₹40,000 p.m.
    Collections to be made on the last day of the month after that on which the goods were sold. Commission at 5% is payable on collection.
  (ii) On the first date of each month, there should be stock to supply all sales of the following month only. Payments to be made on the last date of the month after goods were purchased.
  (iii) Salaries and other field expenses

January to Mach—₹3000 p.m.

April to June—₹5000 p.m.

These are payable on the last day of the month.

Prepare month-wise cash budget for six months ending June. Also, show the budgeted P & L A/c for the said period as on 30 June. Ignore depreciation and tax.

Solution:

Budgeted Profit and Loss Account

for the half year ended 30th June

Dr. **Pro forma P & L Account** *Cr.*

Particulars	Amount ₹	Particulars	Amount ₹
To purchases	3,15,000	By sales	3,80,000
To gross profit	95,000	By closing stock[1]	30,000

Table Contd...

Table Contd...

	4,10,000		4,10,000
To salaries & fixed expenses[4]		By Gross Profit b/d	95,000
	24,000		
To commission on sales (5% of ₹3,80,000)	19,000		
To net profit c/d (Balancing figure)	52,000		
	95,000		95,000

Cash Budget

for the period ended 30th June..............

Particulars	January (₹)	February (₹)	March (₹)	April (₹)	May (₹)	June (₹)
Opening balance receipts	Nil	1,47,000	1,11,000	4000	–	60,000
Issue of equity shares (*Working Note 2*)	6,50,000	–	–	–	–	–
Collections from debtors	–	60,000	60,000	80,000	1,00,000	40,000
(A)	6,50,000	2,07,000	1,71,000	84,000	1,00,000	1,00,000
Payments						
Creditors: Raw materials[3]	–	90,000	60,000	75,000	30,000	30,000
Commission on sales	–	3000	3000	4000	5000	2000
Salaries & fixed expenses	3000	3000	3000	5000	5000	5000
Capital expenditure	5,00,000	–	1,01,000	–	–	–
(B)	5,03,000	96,000	1,67,000	84,000	40,000	37,000
Closing balance (A–B)	1,47,000	1,11,000	4,000	–	60,000	63,000

Working Notes:

1. *Ascertainment of closing stock*

   Since stocks of purchases one month ahead (i.e., before) of sales, i.e., July's stock will be purchased in June, this will appear as an item closing stock.

Sales in July	₹40,000
Less : Gross profit (25% of ₹40,000)	10,000
∴ Closing stock	30,000

2. *Calculation of amount raised from the issue of equity shares*

   We will first calculate month-wise deficit, i.e., excess of payments over receipts (excluding amount raised from issue of equity share) as follows:

(a) January $\left(\frac{\text{Receipt}}{\text{Nil}} - \frac{\text{Payments}}{₹5{,}03{,}000}\right)$	₹5,03,000
(b) February (₹60,000 – ₹96,000)	₹36,000
(c) March (₹60,000 – ₹1,67,000)	₹1,07,000
(d) April (₹80,000 – ₹84,000)	₹4000
(e) May	No deficit
(f) June	No deficit
	₹6,50,000

Thus, ₹6,50,000 worth of equity share capital has to be issued (including premium). Issue of equity shares (including premium) ₹6,50,000 (**make it 130 in place of 100**)

Less: Share premium $\left(\frac{30}{100} \times ₹6{,}50{,}000\right)$	1,50,000
∴ Share capital	5,00,000

3. *Calculation of cash payments for raw materials purchases*
   Since the business starts in January and raw materials have to be purchased one month ahead, i.e., January and February's raw materials must be purchased in January. Payments have to be made in the next month, namely, January and February's stock (both purchased in January) have to be paid in February.

	Month of Sale					
Particulars	**Jan. & Feb. (₹)**	**March (₹)**	**April (₹)**	**May (₹)**	**June (₹)**	**July (₹)**
Sales value	1,20,000	80,000	1,00,000	40,000	40,000	40,000
Less : Gross profit–25%	30,000	20,000	25,000	10,000	10,000	10,000
Purchases	90,000	60,000	75,000	30,000	30,000	30,000

   Similarly, purchases for other months are made and paid for.
4. Salaries and expenses:
   (Jan – March 3000 × 3 = 9,000) + (April – June = 5000 × 3 = 15,000) = 24,000
5. Sales = 60,000 + 60,000 + 80,000 + 1,00,000 + 40,000 + 40,000 = 3,80,000

Problem 37 Flower Ltd. manufactures two products A and B. It is going to prepare its budget for the year ending 31st December 2021. Expectation for the year includes the following:

Particulars	**(₹)**	**(₹)**
(a) Opening balances		
Stock: Raw materials		
A	6800	
B	14,400	

Table Contd...

Table Contd...

(b) Finished Products	A	B
Budgeted sales (units)	10,000	2000
Budgeted selling price (per unit)	₹30	₹50
Opening stock of finished goods (in units)	400	600
Budgeted closing stock (units)	2400	400
(c) Production Details		
(i) Direct Materials	P	Q
Raw materials per unit of production:		
A	5 kg	3 kg
B	2 kg	4 kg
Opening stock of raw materials	4000 kg	4000 kg
Budgeted closing stock	5000 kg	3000 kg
Cost per kg of raw material purchased	₹0.50	₹1
(ii) Director labour—Labour is paid at the rate of ₹2 per hour. Each unit of A requires 3 labour hours and each unit of B requires 5 labour hours		
(iii) Factory overheads—It has been estimated factory overheads will be ₹67,500 including ₹23,500 for depreciation. Factory overheads are absorbed on a direct labour-hour basis.		
(iv) Work-in-progress—This is negligible and can be ignored (i.e., no opening or closing stocks)		
(d) Administration Overheads		
These are assumed to be ₹23,250. They are charged to goods leaving work-in-progress and entering finished goods stock and are absorbed as a percentage of factory cost.		
(e) Selling and Distribution Overheads		
These are estimated to be ₹20,000. They are charged to the cost of sales on the basis of percentage of the selling price.		
(f) Stock Pricing		
Goods are priced on a FIFO basis. Opening stock of raw materials are 4000 kg of P at ₹0.50 and 4000 kg of Q at ₹1.		
(g) Taxation in the year's profit is estimated at ₹30,000. Overdraft interest in the year is expected to be ₹595, ₹500 of which will be paid during the third quarter of the year.		

You are required to prepare the following budgets for the year for Flower Ltd. using absorption costing methods:

(a) Sales budget.
(b) Production budget (quantities only).
(c) Direct labour budget.
(d) Direct materials budget (usage and purchases).
(e) Overhead absorption rate.

(f) Cost of goods sold budget.

(g) Budgeted P&L A/c.

Solution:

(a) Sales Budget

for the year ended 31st December

Product	Quantity (units)	Selling price (₹)	Total amount (₹)
A	10,000	30	3,00,000
B	2000	50	1,00,000
			4,00,000

(b) Production Budget

for the year ended 31st December

Particulars	A (units)	B (units)
Budgeted sales	10,000	2000
Desired closing stock (finished goods)	2400	400
	12,400	2400
Opening stock (finished goods)	(400)	(600)
Units to be produced	12,000	1800

(c) Direct Labour Budget

for the year ended 31st December

Product	Quantity produced (units)	Direct labour hours per unit (hrs)	Total time (hrs)	Hourly wage rate (₹)	Total amount (₹)
A	12,000	3	36,000	2	72,000
B	1800	5	9000	2	18,000
			45,000		90,000

(d) Direct Materials Usage Budget

for the year ended 31st December

Particulars	Materials		Total (₹)
	P (kg)	Q (kg)	
Product A ((i) 12,000 units 5 kg; (ii) 12,000 units 3 kg)	60,000	36,000	

Table Contd...

Table Contd...

Product B (i) 1800 units 2 kg; (ii) 1800 units 4 kg	3600	7200	
Total Direct Material required (a)	63,600	48,200	
Per kg (b)	₹0.50	₹1	
Total Cost of Direct Materials to be (a) × (b)	₹31,800	₹43,200	75,000

(d) Direct Materials Purchase Budget

for the year ended 31st December

Particulars	Materials		Total (₹)
	P (kg)	Q (kg)	
Direct material required to production (Direct material usage budget)	63,600	43,200	
Desired closing stock (raw material)	5000	3000	
Total requirements	68,600	46,200	
Opening stock (raw material)	(4000)	(4000)	
Purchases (a)	64,600	42,200	
Price per kg (b)	₹0.50	₹1.00	
Cost of purchases (a) × (b)	₹32,300	₹42,200	74,500

(e) Factory Overhead Budget (Absorption Rate)

for the year ended 31st December

Particulars	Activity level 45,000 direct labour-hours
Depreciation	23,500
Other Items	44,000
Total	67,500
Overhead absorption rate = $\frac{₹67,500}{45,000 \text{ hrs}}$ = ₹1.50 per direct labour-hour	

(f) Cost of Goods Sold Budget

for the year ended 31st December

Particulars	Amount (₹)
Opening stock of finished goods	
A	6800
B	14,400

Table Contd...

Table Contd...

Particulars		Amount (₹)
Direct materials	75,000	
Direct wages	90,000	
Factory overhead	67,500	
Work costs or factory cost	2,32,500	
Administration overheads	23,250	
Cost of production		2,55,750
Cost of goods available for sale		2,76,950
Less: Closing stock of finished goods		52,140
Cost of goods sold		2,24,810

(g) Budgeted Profit and Loss Statement

for the year ended 31st December

Particulars		Amount (₹)
Sales revenue		4,00,000
Cost of goods sold		2,24,810
Gross margin/Gross profit		1,75,190
Operating expenses :		
Interest	595	
Selling overhead	20,000	20,595
Operating income/Net profit		
Before tax		1,54,595
Income tax		30,000
Net profit after tax		1,24,595

Working Notes:

Calculation of cost of each unit of finished goods

		A		B	
	Cost per unit of input (₹)	Quantity or hours required for each unit	Amount	Quantity or hours required for each unit	Amount (₹)
Material P	0.50	5 kg	2.50	2 kg	1.00
Material Q	1.00	3 kg	3.00	4 kg	4.00
Direct wages	2.00	3 hr	6.00	5 hr	10.00
Factory overhead	1.50	3 hr	4.50	5 hr	7.50

Table Contd...

Table Contd...

Work/Factory cost			16.00		22.50
Add : Administration			1.60		2.25
overhead 10% on factory cost			17.60		24.75

1. Closing stock of finished goods have been valued on the basis of cost of production per unit for the budget year as the problem states that goods are to be priced on "FIFO basis.
2. Administration overhead absorption rate has been calculated as follows:

$$= \frac{₹11{,}625}{₹1{,}16{,}250} \times 100 \times 100 = 10\%$$

Solution:

Details	40000 units		60000 units		70000 units	
	Per unit	Amount	Per unit	Amount	Per unit	Amount
Sales	50	2,00,00,000	50	3,00,00,000	45	3,15,00,000
Variable cost						
Direct materials	15	60,00,000	15	90,00,000	15	1,05,00,000
Direct wages	10	40,00,000	10	60,00,000	10	70,00,000
Factory overheads	8	32,00,000	8	48,00,000	8	56,00,000
S&A overheads	3	1,20,00,000	3	18,00,000	3.15	22,05,000
Total Variable Cost	36	1,44,00,000	36	2,16,00,000	36.15	2,53,05,000
Contribution	14	56,00,000	14	84,00,000	8.85	61,95,000
Fixed cost						
Factory overheads	12	4,80,00,000	8	48,00,000	6.85	4800000
S&A overheads	6	24,00,000	4	24,00,000	3.42	24,00,000
Additional fixed cost	–	–	2.50	15,00,000	2.42	17,00,000
Advertisement cost	–	–	2.00	12,00,000	–	–
Total Fixed Cost	18	72,00,000	16.50	9,00,000	12.70	89,00,000
Total Cost per unit	54	2,16,00,000	52.50	3,15,00,000	48.85	3,42,05,000
Loss	4	1600000	2.50	15,00,000	3.85	27,05,000

Problem 38 Y Ltd. manufactures two products using one type of material and one grade of labour. Shown below is an extract from the company's working papers of the next period's budget:

	Product A	Product B
Budgeted sales (units)	3600	4800
Budgeted material consumption per product (kg)	5	3
Budgeted material cost ₹12 per kg. Standard hours allowed per product budgeted wage rate ₹8 per hour	5	4

Overtime premium is 50% and is payable, if a worker works for more than 40 hours than 40 hours a week, there are 90 direct workers. The target productivity ratio (or efficiency ratio) for the productive hours worked by the direct workers in actually manufacturing the products is 80%; in addition the productive downtime budgeted at 20% of the productive hours worked. There are twelve 5-day weeks in the budget period and it is anticipated that sales and production will occur evenly throughout the whole period. It is anticipated that stock at the beginning of the period will be: Product A 1020 units: Product B 2400 units; Raw material 4300 kg. The target closing stock expressed in terms of anticipated activity during the budget period are : Product A 15 days sales; Product B 20 days sales; Raw material 10 days consumption.

Required : Calculate the material purchases budget and the wages budget for the direct workers, showing the quantities and value, for the next period.

Solution:

Material Purchase Budget (in quantities and value)

Particulars	Product A	Product B	Total
Budgeted production (units)	3480	400	
Material consumption (kg)	17,400 (3480 units × 5 kg)	12,000 (4000 units × 3 kg)	29,400
Add : Closing balance of material (kg)			4900
Less : Anticipated opening balance of material (kg)			4300
Total quantity of material (kg) to be purchased [B + C – D]			30,000
Total value of material to be purchased (₹) (30,000 kg × ₹12)			₹3,60,000

DIRECT WORKERS WAGES BUDGET

(showing hours required and wages paid)

Standard hours for product A (3480 units × 5 hours)	17,400
Standard hours for product B (4000 units × 4 hours)	16,000
Total standard hours	33,400
Standard hours at 80% efficiency ratio (33,400 × 100/80)	41,750
Add: Non-productive downtime (20% × 41750 hours)	8350

Table Contd...

Table Contd...

Total labour hours required [D + E]	50,100
Less: Normal labour hours (90 workers × 60 days × 8 hours)	43,200
Overtime hours available [F – G]	6900
Wages for normal hours (₹) (4,32,000 hours × ₹ 8)	3,45,600
Overtime wages (₹) (6,900 × ₹ 12)	82,800
Total wages [I + J]	4,28,400

Working Notes:

Closing stock of products A and B

Budgeted period of sales (in days) = 12 weeks × 5 days = 60 days

Closing stock of Product A (units) (15 days sales) = $\frac{3600 \text{ units} \times 15 \text{ days}}{60 \text{ days}}$ = 900 units

Closing stock of Product B (units) (20 days sales) = $\frac{4800 \text{ units} \times 20 \text{ days}}{60 \text{ days}}$ = 1600 units

Production Budget (units)

Particulars	Product A	Product B
Sales (units) (60 days)	3600	4800
Add: Closing stock balance	900	1600
Less: Anticipated opening balance	1020	2400
Total number of units to be produced [A + B – C]	3480	4000

Closing balance of material for 10 days of its consumption

$$= \frac{\text{Total material consumption}}{60 \text{ days}} \times 10 \text{ days}$$

$$\frac{29{,}400 \text{ kg}}{60 \text{ days}} \times 10 \text{ days} = 4900 \text{ kg.}$$

Problem 39 Sangam is manufacturing for sale, four models of TV sets. The major components, viz., cabinet, high voltage transformer and the speaker are brought out by the company. Picture tubes for three out of the four models are purchased from other firms. Four cabinet style (A, B, C and D), two kinds of transformers (X and Y), three kinds of speaks and three types of picture tube are assembled in the following ways in the final product:

Model	Cabinet	Transformer	Speaker	Picture Tube
Standard	A @ ₹ 200	X @ ₹ 200	5" Cone @ ₹ 300	OWN
Deluxe	B @ ₹ 300	X @ ₹ 200	5" Cone @ ₹ 300	BEL @ ₹ 1200
Aristocrat	C @ ₹ 500	Y @ ₹ 300	6" Cone @ ₹ 400	BEL @ ₹ 1200
Royal	D @ ₹ 700	Y @ ₹ 300	12" Cone @ ₹ 600	TELTUBE @ ₹ 1600

The company expects the following inventories in hand on 1st July 2021:

Finished sets:

Standards 46: Deluxe 73 : Aristocrat 64; Royal 69.

Sub-assemblies:

Cabinet : Q–30; B–40; C–20; D–25

Transformers : X-31; Y-17.18.

Speakers : 5" Cone - 27; 6" Cone - 47; 12" Cone - 18.

Picture tubes: OWN-20; BEL 17, Teltube-34.

The sales manager estimates that sales for the quarter, July–September 2021, will be:

Model	Standard	Deluxe	Aristocrat	Royal
Quantity	200	600	500	300

The following inventory quantities have been budgeted for 30th September 2021:

Finished sets : 25 in each Model

Sub-assemblies : Cabinet — 15 (each model)

Transformers — 20 (each type)

Speakers — 30 (each type)

Picture tube — OWN — 30; BEL — 40; Teltube — 20

Required: Prepare the production and purchase budgeted for the various items stated above for the quarter July–September 2021:

SARGAM Co.

Production Budget (in units) for July to Sept. 2021

Particulars	Standard	Delux	Aristocrate	Royal
A. Budgeted sales	200	600	500	300
B. *Add:* Closing stock	25	25	25	25
C. *Less:* Opening stock	46	73	64	69
D. Units to be produced (A+B–C)	179	552	461	256

Purchase Budget (In Units and in ₹ (in lakhs)]

Particulars	Cabinets				Transformers		Speakers			Picture Tube	
	A	B	C	D	X	Y	5	6	12	BEL	Tel Tube
A. Budgeted usage	179	552	461	256	731	717	731	461	256	1013	256
B. *Add:* Closing stock	15	15	15	15	20	20	30	30	30	40	20

Table Contd...

Table Contd...

C. *Less:* Opening stock	30	40	20	25	31	17	27	4	18	17	39
D. Units to be purchased	164	527	456	246	720	720	734	444	268	1036	242
E. Unit cost (₹)	200	300	500	700	200	300	300	400	600	1200	1600
F. Total purchases	328	1.581	2.28	1.722	1.440	2.16	2.202	1.776	1.608	12.432	3.872

Problem 40 Food Panda has prepared the following sales budget for the first five months of 2021:

Months	January	February	March	April	May
Sales units	10,800	15,600	12,200	10,400	9800

Inventory of finished goods at the end of every month is to be 25% of sales estimate for the next month. On 1st January, 2021, there were 2700 units of product on hand. There is no work in progress at the end of any month.

Every unit of product requires two types of materials in the following quantities:

Material A — 4 kg, Material B — 5 kg.

Materials equal to one half of the requirement of next month's production are to be in hand at the end of every month. This requirement was also met on 1st January, 2021.

Required : Prepare the following budgets for the quarter ending 31st March, 2021:

(a) Production budget (quantitative), (b) material purchase budget (quantitative).

Solution:

Production Budget

for the quarter ended 31st March, 2021 (quantitative)

Particulars	January	February	March	Total
Budgeted Sales	10,800	15,600	12,200	36,600
Add : Budgeted closing stock	3,900[1]	3052[2]	2600	9550
Total	14,700	18,650	14,800	48,150
Less : Budgeted opening stock	2700	3900	3050	9650
Units to be produced	12,000	14,750	11,750	38,500

1. Closing stock for January = 15,600 × 25% = 3900
2. Closing stock for February = 12,200 × 25% = 3050
3. Closing stock for Mach = 10,400 × 25% = 2600

MATERIAL PURCHASE BUDGET

for the quarter ended 31st March 2021 (quantitative)

Particulars	January	February	March	Total
Material A:				
Budgeted Usage	48,000	59,000	47,000	1,54,000
Add : Budgeted closing stock	29,500	23,500	20,500	73,500
Total	77,500	82,500	67,500	2,27,500
Less : Budgeted opening stock	24,000	29,500	23,500	77,000
Purchases to be made	53,500	53,000	44,000	1,50,500
Material B:				
Budgeted usage	60,000	73,750	58,750	1,92,500
Add : Budgeted closing stock	36,875	29,375	25,625	91,875
Total	96,875	10,315	84,375	2,84,375
Less : Budgeted opening stock	30,000	36,875	29,375	96,250
Purchases to be made	66,875	66,250	55,000	1,88,125

Working Notes:

1. *Computation of Budgeted Consumption*

Particulars	Material A		Material B	
January	(12000* × 4)	48,000	(12,000* × 5)	60,000
February	(14750* × 4)	59,000	(14,750* × 5)	73,750
March	(11750* × 4)	47,000	(11,750* × 5)	58,750
Total		1,54,000		1,92,500

These figures are taken from production budget.

2. *Computation of production and material required in the month of April*

Particulars	Units
Sales	10,400
Budgeted Closing Stock (9800 × 25%)	2450
Less : Budgeted Opening Stock	2600
Production (A + B – C)	10,250
Material required	
Material A (10250 × 4)	41,000
Material B (10250 × 5)	51,250

3. *Computation of Budgeted Closing Stock*

Particulars	Material A		Material B	
	Budgeted Usage 2	Budgeted Closing Stock 3 = 50% of 2	Budgeted Usage 4	Budgeted Closing Stock 5 = 50% of 4
January	59,000	29,500	73,500	36,875
February	47,000	23,500	58,250	29,125
March	41,000	20,500	51,250	25,625
Total		73,750		91,625

Problem 41 X Ltd. manufacturing three products, has the following direct labour requirements for the product:

	Direct labour hours per unit (in minutes)		
Operation	Product 1	Product 2	Product 3
I	18	42	30
II	–	12	24
III	9	6	–

The factory work 8 hours per day, 6 days in a week. Each budget quarter has 13 weeks and in terms of leave, rates holidays and other causes, 124 hours are lost in each quarter. Operations I, II and III have the budgeted nearly wants for workers at ₹16, ₹24 respectively. The budgeted sales of the products during the quatrain are:

Product 1	9000 units
Product 1	15,000 units
Product 1	12,000 units

There were operating stocks of 5000 units of product 2 and 4000 units of Product 3 and it is proposed to have closing stock at the end of the quarter as follows:

Required: Prepare a manpower budget for the quarter, showing for each operation: (i) Direct labour hours a cost, and (iii) Number of workers.

Product 1	1000 units
Product 3	2000 units

Solution:

Manpower budget showing for each operation direct labour hours,
Direct labour cost and number of workers for the quarter ending _____

Particulars	Operation I	Operation II	Operation III	Total
Direct labour hr (Refer to W.N. (ii)]	15,000 hr	6000 hr	2500 hr	23500 hr

Table Contd...

Table Contd...

Particulars	Operation I	Operation II	Operation III	Total
Direct labour cost (₹) (Refer to W.N. (iii)]	2,40,000	1,20,000	60,000	4,20,000
No. of workers (Refer to W.N. (v)]	30 men	12 men	5 men	47 men

Working Notes:

(i) Production Budget for the quarter ending ______

Particulars	Product 1	Product 2	Product 3
Budgeted sales (units)	9000	15,000	12,000
Add: Closing stock (units)	1000	–	2000
Less: Opening stock (units)	5000	–	4000
Budgeted production [A + B – C]	10,000	10,000	10,000

(ii) Budges direct labour hours required in each operation for the quarter ending ______

A Product	B Budgeted Production (units)	C Direct Labour hours per unit	D = B × C/60 Direct Labour Hours required
Operation 1 :			
Product 1	10,000	18 min	3000 hr
Product 2	10,000	42 min	7000 hr
Product 3	10,000	30 min	5000 hr
			15,000 hr
Operation II :			
Product 1	10,000	–	–
Product 2	10,000	12 min	2000 hr
Product 3	10,000	24 min	4000 hr
			6000 hr
Operation III :			
Product 1	10,000	9 min	1500 hr
Product 2	10,000	6 min	1000 hr
Product 3	10,000	–	–
			2500 hrs

(iii) Budgeted labour cost for the quarter ending _____

Operation	Direct Labour hours	Direct Labour hourly Rate	Direct Labour cost (₹)
I	15,000	16	2,24,000
II	6000	20	1,20,000
III	2500	24	60,000

(iv) Computation of net direct labour hours available in a quarter

A. Total number of hours available in a quarter (13 weeks × 6 days × 8 hours)

B. *Less:* Estimated hours lost due to leave, etc.

C. Net available hours

(v) $$\text{No. of workers required} = \frac{\text{Direct labour hours required}}{\text{Net available hours in a quainter}}$$

$$\text{Operation I} = \frac{15000}{500} = 30 \text{ men}$$

$$\text{Operation I} = \frac{6000}{500} = 12 \text{ men}$$

$$\text{Operation I} = \frac{2500}{500} = 5 \text{ men}$$

$$= 47 \text{ men}$$

Problem 42 AC company is engaged in manufacturing two products X and Y. Product X uses one unit of component P and two units of component Q. Product Y uses two units of component P, one unit of component Q and two units of component R. Component R which is assembled in the factory uses one unit of component Q.

Component P and Q are purchased from the market. The company has prepared the following forecast of sales and inventory for the next year.

Particulars	Product X	Product Y
Sales (in units)	80000	150000
At the end of the year	10000	20000
At the beginning of the year	30000	50000

The production of both the products and assembling of the component R will be spread out uniformly through the year. The company at present orders its inventory of P and Q in quantities equivalent to 3 months production. The company has compiled the following data related to two components.

Particulars	P	Q
Price per unit (₹)	20	8
Order placing cost per order (₹)	1500	1500
Carrying cost per annum	20%	20%

Required:

(a) Prepare a budget of production and requirements of components during next year.

(b) Suggest the optimal order quantity of components P and Q.

Solution:

PRODUCTION BUDGET FOR PRODUCT X AND Y

Particulars	X Units	Y Units
A. Budgeted sales	80,000	1,50,000
B. *Add :* Ending inventory at the end of the year	10,000	20,000
C. *Less :* Beginning inventory	30,000	50,000
D. Budgeted production (A + B – C)	60,000	1,20,000

BUDGETED REQUIREMENTS OF COMPONENTS P, Q AND R

Particulars	P	Q	R
For product X: Production 60,000 units			
P: 60,000 × 1 per unit	60,000		
Q: 60,000 × 2 per unit		1,20,000	
Product Y: Production 1,20,000 units			
R: 1,20,000 × 2 per unit	2,40,000		
Q: 1,20,000 1 per unit		1,20,000	
R: 1,20,000 × 2 per unit			2,40,000
For comp R : Production 2,40,000 components			
Q: 2,40,000 × 1 per component R		2,40,000	
Total requirements	3,00,000	4,80,000	2,40,000

(b)

$$\text{EOQ} = \sqrt{\frac{2 \text{ Annual wage} \times \text{Ordering cost per order}}{\text{Carrying cost per unit}}}$$

$$\text{EOQ(P)} = \sqrt{\frac{2 \times 3,00,000 \times 1500}{20 \times 20\%}} = 15,000 \text{ components}$$

$$\text{EOQ(Q)} = \sqrt{\frac{2 \times 4,80,000 \times 1500}{8 \times 20\%}} = 30,000 \text{ components}$$

REVIEW QUESTIONS

1. (a) State the important features of zero-base budgeting.
   (b) Distinguish between fixed and flexible budget.
2. Discuss the steps necessary for the success of budgetary control system in an organisation.
3. Distinguish between zero-base budget and conventional budget.
4. What purpose is served by instituting a budgetary central system in an organisation having both manufacturing and selling activities.
5. Explain briefly the concept of fixed budget.
6. Budget is an aid to management not a substitute for management. Comment.
7. Write notes on:
   (a) Budget manual
   (b) Principal budget factor
   (c) Performance budgeting
   (d) Single and multiple overhead rate
   (e) Flexible budget
   (f) Zero-base budgeting
8. Write short notes on:
   (a) Zero-base budgeting
   (b) Limitation of budget
   (c) Master budget
   (d) Flexible budget
   (e) Profit centre
9. Briefly explain the essentials of an effective budgetary central system.
10. What are the essentials for effective budgeting?

UNSOLVED PRACTICAL QUESTIONS

1. The following information is available from the records of TD Tools Limited for the last six months of 2021 (and of only the sales of January, 2022) in respect of product X:

   (i) Units to be sold in different months are:

Month	Quantity (Unit)
July, 2021	1100
August, 2021	1100
September, 2021	1700
October, 2021	1900

Table Contd...

Table Contd...

November, 2021	2500
December, 2021	2300
January, 2022	2000

(ii) There will be no work-in-progress at the end of the month.

(iii) Finished units equal to half the sales for the next month will be in stock at the end of every month (including June, 2021).

(iv) Budgeted production and production cost for the year ending December 31, 2021 are as under:

Production (units)	₹22,000
Direction material per unit	₹30.00
Direct wages per unit	₹15.00
Total overheads apportioned to the product "X"	₹2,64,000

It is required to prepare:

(a) A production budget for each of the last six months of 2021

(b) A summarised production cost budget for the same period.

[*Ans.* Production units (month-wise): 1000, 1400, 1800, 2200, 2400, 2150; Total production cost: ₹6,29,850]

2. From the following details, prepare a production budget of Alpha Sales Corporation of Punjab for the year ended on 31.3.2020.

Production	Sales (Unit)	Estimated Stock (Unit)	
	[As Per Sales Budget]	01.04.2019	31.03.2020
P	6,00,000	60,000	65,000
Q	4,00,000	22,000	18,000
R	3,50,000	30,000	30,000

[*Ans.* Units to be produced : P 6,05,000, Q 3,96,000, R 3,50,000]

3. Prepare a flexible budget for the overheads of Damyanti Limited from the following data and ascertain the overhead rates based on direct labour hours at 50%, 60% and 70% capacity.

At 60% capacity:

Element of Cost	Amount (₹)
Variable overheads:	
Indirect material	6000
Indirect labour	18,000
Semi-variable overheads:	
Electricity (40% fixed and 60% variable)	30,000

Table Contd...

Table Contd...

Repairs (80% fixed and 20% variable)	3000
Fixed overheads:	
Depreciation	16,500
Insurance	4500
Salaries	
Estimated direct labour hours: 1,86,000	

[***Ans.*** Overhead rates : 0.55; 0.50; and 0.46]

4. A single product company estimated its sales for the next year (quarter-wise) as under:

Quarter	Sale Units
I	30,000
II	37,500
III	41,250
IV	45,000

The opening stock of finished goods is 10,000 units and the company expects to maintain the closing stock of finished goods at 16,250 units at the end of the year. The production pattern in each quarter is based on 80% of the sales of the current quarter and 20% of the sales of the next quarter. The opening stock of raw material in the beginning of the year is 10,000 kg and the closing stock at the end of the year is required to be maintained at 5000 kg. Each unit of finished output requires 2 kg of raw materials.

The company proposes to purchase the entire annual requirement of the raw material in the first three quarters in the proportion and the prices given below:

Quarter	Purchase of raw materials % to total annual requirement in quantity	Price per kg
I	30	2
I	50	3
I	20	4

The value of the opening stock of raw material in the beginning of the year is ₹20,000.

Required: Present the following for the next year (quarter-wise):

(i) Production budget in units

(ii) Raw material consumption in quantity

(iii) Raw material purchase budget in quantity and value

(iv) Priced store ledger card of the raw materials using in first-in-first-out method

[*Ans.* (i) Unit: 31,500; 38,255, 42,000, 48,250; (ii) kg.: 63,000; 7,65,000, 84,000, 96,500; (iii) 95,500 kg. for ₹1,89,000 in Quarter I; 63,000 kg for ₹2,52,000 in Quarter III; (iv) 5000 kg @ ₹4 = ₹20,000]

5. A factory is currently running at 50% capacity and produces 500 units at a cost of ₹90 per unit as per details given below:

Element of Cost	Amount (₹)
Material	50
Labour	15
Factory overheads (6 fixed)	15
Administrative overheads (₹5 fixed)	10

The current selling price is ₹100 per unit. At 60% working, material cost per unit increase by 2% and selling price per unit falls by 2%.

At 80% working, material cost per unit increases by 5% and selling price per unit falls by 2.5%.

Prepare a flexible budget showing profit of the company at 60% and 80% working and give your comments.

[*Ans.* Contribution at 60% is ₹18 per unit, and profit ₹53,000; Contribution at 80% is ₹16 per unit, and profit ₹73,000)

6. Prepare a flexible budget for production at 80 and 100 per cent activity on the following basis of the information provided:

Details	Amount (₹)
Production at 50% capacity (unit)	5000
Direct material	80 per unit
Direct wages	50 per unit
Direct expenses	15 per unit
Works overhead costs	50,000 (50% fixed)
Administration overhead costs	60,000 (60% variable)

[*Ans.* At 80% per unit variable cost: ₹157.20 and fixed cost per unit ₹6125 (Absolute amount; ₹49,000); at 100% per unit variable cost: ₹157.20 and fixed cost per unit ₹4.90 (absolute amount ₹49,000]

7. Data regarding sales, cost and profit at 50% capacity are given below:

Details	Amount (₹)
Sales	50,00,000
Direct cost	20,00,000
Factory overheads	10,00,000
Office overheads	50,00,000
Selling overheads	7,50,000
Profit	7,50,000

Every 10% increase in sales beyond the given capacity of 50% is possible only after reducing the price by one per cent on the base level of 50% capacity. Direct material cost is 25% of the total direct cost at 50% level of capacity. With every 10% increase in capacity above this level, the price of the direct material comes down by 2%. 50% of the factory overheads are fixed and the rest are fully variable. Office overheads are of step character. Every 10% increase in output results in 2% increase in office overheads over 50% capacity. Selling overheads increase in proportion of sales value. Prepare a flexible budget at 80% capacity level.

[*Ans.* Sales ₹7,76,00,000 Profit ₹16,14,000]

8. With the following data for 60% capacity utilisation, prepare a budget for 60%, 80% and 100% capacity:

   Production at 60 capacity : 600 units

   Materials = ₹100; Labour ₹40; Expenses ₹10; Factory overhead – ₹40,000 (40% Fixed); Administration overhead ₹30,000 (60% fixed).

   [*Ans.* ₹1,60,000; ₹1,60,000; and ₹16,000]

9. The income statement Forum Ltd. for the year ended Mar. 31, 2020 is presented below:

	Product X		Product Y		Total	
	Budget	**Actual**	**Budget**	**Actual**	**Budget**	**Actual**
Sales (units)	2000	2800	6000	5600	8000	4400
Total sales of market (units)	–	–	–	–	40,000	45,654
Sales revenue (₹)	6000	7560	12,000	11,760	18,000	19,320
Cost of goods sold (₹)	2400	2800	6000	5880	8400	8680
Fixed costs (₹)	1800	1900	2400	2400	4200	4300
Total cost (₹)	4200	4700	8400	8280	12,600	12,980
Net profit (₹)	1800	2860	3500	3600	5400	6340

Using the above information compute:

(a) Market size variance, (b) Market share variance.

[*Ans.* (a) (₹1,257 (f), (b) ₹877 (A)]

10. The following information is available is respect of Tamaine Chemicals for a week:
   (a) 400 kg of raw materials were actually used in producing product 'EXE'. The purchase cost thereof being ₹24,800. The standard price per kg of raw material is ₹60. The expected output is 12 units of product 'EXE' from each kg of raw material. Raw material price variance and usage variance as computed by cost accountant are ₹800 (adverse) and ₹600 (adverse) respectively.
   (b) The week is of 40 hours. The standard time to produce one unit of 'EXE' is 30 minutes. The standard wage rate is ₹5 per labour hour. The company employs 60 workers who have been paid hourly wage rate as order:

Number of workers:	6	8	46
Hourly wages rate (₹):	4.80	5.20	5.00

(c) Budgeted overheads for a four-week period is ₹81,600. The actual fixed overheads spent during the said week are ₹19,800.

(d) Entire output of 'EXE' has been sold at its standard selling price of 15 per unit.

Required:

(i) Compute the variance relating to labour and overheads.

(ii) Prepare a statement showing total standard costs, standard profit and actual profit for the week

[***Ans.*** LCV ₹316 (A), LRV ₹16 (A), LEV ₹300 (A), TFOCV ₹90 (F) FOVV ₹510 (A), FOEV ₹600 (F)]

11. Following is the standard cost details of a component:

Materials 2 units @ ₹15 ₹30.

Labour 3 hours @ ₹20 ₹60

Total overheads 3 hours @ ₹10 ₹30

During a particular month 10,000 units of the component were produced and the same was found to be at 60% capacity of the budget. In preparing the variance report for the month, the cost accountant gathered the following information:

Labour	₹6,50,000
Variable overhead	₹2,00,000
Fixed overhead	₹3,00,000
Material price variance	₹ 70,000 (A)
Material cost variance	₹ 50,000 (A)
Labour rate variance	₹ 50,000 (F)
Fixed overhead expenditure variance	₹ 50,000 (A)

Required: Calculate (a) Actual material cost incurred, (b) Standard cost of material actually consumed, (c) Labour efficiency variance, (d) Variable OH efficiency variance, (e) Variance OH expenditure variance (f) Fixed OH efficiency variance, (g) Fixed OH capacity, (h) Fixed, (h) OH volume variance.

[***Ans.*** (a) ₹3,50,000 (b) ₹2,80,000 (c) ₹1,00,000 (A) (d) ₹25,000 (A) (e) ₹25,000 (A) (f) ₹25,000 (A) (g) ₹75,000 (A) (h) 1,00,000 (A)

12. The standard cost chart of producing one of hair colour in as follows:

	₹
Direct material	120
A: 12 kg @ ₹10	30
B: 5 kg @ ₹6	15

Table Contd...

Table Contd...

	₹
Direct Wages — 5 hr @ ₹3	35
Fixed production overheads	200
Total standard cost:	50
Standard sale price	250

Fixed production overhead is absorbed on expected annual output of 13,200 units. Actual result for the month of September, 2021 are as under.
Actual production : 1000 units

	₹
Sales 1000 units @ 250	2,50,000
Direct material	1,21,000
A: 11000 kg	28,600
B: 5200 kg	17,500
Direct wages 5500 hr	39,000
Fixed overheads	2,06,100
Gross profit	43,900

Required: Calculate all variances. Material price variance is taken out at the time of receipt of material. Material purchased were: 12,000 kg of A@₹11 & 5,000 kg of B@₹5.50

[***Ans.*** MCV ₹400 (F), MPV ₹8400 (A), MUV ₹8800 (A), MMV ₹1741.18 (F), MYV ₹75,882 (F) Material purchase variance ₹9500 (A), LCV ₹2500 (A), LRV ₹100 (A), LEV = ₹1500 (A), FOEV ₹500 (A), FOV ₹3500 (A), Overhead Efficiency Variance ₹3500 (A)]

13. Hindustan Ltd. provides you the following information:

	Product A	Product B
Sales (in units) as per sales budget:		
1st quarter 2021	2000	4000
2nd quarter 2021	4720	2000
3rd quarter 2021	4320	2500
4th quarter 2021	4960	1500
Stock position on 1.1.2021		
Percentage of 1st quarter 2021 sales	20%	100%
Stock position ending 1st quarter 2021 sales		
Percentage of next quarter's sales	50%	50%
Stock position as on 31.12.2021	4400	2000

Required: Prepare sales budget for the year 2022

[***Ans.*** Unit to be produced qtr-wise: Product A 3960, 4520 6880, 1000, 2250; 2000, 2750]

14. A Toy company provides you the following information:

	Product A	Product B
Material X @ ₹3 per unit		
Material Y @ ₹1 per unit	2 units	2 units
Units to be produced as per	1 unit	2 units
Units to be produced as per		
Production Budget	20,000	8,000
Inventory of raw material:		
	Material X	*Material Y*
Opening stock as on 1.1.2021	24,000 Units	4000 Units
Estimated closing stock as on 31.12.2021	32,000	8000

Required : Prepare direct material usage and purchase budget for the year 2021.

[***Ans.*** Total purchased (units & amt.): Material X: 80,000 units, ₹2,40,000 material Y 40000 units and ₹40,000]

15. Prepare the cash budget for October at 2021 from the information supplied by Shah Agency Trading concern.

(a) Balance Sheet as on 31st March 2021

Liabilities	₹	Assets		₹
Proprietor's capital	2,00,000	Cash		41,000
Outstanding liabilities	34,000	Stock in trade		1,01,000
		Sundry debtors		50,000
		Furniture	50,000	
		Less: Depreciation	10,000	40,000
	2,34,000			2,34,000

Estimate Sales and expenditure on salaries

Months	Sales (₹)	Salaries (₹)
April	60,000	6000
May	1,04,000	7000
June	1,00,000	70,000
July	1,50,000	8000
August	1,80,000	8000
September	70,000	6000
October	50,000	6000
November	50,000	6000

The other monthly expenses are ; rent ₹2000, deprecation ₹2000, misc. expenses ₹1000 and commission 1% of sales.

Of the sales, 80% is on credit and 20% for cash.

70% of the credit sales are collected is one month and the balance is two months. There are no bad debt losses.

Gross margin on sales an average is 30%.

Purchases equal to next month's sales are made every month and they are paid during the month in which they are made.

The firm maintains a minimum cash balance of ₹20,000.

Cash deficiencies are made up by bank loans which are repaid at the earliest available opportunity and cash in excess of ₹30,000 is invested in securities (interest on bank loans and securities is to be ignored).

Outstanding liabilities remain unchanged.

Credit sales in February and March were equal.

[*Ans.* Closing balance: April to August ₹20,000 Sept. to October ₹30,000]

16. ABC Ltd. provides you the following information.

(a) Sales, purchase, etc.

	April (₹)	May (₹)	June (₹)	July (₹)	August (₹)	September (₹)
Cash sales	16,000	24,000	32,000	40,000	48,000	56,000
Collection from debtors	32,000	64,000	96,000	1,28,000	1,60,000	1,92,000
Cash purchases	16,000	24,000	32,000	40,000	48,000	56,000
Payment to creditors	24,000	48,000	72,000	96,000	1,20,000	1,44,000
Payment of expenses	24,000	10,000	15,600	5,900	54,000	40,000

(b) the opening cash balance of ₹20,200 is the minimum cash balance to be maintained.

(c) Any short fall in the minimum cash balance is to be met by bank borrowings in the multiple of ₹10,000 @ 12% pa or by sale of marketable securities in the multiple of ₹20,000. Bank interest on monthly basis is payable on the first date of the subsequent month. Bank interest is payable for a minimum period of a month.

(d) Any surplus cash is to be used to repay the borrowings in the multiple of ₹10,000 or to purchase the marketable securities in the multiple of ₹20,000 [ignore interest on securities received and paid].

Required: Prepare the cash budget for April to September.

[*Ans.* Closing balance: ₹24,000, ₹29,800, ₹28,000, ₹30,000, ₹38,000]

17. P.C.T. Ltd. provides you the following figures for the year 2021.

	Product A	Product B
Sale (in unit) 1st quarter	2500	3200
2nd quarter	5900	1600
3rd quarter	5400	2000
4th quarter	6200	1200
₹24	₹50	
Selling price per unit		
Target for 2022		
Sales quantity increase (decrease)	(20%)	25%
Selling price increase (decrease)	25%	(20%)

Sales area X, Y and Z respectively produce 10%, 20%, 70% of product 'A' sales and 70%, 20% and 10% of produce 'B' sales.

Required : Prepare sales budget for the year 2022.

[*Ans.* Sales: Product A ₹2,40,000, product B ₹2,00,000]

CASE STUDIES

1. Raghvendra is the Controller of Bangalore Laboratories, a manufacturer, and distributor of generic prescription pharmaceuticals. He is currently in the process of preparing the annual budget and reviewing the current business plan. The business unit managers of Banglore prepare and assemble the detailed operating budgets with technical assistance from the corporate accounting staff. The final budgets are then presented by the business unit managers to the corporate executive committee for approval. The corporate accounting staff reviews the budgets for adherence to corporate accounting policies, but no detailed review for reasonableness of the line items within the budget is done.

   Raghvendra is aware that the upcoming year for the company may be a difficult one due to the operation of a major patent and the loss of a loss of a licensing agreement for another product line. He also knows that during the budgeting process, "budgetary slack" is created in varying degrees throughout the organisation. Raghvendra believes this slack has a negative effective on the overall business objective of Banglore Laboratories and should be eliminated where possible.

   Required:

   (a) Define budgetary slack.

   (b) Explain the advantages and disadvantages of budgetary slack from the point of view of each of the following:

      1. The business unit manager who must achieve the budget.
      2. Corporate management.

(c) Raghvendra is considering implementing zero-based budgeting at Banglore Laboratories

1. Define zero-based budgeting.
2. Describe how zero-based budgeting could be advantageous to Bangalore Laboratories a controlling budgetary slack.
3. Discuss the disadvantages Bangalore Laboratories might encounter from using zero-based budgeting.

2. HEL Company is a large multi-division firm with several plans in each division. A comprehensive budgeting system is used for palling operations and measuring performance. The annual budgeting process stars in August, five months prior to the beginning of the fiscal year. At this time, the division manager submits proposal budget for sales, production and inventory level are expenses. Capital expenditure requests also are formalise at this time. The expense budgets include direct labour and all overhead items that are separated into fixed and variable components. Direct material are budgeted separately in developing the production and inventory schedule.

The expense budget for each division are developed from the plans' result, as measured by the percentage variation from an adjusted budget in the first six months of the current year and target expense reduction percentage established by the corporation.

To determine plan percentages, the plan budget for the just completed half-year period is revised to recognise change in operating procedures and costs outside the control of plan management (e.g., labour was rate changes, product style changes, and so forth). The difference between this revised budget and the actual expenses is the controllable variance and is expressed as a percentage of the actual expenses. This percentage is added (if unfavourable) to the corporate target expense reduction percentage. A favourable plant variance and the corporate target reduction was 4% the plant's budget for the next year should reflect costs approximately 6% below this year actual costs.

Next year's final budget for the company, the division, and the plans are adopted after corporate analysis of the proposed budgets and a careful review with each division manager of the changes made by corporate management. Division profit budgets include allocated corporate costs and plant profit budgets include allocated division and corporate costs.

Return on assets is used to measure the performance of divisions and plants. The asset base for a division consists of all assets assigned to the division, including its working capital, and an allocated share of corporate assets. For plants, the assets base includes the assets assigned to the plant plus an allocated portion of the division and corporate assets. Recommendation for promotions and salary increase for the executives of the divisions and plants are influenced by how well actual return on assets compare with the budgeted return on assets.

The plant manager of the Chennai, a major plant in the Southern Division, carefully controls his costs during the first six months so that any improvement appears after the target reduction of appears is established. He accomplishes this by careful planning and timing of his discretionary expenditure.

During 2021, the property adjacent to the Chennai Plant was purchased by HEL Company. This expenditure was not included in the 2021 capital budget. Corporate management decided to divert funds from a project at another plant since the property appeared to be better long-term investment.

Also during 2021, HEL Company experienced depressed sales. In an attempt to achieve budgeted by 6%. In order to accomplish this expense reduction, the Chennai Plant manager reduced preventive maintenance and postponed needed major repairs. Employees who quit were not replaced unless absolutely necessary. Employee training was postponed whenever possible. The raw material, supplies, and finished goods inventories were reduced below normal level.

Required:

(a) Evaluate the budget procedure of HEL Company with respect to its effectiveness for planning and controlling operations.

(b) Is the HEL Company's use of return on assets to evaluate the performance of the Chennai Plant controlling operations.

(c) Analyse and explain the Chennai Plant manager's behaviour during 2021.

3. An effective budget converts the objectives and goals of management into quantified plans. If done correctly, it can serve as a motivating force within the company as well the basis of control and performance evaluation. Creating a budget is essential to the operations of a company.

   Two different approaches to preparing a budget are the imposed budget and the participate budget. The imposed budget is created by top management with minimal input from those individuals who are accountable for budgetary result, the participate budget, in contract, encourages input and accountable individuals directly participate in the budgeting process along with top management.

Required:

(a) Discuss the behavioural implications of the imposed budgetary approach.

(b) 1. Describe at least three benefits of the imposed budgetary approach.

2. Describe at least three potential problems to the organisation can derive form a participate budgetary approach.

(c) Discuss the behavioural impact on operational management employees of participatate budgeting.

4. Nitin, the controller in New Delhi Municipal Corporation, New Delhi recognises the importance of the budgetary process for planning, control, and motivation purposes. He believes that a properly implemented participate budgeting process for planning purposes, subordinates to improve productivity within their particular departments.

Based on this and a management by exception reporting procedure based on that budget will motivate his philosophy, Nitin has implemented the following budget procedures.

- An appropriation target figure is given to each department manager. This amount is the maximum funding that each department can expect to receive in the next fiscal year.
- Department managers develop their individual budgets within the following spending constraints as directed by the controller's staff.
  1. Expenditure requests cannot exceed the appropriation target.
  2. All fixed expenditures should be included in the budget. Fixed expenditure would include such items as contracts and salaries at current levels.
  3. All government project directed by higher authority should be included in the budget in their entirety.
- The controller consolidates the department budget requests from the various departments into one budget that is to be submitted for the entire division.
- Upon final budget approval by the legislature, the controller's staff allocates the appropriation to the various departments on instructions from the division manager. However, a specified percentage of each department's appropriation is held back in anticipation of potential budget cuts and special funding needs. The amount and use of this contingency fund are felt to the discretion of the division manager.
- Each department is allowed to adjust in budget when necessary to operate within the reduced appropriation level. However, as stated in the original directive, specific projects authorised by higher authority must remain intact.
- The final budget is used as the basis of control for a management by exception form of reporting. Excessive expenditures by account for each department are highlighted on a monthly basis. Department managers are expected to account for all expenditures over budget. Fiscal responsibility is an important factor in the overall performance evaluation of department managers.

Nitin believes his policy of allowing the department managers to participate in the budget process and then holding them accountable for their performance is essential, especially during these times of limited resources. He further believes that department managers will be positively motivated to increase the efficiency and effectiveness of their departments because they have provided input into the initial budgetary process and required to justify any unfavourable performance.

Required:

(a) Explain the operational and behavioural benefits that generally are attributed to a participate budgeting process.

(b) Identify deficiencies in Nitin's participate budgetary policy for planning and performance evaluation purpose. For each deficiency identified, recommend how the deficiency can be corrected.

5. TabComp Inc. is a retail distributor for MZB-33 computer hardware and related software and support services. TabComp prepares annual sales forecasts of which the first six months for 2020 are presented below.

TabComp Inc. Sales Forecast, Six Months - 2020

	Hardware Sales		Software	Total
	Units	**(₹)**	**Sales and Support**	**Sale**
January	130	3,90,000	₹1,60,000	₹5,50,000
February	120	3,60,000	1,40,000	5,00,000
March	110	3,30,000	1,50,000	4,80,000
April	90	2,70,000	1,30,000	4,00,000
May	100	3,00,000	1,25,000	4,25,000
June	125	3,75,000	2,25,000	6,00,000
Total	675	20,25,000	9,30,000	29,55,000

Cash sales account for 25 per cent for TabCab's total sales, 30 per cent of the total sales are paid a bank credit card and the remaining 45 per cent are on open account (TabCom's own charge accounts). The cash and bank credit sales are received in the month of the sales. Bank credit card sales are subject to a four per cent discount deducted at the time of the daily deposit. The cash receipts for sale on open account are 70 per cent in the month following the sale, 28 per cent in the second month following the sale, and the remaining are estimated to be uncollectible.

TabComp's month-end inventory requirements for computer hardware units are 30 per cent of the next months sales. A one-month lead time is required for delivery from the manufacture, thus, the store by the first day of the month needed. The computer hardware units are purchased under some time of n/45 measured from the time of the month needed. The computer hardware units are purchased under the computer units is 60 per cent of the selling price.

Required:

(a) Calculate the cash that TabComp Inc. can expect to collect during April 2020. Be sure to show all of your calculations.

(b) TabComp Inc. is determining the MZB-33 computer hardware units that will be ordered on January all of your calculation.

(i) Determine the projected number of computer hardware units that will be ordered.

(ii) Calculate the value of the order that TabComp will place for the these computer hardware units.

(iii) In which month will TabComp pay for these hardware units?

(c) As part of the annual budget process, TabComp Ins, prepares a cash budget by month for the entire year. Explain why a company such as TabComp prepares a cash budget by month for the entire year.

[*Ans.* (a) Total collections ₹4,29,400. (b) (i) 104 (ii) ₹1,87,200 is value of order (iii) Payment will be made on the last day of the 45-day discount period. (c) Monthly cash budgets are prepared in order to plain for cash need]

6. Incence Fashion manufactures and sells fashion goods. The company has four divisions strategically located near all the major markets. Each division operates as an independent responsibility centre and is evaluated at the end the year as an autonomous profit unit.

The management of Reebok is not very happy with the performance of one of its division whose cash budget is presented below. The management believes that the division has not achieved the desired growth and profitability mainly because of its slow collection policy.

Budget statement of cash receipts and cash disbursements for the company for the year ended 30 June 2021.

Particulars	Total (₹)	I Quarter (₹)	II Quarter (₹)	III Quarter (₹)	IV Quarter (₹)
Opening Cash Balance	85,000	20,000	15,000	30,000	20,000
Cash Receipts	60,000	15,000	6,000	26,000	13,000
Total Cash Available	1,45,000	35,000	21,000	56,000	33,000
Cash Disbursement Inventory	25,000	5000	6000	9000	5000
Asset Purchase	60,000	30,000	15,000	5000	10,000
Operating Expenses	1,00,000	40,000	26,000	16,500	17,500
Minimum Cash Balance Required	20,000	5000	5000	5000	5000
Total Cash Needed	1,20,000	45,000	31,000	21,500	22,500
Excess of Cash Available over Cash Disbursement	25,000	(10,000)	(10,000)	34,000	10,500

After a tremendous amount of research, it has been found that some areas of concern noticed by management are:

(a) In preparing the budget, participation from various levels within the organisation.

(b) The revenant people for implementing the budget are not consulted. There are the people who have the ability to control the item that is budgeted, and who will be rewarded according to its accomplishment.

(c) The budget committee has not reviewed the budget to make sure there are no internal inconsistencies.

In the context of this information, discuss how the Reebok's budgeting process could be revised to correct the problem.

CHAPTER

5 Standard Costing and Variance Analysis

MEANING

Standard costing is a managerial tool for planning, decision making, coordination and control of business activities. Efficient and optimal utilisation of resources can take place only when the actual performance is compared with the standards set by the business enterprise. The comparison of actual cost with the standard cost is facilitated by standard costing. It is an integral part of planning and controlling of cost systems in an organisation. The difference between actual and standard cost is known as variance, which is discussed in this chapter. When the actual cost exceeds the standard cost, the variance is said to be unfavourable and when the actual cost is less than the standard cost the variance is termed favourable.

Standard costing is an essential part of overall planning and control system in any organisation. Control means conformance to plans. It entails (i) the setting up of yardsticks or standards of performance, (ii) comparison of actual performance with the standard and (iii) taking remedial measures to set right the deviations. It is one of the tools to control costs. It requires the determination of costs in advance of production. The predetermined costs are compared with actual costs. The difference between the actual costs and the predetermined costs, known as variance, is analysed and investigated to find out the reasons. Variances are reported to the management for taking remedial/corrective measures meant to adhere to predetermined or standard costs.

Standard cost accounting, simply known as standard costing, is an essential part of a control system. In a standard costing system, according to the ICWA, London, "standard costs are prepared and need to clarify the final results of a business, particularly by measurement of the variations of actual costs from standard costs and the analysis of the causes of variations for the purpose of maintaining efficiency by executive action". Wheldon states that "standard costing is a method of ascertaining the costs whereby statistics are prepared to show (a) the standard cost, (b) the actual cost, (c) the difference between these costs, which is termed variance". It consists of the following:

(i) Determination and use of standard cost.

(ii) **Comparison** of actual costs with standard costs and measuring the variances.

(iii) **Controlling** costs by the variance analysis.

(iv) **Reporting** to management for taking necessary action to optimise efficiency.

Standard cost seeks to establish the cost of a product, operations or process under standard operating environment. The aim of standard cost is to eliminate the influence of abnormal changes in prices. It is used as a guide forfeiture decision and action over a period of time. Standard costing is an effective managerial tool for planning, decision-making coordination and control of business. The object of standard cost is to ascertain the quotation and determination of price policy. It is a technique of cost control. For controlling costs, management should not only know actual cost (the cost actually incurred) but also predetermined costs (i.e., the cost that should have been incurred).

Need of Standard Costing. The need of standard casting arises because of the limitations of the historical costing in the field of cost control. Actual costs are meaningful only when they are compared with predetermined costs.

Limitations of the historical costing are enumerated as under:

1. Historical costs do not provide any means of evaluating and comparing performances. Therefore, historical costs are ineffective in cost control.
2. Historical costs do not provide reliable guides to management in the tasks of budgeting, planning and decision making. Costs incurred in the past reflect a situation in a previous period. The conditions prevailing in one period unlikely to recur in another period. Historical costs are not of any help in cost reduction since they contain no standard or goals towards the attainment of which the employee can work.

Historical costing is a system where costs are ascertained once they are incurred. It is a postmortem of the costs. It does not help in finding mistakes and inefficiencies. Due to such limitations of historical costing, the standard costing technique was introduced. Standard costing seeks to establish the cost of a product, operations or process under standard operating conditions. The purpose of standard cost is to ward off the influence of abnormal changes in prices. It is used as a guide for future decision and action over a period of time. Standard costing is an effective managerial tool for planning, decision making, coordination and control of business. It is a system of cost control.

Advantages of Standard Costing

1. Provides a yardstick for comparison of cost.
2. Facilitates planning and controlling of cost systems in an organisation.
3. Variance analysis helps in determining the favourable and unfavourable events.
4. Personnels will try to optimise resource utilisation so that actual cost reducing.
5. Helps management in formulation of cost related policies and decision making.
6. It facilitates timely reporting system.
7. Improves the productivity and creates cost consciousness.
8. Provides the basis for measurement of performance.
9. Facilitates formulation of price and production policies.

Limitations of Standard Costing

1. Quantitative setting up of standards may not be possible in all cases, hence the actual performance cannot be compared with any standard.
2. The set standards may not be correct always.
3. Frequent revision of standards is required in industries which are subject to radical changes, hence revision of standard each time may add to the financial burden of the business.
4. Small firms may not spend on setting of standards as the job is performed by highly specialised staff.
5. Cannot be applied to customer-specific products industry.

Budgetary Control and Standard Costing

Both budgetary control and standard costing techniques are adopted by the business for ascertaining and controlling of cost in the organisation, but the spectrum of budgetary control is wider than standard costing. Standard costing concentrates on cost control but budgetary control concentrates on the overall operation of the business enterprise. However, both aim at the optimal utilisation of resources and minimisation of cost. Budgetary control system can function without standard costing system but standard costing system cannot function without budgetary control. Budgetary control is an extensive exercise concerning the operations of business but standard costing is an intensive activity focusing on controlling of costs.

Standard Costing as a Tool for Management

The technique of standard costing is used for building a proper budgeting and feedback system in the organisation. It helps the management in making correct predictions and provides a criterion for appraising the performance. The management can make use of the standard costing technique for the following purposes:

1. **Cost Awareness.** The atmosphere of cost consciousness is felt by the staff, managerial as well as workmen. The standard costing provides incentives to workers, supervisors and the top executives for efficient work.
2. **Management by 'Exception'.** This principle helps the management in concentrating its attention on cases which are off the standard. The trend of costs is displayed and thus a pattern is provided for the elimination of undesirable factors causing damage to the business.
3. **Corrective Action.** It provides a framework for comparison of actual with standard costs, in terms of different elements separately. It assists in locating the nature and cause of influence on cost and the performance of the firm. Based on analytical study of various factors corrective action is proposed.
4. **Applying the Responsibility Accounting.** Determination of favourable and unfavourable variances and ascertainment of controllability of factors influencing the variances help in fixing responsibility for below par achievement. Thus, standard cost provides a basis for measurement of performance. Actual costs below standard costs indicate efficient performance and vice versa.

5. **Better Future.** An effective and more accurate budget can be built up for the forthcoming period on the basis of knowledge of variations of actual costs and standard costs. As the information is available at the earliest possible time, the capacity to envisage future events is developed.
6. **Improved Productivity.** The operations are scrutinised carefully and inefficiencies are brought to the fore. M3 (i.e., men, machines and materials) is more effectively utilised and the economies can be effected in the business along with enhanced productivity.
7. **Formation of Price and Production Policies.** It provides useful guide to the management in formulating price and production policies in the field of inventory pricing, product pricing, profit planning. It also provides a system of reporting to higher levels of authority to take appropriate decisions.

VARIANCE ANALYSIS

Variance is the deviation of actual from the standard or budgeted. Variance analysis is primarily divided in two categories : Sales variance analysis and cost variance analysis. When the actual cost is less than the standard cost, it is considered to be a favourable variance and when the actual cost is more than the standard cost, the variance is unfavourable. When the variance arises due to factors which are controllable like production time, etc. is known as controllable variance and when the variance arises due to factors which are beyond the control of the management is known as uncontrollable variance.

COST VARIANCES

Cost variance is of three types

1. Material cost variance
2. Labour cost variance
3. Overhead cost variance
   - Variable
   - Fixed

we shall now discuss each of the above variances in detail.

1. Material Cost Variance

The difference between the desired or standard cost of raw material prescribed for a particular level of output and the actual raw material used is known as material cost variance.

Material cost variance

= Standard cost – Actual cost

= (SQ × SP) – (AQ × AP)

where SQ is standard output

SP is standard price

AQ is actual output

and AP is actual price

1a. *Material Price Variance*

MPV = AQ (SP – AP), where AQ = Actual output
SP = Standard price
AP = Actual price

The difference between the price specified and the actual price paid for the raw material used for the actual output level is known as material price variance. It may arise due to change in market price, custom and excise duties; off season purchasing, etc.

1b. *Material Usage Variance*

MUV = SP (SQ – AQ)

The difference between the standard quantity of raw material specified and the actual quantity used, both valued at standard price is known as material usage variance. P arises due to theft, defective tools, sub-standard materials, etc.

Material cost variance = Material price variance + Material usage variance

1bi. *Material Mix Variance (MMV)*

MMV = SP (RSQ – AQ)

where RSQ is raised standard quantity and RSQ = Actual input × Standard proportion

When the actual mix of materials used is different from the standard mix desired, it gives rise to the material mix variance.

1bii. *Material Yield Variance (MYV)*

MYV = SP (SQ – RSQ)

Material usage variance = Material mix variance + Material yield variance

Illustration 1 The cosmetic company produces 100 units of facewash. It uses two raw materials F1 and F2 to produce the face wash. The following information regarding the desired and the actual mix is given below.

Raw Material	Standard	Actual
F1	20 units @ ₹10 each	25 units @ ₹8 each
F2	30 units @ ₹8 each	40 units @ ₹10 each

Calculate the various material variances.

Solution:

1. Material Cost Variance

MCU = SQ × SP – AQ × AP

F1 = (20 × 10) – (25 × 8) = 200 – 200 = Nil

F2 = (30 × 8) – (40 × 10) = 240 – 400 = 160 (UF)

Total material cost variance = Nil + 160 (UP) = ₹160 (UF)

2. Material Price Variance

MPU = AQ (SP – AP)

F1 = 25 (10 – 8) = 50 ₹ (F)

F2 = 40 (8 – 10) = 80 ₹ (UF)

Total material price variance = ₹30 (UF)

3. Material Usage Variance

MUV = SP (SQ – AQ)

F1 = 10 (20 – 25) = ₹ 50 (UF)

F2 = 8 (30 – 40) = ₹ 80 (UF)

Total material usage variance = ₹ 130 (UF)

Check:

Material cost variance = Material price variance = Material usage variance

₹ 160 (UF) = ₹ 30 (UF) + ₹ 130 (UF)

4. Material Mix Variance

MMV = SP (RSQ – AQ)

F1 = 10 (26 – 25) = ₹ 10 (F)

F2 = 8 (39 – 40) = ₹ 8 (UF)

RSQ : Actual quantity of 25 units of F1 and 40 units of F2, which makes 65 units in Total are apportioned in the standard quantity ratio which is 2:3 (20 units of F1: 30—units of F2)

So 65 unit in the ratio 2:3 = 26 units and 39 units respectively.

Total material mix variance = ₹ 2 (F)

5. Material Yield Variance

MYV = SP (SQ – RSQ)

F1 = 10 (210 – 26) = ₹ 60 (UF)

F2 = 8 (30 – 39) = ₹ 72 (UF)

Total material yield variance = 1320 (UF)

Check:

Material usage variance = Material mix variance + Material yield variance

130 (UF) = 2 (F) + 132 (UF)

2. Labour Cost Variance

The difference between the actual and standard labour costs is known as labour cost variance.

$$LCV = SC - AC$$

or LCV = (Standard hours for actual output × Standard rate per hour)

– (Actual hours × Actual rate per hour)

2a. *Labour Rate Variance*

$$LRV = (SR - AR)\ AH \times AQ$$

where, SR = Standard rate per labour hour

AR = Actual rate per labour hour

AH = Actual hour taken to produce one unit

AQ = Actual output

LRV focusses on actual worked hours. The difference between the actual and the standard usage rate is known as labour rate variance. LRV may arise due to reasons like overtime usage payment as overtime usage rate is much higher than the normal rate, hiring of more skilled workers thereby paying them more, etc.

2b. *Labour Efficiency or Labour Time Variance*

$$\text{LEV or LTV} = [(\text{SH} \times \text{AQ}) - (\text{AH} \times \text{AQ})] \text{ SR}$$

where, SH = Standard hour taken to produce one unit

or

$$\text{LEV} = \text{Standard rate (Standard time} - \text{Actual time)}$$

LEV or LTV represents the difference between the hours actually taken by workers for actual output and the hours they should have actually taken for actual output produced.

LEV arises due to money reasons like improper machinery, unskilled labour, lack of supervision, etc.

Labour cost variance = Labour rate variance + Labour efficiency or time variance

2c. *Labour Idle Time Variance*

$$\text{LITV or ITV} = \text{Idle hours} \times \text{Standard usage rate per hour}$$

2d. *Labour Efficiency Variance Revised*

LEV (revised) [(SH × AQ) – AH worked)] SR

$$\text{AH worked} = \text{Actual hours paid for} - \text{Idle time hours.}$$

Labour efficiency or time variance =	Labour efficiency variance revised	+	Labour gang variance

2e. *Labour Gang Variance*

$$\text{LGV} = (\text{RSH} - \text{AH}) \text{ SR}$$

RSH is the standard composition of actual labour hours worked. It is called revised standard hours.

2f. *Labour Yield Variance*

$$\text{LYV} = \text{SC (AY} - \text{SY)}$$

AY is actual yield

And SY is the standard yield for actual hours worked.

Illustration 2 A textile manufacturing unit has three categories of workers—printers, dyers and artisans. The following is the weekly standard and actual data of labour engagement. Calculate the various labour variances.

Information	Printers	Dyers	Artisans
Standard number of workers	32	12	6
Actual number of workers	28	18	4
Standard wage rate/hr	₹16	₹12	₹10
Actual wage rate/hr	₹20	₹15	₹12

The unit works for 9 hours per day and five days a week. 1800 standard labour hours work was done in that period.

Solution: The textile unit functions for 9 hours/day and 5 days in a week

$\Rightarrow 9 \times 5 \quad = 45$ hours/week.

Now standard workers are in the ratio

$$32 : 12 : 6 \Rightarrow 16 : 6 : 3$$

Now Total standard labour hours 1800 shall be divided in the above ratio's which is 1152: 432: 216

Types of Workers*	Standard Cost for Actual Output			Actual Cost for Actual Output		
	Hours	Rate (₹)	Amount (₹)	Hours	Rate (₹)	Amount (₹)
Printers (P)	1152	16	18,432	1260	20	25,200
Dyers (D)	432	12	5184	810	15	12,150
Artisans (A)	216	10	2160	180	12	2160
	1800	–	25,776	2250		39,510

*Total actual workers of all three categories are 28 printers + 18 dyers + 4 artisans = 50 workers.

Now in a week a worker works for 45 hours. So total actual labour hours are 50 × 45 = 2250 hours.

Now this 2250 actual hours produced are divided in the ratio of workers 28 : 18 : 4 which comes to 1260; 810 and 180 respectively.

(i) LCV = SC – AC

P = 18,432 – 25,200 = 6768 (UF)

D = 5184 – 12,150 = 6966 (UF)

A = 2160 – 2160 = Nil

Total LCV = 6768 (UF) + 6966 (UF) + Nil

= 13,734 (UF)

(ii) LRV = AH (SR – AR)

P = 1260 (16 – 20) = 5040 (UF)

D = 810 (12 – 15) = 2430 (UF)

A = 180 (10 – 12) = 360 (UF)

Total LRV = ₹7830 (UF)

(iii) LEV = SR (SH – AH)

P = 16 (1152 – 1260) = 1728 (UF)

D = 12 (432 – 810) = 4536 (UF)

A = 10 (216 – 180) = 360 (F)

Total LEV = ₹5904 (UF)

LCU = LRU + LEU

₹13734 (UF) = ₹7830 (UF) + ₹5904 (UF)

(iv) LGV = SR (RSH – AH)

P = 16 (1440 – 1260) = 2880 (F)

D = 12 (540 – 810) = 3240 (UF)

A = 10 (270 – 180) = 900 (E)

Total LGU = ₹540 (F)

RSH → Total actual hours of 2250 are divided in the ratio of standard hours which is 16 : 6 : 3.

So 2250 were in the ratio 16 : 6 : 3 comes out to 1440 hr : 540 hr : 270 hr.

(v) LEV required = SR (SH – RSH)

P = 160 (1152 – 1140) = 4608 (UF)

D = 12 (432 – 540) = 1296 (UF)

A = 10 (216 – 270) = 540 (UF)

Total LEV Revised = ₹6444 (UF)

LEV = LGU + LEU revised

5904 (UF) = 540 (F) + 6444 (UF)

(vi) LYV is

Standard cost/Unit of output (Standard output – Actual output)

25,776/1800 hr (1800 – 23,250) = ₹6444 (HF)

LYV = LEV Revised

3. *Overhead Variances*

Overhead variance is the difference between the standard overhead cost and actual overhead cost.

VARIABLE OVERHEAD VARIANCES

3a. *Variable Overhead Variance (VOV)*

It is also known as variable overhead cost variance (VOCV)

VOCV = (SVOC × AO) – (AVOC × AO)

VOCV = ROH – AOH

ROH is recovered overheads, AOH is actual overheads

SVOC is standard variable overhead cost

AVOC is actual variable overhead cost

3ai. *Variable Overhead Efficiency Variance (VOEV)*

VOEV = (SHAO – AH) × SVOR/hour

where, SHAO = Standard hours for actual output, AH = Actual hours

3aii. *Variable overhead spending variance (VOSV) or Variable overhead expenditure variance*

VOSV = (Actual hours worked × SVOR) – Actual overhead cost incurred

SVOR is standard variable overhead rate per hour.

VOCV = VOEV + VOSV

FIXED OVERHEAD VARIANCES

3b. *Fixed Overhead Variance (FOV)*

It is also known as fixed overhead cost variance (FOCV).

FOCV = Recovered fixed overheads – Actual fixed overheads = ROH – AOH

$$ROH = SFOR \text{ actual output in units}$$

SFOR is standard fixed overhead rate

3bi. *Fixed Overhead Spending Variance (FOSV)*

$$FOSV = BOH - AOH$$

where, BOH is budgeted fixed overheads

AOH is actual fixed overheads

3bii. *Fixed Overhead Efficiency Variance (FOEV)*

$$FOEV = (SHAO - AH_W)\ SFOR/hour,$$

[SFOR is standard fixed overhead rate per hour]

AH_W is actual hours worked and SHRO is standard hour for actual output

3biii. *Fixed Overhead Volume Variance (FOVV)*

$$FOVV = (SHAO - BH)\ SFOR/hour$$

where BH = Budgeted hours/Time

FOCV = FOSV + FOEV + FOVV

SALES VARIANCES

The difference between actual value of sales and budgeted value of sales is called sales variance. When actual sales are more than budgeted sales it is a favourable situation and vice versa. Sales variance can be studied under two heads.

1. Value or turnover method
   (a) sales revenue value variance
   (b) sale price variance
   (c) sales volume variance.
2. Sales margin or profit method
   (a) sales margin variance
   (b) sales margin price variance
   (c) sales margin volume variance
   (d) sales margin mix variance.

1. Turnover/Value Method

The variance arising out of changes in sales price, sales quantity, sales mix and other factors are analysed by turnover method.

(a) Sales Revenue Value Variance. The difference between the actual sales and budgeted sales is defined as sales revenue value variance. The variance is unfavourable if actual sales are less than the budgeted sales and favourable if the actual sales exceed the budgeted sales.

Sales Revenue Variance = Actual Sales – Budgeted Sales

$$SRV = (AQ \times AP) - (BQ \times SP)$$

(b) Sales Price Variance. Difference in actual selling price and that of the budgeted selling price is known as sales price variance or budgeted sales.

$$SPV = \text{Actual quantity sold (Actual price – Standard price)}$$

$$SPV = AQ\ (AP - SP)$$

where AQ is actual quantity, AP is actual price is SP in standard price.

(c) Sales Volume Variance. The difference in actual quantity sold and budgeted quantity of sales multiplied by the budgeted on standard price causes sales volume variance.

Sales volume variance = Standard price (Actual quantity sold – Budgeted or standard quantity of sales).

$$SW = SP\ (AQ - BQ)$$

Illustration 3 Following is the information of Shiny Lipsticks

Budgeted/Standard Sales			Actual sales		
Quantity (Units)	Price (₹)/unit	Amount (₹)	Quantity (Units)	Price (₹)/unit	Amount (₹)
1000	5	5000	1100	6	6600

Calculate sales variance.

Solution:

1. Sales revenue variance = Actual sales – Budgeted sales

$$SRV = (AQ \times AP) - (BQ \times SP)$$

$$SRV = 6600 - 5000 = ₹\,1600 \text{ (favourable)}$$

2. Sales volume variance = Standard sales price (Actual quantity sold – Budgeted quantity of sales)

$$SVV = SP\ (AQ - BQ)$$

$$SVV = 5\ (1100 \text{ units} - 1000 \text{ units})$$

$$= ₹\,500 \text{ (favourable)}$$

3. Sales price variance

$$SPV = AQ\ (AP - BP)$$

$$SVV = 1100\ (6 - 5)$$

$$= ₹\,1100 \text{ (Favourable)}$$

Check No. 1

Sales revenue variance = Sales price variance + Sales volume variance

$$₹\,1600 = 1100 + 500$$

4. Sales Mix Variance

The mix variance is a part of sales volume variance. It arises due to change effected in standard mix of difference articles sold. It can be either quantity based or value based.

(i) Quantity Based

The case where products are homogenous, this method is followed.

Sales mix variance = (Standard sales – Revised standard sales)

Sales mix variance = Standard price (Actual quantity sold – Revised standard quantity of sales)

Revised standard quantity of sales

The difference between the sales volume and the sales mix variance arising due to difference in quantity sold represents sales quantity variance. It is a part of sales volume variance.

Sales quantity variance = (Revised standard sales – Budgeted sales)

Sales quantity variance = (Revised standard quantity – Budgeted sales quantity)

SQV = SP (RSQ – BQ)

(ii) Value Based

The case where products are not homogeneous, this method is followed. The actual sales at standard prices are to be expressed in budgeted ratio of sales so as to calculate revised standard sales and then these are compared with the standard sales. The outcome of standard sales and budgeted ratio of sales is the revised standard sales.

Budgeted ratio of sales = Budgeted sales of a product / Total budgeted sales

If a standard sales are more than the revised standard sales it means a favourable variance and vice versa.

As the revised standard sales is only a rearrangement of standard sales in the budgeted sales ratio, the total mix variance for all the products taken together is always NIL. The reason behind the rearrangement is product-wise mix variance.

Thus, we can say that the total of revised standard sales is exactly equal to standard sales.

Illustration 4 An ice cream parlour has two flavours – Vanilla and Strawberry

Flavours	Budgeted/ Standard Sales			Actual sales		
	Quantity (Unit)	Price (₹)	Amount (₹)	Quantity (Unit)	Price (₹)	Amount (₹)
Vanilla	200	10	2,000	250	8	2,000
Strawberry	300	8	2,400	100	15	1,500
Total	500		4,400	350		3,500

Solution:

Flavours	Budgeted			Actual			Standard sales = (AQ × BP)
Vanilla	200	10	2,000	250	8	2,000	2500
Strawberry	300	8	2,400	100	15	1,500	800
Total	500		4,400	350		3,500	3300

2. Sales Margin or Profit Method

Difference between total budgeted profit and total actual profit is known as sales margin method.

(a) Total sales margin variance = (Actual margin per unit × Actual quantity sold) – (Standard or budgeted margin per unit × Budgeted or standard quantity of sales)

TSMV = (AM × AQ – (SM or BM – SQ or BQ)

(b) Sales margin price variance = Actual quantity (Actual margin – Standard or budgeted margin)

SMPV = AQ (AM – SM or BM)

(c) Sales margin volume variance = Standard margin per unit × (Actual sales – Budgeted or standard sales)

SMVV = SM (AQ – BQ or SQ)

Sales margin quantity variance = (Standard margin or Budgeted margin) × (Revised standard quantity – Budgeted standard quantity)

SMQV = SM or BM (RSQ – SQ or BQ)

Illustration 5 The following are the data for the month of March 2021 of Greenfield Co-operative.

Product	Budgeted Sales (Unit)	Budgeted Selling Price per unit (₹)	Actual Sales (Units)	Actual Selling Price per unit (₹)
A	2160	12	2240	11
B	1440	5	960	6

You are required to complete:

(i) Sales value variance
(ii) Sales volume variance
(iii) Sales price variance
(iv) Sales mix variance

Under the assumption that are products are non-homogeneous. Calculate the above ratios again with the assumption that the products are homogeneous. [*DU, 2007. Modified*]

Solution: When products are non-homogeneous

Product	Budget			Actual			Standard			Revised standard soles	
	Qty.	Price (₹)	Value	Qty.	Price (₹)	Value	Qty	Price (₹)	Value	Ratio (X)	Value
A	2160	12	25920	2240	11	24640	2240	12	2680	78.26	24793
B	1440	5	7200	960	6	5760	960	5	480	21.74	6887

1. Sales price variance = Actual sales – Budgeted sales

SVV (product A) = 24,640 – 25,920 = ₹ 1280 (UF)

SVV (product B) = 5760 – 7200 = ₹ 1440 (UF)

Total SVV = 1280 (UF) + 1440 (UF) = 2720 (UF)

2. Sales price variance = Actual sales – Standard sales

SPV (product A) = 24,640 – 2680 = ₹ 2240 (UF)

SPV (product B) = 5760 – 4800 = ₹ 7960 (UF)

Total SPV = 2240 (UF) + 960 (F) = ₹ 1280 (UF)

3. Sales price variance = Actual sales – Standard sales

SPV (product A) = 24,640 – 2680 = ₹ 2240 (UF)

SPV (product B) = 5760 – 4800 = ₹ 7960 (UF)

Total SPV = 2240 (UF) + 960 (F) = ₹ 1280 (UF)

4. Sales mix variance = Budged sales – Revised standard sales

SMV (product A) = 26,880 – 24,893 = ₹ 2087 (F)

SMV (product B) = 4800 – 687 = ₹ 2087 (UF)

Total SMV = 2087 (F) + 2087 (UF) = NIL

SOLVED PRACTICAL PROBLEMS

Problem 1 The budgeted and the actual sales for a period in respect of three products are given below:

Budgeted Data

Product	Quantity (Unit)	Price (₹)	Value (₹)
P-1	1600	10	16,000
P-2	1200	20	24,000
P-3	900	30	24,000
			64,000

Actual Data

Product	Quantity (Unit)	Price (₹)	Value (₹)
P-1	2000	12	24,000
P-2	1100	19	20,900
P-3	900	28	25,200
			70,100

Calculate sales variances.

Solution:

Working Notes:

Calculation of revised standard quantity (RSQ):

RSQ total actual quantity × Budgeted proportion (product-wise)

Budgeted proportion (product-wise) = 1600 : 1200 : 800, i.e., 4:3:2

RSQ (P-1) = 4000 × 4/9 = 16,000/9

RSQ (P-2) = 4000 × 3/9 = 12,000/9

RSQ (P-3) = 4000 × 2/9 = 8000/9

Variance computation:

Sales revenue variance = (Actual sales – Budgeted sales)

= 70,100 – 64,000 = ₹6100 (F)

Sales price variance = Actual quantity sold (Actual price – Standard price)

P-1 = 2000(12 – 10) = ₹4000 (F)

P-2 = 1100(19 – 20) = ₹1100 (UF)

P-3 = 900(28 – 30) ₹1800 (UF)

Total sales price variance = ₹1100 (F)

Sales volume variance = Standard sales price (Actual quantity sold – Standard quantity)

P-1 = 10(2000 – 1600) = ₹4000 (F)

P-2 = 20(1100 – 1200) = ₹2000 (UF)

P-3 = 30(900 – 800) = ₹3000 (F)

Total sales volume variance = ₹5000 (F)

Check No. I

Sales value variance sales price variance + Sales volume variance

₹6100 (F) = ₹1100 (F) + ₹5000 (F)

Sales mix variance = Standard sales price (Actual quantity sold – Revised standard quantity)

P-1 = 10(2000 – 16,000/9) = ₹2000/9 (F)

P-2 = 20(1100 – 12,000/9) = ₹14,000/3 (UF)

P-3 = 30(900 – 8000/9) = ₹3000/9 (F)

Total Sales mix Variance = ₹19,000/9 (UF)

Sales quantity variance = Standard sales price (Revised standard qty. – Budgeted sales qty)

P-1 = 10(16,000/9 – 1600) = ₹16,000/9 (F)

P-2 = 20(12,000/9 – 1200) = ₹24,000/9 (F)

P-3 = 30(8000/9 – 800) = ₹24,000/9 (F)

Total quantity variance = ₹64,000/9 (F)

Check No. II

Sales volume variance = Sales mix variance + Spies quantity variance

₹5000 (F) = ₹19,000/9 (UF) + 64,000/9 (F)

Problem 2 Synergy corporation provides the following information for the month of March 2021.

Product	Budget	Budget	Actual	Actual
	Quantity (Unit)	Amount (₹)	Quantity (Unit)	Amount (₹)
P-1	1500	30,000	1200	27,600
P-2	1000	25,000	1200	30,000
P-3	2500	1,12,500	3600	1,51,200
Total	5000	1,67,500	6000	2,08,800

Calculate the following variances

1. Sales mix variance
2. Sales quantity variance
3. Sales price variance, and
4. Sales revenue variance.

Solution:

Working Notes:

Rate or price = Amount divided by Qty

SP (P-1) = 3000/1500 = ₹20

SP (P-2) = 25,000/1000 = ₹25

SP (P-3) = 1,12,500/2500 = ₹45

AP (P-1) = 27,600/1200 = ₹23

AP (P-2) = 30,000/1200 = ₹25

AP (P-3) = 1,51,200/3600 = ₹42

Standard proportion = 1500:1000:2500 OR 0.3:0.2: 0.5

RSQ = AQ × Standard proportion

RSQ(P-1) = 6000 × 0.3 = 1800

RSQ(P-1) = 6000 × 0.2 = 1200

RSQ(P-1) = 6000 × 0.5 = 3000

Sales quantity variance: SMV = SP (AQ – RSQ)

P-1 = 20 (1200 – 1800) = ₹12,000 (UF)

P-2 = 25(1200 – 100) = NIL

P-3 = 45(3600 – 3000) = ₹27,000 (F) Total sales mix variance = ₹12,000 (UF) + NIL + ₹27,000 (F) = ₹15,000 (F)

Sales price variance: SPV = AQ (AP – SP)

P-1 = 1200(23 – 20) = ₹3600 (F)
P-2 = 1200(25 – 25) = NIL
P-3 = 3600(42 – 45) = ₹10,800 (UF)

Total sales price variance = ₹3600 (F) + NIL + ₹10,800 (UF) = ₹7200 (UF)

Sales revenue variance: SRV = (AQ × AP) – (BQ × SP)

P-1 = (1200 × 23) – (1500 × 20) = (27600) – (30000) = ₹2400 (UF)
P-2 = (1200 × 25) – (1000 × 25) = (30000) – (25000) = ₹5000 (F)
P-3 = (3600 × 42) – (2500 × 45) = (151200) – (112500) = ₹38,700 (F)

Total sales revenue variance

₹2400 (UF) + ₹5000 (F) + ₹38,700 (F) + ₹41,300 (F)

Check: SRV = SMV + SQV + SPV

₹41,300 (F) = ₹15,000 (F) + ₹33,500 (F) + ₹7200 (UF)

Problem 3 Compute the following variances from the data given below:

Total sales margin variance

1. Sales margin volume variance
2. Sales margin price variance
3. Sales margin mix variance
4. Sales margin quantity variance

Product	Budgeted quantity (Unit)	Actual Quantity (Unit)	Budgeted Selling price (₹)	Actual Selling price (₹)	Standard Cost per Unit (₹)
P-1	2400	4000	169	136	100
P-2	1600	2000	80	70	50

Solution:

Product	Budgeted sales price per unit (₹)	Standard cost per unit (₹)	Standard sales margin (₹)	Budgeted qty. (₹)	Budgeted profit	Actual sales price (₹)	Actual sales Margin (₹)	Actual sales Qty. (Unit)	Actual profit
P-1	160	100	60	2400	1,44,000	136	36	4000	1,44,000
P-2	80	50	30	1600	48,000	70	20	2000	40,000

Total sales margin = Total actual profit – Total budgeted profit 1,84,000 – 1,92,000 = ₹8,000 (UF)

Sales margin volume variance : SMVV = SM (AQ–BQ)

P-1 = 60(4000 – 2400) = ₹96,000 (F)
P-2 = 30(2000 – 1600) = ₹12,000 (F)

Total sales margin volume variance: ₹96,000 (F) + ₹12,000 (1) = ₹1,08,000 (F)

Sales margin price variance: SMPV = AQ (AM–SM)

P-1 = 4000(36 – 60) = ₹96,000 (UF)

P-2 = 2000(20 – 30) = ₹20,000 (UF)

Total sales margin price variance: ₹96,000(UF) + ₹20,000 (UF) = ₹1,16,000 (UF)

Sales margin mix variance: SMMV = SM (AQ–RSQ)

P-1 = 60(4000 – 3600) = ₹24,000 (F)

P-2 = 30(2000 – 4000) = ₹12,000 (UF)

Total sales margin mix variance: ₹24,000 (F) + ₹12,000 (UF) = ₹12,000 (F)

Sales margin quantity (sub-volume) variance: SMVQ = SM (RSQ–BQ)

P-1 = 60(3600 – 2400) = ₹72,000 (F)

P-2 = 30(2400 – 1600) = ₹24,000 (F) Total sales margin (sub-volume) variance:

= ₹72,000 (F) + ₹24,000 (F)

= ₹96,000 (F)

Alternatively:

Sales margin quantity (sub-volume) variance: SR (AQ–BQ)

= 48(6000 – 4000) = ₹96,000 (F)

Working Note:

Standard proportion = 2400: 1600, i.e., 3:2 CR 0.6:0.4

RSQ = Total actual × Mix standard proportion

RSQ (P-1) = 6000 × 0.6 = 3600

RSQ (P-2) = 6000 × 0.4 = 2400

SR (budgeted profit per unit of budgeted Mix) = 1,92,000/4000 = ₹48

Problem 4 An item requires 10 kg of raw material @ ₹4 per kg for one unit. The actual consumption of material was 12 kg @ ₹4.50 per kg. The actual output was 50 units. Calculate the material cost variances.

Solution:

	(1)	(2)	(3)	(4)
Material	SP × SQ 4 × (10 × 50)	SP × SM 4 × (600)	SP × AQ 4 × (12 × 50)	AP × AQ 4.5 × (12 × 50)
	2000	2400	2400	2700

where SP = Standard price per kg of raw material = ₹4

SQ = Standard quantity of raw material required for actual output.

= Standard quantity of raw material for one unit × Actual output

= 10 × 50 = 500

SM = Standard mix, i.e., total actual quantity of raw material used in standard ratio. In case, one material only, SM = AQ

= 12 × 50 = 600

AQ = Actual quantity of raw material used = 12 × 50 = 600

AP = Actual price per kg of raw material = ₹4.50

1. Material yield variances = (1) – (2)
= (SP × SQ) – (SP × SM)
= 4 × (10 × 50) – 4 × (600)
= 2000 – 2400 = 400 (A)

2. Material mix variance = (2) – (3)
= (SP × SM) – (SP × AQ)
= 4 (600) – 4 × (12 × 50)
= NIL

3. Material price variance = (3) – (4)
= (SP × AQ) – (AP × AQ)
= 4 × (12 × 50) – 4.5 × (12 × 50)
= 300 (A)

4. Material usage variance = (1) – (3)
= (SP × SQ) – (SP × AQ)
= 4 × (10 × 50) – 4 × (12 × 50)
= 400 (A)

5. Material cost variance = (1) – (4)
= (SP × SQ) – (AP × AQ)
= 4 × (10 × 50) – 4.5 × (12 × 50)
= 700 (A)

Verification

Material usage variance = Material yield variance + Material mix variance
= 400 (A) + Nil = 400 (A)

Material cost variance = Material usage variance + Material price variance
= 700 (A)

Problem 5 The standards for a chemical mixture are A 40%, and B 60%. The price is ₹20 per kg and ₹30 per kg for A and B respectively. The standards loss is 10%. During a period 182 kg of output were produced from A 90 kg (₹18 per kg) and B 110 kg (₹34 per kg). Calculate the materials cost variances. [*B.Com. (H)*]

Solution:

Material	(1)	(2)	(3)	(4)
	SP × SQ	SP × SM	SP × AQ	AP × AQ
A	$20 \times \left(\frac{40}{90} \times 182\right)$	$20 \times \left(200 \times \frac{40}{100}\right)$	(20 × 90)	(18 × 90)
B	$30 \times \left(\frac{60}{90} \times 182\right)$	$30 \times \left(200 \times \frac{60}{100}\right)$	(30 × 110)	(34 × 110)
	5257.77	5,200	5,100	5,360

where SP : Standard price per kg of raw material.

Material A = ₹20

Material B = ₹30

SQ : Standard quantity of raw material required for actual output.

Standard quantity of raw material for one unit × actual output.

$$\text{Material A} = \left(\frac{40}{90} \times 182\right)$$

$$\text{Material B} = \left(\frac{60}{90} \times 182\right)$$

SM : Standard mix, i.e., total actual quantity of raw material used in standard ratio = 90 + 110 = 200 in the ratio of 40:60

$$\text{Material A} = \left(200 \times \frac{40}{100}\right)$$

$$\text{Material B} = \left(200 \times \frac{60}{100}\right)$$

AQ : Actual quantity of raw material used.

Material A = 90

Material B = 110

AP : Actual price per kg of raw material.

Material A = ₹18

Material B = ₹34

1. Material yield variance = (1) – (2)

= (SP × SQ) – (SP × SM)

$$\text{Material A} = \left(\frac{40}{90} \times 182\right) - 20 \times \left(200 \times \frac{40}{100}\right) = 17.77\text{ (F)}$$

$$\text{Material B} = \left(\frac{60}{90} \times 182\right) - 30 \times \left(200 \times \frac{60}{100}\right) = 40\text{ (F)}$$

MYV = 57.77 (F)

2. Material mix variance = (2) – (3)

= (SP × SM) – (SP × AQ)

$$\text{Material A} = 20 \times \left(200 \times \frac{40}{100}\right) - (20 \times 90) = 200\text{ (A)}$$

$$\text{Material B} = \left(200 \times \frac{60}{100}\right) - (30 \times 110) = 300\text{ (F)}$$

MMV = 100 (F)

3. Material price variance = (3) – (4)

$$= (SP \times AQ) - (AP \times AQ)$$

Material A = $(20 \times 90) - (18 \times 90)$ = 180 (F)

Material B = $(30 \times 110) - (34 \times 110)$ = 440 (A)

MPV = 260 (A)

4. Material usage variance = (1) – (3)

$$= (SP \times SQ) - (SP \times AQ)$$

Material A = $\left(\frac{40}{90} \times 182\right) - (20 \times 90)$ = 182.23 (A)

Material B = $\left(\frac{60}{90} \times 182\right) - (30 \times 110)$ = 340 (F)

MUV = 157.77 (F)

5. Material cost variance = (1) – (4)

$$= (SP \times SQ) - (AP \times AQ)$$

Material A = $20 \times \left(\frac{40}{90} \times 182\right) - (18 \times 90)$ = 2.23 (A

Material B = $30 \times \left(\frac{60}{90} \times 182\right) - (34 \times 110)$ = 100 (A)

MCV = 102.23 (A)

Problem 6 Calculate the material cost variances from the following information:

	Standards		Actual	
	Qty.	**Price**	**Qty.**	**Price**
M	100 units	₹2.00	215 units	₹1.80
N	200 units	₹1.70	385 units	₹2.00
Less: Wastage	30 units		70 units	
Output	270 unit		530 units	
Actuals				

Solution:

Material	(1)	(2)	(3)	(4)
M	SP × SQ $2 \times \left(\frac{100}{270} \times 530\right)$	SP × SM $2 \times \left(600 \times \frac{1}{3}\right)$	SP × AQ (2 × 215)	AP × AQ (1.8 × 215)

Contd...

Table Contd...

N	$1.7 \times \left(\frac{200}{270} \times 530\right)$	$1.7 \times \left(600 \times \frac{2}{3}\right)$	(1.7 × 385)	(2 × 385)
	1,060	1,080	1,084.5	1,157

where SP : Standard price per kg of raw material.

SQ : Standard quantity of raw material required for actual output.

= Standard quantity of raw material for one unit × Actual output.

SM : Standard mix, i.e., Total actual quantity of raw material used in standard ratio = 215 + 385 = 600 in the ratio of 100 : 200

AQ : Actual quantity of raw material used.

AP : Actual price per kg of raw material.

1. Material yield variances = (1) – (2)

= (SP × SQ) – (SQ × SM)

$$\text{Material M} = 2 \times \left(\frac{100}{270} \times 530\right) - 2 \times \left(600 \times \frac{1}{3}\right) \quad = 7.40\ (A)$$

$$\text{Material N} = 2 \times \left(\frac{200}{270} \times 530\right) - 1.7 \times \left(600 \times \frac{2}{3}\right) \quad = 12.60\ (A)$$

MYV = 20 (A)

2. Material mix variance = (2) – (3)

= (SP × SM) – (SP × AQ)

$$\text{Material M} = 2 \times \left(600 \times \frac{1}{3}\right) - (2 \times 215) \quad = 30\ (A)$$

$$\text{Material N} = 1.7 \times \left(600 \times \frac{2}{3}\right) - (1.7 \times 385) \quad = 25.5\ (F)$$

MMV = 4.50 (A)

3. Material price variance = (3) – (4)

= (SP × AQ) – (AP × AQ)

Material M = (2 × 215) – (1.8 × 215) = 43 (F)

Material N = (1.7 × 385) – (2 × 385) = 115.5 (A)

MPV = 72.5 (A)

4. Material usage variance = (1) – (3)

= (SP × SQ) – (SP × AQ)

$$\text{Material M} = 2 \times \left(\frac{100}{270} \times 530\right) - (2 \times 215) \quad = 37.40\ (F)$$

$$\text{Material N} = 0.7 \times \left(\frac{200}{270} \times 530\right) - (1.7 \times 385) \qquad = 12.90 \text{ (F)}$$

$$\text{MUV} = 24.50 \text{ (A)}$$

5. Material cost variance = 1 – 4

$$= (SP \times SQ) - (AP \times AQ)$$

$$\text{Material M} = 2 \times \left(\frac{100}{270} \times 530\right) - (1.8 \times 216) \qquad = 5.60 \text{ (F)}$$

$$\text{Material N} = 1.7 \times \left(\frac{200}{270} \times 530\right) - (2 \times 385) \qquad = 102.60 \text{ (A)}$$

$$\text{MCV} = 97 \text{ (A)}$$

Problem 7 From the following data, calculate the material cost variances:

Materials	Standards		Actual	
	Qty.	Price	Qty.	Price
A	15	2	10	3
B	30	3	20	6
C	30	6	20	5

Solution:

Material	(1)	(2)	(3)	(4)
	SP × SQ	SP × SM	SP × AQ	AP × AQ
A	(2 × 15)	(2 × 10)	(2 × 10)	(3 × 10)
B	(3 × 30)	(3 × 20)	(3 × 20)	(6 × 20)
C	(6 × 30)	(6 × 20)	(6 × 20)	(5 × 20)
	300	200	200	250

Note: When output is not given, it is assumed that actual output is one unit.

where SP : Standard price per kg of raw material.

SQ : Standard quantity of raw material required for actual output.

= Standard quantity of raw material for one unit × Actual output.

SM : Standard mix, i.e., Total actual quantity of raw material used in standard ratio = 10 + 20 + 20 = 50 in the ratio of 15:30:30

AQ : Actual quantity of raw material used.

AP : Actual price per kg of raw material.

1. Material yield variances = (1) – (2)

$$= (SP \times SQ) - (SP \times SM)$$

Material A = (2 × 15) – (2 × 10) = 10 (F)
Material B = (3 × 30) – (3 × 20) = 30 (F)
Material C = (6 × 30) – (6 × 20) = 60 (F)
MYV = 100 (F)

2. Material mix variance = (2) – (3)
= (SP × SM) – (SP × AQ)
Material A = (2 × 10) – (2 × 10) = Nil
Material B = (3 × 20) – (3 × 20) = Nil
Material C = (6 × 20) – (6 × 20) = Nil
MMV = Nil

3. Material price variance = (3) – (4)
= (SP × AQ) – (AP × AQ)
Material A = (2 × 10) – (3 × 10) = 10 (F)
Material B = (3 × 20) – (6 × 20) = 60 (A)
Material C = (6 × 20) – (5 × 20) = 20 (F)
MPV = 50 (A)

4. Material usage variance = (1) – (3)
= (SP × SQ) – (SP × AQ)
Material A = (2 × 15) – (2 × 10) = 10 (F)
Material B = (3 × 30) – (3 × 20) = 30 (F)
Material C = (6 × 30) – (6 × 20) = 60 (F)
MUV = 100 (F)

5. Material cost variance = (1) – (4)
= (SP × SQ) – (AP × AQ)
Material A = (2 × 15) – (3 × 10) = Nil
Material B = (3 × 30) – (6 × 20) = 30 (A)
Material C = (6 × 30) – (5 × 20) = 80 (F)
MCV = 50 (F)

Problem 8 The standard material cost for 100 kg of chemical 'X' is made up of three components as:

A 30 kg @ ₹4.00 per kg

B 40 kg @ ₹5.00 per kg

C 80 kg @ ₹6.00 per kg

In a batch, 500 kg of chemical 'X' were produced from a mix of A 140 kg (Cost ₹588), B 220 kg (cost ₹1056) and C 440 kg (cost ₹2860). How do the yield, mix and price factor contribute to the variance in the actual per 100 kg of chemical D over the standard cost.

[B.Com. (H)]

Solution:

Material	(1)	(2)	(3)	(4)
	SP × SQ	SP × SM	SP × AQ	AP × AQ
A	$4 \times \left(\frac{30}{100} \times 500\right)$	$4 \times \left(800 \times \frac{3}{15}\right)$	(4 × 140)	(4.2 × 140)
B	$5 \times \left(\frac{40}{100} \times 500\right)$	$4 \times \left(800 \times \frac{4}{15}\right)$	(5 × 220)	(4.80 × 220)
C	$6 \times \left(\frac{80}{100} \times 500\right)$	$6 \times \left(800 \times \frac{8}{15}\right)$	(6 × 440)	(6.5 × 440)
	4000	4266.66	4300	4504

where SP : Standard price per kg of raw material.

SQ : Standard quantity of raw material required for actual output.
= Standard quantity of raw material for one unit × Actual output.

SM : Standard mix, i.e., Total actual quantity of raw material used in standard ratio = 140 + 220 + 440 = 800 in the ratio of 30 : 40 : 80

AQ : Actual quantity of raw material used.

AP : Actual price per kg of raw material.

1. Material yield variances = (1) – (2)
= (SP × SQ) – (SP × SM)

$$\text{Material A} = 4 \times \left(\frac{30}{100} \times 500\right) - 4 \times \left(800 \times \frac{3}{15}\right) = 40\ (A)$$

$$\text{Material B} = 5 \times \left(\frac{40}{100} \times 500\right) - 5 \times \left(800 \times \frac{4}{15}\right) = 66.66\ (A)$$

$$\text{Material C} = 6 \times \left(\frac{80}{100} \times 500\right) - 6 \times \left(800 \times \frac{8}{15}\right) = 160\ (A)$$

$$\text{MYV} = 266.66\ (A)$$

2. Material mix variance = (2) – (3)
= (SP × SM) – (SP × AQ)

$$\text{Material A} = 4 \times \left(800 \times \frac{3}{15}\right) - 5 \times 220 = 80\ (F)$$

$$\text{Material B} = 4 \times 140 - 6 \times \left(800 \times \frac{8}{15}\right) = 33.34\ (A)$$

$$\text{Material C} = 5 \times \left(800 \times \frac{4}{15}\right) - 6 \times 440 \qquad = 80\ (A)$$

MPV = 33.34 (A)

3. Material price variance = (3) – (4)

= (SP × AQ) – (AP × AQ)

Material A = (4 × 140) – (4.2 × 140) = 28 (A)

Material B = (5 × 220) – (4.80 × 220) = 44 (F)

Material C = (6 × 440) – (6.5 × 440) = 220 (A)

MPV = 204 (A)

4. Material usage variance = (1) – (3)

= (SP × SQ) – (SP × AQ)

$$\text{Material A} = 4 \times \left(\frac{30}{100} \times 500\right) - (4 \times 140) \qquad = 40\ (F)$$

$$\text{Material B} = 5 \times \left(\frac{40}{100} \times 500\right) - (5 \times 220) \qquad = 100\ (A)$$

$$\text{Material C} = 6 \times \left(\frac{80}{100} \times 500\right) - (6 \times 440) \qquad = 240\ (A)$$

MUV = 300 (A)

5. Material cost variance = (1) – (4)

= (SP × SQ) – (AP × AQ)

$$\text{Material A} = 4 \times \left(\frac{30}{100} \times 500\right) - (4.2 \times 140) \qquad = 12\ (F)$$

$$\text{Material B} = 5 \times \left(\frac{40}{100} \times 500\right) - (4.80 \times 220) \qquad = 56\ (A)$$

$$\text{Material C} = 6 \times \left(\frac{80}{100} \times 500\right) - (65 \times 440) \qquad = 460\ (A)$$

MCV = 504 (A)

Problem 9 In a manufacturing process the following standards apply:

Standard price	
Raw material A	₹ 10 per kg
Raw material B	₹ 5 per kg
Standard mix	75% A, 25% B (by weight)
Standard yield	90%

In a period the actual costs, usage and output were:

4400 kg of A costing ₹46,500
1600 kg of B costing ₹7850
Output: 5670 kg of product.

The budgeted output for the period was 7200 kg. You are required to compute the material cost variances.

Solution:

Material	(1)	(2)	(3)	(4)
	SP × SQ	SP × SM	SP × AQ	AP × AQ
A	$10 \times \left(\frac{75}{90} \times 5{,}670\right)$	$10 \times \left(6000 \times \frac{75}{100}\right)$	(10 × 4,400)	(10.57 × 4,400)
B	$5 \times \left(\frac{25}{90} \times 5{,}670\right)$	$5 \times \left(6000 \times \frac{25}{100}\right)$	(5 × 1,600)	(4.90 × 1,600)
	55,125	52,500	52,000	54,350

where SP : Standard price per kg of raw material.
SQ : Standard quantity of raw material required for actual output.
Standard quantity of raw material for one unit × actual output
SM : Standard mix, i.e., Total actual quantity of raw material used in standard ratio = 4,400 + 1,600 = 6,000 in the ratio of 75:25
AQ : Actual quantity of raw material used.
AP : Actual price per kg of raw material.

1. Material yield variances = (1) – (2)
= (SP × SQ) – (SP × SM)

$$\text{Material A} = 10 \times \left(\frac{75}{90} \times 5670\right) - 10 \times \left(6{,}000 \times \frac{75}{100}\right) = 2250\ (F)$$

$$\text{Material B} = 5 \times \left(\frac{25}{90} \times 5670\right) - 5 \times \left(6{,}000 \times \frac{25}{100}\right) = 375\ (F)$$

MYV = 2625 (P)

2. Material mix variance = (2) – (3)
= (SP × SM) – (SP × AQ)

$$\text{Material A} = 10 \times \left(6{,}000 \times \frac{75}{100}\right) - (10 \times 4{,}400) = 1000\ (F)$$

$$\text{Material B} = 6 \times \left(6{,}000 \times \frac{25}{100}\right) - (5 \times 1{,}600) = 500\ (A)$$

MMV = 1500 (A)

3. Material price variance = (3) – (4)

= (SP × AQ) – (AP × AQ)

Material A = (10 × 4400) – (10.57 × 4400) = 2508 (A)

Material B = (5 × 1600) – (490 × 1600) = 158 (F)

MPV = 2350 (A)

4. Material usage variance = (1) – (3)

= (SP × SQ) – (SP × AQ)

$$\text{Material A} = 10 \times \left(\frac{75}{90} \times 5670\right) - 10 \times 4400 = 3250\ (F)$$

$$\text{Material B} = 5 \times \left(\frac{25}{90} \times 5670\right) - 6 \times 1600 = 125\ (A)$$

MUV = 3125 (F)

5. Material cost variance = (1) – (4)

= (SP × SQ) – (AP × AQ)

$$\text{Material A} = 10 \times \left(\frac{75}{90} \times 5670\right) - 10.57 \times 4400 = 742\ (F)$$

$$\text{Material B} = 5 \times \left(\frac{25}{90} \times 5670\right) - 4.90 \times 1600 = 33\ (F)$$

MCV = 775 (F)

Problem 10 Infotech Ltd. manufactures a product by mixing three raw materials. For every batch of 100 kg of product, 125 kg of raw materials are used. During a particular month 60 batches were prepared to produce an output of 5600 kg of BXE. The other relevant information was as given below:

	Standard		Actual		
	Mix(%)	Price per kg	Mix (%)	Price per kg	Material purchased
A	50	₹20	60	₹21	5000 kg
B	30	₹10	20	₹8	2000 kg
C	20	₹5	20	₹6	1200 kg

Calculate the material cost variances. [*B.Com. (H)*]

Solution:

Material	(1)	(2)	(3)	(4)
	SP × SQ	SP × SM	SP × AQ	AP × AQ

Table Contd...

Table Contd...

Material	(1)	(2)	(3)	(4)
A	$20 \times \left(7000 \times \frac{5}{10}\right)$	$20 \times \left(7500 \times \frac{5}{10}\right)$	$20 \times \left(7500 \times \frac{6}{10}\right)$	$21 \times \left(7500 \times \frac{6}{10}\right)$
B	$10 \times \left(7000 \times \frac{3}{10}\right)$	$10 \times \left(7500 \times \frac{3}{10}\right)$	$10 \times \left(7500 \times \frac{2}{10}\right)$	$8 \times \left(7500 \times \frac{2}{10}\right)$
C	$5 \times \left(7000 \times \frac{2}{10}\right)$	$5 \times \left(7500 \times \frac{2}{10}\right)$	$5 \times \left(7500 \times \frac{2}{10}\right)$	$6 \times \left(7500 \times \frac{2}{10}\right)$
	97,500	104,500	112,000	118,000

where SP : Standard price per kg of raw material.

SQ : Standard quantity of raw material required for actual output.
= Standard quantity of raw material for One unit × Actual output.

SM : Standard mix, i.e., Total actual quantity of raw material used in standard ratio = 7500 in the ratio of 50 : 30 : 20

AQ : Actual quantity of raw material used.

AP : Actual price per kg of raw material.

Working Notes:

1. Total SQ $= \frac{125}{100} \times 5600$
   = 7000 in the standard ratio of materials.
2. Total AQ = 125 × 60
   = 7500 in the actual ratio.

1. Material yield variances = (1) – (2)
   = (SP × SQ) – (SP × SM)

$$\text{Material A} = 20 \times \left(7000 \times \frac{5}{10}\right) - 20 \times \left(7500 \times \frac{5}{10}\right) = 5000\ (A)$$

$$\text{Material B} = 10 \times \left(7000 \times \frac{3}{10}\right) - 10 \times \left(7500 \times \frac{3}{10}\right) = 1500\ (A)$$

$$\text{Material C} = 5 \times \left(7000 \times \frac{2}{10}\right) - 5 \times \left(7500 \times \frac{2}{10}\right) = 500\ (A)$$

MYV = 7000 (A)

2. Material mix variance = (2) – (4)
   = (SP × SM) – (SP × AQ)

$$\text{Material A} = 20 \times \left(7500 \times \frac{5}{10}\right) - 20 \times \left(7500 \times \frac{5}{10}\right) = 15{,}000\ (F)$$

$$\text{Material B} = 10 \times \left(7500 \times \frac{3}{10}\right) - 10 \times \left(7500 \times \frac{2}{10}\right) = 7500\ (A)$$

$$\text{Material C} = 5 \times \left(7500 \times \frac{2}{10}\right) - 5 \times \left(7500 \times \frac{2}{10}\right) = \text{Nil}$$

$$\text{MMV} = 7500\ (A)$$

3. Material price variance = (3) – (4)

= (SP × AQ) – (AP × AQ)

$$\text{Material A} = 20 \times \left(7500 \times \frac{6}{10}\right) - 21 \times \left(7500 \times \frac{6}{10}\right) = 4500\ (A)$$

$$\text{Material B} = 10 \times \left(7500 \times \frac{2}{10}\right) - 8 \times \left(7500 \times \frac{2}{10}\right) = \text{Nil}$$

$$\text{Material C} = 5 \times \left(7500 \times \frac{2}{10}\right) - 6 \times \left(7500 \times \frac{2}{10}\right) = 1500\ (A)$$

$$\text{MPV} = 6000\ (A)$$

4. Material usage variance = (1) – (3)

= (SP × SQ) – (SP × AQ)

$$\text{Material A} = 20 \times \left(7000 \times \frac{5}{10}\right) - 20 \times \left(7500 \times \frac{6}{10}\right) = 20{,}000\ (A)$$

$$\text{Material B} = 10 \times \left(7000 \times \frac{3}{10}\right) - 10 \times \left(7500 \times \frac{2}{10}\right) = 6000\ (P)$$

$$\text{Material C} = 5 \times \left(7000 \times \frac{2}{10}\right) - 5 \times \left(7500 \times \frac{2}{10}\right) = 500\ (A)$$

$$\text{MUV} = 14{,}500\ (A)$$

5. Material cost variance = (1) – (4)

= (SP × SQ) – (AP × AQ)

$$\text{Material A} = 20 \times \left(7000 \times \frac{5}{10}\right) - 21 \times \left(7500 \times \frac{6}{10}\right) = 24{,}500\ (A)$$

$$\text{Material B} = 10 \times \left(7000 \times \frac{3}{10}\right) - 8 \times \left(7500 \times \frac{2}{10}\right) = 6000\ (F)$$

$$\text{Material C} = 5\left(7000 \times \frac{2}{10}\right) - 6 \times \left(7500 \times \frac{2}{10}\right) = 2000\ (A)$$

$$\text{MCV} = 20{,}500\ (A)$$

Problem 11 The standard mix of a product is as given below:

A	60 units	@ 15 paise per unit
B	80 units	@ 20 paise per unit
C	100 units	@ 25 paise per unit
	240 units	

Ten units of the finished product were obtained from this mix. During a particular month, 10 mixes were completed and the consumption was:

A	640 units	@ 20 paise per unit
B	960 units	@ 15 paise per unit
C	840 units	@ 30 paise per unit

Actual output was 90 units. Calculate the material cost variances.

Solution:

Material	(1)	(2)	(3)	(4)
	SP × SQ	SP × SM	SP × AQ	AP × AQ
A	$0.15 \times \left(\frac{60}{10} \times 90\right)$	$0.15 \times \left(2440 \times \frac{6}{24}\right)$	(0.15 × 640)	(0.20 × 640)
B	$0.20 \times \left(\frac{80}{10} \times 90\right)$	$0.20 \times \left(2440 \times \frac{8}{24}\right)$	(0.20 × 960)	(0.15 × 960)
C	$0.25 \times \left(\frac{100}{10} \times 90\right)$	$0.25 \times \left(2440 \times \frac{10}{24}\right)$	(0.25 × 840)	(0.30 × 840)
	450	508.32	498	524

where SP : Standard price per kg of raw material.

SQ : Standard quantity of raw material required for actual output.

= Standard quantity of raw material for One unit × Actual output.

SM : Standard mix, i.e., Total actual quantity of raw material used in standard ratio = 640 + 960 + 840 = 2,440 in the ratio of 60 : 80 : 100

AQ : Actual quantity of raw material used.

AP : Actual price per kg of raw material.

1. Material yield variances = (1) – (2)

$$= (SP \times SQ) - (SP \times SM)$$

$$\text{Material A} = 0.15 \times \left(\frac{60}{10} \times 90\right) - 0.15 \times \left(2440 \times \frac{6}{24}\right) = 10.50\,(A)$$

$$\text{Material B} = 0.20 \times \left(\frac{80}{10} \times 90\right) - 0.20 \times \left(2440 \times \frac{8}{24}\right) = 18.66\,(A)$$

$$\text{Material C} = 0.25 \times \left(\frac{100}{10} \times 90\right) - 0.25 \times \left(2440 \times \frac{10}{24}\right) = 29.16\,(A)$$

$$\text{MYV} = 58.32\,(A)$$

2. Material mix variance = (2) – (3)

= (SP × SM) – (SP × AQ)

$$\text{Material A} = 0.15 \times \left(2440 \times \frac{6}{24}\right) - (0.15 \times 640) = 4.50\,(A)$$

$$\text{Material B} = 0.20 \times \left(2440 \times \frac{8}{24}\right) - (0.20 \times 960) = 29.33\,(A)$$

$$\text{Material C} = 0.25 \times \left(2440 \times \frac{10}{24}\right) - (0.25 \times 840) = 44.17\,(F)$$

$$\text{MMV} = 10.32\,(F)$$

3. Material price variance = (3) – (4)

= (SP × AQ) – (AP × AQ)

Material A = (0.15 × 640) – (0.20 × 640) = 32 (A)

Material B = (0.20 × 960) – (0.15 × 960) = 48 (F)

Material C = (0.25 × 840) – (0.30 × 840) = 42 (A)

MPV = 26 (A)

4. Material usage variance = (1) – (3)

= (SP × SQ) – (SP × AQ)

$$\text{Material A} = 15 \times \left(\frac{60}{10} \times 90\right) - (0.15 \times 640) = 15\,(A)$$

$$\text{Material B} = 20 \times \left(\frac{80}{10} \times 90\right) - (0.20 \times 960) = 48\,(A)$$

$$\text{Material C} = 0.25 \times \left(\frac{100}{10} \times 90\right) - (0.25 \times 840) = 15\,(F)$$

$$\text{MUV} = 48\,(A)$$

5. Material cost variance = (1) – (4)

= (SP × SQ) – (AP × AQ)

$$\text{Material A} = 0.15 \times \left(\frac{60}{10} \times 90\right) - (0.20 \times 640) = 47\,(A)$$

$$\text{Material B} = 0.20 \times \left(\frac{80}{10} \times 90\right) - (0.15 \times 960) = \text{Nil}$$

$$\text{Material C} = 0.25 \times \left(\frac{100}{10} \times 90\right) - (0.30 \times 840) \qquad = 27\text{ (A)}$$

$$\text{MCV} = 74\text{ (A)}$$

Problem 12 One kilogram of detergent requires two chemicals A and B. The following were the details of detergent for the month of June.

(a) Standard mix Chemical 'A' 50% and Chemical 'B' 50%.
(b) Standard price per kilogram of Chemical 'A' ₹12 and Chemical 'B' ₹15.
(c) Actual input of Chemical 'B' 70 kg.
(d) Actual price per kg of Chemical 'A' ₹15.
(e) Standard normal loss 10% of total input.
(f) Materials cost variance total ₹650 adverse.
(g) Materials yield variance total ₹135 adverse.

You are required to calculate:

(1) Material mix variance (total)
(2) Material usage variance (total)
(3) Material price variance (total)
(4) Actual loss of actual input
(5) Actual input of Chemical 'A'
(6) Actual price per kg of Chemical 'B'.

Solution:

Material	(1)	(2)	(3)	(4)
	SP × SQ	SP × SM	SP × AQ	AP × AQ
A	12 × 50	$12 \times \left(\frac{70 + x}{2}\right)$	12 × 40	15 × 40
B	15 × 50	$15 \times \left(\frac{70 + x}{2}\right)$	15 × 70	y × 70
	1350	945 + 13.5x	1530	600 + 70y

Let the AQ of A is x kg.

$$\text{MYV} = (1) - (2)$$
$$= (\text{SP} \times \text{SQ}) - (\text{SP} \times \text{SM})$$
$$\text{MYV} = 1350 - (945 + 13.5x)$$
$$x = 40 \text{ kg}$$

Substitute this value in columns (3) and (4)

Now, let the AP of B is ₹y.

$$\text{MCV} = (1) - (4)$$
$$= (\text{SP} \times \text{SQ}) - (\text{AP} \times \text{AQ})$$
$$-650 = 1350 - (600 + 70y)$$
$$\Rightarrow \qquad y = 20$$

1. MMU = 1350 – 1485 = 135 (A)
2. MUV = 1350 – 1530 = 180 (A)
3. MPV = 1530 – 2000 = 470 (A)
4. Actual loss = 110 – 100 = 10 kg
5. Actual quantity of A = 40 kg
6. AP of B = ₹20

Problem 13 Ceramic Ltd. makes plastic tiles of standard size of 6" × 6" × 1/8". From the following information you are required to calculate material cost variances.

A standard mix of the compound required to produce an output of 20,000 sq. ft. of tiles 1/8" thick is as follows:

Materials	Qty. (kg)	Price per kg (₹)
A	600	0.90
B	400	0.65
C	500	0.40

During a period, 8 mixes were processed and actual materials consumed were:

A	5000 kg	₹0.85
B	2900 kg	₹0.60
C	4400 kg	₹0.45

[*B.Com. (H)*]

Actual production for the period was 6,20,000 tiles.

Solution:

Material	(1)	(2)	(3)	(4)
	SP × SQ	SP × SM	SP × AQ	AP × AQ
A	$0.9 \times \left(\frac{600}{80,000} \times 6,20,000\right)$	$0.9 \times \left(12,300 \times \frac{6}{15}\right)$	(0.9 × 5000)	(0.85 × 5000)
B	$0.65 \times \left(\frac{400}{80,000} \times 6,20,000\right)$	$0.65 \times \left(12,300 \times \frac{4}{15}\right)$	(0.65 × 2900)	(0.6 × 2900)
C	$0.40 \times \left(\frac{500}{80,000} \times 6,20,000\right)$	$0.40 \times \left(12,300 \times \frac{5}{15}\right)$	(0.4 × 4400)	(0.45 × 4400)
	7750	8200	8145	7970

where SP : Standard price per kg of raw material.

SQ : Standard quantity of raw material required for actual output.

= Standard quantity of raw material for One unit × Actual output.

SM : Standard Mix, i.e., total actual quantity of raw material used in standard ratio = 5000 + 2900 + 4400 = 12,300 in the ratio of 600 : 400 : 500

AQ : Actual quantity of raw material used.

AP : Actual price per kg of raw material.

Working Notes:

$$\text{Area of one tile} = \frac{6'' \times 6''}{12'' \times 12''} = \frac{1}{4} \text{ sq. ft.}$$

$$\text{Total output} = \frac{20{,}000 \text{ sq. ft.}}{\frac{1}{4} \text{ sq. ft}} = 80{,}000 \text{ tiles}$$

1. Material yield variances = (1) – (2)

= (SP × SQ) – (SP × SM)

$$\text{Material A} = 0.9 \times \left(\frac{600}{80{,}000} \times 6{,}20{,}000\right) - 0.9 \times \left(12{,}300 \times \frac{6}{15}\right) = 243 \text{ (A)}$$

$$\text{Material B} = 0.65 \times \left(\frac{400}{80{,}000} \times 6{,}20{,}000\right) - 0.65 \times \left(12{,}300 \times \frac{4}{15}\right) = 117 \text{ (A)}$$

$$\text{Material C} = 0.40 \times \left(\frac{500}{80{,}000} \times 6{,}20{,}000\right) - 0.40 \times \left(12{,}300 \times \frac{5}{15}\right) = 90 \text{ (A)}$$

MYV = 450 (A)

2. Material mix variance = (2) – (3)

= (SP × SM) – (SP × AQ)

$$\text{Material A} = 0.9 \times \left(12{,}300 \times \frac{6}{15}\right) - (0.9 \times 5000) = 72 \text{ (A)}$$

$$\text{Material B} = 0.65 \times \left(12{,}300 \times \frac{4}{15}\right) - (0.65 \times 2900) = 247 \text{ (F)}$$

$$\text{Material C} = 0.40 \times \left(12{,}300 \times \frac{5}{15}\right) \quad (0.4 \times 4400) = 120 \text{ (A)}$$

MMV = 55 (F)

3. Material price variance = (3) – (4)

= (SP × AQ) – (AP × AQ)

Material A = (0.9 × 5000) – (0.85 × 5000) = 250 (F)

Material B = (0.65 × 2900) – (0.6 × 2900) = 145 (F)

Material C = (0.4 × 4400) – (0.45 × 4400) = 220 (A)

MPV = 175 (A)

4. Material usage variance = (1) – (3)

= (SP × SQ) – (SP × AQ)

$$\text{Material A} = 0.9 \times \left(\frac{600}{80{,}000} \times 6{,}20{,}000\right) - (0.9 \times 5000) \quad = 315\ (A)$$

$$\text{Material B} = 0.65 \times \left(\frac{400}{80{,}000} \times 6{,}20{,}000\right) - (0.65 \times 2900) \quad = 130\ (F)$$

$$\text{Material C} = 0.40 \times \left(\frac{500}{80{,}000} \times 6{,}20{,}000\right) - (0.4 \times 4400) \quad = 210\ (A)$$

MUV = 395 (A)

5. Material cost variance = (1) – (4)

= (SP × SQ) – (AP × AQ)

$$\text{Material A} = 0.9 \times \left(\frac{600}{80{,}000} \times 6{,}20{,}000\right) - (0.85 - 5000) \quad = 65\ (A)$$

$$\text{Material B} = 0.65 \times \left(\frac{400}{80{,}000} \times 6{,}20{,}000\right) - (0.6 \times 2900) \quad = 275\ (F)$$

$$\text{Material C} = 0.40 \times \left(\frac{500}{80{,}000} \times 6{,}20{,}000\right) - (0.45 \times 4400) \quad = 430\ (A)$$

MCV = 220 (A)

Problem 14 Cleanmate Ltd. has established the following standard mix for producing 9 gallons of chemical. It mixes 3 raw materials – X, Y and Z.

	₹
5 gallons – Material X at ₹7 per gallon	35
3 gallons – Material Y at ₹5 per gallon	15
2 gallons – Material Z at ₹2 per gallon	4
	54

A standard loss of 10% of input is expected to occur. Actual input was:

Material X – 53,000 gallons at ₹7 per gallon

Material Y – 28,000 gallons at ₹5.30 per gallon

Material Z – 19,000 gallons at ₹2.20 per gallon

Actual output for the period was 92,700 gallons.

Calculate material cost variances. [*B.Com. (H)*]

Solution:

Material	(1)	(2)	(3)	(4)
	SP × SQ	SP × SM	SP × AQ	AP × AQ
X	$7 \times \left(\frac{5}{9} \times 92{,}700\right)$	$7 \times \left(1{,}00{,}000 \times \frac{5}{10}\right)$	(7 × 53,000)	(7 × 53,000)
Y	$5 \times \left(\frac{3}{9} \times 92{,}700\right)$	$5 \times \left(1{,}00{,}000 \times \frac{3}{10}\right)$	(5 × 28,000)	(5.3 × 28,000)
Z	$2 \times \left(\frac{2}{9} \times 92{,}700\right)$	$2 \times \left(1{,}00{,}000 \times \frac{2}{10}\right)$	(2 × 19,000)	(2.2 × 19,000)
	5,56,200	5,40,000	5,49,000	5,61,200

where SP : Standard price per kg of raw material.

SQ : Standard quantity of raw material required for actual output.
= Standard quantity of raw material for Oned unit × Actual output.

SM : Standard mix, i.e., Total actual quantity of raw material used in standard ratio = 53,000 + 28,000 + 19,000 = 1,00,000 in the ratio of 5 : 3 : 2.

AQ : Actual quantity of raw material used.

AP : Actual price per kg of raw material.

1. Material yield variances = (1) – (2)
= (SP × SQ) – (SP × SM)

$$\text{Material A} = 7 \times \left(\frac{5}{9} \times 92{,}700\right) - 7 \times \left(1{,}00{,}000 \times \frac{5}{10}\right) = 10{,}500 \text{ (F)}$$

$$\text{Material B} = 5 \times \left(\frac{3}{9} \times 92{,}700\right) - 5 \times \left(1{,}00{,}000 \times \frac{3}{10}\right) = 4500 \text{ (F)}$$

$$\text{Material C} = 2 \times \left(\frac{2}{9} \times 92{,}700\right) - 2 \times \left(1{,}00{,}000 \times \frac{2}{10}\right) = 1200 \text{ (F)}$$

MYV = 16,200 (F)

2. Material mix variance = (2) – (3)
= (SP × SM) – (SP × AQ)

$$\text{Material A} = 7 \times \left(1{,}00{,}000 \times \frac{5}{10}\right) - 7 \times 53{,}000 = 21{,}000 \text{ (A)}$$

$$\text{Material B} = 5 \times \left(1{,}00{,}000 \times \frac{3}{10}\right) - 5 \times 28{,}000 = 10{,}000 \text{ (F)}$$

$$\text{Material C} = 2 \times \left(1,00,000 \times \frac{2}{10}\right) - 2 \times 19,000 \qquad = 2000\ (F)$$

$$\text{MMV} = 9000\ (A)$$

3. Material price variance = (3) – (4)

$$= (SP \times AQ) - (AP \times AQ)$$

$$\text{Material A} = 7 \times 53,000 - 7 \times 53,000 \qquad = \text{Nil}$$

$$\text{Material B} = 5 \times 28,000 - 5.3 \times 28,000 \qquad = 8400\ (A)$$

$$\text{Material C} = 2 \times 19,000 - 2.2 \times 19,000 \qquad = 3800\ (A)$$

$$\text{MPV} = 12,200\ (A)$$

4. Material usage variance = (1) – (3)

$$= (SP \times SQ) - (SP \times AQ)$$

$$\text{Material A} = 7 \times \left(\frac{5}{9} \times 92,700\right) - (7 \times 53,000) \qquad = 10,500\ (A)$$

$$\text{Material B} = 5 \times \left(\frac{3}{9} \times 92,700\right) - (5 \times 28,000) \qquad = 14,500\ (F)$$

$$\text{Material C} = 2 \times \left(\frac{2}{9} \times 92,700\right) - (2 \times 19,000) \qquad = 3200\ (F)$$

$$\text{MUV} = 7200\ (F)$$

5. Material cost variance = (1) – (4)

$$= (SP \times SQ) - (AP \times AQ)$$

$$\text{Material A} = 7 \times \left(\frac{5}{9} \times 92,700\right) - 7 \times 53,000 \qquad = 10,500\ (A)$$

$$\text{Material B} = 5 \times \left(\frac{3}{9} \times 92,700\right) - 5 \times \left(\frac{3}{9} \times 92,700\right) \qquad = 6100\ (F)$$

$$\text{Material C} = 2 \times \left(\frac{2}{9} \times 92,700\right) - 2.2 \times 19,000 \qquad = 600\ (A)$$

$$\text{MCV} = 5000\ (A)$$

Problem 15 Kriti Ltd. produces an article by blending two basic raw materials. The following standards have been set up for raw material.

Material	Standard Mix	St. Price per kg
A	40%	₹4
B	60%	₹3

The standard loss in processing is 15%. During September 2021 the company produced 1700 kg of finished output. The position of stock and purchases for the month of September 2021 is as under:

Material	Stock on 1-4-2019	Stock on 30-4-2013	Purchases during April 2019	
	kg	kg	kg	Cost (₹)
A	35	5	800	3400
B	40	50	1200	3000

Calculate all material variances assuming FIFO method of issue of materials. The opening stock is to be valued at standard price. [*B.Com. (H)*]

Solution:

Material	(1)	(2)	(3)	(4)
	SP × SQ	SP × SM	SP × AQ	AP × AQ
A	$4 \times \left(\frac{40}{85} \times 1700\right)$	$4 \times \left(2020 \times \frac{4}{10}\right)$	(4 × 830)	$\begin{bmatrix} 4 \times 35 \\ 4.25 \times 795 \end{bmatrix}$
B	$3 \times \left(\frac{60}{85} \times 1700\right)$	$3 \times \left(2020 \times \frac{6}{10}\right)$	(3 × 1190)	$\begin{bmatrix} 2.5 \times 1150 \\ 3 \times 40 \end{bmatrix}$
	6800	6868	6890	6513.75

where SP : Standard price per kg of raw material.

SQ : Standard quantity of raw material required for actual output.

= Standard quantity of raw material for One unit × Actual output.

SM : Standard mix, i.e., Total actual quantity of raw material used in standard ratio = 830 + 1190 = 2020 in the ratio of 40 : 60

AQ : Actual quantity of raw material used.

AP : Actual price per kg of raw material.

Working Notes:

(a) Actual consumption of materials

Material	Op. stock	+	Purchases	–	Closing stock	=	Consumption
A	35 kg	+	800 kg	–	5 kg	=	830 kg
B	40 kg	+	1200 kg	–	50 kg	=	1190 kg

(b) Calculation of actual price per kg

$$\text{Material A} = \frac{3400}{800} = ₹74.25$$

$$\text{Material B} = \frac{3000}{1200} = ₹2.50$$

(c) It is assumed that firm is using FIFO method.

(d) It is assumed that last year also the prices were same as in the current year.

1. Material yield variances = (1) – (2)

= (SP × S) – (SP × SM)

$$\text{Material A} = 4 \times \left(\frac{40}{85} \times 1700\right) - 4 \times \left(2020 \times \frac{4}{10}\right) \qquad = 32\ (A)$$

$$\text{Material B} = 3 \times \left(\frac{60}{85} \times 1700\right) - 3 \times \left(2200 \times \frac{6}{10}\right) \qquad = 36\ (A)$$

MYV = 68 (A)

2. Material mix variance = (2) – (3)

= (SP × SM) – (SP × AQ)

$$\text{Material A} = 4 \times \left(2020 \times \frac{4}{10}\right) - 4 \times 830 \qquad = 88\ (A)$$

$$\text{Material B} = 3 \times \left(2200 \times \frac{6}{10}\right) - 3 \times 1190 \qquad = 66\ (F)$$

MMV = 22 (A)

3. Material price variance = (3) – (4)

= (SP × AQ) – (AP × AQ)

$$\text{Material A} = 4 \times 830 - \begin{bmatrix} 4 \times 35 \\ 4.25 \times 795 \end{bmatrix} \qquad = 198.75\ (A)$$

$$\text{Material B} = 3 \times 1190 - \begin{bmatrix} 2.5 \times 1150 \\ 3 \times 40 \end{bmatrix} \qquad = 575.00\ (F)$$

MPV = 376.25 (F)

4. Material usage variance = (1) – (3)

= (SP × SQ) – (SP × AQ)

$$\text{Material A} = 4 \times \left(\frac{40}{85} \times 1700\right) - 4 \times 830 \qquad = 120\ (A)$$

$$\text{Material B} = 3 \times \left(\frac{60}{85} \times 1700\right) - 3 \times 1190 \qquad = 30\ (F)$$

MUV = 90 (A)

5. Material cost variance = (1) – (4)

= (SP × SQ) – (AP × AQ)

$$\text{Material A} = 4 \times \left(\frac{40}{85} \times 1700\right) - \begin{bmatrix} 4 \times 35 \\ 4.25 \times 795 \end{bmatrix} \qquad = 318.75\ (A)$$

$$\text{Material B} = 3 \times \left(\frac{60}{85} \times 1700\right) - \left[\frac{2.5 \times 1150}{3 \times 40}\right] = 605 \text{ (F)}$$

$$\text{MCV} = 286.25 \text{ (F)}$$

Problem 16 Calculate the labour cost variances from the following:

Standard output	1000 units	Actual hours worked	6000
Standard time for one unit	5 hr	Actual rate per hour	₹3.50
Standard rate per hour	₹4.00	Actual output	1500 units
Time lost	500 hr		

Solution:

Labour	(1)	(2)	(3)	(4)	(5)
	SR × ST 4 × (5 × 1500)	SR × SM (4 × 6000)	SR × AT_W (4 × 6000)	SR × AT_F (4 × 6500)	AR × AT_F (3.50 × 6500)
	30,000	24,000	24,000	26,000	22,750

where SR : Standard rate per labour hour = ₹4

ST : Standard time required for actual output = 5 × 1500 = 7500

SM : Standard mix, i.e., Total actual time worked in standard ratio of workers.

AT_W : Actual time worked = 6000 hr

AT_P : Actual time paid for = 6000 + 500 = 6500

AR : Actual rate per labour hour = ₹3.50

1. Labour revised efficiency variance = (1) – (2)
   = (SR × ST) – (SR × SM)
   = 4 × (5 × 1500) – (4 × 6000)
   = 30,000 – 24,000 = 6000 (F)
2. Labour mix variance = (2) – (3)
   = (SR × SM) – (SR × AT_W)
   = (4 × 6000) – (4 × 6000) = Nil
3. Labour idle time variance = (3) – (4)
   = (SR × AT_W) – (SR × AT_P)
   = (4) × 6000) – (4 × 6500) = 2000 (A)
4. Labour efficiency variance = (1) – (4)
   = (SR × ST) – (SR × AT_P)
   = (4) × (5 × 1500) – (4 × 6500) = 4000 (F)
5. Labour rate variance = (4) – (5)
   = (SR × AT) – (AR × AT_P)
   = (4 × 6500) – (3.50 × 6500) = 3250 (F)
6. Labour cost variance = (1) – (5)

$$= (SR \times ST) - (AR \times AT_P)$$
$$= (4 \times (5 \times 1500) - (3.50 \times 6500) = 7250\ (F)$$

Verification

Labour cost variance = Labour efficiency variance + Labour rate variance

= (4000 (F) + 3250 (F) = 7250 (F)

Problem 17 The budgeted and the actual sale figures for the month February 2021 are given below:

Product	Budget	Budget	Actual	Actual
	Quantity (Unit)	Amount (₹)	Quantity (Unit)	Amount (₹)
P-1	1500	30,000	1250	28,750
P-2	1500	45,000	2000	56,000
P-3	2000	1,00,000	2750	1,48,500
Total	5000	1,75,000	6000	2,33,250

Calculate sales variance using turnover method assuming sales are homogeneous.

Solution:

Working Notes:

Rate or price = Amount divided by quantity

SP (P-1) = 30,000/1500 = ₹20

SP (P-2) = 45,000/1500 = ₹30

SP (P-3) = 1,00,000/2000 = ₹50

AP (P-1) = 28,750/1250 = ₹23

AP (P-2) = 56,000/2000 = ₹28

AP (P-3) = 1,48,500/2750 = ₹54

Standard proportion = 1500 : 1500 : 2000 OR 0.3 : 0.3 : 0.4

RSQ = Total AQ × Standard proportion

RSQ (P-1) = 6000 × 0.3 = 1800

RSQ (P-2) = 6000 × 0.3 = 1800

RSQ (P-3) = 6000 × 0.4 = 2400

Sales revenue variance:

SRV = (AQ × AP) – (SQ × SP)

P-1 = (1250 × 23) – (1500 × 20) = (28,750) – (30,000) = ₹1250 (UF)

P-2 = (2000 × 28) – (1500 × 30) = (56,000) – (45,000) = ₹1000 (F)

P-3 = (2750 × 54) – (2000 × 50) = (1,48,500) – (1,00,000) = ₹48,500 (F)

Total sales revenue variance

= ₹1250 (UF) + ₹11,000 (F) + ₹48,500 (P) = ₹1,16,500 (P)

Sales price variance:

SPV = AQ(AP – SP)

P-1 = 1250(23 – 20) = ₹3750 (F)

P-2 = 2000(28 – 30) = ₹4000 (UF)

P-3 = 2750(54 – 50) = ₹11,000 (F)

Total sales price variance

= ₹3750 (F) + ₹4000 (UF) + ₹1,1,000 (F) = ₹10,750 (F)

Sales volume variance: SMV = SP (AQ–BQ)

P-1 = 20(1250 – 1500) = ₹5000 (UF)

P-2 = 30 (2000 – 1500) = ₹15,000 (F)

P-3 = 50 (2750 – 2000) = ₹37,500

Total sales volume variance

= ₹5000 (UF) + ₹15,000 (F) + ₹37,500 (F)

= ₹47,500 (F)

Check No. I

Sales revenue variance = Sales price variance + Sales volume variance

₹58,250 (F) + ₹10,750 (F) + ₹47,500 (F)

Sales mix variance: SMV SP AQ–RS)

P-1 = 20 (1250 – 1800) = ₹11,000 (UF)

P-2 = 30 (2000 – 1800) = ₹6000 (F)

P-3 = 50 (2750 – 2400) = ₹20,000 (F)

Total sales mix variance

₹11,000 (UF) + ₹6000 (F) + ₹17,500 (F) = ₹12,500 (F)

Sales quantity variance: SQV SP RQ-BQ)

P-1 = 20 (1800 – 1500) = ₹6000 (F)

P-2 = 30 (1800 – 1500) = ₹9000 (F)

P-3 = 50 (2400 – 2000) = ₹20,000 (F)

Total sales quantity variance

= ₹6000 (F) + ₹9000 (F) + ₹20,000 (F) = ₹35,000 (P)

Check No. II

Sales volume variance = Sales mix variance + Sales quantity variance

₹47,500 (F) ₹12,500 (F) + ₹35,000 (F)

Problem 18 The working results of a company for two corresponding years are shown below:

Particulars	Year 1 (₹ in lakhs)	Year 2 (₹ in lakhs)
Sales	1200	1540
Direct material	600	648
Direct wages and variable overheads	360	412
Fixed overheads	160	300
	1120	1360
	80	180

In year 2, there has been an increase in the selling price by 10%. Following are the details of material consumption and utilisation of direct labour hours during the two years.

Particulars	Year 1	Year 2
Direct material consumption in m/t	5,00,000	5,40,000
Direct labour hours	75,00,000	80,00,000

Required

(i) Keeping year 1 as base year, analyse the results of year 2 and work out the amount which each factor has contributed to change in profit.

(ii) Find out the break-even sales for both years.

(iii) Calculate the percentage increase in selling price that would be needed over the sales value of year 2 to earn a might of safety of 45%.

Solution:

(i) Reconciliation statement showing which factor has contributed change in profit

Particulars	Favourable (₹ In lakhs)	Adverse (₹ In lakhs)
A Increase in contribution due to increase in volume (₹280 lakhs – ₹240 lakhs)	40	–
B Sales price variance	140	
C Material usages variance	52	
D Material price variance	–	0
E Direct labour rate variance	–	28
F Direct labour efficiency variance	36	–
G Fixed overhead expenditure variance	–	140
	268	168
Total change in profit	100	

(ii) $$\text{Break-even Sales (Year 1)} = \frac{\text{Fixed cost}}{\text{P/V ratio}} = \frac{₹160 \text{ lakhs}}{(₹240 \text{ lakhs}/₹1200 \text{ lakhs})}$$

$$= ₹800 \text{ lakhs}$$

$$\text{Break-even sales (year 2)} = \frac{₹300 \text{ lakhs}}{(₹480 \text{ lakhs}/₹1540 \text{ lakhs})} = ₹962.50 \text{ lakhs}$$

(iii) **Percentage Increase in Selling Price needed over the Sales Value of year 2 to earn a Margin of Safety of 45% in year 3.**

Variable cost in year 2 = ₹1060 each

Let revised sales be X

Revised contribution = X – ₹1060

If margin of safety to be earned is 45% then break-even point should be 55%

$$\text{BEP (\%)} = \frac{\text{Fixed cost}}{\text{Revised contribution}}$$

$$55\% = \frac{₹300 \text{ lakhs}}{X - ₹1{,}060} \Rightarrow 0.55\,(X - ₹1{,}060 \text{ lakhs}) = ₹300 \text{ lakhs}$$

$$X = ₹1605.46 \text{ lakhs}$$

$$\text{Percentage increase in selling price} = \frac{(₹1605.46 \text{ lakhs} - ₹1540 \text{ lakhs})}{₹1540 \text{ lakhs}}$$

$$= 4.25\%$$

Working Notes:

(i) Budgeted sales in year 2 (taking year 1 as base year)
= ₹15,40,000 × 100/110 = ₹14,00,000

(ii) Budgeted direct material (in year 2) = $\frac{600}{1{,}200} \times 1400$ lakhs = 700 lakhs

(iii) Budgeted direct wages and variable overhead (in year 2) = $\frac{360}{1200} \times 1400 = 420$ lakhs

Problem 19 Standard cost card of a product is as under

Direct materials:		₹
A.	2 kg @ ₹3 per kg	6.00
B.	1 kg @ ₹4 per kg	4.00
Direct wages × Hours @ ₹4 per hour		20.00
Variable overheads × Hours @ ₹1 per unit		5.00
Fixed overheads × Hours @ ₹2 per hour		10.00
Total		45.00
Standard profit		5.00
Standard selling Price		50.00

Budgeted output is 8000 units per month.

In October 2021 the company produced and sold 6000 units. The actual sales value was ₹3,05,000. Direct material consumed was: Material A 14850 kg valued at ₹43,065 and Material B 7260 kg valued at ₹29,750.

The total direct labour hours worked was 32,000 and the wages paid therefore amounted to ₹1,27,500. The direct labour hours actually booked on production was 31,800. Overheads recorded were: Fixed ₹80,600 and variable ₹30,000. Closing work-in-progress was 600 units in respect of which materials A and B were fully issued and labour and overhead were 50% complete. Work-in-progress is valued at standard cost.

Required: Prepare an operating statement.

Solution:

Operating Statement

Particulars			₹
A Budgeted profit (8000 units × ₹5)			40,000
B Sales margin variance			
	(F)	(A)	
S.M. price variance	₹5000		
S.M. volume variance		₹10,000	
Total	5000	10,000	(5000)
C Cost variances:			
Direct materials:	775		
Price		7700	
Yield	110		
Mix			
Direct wages:	500		
Rate		1200	
Yield		800	
Idle time			
Variable overhead:			
Efficiency		300	
Idle time		200	
Expenditure	2,000		
Fixed overhead:			
Efficiency		600	
Idle time		400	
Capacity		16,000	
Expenditure		600	
Total cost variance	3385	27,800	(24,415)
D Actual Profit			10,585

Working Notes:

(i) *Calculation of Material Variance*

Standard Qty. of Material 'A' = (6000 + 600) × 2 = 13200 kg

Standard Qty. of Material 'B' = (6000 + 600) × 1 = 6600 kg

Total standard input = 13200 + 6600 = 19800 kg

Revised Std. Qty. of Material 'A' = $\frac{13200}{19800} \times 22{,}110 = 14{,}740$

Revised Std. Qty. of Material 'B' = $\frac{6600}{19800} \times 22{,}110 = 7370$

Basic Calculations for the Computation of Material Cost Variance

Type of Material	SQ for AO	SP	SQ × SP (1)	AQ	AP	AQ × AP (2)	AQ × AP (3)	RQ	RQ × SP (4)
A	13,200	3	39,600	14,850		43,065	44,550	14,740	44,220
B	6600	4	26,400	7260		29,750	29,040	7370	29,480
	19,800			22,110					
			66,000			72,815	73,590		73,700

A Material cost variance (1 – 2) ₹6,815 (A)

B Material efficient variance (1 – 3) ₹2,000 (A)

C Material yield variance (1 – 4) ₹7,700 (A)

D Material mix variance (3 – 4) ₹110 (F)

E Material price variance (3 – 2) ₹775 (P)

(ii) *Calculation of Labour Cost Variance*

Standard hours = (6000 + 50% of 600) × 5 = 31,500

Basic Calculations for the Computation of Material Cost Variance

SH for AO	SR	SH × SR (1)	AH	AR	AH × AR (2)	AH × SR (3)	RPH	RPH × SR (4)
31,500	4	1,26,000	32,000		1,27,500	1,28,000	31,800	1,27,200

A Labour cost variance (1 – 2) ₹1500 (A)

B Labour efficient variance (1 – 3) ₹2000 (A)

C Labour yield variance (1 – 4) ₹1200 (A)

D Labour idle variance (3 – 4) ₹800 (F)

E Labour rate variance (3 – 2) ₹500 (F)

(iii) *Calculation of Labour Cost Variance*

Basic Calculations for the Computation of Overhead Variance

Name of Overhead	SH for AO	SR	SH × SR (1)	AH	AR	AH × AR (2)	AH × SR (3)	BH	BH × SR (4)	APH	APH × SR (5)
Fixed	31500	2.00	63,000	32,000		80,000	6,46,000	40,000	80,000	31,800	63,600
Variable	31500	1.00	31,500	32,000		30,000	32,000	31,500	31,500	31,800	31,800

A Fixed overhead efficiency variance (1 – 5) ₹600 (A)
B Fixed overhead idle time variance (5 – 3) ₹400 (A)
C Fixed overhead capacity variance (3 – 4) ₹16,000 (A)
D Fixed overhead expenditure variance (4 – 2) ₹600 (A)
E Fixed overhead efficiency variance (1 – 5) ₹300 (A)
F Variable overhead idle time variance (6 – 3) ₹200 (A)
G Variable overhead expenditure variance (3 – 2) ₹2000 (F)
H Total overhead cost variance (A + B + D + E + F + G) = ₹16,100 (A)

(iv) *Calculation of Sales Margin Variance:*

Actual selling price per unit = ₹3,05,000/6000 units = 50.833

Actual margin per unit = Actual selling price – Standard cost
= ₹50.833 – ₹45 = ₹5.833

Basic Calculations for the Computation of Sales Variance

BQ	BM	BQ × BM (1)	AQ	AM	AQ × AM (2)	AQ × AM (3)
8000	5	40,000	6000	5.8333	35,000	30,000

A Sales margin value variance (2 – 1) = ₹5000 (A)
B Sales margin volume variance (3 – 1) = ₹10,000 (A)
C Sales margin price variance (2 – 3) = ₹5000 (F)

Problem 20 S. Ltd. operated a system of standard costing in respect one in its product which of manufactured within a single cost centre, the following information is available.

For one unit of product the standard material input is 20 litres at a standard price of ₹2 per litre. The standard wage rate is ₹5 hours are allowed to produce one unit. Fixed production overhead is absorbed at the rate of 100% of direct wages cost. The material price variance was extracted on purchase.

During the month just ended the following occurred:

Total price paid for material purchased	₹1.95 per litre
Total direct wages cost	₹1,56,000
Fixed production overhead incurred	₹1,58,000

Variance	*Favourable* (₹)	*Adverse* (₹)
Direct material price	8.00	–
Direct material usage	–	5000
Direct labour rate	–	5760
Direct labour efficiency	2760	–
Fixed production overhead expenditure	–	8000

Required: Calculate the following for the month: (i) Budgeted output in unit; (ii) Number of litres purchased; (iii) Number of litres used above standard allowing; and (iv) Actual units produced; (v) Actual hours worked, (vi) Average actual wage rate per hour.

Solution:

(i) *Budgeted output (in units)*

Fixed overhead expenditure = (BH × SR) – AH × AR) – ₹8000
= (BH × ₹6) – ₹1,58,000 BH
= (₹1,58,000 – ₹8000)/6 = ₹25,000

Budgeted output = 25,000/5 = 5000 units

(ii) *Number of Litres Purchased*

Material usage variance = AQ (SP – AP)
₹8000 = AQ (₹2.00 – ₹1.95)
AQ = 1,60,000 Litres

(iii) *No. of Litres used above standard*

Material usage variance SP (SQ – AQ) – ₹5000 = 2(SQ 1,60,000)
SQ = 1,60,000 – (5000/2) = 1,57,500

No. of Litres used above standard allowed

(iv) *Actual number of units produced*

Direct labour cost variance = (SH × SR) – (AH × AR)
₹2760 (F) + ₹5760 (A) = (SH × 6) – ₹1,56,000 ₹3000
= (SH × 6) – 1,56,000 SH
= (1,56,000 – 3000/6 = 25,500

Actual number of units produced = 25,500/5 = 5100

(v) *Actual hours worked*

Direct labour efficiency variance = SR (SH – AH)S
₹2760 = 6 [(5100 × 5) hours

(vi) *Actual wage rate per hour*

$$\text{Direct labour rate variance} = \frac{\text{Actual direct cost}}{\text{Actual hours}} = \frac{₹1,56,000}{25,040} = ₹6.23.$$

Problem 21 A group of workers normally consists of 30 men, 15 women and 10 boys. They are paid at rates per hour as man–₹0.80, woman–₹0.60, boy–₹0.40.

In a normal working week of 40 hours, the gang is expected to produce 2000 units of output.

During the week ended 31 December, the gang consisted of 40 men, 10 women and 5 boys. The actual wages paid were @ ₹0.70, ₹0.65 and ₹0.30 respectively. 1600 units were produced. Four hours were lost due to abnormal idle time.

Calculate (i) Wage variance, (ii) Wage rate variance, (iii) Labour efficiency variance, (iv) Idle time variance (v) Gang composition variance, (i.e., labour mix variance) and (vi) Labour revised efficiency variance, or labour yield variance. [*B.Com. (H)*]

Solution:

Labour	(1)	(2)	(3)	(4)	(5)
	SR × ST	SR × SM	SR × AT_W	SR × AT_P	AR × AT_P
Men	$0.8 \times \left(\frac{30 \times 40}{2000} \times 1600\right)$	$0.8 \times \left(55 \times 36 \times \frac{30}{55}\right)$	0.8 × (40 × 36)	0.8 × (40 × 40)	0.70 × (40 × 40)
Women	$0.6 \times \left(\frac{15 \times 40}{2000} \times 1600\right)$	$0.6 \times \left(55 \times 36 \times \frac{15}{55}\right)$	0.6 × (10 × 36)	0.6 × (10 × 40)	0.65 × (10 × 40)
Boys	$0.4 \times \left(\frac{10 \times 40}{2000} \times 1600\right)$	$0.4 \times \left(55 \times 36 \times \frac{10}{55}\right)$	0.4 × (5 × 36)	0.4 × (5 × 40)	0.30 × (5 × 40)
	1,184	1,332	1,440	1,600	1,440

where SR : Standard rate per labour hour

AT_W : Actual time worked

AT_P : Actual time paid for

AR : Actual rate per labour hour

ST : Standard time required for actual output

SM : Standard mix, i.e.; total actual time worked in standard ratio of workers.

1. Labour revised EV = (1) – (2)

= (SR × ST) – (SR × SM)

$$\text{Men} = 0.8 \times \left(\frac{30 \times 40}{2000} \times 1600\right) - 0.8 \times \left(55 \times 36 \times \frac{30}{55}\right) = 96\text{ (A)}$$

$$\text{Women} = 0.6 \times \left(\frac{15 \times 40}{2000} \times 1600\right) - 0.6 \times \left(55 \times 36 \times \frac{15}{55}\right) = 36\text{ (A)}$$

$$\text{Boys} = 0.6 \times \left(\frac{10 \times 40}{2000} \times 1600\right) - 0.4 \times \left(55 \times 36 \times \frac{10}{55}\right) = 16\text{ (A)}$$

LREV = 148 (A)

2. Labour mix variance = (2) – (3)

$= (SR \times SM) - (SR \times AT_W)$

$$\text{Men} = 0.8 \times \left(55 \times 36 \times \frac{30}{55}\right) - 0.8 \times (40 \times 36) = 288\ (A)$$

$$\text{Women} = 0.6 \times \left(55 \times 36 \times \frac{15}{55}\right) - 0.6 \times (10 \times 36) = 108\ (F)$$

$$\text{Boys} = 0.4 \times \left(55 \times 36 \times \frac{10}{55}\right) - 0.4 \times (5 \times 36) = 72\ (F)$$

LMV = 108 (A)

3. Labour idle time variance = (3) – (4)

$= (SR \times AT_W) - (SR \times AT_P)$

Men = 0.8 × (40 × 36) – 0.8 × (40 × 40) = 128 (A)

Women = 0.6 × (10 × 36) – 0.6 × (10 × 40) = 24 (A)

Boys = 0.4 × (5 × 36) – 0.4 × (5 × 40) = 8 (A)

LITV = 160 (A)

4. Labour efficiency variance = (1) – (4)

$= (SR \times ST) - (SR \times AT_P)$

$$\text{Men} = 0.8 \times \left(\frac{30 \times 40}{2000} \times 1600\right) - 0.8 \times (40 \times 40) = 512\ (A)$$

$$\text{Women} = 0.6 \times \left(\frac{15 \times 40}{2000} \times 1600\right) - 0.6 \times (10 \times 40) = 48\ (F)$$

$$\text{Boys} = 0.4 \times \left(\frac{10 \times 40}{2000} \times 1600\right) - 0.4 \times (5 \times 40) = 48\ (F)$$

LEV = 416 (A)

5. Labour rate variance = (4) – (5)

$= (SR \times AT_P) - (AR \times AT_P)$

Men = 0.8 × (40 × 40) – 0.70 × (40 × 40) = 160 (F)

Women = 0.6 × (10 × 40) – 0.65 × (10 × 40) = 20 (A)

Boys = 0.4 × (5 × 40) – 0.30 × (5 × 40) = 20 (F)

LRV = 160 (F)

6. Labour cost variance = (1) – (5)

$= (SR \times ST) - (AR \times AT_P)$

$$\text{Men} = 0.8 \times \left(\frac{30 \times 40}{2000} \times 1600\right) - 0.70 \times (40 \times 40) = 352\ (A)$$

$$\text{Women} = 0.6 \times \left(\frac{15 \times 40}{2000} \times 1600\right) - 0.65 \times (10 \times 40) = 28 \text{ (F)}$$

$$\text{Boys} = 0.4 \times \left(\frac{10 \times 40}{2000} \times 1600\right) - 0.30 \times (5 \times 40) = 68 \text{ (F)}$$

$$\text{LCV} = 256 \text{ (A)}$$

Problem 22 The direct labour strength of a section of an engineering factory is 100 workers who are paid at the rate of ₹6.00 per day of 8 hours each. The normal production is 1000 pieces per week of 48 hours.

During a particular week an order of 1500 pieces was completed spending in all 7650 hours made up of 6300 hours at normal wages and 1350 hours at overtime wages (double rate). The total wages came to ₹6300. Calculate the labour cost variances.

Solution:

	(1)	(2)	(3)	(4)	(5)
	SR × ST	SR × SM	SR × AT_W	SR × AT_P	AR × AT_P
Labour	$0.75 \times \left(\frac{100 \times 48}{1000} \times 1500\right)$	(0.75 × 7650)	(0.75 × 7650)	(0.76 × 7650)	(0.7 × 7850)
	5400	5737.5	5737.5	5737.5	5355

where SR : Standard rate per labour hour.

ST : Standard time required for actual output.

SM : Standard mix, i.e., Total actual time worked in standard ratio of workers.

AT : Actual time worked.

AT_P : Actual time paid for.

AR : Actual rate per labour hour.

1. Labour revised efficiency variance = (1) – (2)

$$= (\text{SR} \times \text{ST}) - (\text{SR} \times \text{SM})$$

$$= 0.75 \times \left(\frac{100 \times 48}{1000} \times 1500\right) - (0.75 \times 7650)$$

$$= 337.5 \text{ (A)}$$

2. Labour mix variance = (2) – (3)

$$= (\text{SR} \times \text{SM}) - (\text{SR} \times \text{AT}_W)$$

$$= (0.75 \times 7650) - (0.75 \times 7650)$$

$$= \text{Nil}$$

3. Labour idle time variance = (3) – (4)

$$= (\text{SR} \times \text{AT}_W) - (\text{SR} \times \text{AT}_P)$$

$$= (0.75 \times 7650 - (0.75 \times 7650)$$

$$= \text{Nil}$$

4. Labour Efficiency Variance $= (1) - (4)$
$= (SR \times ST) - (SR \times AT_P)$
$= 0.75 \times \left(\frac{100 \times 48}{1000} \times 1500\right) - (0.75 \times 7650)$
$= 337.5$ (A)

5. Labour Rate Variance $= (4) - (5)$
$= (SR \times AT_P) - (AR \times AT_P)$
$= (0.75 \times 7650 - (0.7 \times 7650)$
$= 382.5$ (F)

6. Labour Cost Variance $= (1) - (5)$
$= (SR \times ST) - (AR \times AT_P)$
$= 0.75 \times \left(\frac{100 \times 48}{1000} \times 1500\right) - (0.7 \times 7650)$
$= 45$ (F)

Problem 23 The standard labour employment and the actual labour engaged in a week for the job are as under:

	Skilled	Semi-Skilled	Unskilled
Standard No. of workers	32	12	6
Standard hourly rate	3	2	1
Actual No. of workers	28	18	4
Actual hourly rate	4	3	2

During the 40 hours working week, the gang produced 1800 standard labour hours of work. Compute the labour cost variances. [*B.Com. (H)*]

Solution:

Labour	(1)	(2)	(3)	(4)	(5)
	SR × ST	SR × SM	SR × AT_W	SR × AT_P	AR × AT_P
Skilled	$3 \times \left(1800 \times \frac{32}{50}\right)$	$3 \times \left(2000 \times \frac{32}{50}\right)$	3 × (28 × 40)	3 × (28 × 40)	4 × (28 × 40)
Semi-skilled	$2 \times \left(1800 \times \frac{12}{50}\right)$	$2 \times \left(2000 \times \frac{12}{50}\right)$	2 × (18 × 40)	2 × (18 × 40)	3 × (18 × 40)
Unskilled	$1 \times \left(1800 \times \frac{6}{50}\right)$	$1 \times \left(2000 \times \frac{6}{50}\right)$	1 × (4 × 40)	1 × (4 × 40)	2 × (4 × 40)
	4536	5040	4960	4960	6960

where SR : Standard rate per labour hour

AT_W: Actual time worked

AT_P : Actual time paid for

AR : Actual rate per labour hour

ST : Standard time required for actual output

SM : Standard mix, i.e.; total actual time worked in standard ratio of workers.

1. Labour revised efficiency variance = (1) – (2)

$$= (SR \times ST) - (SR \times SM)$$

$$\text{Skilled} = 3 \times \left(1800 \times \frac{32}{50}\right) - 3 \times \left(2000 \times \frac{32}{50}\right) = 384\ (A)$$

$$\text{Semi-skilled} = 2 \times \left(1800 \times \frac{12}{50}\right) - 2 \times \left(2000 \times \frac{12}{50}\right) = 96\ (A)$$

$$\text{Unskilled} = 1 \times \left(1800 \times \frac{6}{50}\right) - 1 \times \left(2000 \times \frac{6}{50}\right) = 24\ (A)$$

$$\text{LREV} = 504\ (A)$$

2. Labour mix variance = (2) – (3)

$$= (SR \times SM) - (SR \times AT_W)$$

$$\text{Skilled} = 3 \times \left(2000 \times \frac{32}{50}\right) - 3 \times (28 \times 40) = 480\ (F)$$

$$\text{Semi-skilled} = 2 \times \left(2000 \times \frac{12}{50}\right) - 2 \times (18 \times 40) = 480\ (A)$$

$$\text{Unskilled} = 1 \times \left(2000 \times \frac{6}{50}\right) - 1 \times (4 \times 40) = 80\ (F)$$

$$LMV = 80\ (F)$$

3. Labour idle time variance = (3) – (4)

$$= (SR \times AT_W) - (SR \times AT_P)$$

$$= 3 \times (28 \times 40) - 3 \times (28 \times 40) = \text{Nil}$$

$$= 2 \times (18 \times 40) - 2 \times (18 \times 40) = \text{Nil}$$

$$= 1 \times (4 \times 40) - 1 \times (4 \times 40) = \text{Nil}$$

$$\text{LITV} = \text{Nil}$$

4. Labour efficiency variance = (1) – (4)

$$= (SR \times ST) - (SR \times AT_P)$$

$$\text{Skilled} = 3 \times \left(1800 \times \frac{32}{50}\right) - 3 \times (28 \times 40) = 96\ (F)$$

$$\text{Semi-skilled} = 2 \times \left(1800 \times \frac{12}{50}\right) - 2 \times (18 \times 40) = 576 \text{ (A)}$$

$$\text{Unskilled} = 1 \times \left(1800 \times \frac{6}{50}\right) - 1 \times (4 \times 40) = 56 \text{ (F)}$$

$$\text{LEV} = 424 \text{ (A)}$$

5. Labour rate variance = (4) – (5)

$$= (SR \times AT_P) - (AR \times AT_P)$$

$$\text{Skilled} = 3 \times (28 \times 40) - 4 \times (28 \times 40) = 1120 \text{ (A)}$$

$$\text{Semi-skilled} = 2 \times (18 \times 40) - 3 \times (18 \times 40) = 720 \text{ (A)}$$

$$\text{Unskilled} = 1 \times (4 \times 40) - 2 \times (4 \times 40) = 160 \text{ (A)}$$

$$\text{LRV} = 2000 \text{ (A)}$$

6. Labour cost variance = (1) – (5)

$$= (SR \times ST) - (AR \times AT_P)$$

$$= 3 \times \left(1800 \times \frac{32}{50}\right) - 4 \times (28 \times 40) = 1024 \text{ (A)}$$

$$= 2 \times \left(1800 \times \frac{12}{50}\right) - 3 \times (18 \times 40) = 1296 \text{ (A)}$$

$$= 1 \times \left(1800 \times \frac{6}{50}\right) - 2 \times (4 \times 40) = 104 \text{ (A)}$$

$$\text{LCV} = 2424 \text{ (A)}$$

Problem 24 The data obtained from a factory are as follows:

	Men	Women
No. in a standard gang	20	10
Standard rate per hour	0.90	0.80
No. in actual gang	16	14
Actual rate per hour	₹1	₹0.70

In a 48-hour week the gang as actually composed, produced 1200 standard hours. Compute the labour cost variances.

Solution:

Labour	(1)	(2)	(3)	(4)	(5)
	$SR \times ST$	$SR \times SM$	$SR \times AT_W$	$SR \times AT_P$	$AR \times AT_P$
Men	$0.9 \times \left(1200 \times \frac{2}{3}\right)$	$0.9 \times \left(1440 \times \frac{2}{3}\right)$	$0.9 \times (16 \times 48)$	$0.9 \times (16 \times 48)$	$1 \times (16 \times 48)$

Contd...

Table Contd...

Women	$0.8 \times \left(1200 \times \frac{1}{3}\right)$	$0.8 \times \left(1440 \times \frac{1}{3}\right)$	0.8 × (14 × 48)	0.8 × (14 × 48)	0.70 × (14 × 48)
	1040	1248	1228.8	1228.8	1238.4

where SR : Standard rate per labour hour

AT_W : Actual time worked

AT_P : Actual time paid for

AR : Actual rate per labour hour

ST : Standard time required for actual output

SM : Standard mix, i.e.; total actual time worked in standard ratio of workers.

1. Labour revised efficiency variance = (1) – (2)

$$= (SR \times ST) - (SR \times SM)$$

$$\text{Men} = 0.9 \times \left(1200 \times \frac{2}{3}\right) - 0.9 \times \left(1440 \times \frac{2}{3}\right) = 144\ (A)$$

$$\text{Women} = 0.8 \times \left(1200 \times \frac{1}{3}\right) - 0.8 \times \left(1440 \times \frac{1}{3}\right) = 64\ (A)$$

$$\text{LREV} = 208\ (A)$$

2. Labour mix variance = (2) – (3)

$$= (SR \times SM) - (SR \times AT_W)$$

$$\text{Men} = 0.9 \times \left(1200 \times \frac{2}{3}\right) - 0.9 \times (16 \times 48) = 172.8\ (F)$$

$$\text{Women} = 0.8 \times \left(1200 \times \frac{1}{3}\right) - 0.8 \times (14 \times 48) = 153.6\ (A)$$

$$\text{LMV} = 19.2\ (F)$$

3. Labour idle time variance = (3) – (4)

$$= (SR \times AT_W) - (SR \times AT_P)$$

$$\text{Men} = 0.9 \times (16 \times 48) - 0.9 \times (16 \times 48) = \text{Nil}$$

$$\text{Women} = 0.8 \times (14 \times 48) - 0.8 \times (14 \times 48) = \text{Nil}$$

$$\text{LITV} = \text{Nil}$$

4. Labour efficiency variance = (1) – (4)

$$= (SR \times ST) - (SR \times AT_P)$$

$$\text{Men} = 0.9 \times \left(1200 \times \frac{2}{3}\right) - 0.9 \times (16 \times 48) = 28.8\ (F)$$

$$\text{Women} = 0.8 \times \left(1200 \times \frac{1}{3}\right) - 0.80 \times (14 \times 48) = 217.6\ (A)$$

$$\text{LEV} = 188.8\ (A)$$

5. Labour rate variance = (4) – (5)

$$= (SR \times AT_P) - (AR \times AT_P)$$

$$\text{Men} = 0.9 \times (16 \times 48) - 1 \times (16 \times 48) = 76.8\ (A)$$

$$\text{Women} = 0.8 \times (14 \times 48) - 0.70 \times (14 \times 48) = 67.2\ (A)$$

$$\text{LRV} = 9.6\ (A)$$

6. Labour cost variance = (1) – (5)

$$= (SR \times ST) - (AR \times AT_P)$$

$$\text{Men} = 0.9 \times \left(1200 \times \frac{2}{3}\right) - 1 \times (16 \times 48) = 48\ (A)$$

$$\text{Women} = 0.8 \times \left(1200 \times \frac{1}{3}\right) - 0.70 \times (14 \times 48) = 150.4\ (A)$$

$$\text{LCV} = 198.4\ (A)$$

Problem 25 Calculate the labour cost variances from the following

	Standard wages
Grade X	90 labourers at ₹2 per hour
Grade Y	60 labourers at ₹3 per hour
	Actual wages
Grade X	80 labourers at ₹2.50 per hour
Grade Y	70 labourers at ₹2 per hour

Budgeted hours 1000, actual hours 900

Budgeted gross production 5000 units; standard loss 20%,

Actual loss 900 units.

Solution:

Labour	(1)	(2)	(3)	(4)	(5)
	$SR \times ST$	$SR \times SM$	$SR \times AT_W$	$SR \times AT_P$	$AR \times AT_P$
X	$2 \times \left(\frac{1000}{4000} \times 4000 \times \frac{9}{15}\right)$	$2 \times \left(900 \times \frac{9}{15}\right)$	$2 \times \left(900 \times \frac{8}{15}\right)$	$2 \times \left(900 \times \frac{8}{15}\right)$	$2 \times \left(900 \times \frac{8}{15}\right)$
Y	$3 \times \left(\frac{1000}{4000} \times 4000 \times \frac{6}{15}\right)$	$3 \times \left(900 \times \frac{6}{15}\right)$	$3 \times \left(900 \times \frac{7}{15}\right)$	$3 \times \left(900 \times \frac{7}{15}\right)$	$3 \times \left(900 \times \frac{7}{15}\right)$
	2,460	2,160	2,220	2,220	2,040

where SR : Standard rate per labour hour

AT_W : Actual time worked

AT_P : Actual time paid for

AR : Actual rate per labour hour

ST : Standard time required for actual output

SM : Standard mix i.e.; total actual time worked in standard ratio of workers.

1. Labour revised efficiency variance = (1) – (2)

= (SR × ST) – (SR × SM)

$$\text{Grade X} = 2 \times \left(\frac{1000}{4000} \times 4100 \times \frac{9}{15}\right) - 2 \times \left(900 \times \frac{9}{15}\right) = 150\ (F)$$

$$\text{Grade Y} = 3 \times \left(\frac{1000}{4000} \times 4100 \times \frac{6}{15}\right) - 3 \times \left(900 \times \frac{6}{15}\right) = 150\ (F)$$

LREV = 300 (F)

2. Labour mix variance = (2) – (3)

= (SR × SM) – (SR × AT_W)

$$\text{Grade X} = 2 \times \left(900 \times \frac{9}{15}\right) - 2 \times \left(900 \times \frac{8}{15}\right) = 120\ (F)$$

$$\text{Grade Y} = 3 \times \left(900 \times \frac{6}{15}\right) - 3 \times \left(900 \times \frac{7}{15}\right) = 180\ (A)$$

LMV = 60 (A)

3. Labour idle time variance = (3) – (4)

= (SR × AT_W) – (SR × AT_P)

$$\text{Grade X} = 2 \times \left(900 \times \frac{8}{15}\right) - 2 \times \left(900 \times \frac{8}{15}\right) = \text{Nil}$$

$$\text{Grade Y} = 3 \times \left(900 \times \frac{7}{15}\right) - 3 \times \left(900 \times \frac{7}{15}\right) = \text{Nil}$$

LITV= Nil

4. Labour efficiency variance = (1) – (4)

= (SR × ST) – (SR × AT_P)

$$\text{Grade X} = 2 \times \left(\frac{1000}{4000} \times 4100 \times \frac{9}{15}\right) - 2 \times \left(900 \times \frac{8}{15}\right) = 270\ (F)$$

$$\text{Grade Y} = 3 \times \left(\frac{1000}{4000} \times 4100 \times \frac{6}{15}\right) - 3 \times \left(900 \times \frac{7}{15}\right) = 30\ (A)$$

LEV = 240 (F)

5. Labour rate variance = (4) – (5)

= (SR × AT_P) – (AR × AT_P)

$$\text{Grade X} = 2 \times \left(900 \times \frac{8}{15}\right) - 2.5 \times \left(900 \times \frac{8}{15}\right) = 240 \text{ (A)}$$

$$\text{Grade Y} = 3 \times \left(900 \times \frac{7}{15}\right) - 2 \times \left(900 \times \frac{7}{15}\right) = 420 \text{ (F)}$$

$$\text{LRV} = 180 \text{ (F)}$$

6. Labour cost variance = (1) – (5)

$$= (SR \times ST) - (AR \times AT_P)$$

$$\text{Grade X} = 2 \times \left(\frac{1000}{4000} \times 4100 \times \frac{9}{15}\right) - 2.5 \times \left(900 \times \frac{8}{15}\right) = 30 \text{ (P)}$$

$$\text{Grade Y} = 3 \times \left(\frac{1000}{4000} \times 4100 \times \frac{6}{15}\right) - 2 \times \left(900 \times \frac{7}{15}\right) = 390 \text{ (F)}$$

$$\text{LCV} = 420 \text{ (F)}$$

Problem 26 The standard output of 'X' is 25 units per hour in a manufacturing department of a company employing 100 workers. The standard wage rate per labour hour is ₹6.

In a 42-hour week, the department produced, 1040 units of 'X' despite 5% of the time paid was lost due to abnormal reason. The hourly rate actually paid were ₹6.20, ₹6 and ₹5.70 respectively to 10, 30 and 60 workers.

Compute relevant variances.

Solution:

Labour	(1)	(2)	(3)	(4)	(5)
	SR × ST	SR × SM	SR × AT_W	SR × AT_P	AR × AT_P
W_1	$6 \times \left(\frac{100}{25} \times 1040 \times \frac{1}{3}\right)$	$6 \times \left(3990 \times \frac{1}{3}\right)$	$6 \times \left(3990 \times \frac{1}{10}\right)$	$6 \times \left(4200 \times \frac{1}{10}\right)$	$6.2 \times \left(4200 \times \frac{1}{10}\right)$
W_2	$6 \times \left(\frac{100}{25} \times 1040 \times \frac{1}{3}\right)$	$6 \times \left(3990 \times \frac{1}{3}\right)$	$6 \times \left(3990 \times \frac{3}{10}\right)$	$6 \times \left(4200 \times \frac{3}{10}\right)$	$6 \times \left(4200 \times \frac{3}{10}\right)$
W_3	$6 \times \left(\frac{100}{25} \times 1040 \times \frac{1}{3}\right)$	$6 \times \left(3990 \times \frac{1}{3}\right)$	$6 \times \left(3990 \times \frac{6}{10}\right)$	$6 \times \left(4200 \times \frac{6}{10}\right)$	$5.7 \times \left(4200 \times \frac{6}{10}\right)$
	24,960	23,940	23,940	25,200	24,528

where SR : Standard rate per labour hour

AT_W : Actual time worked

AT_P : Actual time paid for

AR : Actual rate per labour hour

ST : Standard time required for actual output

SM : Standard mix, i.e.; total actual time worked in standard ratio of workers.

1. Labour revised efficiency variance = (1) – (2)

$$= (SR \times ST) - (SR \times SM)$$

$$\text{Worker 1} = 6 \times \left(\frac{100}{25} \times 1040 \times \frac{1}{3}\right) - 6 \times \left(3990 \times \frac{1}{3}\right) = 340\ (F)$$

$$\text{Worker 2} = 6 \times \left(\frac{100}{25} \times 1040 \times \frac{1}{3}\right) - 6 \times \left(3990 \times \frac{1}{3}\right) = 340\ (F)$$

$$\text{Worker 3} = 6 \times \left(\frac{100}{25} \times 1040 \times \frac{1}{3}\right) - 6 \times \left(3990 \times \frac{1}{3}\right) = 340\ (F)$$

LREV = 1020 (F)

2. Labour mix variance = (2) – (3)

$$= (SR \times SM) - (SR \times AT_W)$$

$$\text{Worker 1} = 6 \times \left(3990 \times \frac{1}{3}\right) - 6 \times \left(3990 \times \frac{1}{10}\right) = 5586\ (F)$$

$$\text{Worker 2} = 6 \times \left(3990 \times \frac{1}{3}\right) - 6 \times \left(3990 \times \frac{3}{10}\right) = 798\ (F)$$

$$\text{Worker 3} = 6 \times \left(3990 \times \frac{1}{3}\right) - 6 \times \left(3990 \times \frac{6}{10}\right) = 6384\ (A)$$

LMV = Nil

3. Labour idle time variance = (3) – (4)

$$= (SR \times AT_P) - (SR \times AT)$$

$$\text{Worker 1} = 6 \times \left(3990 \times \frac{1}{10}\right) - 6 \times \left(4200 \times \frac{1}{10}\right) = 126\ (A)$$

$$\text{Worker 2} = 6 \times \left(3990 \times \frac{3}{10}\right) - 6 \times \left(4200 \times \frac{3}{10}\right) = 378\ (A)$$

$$\text{Worker 3} = 6 \times \left(3990 \times \frac{6}{10}\right) - 6 \times \left(4200 \times \frac{6}{10}\right) = 756\ (A)$$

LITV = 1260 (A)

4. Labour efficiency variance = (3) – (4)

$$= (SR \times ST) - (SR \times AT_P)$$

$$\text{Worker 1} = 6 \times \left(\frac{100}{25} \times 1040 \times \frac{1}{3}\right) - 6 \times \left(4200 \times \frac{1}{10}\right) = 5800\ (F)$$

$$\text{Worker 2} = 6 \times \left(\frac{100}{25} \times 1040 \times \frac{1}{3}\right) - 6 \times \left(4200 \times \frac{3}{10}\right) = 760\ (F)$$

$$\text{Worker 3} = 6 \times \left(\frac{100}{25} \times 1040 \times \frac{1}{3}\right) - 6 \times \left(4200 \times \frac{6}{10}\right) = 6800\ (A)$$

$$\text{LEV} = 240\ (A)$$

5. Labour rate variance = (4) – (5)

$$= (SR \times AT_P) - (AR \times AT_P)$$

$$\text{Worker 1} = 6 \times \left(4200 \times \frac{1}{10}\right) - 6.2 \times \left(4200 \times \frac{1}{10}\right) = 84\ (A)$$

$$\text{Worker 2} = 6 \times \left(4200 \times \frac{3}{10}\right) - 6 \times \left(4200 \times \frac{3}{10}\right) = 756\ (A)$$

$$\text{Worker 3} = 6 \times \left(4200 \times \frac{6}{10}\right) - 5.7 \times \left(4200 \times \frac{6}{10}\right) = \text{Nil}$$

$$\text{LRV} = 672\ (A)$$

6. Labour cost variance = (1) – (5)

$$= (SR \times ST) - (AR \times AT_P)$$

$$\text{Worker 1} = 6 \times \left(\frac{100}{25} \times 1040 \times \frac{1}{3}\right) - 6.2 \times \left(4200 \times \frac{1}{10}\right) = 5716\ (F)$$

$$\text{Worker 2} = 6 \times \left(\frac{100}{25} \times 1040 \times \frac{1}{3}\right) - 6 \times \left(4200 \times \frac{3}{10}\right) = 760\ (F)$$

$$\text{Worker 3} = 6 \times \left(\frac{100}{25} \times 1040 \times \frac{1}{3}\right) - 5.7 \times \left(4200 \times \frac{6}{10}\right) = 6044\ (A)$$

$$\text{LRV} = 432\ (F)$$

Problem 27 Calculate the fixed overhead cost variances from the following:

	Budget	Actual
No. of working days	20	22
Man hours per day	8000	8400
Time per unit	2 hr	1.5 hr
Overhead cost	₹1,60,000	₹1,68,000

Solution:

Overheads	(1)	(2)	(3)	(4)	(5)
	$SR \times ST$	$SR \times AT_W$	$SR \times RBT$	$SR \times BT$	$AR \times AT_P$
Fixed	$1 \times \left(2 \times \frac{22 \times 8400}{1.5}\right)$	1 × (22 × 8400)	(1 × 1,76,000)	(1 × 1,60,000)	(1,68,000)
	2,46,400	1,84,800	1,76,000	1,60,000	1,68,000

where SR : Standard Rate per hour

ST : Standard time required for actual output

AT_W : Actual time worked

AT_P : Actual time paid for

BT : Standard time for budgeted output

RBT : Revised budgeted time = $\frac{BT}{\text{Budgeted days}} \times$ Actual days

AR : Actual rate per hour

1. F.O. Efficiency variance = (1) – (2)

$= \text{Absorbed overhead–Standard overhead}$

$= (SR \times ST) - (SR \times AT_W)$

$= 1 \times \left(2 \times \frac{22 \times 8400}{1.5}\right) - 1 \times (22 \times 8400)$

$= 61{,}600 \text{ (F)}$

2. F.O. Capacity variance = (2) – (3)

$= \text{Standard overhead – Revised budgeted overhead}$

$= (SR \times AT_W) - (SR \times RBT)$

$= 1 \times (22 \times 8400) - (1 \times 1{,}76{,}000)$

$= 8800 \text{ (F)}$

3. F.O. Calendar variance = (3) – (4)

$= (SR \times RBT) - (SR \times BT)$

$= (1 \times 1{,}76{,}000) - (1 \times 1{,}60{,}000)$

$= 16{,}000 \text{ (F)}$

4. F.O. Expenditure variance = (4) – (5)

$= \text{Budgeted overhead – Actual overhead}$

$= (SR \times AT_P) - (AR \times AT_P)$

$= (1 \times 1{,}60{,}000) - (1{,}68{,}000)$

$= 8000 \text{ (A)}$

5. F.O. Volume variance = (1) – (4)

$= \text{Absorbed overhead – Budgeted overhead}$

$= (SR \times ST) - (SR \times BT)$

$= 1 \times \left(2 \times \frac{22 \times 8400}{1.5}\right) - (1 \times 1{,}60{,}000)$

$= 86{,}400 \text{ (F)}$

6. F.O. Cost variance = (1) – (5)

$= \text{Absorbed overhead – Actual overhead}$

$= (SR \times ST) - (AR \times AT_P)$

$$= 1 \times \left(2 \times \frac{22 \times 8400}{1.5}\right) - 1,68,000$$

$$= 78,400 \text{ (F)}$$

Problem 28 The following information relates to Biotech Ltd.

Normal overhead rate	₹3
Actual hours operated	20,000
Allowed hours for actual production	21,000
Allowed overheads for budgeted hours	₹70,000
Actual overheads	₹72,000

Calculate (a) overhead budget variance (b) volume variance (c) efficiency variance (d) capacity variance (e) total overhead cost variance.

Solution:

Overheads	(1)	(2)	(3)	(4)	(5)
	SR × ST	SR × AT_W	SR × RBT	SR × BT	AR × AT_P
Fixed	3 × 21,000	3 × 20,000	$3 \times \frac{70,000}{3}$	70,000	72,000
	63,000	60,000	70,000	70,000	72,000

where SR : Standard rate per hour

ST : Standard time required for actual output

AT_W : Actual time worked

AT_P : Actual time paid for

BT : Standard time for budgeted output

RBT: Revised budgeted time = $\frac{\text{BT}}{\text{Budgeted days}} \times$ Actual days

AR : Actual rate per hour

1. F.O. Efficiency variance = (1) – (2)
   = (SR × ST) – (SR × AT_W)
   = 3 × 21,000 – 3 × 20,000
   = 3000 (F)
2. F.O. Capacity variance = (2) – (3)
   = (SR × AT) – (SR × RBT)
   = (3 × 20,000) – 70,000
   = Nil
3. F.O. Calendar variance = (3) – (4)
   = (SR × RBT) – (SR × BT)

$= 70{,}000 - 70{,}000$
$= \text{Nil}$

4. F.O. Expenditure variance $= (4) - (5)$
$= (SR \times AT_P) - (AR \times AT_P)$
$= 70{,}000 - 72{,}000$
$= 2000\ (A)$

5. F.O. Volume variance $= (1) - (4)$
$= (SR \times ST) - (SR \times BT)$
$= 3 \times 21{,}000 - 70{,}000$
$= 7000\ (A)$

6. F.O. Cost variance $= (1) - (5)$
$= (SR \times ST) - (AR \times AT_P)$
$= 3 \times 21{,}000 - 72{,}000$
$= 9000\ (A)$

Problem 29 From the following information compute fixed overhead cost, expenditure and volume variance.

Normal capacity is 5000 hours. Budget fixed overhead rate is ₹ 10 per standard hour. Actual level of capacity utilised is 4400 standard hours. Actual fixed overhead ₹ 52,000.

[*B.Com. (H)*]

Solution:

	(1)	(4)	(5)
Fixed overheads	SR × ST (10 × 4400)	SR × BT (10 × 5000)	AR × AT_P (52,000)
	44,000	50,000	52,000

where SR : Standard rate per hour

ST : Standard time required for actual output

AT_W : Actual time worked

AT_P : Actual time paid for

BT : Standard time for budgeted output

RBT: Revised budgeted time $= \dfrac{BT}{\text{Budgeted days}} \times \text{Actual days}$

AR : Actual rate per hour

1. F.O. Expenditure variance $= (4) - (5)$
$= (SR \times AT_P) - (AR \times AT_P)$
$= (10 \times 5000) - (52{,}000)$
$= 2000\ (A)$

2. F.O. Volume variance = (1) – (4)

$$= (SR \times ST) - (SR \times BT)$$
$$= (10 \times 4400) - (10 \times 5000)$$
$$= 6{,}000 \text{ (A)}$$

3. F.O. Cost variance = (1) – (5)

$$= (SR \times ST) - (AR \times AT_P)$$
$$= (10 \times 4400) - (52{,}000)$$
$$= 8000 \text{ (A)}$$

Problem 30 Subway Ltd. has furnished you the following data:

	Budget	Actual (July)
Production in units	20,000	22,000
Fixed overheads	₹30,000	₹31,000
No. of working days	25	27

Budgeted fixed overhead rate is ₹1 per hour. In July, the actual hours worked were 31,500. Calculate overhead cost variances. [*CA, Inter. Adapted*]

Solution:

	(1)	(2)	(3)	(4)	(5)
	$SR \times ST$	$SR \times AT_W$	$SR \times RBT$	$SR \times BT$	$AR \times AT_P$
Fixed overheads	$1 \times \left(\frac{30{,}000}{20{,}000} \times 20{,}000\right)$	$(1 \times 31{,}500)$	$1 \times \left(\frac{30{,}000}{25} \times 27\right)$	$(1 \times 30{,}000)$	$(31{,}000)$
	33,000	31,500	32,400	30,000	31,000

where SR : Standard rate per hour

ST : Standard time required for actual output

AT_W : Actual time worked

AT_P : Actual time paid for

BT : Standard time for budgeted output

RBT : Revised budgeted time $= \dfrac{BT}{\text{Budgeted days}} \times \text{Actual days}$

AR : Actual rate per hour

1. F.O. Efficiency variance = (1) – (2)

$$= (SR \times ST) - (SR \times AT_W)$$
$$= 1 \times \left(\frac{30{,}000}{20{,}000} \times 22{,}000\right) - (1 \times 31{,}500)$$
$$= 1500 \text{ (F)}$$

2. F.O. Capacity variance $= (2) - (3)$

$= (SR \times AT_P) - (SR \times RBT)$

$= (1 \times 31{,}500) - 1 \times \left(\frac{30{,}000}{25} \times 27\right)$

$= 900$ (A)

3. F.O. Calendar variance $= (3) - (4)$

$= (SR \times RBT) - (SR \times BT)$

$= 1 \times \left(\frac{30{,}000}{25} \times 27\right) - (31{,}000)$

$= 2400$ (F)

4. F.O. Expenditure variance $= (4) - (5)$

$= (SR \times AT_P) - (AR \times AT_P)$

$= (1 \times 30{,}000) - (31{,}000)$

$= 1000$ (A)

5. F.O. Volume variance $= (1) - (4)$

$= (SR \times ST) - (SR \times BT)$

$= 1 \times \left(\frac{30{,}000}{20{,}000} \times 22{,}000\right) - (1 \times 30{,}000)$

$= 3000$ (F)

6. F.O. Cost variance $= (1) - (5)$

$= (SR \times ST) - (AR \times AT_P)$

$= 1 \times \left(\frac{30{,}000}{20{,}000} \times 22{,}000\right) - (31{,}000)$

$= 2000$ (F)

Problem 31 The following information was obtained from the records of a clothing company

Overhead cost variance	₹1400(A)
Overhead volume variance	₹1000(A)
Budgeted time	1200 hours
Budgeted overheads	₹6000
Actual rate of recovery of overheads	₹8 per hour

You are required to compute the following: Expenditure variance, actual overheads incurred, actual hours worked, capacity variance, efficiency variance, and standard time for actual production.

Solution:

	(1)	(2)	(3)	(4)	(5)
Fixed Overheads	SR × ST 5 × 1000	SR × AT_W 5 × 800	SR × RBT 5 × 1200	SR × BT 5 × 1200	AR × AT_P 8 × 800
	5000	4000	6000	6000	6400

where SR : Standard rate per hour

ST : Standard time required for actual output

AT_W : Actual time worked

AT_P : Actual time paid for

BT : Standard time for budgeted output

RBT: Revised budgeted time $= \frac{BT}{\text{Budgeted days}} \times$ Actual days

AR : Actual rate per hour

1. F.O. Efficiency variance = (1) – (2)
$= (SR \times ST) - (SR \times AT_W)$
$= (5 \times 1000) - (5 \times 800)$
= 1000 (F)

2. F.O. Capacity variance = (2) – (3)
$= (SR \times AT_W) - (SR \times RBT)$
$= (5 \times 800) - (5 \times 1200)$
= 2000 (A)

3. F.O. Calendar variance = (3) – (4)
$= (SR \times RBT) - (SR \times BT)$
$= (5 \times 1200) - (5 \times 1200)$
= Nil

4. F.O. Expenditure variance = (4) – (5)
$= (SR \times AT_P) - (AR \times AT_P)$
$= (5 \times 1200) - (8 \times 800)$
= 400 (A)

5. F.O. Volume variance = (1) – (4)
$= (SR \times ST) - (SR \times BT)$
$= (5 \times 1000) - (5 \times 1200)$
= 1,000 (A)

6. F.O. Cost variance = (1) – (5)
$= (SR \times ST) - (AR \times AT_P)$
$= (5 \times 1000) - (8 \times 800)$
= 1400 (A)

Problem 32 In Department A of a plant, the following data are submitted for the week ending 31-3-2020

Standard output for 40 hours per week	1400 units
Budgeted fixed overheads for 40 hours per week	₹1400
Actual output	1200 units
Actual hours worked	32
Actual fixed overhead	₹1500

Calculate variances

Solution:

	(1)	(2)	(3)	(4)	(5)
	SR × ST	SR × AT_W	SR × RBT	SR × BT	AR × AT_P
Fixed Overheads	$35 \times \left(\frac{40}{1400} \times 1200\right)$	(35 × 32)	(1 × 1400)	(1 × 1400)	(1500)
	1200	1120	1400	1400	1500

where SR : Standard rate per hour

ST : Standard time required for actual output

AT_W : Actual time worked

AT_P : Actual time paid for

BT : Standard time for budgeted output

RBT : Revised budgeted time = $\frac{BT}{\text{Budgeted days}} \times$ Actual days

AR : Actual rate per hour

1. F.O. Efficiency variance = (1) – (2)

$$= (SR \times ST) - (SR \times AT_W)$$

$$= 35 \times \left(\frac{40}{1400} \times 1200\right) - (35 \times 32)$$

$$= 80\ (F)$$

2. F.O. Capacity variance = (2) – (3)

$$= (SR \times AT_W) - (SR \times RBT)$$

$$= (35 \times 32) - (1 \times 1400)$$

$$= 280\ (A)$$

3. F.O. Calendar variance = (3) – (4)

$$= (SR \times RBT) - (SR \times BT)$$

$$= (1 \times 1400) - (1 \times 1400)$$

= Nil

4. F.O. Expenditure variance = (4) – (5)

$= (SR \times AT_P) - (AR \times AT_P)$

$= (1 \times 1400) - (1500)$

$= 100$ (A)

5. F.O. Volume variance = (1) – (4)

$= (SR \times ST) - (SR \times BT)$

$$= 35 \times \left(\frac{40}{1400} \times 1200\right) - (1 \times 1400)$$

$= 200$ (A)

6. F.O. Cost variance = (1) – (5)

$= (SR \times ST) - (AR \times AT_P)$

$$= 35 \times \left(\frac{40}{1400} \times 1200\right) - (1500)$$

$= 300$ (A)

Problem 33 From the following, calculate the variable overhead cost variances:

	Standard	**Actual**
Production	4000 units	3800 units
Working days	20	21
Variable overhead	₹ 12,000	₹ 15,000

Solution:

	(1)	**(2)**	**(3)**
Variable Overheads	$SR \times ST$ $\left(\frac{1200}{20} \times 20\right)$	$SR \times AT_W$ $\left(\frac{1200}{20} \times 21\right)$	$AR \times AT_P$ (15,000)
	12,000	12,600	15,000

where SR : Standard rate per day

ST : Standard time required for actual output

AT_W : Actual time worked

AT_P : Actual time paid for

AR : Actual rate per day

1. Variable overheads efficiency variance = (1) – (2)

$= (SR \times ST) - (SR \times AT_W)$

$$= \left(\frac{12,000}{20} \times 20\right) - \left(\frac{12,000}{20} \times 21\right)$$

$$= 600 \text{ (A)}$$

2. Variable overhead expenditure variance = (2) – (3)

$$= (SR \times AT_W) - (AR \times AT_P)$$

$$= \left(\frac{12,000}{20} \times 21\right) - (15,000)$$

$$= 2400 \text{ (A)}$$

3. Variance overhead cost variance = (1) – (3)

$$= (SR \times ST) - (AR \times AT_P)$$

$$= \left(\frac{12,000}{20} \times 20\right) - (15,000)$$

$$= 3000 \text{ (A)}$$

Problem 34 In a factory, the standard units of production for the year were fixed at 1,20,000 units and overhead expenditure were estimated to be:

Fixed ₹12,000; variable ₹6000; semi-variable ₹1800.

Actual production during a particular month was 8000 units. Each month has 20 working days.

During the month in question there was one statutory holiday and the actual overhead amounted to:

Fixed ₹1190; variable ₹3480; semi-variable ₹192.

Semi-variable charges are considered to include 60% of fixed nature and 40% of variable nature.

Find out the fixed overhead cost variances and variable overhead cost variances.

Solution:

Standard	Actual
Fixed $\frac{12000}{12} = 1000$	1190
Variable $\frac{6000}{12} = 500$	480

Semi-variable $\frac{1800}{12} = 150$ → 60% fixed = 90; 40% fixed = 60

192 → 60% fixed = 115.2; 40% fixed = 76.80

The fixed and variable part of semi-variable cost is added to the respective fixed and variable overheads.

Therefore,

	Standard	*Actual*
Fixed overheads	1090	1305.20
Variable overheads	560	556.80
Working days	20	19
Output	10,000 units	8000 units

Fixed overhead cost variance

(1)	(2)	(3)	(4)	(5)
SR × ST	SR × AT_W	SR × RBT	SR × BT	AR × AT_P
$\frac{1090}{20} \times \left(\frac{20}{10,000} \times 8000\right)$	$\frac{1090}{20} \times 10$	$\frac{1090}{20} \times \left(\frac{20}{20} \times 19\right)$	$\frac{1090}{20} \times 20$	$\frac{1305.20}{19} \times 19$
872	1035.50	1035.5	1090	1305.20

1. F.O. Efficiency variance = (1) – (2)

$$= (SR \times ST) - (SR \times AT_W)$$

$$= \frac{1090}{20} \times \left(\frac{20}{10,000} \times 8000\right) - \frac{1090}{20} \times 10$$

$$= 163.5\ (A)$$

2. F.O. Capacity variance = (2) – (3)

$$= (SR \times AT_W) - (SR \times RBT)$$

$$= \frac{1090}{20} \times 10 - \frac{1090}{20} \times \left(\frac{20}{20} \times 19\right)$$

= Nil

3. F.O. Calendar variance = (3) – (4)

$$= (SR \times RBT) - (SR \times BT)$$

$$= \frac{1090}{20} \times \left(\frac{20}{20} \times 19\right) - \left(\frac{1090}{20} \times 20\right)$$

$$= 54.5(A)$$

4. F.O. Expenditure variance = (4) – (5)

$$= (SR \times AT_P) - (AR \times AT_P)$$

$$= \frac{1090}{20} \times 19 - \frac{1305.20}{19} \times 19$$

$$= 215.20\ (A)$$

5. F.O. Volume variance = (1) – (4)

$$= (SR \times ST) - (SR \times BT)$$

$$= \frac{1090}{20} \times \left(\frac{20}{10{,}000} \times 8000\right) - \left(\frac{1090}{20} \times 20\right)$$

$$= 218 \text{ (A)}$$

6. F.O. Cost variance = (1) – (5)

$$= (SR \times ST) - (AR \times AT_P)$$

$$= \frac{1090}{20} \times \left(\frac{20}{10{,}000} \times 8000\right) - \left(\frac{1305.20}{19} \times 19\right)$$

$$= 433.2 \text{ (A)}$$

Variable Overhead Cost Variance

	(1)	(2)	(3)
Variable overhead	SR × ST	SR × AT_W	AR × AT_P
	$\frac{560}{20} \times \left(\frac{20}{10{,}000} \times 8000\right)$	$\frac{560}{20} \times 19$	$\frac{556.8}{79} \times 19$
	448	532	556.8

where SR : Standard rate per day

ST : Standard time required for actual output

AT_W : Actual time worked

AT_P : Actual time paid for

AR : Actual rate per day

1. Variable overheads efficiency variance = (1) – (2)

$$= (SR \times ST) - (SR \times AT_W)$$

$$= \frac{560}{20} \times \left(\frac{20}{10{,}000} \times 8000\right) - \frac{560}{20} \times 19$$

$$= 84 \text{ (A)}$$

2. Variable overhead expenditure variance = (2) – (3)

$$= (SR \times AT_W) - (AR \times AT_P)$$

$$= \frac{560}{20} \times 19 - \frac{556.8}{79} \times 19$$

$$= 24.8 \text{ (A)}$$

3. Variance overhead cost variance = (1) – (3)

$$= (SR \times ST) - (AR \times AT_P)$$

$$= \frac{560}{20} \times \left(\frac{20}{10{,}000} \times 8000\right) - \frac{556.8}{79} \times 19$$

$$= 108.8 \text{ (A)}$$

Problem 35 The following standard and actual data in respect of chemical X is made available to you from the records of Fixture Ltd.

Standard Data:		**Total**
Materials	₹	₹
450 kg of material A @ ₹20 per kg	9000	
360 kg of material B @ ₹10 per kg	3600	12,600
810		
−90 kg Normal loss		
720 kg		
Labour : @ per hour		
2400 skilled hours ₹2	4800	
1200 unskilled hours ₹1	1200	
	—	
	Total	18,600
Actual Data:		
Material :		
450 kg of material A @ ₹19 per kg	8550	
360 kg of material D @ ₹11 per kg	3960	12,510
810		
−50 kg Actual loss		
760		
Labour : @ per hour		
2400 skilled hours ₹2.2	5400	
1200 unskilled hours ₹1.25	1500	
Total		19,410

You are required to compute:

(a) Material cost variance
(b) Material price variance
(c) Material yield variance
(d) Labour cost variance
(e) Labour rate variance
(f) Labour yield variance

[*B.Com. (H)*]

Solution:

Material Cost Variances

Materials	(1)	(2)	(3)	(4)
	SP × SQ	SP × SM	SP × AQ	AP × AQ
A	$20 \times \left(\frac{450}{720} \times 760\right)$	$20 \times \left(810 \times \frac{45}{81}\right)$	20 × 450	19 × 450
B	$10 \times \left(\frac{360}{720} \times 760\right)$	$10 \times \left(810 \times \frac{36}{81}\right)$	10 × 360	11 × 360
	13,300	12,600	12,600	12,510

1. Material yield variance = (1) – (2)

$$= (SP \times SQ) - (SP \times SM)$$

$$\text{Material A} = 20 \times \left(\frac{450}{720} \times 760\right) - 20 \times \left(810 \times \frac{45}{81}\right) = 500\ (F)$$

$$\text{Material B} = 10 \times \left(\frac{360}{720} \times 760\right) - 10 \times \left(810 \times \frac{36}{81}\right) = 200\ (F)$$

$$\text{MYV} = 700\ (F)$$

2. Material mix variance = (2) – (3)

$$= (SP \times SM) - (SP \times AQ)$$

$$\text{Material A} = 20 \times \left(810 \times \frac{45}{81}\right) - 20 \times 450 = \text{Nil}$$

$$\text{Material B} = 10 \times \left(810 \times \frac{36}{81}\right) - 10 \times 360 = \text{Nil}$$

$$\text{MMV} = \text{Nil}$$

3. Material price variance = (3) – (4)

$$= (SP \times AQ) - (AP \times AQ)$$

$$\text{Material A} = 20 \times 450 - 19 \times 450 = 450\ (F)$$

$$\text{Material B} = 10 \times 360 - 11 \times 360 = 360\ (A)$$

$$\text{MPV} = 90\ (F)$$

4. Material usage variance = (1) – (3)

$$= (SP \times SQ) - (SP \times AQ)$$

$$\text{Material A} = 20 \times \left(\frac{450}{720} \times 760\right) - 19 \times 450 = 500\ (F)$$

$$\text{Material B} = 10 \times \left(\frac{360}{720} \times 760\right) - 10 \times 360 \qquad = 200\ (F)$$

$$\text{MUV} = 700\ (F)$$

5. Material cost variance = (1) – (4)

$$= (SP \times SQ) - (AP \times AQ)$$

$$\text{Material A} = 20 \times \left(\frac{450}{720} \times 760\right) - 19 \times 450 \qquad = 950\ (F)$$

$$\text{Material B} = 10 \times \left(\frac{360}{720} \times 760\right) - 11 \times 360 \qquad = 160\ (A)$$

$$\text{MCV} = 790\ (F)$$

Labour Cost Variances

Labour	(1)	(2)	(3)	(4)	(5)
	SR × ST	SR × SM	SR × AT_W	SR × AT_P	AR × AT_P
Skilled	$2 \times \left(\frac{2400}{720} \times 760\right)$	2 × 2400	2 × 2400	2 × 2400	2.2 × 2400
Unskilled	$1 \times \left(\frac{1200}{720} \times 760\right)$	1 × 1200	1 × 1200	1 × 1200	1.25 × 1200
	6334	6000	6000	6000	6780

where SR : Standard rate per labour hour

AT_W : Actual time worked

AT_P : Actual time paid for

AR : Actual rate per labour hour

ST : Standard time required for actual output

SM : Standard mix, i.e., total actual time worked in standard ratio of workers.

1. Labour revised efficiency variance = (1) – (2)

$$= (SR \times ST) - (SR \times SM)$$

$$\text{Skilled} = 2 \times \left(\frac{2400}{720} \times 760\right) - 2 \times 2400 \qquad = 267\ (F)$$

$$\text{Unskilled} = 1 \times \left(\frac{1200}{720} \times 760\right) - 1 \times 1200 \qquad = 67\ (F)$$

$$\text{LREV} = 334\ (A)$$

2. Labour mix variance = (2) – (3)

$$= (SR \times SM - (SR \times AT_W)$$

$$\text{Skilled} = 2 \times 2400 - 2 \times 2400 \qquad = \text{Nil}$$

$$\text{Unskilled} = 1 \times 1200 - 1 \times 1200 \qquad = \text{Nil}$$

$$\text{LMV} = \text{Nil}$$

3. Labour idle time variance = (3) – (4)

$$= (SR \times AT_W) - (SR \times AT_P)$$

$$\text{Skilled} = 2 \times 2400 - 2 \times 2400 \qquad = \text{Nil}$$

$$\text{Unskilled} = 1 \times 1200 - 1 \times 1200 \qquad = \text{Nil}$$

$$\text{LITV} = \text{Nil}$$

4. Labour efficiency variance = (1) – (4)

$$= (SR \times ST) - (SR \times AT_P)$$

$$\text{Skilled} = 2 \times \left(\frac{2400}{720} \times 760\right) - 2 \times 2400 \qquad = 267\ (F)$$

$$\text{Unskilled} = 1 \times \left(\frac{1200}{720} \times 760\right) - 1 \times 1200 \qquad = 67\ (F)$$

$$\text{LEV} = 334\ (F)$$

5. Labour rate variance = (4) – (5)

$$= (SR \times AT_P) - (AR \times AT_P)$$

$$\text{Skilled} = 2 \times 2400 - 2.2 \times 2400 \qquad = 480\ (A)$$

$$\text{Unskilled} = 1 \times 1200 - 1.25 \times 1200 \qquad = 300\ (A)$$

$$\text{LRV} = 780\ (A)$$

6. Labour cost variance = (1) – (5)

$$= (SR \times ST) - (AR \times AT_P)$$

$$\text{Skilled} = 2 \times \left(\frac{2400}{720} \times 760\right) - 2.2 \times 2400 \qquad = 213\ (A)$$

$$\text{Unskilled} = 2 \times \left(\frac{1200}{720} \times 760\right) - 1.25 \times 1200 \qquad = 233\ (A)$$

$$\text{LRV} = 446\ (A)$$

Problem 36 From the following data calculate overhead variances:

Fixed overhead	₹ 10,200
Variable overhead	₹ 14,250

Normal capacity 10,000 standard hours.

Budget rate – Fixed overhead ₹ 1 per hour

– Variable overhead ₹ 1.70 per hour

Actual level – 8000 standard hours.

Required : Variable overhead cost variance and fixed overhead cost, budget and volume variances. [*B.Com. (H)*]

Solution:

(i) Variable Overhead Cost Variance

= Recovered Overhead – Actual Overhead

= (SR × ST) – (AR × AT_P)

= 8000 × 1.70 – 14,250 = ₹650 (A)

(ii) Fixed Overhead Cost Variance

= Recovered Overhead – Actual Overhead

= (SR × ST) – (AR × AT_P)

= 1 × 8000 – 10,200 = ₹2200 (A)

(iii) Budget Variance

= Budget Overhead – Actual Overhead

= (SR × BT) – (AR × AT_P)

= 1 × 10,000 – 10,200 = ₹200 (A)

(iv) Volume Variance

= Recovered Overhead – Budget Overhead

= (SR × ST) – (SR × BT)

= ₹8000 – ₹10,000 = ₹2000 (A)

Problem 37 AB Co. operates a system of standard costing in respect of one of its products which is manufactured within a single cost centre. The following information is available.

For one unit of product the standard material input is 20 litres at a standard price of ₹2 per litre. The standard wage rate is ₹6 per hour, and 5 hours are allowed to produce one unit. Fixed production overhead is charged at the rate of 100% of direct wages cost.

During the month just ended the following occurred.

Actual price for material purchased		₹1.95 per litre
Total direct wages cost		₹1,56,000
Fixed production overhead incurred		₹1,58,000
Variances	*Favourable*	*Adverse*
Direct material price	₹8000	–
Direct material usage	–	₹5000
Direct labour rate	–	5760
Direct labour efficiency	2760	–
Fixed overhead expenditure	–	8000

Calculate:

(i) Budgeted output in units

(ii) No. of litres purchased

(iii) No. of litres used above standard allowed

(iv) Actual units produced

(v) Actual hours worked

(vi) Actual wage rate per hour [B.Com. (H)]

Solution:

(i) Let, budgeted output = x

F.O. Expenditure variance = Budgeted fixed overheads – Actual fixed overheads

$= (SR \times BT) - (AR \times AT_P)$

$-8000 = x\,(6 \times 5) - ₹\,1{,}58{,}000$

$30x = 1{,}50{,}000$

$x = 5000$ units

(ii) Number of litres purchased

Let Quantity = x

Material price variance $= (SP \times AQ) - (AP \times AQ)$

$= (2 \times x) - (1.95 \times x)$

$= 8000 = 0.05x$

$= (8000 \div 0.05) = 1{,}60{,}000$

(iii) Number of units used above standard units:

Let, Standard quantity = x

Material usage variance $= (SP \times SQ) - (SP \times AQ)$

$= SP\,(SQ - AQ)$

$-5000 = ₹\,2(x - 1{,}60{,}000)$

$-5000 = 2x - 3{,}20{,}000$

$x = 1{,}57{,}500$

So, extra units allowed = (1,60,000 – 1,57,500) = 2500 units

(iv) Actual units produced

Direct labour cost variance = Labour efficiency variance + Labour rate variance

$= 2760 + (-5760)$

$= 3000$ (A)

Let, Production $= x$

Now, $-3000 = 30x - 1{,}56{,}000$

$30x = 1{,}53{,}000$

$x = 1{,}53{,}000 \div 30 = 5100$ units

(v) Actual hours worked:

Let actual hours $= x$

Labour efficiency variance $= (SR \times ST) - (SR \times AT_P)$

$= SR \times (ST - AT_P)$

$-2760 = ₹\,6\,(5100 \times 5 - x)$

$6x = 1{,}50{,}240$

$x = 25{,}040$

(vi) Actual age rate per hour:

Let, actual wage rate $= x$

$$\text{Labour rate variance} = (SR \times AT_P) - (AR \times AT_P)$$
$$= AT_P \times (SR - AR)$$
$$-5760 = 25{,}040\ (6 - x)$$
$$= 1{,}50{,}240 - 25{,}040x$$
$$= ₹6.23$$

Problem 38 Details regarding a product manufactured by Palm Ltd. for the last one week are as follows:

		₹
Standard cost (for one unit)		
Direct materials	10 units @ ₹1.50	15
Direct wages	5 hours @ ₹8.00	40
Production overheads	5 hours @ ₹10.00	50
Actuals (for whole activity)		
Direct materials	₹ 6435	
Direct wages	₹16,324	
Analysis of variances:		
Direct materials		
Price	₹585 (Adverse)	
Usage	₹375 (Favourable)	
Direct wages (labour)		
Rate	₹636 (Favourable)	
Efficiency	₹360 (Adverse)	
Production overheads		
Expenditure	₹400 (Favourable)	
Volume	₹750 (Favourable)	

You are required to calculate:

(i) actual outputs in units;

(ii) actual price of material per unit;

(iii) actual wage rate per labour hour;

(iv) the amount of production overhead incurred, and

(v) the production overhead efficiency variance. [*B.Com. (H)*]

Solution:

(i) Calculation of actual output units.

$$\text{MCV} = \text{MPV} + \text{MUV}$$
$$= ₹585\ (A) + ₹375\ (F)$$
$$= ₹210\ (A)$$

$$MCV = \text{Standard cost of material for actual output} - \text{Actual Cost}$$
$$= 210\ (A)$$
$$= (SP \times SQ) - (AP \times AQ)$$
$$210\ (A) = SQ \times ₹1.50 - 6435$$
$$210\ (A) + 6435 = 1.50\ SQ$$
$$SQ = \frac{6,225}{1.50} = 4150 \text{ units}$$
$$\text{Actual output} = \frac{\text{Total std. quantity}}{\text{Std. quantity per unit}} = \frac{4150}{10} = 415 \text{ units}$$

(ii) Calculation of actual price of material per unit

$$MPV = (SP \times AQ) - (AP \times AQ)$$
$$585\ (A) = ₹1.50 \times AQ - ₹6435$$
$$585\ (A) + 6435 = 1.50\ AQ$$
$$AQ = \frac{5850}{150} \times 100 = 3900 \text{ units}$$
$$\text{Actual price per unit} = \frac{₹6435}{3900 \text{ units}} = ₹1.65$$

(iii) Calculation of actual wages per hour hour

$$LRV = (SR \times AT_P) - (AR \times AT_P)$$
$$636\ (F) = ₹8 \times AT_P - ₹16,324$$
$$636\ (F) + 16,324 = 8 \times AT_P$$
$$AT_P = 16,960 \div 8 = 2120 \text{ hr}$$
$$\text{Actual wages per labour hour} = \frac{₹16,324}{2120 \text{ hr}} = ₹7.70$$

(iv) Calculation of the amount of production overhead incurred

Production overheads cost variance = Expenditure variance + Volume variance

1150 (F) = 400 (F) + 750 (F)

Production overhead cost variance = Recovered overheads – Actual overheads

= 415 × 5 × 10 – Actual overheads

Actual overheads

= 20,750 – 1150 = ₹19,600

(v) Calculation of production overhead efficiency variance

Production overhead efficiency variance = (Standard hr for actual output – Actual hr) × Standard Overhead rate

= (415 × 5 – 2120) × ₹10 = 450 (A)

Problem 39 Sigma Ltd. furnishes the following information relating to budgeted sales and actual sales for April:

Quantity	Budgeted Price per unit	Actual Quantity	Price per unit	
A	1200	15	880	18
B	800	20	880	20
C	2000	40	2640	38

Calculate the

- sales quantity variance;
- sales mix variance;
- sales price variance; and
- sales value variance.

[*B.Com. (H)*]

Solution:

Sales	(1)	(2)	(3)	(4)
	BP × BQ	BP × BM	BP × AQ	AP × AQ
A	15 × 1200	$15 \times \left(4400 \times \frac{12}{40}\right)$	15 × 880	18 × 880
B	20 × 800	$20 \times \left(4400 \times \frac{8}{40}\right)$	20 × 880	20 × 880
C	40 × 2000	$40 \times \left(4400 \times \frac{20}{40}\right)$	40 × 2640	38 × 2640
	1,14,000	1,25,400	1,36,400	1,33,760

where BP : Budgeted price per unit.

BQ : Budgeted quantity to be solid.

BM : Budgeted mix, i.e., total actual quantity sold in budgeted ratio.

AQ : Actual quantity sold.

AP : Actual price per unit.

1. Sales quantity variances = (1) – (2)

$$= (BP \times BQ) - (BP \times BM)$$

$$\text{Product A} = (15 \times 1200) - 15 \times \left(4400 \times \frac{12}{40}\right) = 1800 \text{ (A)}$$

$$\text{Product B} = (20 \times 800) - 20 \times \left(4400 \times \frac{8}{40}\right) = 1600 \text{ (A)}$$

$$\text{Product C} = (40 \times 2000) - 40 \times \left(4400 \times \frac{20}{40}\right) = 8000\ (A)$$

$$SQV = 14{,}000\ (A)$$

2. Sales mix variance = (2) – (3)

$$= (BP \times BM) - (BP \times AQ)$$

$$\text{Product A} = 15 \times \left(4400 \times \frac{12}{40}\right) - (15 \times 880) = 6600\ (F)$$

$$\text{Product B} = 20 \times \left(4400 \times \frac{8}{40}\right) - (20 \times 880) = \text{Nil}$$

$$\text{Product C} = 40 \times \left(4400 \times \frac{20}{40}\right) - (40 \times 2640) = 17{,}600\ (A)$$

$$SMV = 11{,}000\ (F)$$

3. Sales price variance = (3) – (4)

$$= (BP \times AQ) - (AP \times AQ)$$

$$\text{Product A} = (15 \times 880) - (18 \times 880) = 2640\ (A)$$

$$\text{Product B} = (20 \times 880) - (20 \times 880) = \text{Nil}$$

$$\text{Product C} = (40 \times 2640) - (38 \times 2640) = 5280\ (F)$$

$$SPV = 2640\ (F)$$

4. Sales volume variance = (1) – (3)

$$= (BP \times BQ) - (BP \times AQ)$$

$$\text{Product A} = (15 \times 1200) - (15 \times 880) = 4800\ (F)$$

$$\text{Product B} = (20 \times 800) - (20 \times 880) = 1600\ (A)$$

$$\text{Product C} = (40 \times 2000) - (40 \times 2640) = 25{,}600\ (A)$$

$$SVV = 22{,}400\ (A)$$

5. Sales value variance = (1) – (4)

$$= (BP \times BQ) - (AP \times AQ)$$

$$\text{Product A} = (15 \times 1200) - (18 \times 880) = 2160\ (F)$$

$$\text{Product B} = (20 \times 800) - (20 \times 880) = 1600\ (A)$$

$$\text{Product C} = (40 \times 2000) - (38 \times 2640) = 20{,}320\ (A)$$

$$\text{S value, V} = 19{,}760\ (A)$$

Problem 40 Rustam Ltd. presented the following information:

	Budgeted		Actual	
Quantity	**Price per unit**	**Quantity**	**Price per unit**	
A	1000	2	1800	2.50
B	3000	3	4200	2.75

You are required to calculate the sales quantity variance, sales mix variance, sales price variance and sales value variance.

Solution:

Sales	(1)	(2)	(3)	(4)
	BP × BQ	BP × BM	BP × AQ	AP × AQ
A	(2 × 1000)	$2 \times \left(6000 \times \frac{1}{4}\right)$	(2 × 1800)	(2.5 × 1800)
B	(3 × 3000)	$3 \times \left(6000 \times \frac{3}{4}\right)$	(3 × 4200)	(2.75 × 4200)
	11,000	16,500	16,200	16,050

where BP : Budgeted price per unit.

BQ : Budgeted quantity to be sold.

BM : Budgeted mix, i.e., total actual quantity sold in budgeted ratio.

AQ : Actual quantity sold.

AP : Actual price per unit.

1. Sales quantity variances = (1) – (2)

$$= (BP \times BQ) - (BP \times BM)$$

$$\text{Product A} = (2 \times 1000) - 2 \times \left(6000 \times \frac{1}{4}\right) = 1000\ (A)$$

$$\text{Product B} = (3 \times 3000) - 3 \times \left(6000 \times \frac{3}{4}\right) = 4500\ (A)$$

$$\text{SQV} = 5500\ (A)$$

2. Sales mix variance = (2) – (3)

$$= (BP \times BM) - (BP \times AQ)$$

$$\text{Product A} = 2 \times \left(6000 \times \frac{1}{4}\right) - (2 \times 1800) = 600\ (A)$$

$$\text{Product B} = 3 \times \left(6000 \times \frac{3}{4}\right) - (3 \times 4200) = 900\ (F)$$

$$\text{SMV} = 300\ (F)$$

3. Sales price variance = (3) – (4)

$$= (BP \times AQ) - (AP \times AQ)$$

$$\text{Product A} = (2 \times 1800) - (2.5 \times 1800) = 900\ (A)$$

$$\text{Product B} = (3 \times 4200) - (2.75 \times 4200) = 1050\ (F)$$

$$\text{SPV} = 150\ (F)$$

4. Sales volume variance = (1) – (3)

$$= (BP \times BQ) - (BP \times AQ)$$

Product A = $(2 \times 1000) - (2 \times 1800)$ = 1600 (A)

Product B = $(3 \times 3000) - (3 \times 4200)$ = 3600 (A)

SVV = 5200 (A)

5. Sales value variance = (1) – (4)

$$= (BP \times BQ) - (AP \times AQ)$$

Product A = $(2 \times 1000) - (2.5 \times 1800)$ = 2500 (A)

Product B = $(3 \times 3000) - (2.75 \times 4200)$ = 2550 (A)

S Value V = 5050 (A)

Problem 41 Ford Ltd. furnishes the following information relating to budgeted sales and actual sales for March:

	Budgeted		Actual	
	Quantity	Price per unit	Quantity	Price per unit
A	5000	5	6000	6
B	4000	6	5000	5
C	3000	7	4000	8

Calculate the

- sales quantity variance;
- sales mix variance;
- sales price variance; and
- sales value variance.

[*B.Com. (H)*]

Solution:

Sales	(1)	(2)	(3)	(4)
	BP × BQ	BP × BM	BP × AQ	AP × AQ
A	(5 × 5000)	$5 \times \left(15{,}000 \times \frac{5}{12}\right)$	5 × 6000	(6 × 6000)
B	(6 × 4000)	$6 \times \left(15{,}000 \times \frac{4}{12}\right)$	6 × 5000	(5 × 5000)
C	(7 × 3000)	$7 \times \left(15{,}000 \times \frac{3}{12}\right)$	7 × 4000	(8 × 4000)
	70,000	87,500	88,000	93,000

where BP : Budgeted price per unit.

BQ : Budgeted quantity to be sold.

BM : Budgeted mix, i.e., total actual quantity sold in budgeted ratio.

AQ : Actual quantity sold.
AP : Actual price per unit.

1. Sales quantity variance = (1) – (2)

$$= (BP \times BQ) - (BP \times BM)$$

$$\text{Product A} = (5 \times 5000) - 5 \times \left(15{,}000 \times \frac{5}{12}\right) = 6250 \text{ (A)}$$

$$\text{Product B} = (6 \times 4000) - 6 \times \left(15{,}000 \times \frac{4}{12}\right) = 6000 \text{ (A)}$$

$$\text{Product C} = (7 \times 3000) - 7 \times \left(15{,}000 \times \frac{3}{12}\right) = 5250 \text{ (A)}$$

$$\text{SQV} = 17{,}500 \text{ (A)}$$

2. Sales mix variance = (2) – (3)

$$= (BP \times BM) - (BP \times AQ)$$

$$\text{Product A} = 5 \times \left(15{,}000 \times \frac{5}{12}\right) - (5 \times 6000) = 1250 \text{ (F)}$$

$$\text{Product B} = 6 \times \left(15{,}000 \times \frac{4}{12}\right) - (6 \times 5000) = \text{Nil}$$

$$\text{Product C} = 7 \times \left(15{,}000 \times \frac{3}{12}\right) - (7 \times 4000) = 1750 \text{ (A)}$$

$$\text{SMV} = 500 \text{ (A)}$$

3. Sales price variance = (3) – (4)

$$= (BP \times AQ) - (AP \times AQ)$$

$$\text{Product A} = (5 \times 6000) - (6 \times 6000) = 6000 \text{ (A)}$$

$$\text{Product B} = (6 \times 5000) - (5 \times 5000) = 5000 \text{ (F)}$$

$$\text{Product C} = (7 \times 4000) - (8 \times 4000) = 4000 \text{ (A)}$$

$$\text{SPV} = 5000 \text{ (A)}$$

4. Sales volume variance = (1) – (3)

$$= (BP \times BQ) - (BP \times AQ)$$

$$\text{Product A} = (5 \times 5000) - (5 \times 6000) = 5000 \text{ (A)}$$

$$\text{Product B} = (6 \times 4000) - (6 \times 5000) = 6000 \text{ (A)}$$

$$\text{Product C} = (7 \times 3000) - (7 \times 4000) = 7000 \text{ (A)}$$

$$\text{SVV} = 18{,}000 \text{ (A)}$$

5. Sales value variance = (1) – (4)

$$= (BP \times BQ) - (AP \times AQ)$$

Product A = (5 × 5000) – (6 × 6000) = 11,000 (A)
Product B = (6 × 4000) – (5 × 5000) = 1000 (A)
Product C = (7 × 3000) – (8 × 4000) = 11,000 (A)

Sales value, V = 23,000 (A)

Problem 42 A factory produces two products P and Q. P takes 10 hours to produce and Q requires 16 hours as per the budget. Budgeted production for the month is 600 units of P and 250 units of Q. A month has 25 budgeted days of 8 hours each. During the month, 500 units of P and 400 units of Q were produced. The factory employs 50 workers. They actually worked for 9 hours daily for 24 days.

Calculate: (i) Efficiency ratio; (ii) Activity ratio; (iii) Capacity ratio; and (iv) Calendar ratio. [*B.Com. (H)*]

Solution:

Budgeted days for actual production	= 25 days
Actual days for actual production	= 24 days
Budgeted hours for budgeted production: 50 × 25 days × 8 hr	= 10000 hrs
Actual hours for actual production = 50 × 24 days × 9 hr	= 10800 hrs
Standard hours for actual production:	
Product P = 500 × 10 hr	= 5000 hrs
Product Q = 400 × 16 hr	= 6400 hrs
	= 11400 hrs

$$\text{(i) Efficiency ratio} = \frac{\text{Standard hours for actual production}}{\text{Actual hours worked}} \times 100$$

$$= \frac{11{,}400}{10{,}800} \times 100 = 105.55\%$$

$$\text{(ii) Activity ratio} = \frac{\text{Standard hours for actual production}}{\text{Budgeted hours for budgeted production}} \times 100$$

$$= \text{ST/BT} = \frac{11{,}400}{10{,}000} \times 100 = 114\%$$

$$\text{(iii) Capacity ratio} = \frac{\text{Actual hours worked}}{\text{Budgeted days}} \times 100$$

$$= \frac{10{,}800}{10{,}000} \times 100 = 108\%$$

$$\text{(iv) Calendar ratio} = \frac{\text{Actual days}}{\text{Budgeted days}} \times 100 = 96\%$$

Problem 43 The following are the details regarding production and working hours in a factory during a week:

Budgeted production	88 units
Actual production	75 units
Standard hours per unit	10
Actual working hours	600

Calculate efficiency ratio, activity ratio and capacity ratio.

Solution:

Budgeted hours for budgeted production: 88 × 10 hr = 880 hrs

Actual hours for actual production = 600 hrs

Standard hours for actual production 75 × 10 hr = 750 hrs

$$\text{(i) Efficiency ratio} = \frac{\text{Standard hours for actual production}}{\text{Actual hours worked}} \times 100$$

$$= \frac{750}{600} \times 100 = 125\%$$

$$\text{(ii) Activity ratio} = \frac{\text{Standard hours for actual production}}{\text{Budgeted hours for budgeted production}} = \frac{\text{ST}}{\text{BT}} \times 100$$

$$= \frac{750}{880} \times 100$$

$$= 85.22\%$$

$$\text{(iii) Capacity ratio} = \frac{\text{Actual hours worked}}{\text{Budgeted hours}} \times 100$$

$$= \frac{600}{880} \times 100 = 68.18\%.$$

Problem 44 The following information relates to a company which has installed a standard costing system in its organisation. The standard output and sales for the month of October was 8000 units and the standard cost and profit per unit was as under:

		₹
Direct materials		
A	(2 kg @ ₹ 3 per kg)	6
B	(1 kg @ ₹ 4 per kg)	4
Direct labour	(5 hours @ ₹ 4)	20
Fixed factory overheads	(5 hours @ ₹ 2)	10
Variable factory overheads	(5 hours @ ₹ 1)	5
Total standard cost		45
Standard profit		5
S.P. (standard)		50

In the month of October, the company produced and sold 6000 units. The actual sales were ₹3,05,000. The following costs were incurred:

Direct materials		
A	14,850 kg	₹43,065
B	7260 kg	₹88,750
Direct labour	32,000 hours	₹1,27,500
Fixed factory overheads	(5 hours @ ₹2)	₹80,600
Variable factory overheads	(5 hours @ ₹1)	₹30,000

Closing WIP was 600 units in respect of which materials were fully drawn but labour and overheads to the extent of 50% were incurred. Direct labour hours booked on production were 31,800.

You are required to calculate:

- Cost and sales variances.
- Prepare a statement reconciling the budget profit with the actual profit.

Solution: To compute the output in complete terms, a statement of equivalent production is prepared.

Statement of Equivalent Production

Particulars	Total	Materials		Labour		Overheads	
		Units	%	Units	%	Units	%
Complete Units	6000	6000	100	6000	100	6000	100
Closing WIP	600	600	100	300	50	300	50
		6600		6300		6300	

1. Material cost variances:

	SP × SQ	SP × SM	SP × AQ	AP × AQ
A.	$3 \times (2 \times 6600)$	$3 \times \left(22{,}110 \times \frac{3}{2}\right)$	$3 \times 14{,}850$	43,065
B.	$4 \times (1 \times 6600)$	$4 \times \left(22{,}110 \times \frac{1}{3}\right)$	4×7260	29,750
	66,000	73,700	73,590	72,815

M. yield, V = 7700 (A) Mix = 110 (F) Price = 775 (F)

2. Labour cost variances:

SR × ST	SR × SM	SR × AT_W	SR × AT_P	AR × AT_P
4 × (5 × 6300)	4 × 31,800	4 × 31,800	4 × 32,000	1,27,500
1,26,000	1,27,200	1,27,200	1,28,000	1,27,500

L.E.V. = 1200 (A) Mix = NIL Idle = 800 (A) Rate = 500 (F)

3. Variable overhead variances:

SR × ST	SR × AT_W	AR × AT_P
1 × (5 × 6300)	1 × 31,800	30,000
31,500	31,800	30,000

Eff. = 300 (A) Expenditure = 1800 (F)

4. Fixed overhead variances:

SR × ST	SR × AT_W	SR × RBT	SR × BT	AR AT_P
	2 × (5 × 6300)	2 × 31,800	2 × (5 × 8000)	2 × (5 × 8000)
80,600				
63,000	63,000	80,000	80,000	80,600

Eff. 600 (A) Capacity = 16,400 (A) Calendar = Nil Exp. 600 (A)

5. Sales turnover variances:

BP × BQ	BP × BM	BP × AQ	AP × AQ
50 × 8000	50 × 6000	50 × 6000	3,05,000
4,00,000	3,00,000	3,00,000	3,05,000

Qty. = 1,00,000 (A) Mix = Nil Price = 5000 (F)

Reconciliation Statement as on .....

Particulars		+	–
Budgeted sales @ ₹50		4,00,000	
Sales qty. variance			1,00,000
Sales price variance		5000	
Actual sales		3,05,000	
Less : SC of actual units sold			
DM (6 + 4)	10		
DL	20		

Table Contd...

Table Contd...

V. OH	10	
F.OH	5	
	45	6000 × 45
Budgeted Profit	35,000	
M.Y.V.		7700
M. Mix V	110	
M. Price V	775	
L. Efficiency V		1200
L. Idle V		800
L. Rate V	500	
V. OH Eff. V		300
V. OH Exp. V	1800	
F. OH Eff. V		600
F. OH Capacity V		16,400
F. OH Calendar V		NIL
F. OH Exp. V		600
	38,785	28,200
Actual profit		10,585

Problem 45 The income statement of Grill Ltd. for the first quarter of the current year is given as below:

Sales revenue (18000 units)		7,20,000
Less : Cost of goods sold:		
Direct materials	4,32,800	
Direct labour	1,16,600	
Direct expenses	30,400	
Factory overheads	44,000	
Selling expenses	32,000	6,55,800
Net profit		64,200

The standard output and sales for the period was 20,000 units and the standard cost and profit per unit is as under:

Direct materials (3 units @ ₹ 7.50)	22.5
Direct labour (3 hours @ ₹ 2)	6
Direct expenses	1.5
Fixed factory overheads	1.5
Variable factory overheads	1
Fixed administrative and selling expenses	1.5

Table Contd...

Table Contd...

Total standard cost	34
Standard profit	4
Selling price (standard)	38

Labour was paid at the rate of ₹2.20 per hour and material prices were ₹8 per unit. Factory overheads (actual) include ₹28,000, fixed and the balance amount represents variable. There was no inventory in the beginning or at the end of the year. The company employs labour hour rate as the basis of absorption of fixed overheads.

You are required to calculate:

- Cost, sales and profit variances.
- Prepare a reconciliation statement of profit variances with as many details as possible.

Solution:

1. Material cost variances

SP × SQ	SP × AQ	AP × AQ
$7.5 \times (3 \times 18{,}000)$	$7.5 \times \left(\dfrac{4{,}32{,}800}{8}\right)$	$(8 \times 54{,}100)$
4,05,000	4,05,750	4,32,800

$$\text{Material usage variance} = (SP \times SQ) - (SP \times AQ)$$

$$= [7.5 \times (3 \times 18{,}000)] - \left[7.5 \times \left(\frac{4{,}32{,}800}{8}\right)\right]$$

$$= 750\ (A)$$

$$\text{Material price variance} = (SP \times AQ) - (AP \times AQ)$$

$$= 7.5 \times \left(\frac{4{,}32{,}800}{8}\right) - (8 \times 54{,}100)$$

$$= 27{,}050\ (A)$$

$$\text{Material cost variance} = (SP \times SQ) - (AP \times AQ)$$

$$= 7.5\ (3 \times 18{,}000) - (8 \times 54{,}100)$$

$$= 27{,}800\ (A)$$

2. Labour cost variances

SR × ST	$SR \times AT_P$	$AR \times AT_P$
$2 \times (3 \times 18{,}000)$	$2 \times \left(\dfrac{1{,}16{,}600}{2.2}\right)$	$2.2 \times 53{,}000$
1,08,000	1,06,000	1,16,600

Labour efficiency variance (LEV) = $(SR \times ST) - (SR \times AT_P)$

$$= 2 \times (3 \times 18{,}000) - 2 \times \left(\frac{1{,}16{,}600}{2.2}\right)$$

$$= 2000\ (F)$$

Labour rate variance (LRV) = $(SR \times AT_P) - (AR \times AT_P)$

$$= 2 \times \left(\frac{1{,}16{,}600}{2.2}\right) - 2.2 \times 53{,}000$$

$$= 10{,}600\ (A)$$

Labour cost variance (LCV) = $(SR \times ST) - (AR \times AT_P)$

$$= 2 \times (3 \times 18{,}000) - 2.2 \times 53{,}000$$

$$= 8600\ (A)$$

3. Fixed overhead cost variances: (factory)

SR × ST	SR × AT_W	SR × BT	AR × AT_P
$\frac{1.5}{3} \times (3 \times 18{,}000)$	$\frac{1.5}{3} \times 53{,}000$	$\frac{1.5}{3} \times (3 \times 20{,}000)$	28,000
27,000	26,500	30,000	28,000

Fixed overhead efficiency variance = $(SR \times ST) - (SR \times AT_W)$

$$= \frac{1.5}{3} \times (3 \times 18{,}000) - \left(\frac{1.5}{3} \times 53{,}000\right)$$

$$= 500\ (F)$$

Fixed overhead capacity variance = $(SR \times AT_W) - (SR \times RBT)$

$$= \left(\frac{1.5}{3} \times 53{,}000\right) - \frac{1.5}{3} \times (3 \times 20{,}000)$$

$$= 3{,}500\ (A)$$

Fixed overhead expenditure variance = $(SR \times BT) - (AR \times AT_P)$

$$= \frac{1.5}{3} \times (3 \times 20{,}000) - 28{,}000$$

$$= 2000\ (F)$$

4. Variable OH variances (factory)

SR × ST	SR × AT_W	AR × AT_P
$\frac{1}{3} \times (3 \times 18{,}000)$	$\frac{1}{3} \times 53{,}000$	16,000
18,000	17,667	16,000

Efficiency variance $= (SR \times ST) - (SR \times AT_W)$

$= \frac{1}{3} \times (3 \times 18{,}000) \times \frac{1}{3} \times 53{,}000 = 333$ (F)

Expenditure (budget) variance $= (SR \times AT_W) - (AR \times AT_P)$

$= \frac{1}{3} \times 53{,}000 - 16{,}000 = 1{,}667$ (F)

5. Administration overhead (fixed) cost variances

Absorbed OH	Budgeted OH	Actual OH
1.5 × 18,000	1.5 × 20,000	32,000
27,000	30,000	32,000

Fixed overhead volume variance $= (SR \times ST) - (SR \times BT)$

$= 1.5 \times 18{,}000 - 1.5 \times 20{,}000$

$= 3000$ (A)

Fixed overhead budget variance $= (SR \times BT) - (AR \times AT_P)$

$= 1.5 \times 20{,}000 - 32{,}000 = 2000$ (A)

6. Sales value variances

BP × BQ	BP × AQ	AP × AQ
38 × 20,000	38 × 18,000	40 × 18,000
7,60,000	6,84,000	7,20,000

Sales volume variance $= (BP \times BQ) - (BP \times AQ)$

$= 38 \times 20{,}000 - 38 \times 18{,}000 = 76{,}000$ (A)

Sales price variance $= (BP \times AQ) - (AP \times AQ)$

$= 38 \times 18{,}000 - 40 \times 18{,}000$

$= 36{,}000$ (F)

Reconciliation Statement as on ....

Particulars	+	–
Budgeted Sales Revenue	7,60,000	
Sales revenue variances:		
Price	36,000	
Volume		76,000
Actual sales revenue	7,20,000	
Less : SC of actual units sold		
DM 22.5 × 18,000		4,05,000
DL 6 × 18,000		1,08,000

Table Contd...

Table Contd...

D Exp.		1.5 × 18,000		27,000
Factory OH	– Fixed	1.5 × 18,000		27,000
	– Variable	1 × 18,000		18,000
Administration OH		1.5 × 18,000		27,000
Budgeted Net Profit			1,08,000	
MPV				27,050
MUV				750
LRV				10,600
LTV			2000	
D. Exp. Variance				3400
Fixed OH	– Expenditure		2000	
	– Efficiency		500	
	– Capacity			3500
Variable OH	– Budget		1667	
	– Efficiency		333	
Administration OH	– Budget			2000
	– Volume			3000
			1,14,500	50,300
Actual Profit				64,200

Problems 46 The standard price of a chemical used as raw material is ₹2 per kg. The standard processing cost is ₹1.04 per kg of input. The normal yield of the three products that are produced from the chemical and their selling price are as follows.

Product	*Standard Yield*	*Selling Price per kg*
A	0.50 kg	5
B	0.30 kg	3
C	0.20 kg	2

During the month of October 2021 50,000 kg of the chemical was purchased at a total cost of ₹1,10,000 and the processing cost amounted to ₹53,600. The actual yields were:

A	0.52 kg
B	0.29 kg
C	0.19 kg

Calculate: (a) total standard are actual cost of processing 50,000 kg of chemical; (b) standard cost of processing per unit of products A, B, and C; (c) actual cost of processing per product; (d) standard cost of actual yield of each product; (e) total variance, material price variance, processing cost variance and yield variance.

Solution:

(a) Total standard cost of processing 50,000 kg of chemical

		Standard	*Actual*
Raw material cost (50,000 × ₹2)	=	₹1,00,000	₹1,10,000
Processing (50,000 × ₹1.04)	=	₹52,000	₹53,600
		₹1,52,000	₹1,63,600

The total standard costs of ₹1,52,000 will be apportioned among the various products in the ratios of their sales values as below:

Product (A)	Standard yield for 1 kg of raw material (B)	Selling price per kg (C) ₹	Sales value against the yield of 1 kg of raw material (D) = B × C ₹	Ratio (E)	Standard costs (F) ₹	Standard yield (G) ₹	Per unit standard costs (H) = F/G ₹
A	0.50	5	2.50	25	1,00,000	25,000 kg	4.00
B	0.30	3	0.90	9	36,000	15,000 kg	2.40
C	0.20	2	0.40	4	16,000	10,000 kg	1.60
					1,52,000		

(c) The total actual cost of ₹1,63,600 (i.e., ₹1,10,000 + ₹53,600) will be apportioned in the following ratios:

Product from 1 kg of raw material (A)	Actual yield per kg (B)	Selling price against the yield of 1 kg of raw material (C) ₹	Sales Value (D) = (B) × (C) ₹	Ratio costs (E)	Actual (F) ₹
A	0.52	5	2.60	260	1,10,483
B	0.29	3	0.87	87	36,963
C	0.19	2	0.38	38	16,148
Total					1,63,600

Statement showing the Standard and Actual Costs of the Various Products for the Month of October, 2021

Product	Actual production out of 50,000 kg of raw material	Standard cost per unit ₹	Standard cost per actual output ₹	Actual costs
A	26,000 kg	4.00	1,04,000	1,10,483
B	14,500 kg	2.40	34,800	36,969
C	9500 kg	1.60	15,200	16,148
Total			1,54,000	1,63,600

Total variance is ₹1,54,000 – 1,63,600 = ₹9600 (A). The break-up of this follows:

(i) Material Price Variance: Actual production × (Standard Price – Actual Price)

A	26,000 × (2 – 2.20)	=	₹5200 (A)
B	14,500 (2 – 220)	=	₹2900 (A)
C	9500 × (2 – 2.20)	=	₹1900 (A)
	Total		₹10,000 (A)

Note: Actual Material Cost per kg = 1,10,000/50,000 = ₹2.20

(ii) Yield Variance: Standard Rate × (Actual Yield – Standard Yield)

A	4 × (26,000 – 25,000)	=	₹4000 (F)
B	2.40 × (14,500 – 15,000)	=	₹1200 (A)
C	1.60 × (9500 – 10,000)	=	₹ 304 (A)
	Total		₹2000 (F)

Note: Actual Processing Cost per kg 53,600/50,000 = ₹1.072

Proof: Total variance = Price variance + Yield variance + Conversion cost variance.

OR

₹9600 (A) = ₹10,000 (A) + ₹2000 (F) + ₹1600 (A)

Problem 47 Jumbo Enterprises manufactures one product, and the entire product is soon as it is produced. There are no opening or closing stock are work-in-progress is negligible. The company operates a standard costing system and analysis of variances is made every month. The standard cost card for the product is as follows:

Direct material	0.5 kg @ ₹4 per kg	₹2.00
Direct wages	2 hours @ ₹2 per hour	4.00
Variable overheads	2 hours @ ₹0.30 per hour	0.60
Fixed overheads	2 hours @ ₹3.70 per hour	7.40
Standard cost		14,00
Standard profit		6.00
Standard selling price		20.00

Selling and administration expenses are not included in the standard cost and are deducted from profit as a period cost. Budgeted output for April 2022 was 5100 units. Actual results for April 2022 were as follows:

Production of 4850 units was sold for ₹95,600. Material consumed in production amounted to 2300 kg at a total cost of ₹9800. Labour hours paid for amounted to 8500 hours at a cost of ₹16,800. Actual operating hours amounted to 8000 hours. Variable overheads amounted to 2600. Fixed overhead amounted to ₹42,300. Selling and administration expense amounted to ₹18,000.

Required: Prepare an operating statement for the month ended 30th April, 2022:

Operating statement for the month ending on 30th April 2022

Particulars			₹
A Budgeted profit (5,100 × 6)			30,6000
B Adjustment of variance:	(F)	(A)	
Sales margin variance	₹	₹	
Sales margin price		1400	
Sales margin volume		1500	
Cost variance		600	
Material price	500		
Material usages	200		
Labour rate		1000	
Labour idle time	3400		
Labour efficiency	510		
Variable overhead efficiency		150	
Variable overhead idle time		50	
Variable overhead expenditure			
Fixed overhead efficiency	6290		
Fixed overhead idle time		1850	
Fixed variable capacity		6290	
Fixed overhead expenditure		4560	
	19,900	17,400	(65,000)
Net Effect			
C Actual profit before selling and distribution expenses			24,100
D *Less:* Selling and distribution expenses			18,000
E Actual profit for the month (C–D)			6100

Working Notes:

(i) *Determination of actual profit*

		₹
A Sales		95,600
B Less: Material Cost	9800	
Labour cost	16,800	
Variable overhead	2600	
Fixed overhead	42,300	
Selling and Admn. overhead	18,000	89,500
C actual profit for the month (A–B)		6100

(ii) *Calculation of Material Variance*

Basic Calculations for the Computation of Material Cost Variances

SQ for AO	SP	SQ × SP (1)	AQ	AP	AQ × AP (2)	AP × SP (3)
2425	4	9700	2300		9800	9200

A Material cost variance (1 – 2) = ₹9700 – ₹39,800 = ₹100 (A)

B Material usage variance (1 – 3) = ₹9700 – ₹9,200 = ₹100 (F)

C Material price variance (3 – 2) = ₹9200 – ₹39,800 = ₹100 (A)

(iii) *Calculation of Labour variance*

Basic Calculations for the Computation of Labour Cost Variances

SH for AO	SR	SH × SR (1)	AH	AR	AH × AR (2)	AH × SR (3)	APH	APH × SR (4)
9700	2	19,400	8500		16,800	17,000	8000	16,000

A Labour cost variance (1 – 2) = ₹19,400 – ₹16,800 = ₹2600 (F)

B Labour efficiency variance (1 – 4) = ₹19,400 – ₹16,800 = ₹3400 (F)

C Labour idle time variance (4 – 3) = ₹16,000 – ₹17,000 = ₹1000 (A)

D Labour rate variance (3 – 2) = ₹17,000 – ₹16,800 = ₹200 (F)

(iv) *Calculation of Overhead Variance*

Basic Calculations for the Computation of Overhead Variances

Nature of Overhead	SH for AO	SR	SH × SR (1)	AH	AR	AH × AR (2)	AH × SR (3)	BH	BH × SR (4)	APH	APH × SR (5)
Fixed	9700	3.70	35,890	8500		42,300	31,450	10,200	37,740	8000	29,600
Variable	9700	0.30	2910	8500		2600	2550	8500	2500	8000	2400

A Fixed overheads efficiency variance (1 – 5) = ₹35,890 – ₹29,600 = ₹6290 (F)

B Fixed overheads idle time variance (5 – 3) = ₹29,600 – ₹31,450 = ₹1850 (A)

C Fixed overheads capacity variance (3 – 4) = ₹31,450 – ₹37,750 = ₹2290 (A)

D Fixed overheads expenditure variance (4 – 2) = ₹37,740 – ₹42,300 = ₹4560 (A)

E Variable overhead efficiency variance (1 – 5) = ₹2910 – ₹2400 = ₹510 (F)

F Variable overhead idle time variance (5 – 3) = ₹2400 – ₹2550 = ₹150 (A)

G Variable overheads expenditure variance (3 – 2) = ₹2550 – ₹2600 = ₹50 (A)

H Total overhead cost variance (A + B + C + D + E + G) = ₹6100 (A)

(v) *Calculation of Sales Variance*

Actual selling price per unit = ₹95,600/₹4850 = ₹19.7112

Actual sales margin per unit = Actual selling price – Standard cost per unit

= ₹19.7113 – ₹14.00 = ₹5.7113

Basic Calculations for the Computation of Variances

BQ	BM	BQ × BM (1)	AQ	AM	AQ × AM (2)	AQ × MB
5100	6	30,600	4850	57113	27,700	29,100

A Sales margin value variance (2 – 1) = ₹2,900 (A)

B Sales margin volume variance (3 – 1) = ₹1,500 (A)

C Sales margin price variance (2 – 3) = ₹1,400 (A)

Problem 48 X Ltd. provided following information relating to 1000 units of product 'ZED' during the month of April, 2022:

Standard price per kg of raw material – ₹3

Actual total direct material cost – ₹10,000

Standard direct labour hours – ₹1600

Actual direct labour hours – 1800

Total standard direct labour cost – ₹8000

Standard variable overhead per direct labour hour – ₹1

Standard variable cost per unit of ZED – ₹1600

Actual total variable overheads – ₹1620

The material usage variance is ₹600 adverse and the over all cost variance per unit of ZED is ₹0.07 adverse as compared to the total standard cost per unit of ZED of ₹21.

You are required to complete to the following.

(a) Standard quantity of raw material per unit of ZED; (b) Standard direct labour rate per unit hour; (c) Standard direct material cost per unit of ZED; (d) Standard direct labour cost per unit of ZED; (e) Standard total material cost of the output; (f) Actual total direct labour cost for the output; (g) Material price variance; (h) Labour rate variance; (i) Labour efficiency variance; (j) Variable overhead expenditure variance; and (k) Variable overheads efficiency variance.

Note: Key calculation should form part of the answer.

Solution:

Key Calculations:

		₹	₹
1.	Standard cost of raw material consumed:		21,000
	Total standard cost of ZED (1000 × ₹21)		
	Less: standard cost: Labour	8000	
	Overheads	1600	9600
	Standard cost of material used		11,400

2. Standard cost of raw material per finished unit:
   Total cost of material/output = ₹11,400/1000 units = ₹11.40
3. Standard quantity of raw material per finished unit and total quantity of raw material required:

$$= \frac{\text{Standard cost material per unit}}{\text{Standard rate per kg}} = \frac{₹11.40}{₹3.00} = 3.8 \text{ kg per finished unit}$$

   Total quantity = 3.8 kg × 1000 = 3800 kg
4. Total material cost variance = Standard cost – Actual cost
   = ₹11,400 – ₹10,000 = ₹1400 (F)
5. Actual quantity (AQ) of raw material (in kg):
   Material usage variance = Standard rate × (Standard quantity – Actual quantity)
   or ₹600 (A) = ₹3 × (3800 kg – AQ)
   or 3 AQ = 12,000 kg or AQ = 4000 kg
6. Actual rate of raw material per kg = Actual material cost/Actual quantity
   = ₹10,000/4,000 = 2.50 per kg
7. Standard direct labour rate $= \frac{\text{Standard direct labour cost}}{\text{Standard direct labour hours}}$

$$= \frac{₹800}{1600} = ₹5 \text{ per hour}$$

8.	Actual labour cost and actual rate per hour:		₹21,070
	A Actual total cost 1000 units = 1000 × (₹21 + ₹+ 0.07)	₹10,000	
	B *Less:* Actual cost of material	₹1620	
	Actual variable overheads		₹11,620
	C Actual direct labour cost (A – B)		₹9450
	D Actual direct labour rate per hour = ₹9450/1800		₹5.25

9. Standard labour hours to production one unit = 1600 hours
10. Standard labour cost per unit: 1.6 hr × 5 = ₹8
11. Actual hourly rate of variable overheads:
    = Actual; variable overheads /Actual hours = ₹1,620/1800 = 1.6 hours

Computations:

(a) Standards quantity of raw material per unit of ZED : 8 kg. (*Refer to key calculation 3*)

(b) Standard direct labour rate per hour ₹5 (*Refer to key calculation 7*)

(c) Standard direct material cost per unit of ZED : ₹11.40 (*Refer to key calculation 2*)

(d) Standard direct labour cost per unit of ZED: ₹8 (*Refer to key calculation 10*)

(e) Standard total material cost for the output: ₹11,400 (*Refer to key calculation 1*)

(f) Actual total direct labour cost for the output: ₹9450 (*Refer to key calculation 8*)

(g) Material price variance = Total material cost variance – Material usage variance
= ₹1400 (favorable) – ₹600 (Adverse) = ₹2000 (favourable)

Alternatively,

= Actual quantity (Standard rate – Actual)
= 400 × (₹3 – ₹2.50) = 2000 (favourable)

(h) Labour rate variance = Actual hours × (Standards rate – Actual rate
= 1800 × (₹5 – ₹5.25) = ₹450 (Adverse)

(i) Labour efficiency variance = Standard rate × Hours – Actual hours)
= ₹5 (1600 – 1800) = ₹1000 (Adverse)

(j) Variable overheads expenditure variance
= Actual hours × (Standards rate – Actual rate)
= 1800 (₹1 – 0.90) = ₹180 (favourable)

(k) Variable overhead efficiency variance
= Standards rate (Standards hours – Actual hours)
= ₹1 (1600 – 1800)
= ₹200 (adverse)

Problem 49 Q Limited operates a system of standard costing and in respect of one of its products which is manufactured within a single cost centre, the following information is given.

For one unit of product the standard material input is in litres at a standard price of ₹2.50 per litre. The standard wages rate is ₹ × per hour and 1 unit is produced in 6 hours. Fixed production overhead is absorbed at the rate of 120% of direct wages cost.

During the last four-week accounting period the material price variance was extracted on purchased and the actual price was ₹2.45 per litre. Total direct wages cost was ₹1,21,500. Fixed production overhead incurred was 1,50,000.

Variance:	*Favourable*	*Adverse*
Direct material price	₹8000	
Direct material usage		₹6000
Direct labour rate		₹4500
Direct labour efficiency	3600	
Fixed production overhead expenditure		6000

Required: Calculated for the four-week period: (i) Budgeted output in units, (ii) Number of litres purchased, (iii) Number of litres used above standard, (iv) Actual units produced, (v) Average actual hours worked, and (vi) Average actual wage rate per hour.

Solution:

Basic Calculations:	₹
Standard product cost per unit	40
Material [16 litres @ ₹2.50]	30
Labour [6 hours @ ₹5.06]	30
Fixed production overhead @ ₹120% of labour	160

(i) $$\text{Budgeted output (in units)} = \frac{\text{Budgeted overhead}}{\text{Budgeted overhead per unit}}$$

$$= \frac{₹1,50,000 \times ₹6000}{₹36} = 4000 \text{ units}$$

(ii) $$\text{Number of litres purchased} = \frac{\text{Total direct material price variance}}{\text{Direct material price variance per litre}}$$

$$\frac{8000}{₹2.50 - ₹2.45} = 1,60,000 \text{ units}$$

(iii) Number of litres used above standard allowed

$$= \frac{\text{Total direct material usage variance}}{\text{Standard rate per litre}}$$

$$= \frac{6000}{₹2.50 - ₹2.45} = 2400 \text{ litres}$$

(iv) $$\text{Actual units produced} = \frac{\text{Total standard labour cost of output}}{\text{Standard labour rate per hour}}$$

$$\frac{₹1,121,500 + 3600 - 4500}{₹30} = 4020 \text{ units}$$

(v) $\text{Actual hours worked} = \dfrac{\text{Total standard labour cost of hours}}{\text{Standard labour rate per hour}}$

$$\frac{₹1,121,500 - ₹4500}{5} = 23,400 \text{ hours}$$

(vi) $\text{Average actual wage rate per hour} = \dfrac{\text{Actual labour cost}}{\text{Actual hours worked}} = \dfrac{₹1,21,500}{23,400}$

$$= ₹5.19 \text{ per hour}$$

Problem 50 JS Limited used a full standard cost system with any material. inventory carried at standard, the following data was take from the record of the company for the period ended 31.12.2021:

	₹
Opening raw material inventory	300
Closing raw material inventory	250
Net purchase	410
Material price variance	10(A)
Material usage variance	20(A)
Direct labour cost (Actual)	900
Direct labour cost at standard	840
Actual overhead cost incurred	875
Overhead cost variable	45(F)
Opening work-in-progress inventory	120
Closing work-in-progress inventory	140
Cost of goods sold reported	2,240
Opening finished goods inventory	360

Note: 'F' denotes favourable and 'A' denotes adverse.

You are required to compute: (1) Raw Material purchases at standard; (2) Raw material consumed at actual; (3) Raw material consumed at standard; (4) Labour cost variance; (5) Standard overhead costs; (6) Total manufacturing cost at standard; (7) Cost of products sold to customers; (9) Closing finished goods inventory.

Solution:

1. Raw material purchases at standard

   = Net raw material purchase + Material price variance

   = ₹410 (– ₹10) = ₹400

2. Raw material consumed (at actuals)

   = Opening inventory + Purchase at standard – Closing inventory

   = ₹300 + ₹400 – ₹250 = ₹450

3. Raw material consumed at standard

= Raw material consumed at actual + Usage variance

= ₹450 + (– ₹20) = ₹430

4. Labour cost variance = Standard labour – Actual labour cost

= ₹840 – ₹900 = ₹60 (Adverse)

5. Standard overhead costs = Actual overhead costs incurred + Overhead cost variance

= ₹875 + ₹45 = ₹920.

6. Total manufacturing cost at standard

	₹
Material	430
Labour material	840
Overhead	
	2190

7. Cost of goods manufacturing (at standard)

= Opening WIP + Manufacturing cost at standard – Closing WIP

= ₹120 + ₹2190 – ₹140 = ₹2170

8. Cost of products sold to customers (at standard)

= Cost of good sold reported + Cost variances

= ₹2240 + (– 20 – 10 – 60) + ₹45 = ₹2195

9. Closing finished good inventory (at standard)

= Opening finished goods inventory + Cost of goods manufactured – Cost of product sold to customers

= ₹360 + ₹2170 – ₹2195 = ₹335.

REVIEW QUESTIONS

1. Explain briefly the concept of variance analysis.
2. Examine in brief the shortcomings of the standard cost system.
3. "Standard costing and budgetary control are interrelated but not interdependent". Comment.
4. Describe briefly the managerial uses of variance analysis.
5. Explain the following terms:
   (a) Sales margin mix variance
   (b) Sales margin volume variance
   (c) Sales margin quantity variance
   (d) Sales margin price variable
6. What is sales variance? What are the methods for computing it?

UNSOLVED PRACTICAL QUESTIONS

1. Corma Ltd. produce an article by blending two basic raw materials. The following standards have been set up for raw material.

Material	Standard Mix	Standard price per kg
A	40%	₹4
B	60%	₹3

The standard loss in processing is 15%. During September 2008 the company produced 1700 kg. of finished output. The position of stock and purchases for the month of September 2020 is as under.

Material	Stock on 1-9-2020	Stock on 30-9-2020	Purchased during Sept. 2020	
	Kg.	Kg.	Kg.	Cost ₹
A	35	5	800	3400
B	40	50	1200	3000

Required: Calculate all material variances assuming FIFO method of issue of material. The opening stock is to be valued at standard price.

[*Ans.* MCV ₹286.25 (F), MPV ₹376.25 (F), MUV ₹90 (A), MMV ₹22 (A), MYV ₹68 (A)]

2. Zinger Company manufactures product 'P' by mixing three raw materials. For every 100 kg of P, 125 kg of raw material are used in April there was an output of 5600 kg of P. The standard and actual particulars for April are as follows:

Raw Material	Standard		Actual	
	Mix ₹	Price per kg	Mix ₹	Price per kg
I	50%	40	60%	42
II	30%	20	20%	16
III	20%	10	20%	12

Calculate all material variances assuming actual quantity of material consumed was 7000 kg.

[*Ans.* (a) MCV ₹19,600 (A), MPV ₹5600 (A), MUV ₹14,000 (A), MMV ₹14,000 (A) MYV Nil]

3. Designer Tiles Limited makes plastic titles of standard size of 6" × 6" × 1/8". From the following information, you are required to calculate for direct material:
   (i) The cost variance in total
   (ii) The cost variance subdivided into:
   (a) Price (b) Usage
   (iii) The usage variance analysed to show:
   (a) Mixture (b) Yield

A standard mix of the compound required to produce an output of 20,000 square feet of tiles 8" thick is as follows:

Direct Material	Quantity	Price per kg
A	600 kg	₹0.90
B	400 kg	₹0.65
C	500 kg	₹0.40

During December 2021 mixes were processed and actual material consumed were:

Direct Material	Quantity (tonne)	Price per kg
A	5.00	₹0.85
B	2.90	₹ 0.60
C	4.40	₹ 0.45

Actual production for December was 6,20,000 tiles.

[*Ans.* MCV ₹220 (A), MPV ₹175 (F), MMV ₹55 (F), MYV ₹450 (A)]

4. From the following calculate:
(a) Price variance (b) Usage variance
(c) Mix variance (d) Revised usage variance

Material	Standard			Actual		
	Qty.	Rate	Amt.	Qty.	Rate	Amt.
A	10	2	20	5	3	15
B	20	3	60	10	6	60
C	20	6	120	15	5	75

[*Ans.* MCV ₹20 (A), MUV ₹70 (F), MMV ₹10 (A), MRUV ₹80 (F)]

5. ABC Corp. is producing a standard mix by using 60 kg of material X and 40 kg of material Y. The standard loss of production is 30%. The standard price of X is ₹5 per kg and that of Y. ₹10 per kg. The actual mixture and yield were as follows: X 80 kg @ ₹4.50 per kg, Y 70 kg @ ₹8 per kg, Actual yield is 115 kg.

[*Ans.* MCV ₹230 (F), MPV ₹180 (F): MUV ₹ (F), MMV ₹50 (A): MYV ₹100 (F)]

6. The standard material cost to produce one tonne of chemical X is:
300 kg of material A @ ₹ 10 per kg
400 kg of material B @ ₹ 5 per kg
500 kg of material C @ ₹ 6 per kg
During a period, 100 tonnes of chemical X were produced from the usage of:
35 tonnes of material A at a cost of ₹9000 per tonne
42 tonnes of material B at a cost of ₹6000 per tonne
53 tonnes of material C at a cost of ₹7000 per tonne
Required: Calculate all material cost variances.

[*Ans.* MCV ₹1,38,000 (A), MPV ₹60,000 (A), MUV ₹78,000 (A), MMV ₹11,333 (A) MYV ₹66,667 (A)]

7. From the following data, calculate material mix variance

Material	Standard quantity	Actual quantity	Price per unit
X	50	45	14
Y	40	35	12
Z	30	40	11

Due to shortage of X, it was decided to reduce its consumption by 10 and increase the consumption of Y and Z by 6 and 4 respectively.

[*Ans.* MMV ₹4 (A)]

[**Hint.** Adjust standard quantities]

8. Rang Chemical Ltd. manufactures PXE by mixing three raw materials. For each batch of 100 kg of PXE 125 kg of raw material are used. In much 60 batches are prepared to produce an output of 5600 kg of PXE. The standard and actual particulars for June are as follows:

Raw Material	Standard		Actual		Quantity of raw material
	Mix%	Price per kg ₹	Mix% ₹	Price per kg purchased kg	
A	50	29	60	21	5000
B	30	10	20	8	12000
C	20	5	20	6	12000

Required: Calculate all material variances

[*Ans.* (a) MCV ₹17,500 (A), MPV ₹3000 (A),
MUV ₹14,500 (A), MMV ₹7000 (A)]

9. A manufacturing concern which has adopted standard costing furnishes the following information

Standards

Material for 70 kg finished products	100 kg
Price of material	₹2 per kg

Actual

Output	210000 kg
Material used	280000 kg
Cost of materials	₹5,04,000

[*Ans.* MUV ₹40,000 (F), MPV ₹56,0000 (F), MCV ₹96,000 (F)]

10. Cool Ltd established the following Standard Mix for producing 9 gallon product 'A'.

	₹
5 gallons of material X at ₹7 per gallon	35
3 gallons of material Y at ₹5 per gallon	15
9 gallons of material Z at ₹2 per gallon	4
	₹54

A standard loss of 10% of input is expected to occur. Actual input was as under:
58,000 gallons of material X at a cost of ₹7.00 per gallon
98,000 gallons of material Y at a cost of ₹5.30 per gallon
19,000 gallons of material Z at a cost of ₹2.30 per gallon
Actual output for a period was 92,700 gallons of product A.
Required: Compute all the material cost variances

[***Ans.*** MMV ₹9000 (A), MYV ₹16,200 (F)]

11. The standard cost of a chemical mixture is as follows:
40% material A at 20 per kg
60% material B at 30 per kg
A standard loss of 10% of input is expected in production. The cost records for a period showed the following usage:
90 kg material A at a cost of ₹18 per kg
110 kg material B at a cost of ₹34 per kg
The quantity produced was 182 kg of good product.
Required: Calculate all material cost variances.

[***Ans.*** MCV ₹102.29 (A), MPV ₹260 (A), MUV ₹157.78 (F), MMV ₹100 (F); MYV ₹57.78]

12. 80 kg of material A at a standard price of ₹2 per kg and 40 kg of material B at a standard price of ₹5 per kg were to be used to manufacture 100 kg of a chemical.
During a month, 70 kg of material A priced at ₹2.10 per kg, and 50 kg of material B priced at ₹4.50 per kg were actually used and the output of the chemical was 102 kg.
Required: Calculate all material cost variances.

[***Ans.*** MCV ₹4.80 (A), MPV ₹18 (F), MMV ₹30 (A) MYVP ₹7.20 (F)]

13. The standard cost of a certain chemical mixture 'AB' is :
40% material A at ₹400 per kg
60% material B at ₹600 per kg
A standard loss of 10% is anticipated in production:
The following particulars are available for the month of December.
180 kg of material A has been used at ₹360 per kg
220 kg of material B has been used at ₹680 per kg
The actual production of 'AB' is 369 kg.
Required: Calculate all material variances.

[***Ans.*** (a) MCV ₹1200 (b), MPV ₹10,400 (A), (c) MUV ₹9200 (F), MMV ₹4000 (F); MYV ₹52.00 (F)]

14. From the following particulars, compute:
(a) Material cost variance (b) Material price variance (c) Material usage variance
Quantity of material purchased

Value of material purchased	3000 units
Standard quantity of material required per tonne of output 30 units	₹9000
Standard price of material	₹2.50 per unit
Opening stock of material	Nil
Closing stock of material	500 units
Output during the period	80 tonnes

[*Ans.* MCV ₹1500 (A), MPV ₹1250 (A), MUV ₹250 (A)]

15. A group of 10 skilled and 20 unskilled workers were expected to produce 400 hours of Chemical BXT in an 8-hour day. The standard hourly wage rate was fixed at ₹25 and ₹15 respectively.

Actually, a group of 15 skilled and 10 unskilled workers was deployed and paid for 8-hour day at an hourly wage rate of ₹22 and ₹18 respectively. Two hours were wasted for the entire group due to power failure and only 300 hours of BXT was produced. Your are required to compute:

(i) Labour cost variances; (ii) Labour rate variances; (iii) Idle time variances; (iv) Labour usage variances; (v) Labour mix variances (vi) Labour yield variances.

[*Ans.* LCV ₹780 (A), LRV ₹120 (F); ITV ₹1050 (A); LUV ₹900 (A), LMV ₹400 (A); LYV ₹550 (F)]

16. The following was the composition of the gang of workers in a factory during a particular month, in one of the production departments. The standard composition of workers and wage rate per hour were as below:

Skilled : Two workers at a standard rate of ₹20 per hour each

Semi-skilled : Four workers at a standard rate of ₹12 per each.

Unskilled : Four workers at a standard rate of ₹8 per hour each.

The standard output of the gang was four units per hour of the product. During the month in question, however, the actual composition of the gang and hourly rates paid were as under:

Type of Worker	No. of Workers	Wage rate paid per worker per hour engaged
Skill	2	20
Semi-skilled	3	14
Unskilled	5	10

The gang was engaged for 200 hours during the month, which included 12 hours when no production was possible, due to machine breakdown. 810 units of the product were recorded as output of the gang during the month.

You are required : (a) to compute the standard unit labour cost of the product; (b) to compute the total variance in labour cost during the month; and (c) analyse the variances in (b) above in sub-variances and reconcile.

[*Ans.* LC ₹2100 (A); LRV ₹3200 (A); LEV ₹1100 (F); ITV ₹1440 (A); LYV ₹1740 (F)]

17. A firm gives you the following data:
Standard time per unit 2.5 hours
Actual hours worked 2000 hours
Standard rate of pay ₹2 per hour
25% of the actual hours has been lost as idle time.
Actual output 1000 units
Actual wages ₹4500
Required : Calculate (a) labour rate variance, (b) revised efficiency variance, (c) idle time variance.

[***Ans.*** (a) ₹500 (A), (b) ₹2000 (A), (c) ₹1000 (A)]

18. Standard hours for manufacturing two products M and N are 15 hours per unit and 20 hours per unit respectively. Both products require identical kind of labour and the standard wage rate per hour is ₹5 in a year 10,000 units of M and 15,000 units of N were manufactured. The total of labour hours actually worked were 4,50,500 and the actual wage bill came to ₹23,00,000. This included 1200 hours paid for @ ₹7 per hour and 9400 hours paid for @ ₹7.50 per hour, the balance has been paid at ₹5 per hour. You are required to compute the labour variance.

[***Ans.*** LCV ₹50,000 (A), LEV ₹2500 (A), LRV ₹47,500 (A)]

19. 100 skilled workmen, 40 semi-skilled workmen and 60 unskilled workmen were to work to get a contract job completed within 30 weeks. The standard weekly wages were ₹60, ₹36 and ₹24 respectively. The job was actually completed in 32 weeks by 80 skilled, 50 semi-skilled and 70 unskilled workmen were paid ₹65, ₹40 and ₹20 respectively as wages. Calculate the various labour variance.

[***Ans.*** LCV ₹8800 (A), LRV ₹10,240 (A), LEV ₹1440 (F), LMV ₹19,200 (F), LYV ₹17,760 (A)]

20. The standard labour composition and the actual labour composition engaged during the month are given below:

	Skilled	Semi-skilled	Unskilled
(a) Standard number of workers in a group	30	10	10
(b) Standard wage rate (₹ per hour)	5	3	2
(c) Actual number of workers employed during the month in the group	24	15	12
(d) Actual wage rate per hour (₹)	6	2.5	2

During the month of 200 working hours, the group produced 9600 standard hours of work.

Required: Calculate Wage rate variance, Labour (revised) efficiency, Labour mix variance and Total labour cost variance.

[***Ans.*** Wage rate variance ₹3300 (A); Labour efficiency (revised) variance ₹2400 (A); Labour mix variance ₹3000 (F); Total labour cost variance ₹2700 (A)]

21. A job is scheduled to be completed in 30 weeks with a labour employment of 100 skilled operatives ₹400 semi-skilled operatives and 60 unskilled operatives. The standard weekly wage of each type of operatives are skilled ₹60, 1 semi-skilled ₹36 and unskilled ₹24. The work is actually completed in 32 weeks with a labour force of 80 skilled, 50 semi-skilled and 70 unskilled operatives and the actual weekly wage rates average ₹65 for skilled, ₹40 for semi-skilled and ₹20 for unskilled labour. Analysis the variance in the labour cost due to various reasons.

[*Ans.* LCV ₹8800 (A), LRV ₹10,240 (A), LEV ₹1440 (F), LMV ₹19,200 (F), LREV ₹17,760 (A)]

22. X Ltd. manufacture a particular product, the standard direct labour cost of which is ₹120 per unit whose manufacture involves the following:

Grade of workers	Hours	Rate ₹	Amount ₹
A	30	2	60
B	20	3	60
	50		120

During a period, 100 units of the product were produced, the actual labour cost of which was as follows:

Grade of workers	Hours	Rate ₹	Amount ₹
A	3200	1.50	4800
B	1900	4.00	7600
	5100		12,400

Required: Calculate:

(a) Labour cost variance
(b) Labour rate variance
(c) Labour efficiency variance
(d) Labour mix variance
(e) Labour revised efficiency variance.

[*Ans.* ₹LCV ₹400 (A), LRV ₹300 (A), LEV ₹100 (A), LMV ₹140 (F); LREV ₹240 (A)]

23. A company has a normal capacity of 120 machines, working 8 hours per day of 25 days in a month. The fixed overheads are budgeted at ₹1,44,000 per month. The standard time required to manufacture one unit of product is 4 hours.

In April, the company worked 24 hours of 840 machine hours per day and produced 5305 units of output. The actual fixed overheads were 1,42,000.

Required: Compute all fixed overhead variances.

[*Ans.* FOCV ₹14,680 (A), FOEV ₹2000 (F), FOV ₹16,680 (A), FOEV ₹63,600 (F), FOCV ₹17,280 (A), FOCV ₹5760 (A)]

24. X Ltd. has furnished you the following data:

	Budget	*Actual (July)*
Production in units	20,000	22,000
Fixed overheads	₹30,000	31,000
No. of working days	25	27

Budgeted fixed overhead rate is ₹1 per hour in July, the actual hours worked were 31,500.

[*Ans.* FOCV ₹2000 (F), FOEV ₹1000 (A), FOVV ₹3000 (F), FOCV ₹900 (A), FOEV ₹1500 (F), FOCV ₹2400 (F)]

25. A company operates a standard costing system and showed the following data for the month of March:

	Actual	*Budgeted*
No. of working days	22	20
Man-hours	4300	4000
Overhead rate per hour	–	₹0.50
Hours per unit of output	–	10
Fixed overhead Incurred	₹1800	–
No. of units produced	425	–

Required: Calculate (a) Overhead cost variance, (b) Budgeted variance, (c) Volume variance, (d) Capacity variance, (e) Calendar variance, (f) Efficiency variance.

[*Ans.* OCV ₹325 (F), Budget V ₹200 (F), FOVV ₹150 (F), FOCV ₹50 (A), FOCV ₹200 (F), ROEV ₹25 (A)]

26. Processing of a plant, the following data are submitted for the week ending 31-3-2021.

Standard output for 40 hours per week	1400 units
Budgeted fixed overhead	₹1400
Actual output	1200 units
Actual hours worked	32
Actual fixed overhead	₹1500

Required : Calculate overhead variances.

[*Ans.* FOCV ₹300 (A), FOEV ₹100 (A), FOVV ₹200 (A), FOEV ₹80 (F), FOCV ₹280 (A)]

CASE STUDIES

1. Himalayan Drugs Ltd., a manufacturer of health-care equipment, has been in business for 15 years. Last year, in an effort to better control the costs of their products, the management accountant implemented a standard cost system. Reports are issued monthly for tracking performance, and any negative variances are further investigated.

The production manager complained that the standards are unrealistic, stifle motivation by concentrating only on negative variances, and are out of date too quickly. He noted that his recent switch to a new equipment for a wheelchair has resulted in higher material costs but decreased labour times. The net result was no increase in the total cost of producing the wheelchair. The monthly reports continue to show a negative material variance and a positive labour variance, despite the fact that there are indications that the workers are slowing down.

(a) Describe several ways that a standard cost system strengthens the management in cost control.

(b) Describe at least two reasons why a standard cost system may negatively impact the motivation of production employees.

2. Indian Motors Ltd. has been experiencing declining profit margins and has been looking for ways to increase operating income. It cannot raise selling prices for fear of losing business to its competitors. It must either cut costs or improve productivity. The company uses a standard cost system to evaluate the performance of the assembly department. All negative variances at the end of the month are investigated. The assembly department rarely completes the operations in less time than the standard allows (which would result in a positive variance). Most months, the variance is zero or slightly negative. Reasoning that the application of lower standard costs to the products manufactured will result in improved profit margins, the production manager had recommended that all standard times for assembly operations be drastically reduced. The production manager has informed the assembly personnel that he expects them to meet these new standards.

   Will the lowering of the standard costs (by reducing the time of the assembly operations) result in improved profit margins and increased productivity?

3. Crunchy Chips India (CCI) Ltd., is a specially frozen-food processor located in Punjab, India. Since it founding in 1992, CCI has enjoyed a loyal clientele that is willing to pay premium prices for the high-quality frozen food it prepares from specialised recipes. In the last two years, the company has experienced rapid sales growth in its operating region and had many enquiries about supplying its products on a national basis. To meet this growth, CCI expanded its processing capabilities which resulted in increased production and distribution costs. Furthermore, CCI has been encountering pricing pressures from competitors outside its normal marketing region.

   Because CCI desires to continue its expansion, Raghvendra, Chief Executive Officer, has engaged a consulting firm to assist CCI in determining its best course of action. The consulting firm recommended instituting a standard costing system that would also facilitate a flexible budgeting system to better accommodate the changes in demand that can be expected when serving an expanding market area. Raghvendra met with his management team and explained the consulting firm's recommendations. Raghvendra then assigned the task of establishing standard costs to his management team. After discussing the situation with the respective staffs, the management team met to review the matter.

   Rakesh, purchasing manager, advised that meeting expanded production would necessitate obtaining basic food supplies from other than CCI's traditional sources. This would entail increased raw material and other costs and might result in lower quality supplies. Consequently, these increased costs would need to be made up by the processing department if current costs are to be maintained or reduced.

Ramesh, processing manager, countered that the need to accelerate processing cycles to increase production, coupled with the possibility of receiving lower grade supplies, could be expected to result in a slip in quality and a greater product rejection rate. Under these circumstances, per unit labour utilisation could not be maintained or reduced and forecasting future unit labour content would become very difficult.

Rajiv, production engineer, advised that if equipment is not properly maintained and thoroughly cleaned at prescribed daily intervals, the quality and unique taste of the frozen-food products would probably be affected.

Johnson, Vice-President of sales, stated that if quality could not be maintained, CCI could not expect to increase sales to the levels projected.

When Raghvendra was apprised of the problems encountered by his management team, he advised them that if agreement could not be reached on the appropriate standards, he would arrange to have them set by the consulting firm and everyone would have to live with the results.

Required:

(1) List the major advantages of using a standard costing system.

(2) Identify those who should participate in setting standards, and describe the benefits of their participation in the standard setting process.

(3) What could be the consequences if Raghvendra, Chief Executive Officer, has the standards set by an outside consulting firm?

4. Vikas Mohan is production manager of the Equipment Division of BHEL Ltd. Equipment has limited contact with outside customers and no sales staff. Most of its customers are other divisions of BHEL. All sales and purchases with outside customers are handled by other corporate divisions. Therefore, Equipment is treated as a cost centre for reporting and evaluation purposes rather than as a revenue or profit centre.

Vikas perceives accounting as an historical number generating process that provides little useful information for conducting his job. Consequently, the entire accounting process is regarded as a negative motivational device that does not reflect how hard or how effectively he works as a production manager. Vikas tried to discus these perceptions and concerns with Manish, the controller for the Equipment Division. Vikas told Manish, "I think the cost report is misleading. I know I've had better production over a number of operating periods, but the cost report still says I have excessive costs. Look I'm not an accountant, I'm a production manager. I know how to get a good quality product out. Over a number of years, I've even cut the raw materials used to do it. But the cost report doesn't show any of this. Basically, it's always negative, no matter what I do. There's no way you can win with accounting or the people at corporate headquarters who use those reports".

Manish gave Vikas little consolation. "The accounting system and the cost reports generated by headquarters," Manish stated, "are just part of the corporate game and almost impossible for an individual to change. Although, these accounting reports are pretty much the basis for evaluating the efficiency of your division and the means corporate management uses to determine whether you have done the job they want, you shouldn't worry too much. You haven't been fired yet! Besides these cost reports have been used by BHEL for the last twenty-five years".

Vikas received (from talking to the production manager of the Zinc Division) that most of what Manish said was probably true. However, some minor cost reporting changes for zinc had been agreed to by corporate headquarters. Vikas also knew from the trade grapevine that the turnover of production managers was considered high at BHEL, even though relatively few were fired. Most seemed to end up quitting, usually in disgust, because of beliefs that they were not being evaluated fairly. Typical comments of production managers who have left BHEL are:

- "Corporate headquarters doesn't really listen to us. All they consider are those misleading cost reports. They don't want them changed, and they don't want any supplemental information".
- "The accountants may be quick with numbers, but they don't know anything about production. As it was, I either had to ignore the cost reports entirely or pretend they are important even though they didn't tell how good a job I had done. No matter what they say, about not firing people, negative reports mean negative evaluations. I'm better off working for another company".

A recent copy of the cost report prepared by corporate headquarters for the Equipment Division is shown below. Vikas does not like this report because he believes it fails to properly reflect the division's operations, thereby resulting in an unfair evaluation of performance.

EQUIPMENT DIVISION

Cost Report
For the month of April 2019

	Original Budget (₹)	Actual Cost (₹)	Excess Cost (₹)
Aluminium	4,00,000	4,37,000	37,000
Labour	5,60,000	50,40,000	
Overhead	1,00,000	1,34,000	34,000
Total	10,60,000	11,11,000	71,000

Required:

(a) Comment on Vikas' perceptions of Manish (the controller); corporate headquarters; the cost report; and himself as a production manager. Discuss how his perceptions affect his behaviour and probable performance as a production manager and employee of BHEL.

(b) Identify and explain three changes that could be made in the cost information presented to the production managers that would make the information more meaningful and less threatening to them.

CHAPTER

6 Responsibility Accounting and Transfer Pricing

MEANING

Responsibility accounting is an accounting system under which the manager is delegated decision-making authority and responsibility for each activity within a specific department or division of an organisation.

According to Charles T. Horngreen "Responsibility accounting is a system of accounting that recognises various responsibility centres throughout the organisation and reflects the plan and actions of each of these centres by assigning particular revenues and costs to the one having the pertinent responsibility. It is also called profitability accounting and activity accounting".

ESSENTIALS OF RESPONSIBILITY ACCOUNTING

Responsibility accounting is a responsibility set-up for cost control purposes. It is an approach to cost control that relies on the performance of persons responsible for the implementation of decisions. It is an accounting system designed to control costs by relating executives responsible for their incurrence. Tied closely to the control over costs, this concept emphasises "personalisation of costs by putting questions as to where the cost was incurred and who was responsible for it. The technique seeks to control costs at their starting point by fixing responsibility. Broadly speaking, responsibility accounting is designing the accounting system according to answerability of the managers. The accumulation, classification, measurement and reporting of financial data is so arranged that it promotes the fixing of precise responsibility on the persons within the managerial hierarchy. Horngreh says "Responsibility accounting is a system which is tailored to an organisation so that costs are accumulated and reported by levels of responsibility within the organisation. That is, it focuses attention on people, not things, shifts emphasis from product costing to responsibility accounting. The obvious hypothesis is that since all activities in an enterprise and all items of income, operating costs, other expenses and capital expenditures are the responsibility of some manager, none should be left unassigned. The concept is structured around functional activities for which specific individuals are responsible. One can, therefore, dare say that responsibility accounting as the process of matching the costs and benefits with the unit whose activities led to their achievement.

Insofar as accounting is a financial information system, responsibility accounting could be interpreted as an information system resting with the theory that costs and revenues should be assigned to the manager most responsible for making decisions about them. Higgins makes the point clear when he writes. "In effect, the system personalises the accounting statement by saying, 'Joe, this is what you originally budgeted and this is how you performed for the period with actual operations as compared against you? budget" By definition it is a system of accounting which is tailored to an organisation so that costs are accumulated and reported by levels of responsibility within the organisation. Each supervisory area in the organisation is charged only with cost for which it is responsibility and over which it has control. Thus, the focal point of responsibility accounting is that it looks at each major category of expense and attempts to establish relationship between specific actions and the incurring of costs. Naturally, it extends beyond the normal responsibility and authority of financial management. While a cost accounting system assigns costs primarily for product costing purposes, the main thrust of responsibility accounting is the control of costs at different echelons of management. Within his own area of responsibility; each manager is supreme such that he could make decisions, spend money, investigate the causes of divergence and take whatever corrective action seemed necessary. In view of its reliance on controllability of costs, which commonly are marginal costs, the system is also called "attributable costing", "combined marginal/ absorption costing", "partial absorption costing", "hybrid direct costing", and by way of commendation as "productivity-oriented accounting".

The aforesaid techniques of responsibility accounting apply to all enterprises–big and small, centralised or decentralised, business, non-profit, or governmental. But the system will differ from organisation to organisation because no two organisations can be expected to delegate responsibilities for decision-implementation the same way. The "law of situation" will dictate how the principles should be implemented.

The principles governing the responsibility accounting system may be explained as under:

(1) **Costs should be Traced Directly to the Department**

An example would indicate the point clear. Two production departments may incur transportation costs jointly, but the manager of one production department may have the power to decide about incurrence of the cost. Here, the burden to be shared by the other production department in respect of transportation costs may be unfair. A suitable mechanism of transfer pricing should be evolved so as to charge the other production department, reasonably treating it as an external customer.

(2) **Variances from Budget and Comparison between Budget and Actual Results must be Grounded Firmly in a Discernibly Uniform and Clearly Comparable System of Budgeting and Reporting.**

The responsibility for adhering to standards and the responsibility for any deviations from those standards should also be clearly distinguished. There should be uniformity in preparation and presentation of budgetary and actual data for the sake of comparison.

(3) A clear-cut guideline as to the declaration of responsibility is a prerequisite, otherwise one departmental manager may shrug off the responsibility by passing it over to the other. Confusion as to the shouldering of the responsibility cannot lead in any decisive action by the management.

TECHNIQUES AND PREREQUISITES OF RESPONSIBILITY ACCOUNTING

So many varied techniques have begun to be practised now—under the banner of responsibility accounting that really it has become synonymous with management accounting. It ties accounting, reporting and budgeting to management organisation and responsibilities. The programme engulfs all operating management for which the accounting, cost or budget divisions provide technical assistance. However, there are some points of principles or fundamental aspects of responsibility accounting which are often called its techniques or phases. The four concepts which are basic to the initiation and maintenance of a responsibility accounting system are described below.

1. Once the responsibility centres of a business have been established, the costs and revenues under the control of each responsibility centre must be identified. Only those costs and revenues over which the manager has a definite control can be used in setting standards for his performance. Responsibility accounting has an appeal because it specifies a boundary of operations and distinguishes between controllable and uncontrollable costs. Thus, instead of classifying cost by functions–manufacturing, selling and administrative or as product and period costs, the viewpoint of division here is controllability. The attention is direct towards the individual or the group, and the basic question is who spent the money rather than what the money was spent on. The question 'who did it' is more important than what it was expended upon. A cost is deemed controllable if the head of the responsibility centre under consideration possesses the power to change it by his actions. He exerts spending authority over it such that he can affect (decrease, and possibly, increase) the amount thereof. The manager of a machinery department does influence by his action indirect labour and manufacturing supplies used in his department, but not also salary or the salary of higher executives. Generally, variable costs are charged to a department which are controllable by its manager. In fact, responsibility accounting is married with the technique of direct costing which should better be referred to as variable costing. Such costs as direct materials and direct labour may be easiest to identify as controllable costs. Others such as sales commission and salaries, office costs, and certain elements of manufacturing overhead may also be controllable by the manager. On the other hand, fixed expenses are not controllable, at least, in the short run, by the departmental manager and price, not charged to the responsibility centre. In this connection, the following guidelines should be noted which are available in deciding the appropriate costs to be charged to a person:

(a) Even if the person cannot significantly influence the amount of cost through his own direct action, he may be charged with those elements with which the management desires him to be concerned, so that he will help to influence those who are responsible.

(b) If the person has authority over both the acquisition and the use of the services, he should be charged with the cost of such services. That is, he should have both the acquisition rights and the use rights over the cost.

(c) If the person can significantly influence the amount of cost through his own action, he may be charged with such costs.

2. Control is centred on performance reports, called here responsibility reports, prepared for each responsibility unit. Performance reports constitute the control mechanism, not because they help rectify past mistakes, but because they spur managerial action that prevents future mistakes. The report to each unit shows its expenses, income and capital expenditures in the headings appearing in the account classification, statistics such as volume of work, costs per unit and perhaps man-hour data and number of employees. The questions to be resolved for a report are how often it is to be made, the amount of detail to be presented and the format. In general terms, at successively higher levels in the organisational chain, less and less time is devoted to control and more and more to planning.

Performance reports are feedback reports to assure the follow-through and therewith the ultimate success of the programme. These are addressed to the particular manager who delegated the responsibility. Reports should be simple, attractive and couched in terms understood by the recipients. Presentation can be in the form of statements/graphs, charts or tables. If there is machine-processing, it may force a uniform format for reports turned out in volume. These feedback reports show only the budgeted amount and the variance. This places focus on the variances and management by exception which means that the executive's attention is concentrated on the important deviations from budgeted items. In this way, managers do not waste time on those parts of the reports that reflect the smoothly running phases of performance from the planned or prior performance that is being used as the reference point. Each manager should be informed of deviations within his own area of responsibility so that he can look into the causes and take appropriate action. In essence, a communication system which is designed to aid an enterprise in achieving its cost and profit goals is what is called responsibility accounting. The fact of the matter is that control reports are always comparative, that is, they embody or facilitate comparisons between observed performance and some reference point. In some cases, the comparison may be with a prior time period, in others, the current budgetary plan provides the point of reference. About the extent of details, the guideline is that the factors and variables having a significant impact on decision must be incorporated. But there should be no information overload; too much information cannot be used, it may rather confuse the manager.

3. Flexible Budgeting. Budgeting is the key technique, the cornerstone of cost control procedures. If pre-planning is the heart of the control providing an opportunity for corrective, action, budget is its principal instrument. Fitted to various areas of responsibility, operating budgets express the plans in figures. It is through budgets that responsibility for implementing the decisions made at each level of management is communicated. However, effective responsibility accounting may require more sophisticated budgeting than was previously used. Each manager heading a responsibility centre should prepare or, at least, participate in preparing his budget since he will be held accountable for achieving it. Without a good budget, there is no point in trying to use it as a yardstick. The budget must be based on carefully set objectives and operating plans, not as someone aptly put it, on past history eloquently defended. But it is important that individual's budget is considered an integral part of the overall company budget.

Fixed budgets, flexible budgets and profit planning can all be incorporated into an overall system of responsibility accounting. Fixed budgets offer a medium for overall planning and expression of objectives, and sometimes responsibility reports include comparisons only with fixed budgets. Where work, fixed budget can positively be misleading. It is fallacious to compare results at one activity level with a budget predicted on another level. Flexible budgeting permits comparison of actual costs with budgeted costs that have been geared to changes in production volume.

4. Establishing Responsibility Centres. Responsibility accounting is founded upon responsibility centres. Fixing responsibility for control requires the establishment of definite lines of authority. The organisation chart presents the structure, and following these lines of authority, allows the assignment of cost control responsibility to specific individuals. It is imperative, therefore, that clear-cut lines of authority are drawn by establishing responsibility centres. Responsibility centres represent the sphere of authority or points where decisions have to be implemented. These are generally operating departments or smaller subdivisions used solely for costing. The subdivisions are appropriate for an operating department containing basically different kinds of subsections, some using expensive machinery and other not. This naturally requires an organisational structure where no doubt responsibility for deciding has been decentralised but it has also been specifically fixed for each organisational unit. In fact, an accounting system should parallel the organisation and provide financial and statistical data to evaluate actual results of each supervisor responsible for a function. Costs should be recorded and traced to the individual in the organisation who shoulders primary decision responsibility for an item. The organisational structure should clearly spell out the duties, authority and responsibilities of various managers, foremen, supervisors, departmental and divisional managers, vice-presidents, etc. Hence, before installing a system of responsibility accounting, first an attempt is made to determine the decision points within an organisation, and then the extent and scope of responsibility for each decision point is defined. This responsibility may be limited as one person may be responsible for the labour used in manufacturing a set of equipment in a single department. It may be quite extensive as in the case of a divisional manager who may be responsible for achieving a certain level of profit consistent with the investment under his control.

Preliminaries of Responsibility Accounting

Conceptually, it is an ideal system to ensure cost control, but putting it into practice is difficult. The principal preliminaries are:

(1) The effectiveness of responsibility accounting is determined by how successfully costs can be segregated into controllable and non-controllable categories at each level of management. A manager's performance versus budget can best be measured by evalu-

ating those costs (and revenues) over which he or she has some control. This controllable-uncontrollable dichotomy is crucial for the success of responsibility accounting. It is important, therefore, that costs are segregated for each level, though the fact remains that all costs are controllable at some level. Rent expense, for example, may not be control help at the level of a supervisor but it is so at the level of the plant manager.

(2) A fragile balance must be struck between careful delineation of responsibility on the one hand, and a too rigid separation of responsibility, on the other. Buck passing is a pervasive tendency that is supposedly minimised when responsibility is fixed unequivocally. But often the motivation impact boomerangs. Managers often wear blinders and concentrate more than ever on their individual worlds. Family cooperation is replaced by intracompany competition.

(3) Control of production an of costs is a matter of timing. The effectiveness of control is often in direct proportion to the speed with which a change is recommenced after an unsatisfactory condition is discovered. The performance reports are less effective if they are not available to management immediately after the event in order to improve similar future events. A month and generally even in a week, is to long a period for many off-standard "conditions to remain unchecked and uncorrected. The time interval may prevent positive identification of employees who are responsible for the unsatisfactory work. In addition, there may be many hours and days during which there has been waste and inefficiency in the use of materials and labour representing total losses of some magnitude before corrective measures are taken. It is for this reason that in concerns with enlightened management, daily tabulations of operating results are recorded on blackboards and charts by shifts, cost centres and departments so that employees are informed of their production as contrasted with standards. Daily and weekly accumulation of the results are equal to or better than standards are rewarded through recognition or prizes or bonuses.

(4) Ideally, the organisation itself and its processes must be thoroughly appraised, understood, and altered if necessary, before a system is constructed. That is, the design of a system and the design of an organisational structure are, really inseparable and interdependent. The point is that the most streamlined system is not a substitute for basic organisational ills or management ineptitude. On a practical level, there may be a powerful temptation to separate the design of the system from the design of organisational processes by assuming that the organisational structure is given and therefore not subject to change.

Objectives

The objectives of responsibility accounting are as following:

1. **Measurement of the contribution of a division.** The performance of a responsibility centre can be measured in terms of its efficiency (relationship of inputs to outputs) and effectiveness (relationship between output and the goals of the organisation). A responsibility centre should be both efficient and effective.

2. **Performance evaluation of the individual.** The responsibility accounting is used to measure the performance of the individuals working in an enterprise. This technique allows to measure the performance of an individual along with the performance of the division where he works. In many cases, a division might not have made a satisfactory contribution to the goals of the organisation, but the manager may be judged to have discharged his responsibilities well. In case of a global slowdown, may be the performance of the division has deteriorated but the manager may be rated as efficient in performing his duties by minimising the impact of slow down on the profits of the enterprise.
3. **Goal Congruence.** Divisional performance measurement should be designed in such a way that it motivates the people to achieve their individual goals though the achievement of the organisational goals. This goal congruence may be made possible by introducing a system of incentives.

Responsibility Centres

Responsibility accounting mainly focuses on the responsibility centres. A responsibility centre is a subunit of an organisation which may be an individual or a segment of the organisation for which the performance is measured. The responsibility centre can be a big department like manufacturing department or a small unit like accounts department of the enterprise. The important criteria for creating a responsibility centre is that the unit of an organisation should be separable and identifiable for operating purposes and its performance should be measurable. The manager of each division is responsible only for those activities of that responsibility centre which are under his influence.

For the purpose of measuring the financial performance, the divisions of a firm may be classified according to the type of financial data used in the measurement of performance. Accordingly, the responsibility centres may be classified into: (1) revenue centre, (2) cost centre, (3) profit centre, and (4) investment centre.

Revenue Centre

A revenue centre is a segment of the organisation, which is primarily responsible for the revenue generation. A revenue centre manager has no control over the costs, investment in assets, etc. The performance of a revenue centre is measured by comparing the actual revenue with the budgeted revenue.

Cost/Expense Centre

A cost centre is the particular segment of the organisation, which has been assigned the task of incurring and controlling the costs only. This department does not generate any revenues and therefore, the performance of such a centre is measured in terms of costs incurred by the division. The cost centre managers are responsible only for the costs that are controllable by them. The actual cost incurred is compared with the costs planned to be incurred and the variation in cost is taken as an indicator of efficiency of the divisional manager.

However, the cost of operating the division, fixed or variable, should be directly traceable to it. A manager is not responsible for costs common to several divisions and allocated among them on some arbitrary basis. These costs are not controllable by the manager and therefore, he cannot be held responsible for its occurrence.

These type of responsibility centres are useful for performance evaluation in the cases where (a) the output cannot be measured reliably in monetary term (legal department, accounting department, public relations department) and (b) the responsibility of the manager is to produce the stated quantity of output at the lowest feasible cost.

Profit Centre

A profit centre is a segment of the organisation whose manager is responsible for both revenues and costs. In a profit centre, the manager has the authority and the responsibility to make the decisions that affect both costs and revenues (and thus profit) for the division.

The performance of the manager is evaluated by comparing the expected profits with the actual profits. This criteria of performance measurement is significant because—

1. profit is a combined measure of both efficiency and effectiveness; and
2. it motivates the workers to take the decisions about input and output to maximise the profits.

Although the profit centre basis is superior to the expense centre as a basis of divisional performance measurement, this approach suffers from a few operational difficulties.

1. It cannot be used for all responsibility centres.
2. Measurement of expenses is not always precisely possible.
3. Problem of transfer pricing : In certain organisations, the profit centres may be selling the products within the company to other divisions. The price to be charged for the products transferred to the other departments within the organisation creates the problem in the revenue measurement.

Investment Centre

One of the limitations of profit centre is that it does not consider the amount of investments required to generate the profits. The measurement of performance in an investment centre is based on the relationship between profits and the amount of assets employed in generating those profits. There are two ways to measure the financial performance of an investment:

(a) Return on investment
(b) Residual income.

(a) Return on Investment (ROI)

The performance of a division is measured in terms of actual ROI achieved in relation to the expected ROI. ROI measures profit in relation to the investments required to generate those profits.

$$\text{ROI} = \frac{\text{Divisional profit}}{\text{Divisional investment}} \times 100$$

The earning power of the division depends on the combination of two factors: (1) profitability on sales as reflected in the net profit margin and (2) the profitability of investment, which is revealed by the investment turnover. The term investment may refer to total assets, capital employed or shareholders equity.

$$\text{Earning power} = \text{Net profit margin} \times \text{Investment turnover}$$

$$= \frac{\text{Net profit}}{\text{Sales}} \times \frac{\text{Sales}}{\text{Total assets}}$$

An organisation can improve the return on investment either by the improving the net profit margin or by increasing the turnover with the same amount of investment. It implies that the performance of a firm/segment can be improved either by increasing the profit margin per rupee of sales or by generating more sales volume per rupee of investment. Which method is selected to improve the profits depends on the position of the firm in the industry. In case of severe competition in the market when margins are difficult to increase, the better utilisation of assets by creating more volume of sales is the right strategy. ROI criteria present the overall picture of the performance of the segment and also enable the firm to identify the factors which have a bearing on the profitability.

This criterion of performance measurement was first used by Du Pont Company in U.S.A. This can be explained with the help of following example.

Assume there are two divisions, A and B, each having total assets amounting to ₹ 2,00,000 and average net profit of 10%, i.e., ₹ 10,000 each. Division A has sales of ₹ 2,00,000 whereas the sales of the division B aggregate ₹ 20,00,000. The earning power of the two firms may be computed as:

	Department A	*Department B*
Net sales	₹ 2,00,000	₹ 20,00,000
Net profit	₹ 20,000	₹ 20,000
Total assets	2,00,000	2,00,000
N.P. ratio (1)	10%	1%
Investment turnover (2)	1 times	10 times
ROI (1) × (2)	10%	10%

It is clear from the above table that earning power of the two departments is identical. While the department A has a higher profit margin, the department B has higher investment turnover. Both the departments may improve their performance by generating more sales per rupee of investment or by increasing the profit margin per rupee of sales.

The two components of ROI, namely, the profit margin and investment turnover individually do not give an overall view as the former ignores the profitability of investment and the latter fails to consider the profitability on sales.

The ROI criterion offers the following advantages:

1. ROI is a measure of relative performance and therefore can be used to compare the firms of different sizes.
2. Most acceptable measure of performance as it is easy to understand and interpret.
3. Encourages the managers to optimally use the assets.

ROI suffers from the following limitations:

1. **Defining investments:** The investments may have the different meanings in the different cases. Investments may refer to total assets, capital employed or shareholders fund.
2. **Problem of allocation:** The problem of allocation of common assets among the different divisions arise because each divisional incharge would like to share minimum cost in the common costs.
3. Treatment of assets which are currently idle.
4. Investments expected to generate more profits are selected which may sometimes increase the risk level of the enterprise.
5. Investments good for the division may not always be good for the firm as a whole.
6. Problems of valuation arise regarding the criteria for valuation of assets—book value, original cost or the current replacement cost. ROI based on the replacement cost of the assets provides the best measure of current performance. Its weakness, however, is that replacement cost is difficult to determine and may require subjective assessment.
7. Managers may be reluctant to invest in new opportunities which offer less than the current ROI as it will reduce the overall ROI of the division. However, this new opportunity may have the ROI more than the minimum required.

(b) Segments Residual Income (RI)

The performance of a division may be measured in terms of residual income, which tries to overcome some of the problems of ROI method.

RI = Operating income of the division – Imputed capital charge

= Divisional profit – (Cost of capital × Investment base)

For a particular firm, if the divisional profit is ₹ 50,000, investment ₹ 5,00,000 and cost of capital charge of 8%, the RI may be computed as—

RI = ₹ 50,000 – (8% × ₹ 5,00,000)

= ₹ 50,000 – ₹ 40,000

= ₹ 10,000

Now the firm has an opportunity to increase the investments by ₹ 2,00,000, available at the rate of 9%. This will increase the division's profit by ₹ 25,000. Residual income from the additional investment of ₹ 2,00,000 will be

RI = ₹ 25,000 – (9% × ₹ 2,00,000)

= ₹ 7000

Therefore, after making additional investment, the total residual income of the division will be ₹ 17,000. Thus, the additional investment may be considered.

The method offers the following advantages:

1. Encourages the investment in the assets, which are earning more than the required rate of return.
2. It allows the different rates for the different divisions/assets.
3. Managers understand the opportunity cost of the funds.
4. Charging each division with the cost of capital ensures that the decisions taken by the different departments are in line with the overall objectives of the organisation.

The method suffers from the following limitations:

1. Problems of measuring the income and investment are present in this method also.
2. Deciding the required rate of return is a difficult task.

Prerequisites of Responsibility Accounting

The responsibility accounting, which is tailored according to the requirements of a particular organisation, makes the following assumptions:

1. Each responsibility centre should be capable of being identified for which the managers should be held responsible.
2. Managers are responsible only for those items over which they can exercise some control.
3. Managers should actively participate in the establishment of goals and budgets against which the performance is to be compared
4. Performance reports should contain only significant information relating to each responsibility centre.
5. Responsibility managers should try to achieve the targets for their area of responsibility only.

Advantages of Responsibility Accounting

The benefits of responsibility accounting are many and varied. These are well explained by the statement: "A man will go out of his way to make a plan work if he feels that it is his own creation rather than something that has been forced upon him. He often finds ways and means of effecting savings that the front office would never dream of". The main benefits may be spelt out as below:

1. Since responsibility accounting, hinges on the redesigning of the corporate organisation, it paves way for the delegation of authority and placement of responsibility. In a business of modern size and complexity, neither planning nor control can be effective unless the management has worked out a satisfactory method of decentralisation.
2. Since the emphasis of responsibility accounting is on decentralisation of authority and delineation of objectives, the system of Management by Objectives (MBO) gets established. The heads of divisions/departments understand quite clearly what is expected of them which enables the top to exercise managerial action. Predetermined objectives

hold them accountable for target attainments in their respective cost centres. Deficient and potential areas of managers' performance are identified for necessary action.

3. When an organisation designs its accumulation and reporting system on the basis of areas of responsibility, its management is able to relate efforts and achievements, responsibility accounting is the process of machining the costs and benefits with the unit (and manager) whose activities led to their achievement. If the assignment of responsibility for costs and benefits has been strictly defined, it shall be difficult for individual managers to pass the buck when unfavourable results appear.
4. An organisation in which there is clearly defined authority and corresponding placement or responsibility, it identifies the area of the unsatisfactory operating condition. Such a system immediately draws attention towards the off-standard condition which forms the basis for an investigation into the reasons, resulting hopefully, in remedy and correction.
5. A business in unlikely to continue to operate at a profit even with the existence of high monetary rewards for employees. The rewards for work must include not only economic incentives but also those which stem from participating, from doing a good job, from belonging, These are the characteristics of morale and necessary ingredients of efficient performance, Considerable frustration will be generated over the results of a decision in which he had no opportunity to participate.
6. Divisionalisation of organisation facilitates responsibility-authority-accountability relationship.
7. Efficiency of managers enhances since the establishment of responsibility centres helps them to focus on the requirements of a particular centre.
8. Periodic evaluation of the jobs helps the management in framing of pricing and cost policies.
9. Reduces wastages of resources.
10. Managers can take remedial measures by comparing the performance of different centres.
11. Helps the organisation to adopt itself to the changing environment.

Limitations of Responsibility Accounting

1. Particular responsibility centre may not be acting in the overall interest of the organisation.
2. Responsibility accounting is difficult to apply in organisations where division of departments and segments is not clearly defined.
3. Conflict of interest between a particular responsibility centre and the organisation.

Transfer Pricing

"Transfer price" is the price at which the product is transferred from one division to the other. A multi-divisional company often faces the problem of pricing when the goods and services are transferred from one division to another. The price at which goods are transferred to other divisions called 'transfer price' directly impacts their performance. The price charged by the selling division affects the profit of both the divisions. For the selling division, a higher price increases the profit but at the same time increases the cost of the buying division and thereby adversely affects its performance.

AIM/OBJECTIVES OF TRANSFER PRICE POLICY

A correct transfer pricing policy should aim at—

1. Correct measurement of divisional performance.
2. Motivating the divisional managers to maximise the profitability of their divisions and also that of the organisation as a whole.
3. Maintaining the divisional autonomy and authority. Managers should be given autonomy to fix the transfer prices rather than dictating it.
4. Align the interest of the division with the objectives of the organisation.
5. Ensuring harmony between all the division.
6. No favourtism to any particular division.

Methods of Transfer Pricing

The different methods of transfer pricing are as given below:

(1) Market based prices

(2) Cost based prices

- (a) Marginal cost
- (b) Full cost
- (c) Full cost plus profit margin
- (d) Standard full cost

(3) Negotiated prices

Methods of Transfer Pricing

- (1) Cost based prices
  - (a) Marginal cost
  - (b) Full cost
  - (c) Full cost plus profit
  - (d) Standard cost
- (2) Market based prices
- (3) Negotiated prices

(1) Market based Prices

In this method, the market price of the product is taken as transfer price between two divisions. The transfer of goods at market price allows the realistic evaluation of the performance of the division. In case, the other division has to buy the goods from the market, the costs will remain same for it. Divisional profits are therefore likely to be similar to the profits that would be calculated if the divisions were separate organisations. Market based prices are based on the concept of opportunity cost.

(2) Cost based Prices

When it is not possible to find the competitive market price, cost based methods are used as the basis for transfer prices. Cost based transfer prices may be in different forms such as marginal cost, full cost, full cost plus profit and standard cost.

(a) **Marginal Cost.** In this approach, the goods are transferred to other divisions at the marginal cost of the products. This kind of transfer pricing is relevant only for the short-term decisions. In this case, the division becomes only a cost centre and never earns the profit.

(b) **Full Cost.** In this, transfer price is based on the full cost of the product. In this method, there is no incentive for the selling division as only the costs are allowed to be recovered and no profit is made.

(c) **Full Cost Plus Profit.** In this, the product is transferred to other divisions at price which consists of recovery of full cost plus a profit margin. Full cost plus profit margin approach overcomes the weaknesses of full cost basis transfer pricing system. The selling division generates profit and contributes to the profit of the company as a whole. Sometimes deciding about the mark up creates problem but target return on investment may be considered for it.

(d) **Standard Costs.** When goods are transferred to other divisions and pricing is based on actual cost, the inefficiencies of the selling division are also passed on to the buying division. The performance of buying division gets unduly affected. To create the accountability of the selling division, standard costs are usually used as a basis for transfer pricing in cost based systems.

(3) Negotiated Prices

As the name suggests. It is the negotiated price between the divisions. Under negotiated prices, the managers of both the divisions are allowed to negotiate about the prices at which the products are to be transferred. Generally, this price use to be less than the market price and the benefit is shared by both the divisions. However, negotiated prices approach may waste efforts, time and resources in the negotiating process The prices will depend more on the ability of the manager to negotiate rather than other factors.

SOLVED PRACTICAL PROBLEMS

Problem 1 A unit of ABZ Ltd. has currently a net income of ₹ 1,00,000 p.a. generated from an investment of ₹ 5,00,000; the company requires a minimum ROI of 16.5%. A proposal for a new project requires an investment of ₹ 1,00,000 and will yield ₹ 8,800. Evaluate the project using (a) ROI and (b) residual income.

Solution:

(a) $$\text{ROI} = \frac{\text{Divisional profit}}{\text{Divisional investment}} \times 100$$

Particulars	Existing	Proposed
Net Income	1,00,000	1,08,800
Investment	5,00,000	6,00,000
ROI	20%	18.13%

The proposal may be rejected as ROI falls from the existing 20% to 18.13%.

(b) *Residual income:*

Details	Existing	Proposed
Net income	1,00,000	1,08,800
Less : Imputed cost @ 16.5%	82,500	99,000
Residual Income	17,500	9800

The proposal should be rejected as the residual income has gone down.

Problem 2 Divisions A and B are both considering an outlay on new investment projects.

	Division A	*Division B*
Investment	₹5,00,000	₹5,00,000
Net income on new investment	80,000	55,000
Current ROI	17%	10%

Company's cost of capital is 14%. Should the company accept the project or not?

Solution: *ROI approach:*

$$\text{ROI} = \frac{\text{Net income}}{\text{Investment}} \times 100$$

$$\text{Division A} = \frac{80{,}000}{5{,}00{,}000} \times 100 = 16\%$$

$$\text{Division B} = \frac{55{,}000}{5{,}00{,}000} \times 100 = 11\%$$

Division A should reject the new project as ROI 16% is less than the current ROI of 17%. Division B may accept the project as the ROI is 11% which is higher than the current ROI of 10%.

RI approach :

	Division A	*Division B*
Investment	₹5,00,000	₹5,00,000
Net income on new investment	80,000	55,000
Less : Imputed cost of capital 14%	70,000	70,000
Residual income	10,000	(15,000)

Division A should accept the investment as it gives the RI of ₹10,000 and Division B should reject it because it will give a loss of ₹15,000.

Problem 3 The following information relates to budgeted operations of Division C of a manufacturing company.

	(₹)
Sales (50,000 units at ₹ 10)	5,00,000
Less : Variable costs @ ₹ 5 per unit	2,50,000
Contribution margin	2,50,000
Less : Fixed costs	1,75,000
Divisional profit	75,000

The amount of divisional investment is ₹ 3,00,000 and the minimum desired rate of return on the investment is the cost of capital of 20%.

You are required to (i) calculate divisional expected ROI, (ii) calculate divisional expected RI and (iii) the divisional manager has an offer to sell 10000 units at 8 per unit. Variable cost per unit would be the same as budgeted, but fixed costs would increase by ₹ 5000. Additional investment of ₹ 50,000 would also be required. If the offer is accepted, what would be the impact on RI?

Solution:

(i)

$$\text{ROI} = \frac{\text{Divisional profit}}{\text{Divisional investment}} \times 100$$

$$= \frac{₹75{,}000}{₹3{,}00{,}000} \times 100 = 25\%$$

(ii)

$$\text{RI} = \text{Divisional profit} - \text{Minimum desired rate of return}$$

$$= ₹75{,}000 - (20\% \times ₹3{,}00{,}000)$$

$$= ₹75{,}000 - 60{,}000$$

$$\text{RI} = ₹15{,}000$$

The desired rate of return is 20% but the division C is expecting to achieve an ROI of 25%. The expected profit of ₹ 75,000 is more than the ₹ 60,000 minimum return required, resulting in the positive of ₹ 15,000 residual income.

(iii) Offer to sell additional 10,000 units

Particulars	Original budget	Additional budget	Total
	₹	₹	₹
Sales	5,00,000	80,000	5,80,000
Less : Variable costs	2,50,000	50,000	3,00,000
Contribution	2,50,000	30,000	2,80,000
Less : Fixed costs	1,75,000	5000	1,80,000
Divisional profit	75,000	25,000	1,00,000
Less : Cost of capital (20%)	30,000	10,000	40,000
Residual income	45,000	15,000	60,000

The target residual income increases from ₹45,000 to ₹60,000 as a result of the new offer.

Problem 4 Delta Ltd. fixes the inter-divisional transfer prices for its products on the basis of cost plus on estimated return on investment in its divisions. The relevant particulars of the budget for the Division 'A' for the year is given below:

Particulars	Amount (₹)
Fixed assets	2,00,000
Current assets (other than cash at bank)	1,00,000
Cash at bank	50,000
Yearly fixed cost for the division	2,00,000
Variable cost per unit	10
Budgeted volume of production per year (in units)	50,000
Desired return on investment	30%

You are required to determine the transfer price for Division 'A'.

Solution:

Investment in division A = (Fixed assets + Current assets)
= ₹(2,00,000 + 1,00,000 + 50,000)
= ₹3,50,000

Return on investment (desired return) = 30% of ₹3,50,000 = ₹1,05,000

Budgeted volume of production per year = 50,00,000 units

$$\text{Profit margin per unit} = \frac{1,05,000}{50,000} = 2.10$$

Transfer price for Division 'A'

	₹
Variable cost per unit	10.00
Fixed cost per unit 2,00,000/₹50,000	4.00
Profit margin per unit 1,05,000/50,000	2.10
Transfer price per unit	16.10

Problem 5 CK Textiles is a multi-product company. Product X division within the company handles a specific product and has a target of a long-run rate of return of 20%. Product X Division will charge its unit selling price as necessary to provide this return. The following data are available for the division and its products:

Variable cost per unit	₹50
Total annual fixed costs	₹3,05,000
Long run normal demand	10,000 units each year
Operating assets owned by the division	₹3,50,000

You are required to: (a) compute the per unit selling price that will provide the desired rate of return, and (b) Assume that actual sales fluctuate from 9000 units to 11,000 units. Compute the profit margin, investment turnover and ROI that would be realised on sales at 9000 units, 10,000 units and 11,000 units level of activity [assuming the S.P. to be same as computed in part (a)].

Solution:

(a) *Total Sales Value of 10,000 units*

Variable cost (₹ 50 × 10,000)	=	₹ 5,00,000
Fixed cost	=	3,05,000
Return @ 20%		
3,50,000 ×	=	70,000
Total sales value		8,75,000

$$\text{Selling price per unit} = \frac{8{,}75{,}000}{10{,}000 \text{ units}} = ₹\,87.50$$

(b) *Calculation of Profit Margin, Investment Turnover and ROI*

Particulars	9000 units	10000 units	11000 units
Sales @ ₹ 87.50 per unit	7,87,500	8,75,000	9,62,000
Variable cost @ ₹ 50 per unit	4,50,000	5,00,000	5,50,000
Fixed costs	3,05,000	3,05,000	3,05,000
Total cost	7,55,000	8,05,000	8,55,000
Net profit	32,500	70,000	1,07,500
Profit margin $\frac{\text{Net profit}}{\text{Sales}} \times 100$	$\frac{32{,}500}{7{,}87{,}500} \times 100$ = 4.126%	$\frac{70{,}000}{8{,}75{,}000} \times 100$ = 8%	$\frac{1{,}07{,}500}{9{,}62{,}500} \times 100$ = 11.168%
Investments turnover ratio $\frac{\text{Sales}}{\text{Assets}}$	$\frac{7{,}87{,}500}{3{,}50{,}000}$ = 2.25	$\frac{8{,}75{,}000}{3{,}50{,}000}$ = 2.50	$\frac{9{,}62{,}500}{3{,}50{,}000}$ = 2.75
ROI	4.126 × 2.25 = 9.28%	8 × 2.50 = 20%	11.168 × 2.75= 30.71%

Problem 6 Pharma company facing stiff competition from new MNCs. Its operating income margin has been declining steadily for the past several years. The company has been forced to lower prices so that it can maintain its current market share. The operating results for the past three years are as follows:

Particulars	Year 1	Year 2	Year 3
Sales	₹ 10,00,000	₹ 9,50,000	₹ 9,00,000
Net operating income	1,20,000	1,04,500	94,500
Average assets	15,00,000	15,00,000	15,00,000

For the forthcoming year, the company is restructuring its entire production activities to reduce the costs. It estimates that (i) inventories will be reduced by 70 per cent during the first year of operations, (ii) a 20 per cent reduction in the average operating assets of the company and (iii) also estimates that sales and operating income will be restored to year 1 levels because of simultaneous reductions in operating expenses and selling prices.

You are required to :

(i) Compute the ROI, profit margin, and investment turnover for three years.

(ii) Assuming that the sales and operating income were achieved in the forthcoming year as expected but inventories remained at the same level as in year 3, compute the expected ROI, profit margin and investment turnover. Explain why the ROI increased over the year 3 level.

Solution:

		Year 1	Year 2	Year 3
(i) ROI	=	$\frac{₹1,20,000}{₹15,00,000} \times 100$	$\frac{₹1,04,500}{₹15,00,000} \times 100$	$\frac{₹94,500}{₹15,00,000} \times 100$
	=	8.00%	= 6.97%	= 6.30%
Profit Margin	=	$\frac{₹1,20,000}{₹10,00,000} \times 100$	$\frac{₹1,04,500}{₹9,50,000} \times 100$	$\frac{₹94,500}{₹9,00,000} \times 100$
	=	12.00%	= 11.00%	= 10.50%
Investment Turnover	=	$\frac{₹10,00,000}{₹15,00,000} \times 100$	$\frac{₹9,50,000}{₹15,00,000} \times 100$	$\frac{₹9,00,000}{₹15,00,000} \times 100$
	=	0.67	= 0.63	= 0.60

(ii)

$$\text{ROI} = \frac{\text{Divisional profit}}{\text{Divisional investment}} \times 100$$

$$= \frac{₹1,20,000}{₹15,00,000} \times 100 = 8\%$$

$$\text{Profit Margin} = \frac{\text{Net profit}}{\text{Sales}} \times 100$$

$$= \frac{₹1,20,000}{₹10,00,000} \times 100 = 12\%$$

Problem 7 The performance of Fabric Mart for the year 2020 is as follows:

Details	Designing Department	Fabric Department	Packing Department
Sales	20,000	10,000	15,000
Operation profit	3000	800	1000
Investment	15,000	6000	8000

Rank the performance of these departments using return on investment and profit merging percentage method.

Solution:

Department	ROI	Profit Margin
1. Designing	3000/15,000 × 100 = 20%	3000/20,000 × 100 = 15%
2. Fabric	800/6000 × 100 = 13.3%	800/10,000 × 100 = 8%
3. Packing	1000/8000 × 100 = 12.5%	1000/15,000 × 100 = 6.67%

According to return on investment method and profit margin method, designing department is the best performer. Fabric department comes next and last is packing department.

In this question both returns on investment and profit margin method is giving the same result. However, if the results differ then the ROI method should be followed as it is a better performance measurement method because it relates profits to the investment required to generate those profit.

Problem 8 The details of monitor department of LCD manufacturing company are as follows:

Details	*Amount (₹)*
Sale (1000 units @ ₹10)	10,000
Variable cost @ ₹1/unit	1000
Fixed cost	4000

The Investment is ₹20,000 and the target rate of return on investment is 30%.

Calculate the ROI and residual income of the monitor department. If the department sells additional 200 units, additional investment of ₹500 would be required. What would be its impact on residual income.

Solution:

1. $\text{ROI} = \dfrac{\text{Profit}}{\text{Capital invested}}$

   Calculation of profit

	(₹)
Sales	10,000
Less : Variable cost	1000
Contribution margin	9000
Less : Fixed cost	4000
Profit of monitor department	5000

$$\text{ROI} = \frac{5000}{20,000} \times 100 = 25\%$$

2. Residual Income

   = Profit of monitor department – Target profit

   = (5000) – (30% of 20,000)

   = (5000) – 6000) = (1000)

The residual income of the monitor department is negative since the return on investment is less than the target profit.

Now, when the department sells additional 200 units, following shall be the position

Details	Existing Amount	Additional Amount	Total
Sales	10,000	2000	12,000
Less : Variable Cost	1000	200	1200
	9000	1800	10,800
Less : Fixed Cost	4000	–	4000
Decisional Profit	5000	1800	6800
Less : Target Profit @ 30%	6000	150 (30% of 500)	6150
Residual Income	(1000)	1650	650

In the existing situation the residual income is negative ₹1000. However, if the additional 200 units are hold, the residual income is generated and overall impact is generation of ₹650 residual income.

REVIEW QUESTIONS

1. Define and explain responsibility accounting. What are the pre-requisites for introducing responsibility accounting in a company?
2. (i) Explain the essential ingredients of the system of responsibility accounting.
   (ii) What are the criteria for evaluating the performance of a division?
3. Write notes on the following as used in responsibility accounting.
   (i) Cost centre
   (ii) Revenue centre
   (iii) Profit centre
   (iv) Return of investment (ROI) as a measure of performance.

UNSOLVED PRACTICAL QUESTIONS

1. For B Pharma Ltd. the operating performance of the three divisions of a Standard Mart for the year is as under:

Details	Division I (₹)	Division II (₹)	Division III (₹)
Sales	10,00,000	1,20,00,000	1,80,00,000
Operating profit	60,000	3,00,000	65,000
Investment	5,00,000	4,00,000	50,00,000

(a) Using the operating margin percentage as the criterion, which is the most profitable division?

(b) Using the rate of return on investment as the criterion, which is the most profitable division?

(c) Which of the two measures do you think gives the better indication of overall?

[*Ans.* (a) Ranking I, III and II (b) Ranking III, I and II
(c) ROI is a better measure of operating performance]

2. Koohinoor Ltd. is divided into three segments A, B and C. All the divisions were formed in the same year. Top management desires to determine which of the divisions is the most profitable. The following data have been furnished for your analysis:

Details	Division		
	A (₹)	B (₹)	C (₹)
Net income before taxes	10,000	11,100	16,000
Investment (gross)	50,000	60,000	1,00,000
Investment (net)	25,000	30,000	50,000

Prepare rankings of the three divisions using ROI and RI with a capital charge of 12% that each manager might use to assert that this is the most profitable division. (All calculations are to be made on the basis of net investments).

[*Ans.* ROI: A—₹ 40%; B—₹ 37%, C—₹ 32:
RI: C—₹ 10,000 B—₹ 7,500; A—₹ 7,000]

3. The following information is submitted in respect of division X of a manufacturing Daawat Ltd.

Details	*Amount (₹)*
Sales (50,000 units @ ₹ 20 per unit)	10,00,000
Less : Variable cost @ ₹ 14 per unit	7,00,000
Contribution	3,00,000
Less : Fixed cost	2,20,000
Divisional profit	80,000

The amount of divisional investment is ₹ 5,00,000 and the target rate of return investment is 20%. Find out the following:

(i) Calculate ROI of division X

(ii) Calculate residual income of division X

(iii) The company has an offer to sell 10,000 units at ₹ 18.40 per unit. Variable cost per unit would be the same as budgeted, but fixed costs would increase by ₹ 12,000. Additional investment of ₹ 50,000 would also be required. Find out the effect on residual income.

[*Ans.* (a) ROI = 16%, (b) Residual Income = ₹ 20,000,
(c) The RI increases to positive 4000 from a loss of ₹ 20,000]

CASE STUDIES

1. Electronics division has the opportunity to invest in two projects for the coming year, namely, fax machine and a mobile game player. The outlay required for each investment, the rupee returns, and the ROI is as follows:

Particulars	Fax Machine (₹)	Mobile Game Player (₹)
Investment	1,20,00,000	60,00,000
Operating income	13,00,000	6,40,000
ROI (%)	15	16

The division is currently earning a ROI of 18 per cent, using operating assets of ₹75 million, operating income on the current investment is ₹13.5 million. The division has approval to request up to ₹15 million in new investment capital. The company requires that all investments earn at least 11 per cent (this rate represents the amount the corporation must earn to cover the cost of acquiring the capital). The weighted cost of capital for the company is 12 per cent.

(a) Calculate the ROI for the division for each of the following scenarios : (i) invest in the fax machine; (ii) invest in the mobile game player; (iii) invest in both; and (iv) invest in neither. Which option would the divisional manager choose? In addition also calculate the EVA for the answering machine and the video game player. Also calculate the EVA for the division if neither investment is made. If the manager is evaluated on the basis of EVA, what choice of investments (fax machine, mobile games, neither or both) will be made? Why?

2. The Whirlpool Electric Company is facing stiff competition for the last few years from imported goods. Its income and profits had been declining steadily for the past several years and the company had been forced to adopt several measures in order to maintain its market share. The company had been toying with various alternatives and the companies marketing manager has suggested an alternative that will help revive the profits and the market share of the company in the coming years.

The marketing manager of the Whirlpool Electric Company has come up with a proposal for the manufacture of top-of-the-line freezers. The product will be new in a competitive industry. Their production of a top-of-the-line freezer employs assets of ₹5,08,00,000. Whirlpool hopes to achieve a return on assets employed of 25 per cent. Manufacturing and sales cost information is as follows:

Particulars	Freezers (per Unit)
Total variable cost (₹)	280
Total fixed costs (₹)	120
Total cost per unit (₹)	400
Unit sales and production volume	6,000

The company has asked you to calculate the minimum sales price that they need to charge to achieve the desired rate of return on assets employed at the given sales volume. After a few months, the company is interested in diversifying its operations. If the freezers produced are just one of the many product lines and Whirlpool still desires a 25 per cent rate of return on asses employed:

(a) Calculate the markup percentage on cost with the given facts.

(b) What price would Whirlpool set for the freezer if the markup on cost calculated is 30 per cent?

Glossary

EXTRACTS FROM TERMINOLOGY ISSUED BY CIMA (LONDON)

1. **Absorption costing :** The procedure which charges fixed as well as variable overhead to cost units.
2. **Avoidable costs :** The specific costs of an activity or sector of a business which would be avoided if that activity or sector did not exist
3. **Break-even Chart :** A chart which indicates approximate profit or loss at different levels of sales volume within a limited range.
4. **Break-even Point :** The level of activity at which there is neither profit nor loss. It can be ascertained by using break-even chart or by calculation.
5. **Budget :** A plan expressed in money. It is prepared and approved prior to the budget period and may show income, expenditure, and the capital to be employed. May be drawn up showing incremental effects on former budgeted or actual figures, or be compiled by zero based budgeting.
6. **Budget Centre :** A section of an entity for which control may be exercised and budgets prepared.
7. **Budget Cost Allowance/Flexed Budget :** The budgeted cost ascribed to the level of activity achieved in a budget centre in a control period. It comprises variable costs in direct proportion to volume achieved and fixed costs as proportion of the annual budget.
8. **Budget Period :** The period for which a budget is prepared and used, which may then be sub-divided into control periods.
9. **Budgetary Control :** The establishment of budgets relating to the responsibilities of executives to the requirements of a policy, and the continuous comparison of actual with budgeted results, either to secure by individual action the objectives of that policy or to provide a basis for its revision.
10. **Cash Flow Budget :** A detailed budget of cash income and expenditure incorporating both revenue and capital items. In Government accounting, budgets for cash expenditure are referred as cash limits.
11. **Contribution :** Sales value less variable cost of sales. It may be expressed as total contribution, contribution per unit or as a percentage of sales.

12. **Contribution Centre :** A profit centre whose expenditure is reported on a marginal or direct cost basis.
13. **Cost (as a noun) :** The amount of expenditure (actual or notional) incurred on or attributable to a specific thing or activity.

    (As a verb) : To ascertain the cost of a specified thing or activity. The word 'cost' can rarely stand alone and should be qualified as to its nature and limitation.
14. **Cost Behaviour :** The way in which costs of output are affected by fluctuations in the level of activity. When cost behaviour is not obvious, it may be determined by regression techniques or by a scatter graph.
15. **Cost Benefit Analysis :** Measuring resources used in an activity and comparing them with the value of benefits.
16. **Cost Reduction :** The reduction in unit cost of goods or services without impairing suitability for the use intended.
17. **Cost Unit :** A unit of product or service in relation to which costs are ascertained.
18. **Cost-Volume-Profit Analysis (CVP) :** The study of the effect on future profit of changes in fixed cost, variable cost, sales price, quantity and mix.
19. **Decision Driven Costs :** Those costs incurred following policy decisions which continue to be incurred until the decisions are altered. They do not vary with changes in output or with operational activities.
20. **Differential/Incremental Costs :** The difference in total cost between alternatives, calculated to assist decision making.
21. **Flexible Budget :** A budget which, by recognising the difference between fixed, semi-variable and variable cost is designed to change in relation to the level of activity attained.
22. **Forecasting :** The identification of factors and quantification of their effect on an entity, as a basis for planning.
23. **Historical Cost :** The actual cost of acquiring assets, goods and services.
24. **Ideal Standard :** A standard which can be attained under the most favourable conditions, with no allowance for normal losses, waste and machine downtime. Also known as potential standard.
25. **Investment Centre :** A profit centre the performance of which is measured by its return on capital employed.
26. **Limiting Factor or Key Factor :** Anything which limits the activity of an entity. An entity seeks to optimise the benefit it obtains from the limiting factor. Examples are: shortage of supply of a resource and a restriction on sales at a particular price.
27. **Marginal Cost :** The cost of one unit of product or service which would be avoided if that unit were not produced or provided.
28. **Marginal Costing :** The accounting system in which variable costs are charged to cost units and fixed costs of the period are written off in full against the aggregate contribution. Its special value is in decision making.
29. **Opportunity Cost :** The value of a benefit sacrificed in favour of an alternative course of action.

30. **Principal Budget Factor :** A factor which will limit the activities of an undertaking and which is taken into account in preparing budgets.
31. **Profit Centre :** A part of a business accountable for costs and revenues. It may be called business centre, business unit, or strategic business unit.
32. **Relevant Costs :** Costs appropriate to a specific management decision.
33. **Responsibility Centre :** A unit of function of an organisation headed by a manager having direct responsibility for its performance.
34. **Revenue Centre :** A centre devoted to raising revenue with no responsibility for production, e.g., sales centre. Often used in a not-for-profit organisation.
35. **Rolling Budget :** A budget continuously updated by adding a further period, say a month or quarter and deducting the earliest period. Beneficial where future costs and/or activities cannot be forecasted reliably.
36. **Semi-variable/semi-fixed cost/mixed cost :** A cost containing both fixed and variable components and which is thus partly affected by fluctuations in the level of activity.
37. **Standard :** A pre-determined measurable quantity set in defined conditions.
38. **Standard Cost :** A standard expressed in money. It is built up from an assessment of the value of cost elements. Its main uses are providing bases for performance measurement, control by exception reporting, valuing stock and establishment of selling prices.
39. **Standard Time :** The total time in which a task should be completed at standard performance, i.e., basic time plus contingency allowance plus relaxation allowance.
40. **Value Added :** Sales value less the cost of purchased materials and services. This represents the worth of an alteration in form, location or availability of a product or service.
41. **Value Analysis :** A systematic interdisciplinary examination of factors affecting the cost of a product or service, in order to devise means of achieving the specified purpose most economically at the required standard of quality and reliability.
42. **Variable Cost :** Cost which tends to vary with the level of activity.
43. **Variance :** Difference between planned, budgeted or standard cost and actual cost and similarly for revenue.
44. **Variance Accounting :** A method by which planned activities (quantified in budgets, standard costs, standard sales and standard profits) are compared with actual results. Provides information for variance analysis.
45. **Variance Analysis :** The analysis of performance by means of variances. Used to promote management action at the earliest possible stages.
46. **Variance Budget :** Difference between budget and actual cost for each cost in a budget and for revenue where appropriate. In flexible budgeting, it is the difference between each flexible budget value and actual value.
47. **Zero Based/Priority Based Budgeting :** A method of budgeting whereby all activities are revaluated each time a budget is set. Discreet levels of each activity are valued and a combination chosen to match funds available.

Select Bibliography

Anderson, D.L. and D.L. Raun, *Information Analysis in Management Accounting* (Santa Barbara, John Wiley), 1978.

Anderson, W.T., C.A. Moyer and AJR. Wyatt, (Ed.), *Accounting: Basic Financial, Cost and Control Concepts* (New York, John Wiley), 1965.

Anthony, R.N., *Management Accounting: Text and Cases* (Illinois, Irwin), 1970,

___________, *Accounting: Text and Cases* (New Delhi, Tata McGraw-Hill), 1995

___________, and J. Dearden, *Management Control Systems: Text and Cases* (Illinois, Irwin), 1980.

___________, and V Govindarajan, *Management Control Systems,* (New Delhi, Tata McGraw-Hill), 1998.

___________, and J.S., Reece, *Management Accounting Principles*, (Bombay, Taraporewala), 1980.

___________, and R.I. Herzlmger, *Management Control in Non-Profit Organisations* (Illinois, Irwin), 1980.

___________, and G.A. Welsch, *Fundamentals of Management Accounting*, (Illinois, Irwin), 1981.

Baxter, W.T. and S. Davidson (Eds.), *Studies in Accounting, (London, England Institute of Chartered Accountants)*, 1977.

Bierman, H., Jr. and A. R. Drebin, *Management Accounting,* (New York, Macmillan), 1976.

Bierman, H., Jr and S. Smidt, *The Capital Budgeting Decision*, (London, Macmillan), 1975.

Boer, G., *Direct Cost and Contribution Accounting*, (London, John Wiley), 1974.

Brown, J.L., and L. R. Howard, *Principles and Practice of Management Accountancy*, (London, English Language Book Society), 1975.

Brown, R.G., *Decision Rules for Inventory Management*, (New York, Holt, Rinehart and Winston), 1963.

Bruns, W.J. and D.T. Decoster, *Accounting and its Behavioural Implications*, (New York, McGraw-Hill), 1969.

Bull, R.J., *Accounting in Business*, (London, Butterworths), 1980.

Chatfield, M. and D. Neilson, *Cost Accounting*, (New York, Harcourt Brace Jovanovich, Inc.), 1983.

Copeland, R.M. and P.E. Dascher, *Management Accounting*, (New York, John Wiley), 1978.

Crowningshield, G.R. and K.A Gorman, *Cost Accounting: Principles and Managerial Applications*, (Boston, Houghton Mifflin Company), 1979.

Cushing, B.E., *Accounting Information Systems and Business Organisation*, (London, Addison Wesley), 1978.

Davidson, S. and R.L. Weil (Eds.) *Handbook of Modem Accounting*,' (New York, McGraw-Hill), 1977.

__________, *Handbook of Cost Accounting*, (New York, McGraw-Hill), 1978.

Dearden, J., *Cost Accounting and Financial Control Systems*, (California, Addison-Wesley Pub. Co.), 1976.

Dearden, J. and J. Shank, *Financial Accounting and Reponing*, (New Jersey, Prentice-Hall), 1975.

Decoster, *D.T. and E.L. Schafer, Management Accounting: A Decision Emphasis*, (New York, John Wiley), 1979.

Fertig, P. and Others, *Using Accounting Information: An Introduction*, (New York, Harcourt), 1971.

Fouike, R.A., *Practical Financial Statement Analysis*, (Illinois, Irwin), 1976.

Garrison, R.H. *Management Accounting, Concepts for Planning, Control, and Decision Making*, (Business Publishers, Texas), 1976.

Garrison, R.H. and Eric Noreen, *Managerial Accounting*, (New York, McGraw-Hill), 1997.

Gibbs, G., *Accounting for Management Decisions*, (Scranton, International Textbook), 1968.

Gordon, M.J. and G. Shillinglow, *Accounting: A Management Approach*, (Illinois, Irwin), 1974.

Greener, M., *Between the Lines of the Balance Sheet,* (London, Pergamon Press), 1968.

Hartley, R.V., *Cost and Managerial Accounting*, (Boston, Allyn and Bacon, Inc.), 1983.

Helfert, E.H., *Techniques for Financial Analysis*, (Illinois, Irwin), 1997.

Horngren, C.T., *Accounting for Management Control*, (New Jersey, Prentice-Hall), 1978.

__________, *Cost Accounting: A Managerial Emphasis*, (New Delhi, Prentice-Hall), 1997.

Horngren, C.T. and G.L. Sundlem, *Introduction to Management Accounting*, (New Delhi, Prentice-Hall), 1990.

Institute of Chartered Accountants, *Standard Costing: An Introduction to the Accounting Process,* (London), 1956.

Institute of Chartered Accountants in England and Wales, *Recommendations on Accounting Principle* 1975.

Kaplan, R.S., *Advanced Management Accounting*, (New Delhi, Prentice-Hall), 1988.

Keith, L., *Accountancy: A Management Perspective*, (Englewood Cliffs, Prentice-Hall), 1980.

Khan M.Y. and P.K. Jain, *Financial Management, Third Edition*, (New Delhi, Tata McGraw-Hill), 1999.

Laidler, E., *Variance Accounting*, (London, Mcmillan), 1976.

Matz, A. and M.F. Usry, *Cost Accounting: Planning and Control*, (Ohio, South Western Publishing Company), 1976.

Maner, M.W., *Cost Accounting*, (New York, McGraw-Hill), 1997.

Meigs, R.F., *Accounting: The Basis for Business Decisions,* (McGraw-Hill, New York), 1996.

Metcalf, R.W. and P.L. Titard, *Principles of Accounting*, (Philadelphia, W.B. Saunder), 1976.

Moore, C.L. and R.K., Jaedicke, *Managerial Accounting,* (New York, South Western Publishing Company), 1976.

Morse, D., *Managerial Accounting*, (New York, McGraw-Hill), 1997.

Moscove, S.A. et. al., *Cost Accounting with Managerial Applications* (Boston, Houghton Mifflin Company), 1985.

Mariarity, S. and C.P. Alien, *Cost Accounting* (New York, Ilaper and Row), 1984.

Mayer, J.N., *Financial Statement Analysts*, (New Jersey, Prentice-Hall), 1969.

National Association of Accountants, *Statement on Management Accounting Practices*, (New York, NAA), 1971.

__________, *Managing the Cash Flow*, 1974.

__________, *Developing and Reporting of Variances*, 1962.

__________, *Direct Costing*, 1953.

__________, *Separating and Using Costs as Fixed and Variable*, 1960.

__________, *Applications of Direct Costing*, 1961.

__________, *Cost-Volume-Profit Relationships*, 1962.

__________, *Accounting for Costs of Capacity*, 1963.

__________, *Product Costs for Pricing Purposes*, 1953.

__________, *Analysis of Non-manufacturing Costs for Managerial Decisions*, 1951.

Osteryoung, J.S., *Capital Budgeting: Long-term Asset Selection*, (Columbus, Offio, Grid), 1979.

Pierced, G.J., *Measurement of Capital Employed* (Londoit, Business Books), 1972.

Rayburn, L.Q., *Principles of Cost Accounting: Managerial Applications*, (Homewood, Illinois, Irwin), 1983.

Shillingipw, G., *Managerial Cost Accounting*, (Illinois, Irwin), 1977.

__________, *Cost Accounting: Analysis and Control*, (Illinois, Irwin), 1967.

Thacker, R.J., *Introduction to Modern Accounting*, (New Jersey, Prentice-Hall), 1977.

__________, and R.L. Smith, *Modern Management Accounting*, (Reston, Reston Publishing Company), 1977.

Tracy, J.F., *Fundamentals of Management Accounting*, (New York, John Wiley), 1976.

Willsmore, A.W., *Accounting for Management Control*, (London, Pitman), 1971.

Woelfel, C.J., *Accounting: An Introduction*, (California, Goodyear Publishing Company), 1977.

Wood, F., *Business Accounting*, (London, English Language Book Society and Longman Group), 1979.

Zimmerman, J., *Accounting for Decision Making and Control*, (New York, McGraw-Hill), 1997.

Index